Lecture Notes in Computer Science 12809

More information about this subseries at http://www.springer.com/series/7410

Jianying Zhou · Chuadhry Mujeeb Ahmed ·
Lejla Batina · Sudipta Chattopadhyay ·
Olga Gadyatskaya · Chenglu Jin ·
Jingqiang Lin · Eleonora Losiouk ·
Bo Luo · Suryadipta Majumdar ·
Mihalis Maniatakos · Daisuke Mashima ·
Weizhi Meng · Stjepan Picek ·
Masaki Shimaoka · Chunhua Su ·
Cong Wang (Eds.)

Applied Cryptography and Network Security Workshops

ACNS 2021 Satellite Workshops
AIBlock, AIHWS, AIoTS, CIMSS, Cloud S&P, SCI, SecMT, and SiMLA
Kamakura, Japan, June 21–24, 2021
Proceedings

Springer

Editors
Jianying Zhou
Singapore University of Technology and Design
Singapore, Singapore

Lejla Batina
ICIS
Radboud University
Nijmegen, The Netherlands

Olga Gadyatskaya
LIACS
Leiden University
Leiden, The Netherlands

Jingqiang Lin
University of Science and Technology of China
Hefei, China

Bo Luo
University of Kansas
Lawrence, KS, USA

Mihalis Maniatakos
New York University
Abu Dhabi, United Arab Emirates

Weizhi Meng
Technical University of Denmark
Kongens Lyngby, Denmark

Masaki Shimaoka
SECOM Co., Ltd.
Tokyo, Japan

Cong Wang
City University of Hong Kong
Hong Kong, Hong Kong

Chuadhry Mujeeb Ahmed
University of Strathclyde
Glasgow, UK

Sudipta Chattopadhyay
Singapore University of Technology and Design
Singapore, Singapore

Chenglu Jin
Centrum Wiskunde & Informatica
Amsterdam, The Netherlands

Eleonora Losiouk
University of Padua
Padua, Italy

Suryadipta Majumdar
CIISE
Concordia University
Montréal, Canada

Daisuke Mashima
Illinois at Singapore Pte Ltd
Singapore, Singapore

Stjepan Picek
Delft University of Technology
Delft, The Netherlands

Chunhua Su
University of Aizu
Aizu-Wakamatsu, Japan

ISSN 0302-9743 ISSN 1611-3349 (electronic)
Lecture Notes in Computer Science
ISBN 978-3-030-81644-5 ISBN 978-3-030-81645-2 (eBook)
https://doi.org/10.1007/978-3-030-81645-2

LNCS Sublibrary: SL4 – Security and Cryptology

This Springer imprint is published by the registered company Springer Nature Switzerland AG
The registered company address is: Gewerbestrasse 11, 6330 Cham, Switzerland

Preface

This proceedings contains the papers selected for presentation at ACNS 2021 satellite workshops, which were held in parallel with the main conference (the 19th International Conference on Applied Cryptography and Network Security) during June 21–24, 2021. The event was planned to be held in Kamakura, Japan. Due to the ongoing COVID-19 crisis, we decided to organize it virtually again to ensure the safety of all participants.

ACNS initiated four satellite workshops successfully in 2019 and expanded to seven in 2020. Each workshop provided a forum to address a specific topic at the forefront of cybersecurity research. In response to this year's call for workshop proposals, another new workshop was launched besides the existing seven workshops.

- AIBlock: 3rd ACNS Workshop on Application Intelligence and Blockchain Security, chaired by Weizhi Meng and Chunhua Su
- AIHWS: 2nd ACNS Workshop on Artificial Intelligence in Hardware Security, chaired by Stjepan Picek and Lejla Batina
- AIoTS: 3rd ACNS Workshop on Artificial Intelligence and Industrial IoT Security, chaired by Daisuke Mashima and Chuadhry Mujeeb Ahmed
- CIMSS: 1st ACNS Workshop on Critical Infrastructure and Manufacturing System Security, chaired by Chenglu Jin and Michail Maniatakos
- Cloud S&P: 3rd ACNS Workshop on Cloud Security and Privacy, chaired by Suryadipta Majumdar and Cong Wang
- SCI: 2nd ACNS Workshop on Secure Cryptographic Implementation, chaired by Jingqiang Lin and Bo Luo
- SecMT: 2nd ACNS Workshop on Security in Mobile Technologies, chaired by Eleonora Losiouk and Olga Gadyatskaya
- SiMLA: 3rd ACNS Workshop on Security in Machine Learning and its Applications, chaired by Sudipta Chattopadhyay

This year, we received a total of 49 submissions. Each workshop had its own Program Committee (PC) in charge of the review process. These papers were evaluated on the basis of their significance, novelty, and technical quality. The review process was double-blind. In the end, 26 papers were selected for presentation at the eight workshops, resulting in an acceptance rate of 53%.

ACNS also gave a Best Workshop Paper Award. The winning papers were selected from the nominated candidate papers from each workshop. The following two papers shared the ACNS 2021 Best Workshop Paper Award.

- Abdullah Albalawi, Vassilios Vassilakis, and Radu Calinescu. "Memory Deduplication as a Protective Factor in Virtualized Systems" from the Cloud S&P Workshop

– Aozhuo Sun, Bingyu Li, Huiqing Wan, and Qiongxiao Wang. "PoliCT: Flexible Policy in Certificate Transparency Enabling Lightweight Self-Monitor" from the SCI Workshop

Besides the regular papers being presented at the workshops, there were also 15 invited talks.

– "Towards Better Large-Scale Consensus Protocols" by Pawel Szalachowski from Google, USA, and "Long-term Availability of Crypto Currencies: Security and Privacy against Quantum-Attacks" by Kouichi Sakurai from Kyushu University, Japan, at the AIBlock workshop
– "Internet of Threats: Federated Anomaly Detection in IoT and Challenges" by Ahmad-Reza Sadeghi from TU Darmstadt, Germany, and "Machine Learning for Hardware Security: Standing on the Shoulders of Giants" by Fatemeh Ganji, Worcester Polytechnic Institute, USA, at the AIHWS workshop
– "Sensor and Process Fingerprinting in Industrial Control Systems" by Martin Ochoa from Appgate, Colombia, and "ML-based Assessment of the Resilience of Autonomous Vehicles" by Ravi Iyer from UIUC, USA, at the AIoTS workshop
– "HACK∃D: Challenges and Solutions for Cybersecurity in Digital Manufacturing" by Nikhil Gupta from New York University, USA, and "Cross-Layer Security of Embedded and Cyber-Physical Systems" by Mohammad Al Faruque from the University of California, Irvine, USA, at the CIMSS Workshop
– "Trusting Outsourced Computation" by Rei Safavi-Naini from the University of Calgary, Canada, and "Secure Network Measurement as a Cloud Service" by Xingliang Yuan from Monash University, Australia, at the Cloud S&P workshop
– "Understanding and Demystifying Bitcoin Mixing Services" by Yajin Zhou from Zhejiang University, China, at the SCI workshop
– "Analyzing and Designing the Security of a Mobile Platform" by Soteris Demetriou from Imperial College London, UK, "Why is Hard to Secure Mobile Proximity Services" by Daniele Antonioli from EURECOM, France, and "From 4G to 5G Security Challenges" by Katharina Kohls from Radboud University, the Netherlands, at the SecMT workshop
– "Adversarial Attacks in ML-Enabled Systems" by Michail Papadakis from Luxembourg University, Luxembourg, at the SiMLA workshop

ANCS included a poster session for the first time in 2021, which was chaired by Masaki Shimaoka. Four posters were included in the proceedings as well, in the form of extended abstracts.

ACNS 2021 workshops were made possible by the joint efforts of many individuals and organizations. We sincerely thank the authors of all submissions. We are grateful to the program chairs and PC members of each workshop for their great effort in providing professional reviews and interesting feedback to authors in a tight time schedule. We thank all the external reviewers for assisting the PC in their particular areas of expertise. We also thank General Chairs Chunhua Su and Kazumasa Omote and the organizing team members of the main conference as well as each workshop for their help in various aspects.

Last but not least, we thank everyone else, speakers and session chairs, for their contribution to the program of ACNS 2021 workshops. We are glad to see that these workshops have become an important part of ACNS and provide a stimulating platform to discuss open problems at the forefront of cybersecurity research.

June 2021

Jianying Zhou
ACNS 2021 Workshop Chair

Organization

AIBlock 2021

Third ACNS Workshop on Application Intelligence and Blockchain Security

June 22, 2021

General Chair

Man Ho Au	The University of Hong Kong, China

Program Chairs

Weizhi Meng	Technical University of Denmark, Denmark
Chunhua Su	University of Aizu, Japan

Program Committee

Konstantinos Chalkias	Novi/Facebook, USA
Mauro Conti	University of Padua, Italy
Jintai Ding	University of Cincinnati, USA
Dieter Gollmann	Hamburg University of Technology, Germany
Georgios Kambourakis	University of the Aegean, Greece
Debiao He	Wuhan University, China
Mario Larangeira	Tokyo Institute of Technology/IOHK, Japan
Wenjuan Li	The Hong Kong Polytechnic University, China
Jiqiang Lu	Beihang University, China
Felix Gomez Marmol	University of Murcia, Spain
Kouichi Sakurai	Kyushu University, Japan
Jun Shao	Zhejiang Gongshang University, China
Claudio Juan Tessone	Swiss Federal Institute of Technology, Switzerland
Ding Wang	Nankai University, China
Qianhong Wu	Beihang University, China

AIHWS 2021

Second ACNS Workshop on Artificial Intelligence in Hardware Security

June 21, 2021

Program Chairs

Lejla Batina	Radboud University, the Netherlands
Stjepan Picek	Delft University of Technology, the Netherlands

Program Committee

Shivam Bhasin	Nanyang Technological University, Singapore
Ileana Buhan	Radboud University, the Netherlands
Chitchanok Chuengsatiansup	The University of Adelaide, Australia
Lukasz Chmielewski	Radboud University, the Netherlands
Elena Dubrova	KTH Royal Institute of Technology, Sweden
Fatemeh Ganji	Worcester Polytechnic Institute, USA
Naofumi Homma	Tohoku University, Japan
Dirmanto Jap	Nanyang Technological University, Singapore
Alan Jovic	University of Zagreb, Croatia
Liran Lerman	Thales Belgium, Belgium
Eleonora Losiouk	University of Padova, Italy
Luca Mariot	Delft University of Technology, the Netherlands
Nele Mentens	Katholieke Universiteit Leuven, Belgium, and Leiden University, the Netherlands
Debdeep Mukhopadhyay	IIT Kharagpur, India
Naila Mukhtar	Macquarie University, Australia
Kostas Papagiannopoulos	NXP Semiconductors, Germany
Guilherme Perin	Delft University of Technology, the Netherlands
Kazuo Sakiyama	The University of Electro-Communications, Japan
Shahin Tajik	Worcester Polytechnic Institute, USA
Vincent Verneuil	NXP Semiconductors, Germany
Nikita Veshchikov	NXP Semiconductors, Belgium

Publicity Chair

Marina Krcek	Delft University of Technology, the Netherlands

AIoTS 2021

Third ACNS Workshop on Artificial Intelligence and Industrial IoT Security

June 22, 2021

Program Chairs

Daisuke Mashima	Illinois at Singapore Pte Ltd, Singapore
Chuadhry Mujeeb Ahmed	University of Strathclyde, UK

Organizing Chairs

Sridhar Adepu	SUTD, Singapore
John Henry Castellanos	SUTD, Singapore
Xin Lou	Illinois at Singapore Pte Ltd, Singapore

Program Committee

Anand Agrawal	NYU Abu Dhabi, UAE
Yao Chen	Illinois at Singapore Pte Ltd, Singapore
Yao Cheng	Huawei International Pte Ltd, Singapore
Mina S. Guirguis	Texas State University, USA
Zhongyuan Hau	Imperial College London, UK
Venkata Reddy	IIPE-Visakhapatnam, India
Jorjeta Jetcheva	San Jose State University, USA
Chitra Javali	Institute for Infocomm Research (I2R), Singapore
Nandha Kumar Kandasamy	SUTD, Singapore
Eunsuk Kang	CMU, USA
Eleonora Losiouk	University of Padua, Italy
Kazuhiro Minami	The Institute of Statistical Mathematics, Japan
Takashi Onoda	Aoyama Gakuin University, Japan
Tohid Shekari	Georgia Tech, USA
Ryan Shah	University of Strathclyde, UK
Yoriyuki Yamagata	AIST, Japan
Riccardo Taormina	TU Delft, the Netherlands
Takeshi Sugawara	The University of Electro-Communications, Japan

CIMSS 2021

First ACNS Workshop on Critical Infrastructure and Manufacturing System Security

June 21, 2021

Program Chairs

Chenglu Jin	CWI Amsterdam, the Netherlands
Michail Maniatakos	New York University Abu Dhabi, UAE

Publicity Chair

Zheng Yang	SUTD, Singapore

Program Committee

Irfan Ahmed	Virginia Commonwealth University, USA
Mohammad Al Faruque	University of California Irvine, USA
Cristina Alcaraz	University of Malaga, Spain
Binbin Chen	SUTD, Singapore
Long Cheng	Clemson University, USA
Soumyajit Dey	Indian Institute of Technology, Kharagpur, India
Jairo Giraldo	University of Utah, USA
Charalambos Konstantinou	Florida State University, USA
Andres Murillo	SUTD, Singapore
Awais Rashid	University of Bristol, UK
Marco Rocchetto	V-Research, Italy
Carlos Rubio-Medrano	Texas A&M University - Corpus Christi, USA
Alexandru Stefanov	Delft University of Technology, the Netherlands
Riccardo Taormina	Delft University of Technology, the Netherlands
Richard J. Thomas	University of Birmingham, UK
Nektarios Tsoutsos	University of Delaware, USA
Edgar Weippl	SBA Research, Austria
Mark Yampolskiy	Auburn University, USA
Zheng Yang	SUTD, Singapore
Stefano Zanero	Politecnico di Milano, Italy
Saman Zonouz	Rutgers University, USA

CLOUD S&P 2021

Third ACNS Workshop on Cloud Security and Privacy

June 24, 2021

SCI 2021

Second ACNS Workshop on Secure Cryptographic Implementation

June 23, 2021

Program Chairs

Jingqiang Lin	University of Science and Technology of China, China
Bo Luo	The University of Kansas, USA

Publication Chair

Jun Shao	Zhejiang Gongshang University, China

Publicity Chairs

Le Guan	University of Georgia, USA
Debiao He	Wuhan University, China

Program Committee

Bo Chen	Michigan Technological University, USA
Fu Chen	Central University of Finance and Economics, China
Jiankuo Dong	Nanjing University of Posts and Telecommunications, China
Johann Großschädl	University of Luxembourg, Luxembourg
Le Guan	University of Georgia, USA
Debiao He	Wuhan University, China
Bingyu Li	Beihang University, China
Fengjun Li	The University of Kansas, USA
Di Ma	ZDNS, China
Yuan Ma	Chinese Academy of Sciences, China
Jun Shao	Zhejiang Gongshang University, China
Ruisheng Shi	Beijing University of Posts and Telecommunications, China
Zhiguo Wan	Shandong University, China
Ding Wang	Nankai University, China
Juan Wang	Wuhan University, China
Jun Xu	Stevens Institute of Technology, USA
Li Yang	Xidian University, China
Fan Zhang	Zhejiang University, China
Fangyu Zheng	Chinese Academy of Sciences, China

Additional Reviewers

Yanbin Li	Nanjing Agricultural University, China
Zhen Zhou	Wuhan University, China
Haoyang An	Wuhan University, China

SecMT 2021

Second ACNS Workshop on Security in Mobile Technologies

June 23, 2021

Program Chairs

Eleonora Losiouk	University of Padua, Italy
Olga Gadyatskaya	Leiden University, the Netherlands

Program Committee

Kevin Allix	University of Luxembourg, Luxembourg
Marco Casagrande	University of Padua, Italy
Lorenzo Cavallaro	King's College London, UK
Guozhu Meng	Institute of Information Engineering, Chinese Academy of Sciences, China
Veelasha Moonsamy	Ruhr University Bochum, Germany
Georgios Portokalidis	Stevens Institute of Technology, USA
Giovanni Russello	University of Auckland, New Zealand
Andrea Saracino	Consiglio Nazionale delle Ricerche, Italy
Riccardo Spolaor	Shandong University, China
Flavio Toffalini	Singapore University of Technology and Design, Singapore
Rolando Trujillo	Deakin University, Australia
Luca Verderame	University of Genova, Italy

SiMLA 2021

Third ACNS Workshop on Security in Machine Learning and its Applications

June 24, 2021

Program Chair

Sudipta Chattopadhyay	Singapore University of Technology and Design, Singapore

Web Chair

Sakshi Udeshi	Singapore University of Technology and Design, Singapore

Program Committee

Chris Poskitt	Singapore Management University, Singapore
Shuhao Zhang	Singapore University of Technology and Design, Singapore
Wenrui Diao	Shandong University, China
Jingyi Wang	Zhejiang University, China
Ezekiel Soremekun	University of Luxembourg, Luxembourg
Shuang Liu	Tianjin University, China
Kehuan Zhang	The Chinese University of Hong Kong, Hong Kong

Contents

AIBlock - Application Intelligence and Blockchain Security

AIHWS - Artificial Intelligence in Hardware Security

AIoTS - Artificial Intelligence and Industrial IoT Security

CIMSS - Critical Infrastructure and Manufacturing System Security

Cloud S&P - Cloud Security and Privacy

SCI -Secure Cryptographic Implementation

Short Paper

AIBlock - Application Intelligence and Blockchain Security

Shaping Blockchain Technology for Securing Supply Chains

Yong Zhi Lim[1,2(✉)], Jianying Zhou[1], and Martin Saerbeck[2]

[1] Singapore University of Technology and Design, Singapore, Singapore
yongzhi_lim@mymail.sutd.edu.sg, jianying_zhou@sutd.edu.sg

[2] Digital Service Centre of Excellence, TÜV SÜV Asia Pacific, Singapore, Singapore
{yong-zhi.lim,martin.saerbeck}@tuvsud.com

Abstract. Purchases in supply chains involve a network of suppliers, manufacturers, logistics or even customers needed for the procurement of goods or services. These are needed to operate a supply chain efficiently and allow timely deliverables to consumers. In our work, we identify and map a typical business process to demonstrate how we can securely allow participants to interact with smart contracts and discover potential use cases for supply chains.

Keywords: Blockchain · Smart contracts · Supply chains

1 Introduction

The rise of Blockchain is arguably attributed to the use of *Bitcoin* for financial transactions. It currently has the world's highest market cap and is the costliest cryptocurrency to date [1]. Its hype has evolved over the past decade and seen the rise of different consensus algorithms, with claims of providing higher hash rates and transactions per second.

As businesses continue to embrace and migrate towards digitization of services, P2P DLT (peer-to-peer distributed ledger technology) or blockchain plays a crucial role and has seen growing interest in adapting it with discovery and deployment of potential use cases in the supply chain sector.

Supply chains, used interchangeably with Supply Chain Management (SCM), is a network of carriers and sellers to allow procurement of goods or services to buyers. This process is constantly optimized over time to save costs and allows for a quicker production cycle.

Cryptocurrencies are not the only reason for the adoption of blockchain technology. A blockchain-enabled supply chain will provide security, transparency, authenticity and trustworthiness [19]. However, the technology is not entirely foolproof, being susceptible to various attacks. This creates a barrier for any supply chain wishing to adapt blockchains. We study existing industry standards to identify and adopt best practices to protect the blockchain.

J. Zhou et al. (Eds.): ACNS 2021 Workshops, LNCS 12809, pp. 3–18, 2021.
https://doi.org/10.1007/978-3-030-81645-2_1

Previous studies which have claimed to successfully deploy a blockchain in supply chains are private in nature, due to the usage of a permissioned blockchain [6]. On the contrary, this defeats the purpose of transparency despite transactions being traceable and with little to none industry-specific knowledge for secure implementation by other parties. To date, most literature describe the benefits of deploying a blockchain but with a lack of practical implementations.

In this paper, we include the identification and mapping of a typical business process to demonstrate how an electronic bill of lading (eBL), which bridges several standards, coded in *Solidity* that allows participants in *Ethereum* to interact with smart contracts and discover potential use cases for supply chains. We also identify current attacks on smart contracts and challenges ahead.

2 Background

2.1 Current State of Purchases in Supply Chains

Purchases in supply chains involve a network of suppliers, manufacturers, logistics or even customers needed for the procurement of goods or services. From the procurement of raw materials, these are needed to operate a supply chain efficiently and allow timely deliverables to consumers. Figure 1 briefly shows how a supply chain perform procurement of raw materials that is supplied by its vendors, going through several processes to manufacture and package the goods, before transportation and reaching out to its consumers.

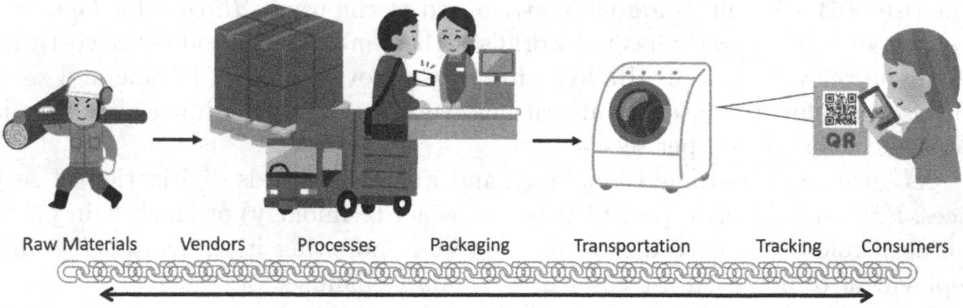

Fig. 1. A Typical Supply Chain Process. Images under free-use from https://www.irasutoya.com by Takashi Mifune

2.2 Procure-to-Pay Process

A typical procure-to-pay process in supply chains (reflected in Fig. 2) generally consist of the following procedures involving 3 parties, the buyer $\mathbb{B}$, seller $\mathbb{S}$ and carrier $\mathbb{C}$:

1. $\mathbb{B}$'s purchasing department creates a Purchase Order (PO) in its ERP (Enterprise Resource Planning) system and sends it to $\mathbb{S}$. The PO contains important information on:
   (a) Items for purchase (item description, item part number, order quantity, unit price, currency, total value, discounts, etc.)
   (b) Delivery instructions (delivery address, delivery date, incoterms, etc.)
   (c) Procurement references (purchase requisition number, quotation number, etc.)
   (d) Other information (buyer and seller information, payment terms, etc.)
2. $\mathbb{S}$ acknowledges receipt and acceptance of the PO by returning a signed copy to $\mathbb{B}$.
3. $\mathbb{S}$ prepares the item together with a copy of the Delivery Order (DO) and Packing List (PL). Upon notice from $\mathbb{S}$, $\mathbb{C}$ arranges for shipment. $\mathbb{C}$ also shares a copy of the Air Waybill (AWB) or the Bill of Lading (BL) with $\mathbb{S}$.
4. Once the item is delivered to the designated address in $\mathbb{B}$'s warehouse, the warehouse personnel then inspects item and tallies it with the DO. The DO is signed physically to acknowledge receipt of the item that it is in good order and condition. The Goods Receipt (GR) is also done in $\mathbb{B}$'s ERP system.
5. $\mathbb{S}$ sends a copy of the invoice to $\mathbb{B}$'s purchasing department. Some business practices may require additional approval on the invoice depending on the $\mathbb{B}$'s internal processes.
6. The invoice is then submitted to $\mathbb{B}$'s accounting department for processing. The accounting personnel checks and verifies invoice against the GR and PO information, which is part of the *three-way matching process*. The invoice is recorded in $\mathbb{B}$'s ERP system and contains information such as billing name and address, delivery address, invoice number and date, PO number, payment terms, item description and part number, quantity, unit price, currency, item amount, tax amount, $\mathbb{S}$'s bank information, etc.
7. Lastly, the invoice is scheduled and due for payment according to agreed payment terms. $\mathbb{B}$'s accounting personnel prepares and processes payment by cash, checks or bank transfers after approved internally. A copy of the payment detail/advice is sent to $\mathbb{S}$ to match receipts.

Standards. According to the United States Code of Federal Regulations (CFR) Title 49, the bill of lading (BL) is a critical document that legally binds the buyer and seller with all relevant shipment information (e.g. addresses, reference numbers, shipping mark, etc.) [3,28]. As we push towards standardizations, alignment with the UNCITRAL (United Nations Commission on International Trade Law) Model Law on Electronic Transferable Records (MLETR) is crucial to ensure a common acceptance and quicker adoption by all [14].

Trade Terms. Better known as International Commercial Terms (Incoterms), trade terms are globally recognized terms by the International Chamber of Commence (ICC) for international trade [15]. It provides rules for trading and the sale of goods. In its most current iteration, ICC has defined 11 terms: *Ex-Works*

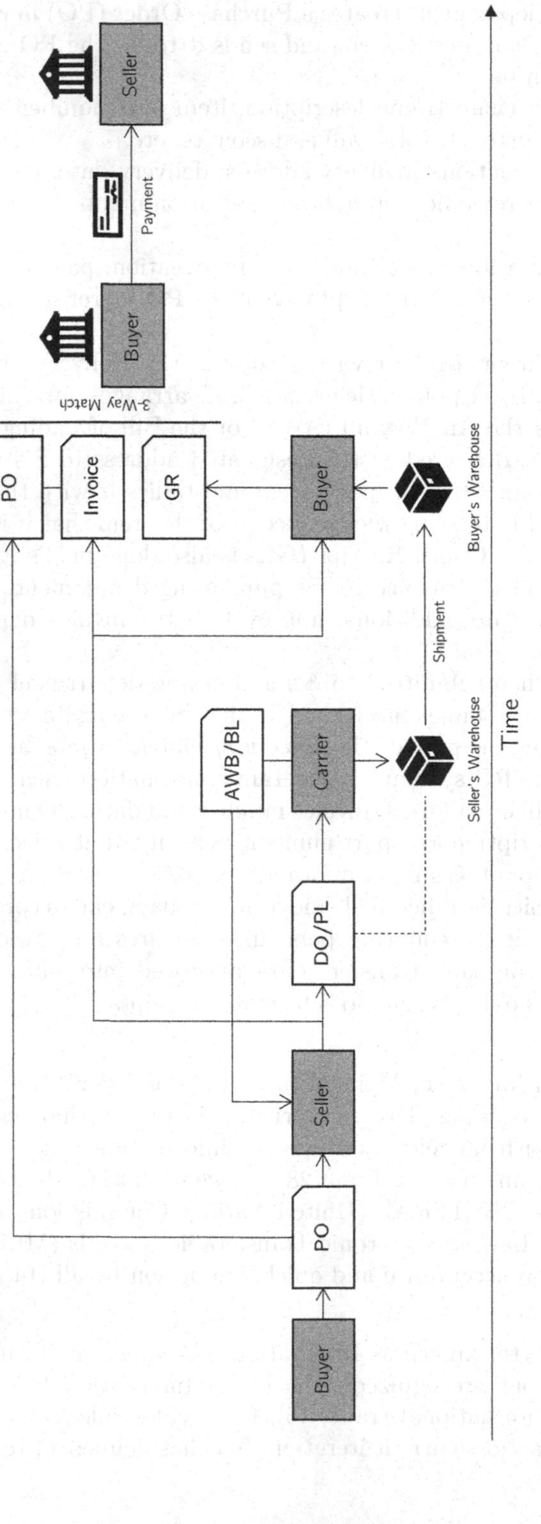

Fig. 2. A Typical Procure-to-Pay Process in the Supply Chain

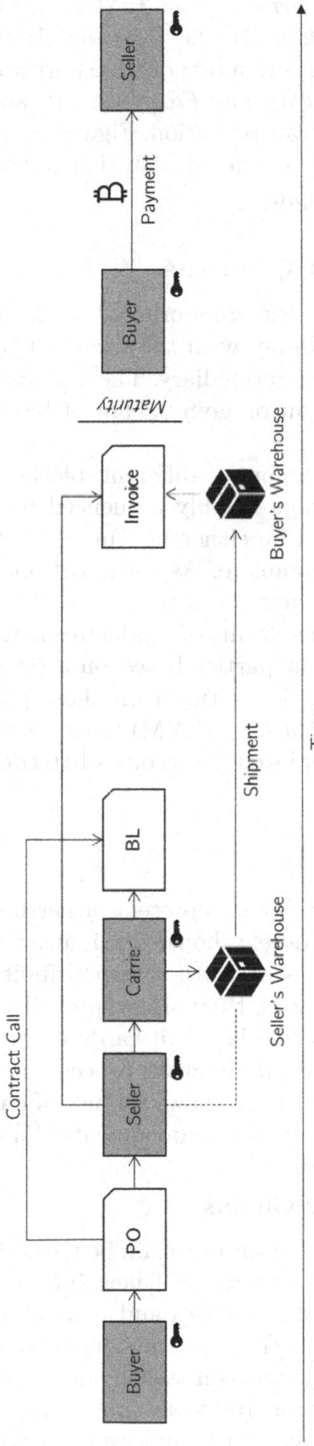

Fig. 3. A Blockchain-Enabled Process in the Supply Chain

(EXW), *Free Carrier* (FCA), *Carriage Paid To* (CPT), *Carriage And Insurance Paid To* (CIP), *Delivered At Place* (DAP), *Delivered At Place Unloaded* (DPU), *Delivered Duty Paid* (DDP) for any mode of transport and *Free Alongside Ship* (FAS), *Free On Board* (FOB), *Cost and Freight* (CFR) and *Cost, Insurance and Freight* (CIF) for sea & inland transportation. Figure 4 clearly indicates the rules which define the liabilities and transfer of risk that fall between the buyer and seller should an issue with shipping arise.

2.3 Blockchain and Smart Contracts

Although not made explicit in *Bitcoin*'s original work, a blockchain claims to facilitate a secure payment gateway with the use of digital signatures between parties, without the need of an intermediary. These transactions are then timestamped and hashed to create an on-going chain of blocks, hoping to outpace attackers [35].

The differentiating factor amongst different blockchains is perhaps their choice of smart contract language. Highly influenced by *Javascript*, it aims to have high readability and could be either be Turing (*Solidity* in *Ethereum*) or non-Turing (*Bitcoin* Scripts) complete. As such, *Bitcoin* does not allow loops, recursion or termination by its own.

Smart contracts are electronic forms of legal agreements which can automate decisions made between different parties based on a set of promises, including protocols within which the parties perform on these promises [42]. *Ethereum* deploys the *Ethereum Virtual Machine* (EVM) to execute these scripts. Once its source code is compiled and deployed, it becomes bytecode and is stored on the blockchan for retrieval.

2.4 Non-Fungible Tokens

Widely known as *ERC-721*, NFTs can represent ownership over digital (e.g. virtual collectables), physical assets (e.g. houses, unique artwork) or even negative value assets (e.g. loans, burdens and other responsibilities) [45]. An example first implemented by *CryptoKitties*, they are cryptocollectibles which represent a real-world analogy to assets like baseball cards or fine art [22]. In our use case, documents involved in the supply chain process, such as the bill of lading (BL) can be represented as a NFT. It allows the use of `safeTransfer`, `approve` functions and tracking of distinguishable documents [45].

2.5 Blockchain for Supply Chains

Can the use of smart contracts in a supply chain be trusted by its buyers, carriers and sellers? In today's digital age, we still lack information sharing between organizations due to centralized databases and manual exchanges of electronic documents. Supply chains can leverage on the benefits of a blockchain to enable greater speed and transparency between stakeholders. We introduce the use of smart contracts to disrupt the procure-to-pay process in supply chains. However, current threats on smart contracts exists and we must address them.

Incoterm		Transfer of Risk	Liabilities											
			Export Packaging	Loading Charges	Delivery to Port/Place	Export Duty, Taxes & Custom Clearance	Origin Terminal Charges	Loading on Carriage	Carriage Charges	Insurance	Destination Terminal Charges	Delivery to Destination	Unloading at Destination	Import Duty, Taxes & Custom Clearance
Any Mode of Transport														
Ex-Works	EXW	At Buyer's Disposal	S	B	B	B	B	B	B	*	B	B	B	B
Free Carrier	FCA	On Buyer's Transport	S	S	S	S	B	B	B	*	B	B	B	B
Carriage Paid To	CPT	At Carrier	S	S	S	S	S	S	S	*	S	B	B	B
Carriage And Insurance Paid To	CIP	At Carrier	S	S	S	S	S	S	S	S	S	B	B	B
Delivered At Place	DAP	At Named Place	S	S	S	S	S	S	S	*	S	S	B	B
Delivered At Place Unloaded	DPU	At Named Placed Unloaded	S	S	S	S	S	S	S	*	S	S	S	B
Delivered Duty Paid	DDP	At Named Place	S	S	S	S	S	S	S	*	S	S	B	S
Sea & Inland Transportation														
Free Alongside Ship	FAS	Alongside Ship	S	S	S	S	S	B	B	*	B	B	B	B
Free On Board	FOB	Onboard Vessel	S	S	S	S	S	S	B	*	B	B	B	B
Cost and Freight	CFR	Onboard Vessel	S	S	S	S	S	S	S	*	B	B	B	B
Cost, Insurance and Freight	CIF	Onboard Vessel	S	S	S	S	S	S	S	S	S	B	B	B

B: Buyer
S: Seller
Asterisk: Negotiable

Fig. 4. Incoterms 2020

3 Design and Implementation

To fully automate the procure-to-pay process in supply chains on the blockchain, we introduce `supplyInvoice`, a smart contract. We show the proposed simplified process in Fig. 3 should a blockchain be deployed for the supply chain. As such, all required information should be obtained from the bill of lading (BL). The BL and invoice are forms of NFTs, which tags itself as a digitized legal document on the blockchain.

Current known open implementations with eBL or invoices exists in [10] and [4] using *Solidity* but not with any standardization, tokenization or use with trade terms.

With specified trade terms in the BL, `supplyInvoice` is able to automatically execute the liabilities should a problem in the shipping process occur. This punishes parties once the liability falls under them and the goods have been transferred (e.g. goods have left seller, goods out for delivery). Several assumptions are made to complete this process: 1) parties perform immediate monetary transfer (no delayed payment terms), 2) no involvement of escrows (third-party) and 3) only honest parties are involved.

3.1 Data Structures

Order. contains necessary information to facilitate communication, payment and successful shipment of goods between the buyer $\mathbb{B}$, seller $\mathbb{S}$ and carrier $\mathbb{C}$. The following structure contains:

- `buyer` address to digital wallet to facilitate payment
- `seller` address to digital wallet to facilitate payment
- `referenceNumber` an unique identifier to allow tracing and easy reference
- `tradeTerms` stipulated in Sect. 2.2 to clearly define liabilities
- `shippingMark` an identifier labelled on the shipped product

3.2 Business Logic

Mapping `supplyInvoice` described in Sect. 2.2, the following function prototypes provide a simplified process to complete a typical procure-to-pay process for interaction in the blockchain.

- `createOrder` is created by $\mathbb{B}$ for the initial order and prompts to populate all necessary fields in the `order` struct to facilitate procurement of goods or services.
- `createInvoice` acknowledges the newly created order and prompts $\mathbb{S}$ to prepare goods for shipment. Prepare payment for $\mathbb{C}$.
- `createLading` is created by $\mathbb{C}$ the BL for the shipping process.
- `assignTradeTerms` assigns the rules and define liabilities between $\mathbb{B}$ and $\mathbb{S}$.
- `negotiateTradeTerms` negotiates specific liabilities between $\mathbb{B}$ and $\mathbb{S}$ for negotiable incoterms stipulated in Fig. 4.

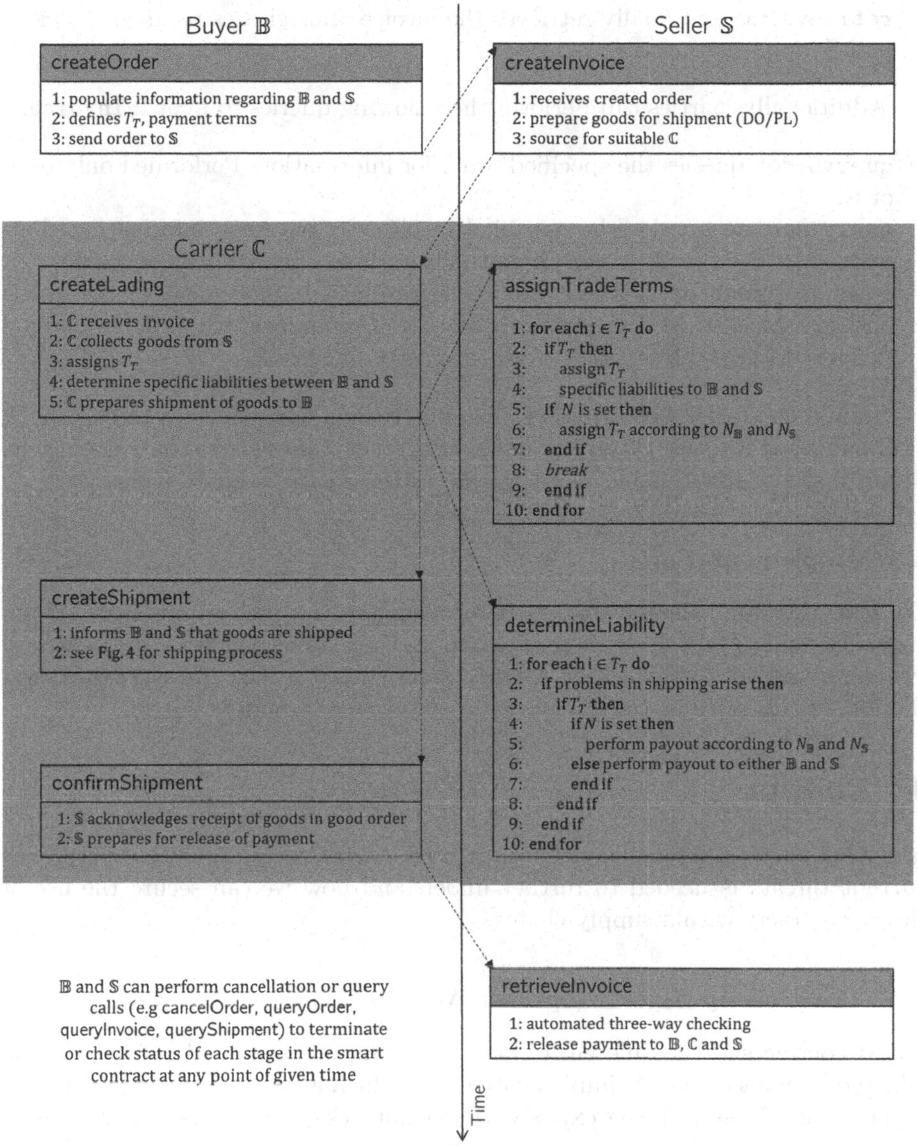

Fig. 5. Automated process in `supplyInvoice` involving 3 different parties, buyer 𝔹, seller 𝕊 and carrier ℂ. A solid line is represented with time, whereas dotted lines represent a typical flow occurring in the smart contract.

- `determineLiability` determines the final liability, should an issue with the shipping occur.
- `confirmShipment` confirms the completion of the shipping process, provided 𝕊 acknowledges receipt of the goods in good order.

- `retrieveInvoice` finally retrieves the invoice and releases payment for $\mathbb{B}$, $\mathbb{C}$ and $\mathbb{S}$, upon maturity.

Additionally, parties can perform the following queries to `supplyInvoice`:

- `queryOrder` queries the specified order for information. Performed only by $\mathbb{B}$ or $\mathbb{S}$.
- `queryInvoice` queries the specified invoice for payment information. Performed by $\mathbb{B}$, $\mathbb{C}$ or $\mathbb{S}$. Access is mutually exclusive between these parties.
- `queryShipment` obtains information regarding the movement of the goods and at which stage is it currently at (e.g. Preparation for export, loading, delivery to port/place, etc.). Performed only by $\mathbb{B}$ or $\mathbb{S}$.

Should the order fail to materialize due to non-agreement of terms, the $\mathbb{B}$ or $\mathbb{S}$ can issue a cancellation via `cancelOrder` or `cancelInvoice` respectively. Figure 5 shows how this business logic is carried out between $\mathbb{B}$, $\mathbb{C}$ and $\mathbb{S}$.

3.3 Implementation

To test this implementation, we wrote `supplyInvoice` in *Solidity.*[1] Using *Ganache* and *Truffle*, we were able to test its functionalities in a private *Ethereum* network. To further solidify security, we utilize the `SafeMath` and the `ERC721` libraries in *OpenZeppelin* to ensure best practices [7].

4 Threats

Although such an implementation may seem robust, a comprehensive study of current threats is needed to further understand how we can secure the use of smart contracts within supply chains.

4.1 Analysis on Smart Contract Attacks

Smart contracts are no different from a usual computer application. They can be affected by bugs or poorly implemented code which allow attackers to exploit or bypass rules. Despite being exposed to cyberattacks in the past, the *Ethereum* blockchain sets an example of a robust and secure network. It is covered in many peer-reviewed research with its security vulnerabilities documented in great detail. Past attacks include The Decentralized Autonomous Organization (*TheDAO*) attack [44] and the Parity Wallet hack [38] were key examples of reentrancy and access control issues that costed *11.5M ETH* (50M USD in 2016) and *150k ETH* (30M USD in 2017) respectively.

Additional vulnerabilities include arithmetic issues (integer underflow or overflow), unchecked return calls, denial of service (DoS), pseudo-randomness, front-running, timestamp dependence and off-chain issues [36]. In light of these

[1] https://github.com/limyz/supplyInvoice.

issues, researchers are tackling these vulnerabilities by analysing the bytecode statically or dynamically or through the study of current transactions performed in *Ethereum*. Many overlapping vulnerabilities which these tools can solve proves the difficulty working between *Solidity* and EVM bytecode.

Static Analysis is performed prior to deployment as bytecode to the EVM. *Oyente*, uses symbolic execution to check for transaction-ordering, timestamp dependence, mishandled exceptions and reentrancy [32]. *ZEUS* uses formal verification for analyzing safety properties of smart contracts [30]. *Maian* checks for unrestricted smart contract actions [37]. *Securify* on the other hand, checks security properties of the EVM bytecode of smart contracts [43]. *Vandal* introduces a framework for detecting security vulnerabilities in smart contract bytecode rapidly, outperforming Oyente, EthIR [18], Mythril [34], and Rattle [41]. *Vandal* extracts logic relations from smart contract bytecode for logic-based analysis [20]. *ETHBMC* is able to capture inter-contract relations, cryptographic hash functions, and memcopy-style operations in smart contracts and claims to be faster than Maian and teEther [23].

Dynamic Analysis is performed at runtime after deployment to the EVM. *ContractFuzzer* uses fuzzing, restricted to the Application Binary Interface (ABI) specifications to find vulnerabilities in smart contracts [29]. *Sereum* prevent reentrancy attacks without requiring any semantic knowledge of the contract [40]. *ECfChecker* dynamically checks if the Effectively Callback Free (ECF) object is feasible and executable [26]. *teEther* actively locates an exploit for a contract given only its binary bytecode [31]. More recently, *TXSPECTOR* [47] and [17] leverages on *Datalog*, a language implementing first-order logic with recursion [27], which allows scalability to detect smart contract vulnerabilities.

Furthermore, an evolving online approach to detect smart contracts attacks include *SODA*, which developed 8 applications containing attack detection methods exploiting major vulnerabilities [21] and *EVMPatch*, which features a bytecode rewriting engine which hardens smart contracts [16].

Despite having research directions dictating the discovery and protection of vulnerabilities in smart contracts, it is still difficult to prevent zero-day vulnerabilities from occurring. Potential research directions in smart contracts analysis is growing and desired to further make the use of them secure.

4.2 Privacy Concerns

NFTs are not enumerable as a private registry of property ownership, or a partially-private registry. As such, privacy cannot be attained because an attacker can simply call `ownerOf` for every possible `tokenId` [45].

However, there is a trade-off in between determining privacy, transparency and the choice of processing these off-chain or the use of permissioned blockchains. By leveraging on existing standards for digitalization of documents in Sect. 2.2, use of such an implementation promotes openness and quicker adoption as supposed to a permissioned blockchain; where only invited users are allowed access. Future implementations to *Eth2* may provide a more robust implementation to increase privacy using zero-knowledge proofs such as *zk-SNARKs* (Zero-Knowledge Succinct Non-Interactive Argument of Knowledge, used in *ZCash*) or *zk-STACKs* (Zero-Knowledge Succinct Transparent Argument of Knowledge) [13].

5 Challenges

Despite growing threats, several challenges also exist in overcoming barriers for the adoption of blockchains in businesses, specifically discovering use cases for supply chains.

5.1 Rising Gas Costs

Gas fees exist in *Ethereum* to help keep the network secure by charging a fee for every computation that is executed. This prevents accidental or intentional infinite loops or other computational wastage and serves as a limit to the number of computational steps of code it can execute. Denoted in *Gwei*, each *Gwei* is equal to 10^{-9} *ETH* [5].

As of writing, average gas costs having risen over 700% to almost 200 *Gwei* from over a year ago [46]. This makes written smart contacts with large number of lines of code computationally expensive and impractical for execution in the network. Despite having *MadMax* to detect gas-focused vulnerabilities [25], *EIP-1559* will include a transaction pricing mechanism that dynamically expands/contracts block sizes along with the introduction of *Eth2* [2]. As *Ethereum* is currently in transition towards *Eth2*, we have yet to see how this will greatly affect implementations [11].

Additionally, permissioned blockchains may choose not to employ costing to deploy smart contracts onto the network. This may be counterintuitive for an already invited small pool of users in a permissioned blockchain to constantly innovate due to the lack of rewards. Implementations within a permissioned blockchain may not be easily audited or standardized since it is not made known to the public domain. A comparison with cost may prove difficult but permissioned blockchains do not have digital currencies and means to transact directly.

5.2 Integration

As smart contracts require a definite solution, it is difficult to code in accordance to current regulatory obligations, governance or standards that needs interpretability by humans.

Overall Security in Blockchain. As mentioned earlier in Sect. 4, tackling the security of smart contacts is simply a part of the blockchain ecosystem. We will need to study and consider the greater impact of verifying the source of the information that is being recorded into the blockchain [39] and the growing concern of APTs (Advanced Persistent Threats) [9].

Interoperability with ERP Systems. *SAP SE*, a german multinational company popularly known for its ERP software, has various application programming interfaces (APIs) with which one can access data within its systems [8]. However, in its community forums, *SAP* has limited smart contract functionality with *Hyperledger Fabric* or *Multichain* and has seen obsolescence [33]. This further challenges how interactivity and exchanges can occur between deeply ingrained proprietary accounting systems and evolving blockchain technologies.

Unique Use Cases. Although the presented workflow may apply to most common supply chains, customization might be required to better fit use cases. Such implementations may include custom clearances, dangerous goods, insurance claims, taxation or any additional special rules or regulations. The existing smart contract can be modified and extended so it can be upgraded while preserving their address, state, and balance [12].

5.3 Cross-Contracts on Different Blockchains

Even though the electronic bill of lading (eBL) can be adopted into a non-fungible token (NFT), some blockchains may not be capable of accepting such tokens due to non-compliance of the *ERC-721* standard. This also includes the deployment of smart contracts, which different blockchains require to be rewritten into another language for proper compilation and use. A possible direction for this is to utilize the *Inter-Blockchain Communication* (IBC) protocol in *Cosmos* [24].

5.4 Framework

There is a current lack of an agnostic framework which determines the characteristics of deploying a secure blockchain in the supply chain. Potential metrics could cover feasibility, performance and pruning requirements.

6 Conclusion

Our work has demonstrated how we can map a typical business process to the *Ethereum* blockchain by writing smart contracts in *Solidity*. This agnostic approach not only provides a secure supply chain but also simplifies and automates several processes to facilitate greater transparency and ease of access to various parties via the use of smart contracts. We identified existing problems and challenges for adoption and also provide potential future research directions to enable blockchain for supply chains.

References

1. BTCBUSD—Binance Spot. https://www.binance.com/en/trade/BTC_BUSD
2. EIP-1559 - Fee market change for ETH 1.0 chain. https://github.com/ethereum/EIPs/blob/master/EIPS/eip-1559.md
3. Electronic Code of Federal Regulations (eCFR). https://www.ecfr.gov/cgi-bin/text-idx?SID=6885de90742b035794f3c377745ff932&mc=true&node=pt49.5.375&rgn=div5
4. fabiojose/ethereum-ex. https://github.com/fabiojose/ethereum-ex
5. Gas and fees—ethereum.org. https://ethereum.org/en/developers/docs/gas/
6. IBM Food Trust - Blockchain for the world's food supply. https://www.ibm.com/blockchain/solutions/food-trust
7. OpenZeppelin. https://openzeppelin.com
8. SAP API Business Hub. https://api.sap.com
9. Security Advisory for SolarWinds. https://www.solarwinds.com/securityadvisory
10. Smart0tter/tradefinance. https://github.com/Smart0tter/TradeFinance
11. The Eth2 upgrades—ethereum.org. https://ethereum.org/en/eth2/
12. Upgrading smart contracts - OpenZeppelin Docs. https://docs.openzeppelin.com/learn/upgrading-smart-contracts
13. ZK-STARKs - EthHub. https://docs.ethhub.io/ethereum-roadmap/layer-2-scaling/zk-starks/
14. UNCITRAL Model Law on Electronic Transferable Records—United Nations Commission On International Trade Law (2017). https://uncitral.un.org/en/texts/ecommerce/modellaw/electronic_transferable_records
15. Incoterms 2020 - ICC - International Chamber of Commerce (2020). https://iccwbo.org/resources-for-business/incoterms-rules/incoterms-2020/
16. EVMPatch: timely and automated patching of ethereum smart contracts. In: 30th USENIX Security Symposium (USENIX Security 21). USENIX Association, Vancouver, B.C., August 2021. https://www.usenix.org/conference/usenixsecurity21/presentation/rodler
17. Smart contract vulnerabilities: vulnerable does not imply exploited. In: 30th USENIX Security Symposium (USENIX Security 21). USENIX Association, Vancouver, B.C., August 2021. https://www.usenix.org/conference/usenixsecurity21/presentation/perez
18. Albert, E., Gordillo, P., Livshits, B., Rubio, A., Sergey, I.: EthIR: a framework for high-level analysis of ethereum bytecode. CoRR abs/1805.07208 (2018). http://arxiv.org/abs/1805.07208
19. Azzi, R., Chamoun, R.K., Sokhn, M.: The power of a blockchain-based supply chain. Comput. Ind. Eng. **135**, 582–592 (2019)
20. Brent, L., et al.: Vandal: a scalable security analysis framework for smart contracts. CoRR abs/1809.03981 (2018). http://arxiv.org/abs/1809.03981
21. Chen, T., et al.: SODA: a generic online detection framework for smart contracts. In: 27th Annual Network and Distributed System Security Symposium, NDSS 2020, San Diego, California, USA, 23–26 February 2020. The Internet Society (2020). https://www.ndss-symposium.org/ndss-paper/soda-a-generic-online-detection-framework-for-smart-contracts/
22. CryptoKitties: Cryptokitties—technical details. https://www.cryptokitties.co/technical-details

23. Frank, J., Aschermann, C., Holz, T.: ETHBMC: a bounded model checker for smart contracts. In: 29th USENIX Security Symposium (USENIX Security 20), pp. 2757–2774. USENIX Association, August 2020. https://www.usenix.org/conference/usenixsecurity20/presentation/frank
24. Goes, C.: The Interblockchain Communication Protocol: An Overview (2020)
25. Grech, N., Kong, M., Jurisevic, A., Brent, L., Scholz, B., Smaragdakis, Y.: Madmax: surviving out-of-gas conditions in ethereum smart contracts. Proc. ACM Program. Lang. **2**(OOPSLA) (2018). https://doi.org/10.1145/3276486
26. Grossman, S., et al.: Online detection of effectively callback free objects with applications to smart contracts. CoRR abs/1801.04032 (2018). http://arxiv.org/abs/1801.04032
27. Immerman, N.: Descriptive Complexity. Springer, Heidelberg (1999). https://doi.org/10.1007/978-1-4612-0539-5
28. International Cargo Express: Bill Of Lading Explained: The Complete Beginner's Guide (2019). https://www.icecargo.com.au/bill-of-lading
29. Jiang, B., Liu, Y., Chan, W.K.: ContractFuzzer: fuzzing smart contracts for vulnerability detection. In: Proceedings of the 33rd ACM/IEEE International Conference on Automated Software Engineering. ASE 2018, pp. 259–269. Association for Computing Machinery, New York (2018). https://doi.org/10.1145/3238147.3238177
30. Kalra, S., Goel, S., Dhawan, M., Sharma, S.: ZEUS: analyzing safety of smart contracts. In: 25th Annual Network and Distributed System Security Symposium, NDSS 2018, San Diego, California, USA, 18–21 February 2018. The Internet Society (2018). http://wp.internetsociety.org/ndss/wp-content/uploads/sites/25/2018/02/ndss2018_09-1_Kalra_paper.pdf
31. Krupp, J., Rossow, C.: Teether: gnawing at ethereum to automatically exploit smart contracts. In: 27th USENIX Security Symposium (USENIX Security 18), pp. 1317–1333. USENIX Association, Baltimore, MD, August 2018. https://www.usenix.org/conference/usenixsecurity18/presentation/krupp
32. Luu, L., Chu, D.H., Olickel, H., Saxena, P., Hobor, A.: Making smart contracts smarter. In: Proceedings of the 2016 ACM SIGSAC Conference on Computer and Communications Security. CCS 2016, pp. 254–269. Association for Computing Machinery, New York (2016). https://doi.org/10.1145/2976749.2978309
33. Misiorek, G.: SAP Hyperledger Retirement - SAP Q&A (2021). https://answers.sap.com/questions/13220261/sap-hyperledger-retirement.html
34. Mueller, B.: b-mueller/smashing-smart-contracts: Write-ups on security analysis of Ethereum smart contracts using symbolic execution and constraint solving (2018). https://github.com/b-mueller/smashing-smart-contracts
35. Nakamoto, S.: Bitcoin: a peer-to-peer electronic cash system. Technical report, Manubot (2019). https://git.dhimmel.com/bitcoin-whitepaper
36. NCC Group: Decentralized Application Security Project (DASP) - Top 10 (2018). https://dasp.co/
37. Nikolic, I., Kolluri, A., Sergey, I., Saxena, P., Hobor, A.: Finding the greedy, prodigal, and suicidal contracts at scale. CoRR abs/1802.06038 (2018). http://arxiv.org/abs/1802.06038
38. Palladino, S.: The Parity Wallet Hack Explained - OpenZeppelin blog (2017). https://blog.openzeppelin.com/on-the-parity-wallet-multisig-hack-405a8c12e8f7/
39. Reyna, A., Martín, C., Chen, J., Soler, E., Díaz, M.: On blockchain and its integration with IoT. Challenges and opportunities. Future Gener. Comput. Syst. **88**, 173–190 (2018). https://doi.org/10.1016/j.future.2018.05.046, https://www.sciencedirect.com/science/article/pii/S0167739X17329205

40. Rodler, M., Li, W., Karame, G.O., Davi, L.: Sereum: protecting existing smart contracts against re-entrancy attacks (2018). http://arxiv.org/abs/1812.05934
41. Stortz, R.: crytic/rattle: evm binary static analysis. https://github.com/crytic/rattle
42. Szabo, N.: Smart contracts: building blocks for digital markets. https://www.fon.hum.uva.nl/rob/Courses/InformationInSpeech/CDROM/Literature/LOTwinterschool2006/szabo.best.vwh.net/smart_contracts_2.html
43. Tsankov, P., Dan, A., Drachsler-Cohen, D., Gervais, A., Bünzli, F., Vechev, M.: Securify: practical security analysis of smart contracts. In: Proceedings of the 2018 ACM SIGSAC Conference on Computer and Communications Security. CCS 2018, pp. 67–82. Association for Computing Machinery, New York (2018). https://doi.org/10.1145/3243734.3243780
44. Vessenes, P.: Deconstructing the DAO attack: A brief code tour (2016). https://vessenes.com/deconstructing-thedao-attack-a-brief-code-tour/
45. Entriken, W., Shirley, D., Evans, J., Sachs, N.: EIP-721: ERC-721 Non-Fungible Token Standard. https://eips.ethereum.org/EIPS/eip-721
46. YCharts: Ethereum Average Gas Price. https://ycharts.com/indicators/ethereum_average_gas_price
47. Zhang, M., Zhang, X., Zhang, Y., Lin, Z.: TXSPECTOR: uncovering attacks in ethereum from transactions. In: 29th USENIX Security Symposium (USENIX Security 20), pp. 2775–2792. USENIX Association, August 2020. https://www.usenix.org/conference/usenixsecurity20/presentation/zhang-mengya

The Obfuscation Method of User Identification System

Jing Xu[1](✉), Fei Xu[2], and Chi Xu[3]

[1] School of Computer and Communication Engineering, University of Science and Technology Beijing, Beijing, China
xj2018@ustb.edu.cn

[2] China Center for International Economic Exchanges, Beijing, China

[3] China Merchants Bank, Beijing, China

Abstract. The research on the identification of network users has been continuous, and methods and algorithms emerge in endlessly. Of course, it solves the problem that it is difficult to identify the identity of network interactive users. Yet, user identification raises questions about user privacy. In the last paper [[, we proposed a user identification method based on Mining Web Usage Profiles from Proxy Logs. For the previous user identification system, we study that which degree the surfing behavior must be obfuscated to prevent identification. Furthermore, we investigate directions in how far a user can hide her identity by obfuscating her web usage pattern through adding or hiding random HTTP connections. In experimental evaluation, we examine the time-period being necessary to obfuscate an identity based on a two-week log file being provided by our industrial partners.

Keywords: User identification · Additive · Subtractive · Obfuscation

1 Introduction

Surfing the World Wide Web (WWW) and using other HTTP-based services is one of the most common applications of connected devices such as personal computers and smart phones. A user connects to a variety of HTTP services and web sites. In last paper [1], we explore the thesis that the portfolio of HTTP connections can be used as an individual fingerprint which allows to reveal the identity of a user.in this paper, we study how to confuse user identity and protect their privacy under this condition.

The identification of users on the web has a plethora of applications, both beneficial, such as marketing and security applications, as well as detrimental applications jeopardizing the privacy of individuals.

For example, we might identify a user u that has recently booked a plane to Budapest who is interested in database research. This information might be used to direct targeted

This work funded by the Fundamental Research Funds for the University of Science and Technology Beijing under Grant FRF-TP-19-016A1 and the National Key R&D Plan Program of China (2019QY(Y)0601).

J. Zhou et al. (Eds.): ACNS 2021 Workshops, LNCS 12809, pp. 19–26, 2021.
https://doi.org/10.1007/978-3-030-81645-2_2

advertisements at that user, such as advertising specific hotels located in close vicinity to a corresponding research conference. In security applications, being able to find anomalies in user behavior can be used to identify misuse of user accounts. Consider an unauthorized individual pretending the identity of another user by stealing a password. In this case, a sudden, drastic and significant change of user behavior and interests may indicate that the account is misused and the account owner should be contacted on a safe channel to check the account and change the password. At the same time, the identification of users may put the identity of individuals at risk. For instance, by learning the behavior of user u, it might be possible to identify, and thus track the physical location, of u against their will.

In the previous work of user identification, we proposed a method to aggregate the proxy server logs into each user's Web usage profile, given a training data set of HTTP connections for which the corresponding user is known. We can use the learned Web usage profile to identify users accessing the web from a new unknown device. In this paper, for this kind of user identification method, in order to reduce the privacy threat brought by the user identification scheme, we study how to blur the web usage pattern, so as to prevent the identification of users in the scene of invasion of personal privacy.

The rest of the paper is organized as follows: Sect. 2 describes related work. Section 3 discusses privacy issues and provides solutions to obfuscate web usage profiles. The results of our experimental evaluation are described in Sect. 4. And in Sect. 5, we summarize our approach and name directions for future work.

2 Related Work

The authors of [2] use a clustering model gained from click stream patterns to classify new sessions. Their solution offers a more sophisticated approach to classify new user sessions having the same IP. In this work however, we assume that a session is simply defined by an IP address and a consecutive time window. The authors of [3, 4] use a heuristic to identify users over a larger period of time by taking advantage from the information in agent logs, e.g. The authors in [5] investigate user web search click streams on a larger scale by extracting client-side logs and reconstructing the users' query sessions. The log entries record the web traffic between a large research network and the Internet. In [6] the authors present a scalable platform based on a Hadoop cluster for click stream analysis. However, their evaluation is focused on session, i.e. the identification of user sessions and click counts by analyzing click streams. [7] Makes another Big Data approach. Their use-case is identifying incidents that might affect the network security utilizing log data created by network services and hosts including a web proxy server. In [8], they detect user access transactions from a proxy log file, in order to create web access prediction models.

The authors in [9] intend to preserve relationship privacy between two users one of whom can even be identified in the released OSN data. They define the l-diversity anonymization model to preserve users' relationship privacy and devise two algorithms to achieve the l-diversity anonymization - one only removes edges while the other only inserts vertices/edges for maintaining as many topological properties of the original social networks as possible, thus retaining the utility of the published data for the third-parties. In [10], they propose a location privacy obfuscation protocols, called Appointment Card Protocol (ACP), utilizing social ties between users. To facilitate the obfuscation operations of queries, we introduce the concept called Appointment Card (AC). [11] propose a secure distance comparison protocol. Furthermore, and present a privacy-preserving location-sharing scheme (PPLS), which allows users to build more complex access control policies.

In all of this article, if the same IP address is used for two different operating systems or browsers, it is assumed that two different users accessed the web sharing the same IP address. Our problem differs from theirs. Previously, we tried to identify users only based on their HTTP communication links, and on the basis of user identification method, we carried out fuzzy processing to prevent identification.

3 Obfuscation Method

In this section, we discuss the privacy aspect of user identification. Given that somebody has already constructed a web usage profile of a given user, it is possible to identify this user on any other device. For example, if a session being recorded by a tracking cookie is complete enough, a web usage profile can be used to predict the actual per-son currently surfing the net. While this is usually used to cater targeted advertisement tailored to the perceived interests to the user, more malicious applications are possible too. Besides the usual privacy concerns, stalking the web traffic, one can create a list of the services used and try to get access data. Knowing the web usage profile of a user can also be instrumented to implement a scoring system where certain interests defined via URLs and domain names are interpreted as positive or negative to the linked individual.

To mitigate these kinds of threats, we now want to examine methods to help the user to hide his or her identity. To make user identification more inaccurate, a user can obfuscate his behavior for sessions where he or she wants to be anonymous. Session obfuscation can be basically achieved by two approaches: adding additional (fake) HTTP connections or hiding HTTP connections.

3.1 Additive Obfuscation

In this approach, a user opens up additional HTTP connections to obfuscate his common pattern of web usage. Technically, this might be implemented by installing a browser addon that opens up a new HTTP connection to random websites from time to time. Let us note that browser addons are just an example how to do the obfuscation on a technical level. To hide the identity of the user, we should select target domains increasing the similarity to other users and access them sufficiently often to change the characteristic of the web usage profile of the current session. The drawback of this approach is that generates additional network traffic. We will measure the additional traffic as percentage of additional HTTP connections relative to the ordinary amount of connections in the session. Figure 1 depicts the principle of additive obfuscation. Formally, we describe the approach as follows (Fig. 2):

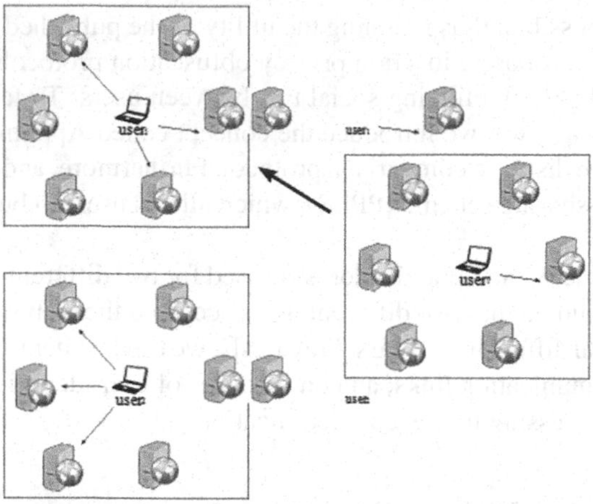

Fig. 1. Illustration on additive obfuscation-shows identification without obfuscation

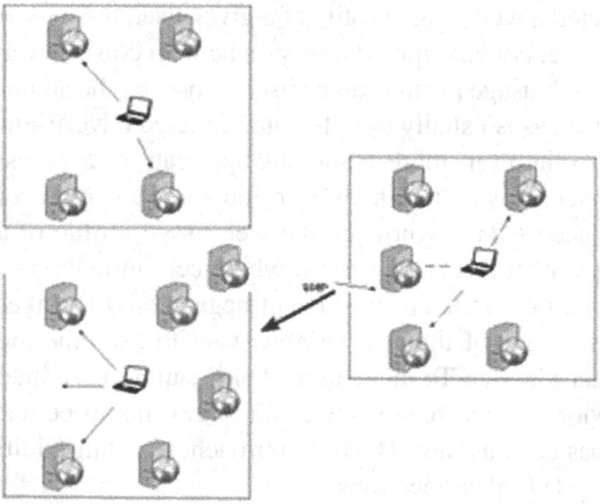

Fig. 2. Illustration on additive obfuscation-the session is obfuscated and therefore, misclassified

Definition 1 (Additive Obfuscation). Given a user identification function $I : DB^* \rightarrow u$ and given a new session $S(a, \tau)$ of user u_S having IP-address a during time interval τ.Let l be an integer denoting a budget of domains that can be added to $S(a, \tau)$ in order to mask the identity of u_S. The task of additive obfuscation is to find an obfuscated session $S_w(a, \tau)$ such that $I(S_w(a, \tau) \cup S(a, \tau)) \neq u_S$ subject to $S_w(a, \tau) \leq l$.

Obviously, the success of additive obfuscation depends on the set of compared web usage profiles. Given the number of additional HTTP connections l, we want to find a strategy maximizing the similarity to other user profiles. This strategy basically consists of two parts: choosing a set of suitable target hosts and deciding how much traffic is used for one host. Let us note that the points in time to access a target domain as well as the particular URL within the host might play a role to successful obfuscation in general.

However, we do not further follow these aspects because both problems do not play any role w.r.t. the methods for user identification in this paper. Furthermore, there are obvious technical solutions like mimicking the access frequencies in the original session and crawling within a domain to solve these problems.

The first interesting question when selecting a strategy is the selection of target hosts. We argue to use frequently visited domains, which can be found in public web access statistics. A frequent domain has a much higher probability to appear in the web usage profiles of other users and thus, adding a frequent domain should increase the similarity to more other users than a rare domain. Of course, we should not add traffic to any domain which is accessed by the user anyway. By adding a new domain, we additionally decrease the similarity to the correct web usage profile which is also important for obfuscating the current session. The next question is the amount of HTTP connections to any selected domain. Another open question is the frequency of selected domains.

In the following, we will propose a method to construct an obfuscation set $D_{obf} = \{(d_1, l_1), (d_2, l_2), \cdots (d_m, l_m)\}$ where d_i is a selected domain and l_i is the amount of assigned connections. As mentioned before, we first of all need a ranking of popular domains $D_{pop} = \{(d_1, r_1), (d_2, r_2), \cdots (d_m, r_m)\}$ where d_i represents a domain and r_i is a ranking based on public access statistics. The amount of domains m must be sufficiently large to allow finding suitable new hosts. Furthermore, we assume to have access to the web usage profile $P(u)$ of the user whose identity we want to hide. For example, the information about frequently accessed domains can be collected by the same addon performing the obfuscation. We propose to construct D_{obf} in the following way: We first decide on a number of newly added domains h. Then we select the h most popular domains in $D_{pop} \notin P(u)$. After selecting h new domains, we now need to determine the amount l_i for each selected domain d_i. A basic strategy assigns $\frac{l}{h}$ connections to each domain. A second strategy is to assign more connections to domains that are more popular as follows,

$$c_i = l \ldots \frac{r_i}{\sum_{j=1}^{h} r_j}.$$

3.2 Subtractive Obfuscation

As mentioned before, a second way to obfuscate a session is to avoid direct access to some of the typical domains. Technically, this is possible by using a VPN server outside the LAN of the proxy. Though routing all traffic via an outside VPN connection will directly avoid any tracking by analyzing user sessions, using a VPN server at an outside organization might be connected to additional cost. Another drawback is that routing traffic via a VPN server is usually slower because all traffic has to be routed through this bottleneck. Another argument against routing the complete traffic over an outside VPN connection is that it might raise suspicion. In other words, it is obvious that the user tries to hide his web profile. Finally, in some cases using the company proxy is mandatory because access to certain services, e.g. online access to electronic publisher services, are often only possible by using the proxy. Thus, hiding the complete traffic might not be an option and a strategy is needed to select the domains that should be accessed via a VPN server.

To evaluate the effort for subtractive obfuscation, we measure the number of domains which have to be accessed via an VPN connection. Thus, we have to hide h domains in the session $S(a, \tau)$ we want to obfuscate. A simple solution is to decide on the percentage of domains and then randomly hide the complete traffic for this host via the VPN connection. A more sophisticated method to select the domains is to weight the probability of hiding a domain based on the popularity of the domain. For this technique, we should weigh less popular domains higher than popular ones. Since many other users visit a popular domain, it reveals less about the identity of the user. However, a rather unpopular domain being visited on a regular basis is much more useful for user identification. To increase the likelihood that unpopular domains are obfuscated, we try to find popularity values for all visited domains. If we find popularity information r_i for domain d_i, we weight the likelihood that this host is obfuscated by $\frac{1}{r_i}$.

4 Experimental Evaluation

To evaluate our techniques for obfuscation, we use our best performing classifier - NN with one aggregated instance per user. Before aggregation, each instance is preprocessed by applying a log function on session counts. The classification accuracy with this approach on the day sessions is about 90%. To demonstrate the effect of obfuscation, we apply the obfuscation beforehand to each test session, classify with all necessary previous steps and measure the classification accuracy on the entire test set.

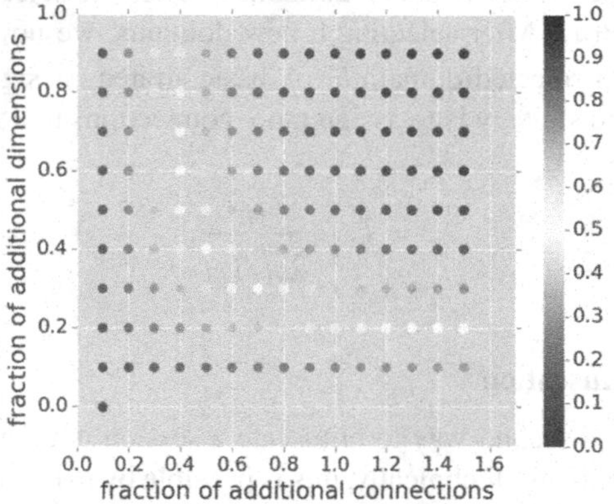

Fig. 3. Obfuscation, host selected based on popularity, connections distributed to the new domains according to popularity

Figure 3 shows results of our method for additive obfuscation. As an estimation of popularity score, we use the global frequency of accesses for each domain. Domains are sorted by popularity in descending order. For each test session, we find the most popular domains not being contained in the session and add them to the session. The connections are distributed to the domains proportionally to the global frequency of the domain. Thus, more popular domains get more connections. Let us note that for the sake of simplicity connections can be also distributed uniformly to the domains, the result is slightly affected. As can be seen in Fig. 4, only with 40% more connections our method decreases prediction quality from 90% to 50%. When adding twice as much traffic, the predictions become impossible.

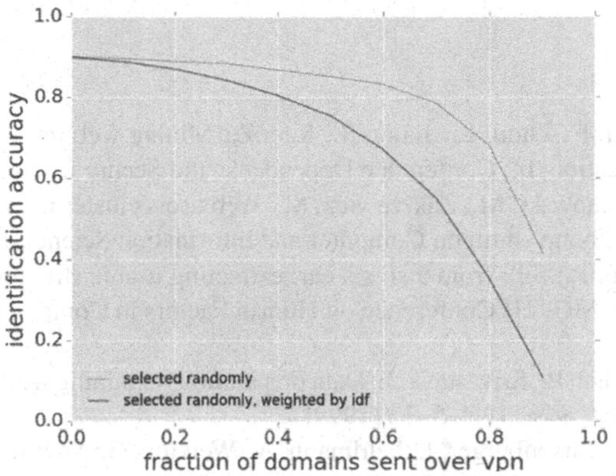

Fig. 4. Obfuscation, domains subtraction

Figure 4 presents the results of subtractive obfuscation. To simulate VPN traffic, forwarding to particular domains we simply remove connections of corresponding domains from the test sessions and compute the classification accuracy. The x-axis shows the fraction of domains removed from test sessions and the y-axis the resulting accuracy. We compare two different approaches here. In the first case, the domains to forward over VPN are selected randomly. In the second case, amongst all domains accessed by users, we give preference to the globally least popular domains. Our intuition here is that globally rarely visited domains explain users best and therefore increase their similarity with their profiles and decrease the similarity to others. Therefore, to increase the chance of removing rare domains, we weight all domains with the inverse of their frequency smoothed by log (idf). As can be seen in Fig. 3, the idf-weighted selection achieves better results. However, to decrease the prediction accuracy to 50%, we still need to hide about 70% of the domains.

5 Conclusion

In this paper, based the method that use of HTTP traffic to identify users [1], we introduce additive and subtractive user obfuscation to prevent the classifiers from finding out the identity of the users. Our experiments indicate that user identification is possible with more than 90% prediction accuracy based on aggregated web usage profiles and nearest neighbor classification. Furthermore, the additive approach to obfuscation showed great promise by lowering the prediction quality to less than 50% by adding approximately 50% of the HTTP connections in the original sessions.

For future work, we plan to examine the use of more sophisticated identification and obfuscation. Finally, we want to examine the performance of web usage profiles under open world conditions where the user behind observed sessions could be unknown, more closely.

References

1. Xu, J., Xu, F., Ma, F., Zhou, L., Jiang, S., Rao, Z.: Mining web usage profiles from proxy logs: user identification. In: Conference Dependable and Secure Computing. IEEE (2021)
2. Morzy, T., Wojciechowski, M., Zakrzewicz, M.: Web users clustering. In: Proceedings of the 15th International Symposium on Computer and Information Sciences, pp. 374–382 (2000)
3. P. Pirolli, J.P., Rao, R.: Silk from a sow's ear: extracting usable structures from the web. In: Proceedings of the SIGCHI Conference on Human Factors in Computing Systems, pp. 118–125. ACM (1996)
4. Cooley, R., Mobasher, B., Srivastava, J.: Data preparation for mining world wide web browsing patterns. Knowl. Inf. Syst. **1**(1), 5–32 (1999)
5. Kammenhuber, N., Luxenburger, J., Feldmann, A., Weikum, G.: Web search clickstreams. In: Proceedings of the 6th ACM SIGCOMM Conference on Internet Measurement, pp. 245–250 (2006)
6. Li, B., Mazur, E., Diao, Y., McGregor, A., Shenoy, P.: A platform for scalable one-pass analytics using mapreduce. In: Proceedings of the 2011 ACM SIGMOD International Conference on Management of Data, pp. 985–996 (2011)
7. Yen, T.-F., et al.: Beehive: large-scale log analysis for detecting suspicious activity in enterprise networks. In: Proceedings of the 29th Annual Computer Security Applications Conference, pp. 199–208. ACM (2013)
8. Lou, W., Liu, G., Lu, H., Yang, Q.: Cut-and-pick transactions for proxy log mining. In: Jensen, C.S., et al. (eds.) EDBT 2002. LNCS, vol. 2287, pp. 88–105. Springer, Heidelberg (2002). https://doi.org/10.1007/3-540-45876-X_8
9. Li, N., Zhang, N., Das, S.K.: Relationship privacy preservation in publishing online social networks. In: Proceedings IEEE 3rd International Conference Privacy Security Risk Trust/IEEE 3rd International Conference Social Compute, p 443–450 (2011)
10. Junggab, S., Donghyun, K., Alam, B., et al.: Privacy enhanced location sharing for mobile online social networks. IEEE Trans. Sustainable Comput., 1 (2018)
11. Xu, C., Xie, X., Zhu, L., et al.: PPLS: a privacy-preserving location-sharing scheme in mobile online social networks. Sci. China Inf. Sci. **63**(3) (2020)

Proof of Assets in the Diem Blockchain

Panagiotis Chatzigiannis[1(✉)] and Konstantinos Chalkias[2]

[1] George Mason University, Fairfax, USA
pchatzig@gmu.edu
[2] Novi Financial/Facebook Research, Menlo Park, USA

Abstract. A great challenge for distributed payment systems is their compliance with regulations, such as anti-money laundering, insolvency legislation, countering the financing of terrorism and sanctions laws. After Bitcoin's MtGox scandal, one of the most needed auditing functionalities for financial solvency and tax reporting purposes is to prove ownership of blockchain reserves, a process known as Proof of Assets (PoA). This work formalizes the PoA requirements in account-based blockchains, focusing on the unique hierarchical account structure of the Diem blockchain, formerly known as Libra. In particular, we take into account some unique features of the Diem infrastructure to consider different PoA modes by exploring time-stamping edge cases, cold wallets, locked assets, spending-ability delegation and account pruning, among the others. We also propose practical optimizations to the byte-size of PoA in the presence of light clients who cannot run a full node, including skipping *Validator* updates, while still maintaining the 66.67% Byzantine fault tolerance (BFT) guarantee.

Keywords: Diem blockchain · Solvency · Tax reporting · Light clients

1 Introduction

During the last decade, many distributed payment systems have emerged as an alternative to centralized banking. While blockchains were initially in anarchy, the need for regulation became apparent to ensure their compliance with laws, regulations and tax reporting. One aspect of such requirement is Proof of Assets (PoA), a fundamental part for proving financial solvency on behalf of custodial wallets [22,24], also known as Virtual Asset Providers (VASPs). Briefly, it is a cryptographic evidence that the organization possesses sufficient assets which, combined with its proved liabilities, offers the so called Proof of Solvency (PoSolv). The need of such proofs became even more apparent after infamous cryptocurrency exchange collapses, such as MtGox [25,37] or even the recent withdrawals suspension from OKEx [4].[1]

---

[1] Panagiotis Chatzigiannis did part of this work during an internship at Novi Financial/Facebook Research.

J. Zhou et al. (Eds.): ACNS 2021 Workshops, LNCS 12809, pp. 27–41, 2021.
https://doi.org/10.1007/978-3-030-81645-2_3

Our work focuses on practical PoA solutions in the Diem blockchain, however parts of our proposal apply to other systems as well. As regulatory compliance, transparency and fund safety are among the top priorities for Diem [13], PoA should be an important feature to achieve a safer wallet ecosystem. Diem's unique hierarchical account model differs from other blockchains and allows for several different PoA types that are not possible in other platforms. Our goal is to formalize and explore many different types of asset proofs in the Diem blockchain. Additionally, as we will show, Diem's PoA, in combination to Know-Your-Customer (KYC) identity verification, can also be useful to mitigate tax evasion, something that is not straight-forward in other blockchains where one can deny ownership of an address. In Diem, wallet addresses are pinned to particular entities, and thus VASPs cannot hide their owned assets on purpose.

In the following, we provide a summary of related work, a detailed analysis of PoA variants handcrafted to Diem's design, and finally practical recommendations for proof compression, aiming to make it more friendly for light (potentially mobile) clients.

1.1 Related Work

Bitstamp's Proof of Reserves [1] was one of the first attempts to provide evidence of a custodial wallet's total assets through an interactive protocol with a third party auditor. The process was to prove account-key ownership by signing over a provided random message; briefly, the ability to sign over a challenge string implies control and ownership of the account(s).

Provisions [24] presented a protocol based on zero-knowledge (ZK) proofs to prove assets, as part of a more general scheme to prove solvency. Its focus was to hide which accounts are owned by the audited entity. Briefly, the organization would form an anonymity set by adding random accounts from the public blockchain to those it already controls, and then prove (in ZK) that it knows a set of private keys that add up to or exceed some amount. Unfortunately, Provisions' custom ZK protocol cannot work with *hashed* public keys (which account for the majority of today's on-chain addresses), or with privacy-preserving cryptocurrencies (such as ZCash [32]) and its protocol's efficiency is linear to the size of anonymity set; thus, it cannot practically apply to most of today's blockchains. However, it is still considered the most sophisticated PoA solution to this day[2].

MProve [26] implemented a PoA algorithm tailored to Monero [41]. Since ring signature obfuscation does not allow for directly applying the Provisions PoA, its approach was to prove that the key images of the addresses controlled by the organization have not previously appeared on the blockchain. As PoA protocols are susceptible to collusion, MProve provides a proof of non-collusion as well by leveraging the one-time nature of key images. Unfortunately, this exposes the sender's identity when these key images are spent, potentially enabling tracing of transactions which breaks Monero's advertised privacy guarantees.

[2] One could use a generic ZK system; however proving costs might be prohibitive in practice for Diem's ZK-unfriendly Pure-Ed25519-with-SHA512 signatures (including multi-sig); even with the latest recursive ZK proof schemes [27].

Wang et al. [42] proposed a scheme for a buyer proving assets to a vendor before finalizing a deal, using the transaction's details as a "challenge", which however is limited to a "buyer-vendor" use-case without any privacy characteristics. More importantly, it does not preserve the prover's privacy against the verifier (or regulator) as strongly as Provisions.

Blockstream's proof of reserves [39] consists of signing an "invalid" Bitcoin transaction for each owned Unspent Transaction Output (UTXO). This transaction cannot be published to the blockchain, however still degrades the organization's privacy against the auditor. A similar approach is followed by Kraken cryptocurrency exchange [3]. The main advantage of this method is that hardware security module (HSM) or cold wallet implementations do not need an extra logic for signing PoA payloads and thus, it is directly backwards compatible with existing custodial wallets.

Ethereum [7] proposed a different payload format when signing a message other than a valid transaction[3]. The purpose of this distinction is to ensure that one should not accidentally sign a transaction masqueraded as a message nonce. In our PoA case, this prevents an auditor from maliciously picking a hash of a transaction as an audit-nonce, which if signed, it could be submitted on chain without the user knowing. Also, Iconomi's proof of reserves [6] proved key ownership to Deloitte (auditor) through either signed nonces or predefined transactions from the proving addresses.

Finally, a recent work [23] provided definitions and systematization for several payment systems, including those offering PoA functionalities, and compared them in terms of their properties and efficiency.

2 Diem Architecture

2.1 Keys and Accounts

Diem [13] is an account-based blockchain payment system, currently maintained by a permissioned set of *Validators* which participate in its BFT-based consensus protocol [15]. Although there are no built-in privacy preserving protocols for its account states and transactions, due to its permissioned nature, all public queries (including blockchain correctness verifications) are proxied through *full nodes*, which have the same view of the blockchain as *Validators*, but without participating in consensus. Compared to traditional cryptocurrencies, Diem provides the following features:

- *Authentication* keys, known as *auth_keys*, are hashed versions of account public keys, however they can be rotated independently as a proactive or reactive measure to defend against possible key loss. This means that unlike Ethereum, a key rotation does not imply change of address.
- Diem natively supports single Pure Ed25519 [33] or threshold multi-sig (*k-out-of-n* up to $n = 32$) *auth_keys*.

[3] Ethereum's message signing uses a flag prefix, to ensure an invalid transaction: *sign(keccak256 "\ x19Ethereum Signed Message:\n" + len(message) + message))*.

- There exists the concept of *withdraw capability*, where the permission to spend can be *delegated* to a different account. This implies that the spending key does not necessarily reside in the state of each address.
- It also supports the *key-rotation capability* where users can give permission to other accounts to update their *auth_keys*. This is useful for wallets where one can still refer to another *cold* address to gain access back to their account in case of accidental *hot auth_key* key loss.
- Account roles define the account owner's authority in the system. A unique characteristic of Diem is its hierarchical role-based access control [11]. Unlike Bitcoin and Ethereum, especially for VASPs, there exist a KYC-ed parent and child accounts as shown in Fig. 1.

2.2 Hierarchical Model

For the purposes of this work, we focus on Diem roles most commonly related to PoA: ParentVASP and ChildVASPs. A ParentVASP represents the primary account of a regulated custodial wallet, while multiple ChildVASPs can be created by ParentVASP accounts[4]. In Diem, a PoA will be requested from the ParentVASP , and these proofs should include all of their children's assets as well. Although not privacy-preserving, due to the well-defined linkability of the accounts belonging to the same entity, hiding owned addresses is not possible for KYC-ed VASPs. In Sect. 4.1 we provide details about the PoA related Diem data structures.

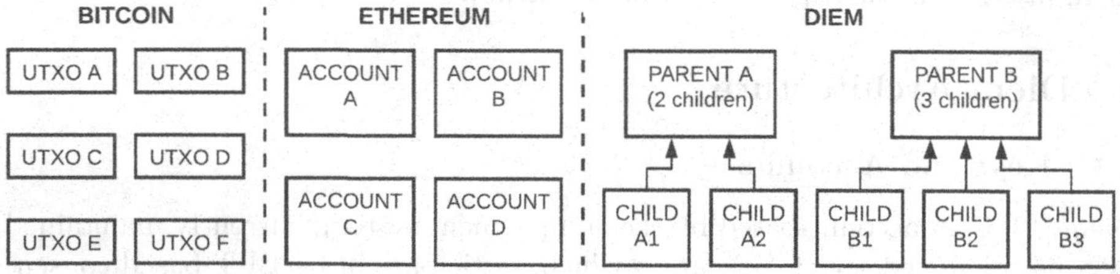

Fig. 1. Address structure in different blockchains.

As an account-based system, Diem associates each account A with a value v_j at each block j. We denote by A^P and A^C accounts with ParentVASP and ChildVASP roles, respectively. An A^P can be linked to n accounts $A_1^C, A_2^C, ...A_n^C$. There is a relation F which maps each child to its parent account, i.e. $F(A^{C_i}) = A^P$. Note however that no inverse relation exists in Diem, i.e. the parent's state does not include a relation $F^{-1}(A^P) = [A^{C_1}, A^{C_2}, ..., A^{C_n}]$. This was probably a design decision to not allow parent account states growing indefinitely when more children are added, because for a large n that map would require significant storage space.

[4] Note that in Diem a ChildVASP is not allowed to have any other children itself.

However, the data structure for A^P *does* include the cardinality n, a very important property to later ensure no child is missing in the proofs. Note that although a ParentVASP can create ChildVASPs, this does not necessarily mean that it controls the keys of its children, and ChildVASPs can transact independently. Of course, nobody prevents wallets from reusing the same key in multiple accounts or apply a BIP32 deterministic key derivation [34]. That said, the hierarchy is mainly enforced for KYC-ed account linking and splitting the risk of a key compromise attack; it also allows for different key and asset management policies, such as cold, warm and hot wallets or transaction sharding and parallelization[5].

2.3 Diem Proof of Assets

Generally, a PoA in Diem implies showing that a ParentVASP account is in possession of assets of some specific currency(ies) value. However, there is a subtle distinction on how to actually show this. One could merely use existing blockchain data structures, and sum the values of a ParentVASP and all of its ChildVASP accounts, based on account *ownership*. While straightforward, this proof does not provide key possession guarantees at the time of the auditing taking place. For instance, account holders might have lost access to their keys, which would make them unable to spend their assets. Therefore, we distinguish between the following two PoA types for a query on account A^P for a block j:

Soft PoA: This proof is non-interactive, and a user (a third party auditor or even a light client) can obtain it at any time and for any block j via a series of blockchain requests to potentially untrusted nodes. Its simple goal is to provably present the total balance for all accounts belonging to the audited entity. No proof-of-knowledge of the spending key is required (and thus the name *soft*), however the parent account is linked with the KYC-ed entity; no other entity can claim this address's balance, and thus some applications might tolerate *soft* proofs. We highlight that this is only possible in Diem due to its hierarchical identity-address binding which makes collusion more difficult and traceable; a *WalletA* cannot just temporarily borrow its private key to a *WalletB* (an on-chain transaction should happen posing the risk of being censored). Such a proof is constructed by showing the following:

1. Given a genesis or any known checkpoint state with Merkle root r_G, prove that the Merkle root r_j is valid (see Sect. 4.1 for details on these data structures). In practice, the auditor will pick the block j for which the PoA is needed. Note that in Diem, this can be shown using a series of epoch change proofs to get the validator-set at block j.
2. For r_j, provide Merkle inclusion proofs for both parent A^P and its children $A^C_1, .., A^C_n$ account states.

[5] While typical account-based systems require a sequence-id to prevent replay attacks, Diem's hierarchical model enables parallelization at the entity level, due to each child maintaining its own sequence-id.

3. All related account state balances (i.e. $A^P, A_1^C, .., A_n^C$) sum up to a value V. In PoSolv, this V is typically compared against proofs of liabilities [22].
4. $F(A_i^C) = A^P, \forall i \in (1, ..n)$, where n is the cardinality in account state A^P. This ensures that no child is accidentally or purposely omitted from the list.

Hard PoA: A *hard* PoA is requiring a key-ownership proof on top of *soft* proofs, usually via signing. To prevent replay attacks, the protocol should require each account to sign over some random challenge. Note that it is acceptable to sign with the *auth_key* (or a delegated key via withdraw capability), valid at a requested block in the past or the most recent one. We refer to these two types as *dated*-hard PoA and *live*-hard PoA, respectively (further discussed in Sect. 4).

3 Implementation Considerations

3.1 What Message to Sign?

As previously discussed, *hard* PoA simulates a proof of key-possession by signing over a challenge r to prevent replays. This can either be a "special" hard PoA transaction, included as metadata, or even run off-chain. Options for r include any combination of the following:

- a random string interactively provided by the auditor.
- the hash of the block (or state snapshot) at height $(j - 1)$. Note that Diem has the concept of transaction *version*, which is a monotonically increasing integer for all of the on-chain transactions. The latter means that one can even take a snapshot at the middle of the block, but typically, when we refer to height we imply the *version* number of the last transaction in a block.
- the latest Bitcoin block or from other robust proof-of-work blockchains (thus, use an external reference for randomness). However that would require running a mini light client as a smart contract or trust an Oracle service that could verify correctness of the external seed input.
- the output of a distributed randomness generation protocol (such as RandHound [40]), which can even be run by Diem *Validators* at each block.
- other publicly verifiable sources of randomness which embed timestamp information [30], such as the closing stock prices in the stock market, weather conditions in major cities etc., ideally with the use of verifiable delay functions (VDFs) [17].

However, some of the above randomness sources are susceptible to collusion attacks. For instance, the auditor and the ParentVASP might collude on the provided randomness in advance, or consensus *Validators* might agree to form a predictable block in Diem (this might be tolerated by the BFT assumption). Therefore we prefer a combination of external verifiable randomness and the RoundHound protocol ran from *Validators* which can offer better transparency guarantees. In short, we need a verifiable random and fresh challenge to ensure that the prover could not have predicted and pre-signed it long ago.

While hard PoA could also be automated to be executed at some predetermined times, the above randomness or challenges need to be unpredictable to prevent misbehavior. Note however that unpredictability is weaker than being "bias-proof", a property required by other use-cases (e.g. lottery protocols). For instance, in a lottery protocol an attacker's goal could be to increase the probability of outputting a string that ends in 0. However in the case of hard PoA, biasing the result in this way would have no benefit for the attacker as we're only interested on signing over a fresh unpredictable challenge. More information on what data to-be-signed offers the above freshness and unpredictability properties is provided in Sect. 4.3.

3.2 Various PoA Considerations

Account State Pruning: Many blockchain systems (including Diem) conserve space by pruning old account states, but still keeping the state's hash to preserve the system's security. Therefore, if the latest blockchain height is m and a PoA is requested for some height $j < m$, the full account state containing a balance v_j might not be available on-chain. In this case, the account's state would have to be recovered by a full-node who maintains the full history. Validating the provided pruned state is easy; we just check if the state's hash-output equals the blockchain-maintained hash value for this account.

Cold Wallets and Valet Keys: Hard PoA might be cumbersome when air-gapped wallets are involved, as performing such an operation would require bringing keys out of cold storage. The process sometimes requires expensive ceremonies, i.e. when the key resides in HSM modules or physical vaults, or when it is split between several parties. A possible approach to improve usability could be a) embedding PoA operations in HSM or b) using valet keys as defined in [5].

Incentives: When proving solvency, malicious auditees might collude to temporarily prove assets *greater* than some value that represents their off-chain liabilities. On the other hand, other auditees might try to *hide* assets on purpose (e.g. for tax evasion purposes). This would be a problem in any system other than Diem, where the auditee could simply claim loss or non-knowledge of some key, and complex blockchain analysis techniques (e.g. clustering) would have to be deployed to prevent such behavior. However Diem's hierarchical, KYC-ed account model mitigates this.

Locked Assets: In our model we do not consider locked on-chain assets, i.e., for future atomic swaps or side-chain smart contracts (locked assets are not supported by Diem yet). In fact, proving solvency by taking locked assets into account is an open research challenge in every blockchain, as discussed in the recent ZKProof 2020 workshop [22].

4 Diem-Specific Implementation Considerations

4.1 Primitives and Soft PoA Implementation in Diem

Sparse Merkle Trees: Recall a Merkle tree [36] is a binary tree constructed by a collision-resistant hash function h, providing logarithmic proofs with logarithmic complexity. Sparse Merkle trees share the same philisophy, however tree-leaves do not contain the accumulated elements themselves but serve to form an "index" of the element along with its path to the root. This enables them to provide proofs of non-membership, where non-accumulated elements can simply end to a placeholder value to maintain tree balance. However, as these class of Merkle trees are intractably large, we can also represent them by omitting sub-trees that only contain placeholder values. Diem uses a variant of Sparse Merkle trees (Jellyfish Merkle trees [28]) which enables shorter inclusion/exclusion proof sizes while still providing collision resistance.

In Diem, transactions are accumulated in a Merkle tree, which in turn contains roots of sparse Merkle trees that represent the state of all accounts as the transaction gets executed [12,13]. The top Merkle tree root defines the block hash and is signed by the *Validators* participating in the consensus (at least 66.67% of them should sign) as transactions are processed and account states are modified accordingly. We describe specific data structure format in Diem below.

Diem Data Structures [8,9]**:** In Diem, account states are represented as an `AccountStateBlob` which includes, among others, the address, balance for each currency and account role (i.e., ParentVASP or ChildVASP). These account states are stored in a sparse Merkle tree called `TransactionInfo`. In turn, this sparse Merkle tree's root hash `state_root_hash` represents all of the accounts' global state at the end of a specific transaction.

In turn, the *most recent* `TransactionInfo` root in an blockchain version, along with the epoch number corresponding to the current *Validator* set and a timestamp, are encapsulated in a `BlockInfo` data structure. This data structure along with a hash value of the consensus Quorum Certificate is encapsulated in a `LedgerInfo` Merkle tree. Note that a version's most recent Transaction (e.g. transaction T4 in Fig. 2), effectively defines the global state of all accounts for that version.

Finally, `LedgerInfo` along with consensus signatures by the current *Validator* set is encapsulated in a `LedgerInfoWithSignatures` data structure, making it acceptable by anyone trusting Diem's BFT assumptions.

Proofs: A core object for implementing Diem soft PoA is the `AccountStateProof` data structure. This contains a sparse Merkle tree proof (`SparseMerkleProof`) for a `TransactionInfo` object, which in turn is verified by a `TransactionInfoWithProof` proof for the Merkle tree. A second crucial element is `EpochChangeProof`, which includes the list of signatures involved in *Validator* set updates. Through these built-in proof functionalities in Diem, we implemented a CLI Soft PoA functionality [10] which returns total on-chain assets owned by Diem ParentVASPs.

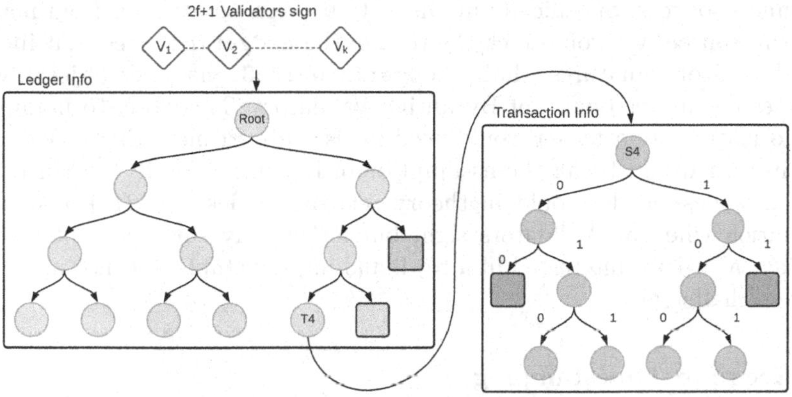

Fig. 2. Diem data structure overview.

4.2 Random Challenge Consistency

It is recommended, especially when BIP32 [34] is applied or the same key is used between accounts, that r should be the same across all signed messages to minimize proof size. However, as keys in Diem are rotated regularly (discussed in Sect. 2.1), there are two options for signing a hard PoA for time[6] t: a) use an authentication key that was valid at a past instance t, and b) use the most recent authentication key (which will be linked to the key at t using a chain of rotations). While both PoA types are acceptable for proving asset control at t, the latter version is stronger as it also shows key control for a more recent time $t + \Delta$. A reason for picking a slightly older t might be to reduce the probability of wallet collusion; if one does not know for which t they will be audited, temporarily borrowing private keys from other wallets is riskier. It is highlighted though that wallet providers might have deleted old account keys, and thus a t closer to the current time/block should be preferred, unless there is a reason not to, e.g. for proving assets exactly at the end of a calendar year.

In any case, we refer to the above two hard PoA types as *dated*-hard PoA and *live*-hard PoA respectively. We mention that especially for cold wallets, it is advised the auditee signs and rotates the keys simultaneously to ensure some additional (although not complete [20]) post-quantum security, due to publishing hashed keys.

---

[6] We assume t is in the past. While it could be possible to make a PoA request for some time in the future in advance, this enables several collusion attack vectors not addressed in this paper.

4.3 Signed Block Hashes as Randomness

In the previous section we discussed that block hashes can be used as a randomness source to sign a hard PoA message, preferably in combination with other randomness sources. Specifically in Diem, to prevent an attacker from manipulating this source, we would pick the root of the `LedgerInfo` tree that includes $2f+1$ Validator signatures (thus a `LedgerInfoWithSignatures` object), where f denotes the upper bound of Byzantine Validators. Therefore, to manipulate this information, an attacker would need to also subvert more than f Validators which in turn would break the assumption of Byzantine Fault Tolerance. Note that a dishonest leader could in theory selectively pick any $2f+1$ signature combination when all Validators sign, but fortunately this does not give any advantage as we are interested in a fresh and unpredictable, but not necessarily unbiased, challenge.

4.4 Accurate Timestamping

Diem's blocks use monotonically increasing timestamps. This implies that (unlike other blockchains) one could use a time reference t instead of a block-height j. In addition, all PoA elements should be consistent for a specific block, with the proof showing the total assets for a *snapshot* of the *same* blockchain height (or timestamp) across all ParentVASP and ChildVASPs. If a variation in height was allowed, malicious provers could move assets among their accounts in neighboring blocks and falsely claim assets greater that those actually owned.

Also, as mentioned before, Diem uses "versions" rather than "blocks-heights", with each transaction resulting in a unique, incremental version. Therefore, as each block has subsequently a *range* of versions, the account states in the latest version in a block need to be retrieved [28]. This can be implemented through appropriate GetVersionByTimestamp() and GetStateByVersion() functionalities, which would return the blockchain version for some specific timestamp and the blockchain state for some version respectively. Note that as shown in Fig. 2, the latest transaction in an epoch should be considered (transaction T4) for all account state proofs, and prove that the immediate next transaction belongs to the next epoch. This ensures that account proofs are provided after all transactions in the block have been considered.

4.5 Compression

Signature Compression: Signatures and public keys account for the largest part of a PoA payload. Actually, there exist three types of signatures:

1. *Validator* signatures over the block data.
2. account signatures for every transaction in a block.
3. key-possession-proof signatures for each auditee key (potentially delegated).

In PoA we are interested in the first and third signature types. Compression can be achieved though various techniques, but some of them require a Diem protocol update and thus, they cannot be applied directly. Examples include having the *Validators* running interactive multi-sig protocols, such as Musig2 [38] and FROST [35], or supporting BLS signatures [18], which allows for aggregation to a single signature (although we still need the public keys). Solutions not requiring a protocol update include the SNARKs [31], STARKs [27] or the recent non-interactive EdDSA half-aggregation [21]. However, for auditee signatures over a challenge, the prover, who controls all of the keys, can simulate a Musig2 in-the-head or apply the Schnorr batching technique of [29].

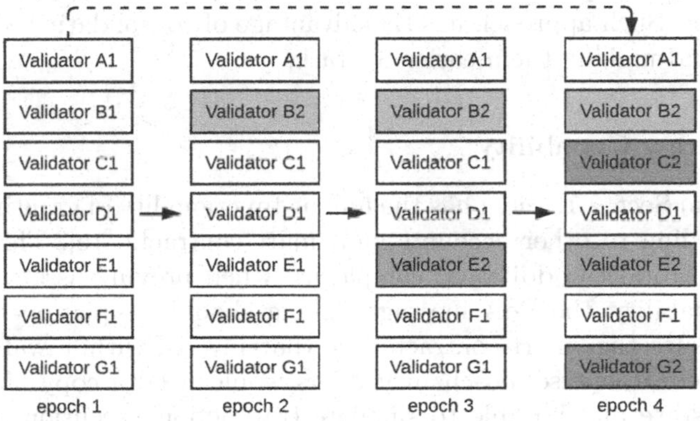

Fig. 3. Epoch skipping optimization.

Epoch Proof Compression: At the moment, Diem's epoch-change proofs are sent in raw format, without tackling duplication between epochs. We present an easy to implement partial compression method without advanced ZK protocols.

Normally, to verify epoch changes, where at least one *Validator* rotates its key, we have to verify all intermediate epochs from the last known checkpoint. However we can skip epoch verifications if less than 1/3 *Validators* have been updated, and only require to "jump" to an epoch where a sufficient number of *Validators* have changed (concept shown in Fig. 3). Note however that this optimization is incompatible with long range attack prevention [14]; still, this might be tolerable in some threat models. We can further optimize epoch proofs by only considering the required $2f+1$ signatures (omit the rest) along with their key rotation operations, even when all *Validators* have signed.

4.6 Multiple Currencies

Note that Diem might support several currencies, and asset proofs might be required across all of them. Our recommendation is that PoA should run per currency (but again for the same height). Converting all currencies to a single one using the current exchange rate is not advised for PoSolv purposes [22], as there are examples of extreme volatility (i.e., the case of Swiss franc cap removal on Jan 15, 2015 [19]).

4.7 PoA Transaction Type

In general, as an alternative to a carefully signed message that is distinguishable from a regular transaction by design [2], transferring some amount (or even a zero amount) to a (designated) address would also work for PoA purposes, especially if one wants on-chain PoA recording. In Diem, a hard PoA could also be executed through a special transaction type, with the sole purpose of signing a message, however such "NO-OP" transactions are not yet implemented. Fortunately, Diem allows sending funds to self, which is one way to implement hard PoA. Another option would be to send some amount to a pre-determined "sink" account. Such approach has the advantage of consolidating all associated PoA events and making them easier to track.

4.8 Withdraw Capability

As discussed in Sect. 2.1, Diem has the unique functionality of granting the capability of spending to other accounts and smart contracts [16]. This delegation mechanism introduces additional complexity when proving assets. Because of withdraw capability, the PoA message signing should happen on-chain, which would make sure the smart-contract logic that involve withdrawal capabilities would execute. Otherwise, off-chain verifiers would need a copy of the current blockchain's state and be able to simulate transaction execution in this copy, which would make the whole process expensive or cumbersome. Another issue is related to potentially incompatible implementations of custom withdraw capability logic (smart-contract), because currently there is no enforcement of requiring additional metadata (which in our case is required to attach the random challenge).

5 Conclusion

We presented several considerations for implementing proof of assets in the Diem blockchain. By taking advantage of Diem's native hierarchical account structure, two major policies of asset proofs have been analyzed: *soft* PoA, which can be executed at any time without interaction with account holders, and *hard* PoA which provide extra assurance that account holders are in control of their keys. However, the latter requires a more carefully planned, coordinated interaction.

All of our proofs rely on widely-used cryptographic primitives with standard assumptions (i.e. signatures and Merkle proofs). We discuss several edge-cases that should be taken into account when designing PoA protocols in a hieararchical, KYC-ed, account-based blockchain system (e.g. timestamping and consistency), and propose practical solutions, including options for fresh and unpredictable proof of key-possession challenges. Finally, we propose easy to implement optimizations (e.g. signature and epoch change proof compression), while still remaining compatible to the underlying Diem blockchain.

Acknowledgement. We thank Philip Hayes, David Wolinsky, Alden Hu and Valeria Nikolaenko for their implementation contributions, Riyaz Faizullabhoy for custody related hints, Dmitry Korneev and Adeniyi Abiodun for their input on needed regulation and compliance, and finally Sam Blackshear and Tim Zakian for enabling the required Move-language API regarding parent-children Diem account linking.

References

1. Bitstamp proof of reserves. https://www.bitstamp.net/s/documents/Bitstamp_proof_of_reserves_statement.pdf
2. Ethereum wiki (archive.org). https://web.archive.org/web/20190613115908if_/github.com/ethereum/wiki/wiki/JSON-RPC#eth_sign
3. Kraken proof of reserves. https://www.kraken.com/en-us/proof-of-reserves-audit
4. Okex suspends withdrawals, says key holder not available due to cooperation with investigation. https://www.coindesk.com/okex-suspends-withdrawals
5. Provisions: Privacy-preserving proofs of solvency for bitcoin exchanges. Real World Crypto 2016. https://rwc.iacr.org/2016/Slides/Provisions
6. Proof of solvency technical overview (2018). https://medium.com/iconominet/proof-of-solvency-technical-overview-d1d0e8a8a0b8
7. Ethereum wiki (2019). https://web.archive.org/web/20190613115908if_/github.com/ethereum/wiki/wiki/JSON-RPC#eth_sign
8. Diem authenticated data structure specification (2021). https://github.com/diem/diem/blob/main/specifications/common/authenticated_data_structures.md
9. Diem data structures specification (2021). https://github.com/diem/diem/blob/main/specifications/common/data_structures.md
10. Diem proofs of assets (2021). https://github.com/diem/diem/blob/main/client/assets-proof/README.md
11. Diem roles and permissions (2021). https://dip.diem.com/dip-2/
12. Diem storage module (2021). https://github.com/diem/diem/tree/master/storage
13. Amsden, Z., et al.: The libra blockchain (2020). https://diem-developers-components.netlify.app/papers/the-diem-blockchain/2020-05-26.pdf
14. Azouvi, S., Danezis, G., Nikolaenko, V.: Winkle: foiling long-range attacks in proof-of-stake systems. In: Proceedings of the 2nd ACM Conference on Advances in Financial Technologies, pp. 189–201 (2020)
15. Baudet, M., et al.: State machine replication in the libra blockchain. The Libra Assn., Technical report (2019)
16. Blackshear, S., Wilsion, B., Zakian, T.: Diem improvement proposal 11 (2021). https://dip.diem.com/dip-11/
17. Boneh, D., Bonneau, J., Bünz, B., Fisch, B.: Verifiable delay functions. In: Annual International Cryptology Conference, pp. 757–788. Springer (2018)
18. Boneh, D., Lynn, B., Shacham, H.: Short signatures from the Weil pairing. In: Boyd, C. (ed.) ASIACRYPT 2001. LNCS, vol. 2248, pp. 514–532. Springer, Heidelberg (2001). https://doi.org/10.1007/3-540-45682-1_30
19. Breedon, F., Chen, L., Ranaldo, A., Vause, N.: Judgement day: algorithmic trading around the swiss franc cap removal (2018)
20. Chalkias, K., Brown, J., Hearn, M., Lillehagen, T., Nitto, I., Schroeter, T.: Blockchained post-quantum signatures. In: 2018 IEEE Blockchain, pp. 1196–1203. IEEE (2018)
21. Chalkias, K., Garillot, F., Kondi, Y., Nikolaenko, V.: Non-interactive half-aggregation of EdDSA and variants of Schnorr signatures. CT-RSA (2021)

22. Chalkias, K., Lewi, K., Mohassel, P., Nikolaenko, V.: Distributed auditing proofs of liabilities. Cryptology ePrint Archive, Report 2020/468 (2020). https://eprint.iacr.org/2020/468
23. Chatzigiannis, P., Baldimtsi, F., Chalkias, K.: SoK: auditability and accountability in distributed payment systems. Cryptology ePrint Archive, Report 2021/239 (2021). https://eprint.iacr.org/2021/239
24. Dagher, G.G., Bünz, B., Bonneau, J., Clark, J., Boneh, D.: Provisions: privacy-preserving proofs of solvency for bitcoin exchanges. In: Ray, I., Li, N., Kruegel, C. (eds.) ACM CCS 2015, pp. 720–731. ACM Press, October 2015. https://doi.org/10.1145/2810103.2813674
25. Decker, C., Wattenhofer, R.: Bitcoin transaction malleability and MtGox. In: Kutyłowski, M., Vaidya, J. (eds.) ESORICS 2014, Part II. LNCS, vol. 8713, pp. 313–326. Springer, Heidelberg (2014). https://doi.org/10.1007/978-3-319-11212-1_18
26. Dutta, A., Vijayakumaran, S.: MProve: a proof of reserves protocol for monero exchanges. In: 2019 IEEE European Symposium on Security and Privacy Workshops, EuroS&P Workshops 2019, Stockholm, Sweden, 17–19 June 2019, pp. 330–339. IEEE (2019). https://doi.org/10.1109/EuroSPW.2019.00043
27. Gabizon, A., et al.: Plumo: towards scalable interoperable blockchains using ultra light validation systems. ZKProof (2020)
28. Gao, Z., Hu, Y., Wu, Q.: Jellyfish Merkle tree (2021). https://developers.diem.com/papers/jellyfish-merkle-tree/2021-01-14.pdf
29. Gennaro, R., Leigh, D., Sundaram, R., Yerazunis, W.: Batching Schnorr identification scheme with applications to privacy-preserving authorization and low-bandwidth communication devices. In: Lee, P.J. (ed.) ASIACRYPT 2004. LNCS, vol. 3329, pp. 276–292. Springer, Heidelberg (2004). https://doi.org/10.1007/978-3-540-30539-2_20
30. Gjermundrød, H., Chalkias, K., Dionysiou, I.: Going beyond the coinbase transaction fee: alternative reward schemes for miners in blockchain systems. In: Proceedings of the 20th Pan-Hellenic Conference on Informatics, pp. 1–4 (2016)
31. Groth, J.: On the size of pairing-based non-interactive arguments. In: Fischlin, M., Coron, J.-S. (eds.) EUROCRYPT 2016. LNCS, vol. 9666, pp. 305–326. Springer, Heidelberg (2016). https://doi.org/10.1007/978-3-662-49896-5_11
32. Hopwood, D., Bowe, S., Hornby, T., Wilcox, N.: Zcash protocol specification. San Francisco, CA, USA, GitHub (2016)
33. Josefsson, S., Liusvaara, I.: RFC 8032: Edwards-Curve Digital Signature Algorithm (EdDSA), January 2017. https://doi.org/10.17487/RFC8032
34. Khovratovich, D., Law, J.: Bip32-ed25519: hierarchical deterministic keys over a non-linear keyspace. In: 2017 IEEE European Symposium on Security and Privacy Workshops (EuroS&PW), pp. 27–31. IEEE (2017)
35. Komlo, C., Goldberg, I.: FROST: flexible round-optimized Schnorr threshold signatures. Cryptology ePrint Archive, Report 2020/852 (2020). https://eprint.iacr.org/2020/852
36. Merkle, R.C.: A digital signature based on a conventional encryption function. In: Pomerance, C. (ed.) CRYPTO 1987. LNCS, vol. 293, pp. 369–378. Springer, Heidelberg (1988). https://doi.org/10.1007/3-540-48184-2_32
37. Moore, T., Christin, N.: Beware the middleman: empirical analysis of bitcoin-exchange risk. In: Sadeghi, A.-R. (ed.) FC 2013. LNCS, vol. 7859, pp. 25–33. Springer, Heidelberg (2013). https://doi.org/10.1007/978-3-642-39884-1_3
38. Nick, J., Ruffing, T., Seurin, Y.: Musig2: simple two-round Schnorr multi-signatures. Cryptology ePrint Archive, Report 2020/1261 (2020). https://eprint.iacr.org/2020/1261

39. Roose, S.: Standardizing bitcoin proof of reserves. https://blockstream.com/2019/02/04/en-standardizing-bitcoin-proof-of-reserves/
40. Syta, E., et al.: Scalable bias-resistant distributed randomness. In: 2017 IEEE Symposium on Security and Privacy, pp. 444–460. IEEE Computer Society Press, May 2017. https://doi.org/10.1109/SP.2017.45
41. Van Saberhagen, N.: Cryptonote v 2.0 (2013). https://cryptonote.org/whitepaper.pdf
42. Wang, H., He, D., Ji, Y.: Designated-verifier proof of assets for bitcoin exchange using elliptic curve cryptography. Future Gener. Comput. Syst. **107**, 854–862 (2020)

An Identity-Based Blind Signature Scheme with Message Recovery from Pairings

Yihong Wen[1], Cong Peng[2], Shicheng Wang[1], Li Li[2], and Min Luo[2](✉)

[1] The 54th Research Institute of China Electronics Technology Group Corporation, Shijiazhuang, China

[2] School of Cyber Science and Engineering, Wuhan University, Wuhan, China
{cpeng,lli,mluo}@whu.edu.cn

Abstract. As a variant of digital signature schemes, the blind signature enables that the signer signs a message without knowing its content. In identity-based cryptography, many blind signature schemes have been proposed. Among them, Verma *et al.* designed an identity-based blind signature scheme with message recovery (IDBS-MR). Unfortunately, after our cryptanalysis, their scheme cannot satisfy untraceability, which enables the signer to break the anonymity of users by tracking the previous signature transmission scripts. To solve the problem, we construct a new IDBS-MR scheme using the bilinear pairing and demonstrates that the proposed scheme has blindness, untraceability, and unforgeability in the random oracle model. Performance results show that compared with Verma *et al.*'s scheme, the proposed scheme has the same computation costs in views of signers, twice computation costs in views of users, but reduces 36% computation costs in views of verifiers.

Keywords: Blockchain · Blind signature · Message recovery · Pairing

1 Introduction

With the emergence of blockchain technologies, distributed electronic cash systems, such as Bitcoin [1], Ethereum [2], Zerocash [3], have become increasingly pervasive. Security and privacy are the main properties for users to employ electronic cash systems. For this purpose, the electronic cash system needs to guarantee the following security: 1) *Unforgeability.* Nobody can expenditure the user's coins without the user's permission. 2) *Anonymity.* Nobody can trace the spending transaction record to the user who initiated it. Various cryptography primitives have been used to guarantee these two properties, such as *ring signatures* [4], *group signatures* [5], *blind signatures* [6].

The concept of *blind signature (BS)* was firstly introduced by Chaum [6], and the core idea is that the signer signs a message without knowing its content. Typically, there are two roles participated in the scheme: *the signer* and *the*

J. Zhou et al. (Eds.): ACNS 2021 Workshops, LNCS 12809, pp. 42–55, 2021.
https://doi.org/10.1007/978-3-030-81645-2_4

user. The user wants to generate the message-signature pair without knowing the private key, while the signer needs to use the private key to sign the blind message sent by the user. And, the signer is unable to link any signature to the previous signature transmission script, so the blind signature scheme provides user anonymity inherently and has been widely used in e-voting, e-commerce, e-payment [6–8].

To better employ blind signature, the following problems need to be solved:

- *How to authenticate the user's public key.*
- *How to reduce the message-signature pair size.*

For the first problem, the traditional approach is using *Public Key Infrastructure (PKI)*, in which the certificate authority provides a valid certificate to bind the user's identity and public key. This turns out to be even more problematic because the management and use of certificates require an excessive number of system resources. Using *identity-based cryptography (IBC)* [9] is an alternative and advantageous approach to treat the user identity as the public key. In identity-based cryptosystems, the *Key Generator Center (KGC)* has super privileges to initialize system parameters (including the master key pair) and generate the private key corresponding to the user identity.

For the second problem, the *message recovery signatures (MRS)* is a practical signature technique that can hide all or part of the message in the signature value and recover it after verification. In the traditional signature scheme, the signed message is transmitted to the verifier together with the signature and requires additional bandwidth for transmission. To avoid transmitting the signed message, Nyberg *et al.* [10] first proposed the concept of embedding messages into signatures. Follow this idea, the message-signature pair is converted to one signature, and the total bit length transmitted is reduced.

Recently, a new type of blind signature [11–16] has been proposed, called *identity-based blind signature with message recovery (IDBS-MR)*, in which the IBC and MRS technologies are combined to enhance the practicability of blind signature. However, untraceability has rarely been studied directly so that the user anonymity is not valid for the signer. This paper aims to provide a new IDBS-MR scheme that can achieve blindness, untraceability, and unforgeability properties.

Contributions. Firstly, we present an efficient attack method to break the untraceability of Verma *et al.*'s scheme. Then, we utilize the bilinear pairing to construct a new IDBS-MR scheme, which is secure under the random oracle model. Finally, performance results show that our scheme has the same computation costs as other schemes in views of signers, twice computation costs as much as other schemes in views of users, but reduces 36% computation costs in views of verifiers.

Organization. Section 2 reviews some previous works on identity-based blind signatures. The concept, framework and security model of the identity-based blind signature are introduced in Sect. 3. In Sect. 4, we analyze Verma *et al.*'s scheme [15] and provide an effective attack method. The proposed IDBS-MR scheme is introduced in Sect. 5. Section 6 and 7 analyze the security and performance of the proposed scheme. Section 8 concludes this paper.

2 Related Work

After Chaum's work [6], various types of blind signature schemes have been proposed, such as RSA-based blind signature [17], identity-based blind signature [18–28], certificateless blind signature [29]. Focusing on the identity-based blind signature (IDBS) scheme, Zhang *et al.* [18] proposed the first IDBS scheme in 2002, then improved in [19]. However, Huang *et al.* [20] and Mao *et al.* [21] cryptanalysed Zhang *et al.*'s scheme [19] and concluded that their scheme is linkable and insecure. Subsequently, some improved schemes [22–25] based on bilinear pairings have been proposed. In 2011, Hu *et al.* [26] proposed a pairing-based IDBS scheme and proved its security without the random oracle. Also, Xu *et al.* [27] designed a unlinkable IDBS scheme based on bilinear pairings. In addition, He *et al.* [28] proposed a pairing-free identity-based blind signature scheme without bilinear pairings in 2011, which greatly improves the computation efficiency and guarantees the user anonymity.

In terms of working with the message recovery mechanism, a few identity-based blind signature schemes with message recovery have been designed [11–16]. In 2005, Han *et al.* [11] utilized modified Weil/Tate pairings to construct a blind message recovery scheme with improved key size. Later, Inspired by Zhang *et al.*'s scheme [24], Elkamchouchi *et al.* [12] designed an improved scheme with less bandwidth adapting the short message scenario. Diao *et al.* [13] designed a new blind scheme to support proxy signature and message recovery mechanism. Recently, James *et al.* [14] and Verma *et al.* [15] proposed an identity-based blind message recovery signature scheme by using pairings, respectively. However, their scheme cannot provide untraceability so that it is insecure against malicious signers, as shown in Sect. 4. Thus, the overall goal of this work is to design a untraceable and provably secure IDBS-MR scheme.

3 Preliminaries

To begin, we review the definition of bilinear pairings and introduce the system model and security model of the IDBS-MR scheme. Some notations are listed in Table 1.

3.1 Bilinear Pairings

Define the mapping e as $e : \mathbb{G}_1 \times \mathbb{G}_2 \rightarrow \mathbb{G}_T$, where the domain are two cyclic additive groups $(\mathbb{G}_1, +)$, $(\mathbb{G}_2, +)$ and the codomain is a cyclic multiplicative group $(\mathbb{G}_T, \cdot)$. Denote P_1 and P_2 as the generator of the primes order q in $\mathbb{G}_1$ and $\mathbb{G}_2$, respectively. Let $g = e(P_1, P_2)$. e is a bilinear pairing, if the following condition holds:

- Computability. $e(P, Q)$ is computational easy for any $P \in \mathbb{G}_1$, $Q \in \mathbb{G}_2$.
- Bilinearity. $e(aP, bQ) = e(P, Q)^{ab}$ for any $P \in \mathbb{G}_1$, $Q \in \mathbb{G}_2$ and $a, b \in \mathbb{Z}_q^*$.
- Non-degeneracy. There exists $P \in \mathbb{G}_1$ and $Q \in \mathbb{G}_2$ such that $e(P, Q) \neq 1_{\mathbb{G}_T}$, where $1_{\mathbb{G}_T}$ is the identity element of $\mathbb{G}_T$.

Table 1. Notations

Notations	Descriptions
KGC	The key generator center
$\mathbb{G}_1, \mathbb{G}_2$	The cyclic additive group
$\mathbb{G}_T$	The cyclic multiplicative group
λ	The security parameter
p, q	The large primes
xP	The scalar multiplication in $\mathbb{G}_1$ or $\mathbb{G}_2$ with the scalar x
$\|q\|$	The bit length of q
$\|x\|_{l_1}$	The left l_1 bits of x
$\|x\|_{l_2}$	The right l_2 bits of x
$a\|\|b$	Concatenation of two bit string a and b
m	The message
σ	The signature

As the cornerstone of security, we assume the following problems are computational hard problems:

- Discrete Logarithm (DL) Problem. Given $P, Q \in \mathbb{G}_i$ ($i \in \{1, 2\}$), find an integer $x \in \mathbb{Z}_q^*$ such that $Q = xP$.
- τ-Strong Diffie-Hellman (τ-SDH) Problem. Given $P, xP, x^2P, \cdots, x^\tau P \in \mathbb{G}_1$ and $Q, xQ, x^2Q, \cdots, x^\tau Q \in \mathbb{G}_2$, find a pair $(c, \frac{1}{c+x}P) \in \mathbb{Z}_q \times \mathbb{G}_1$ for any c.

3.2 System Model

There exists four roles in the IDBS-MR scheme: the *key generator center*, the *user*, the *signer* and the *verifier*. KGC is responsible for initializing system parameters (including the master key pair) and generate the private key corresponding to the signer's identity. During the signature generation phase, the user selects the message to be signed and interacts with the signer through a blind signature protocol to generate a valid signature. Anyone can act as a verifier to check whether a signature is a valid signature of a signer and extract messages from it.

Typically, the IDBS-MR scheme consists of four polynomial-time algorithm: the *system setup algorithm* Setup, the *key extraction algorithm* KeyExtract, the *blind signing algorithm* BlindSig and the *blind verification algorithm* BlindVrf. The details are described as follows:

- $(\mathsf{par}, \mathsf{msk}) \leftarrow \mathsf{Setup}(\lambda)$: The system setup algorithm is run by KGC, which takes a security parameter λ as input and outputs the system parameter par, the master secret key msk and the master public key mpk.
- $\mathsf{usk} \leftarrow \mathsf{KeyExtract}(\mathsf{msk}, ID)$: The key extraction algorithm is run by KGC, which takes a signer's identity ID as input and outputs the signer's private key usk.

- $\sigma \leftarrow$ BlindSig(usk, m): The blind signing algorithm is run by the signer and the user. Firstly, the user blinds the original message m with some blind factors and sends the blind message to the signer. Then, the signer uses its private key usk to sign the blind message and returns the blind signature to the user. Finally, the user unblinds the blind signature to obtain the signature σ of the original message.
- $m/\perp \leftarrow$ BlindVrf(ID, σ): The blind verification algorithm is run by the verifier, which takes a signer's identity ID and a signature σ as inputs, and outputs the hidden message m or the symbol $\perp$. If the signature is valid, the message m will be output; Otherwise, the symbol $\perp$ will be output.

For brevity, we assume that par includes the master public key and is the implicit input to other algorithms.

3.3 Security Model

From the security perspective, the IDBS-MR scheme must satisfy the following requirements:

- *Correctness.* A legitimately generated signature can always be accepted and its hidden message can always be extracted by any verifier.
- *Unforgeability.* For any message, no one can generate its valid signature except the signer.
- *Blindness.* When the user does not publish the message-signature pair, the signer has no ability to know what the message is and when it was signed.
- *Untraceability.* Even if the user publishes all message-signature pairs, the signer has no ability to link a published signature to one previous blind signing interaction process.

If the signer can retrieve valid information about the original message from the blinded message, then it can easily trace the blind signing process when the message is published. Obviously, untraceability is a stronger security property than blinding. Consider all hash functions in the IDBS-MR scheme as hash oracles, we can describe the security model of unforgeability and untraceability as follows:

Definition 1 (Unforgeability). *The IDBS-MR scheme is unforgeable if all PPT adversary win the EUF-Game with negligible probability, i.e.* $Adv_{\mathcal{A}}^{EUF} < \epsilon$. *The adversary $\mathcal{A}$ (i.e. the forger) and the challenger $\mathcal{C}$ (i.e. KGC and the signer) play the EUF-Game as follows:*

1. *Setup. $\mathcal{C}$ initializes system parameters* par *and the master secret key* msk. *Then, $\mathcal{C}$ sends* par *to $\mathcal{A}$.*
2. *Query. $\mathcal{A}$ can adaptively make the following queries to $\mathcal{C}$:*
   - *Hash queries. When $\mathcal{A}$ queries a hash value of some inputs, $\mathcal{C}$ returns a certain value to $\mathcal{A}$.*

- *Key extract queries. When $\mathcal{A}$ queries the private key of an identity ID_i, $\mathcal{C}$ returns a private key d_{ID_i} to $\mathcal{A}$.*
- *Sign queries. When $\mathcal{A}$ queries the signature of a message m_i and a signer's identity ID_i, $\mathcal{C}$ returns a signature σ_i to $\mathcal{A}$.*

3. *Forge. $\mathcal{A}$ outputs a signature σ with a signer's identity ID^*, where ID^* has not been queried in the key extract queries and (m^*, ID^*) has not been queried in the sign queries.*
4. *If σ^* is a valid signature and m^* is the hidden message in σ^*, $\mathcal{A}$ wins the game. The advantage is denoted as*

$$Adv_{\mathcal{A}}^{EUF} = Pr[\mathsf{BlindVrf}(ID^*, \sigma^*)] < \epsilon.$$

Definition 2 (Untraceability). *The IDBS-MR scheme is untraceable if all PPT adversary win the IND-Game with negligible probability, i.e. $Adv_{\mathcal{A}}^{IND} < \epsilon$. The adversary $\mathcal{A}$ (i.e. the signer) and the challenger $\mathcal{C}$ (i.e. the honest user) play the IND-Game as follows:*

1. *$\mathcal{A}$ sends two adaptive chosen message $\{m_0, m_1\}$ to $\mathcal{U}$.*
2. *$\mathcal{U}$ randomly chooses a bit $b \in \{0,1\}$ and executes the blind signature generation algorithm with $\mathcal{A}$ in order of $\{m_b, m_{1-b}\}$ to obtain two signature $\{\sigma_b, \sigma_{1-b}\}$. Then, $\mathcal{U}$ sends (m_0, σ_1) and (m_1, σ_1) to $\mathcal{A}$.*
3. *$\mathcal{A}$ outputs a bit $b' \in \{0,1\}$ to guess that $m_{b'}$ is the first signed message.*
4. *If $b = b'$, $\mathcal{A}$ wins the game. The advantage is denoted as*

$$Adv_{\mathcal{A}}^{IND} = |Pr[b = b'] - \frac{1}{2}| < \epsilon.$$

4 Review and Analysis of Verma et al.'s Scheme

In this section, we briefly review Verma *et al.*'s scheme [15] and present an effective attack method on untraceability.

4.1 Review of Verma et al.'s Scheme

Firstly, we briefly review Verma *et al.*'s scheme [15]. As described in Sect. 3.2, the scheme consists of the following algorithms:

- Setup: Taking a security parameter λ as input, KGC generates a master secret key $\mathsf{msk} = s$ and public parameters $\mathsf{par} = \{\mathsf{pp_{bp}}, l_1, l_2, H_1, H_2, F_1, F_2, P_{pub}\}$, where $\mathsf{pp_{bp}} = \{\mathbb{G}_1, \mathbb{G}_2, \mathbb{G}_T, P_1, P_2, q, e, g\}$ are the bilinear pairing parameters. The hash functions are defined as $H_1 : \{0,1\}^* \to \mathbb{Z}_q^*$, $H_2 : \mathbb{G}_T \to \{0,1\}^{|q|}$, $F_1 : \{0,1\}^{l_2} \to \{0,1\}^{l_1}$ and $F_2 : \{0,1\}^{l_1} \to \{0,1\}^{l_2}$. Also, $P_{pub} = sP_2$ is the master public key where s is the master secret key randomly chosen in $\mathbb{Z}_q^*$.
- $\mathsf{KeyExtract}$: Taking a signer's identity $ID \in \{0,1\}^*$ as input, KGC computes the signer's private key as $d_{ID} = (s + H_1(ID))^{-1}P_1$.
- $\mathsf{BlindSig}$: Given a message $m \in \{0,1\}^{l_2}$, the signer and the user process the follow steps to generate the signature σ.

  - Committing. The signer chooses a random integer $r \leftarrow_{\$} \mathbb{Z}_q^*$ and sends $R = rP$ to the user.
  - Blinding. The user computes $u = F_1(m)||(F_2(F_1(m)) \oplus m)$, $w = e(\alpha R + \beta P_1, P_2)$ and $v = u \oplus H_2(w)$, where α and β are two random integer chosen in $\mathbb{Z}_q^*$. Then, the user sends $\tilde{v} = \alpha^{-1}(v + \beta) \mod q$ to the signer.
  - Signing. The signer sends $\tilde{S} = (r + \tilde{v})d_{ID}$ to the user.
  - Unblinding. The user computes $S = \alpha\tilde{S}$ and outputs $\sigma = (v, S)$ as the signature of the message m.
- BlindVrf: Taking a signature $\sigma' = (v', S')$ as input, the verifier computes $w' = e(S', P_{pub} + H_1(ID)P_2) \cdot e(P_1, P_2)^{-v'}$, $u' = v' \oplus H_2(w')$. Then, the user computes $m' = F_2(|u'|_{l_1}) \oplus |u'|_{l_2}$ and checks whether $|u'|_{l_1} = F_1(m')$. If equals, the signature is valid and m' is the extracted message. Otherwise, abort with the symbol $\perp$.

4.2 Weakness of Verma et al.'s Scheme

Next, we present an effective attack method to break the untraceability of Verma *et al.*'s scheme [15].

Firstly, the signer creates two empty lists L_1, L_2 and updates them for different situations. When the signer executes the blind signature algorithm, the signer needs to record the tuple $(r_i, \tilde{v}_i, \tilde{S}_i)$ into the list L_1. When the user publishes a message signature, the signer updates the tuple (m_j, v_j, S_j) to the list L_2.

Then, the signer computes $Q_{ID} = P_{pub} + H_1(ID)P_2$ and matches tuples of two lists by the traversing method, e.g. i-th tuple of L_1 match with j-th tuple of L_2, and performs the following operation:

$$\begin{cases} x_1 = e((r_i + \tilde{v}_i)^{-1} S_j, Q_{ID}), \\ x_2 = x_1^{\tilde{v}_i} \cdot e(P_1, -v_j P_2), \\ x_3 = x_1^{r_i} \cdot x_2. \end{cases} \tag{1}$$

Finally, the signer checks whether $v_j = H_2(x_3) \oplus u_j$. If holds, the j-th tuple in L_2 is the message and signature of i-th tuple in L_1. Since, only if the corresponding signature of $(r_i, \tilde{v}_i, \tilde{S}_i)$ is (m_j, v_j, S_j), we can ensure that

$$\begin{aligned} x_1 &= e((r_i + \tilde{v}_i)^{-1} \alpha_j (r_j + \tilde{v}_j) d_{ID}, Q_{ID}) \\ &= e(P_1, P_2)^{\alpha_j \cdot (r_i + \tilde{v}_i)^{-1} \cdot (r_j + \tilde{v}_j)} = e(P_1, P_2)^{\alpha_j}, \\ x_2 &= e(\alpha_j P_1, P_2)^{\alpha_i^{-1} \cdot (v_i + \beta_i)} \cdot e(P_1, P_2)^{-v_j} \\ &= e(P_1, P_2)^{\alpha_j \cdot \alpha_i^{-1} \cdot (v_i + \beta_i) - v_j} = e(P_1, P_2)^{\beta_j}, \\ x_3 &= x_1^{r_i} \cdot x_2 = e(\alpha_j R_j + \beta_j P_1, P_2) = w_j, \end{aligned} \tag{2}$$

where $\{\alpha_i, \beta_i, r_i, v_i, \tilde{v}_i\} = \{\alpha_j, \beta_j, r_j, v_j, \tilde{v}_j\}$. Obviously, if x_3 is matching with the tuple (m_j, v_j, S_j), the equation $v_j = H_2(x_3) \oplus u_j$ must hold.

In terms of efficiency, the signer only needs to traverse the list L_2 to track all the signatures. Thus, using the above method, the signer can determine when each signature was signed by itself, thereby break the untraceability.

5 Our Proposed Scheme

Signer		User
Choose $r \leftarrow_\$ \mathbb{Z}_q^*$. Compute $R = rP_1$.	$\xrightarrow{R}$	Choose $\alpha, \beta \leftarrow_\$ \mathbb{Z}_q^*$. Compute $u = F_1(m)\|(F_2(F_1(m)) \oplus m)$, $w_1 = e(\alpha R + \beta P_1, P_2)$, $w_2 = e(\beta \cdot P_1, H_1(ID)P_2 + P_{pub})$, $w = w_1 \cdot w_2$, $v = u \oplus H_2(w)$,
	$\xleftarrow{\tilde{v}}$	$\tilde{v} = \alpha^{-1}(v - \beta) \mod q$.
Compute $\tilde{S} = (r - \tilde{v})d_{ID}$.	$\xrightarrow{\tilde{S}}$	
		Compute $S = \alpha \cdot \tilde{S} + \beta \cdot P_1$. Output $\sigma = (v, S)$.

Fig. 1. The blind signature generation phase.

The algorithms of our IDBS-MR scheme are described as follows:

1. Setup: KGC executes the following steps to initialize system with a security parameter λ:
   (a) Choose a bilinear pairing parameters, denoted as $\mathsf{pp_{bp}} = \{\mathbb{G}_1, \mathbb{G}_2, \mathbb{G}_T, P_1, P_2, q, e, g\}$.
   (b) Choose four hash function satisfying that $H_1 : \{0,1\}^* \to \mathbb{Z}_q^*$, $H_2 : \mathbb{G}_T \to \{0,1\}^{|q|}$, $F_1 : \{0,1\}^{l_2} \to \{0,1\}^{l_1}$ and $F_2 : \{0,1\}^{l_1} \to \{0,1\}^{l_2}$.
   (c) Select a random integer $s \leftarrow_\$ \mathbb{Z}_q^*$ as the master secret key and compute the master public key $P_{pub} = s \cdot P_2$.
   (d) Publish the system parameters as $\mathsf{par} = \{\mathsf{pp_{bp}}, l_1, l_2, H_2, H_1, F_1, F_2, P_{pub}\}$ and keep $\mathsf{msk} = s$ as secret.
2. KeyExtract: Given an identity $ID \in \{0,1\}^*$, KGC computes the signer's private key as $d_{ID} = (s + H_1(ID))^{-1} \cdot P_1$ and sends it to the user.
3. BlindSig: The signer and the user follow the steps given below to generate the signature of a given message $m \in \{0,1\}^{l_2}$ (see Fig. 1):
   - *Committing.* The signer randomly picks up an integer $r \leftarrow_\$ \mathbb{Z}_q^*$ and sends $R = rP_1$ to the user.
   - *Blinding.* The user randomly picks up two integers $\alpha, \beta \leftarrow_\$ \mathbb{Z}_q^*$ and computes $u = F_1(m)\|(F_2(F_1(m)) \oplus m)$, $w_1 = e(\alpha R + \beta P_1, P_2)$, $w_2 = e(\beta \cdot P_1, H_1(ID)P_2 + P_{pub})$, $w = w_1 \cdot w_2$ and $v = u \oplus H_2(w)$. Then, the user sends $\tilde{v} = \alpha^{-1}(v - \beta) \mod q$ to the signer.
   - *Signing.* The signer sends $\tilde{S} = (r - \tilde{v})d_{ID}$ to the user.
   - Unblinding. The user computes $S = \alpha \cdot \tilde{S} + \beta \cdot P_1$ and outputs $\sigma = (v, S)$ as the signature.
4. BlindVrf: Taking a signature $\sigma' = (v', S')$ as input, the verifier computes $w' = e(S', H_1(ID)P_2 + P_{pub}) \cdot g^{v'}$, $u' = v' \oplus H_2(w')$ and $m' = F_2(|u'|_{l_1}) \oplus |u'|_{l_2}$. Then, the user checks whether $|u'|_{l_1}$ equals to $F_1(m')$. If equals, the signature is valid and m' is the extracted message. Otherwise, the signature is invalid.

Correctness. Obviously, the following equation holds

$$\begin{aligned} w' &= e(S', H_1(ID)P_2 + P_{pub}) \cdot g^{v'} \\ &= e(\alpha \cdot \tilde{S} + \beta \cdot P_1, H_1(ID)P_2 + P_{pub}) \cdot g^{v} \\ &= e(\alpha \cdot \tilde{S}, H_1(ID)P_2 + P_{pub}) \cdot w_2 \cdot g^{v} \\ &= g^{\alpha r + \beta - v} \cdot w_2 \cdot g^{v} \\ &= w_1 \cdot w_2 = w \end{aligned} \quad (3)$$

Thus, $u' = v' \oplus H_2(w') = u \oplus H_2(w) \oplus H_2(w') = u$. Hence, $|u|_{l_1} = F_1(m)$ and $m = F_2(|u|_{l_1}) \oplus |u|_{l_2}$ hold. So, the correctness have been proved.

6 Security Analysis

In this section, we prove the blindness, untraceability and unforgeability of the proposed scheme according to the security mode defined in Sect. 3.3.

Firstly, in the BlindSig algorithm, the signer can only get the tuple $(r, w_1, \tilde{v}, \tilde{S})$. By comparing v and $\tilde{v}$, it can be find that $\tilde{v}$ is blinded by the random factor α and β. In addition, both v and $\tilde{v}$ are uniformly distributed in $\mathbb{Z}_q$, so the signer cannot obtain any information about v from $\tilde{v}$, and thus cannot get any bit of the message hidden in v. Next, we will demonstrate the untraceability of the scheme in the following theorem.

Theorem 1. *The proposed scheme satisfies the untraceability property.*

Proof. Note that for any tuple $\{r_i, \tilde{v}_i\}$ and any tuple $\{m_j, v_j, S_j\}$, there must exist an unknown and unique tuple (α, β) that makes the signer's temporary data match the user's signature data, so as to simulate a real blind signing process.

By observing the blind signature generation phase, the signer's tuple $\{r, \tilde{v}\}$ and the signature tuple $\{m, v, S\}$ need to satisfy the following equation relations:

$$v = u \oplus H_2(e(S, H_1(ID)P_2 + P_{pub}) \cdot g^{v}), \quad (4)$$

$$\tilde{v} = \alpha^{-1}(v - \beta) \mod q, \quad (5)$$

$$S = \alpha \cdot \delta \cdot (r - \tilde{v})P_1 + \beta \cdot P_1, \quad (6)$$

where $\delta = (s + H_1(ID))^{-1}$.

From Eq. 5 and 6, we substitute the tuple $\{r_i, \tilde{v}_i\}$ and $\{m_j, v_j, S_j\}$ to establish the following equation

$$\begin{cases} v_j P_1 = \tilde{v}_i \cdot \alpha P_1 + \beta P_1, \\ S_j = \delta \cdot (r_i - \tilde{v}_i) \cdot \alpha P_1 + \beta P_1 \end{cases} \quad (7)$$

In the cyclic additive group $\mathbb{G}_1$, there exists a unique solution $(\alpha P_1, \beta P_1)$ for Eq. 7 since δ is deterministic. Although the solution (α, β) cannot be calculated from the existing tuples, it does exist. Then, if Eq. 7 holds, Eq. 4 also holds since m_j, v_j, S_j haven't changed anything. Thus, (α, β) must exist.

Finally, assume that the adversary $\mathcal{A}$ obtains two signature data $\{m_0, v_0, S_0\}$ and $\{m_1, v_1, S_1\}$. For any tuple $\{r_i, \tilde{v}_i\}(i \in \{0,1\})$, there will always exist a unique tuple (α, β) that matches a signature (either $\{r_0, \tilde{v}_0\}$ or $\{r_1, \tilde{v}_1\}$). Even though $\mathcal{A}$ has infinite computing power, $\mathcal{A}$ outputs a correct value b' with a probability exactly $\frac{1}{2}$. So, the scheme is untraceable.

In the following theorem, we follow the security model of the identity-based signature scheme in [30] and utility the forking lemma [31] to proof the unforgeability of our scheme.

Theorem 2 (Unforgeability). *The proposed scheme is secure in the secure model of existential unforgeability against chosen-message attacks.*

Proof. For a given τ-SDH problem instance $(P, \alpha P, \alpha^2 P, \cdots, \alpha^\tau P, Q, \alpha Q, \alpha^2 Q, \cdots, \alpha^\tau Q)$, $\mathcal{C}$ aims to find a pair $(c, \frac{1}{c+\alpha}P)$, where $c \in \mathbb{Z}_q$. To solve this problem, $\mathcal{C}$ interacts with $\mathcal{A}$ as follows:

Setup phase. $\mathcal{C}$ generates the system parameter $\{P_1, P_2\}$, the master key pair $(P_{pub}, \perp)$ as follows:

1. $\mathcal{C}$ randomly selects $\tau - 1$ integers $\omega_1, \omega_2, \cdots, \omega_{\tau-1} \in \mathbb{Z}_q^*$ and computes the coefficients $c_0, c_1, \cdots, c_{\tau-1} \in \mathbb{Z}_q^*$ of the polynomial $f(z) = \prod_{i=1}^{\tau-1}(z + \omega_i)$.
2. $\mathcal{C}$ sets the generator $P_2 = \sum_{i=0}^{\tau-1} c_i(\alpha_i Q) \in \mathbb{G}_2$ and computes the generator $P_1 = \sum_{i=0}^{\tau-1} c_i(\alpha_i P) = f(\alpha)P \in \mathbb{G}_1$.
3. $\mathcal{C}$ sets the master public $P_{pub} = \sum_{i=1}^{\tau} c_{i-1}(\alpha_i Q)$ so that $P_{pub} = \alpha P_2$ although α is unknown.
4. For $1 \leq i \leq \tau - 1$, $\mathcal{C}$ computes the coefficients of the polynomial $f_i(z) = f(z)/(z + \omega_i) = \sum_{i=0}^{\tau-2} d_i z^i$ and

$$\frac{1}{\alpha + \omega_i} P_2 = \frac{f(\alpha)}{\alpha + \omega_i} = \sum_{i=0}^{\tau-2} d_i \psi(\alpha^i Q).$$

5. $\mathcal{C}$ stores the precomputed pairs $(\omega_i, \frac{1}{\alpha+\omega_i}P_2)(1 \leq i \leq \tau - 1)$ in the list L_ω and sends $\{P_1, P_2, P_{pub}\}$ to $\mathcal{A}$.

Query Phase. $\mathcal{C}$ makes the following response to $\mathcal{A}$'s queries:

- H_1-queries. On input an identity ID_i, $\mathcal{C}$ randomly selects an integer $\omega^* \leftarrow_\$ \mathbb{Z}_q^*$ if $ID_i = ID^*$ and return ω^* to $\mathcal{A}$. Otherwise, $\mathcal{C}$ picks an unused w_i in the list L_ω and return it. Then, $\mathcal{C}$ stores (ID_i, w_i) or (ID^*, w^*) into the list L_1.
- H_2-queries. On input an element $w \in \mathbb{G}_T$, $\mathcal{C}$ randomly selects an integer $y \leftarrow_\$ \mathbb{Z}_q^*$ if w have not been queries. Otherwise, $\mathcal{C}$ picks the matching pair (w, y) in the list L_2 and returns y. Then, $\mathcal{C}$ updates L_2 with the tuple (w, y).
- Key extract queries. On input a identity ID, if $ID = ID_i \in \{ID_1, ID_2, \cdots\}$, $\mathcal{C}$ finds the matching pair (ID_i, w_i) from L_1 and returns the pre-computed element $\frac{1}{\alpha+\omega_i}P_2$ from L_ω. If $ID = ID^*$, aborts.

- Sign queries. On input a message-identity pair (m, ID), if $ID \neq ID^*$, $\mathcal{C}$ randomly selects $S \leftarrow_\$ \mathbb{G}_1$, $v \leftarrow_\$ \mathbb{Z}_q^*$ and computes $w = e(S, H_1(ID)P_2 + P_{pub}) \cdot g^v$, $u = F_1(m)||(F_2(F_1(m)) \oplus m)$ and $y = u \oplus v$. Then, $\mathcal{C}$ stores (w, y) into L_2.

Forge Phase. Based on the forking lemma [31], if $\mathcal{A}$ can forge a signature pair (ID^*, w, v, S), $\mathcal{C}$ can build an algorithm that requests $\mathcal{A}$ to forge a sufficient number of time on input ID^* and outputs two suitable pairs (m, w, v_1, S_1) and (m, w, v_2, S_2) where $v_1 \neq v_2$. Thus, $\mathcal{C}$ can make the following reduction:

If both pairs can pass the verification of the BlindVrf algorithm, the relation $e(S_1, Q_{ID}) \cdot g^{v_1} = e(S_2, Q_{ID}) \cdot g^{v_2}$ where $Q_{ID} = H_1(ID)P_2 + P_{pub}$. Then,

$$e((v_2 - v_1)^{-1}(S_1 - S_2), Q_{ID}) = g,$$

and $T^* = (v_2 - v_1)^{-1}(S_1 - S_2) = \frac{1}{\alpha+\omega^*}P_1$. $\mathcal{C}$ computes the coefficient of the polynomial $f(z)/(z + \omega^*) = \gamma_{-1}\frac{1}{\alpha+\omega^*} + \sum_{i=0}^{\tau-2} \gamma_i z^i$ and

$$\frac{1}{\alpha + \omega^*}P = \frac{1}{\gamma_{-1}}(T^* - \sum_{i=0}^{\tau-2} \gamma_i(\alpha^i P)).$$

Finally, $\mathcal{C}$ obtains a solution $(\omega^*, \frac{1}{\alpha+\omega^*}P)$ to solve the given problem instance. If $\mathcal{A}$ can forge a signature in a time t with the advantage $\epsilon \geq 10(q_s+1)(q_s+q_h)/2^\lambda$, $\mathcal{C}$ can solve the τ-SDH problem in time

$$t' < 120686 q_{h_2}(t + O(q_s \tau_p))/(\epsilon(1 - q/2^\lambda)) + O(q^2 \tau_{mult}).$$

7 Performance Evaluation

In this section, we discuss the performance of our proposed scheme with existing IDBS-MR schemes in terms of computation cost and communication cost. Note that the traditional identity-based blind signature schemes need transmit the message-signature pair to the verifier while the IDBS-MR scheme only transmit the signature to reduce the communication cost. In addition, we employ the same secure parameter $\lambda = 128$ and elliptic curve parameters "BN-256" [32] to evaluate the performance. Thus, the bit length of an element in a group $(\mathbb{Z}_q, \mathbb{G}_1, \mathbb{G}_2, \mathbb{G}_T)$ is determined, i.e. $|\mathbb{Z}_q| = 256$, $|\mathbb{G}_1| = 512$, $|\mathbb{G}_2| = 1024$, and $|\mathbb{G}_T| = 3072$.

Then, we utilize the RELIC library [33] to implement cryptographic primitives on a Laptop with Intel(R) Core(TM) i7-8850U 2.00 GHz processor, 8 GB RAM and Window 10 (64 bit) operating system. Some primary operations are benchmarked and the statistical results are given in the Table 2.

In Table 3, we compare the computation costs of our scheme and other schemes [14,15]. For our scheme, the computation cost of the signer and the user is $2T_{pm1} \approx 0.286$ ms and $2T_{bp} + T_{pm2} + 3T_{pm1} + T_{mi} \approx 3.645$ ms, respectively, while the computation cost of the verifier is $T_{bp} + T_{te} + T_{pm2} \approx 2.624$ ms.

Table 2. Execute time of primary operations (ms)

Notations	Operations	Costs
T_{mi}	Inversion operation in $\mathbb{Z}_q$	0.023
T_{pa1}	Point addition in $\mathbb{G}_1$	0.002
T_{pm1}	Point multiplication in $\mathbb{G}_1$	0.143
T_{pa2}	Point addition in $\mathbb{G}_2$	0.003
T_{pm2}	Point multiplication in $\mathbb{G}_2$	0.229
T_{bp}	Bilinear pairing operation	1.482
T_{te}	Exponentiation operation in $\mathbb{G}_T$	0.913
T_h	Hash operation with 3072 bits input	0.003

Table 3. Computations costs of different entities (ms)

Schemes	Costs of the signer	Costs of the user	Costs of the verifier
Our scheme	$2T_{pm1} \approx 0.286$ ms	$2T_{bp} + T_{pm2} + 3T_{pm1} + T_{mi} \approx 3.645$ ms	$T_{bp} + T_{te} + T_{pm2} \approx 2.624$ ms
Verma *et al.*'s scheme [15]	$2T_{pm1} \approx 0.286$ ms	$T_{bp} + 2T_{pm1} + T_{mi} \approx 1.791$ ms	$2T_{bp} + T_{te} + T_{pm2} \approx 4.106$ ms
James *et al.*'s scheme [14]	$2T_{pm1} \approx 0.286$ ms	$T_{bp} + 2T_{pm1} + T_{mi} \approx 1.791$ ms	$2T_{bp} + T_{pm2} \approx 3.193$ ms

From Table 3, it is clear that our scheme is equals to Verma *et al.* scheme [15] and James *et al.* scheme [14] in terms of the cost of the signer. However, in terms of the cost of the user, our is significantly slower than the other two since it exists an extra bilinear pairing operation. In terms of the cost of the verifier, our scheme is faster than [15] and [14] since it replace the pairing operation with the exponentiation operation in $\mathbb{G}_T$.

In terms of signature size, the three schemes compared are all in the form of (v, S) where v is an element in $\mathbb{Z}_q$ and S is an element in $\mathbb{G}_1$. So, the signature size is both $|\mathbb{Z}_q| + |\mathbb{G}_1| = 768$ bits. In terms of communication costs, the data transmitted for each signature is $(R, \tilde{v}, \tilde{S})$, and its size is $2 * |\mathbb{Z}_q| + |\mathbb{G}_1| = 1024$ bits. Thus, our scheme is the same as the other two in the communication view.

8 Conclusion

This paper proposed an untraceable identity-based blind signature with message recovery and demonstrated that it can achieve the expected blindness, untraceability and unforgeability. Through performance comparison with other schemes, the computation cost of the user has increased in our scheme, but that of the signer remains the same with others. In views of the verifier, the computation cost is significantly reduced. However, the proposed scheme is only suitable for scenarios with a small amount of data since the bit-length of supported messages is short. In the future, a pairing-free IDBS-MR scheme is waiting to be proposed since the pairing operation needs high computation costs.

References

1. Nakamoto, S.: Bitcoin: a peer-to-peer electronic cash system. Technical report, Manubot (2019)
2. Wood, G., et al.: Ethereum: a secure decentralised generalised transaction ledger. Ethereum Project Yellow Paper **151**(2014), 1–32 (2014)
3. Sasson, E.B., et al.: Zerocash: decentralized anonymous payments from bitcoin. In: 2014 IEEE Symposium on Security and Privacy, pp. 459–474. IEEE (2014)
4. Sun, S.-F., Au, M.H., Liu, J.K., Yuen, T.H.: RingCT 2.0: a compact accumulator-based (linkable ring signature) protocol for blockchain cryptocurrency monero. In: Foley, S.N., Gollmann, D., Snekkenes, E. (eds.) ESORICS 2017. LNCS, vol. 10493, pp. 456–474. Springer, Cham (2017). https://doi.org/10.1007/978-3-319-66399-9_25
5. Camenisch, J.: Group signature schemes and payment systems based on the discrete logarithm problem. Ph.D. thesis, ETH Zurich (1998)
6. Chaum, D.: Blind signatures for untraceable payments. In: Chaum, D., Rivest, R.L., Sherman, A.T. (eds.) Advances in Cryptology, pp. 199–203. Springer, Boston, MA (1983). https://doi.org/10.1007/978-1-4757-0602-4_18
7. Chang, C.-C., Lee, J.-S.: An anonymous voting mechanism based on the key exchange protocol. Comput. Secur. **25**(4), 307–314 (2006)
8. Delaune, S., Kremer, S., Ryan, M.: Coercion-resistance and receipt-freeness in electronic voting. In: 19th IEEE Computer Security Foundations Workshop (CSFW 2006), pp. 12-pp. IEEE (2006)
9. Shamir, A.: Identity-based cryptosystems and signature schemes. In: Blakley, G.R., Chaum, D. (eds.) CRYPTO 1984. LNCS, vol. 196, pp. 47–53. Springer, Heidelberg (1985). https://doi.org/10.1007/3-540-39568-7_5
10. Nyberg, K., Rueppel, R.A.: A new signature scheme based on the DSA giving message recovery. In: Proceedings of the 1st ACM Conference on Computer and Communications Security, pp. 58–61 (1993)
11. Han, S., Chang, E.: A pairing-based blind signature scheme with message recovery. Int. J. Inf. Technol. **2**(4), 187–192 (2005)
12. Elkamchouchi, H.M., Abouelseoud, Y.: A new blind identity-based signature scheme with message recovery. IACR Cryptology ePrint Archive, 2008:38 (2008)
13. Diao, L., Gu, J., Yen, I.-L.: A new proxy blind signature scheme with message recovery. Inf. Technol. J. **12**(21), 6159 (2013)
14. James, S., Gowri, T., Babu, G.V., Reddy, P.V.: Identity-based blind signature scheme with message recovery. Electr. Comput. Eng. **7**(5), 2088–8708 (2017)
15. Verma, G.K., Singh, B.B.: Efficient identity-based blind message recovery signature scheme from pairings. IET Inf. Secur. **12**(2), 150–156 (2017)
16. James, S., Gayathri, N.B., Reddy, P.V.: Pairing free identity-based blind signature scheme with message recovery. Cryptography **2**(4), 29 (2018)
17. Cao, T., Lin, D., Xue, R.: A randomized RSA-based partially blind signature scheme for electronic cash. Comput. Secur. **24**(1), 44–49 (2005)
18. Zhang, F., Kim, K.: ID-based blind signature and ring signature from pairings. In: Zheng, Y. (ed.) ASIACRYPT 2002. LNCS, vol. 2501, pp. 533–547. Springer, Heidelberg (2002). https://doi.org/10.1007/3-540-36178-2_33
19. Zhang, F., Kim, K.: Efficient ID-based blind signature and proxy signature from bilinear pairings. In: Safavi-Naini, R., Seberry, J. (eds.) ACISP 2003. LNCS, vol. 2727, pp. 312–323. Springer, Heidelberg (2003). https://doi.org/10.1007/3-540-45067-X_27

20. Huang, Z., Chen, K., Wang, Y.: Efficient identity-based signatures and blind signatures. In: Desmedt, Y.G., Wang, H., Mu, Y., Li, Y. (eds.) CANS 2005. LNCS, vol. 3810, pp. 120–133. Springer, Heidelberg (2005). https://doi.org/10.1007/11599371_11
21. Mao, J.: Linkability analysis of some blind signature schemes. In: Wang, Y., Cheung, Y., Liu, H. (eds.) CIS 2006. LNCS (LNAI), vol. 4456, pp. 556–566. Springer, Heidelberg (2007). https://doi.org/10.1007/978-3-540-74377-4_58
22. Kalkan, S., Kaya, K., Selcuk, A.A.: Generalized ID-based blind signatures from bilinear pairings. In: 2008 23rd International Symposium on Computer and Information Sciences, pp. 1–6. IEEE (2008)
23. Fan, C.-I., Sun, W.-Z., Huang, V.S.-M.: Provably secure randomized blind signature scheme based on bilinear pairing. Comput. Math. Appl. **60**(2), 285–293 (2010)
24. Zhang, L., Hu, Y., Tian, X., Yang, Y.: Novel identity-based blind signature for electronic voting system. In: 2010 Second International Workshop on Education Technology and Computer Science, vol. 2, pp. 122–125. IEEE (2010)
25. Shakerian, R., MohammadPour, T., Kamali, S.H., Hedayati, M.: An identity based public key cryptography blind signature scheme from bilinear pairings. In: 2010 3rd International Conference on Computer Science and Information Technology, vol. 7, pp. 28–32. IEEE (2010)
26. Hu, X., Wang, J., Yang, Y.: Secure ID-based blind signature scheme without random oracle. In: 2011 International Conference on Network Computing and Information Security, vol. 1, pp. 245–249. IEEE (2011)
27. Xu, G., Xu, G.: An ID-based blind signature from bilinear pairing with unlinkability. In: 2013 3rd International Conference on Consumer Electronics, Communications and Networks, pp. 101–104. IEEE (2013)
28. He, D., Chen, J., Zhang, R.: An efficient identity-based blind signature scheme without bilinear pairings. Comput. Electr. Eng. **37**(4), 444–450 (2011)
29. Khan, M.A., Qureshi, I.M., Ullah, I., Khan, S., Khanzada, F., Noor, F.: An efficient and provably secure certificateless blind signature scheme for flying ad-hoc network based on multi-access edge computing. Electronicsd **9**(1), 30 (2020)
30. Barreto, P.S.L.M., Libert, B., McCullagh, N., Quisquater, J.-J.: Efficient and provably-secure identity-based signatures and signcryption from bilinear maps. In: Roy, B. (ed.) ASIACRYPT 2005. LNCS, vol. 3788, pp. 515–532. Springer, Heidelberg (2005). https://doi.org/10.1007/11593447_28
31. Pointcheval, D., Stern, J.: Security arguments for digital signatures and blind signatures. J. Cryptol. **13**(3), 361–396 (2000)
32. Devegili, A.J., Scott, M., Dahab, R.: Implementing cryptographic pairings over Barreto-Naehrig curves. In: Takagi, T., Okamoto, T., Okamoto, E., Okamoto, T. (eds.) Pairing 2007. LNCS, vol. 4575, pp. 197–207. Springer, Heidelberg (2007). https://doi.org/10.1007/978-3-540-73489-5_10
33. Aranha, D.F., Gouvêa, C.P.L., Markmann, T., Wahby, R.S., Liao, K.: RELIC is an Efficient LIbrary for Cryptography. https://github.com/relic-toolkit/relic

AIHWS - Artificial Intelligence in Hardware Security

A Good Anvil Fears No Hammer: Automated Rowhammer Detection Using Unsupervised Deep Learning

Anirban Chakraborty(✉), Manaar Alam, and Debdeep Mukhopadhyay

Indian Institute of Technology, Kharagpur, Kharagpur, India
{anirban.chakraborty,alam.manaar}@iitkgp.ac.in, debdeep@cse.iitkgp.ac.in

Abstract. The Rowhammer bug has exposed a severe reliability issue in modern commodity-grade DRAM modules where repeated accesses to a particular row can cause bit-flips in its adjacent rows. It is a prime example where a reliability issue can lead to a practical security vulnerability that can aid an adversary to mount an array of local and remote attacks to jeopardize a system completely. Although several security countermeasures have been proposed, recent attacks show that they are not sufficient enough to completely mitigate Rowhammer vulnerability. In this paper, we attempt to take a novel approach by using the DRAM access patterns generated by benign processes to train an *unsupervised* Deep Learning model. The objective of the model is to analyze the memory access patterns of processes which suffer from high last level cache miss rate and classify it as either benign or anomaly with high accuracy. We also introduce a reverse-engineering module in our approach to uncover the DRAM bank addressing functions (which are not available publicly) based on a novel bin-partitioning algorithm. We further show that our detection methodology can reliably detect a Rowhammer process with 97% accuracy. In a more general context, we show that a suitable combination of deep learning and reverse engineering of physical addresses can help to detect Rowhammer attacks successfully.

Keywords: Rowhammer · Deep learning application · Autoencoder

1 Introduction

One of the fundamental components of modern computing systems is the physical memory which plays a key role in determining the overall performance and reliability of the system. The requirement for enhanced performance and enlarged memory capacity led the hardware manufacturers to increase the density of memory modules via technological scaling. Although this trend of increasing memory density lowered the cost-per-bit, it created severe reliability and security issues in hindsight. As more and more electronic components are crammed into a small physical space, the memory cells became highly vulnerable to circuit failures. These seemingly benign circuit failures can lead to serious security issues where

J. Zhou et al. (Eds.): ACNS 2021 Workshops, LNCS 12809, pp. 59–77, 2021.
https://doi.org/10.1007/978-3-030-81645-2_5

a malicious attacker can exploit them to leak sensitive data and even jeopardise the system altogether.

The *Rowhammer bug*, introduced by Kim et al. [12] in 2014, is one of the most prominent effect of these circuit-level failures. It is a phenomenon observed when repeated accesses to a particular row of modern Dynamic Random Access Memory (DRAM) chips cause the cells in adjacent rows to lose charge and thereby induce bit flips. Subsequent works have established that most commodity-grade DDR3 and DDR4 DRAM modules are vulnerable to the Rowhammer bug. The phenomenon is attributed to the fact that DRAM cells are closely packed where circuit level cell-to-cell interference causes *disturbance errors* which results in some of the cells to lose charge. Although it was introduced as a reliability issue that could have implications on data integrity, subsequent works have shown that the Rowhammer bug can be exploited to carry out a number of critical security and privacy breaches. Some of the well known threats include taking over remote systems using Javascript-enables websites [9,18], escaping from sandbox environments [13], cross-VM hypervisor privilege escalation attacks [23], attacks on mobile devices [19], key extraction from ciphers like AES [6], RSA [4,24], etc.

One of the striking features, or rather side-effect, of Rowhammer is high cache miss rate. To conduct Rowhammer, one needs to access DRAM rows repeatedly, bypassing the cache memory every time. This leads to high cache miss events which are logged into CPU's Hardware Performance Counters (HPCs). HPCs are extensively used in the literature to detect anomalies in a system [1,21]. Researchers have also tried to develop software-based countermeasures utilizing HPCs to detect probable Rowhammer attacks [2,3]. However, they suffer from high false positives where many benign programs were mis-classified as potentially malicious. It must be noted that fault induced by Rowhammer operation is not entirely random and unpredictable. It is heavily related to device physics and needs a number of necessary criterion to be fulfilled (discussed later in Sect. 2) to induce exploitable faults[1]. Moreover, Rowhammer induced bit-flips are dependent on memory access patterns and not a randomly occurring event [15]. Also, the bit-flips are repeatable, i.e., bit-flips tend to occur at particular locations repeatedly. In other words, not all memory cells are susceptible to Rowhammer faults in a particular DRAM module. The memory access patterns generated by malicious Rowhammer programs are complex in the sense that they are abstracted by the virtual to physical address translation mechanism of the processor. The actual physical locations in the DRAM, in terms of bank and row indices, accessed by a malicious program are difficult to extract.

The central idea of this paper is to utilize HPCs to monitor the last level cache (LLC) misses and if a process is found to produce high LLC miss rate then we use *unsupervised* Deep Learning based approach to identify whether the process is malicious or benign in terms of its memory access patterns. In other words, our proposed tool tries to detect the access patterns which might lead to successful Rowhammer faults with high accuracy that can be implemented on any

[1] We define exploitable faults as those bit-flips which can lead to security or confidentiality issue. Not all bit-flips can be exploited by an adversary to exploit a system.

standard machine without any need to make hardware or system modification. Recently Chakraborty et al. proposed a Deep Learning based detection mechanism [7] to detect Rowhammer attempts where they used supervised learning to train a system. However, the major assumption and a restriction in some sense with the supervised approach is that, the user has to train the model with both positive and negative examples before deploying it on any standard system. In order to do that, the user must run monitored Rowhammer attacks on the particular system to generate both benign and malicious memory access patterns and also requires to have sufficient knowledge about the underlying memory module (in particular, DRAM bank addressing functions[2]). It is worth mentioning that such a solution might not be a feasible one for an amateur user albeit providing high accuracy and certainly limits the usage boundary of the solution. Also, it is infeasible to generate all kinds of Rowhammer access patterns, which is a requisite for training a supervised learning model. In this paper, we propose a more generic and fully automated solution. We approach the problem as *analogous to anomaly detection problem* where benign access patterns are considered as normal and Rowhammer-inducing access patterns are considered anomalies. In order to facilitate this anomaly detection, we use an unsupervised model, a CNN-based Autoencoder as it has recently been shown to be an efficient tool in anomaly detection problem [1,14]. We further remove the requirement of system knowledge by incorporating a reverse-engineering module in our tool that unearths the bank addressing function and subsequently uses that knowledge to aid the detection mechanism. The automated reverse engineering of the DRAM addressing functions provides a system-independent generic solution.

Related Works

A number of countermeasures, both hardware and software based, have been proposed to tackle the Rowhammer bug. However, modifying underlying hardware might not always be a favourable solution, more specifically for already deployed vulnerable systems. ANVIL [3] was proposed as a software-based solution that monitors Last Level Cache (LLC) miss rates using HPCs to detect Rowhammer attempts and selectively activate specific rows in the DRAM. However, it requires a kernel-level modification which might not be feasible to all the users. Also, it suffers from high false positive (for example, motion search in video encoding which can lead to high cache misses [11]). Countermeasures in [5,22] proposed to protect sensitive memory pages by modifying the physical memory allocation subsystem of the Operating System such that user-level pages are not placed adjacent to system pages. However, such attacks can only stop certain types of attack like privilege escalation, escaping from sandboxed environment. But attacks such as [4,6] can still be carried out even with these countermeasures in place as they target user-level applications. Another notable software-based detection mechanism proposed

[2] Given a physical address, its actual location in DRAM is defined by a set of functions which maps a physical address to particular rank, bank and row numbers, which is architecture dependent.

in [20] uses a sliding window protocol and dynamic skewed hash tree but requires a checker and an on-chip memory, thereby requiring changes in memory controller. A machine learning based approach was proposed in [2] where the authors analyzed the cache-miss rates of a process extracted from low-level hardware events to generate identifiable access patterns. However, a major drawback of this approach is its susceptibility to noise and significantly higher chances of false positives. A supervised deep-learning based detection tool was proposed in [7] which requires an user to train the model on their own system using both benign and malicious memory access patterns.

Our Contributions

In this work, we introduce an unsupervised Deep Learning based Rowhammer detection tool which *does not require any hardware or kernel-level modification.* In short, it can be used as a standalone tool on any target system without any specific requirement of prior knowledge of the underlying hardware. The major strength of this tool lies in the fact that it incorporates an automated reverse-engineering module that tries to recover the DRAM bank addressing functions using timing channels manifested due to row-buffer collisions. The knowledge of these bank addressing functions make it feasible to map the physical addresses to its corresponding locations in DRAM in terms of bank and row indices for any given processor and DRAM. From this perspective, our tool offers a generic and system-independent solution compared to the work proposed in [7]. Further, we explore the feasibility and efficacy of using unsupervised Deep Learning techniques to detect potentially malicious complex access patterns of programs accessing the memory. In particular, we use CNN-based Autoencoder to identify probable Rowhammer attempts which are categorized as anomalous access patterns by the tool. *To the best of our knowledge, this is the first work which provides a fully-automated unsupervised diagnostic tool using CNN-based Autoencoders that analyzes DRAM access patterns to detect Rowhammer attacks.*

Organisation

The rest of the paper is organized as follows: Sect. 2 provides the necessary background information. In Sect. 3, we discuss the reverse engineering of the DRAM bank addressing functions of the underlying hardware and generate the access patterns by mapping each physical address into its corresponding bank and row indices. In Sect. 4, we present our proposed detection methodology along with the assumed threat model for our detection. Section 5 provides the experimental setup that has been used for this work along with all the implementation details and evaluation results. Finally, we conclude in Sect. 6.

2 Preliminaries

In this section, we provide a brief and necessary background on DRAM Architecture, the Rowhammer Bug, Hardware Performance counters and CNN-based Autoencoders which are used in this work.

2.1 DRAM Architecture

The Dynamic Random Access Memory (DRAM) constitute the main memory subsystem along with the on-chip memory controller. The interchange of data between the processor and DRAM is done through system bus under the control of memory controller. The DRAM cards or modules, known as Dual Inline Memory Modules (DIMM), are connected to the system through physical slots known as *channels*. The memory cells, composed of transistors and capacitors, are the fundamental units of physical memory that store data in form of electric charge. These memory cells are arranged in rows and columns into two-dimensional arrays known as *banks* residing on either side of the DIMM, collectively called *ranks*. All the rows in a bank are connected to a *row-buffer* which holds data from most recently accessed row. When a certain memory address is referenced, the memory controller first checks the row-buffer in the particular bank. If the required data is not present in the row-buffer, the contents of the row-buffer is transferred back to its original row and the requested data is brought into the row-buffer. Therefore, if two different rows from the same bank are referenced, it leads to the above mentioned situation called *row-buffer collision*.

2.2 The Rowhammer Bug

Due to constant scaling down of electrical components that constitute a DRAM cell, a large number of memory cells can be accommodated in smaller physical space inside DRAM banks. However, due to its closely packed architecture, DRAM cells tend to interact among themselves leading to electromagnetic coupling effects. When a particular DRAM row is accessed in high frequency and in a repeated manner, the cells in the neighbouring rows tend to lose their charge, thereby inducing bit-flips in them, i.e., a memory cell holding logical '1' is converted to '0'. This phenomenon is known as *Rowhammer* which has been exploited to launch a number of security attacks in the past. In the normal operation, the rows are periodically refreshed at a specific interval such that the cells do not lose charge. However, if selective DRAM rows are accessed in a frequent and consistent manner, such that multiple accesses are made to the different rows in the same bank within the *refresh interval*, bypassing the cache memory for every access, then bit-flips can be induced with high probability. Governed by the device physics, the sequences of accesses to different rows in the DRAM creates complex patterns that induces the bit-flips. It must be noted that any random access might not be enough to create the Rowhammer effect.

2.3 Hardware Performance Counters

Hardware Performance Counters (HPCs) are a set of special-purpose registers present in modern processors as a part of performance monitoring unit (PMU) to monitor performance-related hardware and software events. The event-based performance information helps to understand how a particular process affects the hardware and software behavior of the system. The number of registers and the hardware events supported varies across processor models and microarchitectures. HPC-based profiling tools are present in almost all modern operating systems (OS). Linux uses *perf_event* subsystem to read the HPC values from kernel space. The *perf_event* operates in two modes - counting and sampling. In counting mode, the profiling tool enables HPCs at the start of a software module's execution and read the values only at the end of its execution. Whereas in sampling mode, the HPC values are read dynamically at a pre-defined interval.

2.4 CNN-Based Autoencoder

Autoencoder (AE) is a type of neural network used for unsupervised learning where it is trained to copy its input to its output approximately. A Convolutional Neural Network (CNN)-based AE consists of two modules: *Encoder* and *Decoder*. The Encoder is a CNN model that maps an input data to a vector representation of fixed dimensionality, and the Decoder is another CNN model that tries to reconstruct the input from the fixed vector representation. CNNs belong to a specific family of neural networks where multiple layers are stacked one after another in a particular order to create the model. The layers belong to the three main categories -

- *Convolution layer*: performs a series of *convolution* operations by sliding a set of *filters* or *kernels* over the inputs during the forward computation phase. The output, known as *feature maps*, shows the locations of the features detected on the input data. An *activation function* is applied after each convolution operation to determine the important features.
- *Pooling Layer*: a non-linear sub-sampling layer that helps in reducing the computation complexity and enhances the robustness of the model. A sliding window over the input data provides the mean (*Average Pooling*) or maximum (*Max Pooling*) as the output.
- *Fully Connected layer*: the final layer in the model that combined the outputs from each neuron from the last convolution or pooling layer and provides as output the probability distribution over the classes.

It is worth mentioning that the filter weights in the convolution layer are randomly assigned initially, which are learned by trying to minimize the overall loss[3] during the backward computation phase using the *back-propagation* algorithm.

The primary goal of an AE is to induce a representation for a set of input data by learning an approximate identity function. Let us consider an input data $\mathcal{X} \in \mathbb{R}^d$ of dimension d. Let us assume that we have a set $\mathcal{S}_T$ of such input data, which we call the *training data*. The Encoder and the Decoder are jointly trained for each $\mathcal{X} \in \mathcal{S}_T$ to obtain a fixed length vector representation $\mathcal{F}$, where $\mathcal{F} \in \mathbb{R}^n$ is an n-dimensional vector and $n < d$. The vector $\mathcal{F}$ represents the common characteristic existing in the training data. Since, the AE learns an *approximate* identity function, it will incur some errors while reproducing the target output

[3] Loss quantifies the average prediction error of the network. A decreasing loss indicates that the network is properly learning.

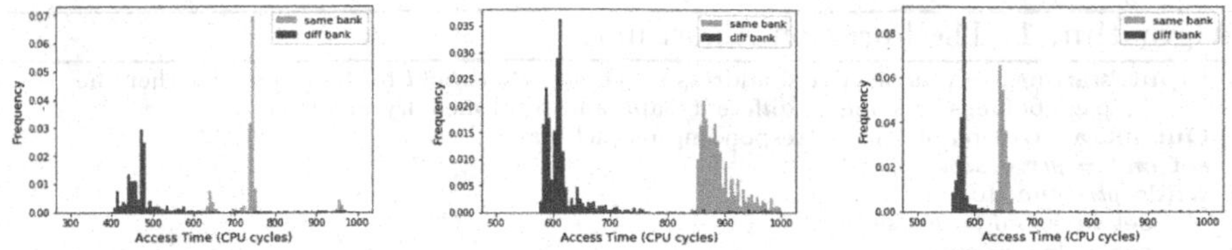

(a) IvyBridge platform (b) KabyLake platform (c) Broadwell Platform

Fig. 1. Access times in CPU cycles for different processors (a) Intel i5-3330, (b) Intel i7-7700 and (c) Intel Xeon-E5-2690v4

for a given input. Let, for an input $\mathcal{X}$, the reconstructed data is $\mathcal{X}' \in \mathbb{R}^d$. The error while generating $\mathcal{X}'$ from $\mathcal{X}$ is termed as *Reconstruction Error*. The reconstruction errors for all the sequences in $\mathcal{S}_T$ is $\mathcal{L} = \sum_{\mathcal{X} \in \mathcal{S}_T} \|\mathcal{X} - \mathcal{X}'\|^2$. The learning goal of the AE is to minimize these errors for all the input samples.

3 Mapping Virtual Addresses to DRAM Banks

In order to successfully induce faults in a DRAM row using Rowhammer, a process has to repeatedly access its adjacent rows with high frequency. However, each process has its own virtual address space which is translated into physical addresses by the Memory Management Unit (MMU) and subsequently mapped into actual physical locations in DRAM chips. The virtual to physical address mapping can be obtained by accessing `pagemap`[4]. Although the knowledge of physical address can aid in making Rowhammering more precise, a correct DRAM address mapping will help to induce more faults in considerably lesser time. Although these DRAM mappings are publicly available for AMD processors, Intel does not publish these details. DRAMA [16] was the first generic tool that attempted to reverse-engineer the DRAM addresses using a hardware-based and a software-based approach. The hardware based approach needs physical probing of the memory bus, thereby restricting its usage to possibility of template-formation for the target systems. The software approach, although does not require any physical access to the system, uses a brute-force approach to generate all possible linear combinations of the physical bits. These blind selection of physical addresses makes the software approach inefficient (taking long time) and often unable to produce correct results with high confidence.

The DRAM mapping function should be efficient and provide correct result in a single run in order to make our diagnostic tool fully automated. Therefore, we introduce a novel *bin partitioning* algorithm to partition the available virtual address space into hypothetical *bins* where each bin corresponds to a DRAM bank. The bin partitioning step heavily refines the number of physical addresses which will be used to verify the generated bank mapping functions. In the next step, we

[4] `pagemap` is an interface provided in Linux that allows userspace programs to access page table and related information for a particular process.

Algorithm 1: The Partition Algorithm

```
Input: starting address of virtual address space ptr, threshold to determine whether the
       page belongs to same or different bank and total memory allocated size
Output: a partition of bins corresponding to each bank
set end := ptr + size
while ptr<end do
    set inserted := False
    set addr1 := ptr
    set addr2 := ptr + pagesize
    if first page then
        bin0 := bin0 ∪ addr1
        access_time := Access_time(addr2)
        if access_time >threshold then
            bin0 := bin0 ∪ addr2
        else
            bin1 := bin1 ∪ addr2
        end
    else
        for i = 0 to no. of banks do
            if bin_i ≠ φ then
                access_time := Access_time(addr1)
                if access_time >threshold then
                    bin_i := bin_i ∪ addr1
                    set inserted = True
                end
            end
        end
        if inserted = False then
            for i = 0 to no. of banks do
                if bin_i = φ then
                    bin_i := bin_i ∪ addr2
                    break
                end
            end
        end
    end
    ptr = ptr + pagesize
end
```

reconstruct the mapping functions from physical address bits by generating linear Boolean functions and checking them against each bin. The idea is that since each bin corresponds to one single bank, all the addresses in a bin should show similar results for the correct function.

3.1 Partitioning Available Virtual Address Space

Algorithm 1 shows the bin partitioning method based on timing difference observed due to row-buffer collision in DRAM. The algorithm starts by allocating a large memory space (for example, 1 GB) and filling the entire memory space with all 1's. Filling memory with some meaningful data will ensure that all the virtual pages are actually mapped to some physical page frame. A page is a block of virtual addresses which is mapped into a physical page frame consisting of contiguous addresses. Thus, within a page, all the addresses are contiguously located in the physical memory. Also, a single page can reside inside one row. So, we traverse through the virtual memory space in page by page manner. We

Algorithm 2: The Bank Addressing Algorithm

```
Input: B := set of bins generated by Algorithm 1
Output: C := set of bank mapping functions
set F := list of all linear Boolean functions
set C := ∅
for bin ∈ B do
    foreach pair < p1, p2 > ∈ bin do
        for f ∈ F do
            if f(p1) = f(p2) then
                C := C ∪ f
            end
        end
    end
end
remove_redundant(C)
return C
```

dynamically create a number of storage containers and call them *bins* where each bin will correspond to a particular bank. Initially all bins are empty. For the first page, we put it in bin_0. We pick up the next page; access the starting address (or any valid offset for that matter) from the first page and second page sequentially and note the access times. It must be noted that after every pair of accesses, the cache must be flushed so that all the accesses are served from the DRAM. Now, if the access time for the second page is more than some pre-defined threshold (can be determined from the graphs in Fig. 1), that would mean the pair of accesses have resulted in a row-buffer conflict. So, the pair of page frames, corresponding to the virtual pages accessed, might be located in the *same bank but different row*, resulting in a row buffer collision during the access. In that case, we put the second page in the same bin as the first one, i.e., bin_0. Whereas, if the access time is less than the threshold, we put it in the next bin, i.e., bin_1. After this step, either bin_0 has two elements or both bin_0 and bin_1 have one element each. Now, we sequentially take one page at a time from the virtual memory space starting from third page (the first and second page has already been placed in correct *bins*). We run a loop with index i which goes from 0 to the number of banks available in the DIMM. For each page, we check if the ith bin is empty or not. If it has atleast one element, we pick any element from the bin and access both the pages one after another, similar to the way we did in the first case. Again the timing details are noted and if the difference in access times is greater than the threshold, we conclude that both the pages belong to the same bank, else the process continues for other bins. If no such bin is found, the page is inserted into a new bin. After the entire virtual space is traversed page by page, all the bins will have pages that belong to a particular bank. Once the entire allocated address space have been traversed as mentioned above, the pages belonging to each bank will reside in one of the *bins*.

3.2 Deriving Bank Index Mapping Function

In the previous subsection, we utilized the timing channel created by row-buffer collision to partition the address space into a number of bins - each bin representing a bank in the installed DIMM. Since all the physical addresses in a particular bin belong to one bank, all the addresses must provide same result when applied to the correct bank mapping linear Boolean function [25]. We note that in a system having M GB (m bits) of memory, the maximum number of bits of physical address required to uniquely address all the memory locations will be $\log_2 m$. We further note that the lower 6 bits are used for addressing within a cache-line (assuming a 64-bit machine). In other words, the bits higher than $\log_2 m$ and last 6 bits from least significant bit (LSB) position do not contribute to bank addressing and thus can be ignored. With this knowledge we proceed to generate a set of candidate linear Boolean functions as discussed in Algorithm 2. For each pair of addresses in a bin, we apply all possible linear Boolean functions to check whether they generate same result. Finally, we obtain a set of linear Boolean functions that produced the same result for all the addresses in each bin. It is to be further noted that the set of linear functions might contain two functions f, g such that g contains all the literals that are already present in f. In such case, we remove the redundancy by rejecting g and accepting only function f. Figure 2 shows the overall reverse engineering process as described in Algorithm 1 and Algorithm 2.

3.3 Generation of Access Patterns

A process running on a system accesses the allocated memory using its own virtual address space. The virtual addresses accessed by a process does not directly reflect the actual physical locations activated in the DRAM. In the previous subsections (Sect. 3.1 and Sect. 3.2), we discussed how virtual addresses can be mapped to its corresponding bank and row indices with the help of the reverse-engineering module. The knowledge of DRAM bank addressing functions and access to `pagemap` enables us to generate the dataset required by the deep-learning based *analyzer* to learn the complex features of the access patterns. The generic Rowhammer attack technique requires the adversary to allocate a sufficiently large amount of memory and randomly select a fixed set of addresses to *hammer* at every iteration. Without loss of generality, we assume that a set of n randomly chosen addresses from the virtual address space is used every time for hammering and m number of such sets constitute an *episode*. Therefore, in each episode the adversary tries out $m \times n$ different addresses, with each address being accessed multiple times. After execution of each episode, the adversary checks whether the bit-flip is achieved. If not, the process is continued keeping the values of m and n fixed, unless a fault is detected. We consider an episode of $m \times n$ addresses as one iteration of the attack[5]. The tool transforms or encodes these $m \times n$ addresses into unique tuples (r_i, b_i) of row number r_i and bank number b_i $\forall i \in (m \times n)$. To constitute the dataset for the deep-learning based model, the tool creates a 3-dimensional $m \times n \times 2$ matrix where each address is identified by its row number r_i and bank number b_i.

[5] In our experimental setup, we have empirically selected m as 10 and n as 8.

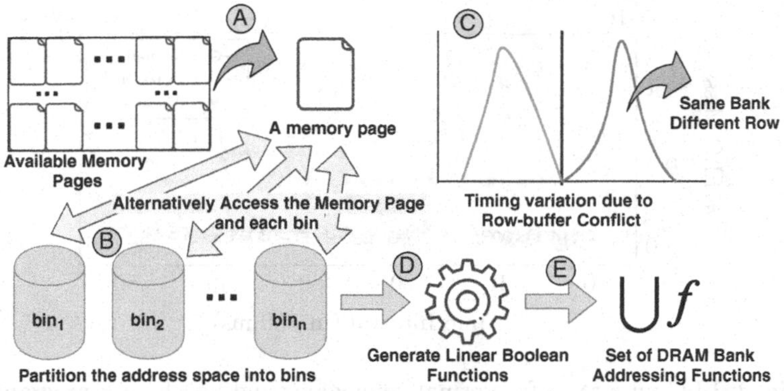

Fig. 2. Reverse Engineering of DRAM Bank addressing functions. (A) A single memory page from the available address space is selected. (B) Alternatively access the contents of each bin and the memory page. (C) Based on row buffer timing channel, put the page into correct bin. (D) Once the entire memory has been partitioned into bins, generate linear Boolean functions as candidates for Bank Addressing function. (E) Set of DRAM Bank Addressing Functions

4 Proposed Unsupervised Detection Methodology

In this paper, we follow a detection methodology similar to the one proposed by Chakraborty et al. [7]. However, our proposed tool incorporates a reverse-engineering module (as discussed in Sect. 3) which makes it generic and system-independent and uses unsupervised learning to analyze the access patterns. The major advantage of using unsupervised learning is that any system can be modelled using benign processes (e.g. benchmark programs), therefore alleviating the need for labelled dataset, and any attempt for Rowhammer access will be categorized as anomaly.

The overall detection methodology can be categorized into two phases: *offline phase* and *online phase*. In the offline phase, the tool will generate *significantly large* benign patterns of DRAM accesses, which represents the legitimate behavior of the target system. These access patterns are pre-processed to transform them into suitable datasets to feed into a deep learning based *analyzer* in order to learn intricate internal features. The entire process of extracting the access pattern and learning of these features is termed as offline phase and needs to be performed only once. In the online phase, the trained analyzer is fed with the addresses of unknown process to predict whether the access patterns will lead to a bit flip. The entire operation is composed of the following five steps.

1. **Access:** It is the first step where different actors are involved in either phases. In the offline phase, the tool itself acts as an actor where it generates large amount of benign access patterns. These access patterns can be generated by any memory-intensive benchmark program. Whereas, an unknown process (malicious or benign) is the actor in the online phase, where it tries to make random accesses to DRAM rows.

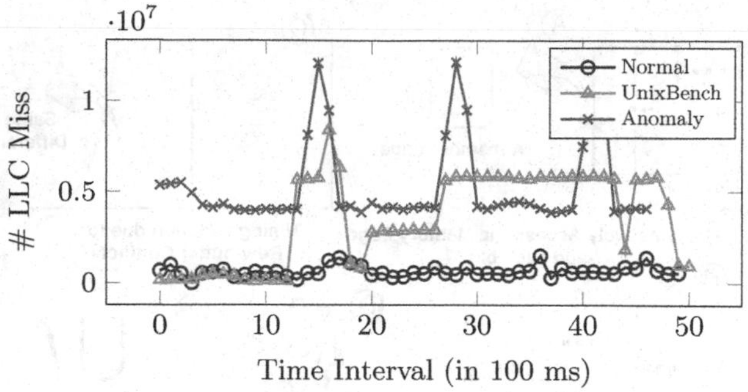

Fig. 3. LLC miss rates for normal, anomalous and benchmark program

2. **AddressMap:** This step is common for both offline and online phases. The tool acquires the virtual addresses accessed by the processes and translates them into corresponding physical addresses using `pagemap`[6].
3. **AccessMap:** The physical addresses thus acquired are mapped to bank and row numbers in the DRAM using the reverse-engineering approach discussed in Sect. 3. These (bank, row) pairs corresponding to each physical address constitute the access pattern data for the analyzer. Both offline and online phases contain this step.
4. **DataPreparation:** The (bank, row) pairs corresponding to each physical address are transformed into a suitable form to feed into the deep-learning based analyzer. The *dataset* produced in this step consists of the sequence of accessed virtual addresses, which we refer to as 'access patterns', is used for *training* in offline phase and *prediction* in online phase
5. **Authorization:** This step is only available in online phase where the analyzer tries to determine whether the probable adversary is a malicious process (i.e., trying to conduct Rowhammer attack) based on its access pattern.

4.1 Identification of a Probable Adversary

As already discussed earlier, Rowhammering process generally leads to high cache miss rate as the adversarial process tries to bypass the cache by flushing it after every access. Additionally, two different rows in the same bank must be accessed such that row-buffer collision takes place and the respective rows are activated. These conditions lead to a high cache miss rate which can be observed by monitoring the cache-miss event of the Hardware Performance Counters (HPC). Linux provides `perf` tool which can dynamically monitor the HPC values at given intervals. We use the following command to monitor the `cache-misses` event at every 100 ms for an executable.

```
perf stat -e cache-misses -I 100 <executable>
```

[6] Assuming the tool has admin privilege, which is a practical assumption for a diagnostic tool, itś able to access `pagemap` in modern Linux kernels.

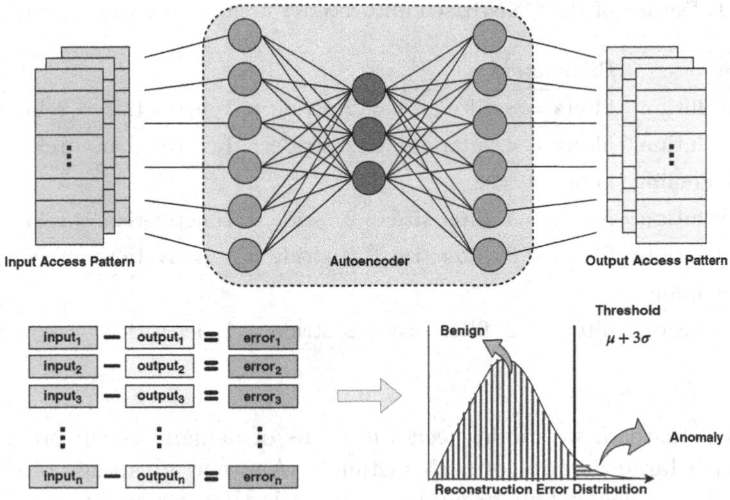

Fig. 4. Overview of the unsupervised analyzer

At first we construct a distribution of LLC miss rates from the values provided by `perf` tool when the system is running under normal load. Based on the values, we empirically select a threshold to segregate potential adversarial process from benign processes. Figure 3 shows the last level cache miss statistics under three operational conditions - (a) the system is under normal load, (b) a Rowhammer process running in the system, classified as anomaly, (c) running UnixBench [17] benchmark suite. As clearly evident, a Rowhammer process has high cache miss rate in comparison to a benign one. Also note that the benchmark program, which is a benign process, suffers from high LLC miss rate.

4.2 Analyzer: Determining Rowhammer Process

Once a probable Rowhammer adversary has been identified, the tool starts recording the virtual addresses accessed by the suspicious process. As discussed in Sect. 3.3, a special 3-dimensional dataset containing the information of all the addresses accessed in an *episode* in terms of row and bank indices of DRAM is generated. This dataset is fed to the analyzer to learn the complex patterns created by the sequence of accesses made by the suspicious process. The deep-learning based analyzer undertakes different roles in offline and online phases which we discuss below.

Offline Phase: In the offline phase, the analyzer obtains abundant data of benign access patterns. Then it trains a CNN based Autoencoder using this benign patterns to learn intricate features present in the data in order to develop a generalized anomaly detection strategy. We avoid modeling access patterns of rowhammer programs as there can be a potential new one whose access pattern

Table 1. Details of the CNN-based autoencoder architecture used in our study

Layers	Parameters
Convolution	filters = 8, filter size = 2, stride = 1, activation = relu
Convolution	filters = 4, filter size = 2, stride = 1, activation = relu
Max Pooling	pool size = 2
Convolution	filters = 4, filter size = 2, stride = 1, activation = relu
Convolution	filters = 8, filter size = 2, stride = 1, activation = relu
Upsampling	size = 2
Convolution	filters = 2, filter size = 2, stride = 1, activation = sigmoid

is unknown. Instead, we model access patterns of benign system programs, as we can get a large number of such instances. Another advantage of detecting anomalies by modeling benign access patterns is that we do not need labeled dataset since any activity with unusual access patterns crossing an empirically calculated threshold can be detected as an anomaly. Thus, we use an unsupervised learning strategy to detect these anomalies. The training is performed as discussed in Sect. 2.4 and the details of the training parameters are provided in Sect. 5.2. Intuition behind the anomaly detection is that the Autoencoder is only shown benign access patterns during the training phase and learned to reconstruct them. However, when an anomalous access pattern is given as an input to the Autoencoder, it will not be able to reconstruct it accurately, and hence would lead to higher reconstruction errors in comparison to the normal sequences. In order to quantify the threshold for detecting anomalous activities, we calculate reconstruction error distribution ($\mathcal{E}$) for some unknown samples of benign access patterns, which are not used in the training phase. Since the unknown samples belong to benign access patterns, according to the 3σ rule of thumb[7], all the error values in $\mathcal{E}$ should lie within three standard deviations of the mean. Hence, we set the threshold ($\mathcal{E}_t$) for reconstruction error as $\mathcal{E}_t = \mu_{\mathcal{E}} + 3 \times \sigma_{\mathcal{E}}$, where $\mu_{\mathcal{E}}$ and $\sigma_{\mathcal{E}}$ are mean and standard deviation of distribution $\mathcal{E}$. Thus, for an unknown access pattern, if the reconstruction error is greater than $\mathcal{E}_t$, we state that the access pattern belongs to an anomalous observation.

Online Phase: In the online phase, the analyzer tries to determine whether the access pattern from some unknown process belongs to a benign or malicious one. The analyzer uses the trained CNN based Autoencoder to calculate the reconstruction error e for that particular pattern. The analyzer allows the process to execute if $e < \mathcal{E}_t$ and blocks it from executing otherwise. Figure 4 depicts the overall working principle of the Analyzer. The Autoencoder tries to reconstruct the output patterns from the input access patterns, learning the important features of the input dataset in the process. The reconstruction error is given by

[7] The three sigma rule states that all the data points will lie within three standard deviations of the mean with 99.7% probability.

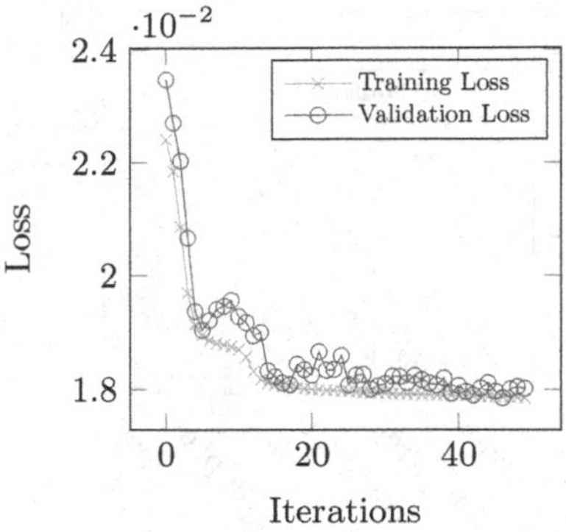

Fig. 5. Training and validation loss of the autoencoder

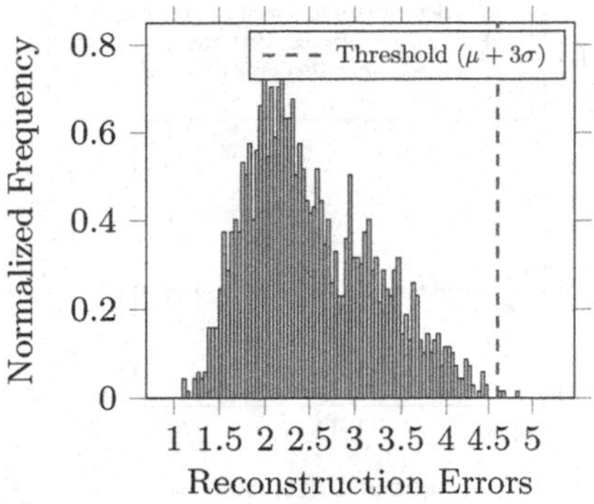

Fig. 6. Reconstruction error distribution of benign inputs

$error_i = (input_i - output_i)\ \forall i$. The threshold set by $\mu + 3\sigma$ helps in separating out anomalous access patterns from the benign ones.

5 Experimentation and Results

In this section, we provide the details of our experimental setup and the implementation details of the CNN-based Autoencoder. Further, we evaluate the efficiency and accuracy of the proposed detection methodology.

5.1 Experimental Setup

We validated our proposed methodology on a standard Desktop computer running on Intel i5-3330 processor and Ubuntu 14.04 (4.13.0-36-generic kernel)[8]. It has Hynix DDR3 DRAM of 4GB capacity. We used `Keras` [8] deep learning library to implement the CNN model. In order to reduce the training time we execute the offline training in an NVIDIA `Quadro K620` GPU[9].

5.2 Implementation Details of CNN-Based Autoencoder

The network architecture and the training parameters for our CNN-based Autoencoder model are presented in Table 1. We use *Batch Normalization* after every *Convolution Layer* (except for the last layer) in order to increase the stability of the network and speedup the training process. This layer also helps to prevent the model from *overfitting*[10]. We used *Mean Square Error* as loss function with batch size of 10 and learning rate of 0.0001. Further, we used *Adam's Optimizer* with $\beta_1 = 0.9$, $\beta_2 = 0.999$, $\epsilon = 1e^{-8}$ and no learning rate decay.

[8] We would like to emphasise that the detection tool is system-independent and can be employed on any standard x86 and Linux based machine.

[9] The offline training can also be done on the CPU of the target system.

[10] A phenomenon where the neural network actually *memorizes* the data instead of learning the targeted features.

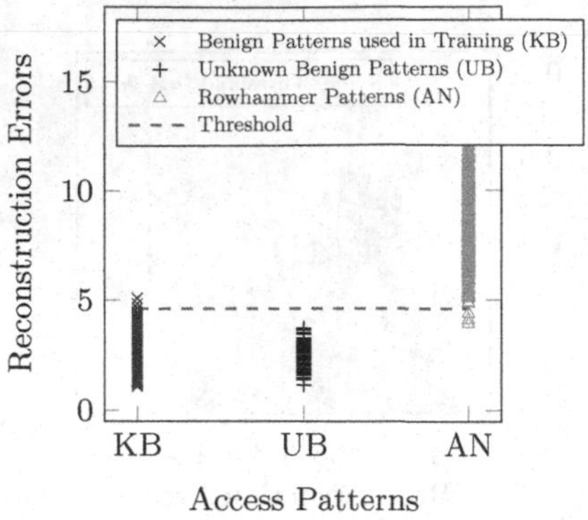

Fig. 7. Reconstruction errors of different access patterns

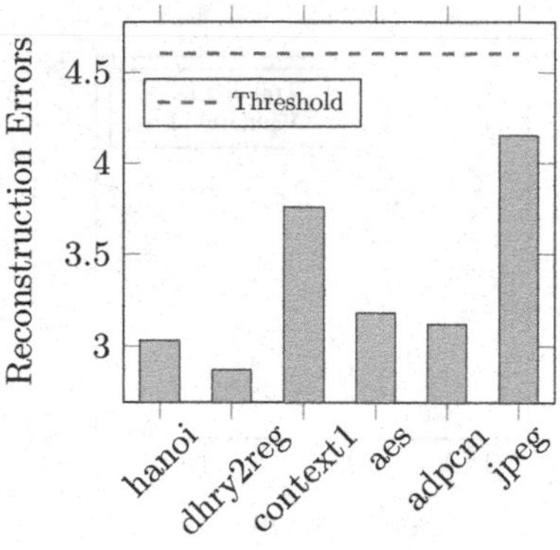

Fig. 8. Reconstruction errors of different benchmark programs

5.3 Evaluation of Autoencoder

We used the obtained dataset as discussed in Sect. 3.3 to train our CNN-based Autoencoder model. Figure 5 shows the plots for both training and validation loss. We can observe that the *training loss* decreases gradually with each iteration signifying the Autoencoder model is able to learn the complex features of the dataset. Moreover, the *validation loss*[11] also decreases along with the training loss, which implies that the model is not overfitting. The decision of the Autoencoder for an unknown input being benign or anomaly depends on a threshold of reconstruction error $\mathcal{E}_t$, as we discussed in Sect. 4.2. The reconstruction error distribution for an abundant of unknown benign examples which are not used in training are shown in Fig. 6. The value of $\mathcal{E}_t$ in our experimental setup after applying 3σ analysis came out to be approximately 4.6404.

The performance results of the Autoencoder model can be seen in Fig. 7. The model was trained using known benign access patterns and based on the reconstruction error, a threshold has been set. Then the model was tested for both benign and anomalous access patterns. All the benign patterns have been correctly classified, thereby having no false positive. The anomalous patterns have been correctly identified with an accuracy of 97%. We further tested our model on a number of benchmark programs from two popular Linux system benchmarking suites - UnixBench [17] and CHStone [10]. The reconstruction error values for some of the programs have been shown in Fig. 8. All the tested programs have been identified as benign by our Autoencoder model. It is also worth mentioning that `jpeg` program of CHStone benchmark suite showed a high reconstruction error but it's well within the threshold for the Autoencoder to classify it as a benign process.

[11] Validation loss is obtained by feeding the model with unknown data which is not used for the training.

5.4 Detection Time

The dataset preparation step requires on average 1500 ms to generate the dataset of access patterns from the virtual addresses accessed by an unknown process. The dataset is then passed to the AE-based analyzer which takes around 43.143 ms to process the patterns. Therefore, the average time required to detect a probable Rowhammer process and eventually block it from further progressing is around 1543.143 ms on our experimental platform. In other words, it takes approximately 1.5 s to detect a Rowhammer process from the start of its execution. It is worth mentioning that Rowhammer, being a probabilistic method, takes around 20 s on our experimental setup to successfully induce a bit flip. Hence, the overall detection time of our proposed tool is much less than the time taken by an adversary to induce faults using Rowhammer.

5.5 Discussion

One of the requisite properties to achieve success in any Rowhammer based attack is to access the same bank different row (SBDR) DRAM cells rapidly. Hence, the DRAM access patterns for these attack processes include both *spatial* and *temporal* characteristics. Moreover, it has already been shown that the DRAM access patterns for such attack processes are not entirely random [15]. The proposed unsupervised detection methodology models the access patterns of benign applications that execute in a target system. The benign access patterns mostly neither have spatial characteristics nor temporal characteristics as the DRAM access requests for such processes depend on the availability of rows and banks in DRAM modules. However, a Rowhammer adversary targets particular cells in the DRAM modules, thereby forming distinguishable characteristics in the access patterns. These patterns help our proposed methodology to detect Rowhammer attacks efficiently. An adversary can attempt to develop a Rowhammer attack by removing both spatial and temporal characteristics from the access patterns to defeat the proposed detection mechanism. However, this approach will increase the failure rate of the Rowhammer attack as the process will not be able to maintain SBDR paradigm that emphasizes the robustness of the proposed methodology.

6 Conclusion

In this paper, we presented an automated unsupervised deep learning based diagnostic tool that can detect Rowhammer attacks even before their completion with considerably high accuracy. In order to make the tool generic, we incorporated an improvised reverse engineering module to uncover the physical address to DRAM bank and row mapping. These mappings help the tool to accurately identify physical locations in the memory in terms of bank and row indices. The overall detection process can be divided into two parts - dataset generation and analyzing the patterns. The tool continuously monitors the HPCs to identify programs that result in a high LLC rate and simultaneously gathers the virtual addresses for such programs. Once the virtual addresses (termed as access patterns) are obtained, they are fed to the analyzer. The analyzer is powered by a CNN-based Autoencoder which has been trained using benign access patterns. Thus, whenever a Rowhammer process tries to access the memory because of its temporal and spatial characteristics, the analyzer classifies it as an anomaly.

Acknowledgement. This work was partially supported by Department of Science and Technology, Government of India under the Swarnajayanti Fellowship program and Information Security Education and Awareness (ISEA), MeitY, Government of India.

References

1. Alam, M., Bhattacharya, S., Dutta, S., Sinha, S., Mukhopadhyay, D., Chattopadhyay, A.: RATAFIA: ransomware analysis using time and frequency informed autoencoders. In: IEEE HOST, pp. 218–227 (2019)
2. Alam, M., Bhattacharya, S., Mukhopadhyay, D., Bhattacharya, S.: Performance counters to rescue: A machine learning based safeguard against micro-architectural side-channel-attacks. IACR Cryptology ePrint Archive **2017**, 564 (2017)
3. Aweke, Z.B., Yitbarek, S.F., Qiao, R., Das, R., Hicks, M., Oren, Y., Austin, T.: ANVIL: software-based protection against next-generation rowhammer attacks. ACM SIGPLAN Notices **51**(4), 743–755 (2016)
4. Bhattacharya, S., Mukhopadhyay, D.: Curious case of rowhammer: flipping secret exponent bits using timing analysis. In: Gierlichs, B., Poschmann, A.Y. (eds.) CHES 2016. LNCS, vol. 9813, pp. 602–624. Springer, Heidelberg (2016). https://doi.org/10.1007/978-3-662-53140-2_29
5. Brasser, F., Davi, L., Gens, D., Liebchen, C., Sadeghi, A.R.: Can't touch this: software-only mitigation against rowhammer attacks targeting kernel memory. In: USENIX Security 2017, pp. 117–130 (2017)
6. Chakraborty, A., Bhattacharya, S., Saha, S., Mukhopadhyay, D.: Explframe: exploiting page frame cache for fault analysis of block ciphers. In: DATE, pp. 1303–1306 (2020)
7. Chakraborty, A., Alam, M., Mukhopadhyay, D.: Deep learning based diagnostics for rowhammer protection of dram chips. In: IEEE ATS, pp. 86–865. IEEE (2019)
8. Chollet, F.: Building autoencoders in keras. The Keras Blog (2016)
9. Gruss, D., Maurice, C., Mangard, S.: Rowhammer.js: a remote software-induced fault attack in JavaScript. In: Caballero, J., Zurutuza, U., Rodríguez, R.J. (eds.) DIMVA 2016. LNCS, vol. 9721, pp. 300–321. Springer, Cham (2016). https://doi.org/10.1007/978-3-319-40667-1_15
10. Hara, Y., Tomiyama, H., Honda, S., Takada, H., Ishii, K.: Chstone: a benchmark program suite for practical c-based high-level synthesis. In: 2008 IEEE International Symposium on Circuits and Systems, pp. 1192–1195. IEEE (2008)
11. Herath, N., Fogh, A.: These are not your grand daddys CPU performance counters-CPU hardware performance counters for security. Black Hat Briefings (2015)
12. Kim, Y., et al.: Flipping bits in memory without accessing them: an experimental study of dram disturbance errors. In: ACM SIGARCH Computer Architecture News, vol. 42, pp. 361–372. IEEE Press (2014)

13. Seaborn, M., Dullien, T.: Exploiting the dram rowhammer bug to gain kernel privileges (2015). https://googleprojectzero.blogspot.com/2015/03/exploiting-dram-rowhammer-bug-to-gain.html
14. Malhotra, P., Vig, L., Shroff, G., Agarwal, P.: Long short term memory networks for anomaly detection in time series. In: Proceedings, p. 89. Presses universitaires de Louvain (2015)
15. Mutlu, O., Kim, J.S.: Rowhammer: a retrospective. IEEE Trans. Comput.-Aided Des. Integrated Circ. Syst. **39**(8), 1555–1571 (2019)
16. Pessl, P., Gruss, D., Maurice, C., Schwarz, M., Mangard, S.: DRAMA: exploiting dram addressing for cross-CPU attacks. In: USENIX Security, pp. 565–581 (2016)
17. Smith, B., Grehan, R., Yager, T., Niemi, D.: Byte-unixbench: a Unix benchmark suite. Technical report (2011)
18. Tatar, A., Konoth, R.K., Athanasopoulos, E., Giuffrida, C., Bos, H., Razavi, K.: Throwhammer: Rowhammer attacks over the network and defenses. In: USENIX ATC, pp. 213–226 (2018)
19. Van Der Veen, V., et al.: Drammer: deterministic rowhammer attacks on mobile platforms. In: ACM CCS, pp. 1675–1689. ACM (2016)
20. Vig, S., Bhattacharya, S., Mukhopadhyay, D., Lam, S.K.: Rapid detection of rowhammer attacks using dynamic skewed hash tree. In: HASP, p. 7. ACM (2018)
21. Wang, X., Karri, R.: Numchecker: detecting kernel control-flow modifying rootkits by using hardware performance counters. In: ACM/EDAC/IEEE DAC, pp. 1–7. IEEE (2013)
22. Wu, X.C., Sherwood, T., Chong, F.T., Li, Y.: Protecting page tables from rowhammer attacks using monotonic pointers in dram true-cells. In: ASPLOS, pp. 645–657 (2019)
23. Xiao, Y., Zhang, X., Zhang, Y., Teodorescu, R.: One bit flips, one cloud flops: cross-VM row hammer attacks and privilege escalation. In: USENIX Security, pp. 19–35 (2016)
24. Zhang, F., et al.: Persistent fault analysis on block ciphers. IACR TCHES, pp. 150–172 (2018)
25. Zhang, Z., Zhu, Z., Zhang, X.: Breaking address mapping symmetry at multi-levels of memory hierarchy to reduce dram row-buffer conflicts. JILP **3**, 29–63 (2001)

Model Evasion Attacks Against Partially Encrypted Deep Neural Networks in Isolated Execution Environment

Kota Yoshida(✉) and Takeshi Fujino

Ritsumeikan University, Shiga, Japan
ri0044e@ed.ritsumei.ac.jp, fujino@se.ritsumei.ac.jp

Abstract. It is important to hide DNN models from adversaries not only for protecting intellectual property but also for preventing attacks. Isolated execution environments (IEEs) are necessary to protect the DNN model in an edge device. Conventional studies on DNN inference in IEEs have focused on model confidentiality and not the threat of model evasion attacks. If some of the model parameters or intermediate results are leaked to adversaries, model evasion attacks may occur even if the confidentiality of the model is secured. In this work, we performed attacks against partially encrypted DNN models that are executed on IEEs. In an existing proposal, a feature extractor of the model is executed in a normal world and a classifier is executed in a secure enclave, but there is still a threat that an adversary may perform a gradient-based model evasion attack against a feature extractor. We performed gradient-based model evasion attacks against the feature extractor more efficiently by preparing multiple guide images. Our results clarified that all parameters on the feature map should be kept secret by the parameter encryption. In addition, we consider another risk case where calculated values on the feature extractor are stored in the unencrypted memory and demonstrated the gradient estimation-based model evasion attack by exploiting the intermediate feature maps. Our results indicate that both DNN model parameters and intermediate feature maps should be concealed not only for protecting intellectual property but also for preventing model evasion attacks.

Keywords: Model evasion attack · Adversarial examples · Trusted execution environment · Deep neural network

1 Introduction

Trained deep neural networks (DNNs) are widely used in various tasks such as image recognition. DNNs require high costs for training, including the domain knowledge to optimize the model architecture, a huge dataset that is annotated by hand, and computing the resources to calculate parameter optimization. Therefore, a trained DNN model that is implemented in commercial services is quite valuable.

J. Zhou et al. (Eds.): ACNS 2021 Workshops, LNCS 12809, pp. 78–95, 2021.
https://doi.org/10.1007/978-3-030-81645-2_6

Information of DNN models, especially model architectures and parameters, is also valuable to adversaries. In a white-box scenario, which assumes an adversary knows information about the DNN models, various threats have been reported. The model inversion attack estimates training data that include confidentiality and privacy from DNN models. The model evasion attack calculates a perturbation and then adds it to an input, which is called an adversarial example. This adversarial example causes misrecognition.

It is important to hide DNN models from adversaries not only for protecting intellectual property but also for preventing attacks. Homomorphic encryption [5,18], multi-party computing [9], and isolated execution [6,13] all allow calculations while hiding the DNN model from adversaries. While isolated execution is a promising choice in an edge device, isolated execution environments (IEEs) have limited computing resources and it is difficult to unroll all operations of the DNN model inferences onto an enclave. Hanzlik et al. [6] proposed dividing the DNN model inference operations into individual layers and then executing them layer-by-layer on the enclave, but the calculation time is longer than in a normal environment. Schlogl et al. proposed eNNclave, where transfer learning enables splitting the DNN model into normal (feature extractor) and confidential (classifier) parts. The normal part of the DNN model is executed in the normal world, and the confidential part is executed in the secure enclave. This enables faster inference because it can use the abundant computational resources in the normal world (e.g., GPUs). While promising, these studies have focused on model confidentiality and did not consider model evasion attacks. Model evasion attacks are possible without all of the information about models. As such, attacks may occur when a part of the information is leaked even if it is not enough to restore the entire model.

In this paper, we focus on IEEs and model evasion attacks. We investigate which information of the DNN model inference should be hidden from adversaries to prevent the attacks by using IEEs. We assume that a feature extractor is leaked if it is executed in the normal world. We evaluate gradient-based model evasion attacks against the feature extractor on an eNNcalve scenario. We assume that intermediate feature maps are leaked if they are stored in the normal world memory in plain text when an enclave switches the processing layer. We evaluate gradient estimation-based model evasion attacks with the intermediate feature maps.

Our contributions are as follows.

- We studied model evasion attacks against DNN models that are partially executed on IEEs.
- We found a more efficient method for gradient-based model evasion attacks against a feature extractor by preparing multiple guide images. The guide images mean that images acquired from the guide (the adversary's misclassification target) class.
- We performed gradient estimation-based model evasion attacks with an intermediate feature map. In this scenario, all model parameters are hidden but the calculated intermediate values (i.e., feature maps) are accessible by the

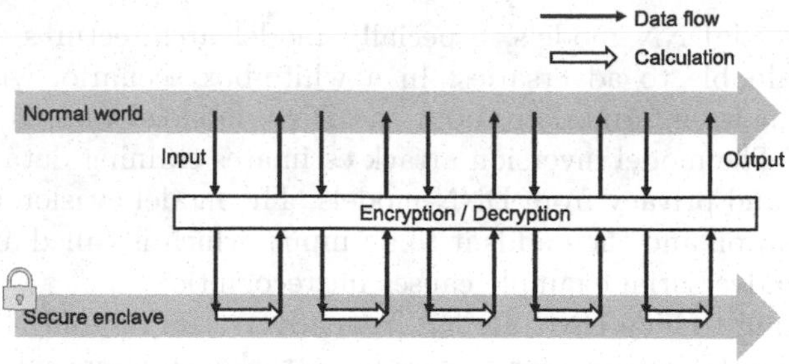

Fig. 1. Overview of MLCapsule [6].

adversary. The experimental results indicate that the intermediate values, as well as the model parameters, should be hidden from the adversary.

2 Related Works

2.1 DNN Model Inference on IEEs

Hanzlik et al. [6] proposed MLCapsule, where a DNN model provider protects the intellectual property of ML services and clients perform inference offline. Figure 1 shows an overview of MLCapsule. All DNN model parameters, such as weight and bias, are encrypted. The user interacts with the provider and sets up a secure enclave. A part of the layers is loaded and decoded on the enclave, and inference is performed. The internal state of the DNN inference is encrypted and stored in the normal world. The user repeats operations for each layer and obtains the result of the inference. Generally, the enclave can not use an inference accelerator, and cryptographic operations cause an increase in processing time.

Schlogl et al. proposed eNNclave [13] for improving DNN model inference speed on IEEs. eNNclave assumes that a DNN model is trained by transfer learning, an overview of which is shown in Fig. 2. Transfer learning diverts a feature extractor of a trained public model to other tasks. It is performed in the following steps.

1. Extract a feature extractor from a trained public model.
2. Add a classifier to the feature extractor and initialize.
3. Fix the parameters of the feature extractor and train the classifier.

Note that the feature extractor of the transferred model is the same as the public model's one. Figure 3 shows an overview of eNNclave. In this scenario, secret information on the target task after transfer learning is only included in the classifier. Schlogl et al. claimed that the feature extractor of the transferred model was public information and the transferred model information could be sufficiently hidden by executing only the classifier in the secure enclave. The feature etractor can be executed in the normal world without encryption and accelerated by GPUs.

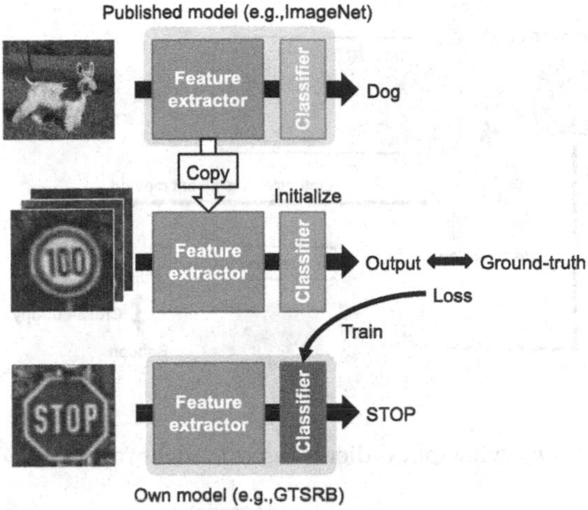

Fig. 2. Overview of transfer learning.

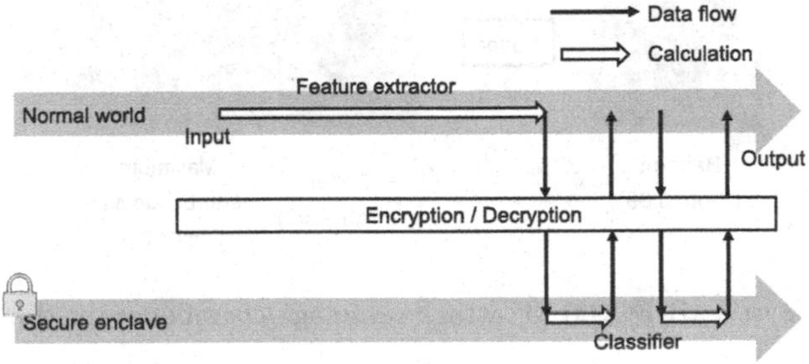

Fig. 3. Overview of eNNclave [13].

2.2 Model Evasion Attacks

The purpose of model evasion attacks on image classification tasks is to calculate perturbations that cause misclassification. An input image with perturbation is called an adversarial example. Scenarios in which an adversary specifies a misclassification target class are called a targeting attack.

If an adversary knows all target model architecture and parameters, it can calculate an adversarial example by calculating a gradient of an input (source) image with respect to an adversarial target (guide) class. This is a white-box scenario. In this paper, we call such an attack a gradient-based model evasion attack. The fast gradient sign method (FGSM) [4] and the momentum iterative FGSM (MI-FGSM) [3], which is an improved version of FGSM, are typical methods of the model evasion attack. An overview of the gradient-based attack is shown in Fig. 4. Adversarial examples by targeted MI-FGSM (TMI-FGSM) are calculated by the following equations:

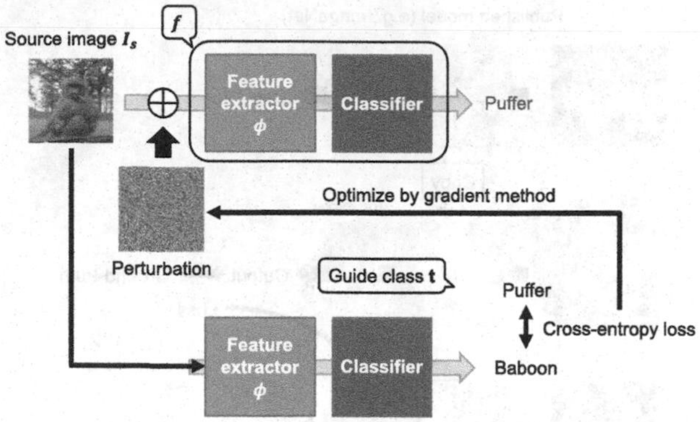

Fig. 4. Overview of gradient-based model evasion attack.

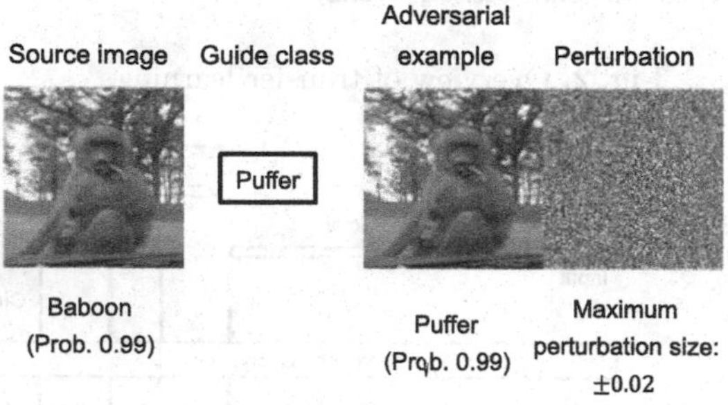

Fig. 5. Example of TMI-FGSM [3] attack on image classifier trained by ImageNet.

$$
\begin{aligned}
I_{adv}^{0} &= I_s \\
I_{adv}^{k+1} &= clip(I_{adv}^{k} - \alpha \times sign(m^{k+1})),
\end{aligned}
\tag{1}
$$

$$
\begin{aligned}
m^{0} &= 0 \\
m^{k+1} &= m^{k} + \frac{\nabla_{I_{adv}^{k}} J(f(I_{adv}^{k}), t)}{||J(f(I_{adv}^{k}), t)||_1},
\end{aligned}
\tag{2}
$$

where I_{adv} is an adversarial example, I_s is a source image, t is an adversarial target class, k is the number of iterations, α is the step size, function $clip(a)$ clips input a into $a \in [0, 1]$, function $sign(a)$ calculates the sign of input a, function $f(a)$ is a DNN model that calculates the classification result from input image a, and function $J(a, b)$ calculates the cross-entropy between a and b. A result of a TMI-FGSM attack against an image classifier trained by ImageNet is shown in Fig. 5.

In the gradient-based model evasion attack, an adversary does not necessarily need to know all the architecture and parameters of the target model. If an adversary knows only the architecture and parameters of the feature extractor

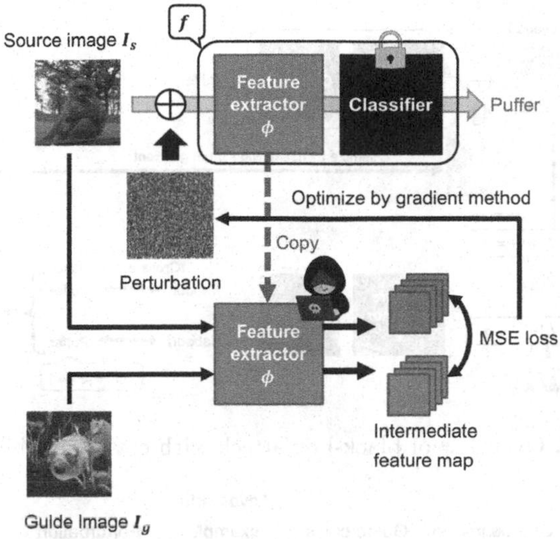

Fig. 6. Overview of gradient-based model evasion attack against feature extractor.

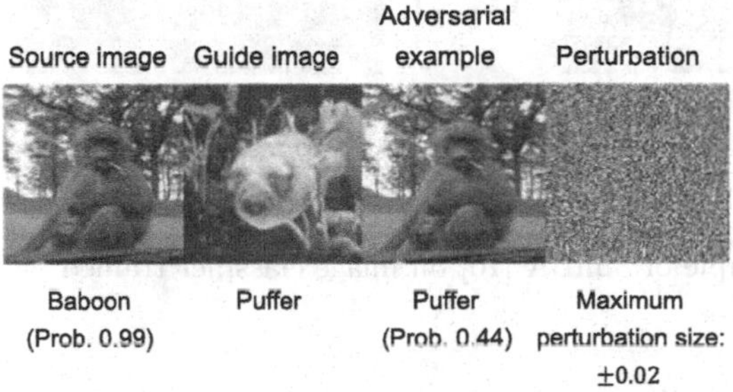

Fig. 7. Example of TMI-FGSM against feature extractor from an image classifier trained by ImageNet.

of the target model, it can calculate an adversarial example by calculating a gradient of the source image with respect to the distance between the intermediate feature map of the source and guide images [7,8,12,17]. The guide images mean that images acquired from the guide (the adversary's misclassification target) class. In this attack, instead of improving the probability of the guide class, the adversary calculates the perturbation to bring the intermediate representation (feature map) of the source image closer to the intermediate representation of the guide image. In this paper, we call this attack a gradient-based model evasion attack against a feature extractor. Wang et al. pointed out that a DNN model trained with transfer learning is vulnerable to this attack [17]. Inkawhich et al. extended TMI-FGSM to against feature extractor [8]. An adversarial example by the extended TMI-FGSM is calculated by replacing Eq. 2 with Eq. 3 (Fig. 6):

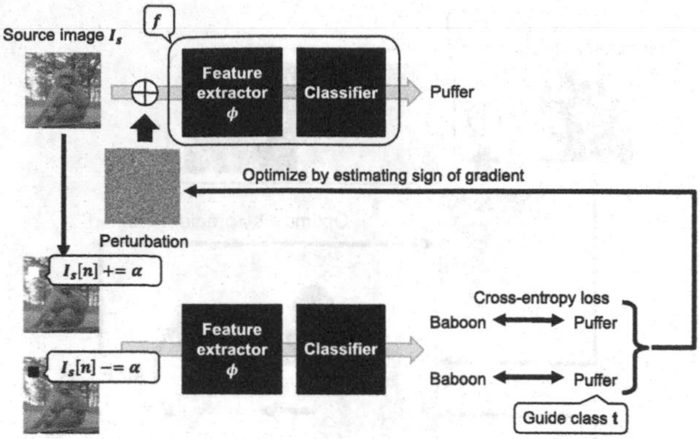

Fig. 8. Overview of black-box attack with class probability.

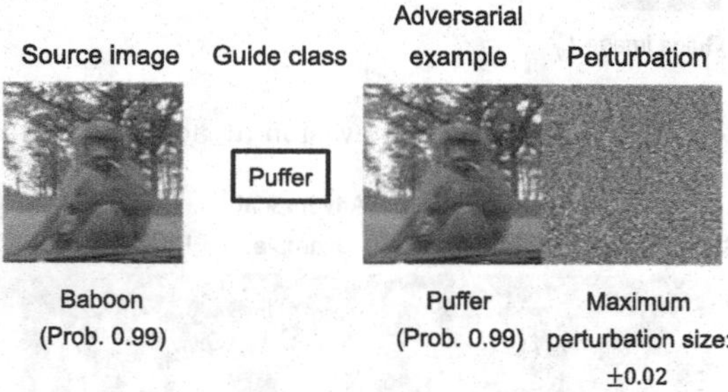

Fig. 9. Example of SimBA [10] on image classifier trained by ImageNet.

$$m^0 = 0$$
$$m^{k+1} = m^k + \frac{\nabla_{I^k_{adv}} MSE(\phi(I^k_{adv}), \phi(I_g))}{||MSE(\phi(I^k_{adv}), \phi(I_g))||_1}, \quad (3)$$

where function $MSE(a, b)$ calculates a mean squared error between a and b, function $\phi(a)$ is a feature extractor that calculates an intermediate feature map by input image a, and I_g is a guide image that belongs to a guide class. A result of a TMI-FGSM attack against feature extractor of an image classifier trained by ImageNet is shown in Fig. 7.

If an adversary does not know the target model architecture or parameters but has access to the classification result, it can calculate an adversarial example by estimating a gradient of a source image with respect to a guide class probability [1,10,14]. In this paper, we call this attack a gradient estimation-based model evasion attack. The adversary estimates the gradient of the source image from the change in output probability when the source image is changed slightly. A simple black-box attack (SimBA) [10] is a typical method of the model evasion attack. Algorithm 1 is an algorithm of SimBA. Figure 8 shows an overview of

Algorithm 1. Simple black-box attack (SimBA) [10]

Input: Source image I_s, Guide class t, Number of image pixels N,
Perturbation parameter α, DNN model f, Cross-entropy function J
Output: Adversarial example I_{adv}

```
I_adv = I_s
for n=0 to N-1 do
    x' = I_adv
    x'[n] = I_adv[n] + α
    p+ = J(f(x'), t)
    x' = I_adv
    x'[n] = I_adv[n] − α
    p− = J(f(x'), t)
    if p+ < p− then
        I_adv[n] = I_adv[n] + α
    else if p+ > p− then
        I_adv[n] = I_adv[n] − α
    else
        I_adv[n] = I_adv[n] + 0
    end if
    I_adv = clip(I_adv)
end for
return I_adv
```

Table 1. Related model evasion attacks and this work.

Gradient-based		Gradient estimation-based	
Whole model	Feature extractor	Class probability	Intermediate feature-map
FGSM [4] MI-FGSM [3]	Sabour et al. [12] Wang et al. [17] Huang et al. [7] Extended MI-FGSM [8] Extended MI-FGSM with multiple guide images (Sect. 3)	SimBA [10] Bhagoji et al. [1] Senzaki et al. [14]	Extendetd SimBA (Sect. 5)

the targeted SimBA. A result of the SimBA against an image classifier trained by ImageNet is shown in Fig. 9.

In this paper, we improve the TMI-FGSM against a feature extractor [8] by using multiple guide images in Sect. 3. In Sect. 4, we evaluate the TMI-FGSM against a feature extractor on eNNclave scenario [13]. In Sect. 5, we extend SimBA from class probability-based to intermediate feature map-based and evaluate the attack in the MLCapsule scenario [6] when the feature map is not encrypted. Table 1 lists the related methods and this work.

3 Gradient-Based Model Evasion Attacks Against Feature Extractor with Multiple Guide Images

In this section, we evaluated a gradient-based model evasion attack against feature extractor. Conventional works have assumed just one guide image, but we performed the attack using multiple guide images.

3.1 Experimental Setup

We used an image classification DNN model with VGG-16 architecture [15] trained by ImageNet [2]. The model had 13 convolution layers in the feature extractor and three fully connected layers in the classifier. The model was pre-trained and published on Pytorch [11]. The top-1 accuracy of the model was 71.6%.

We extended the TMI-FGSM against feature extractor [8] to calculate adversarial examples by applying Eq. 4 instead of 3. The equation minimizes the distance between the intermediate feature map by adversarial examples I_{adv} and the mean of intermediate feature maps by guide images I_g, as

$$\begin{aligned} m^0 &= 0 \\ m^{k+1} &= m^k + \frac{\nabla_{I^k_{adv}} MSE(\phi(I^k_{adv}), \frac{1}{S}\sum_{s=1}^{S}\phi(I^s_g))}{||MSE(\phi(I^k_{adv}), \frac{1}{S}\sum_{s=1}^{S}\phi(I^s_g))||_1}, \end{aligned} \tag{4}$$

where S is the number of guide images and I^s_g is an s-th guide image.

We set 100 pairs of source images and multiple guide images. The brightness value of each image was normalized to the range of 0 to 1. We acquired a feature map from the 13th convolution layer output of the model. We evaluated the classification accuracy and the success rate of the targeted attack while increasing perturbation limits from ± 0.01 to ± 0.2. The classification accuracy is a ratio of the created adversarial examples that are classified into the correct (source) class. The success rate is a ratio of the created adversarial examples that are classified into the guide class. Note that not all samples behave as adversarial examples due to the limited amount of perturbation applied to the input image.

3.2 Experimental Results

Figure 10 shows the classification accuracy and the success rate of the targeted attack for each number of guide images. The results of the TMI-FGSM attack [3] and random noise attack which adds uniformed random noise to input images are also shown in the figures for comparison.

As shown in Fig. 10(a), the TMI-FGSM against feature extractor significantly reduced the classification accuracy, similar to using whole model. There was no difference in attack efficiency depending on the number of guide images. In (b), the TMI-FGSM against feature extractor with only one guide image achieved the targeted attack success rate of about 80%. The success rate of the attack

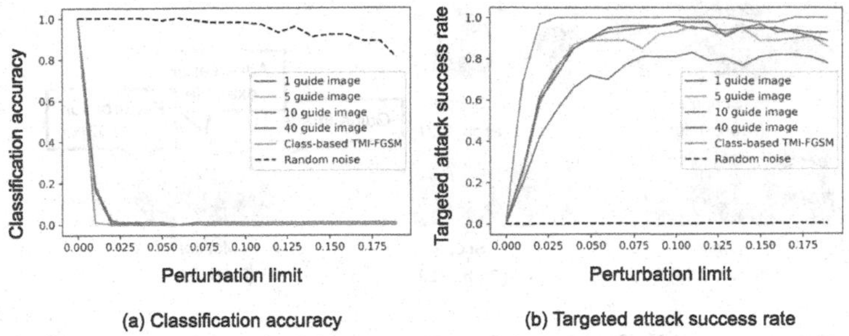

Fig. 10. (a) Classification accuracy and (b) success rate of targeted attack for each number of guide images.

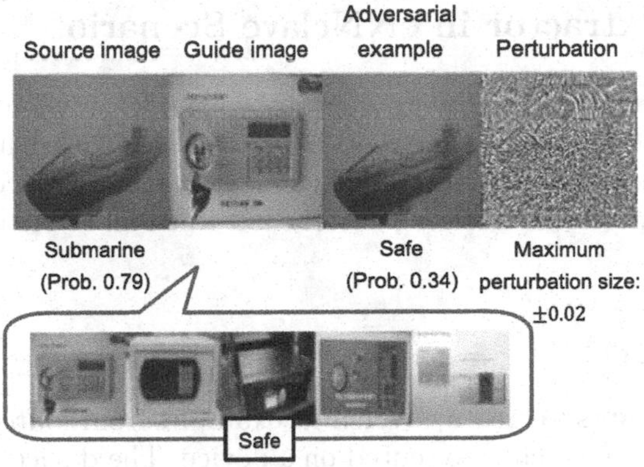

Fig. 11. Results of TMI-FGSM against feature extractor using five guide images.

was significantly improved when the number of images was increased from one to five. We improved the success rate to about 98% with 40 guide images. Thus, the success rate of the targeted attack was increased by increasing the number of guide images. However, a success rate comparable to the attack against the whole model was not achieved when the perturbation amount was low. There was almost no difference in attack efficiency depending on the number of guide images when there were five or more guide images.

Figure 11 shows an example of the TMI-FGSM against feature extractor using five guide images. The source image is from the submarine class and the guide image is from the safe class. The adversarial example was classified into the safe class. Figure 12 shows examples of the attack using one of these guide images. The targeting attack was not successful even if one of the guide images was used. However, the targeting attack was successful by averaging the feature maps of these five guide images, as shown in Fig. 11. This is a rare case but it indicates that an attack with multiple guide images can improve the success rate even if the attack with a single guide image has failed.

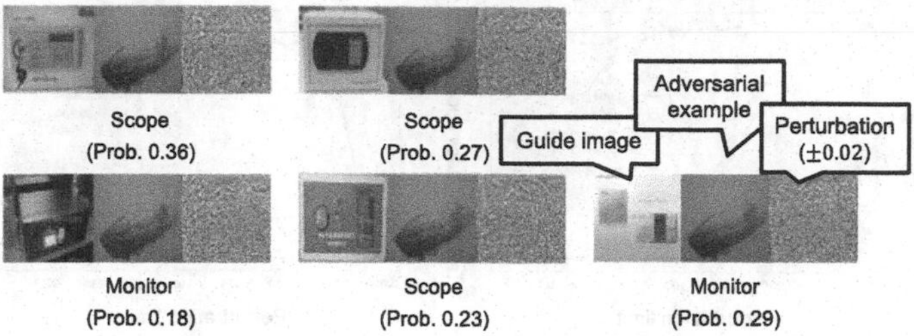

Fig. 12. Results of TMI-FGSM against feature extractor using one guide image.

4 Gradient-Based Model Evasion Attacks Against Feature Extractor in eNNclave Scenario

In this section, we performed a gradient-based model evasion attacks against feature extractor in eNNclave scenario [13]. We investigated how many layers could be placed in the normal world. When more layers are placed in the normal world, the device performs inference faster than when all layers are placed in the secure enclave.

4.1 Threat Model

An adversary attempts to create adversarial examples from source images against a target DNN model which is executed on a device. The device is designed with eNNclave scenario. The target DNN model is trained with transfer learning, and the feature extraction layer is the same as a public model's one. Users of the device, including the adversary, input a source image to the device and the device returns the classification result by the DNN model. Here, since the classification result returns only with the low-precision probability or the label name of the Top-1 class, the gradient estimation-based model evasion attacks with class probability cannot be performed [1,14]. The device calculates the feature extraction layer on the normal world application and inputs the result (intermediate feature map) to the enclave application. The enclave application calculates the classification layer and returns the modified classification result to the normal world application.

The goal of the adversary is to reduce the classification accuracy of the target model by adversarial examples and/or to classify an adversarial example into a certain guide class. The adversary can freely peep into the memory space managed by the normal world. When the DNN model inference is executed in the normal world, the adversary can read the DNN model structures and parameters. The adversary can not read or write to the memory space managed by the secure world (enclave).

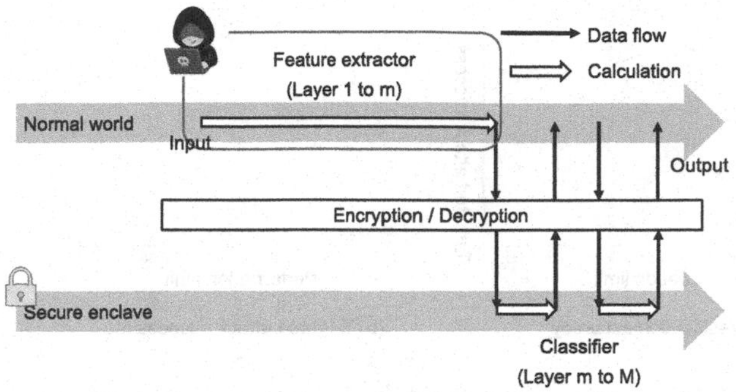

Fig. 13. Overview of our evaluation scenario based on eNNclave.

4.2 Experimental Setup

We assumed that the number of layers from the DNN model was M and that the layers from the first to m-th operated in the normal world while the remaining ones operated in the secure enclave. The adversary could steal the first to m-th layers as a feature extractor and perform an attack against it. Figure 13 shows an overview of our evaluation scenario based on eNNclave.

We trained a DNN model for a GTSRB traffic sign classification task [16] from the VGG-16 ImageNet classification model by using transfer learning. The model achieved a classification accuracy of 90.3%. We set 100 pairs of source images and ten guide images and then performed the attack. We evaluated the classification accuracy and the success rate of the targeted attack while increasing the perturbation limits from ±0.01 to ±0.2.

4.3 Experimental Results

Figure 14 shows the classification accuracy and the success rate of the targeted attack for each number of guide images. The results of TMI-FGSM against the whole model and random noise attack which adds uniformed random noise to input images are also shown in the figures for comparison. A result of the TMI-FGSM attack against feature extractor (m = 13) is shown in Fig. 15.

As we can see in Fig. 14(a), it was difficult to decrease the classification accuracy of the model when the adversary was able to use only shallow layers. However, the attack degraded the accuracy more efficiently than random noise even if the adversary knew only the first convolution layer (i.e., m was one). In (b), it was easier for the adversary to fool the model when more layers were executed in the normal world (i.e., m was more than nine).

The adversary has access to the model parameters if the calculations are carried out in the normal world. These experimental results show that the adversary can perform a gradient-based model evasion attack against the feature extractor even if it only knows the first several layers of the model parameters.

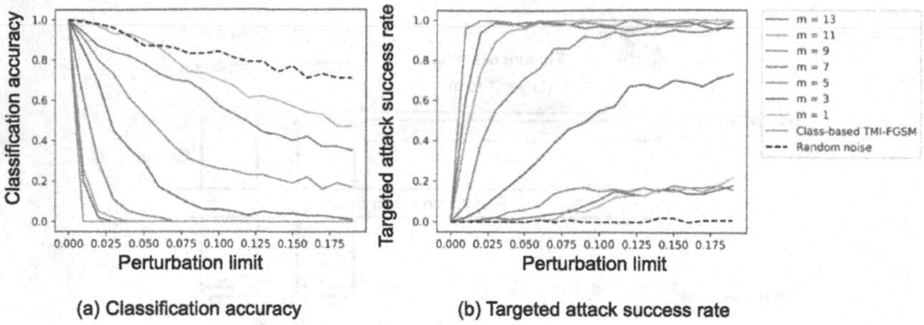

Fig. 14. (a) Classification accuracy and (b) success rate of targeted attack for each adversary's accessible layers m.

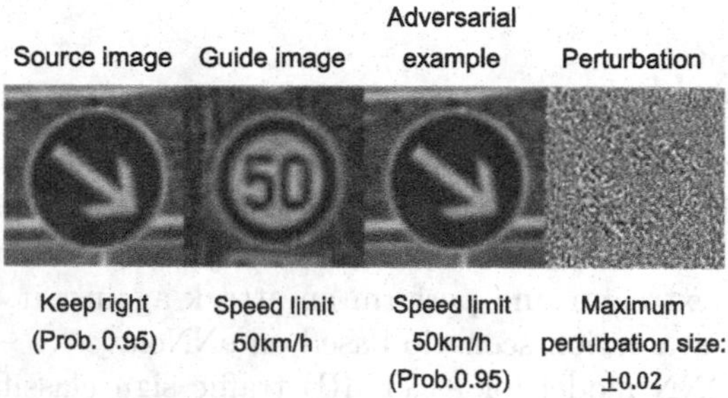

Fig. 15. Results of TMI-FGSM against feature extractor (m = 13) using 10 guide images.

5 Gradient Estimation-Based Model Evasion Attacks with Feature Maps

In this section, we evaluated a gradient estimation-based model evasion attacks with feature maps. We assumed that intermediate feature maps were stored in the normal world memory with plain text while the secure enclave switched the calculation layer. An adversary could attack by using a feature map from each calculation layer output.

5.1 Threat Model

(9) An adversary attempts to create adversarial examples from source images against a target DNN model which is executed on a device. The device is designed with MLCapsule scenario. Users of the device, including the adversary, input a source image to the device and the device returns the classification result by the DNN model. (9, 10, 12) Here, since the classification result returns only with the low-precision probability or the label name of the Top-1 class, the gradient estimation-based model evasion attacks with class probability cannot be performed [1,14]. (9) The device calculates the DNN model inference process layer-by-layer on the enclave application. The enclave application calculates a layer and

Algorithm 2. Extended SimBA for exploiting feature map. Parts that differ from SimBA are highlighted in red.

Input: Source image I_s, Guide images I_g, Number of guide images S, Number of image pixels N,
Perturbation parameter α, DNN model f, Feature extractor ϕ
Output: Adversarial example I_{adv}

```
I_adv = I_s
for n=0 to N-1 do
    x' = I_adv
    x'[n] = I_adv[n] + α
    p+ = MSE(φ(x'), 1/S Σ_{s=1}^{S} φ(I_g^s))
    x' = I_adv
    x'[n] = I_adv[n] − α
    p− = MSE(φ(x'), 1/S Σ_{s=1}^{S} φ(I_g^s))
    if p+ < p− then
        I_adv[n] = I_adv[n] + α
    else if p+ > p− then
        I_adv[n] = I_adv[n] − α
    else
        I_adv[n] = I_adv[n] + 0
    end if
    I_adv = clip(I_adv)
end for
return I_adv
```

temporarily stores intermediate feature maps into normal world memory space for preparing the next layer. Each intermediate feature map is not encrypted.

The goal of the adversary is to reduce the classification accuracy of the target model by adversarial examples and/or to classify an adversarial example into a certain guide class. The adversary can freely peep into the memory space managed by the normal world. When the intermediate feature map is stored in the normal world memory space, the adversary can read the feature map. The adversary can not read or write to the memory space managed by the secure world (enclave). Thus, the adversary can not obtain the DNN model structure and parameters, the adversary only exploits the feature map.

5.2 Attack Methodology

Algorithm 2 shows our gradient estimation-based model evasion attack with feature maps. It is an extended method from class probability-based SimBA to exploiting feature maps. An adversary inputs source image I_s and some guide images I_g and obtains intermediate feature maps $\phi(I_s)$ and $\phi(I_g)$. The adversary changes the pixels of the source image in the plus and minus directions, respectively, and measures the distance between $\phi(I_s)$ and $\phi(I_g)$. The adversary estimates a gradient of a source image with respect to the distance and selects the perturbation of the pixel.

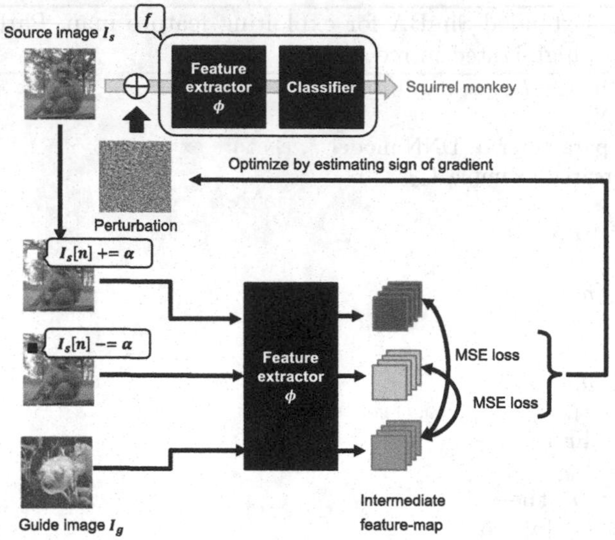

Fig. 16. Overview of gradient estimation-based model evasion attack with feature maps

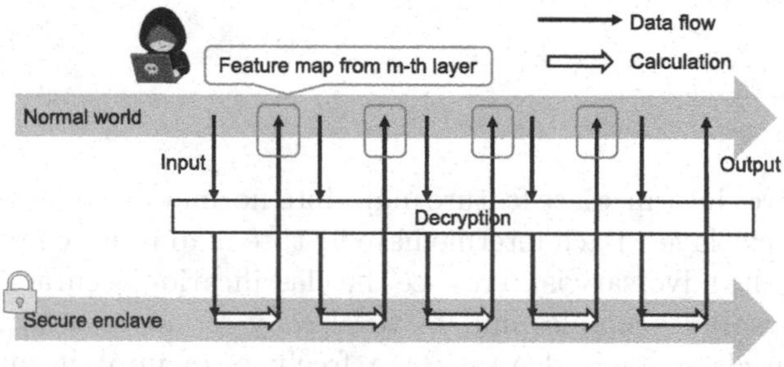

Fig. 17. Overview of our gradient estimation-based model evasion attack scenario based on MLCapsule.

Figure 16 shows an overview of the gradient estimation-based model evasion attack with feature maps. The adversary can not obtain a feature extractor but can obtain an intermediate feature map from each calculation layer. The adversary chooses the perturbation of each pixel on the basis of the MSE loss between the intermediate feature map of the input image with tampered pixel and guide images (Fig. 17).

5.3 Experimental Setup

We prepared the same DNN model for traffic sign recognition as Sect. 4.2. We assumed an adversary could obtain intermediate feature maps from each output of the 1st, 7th, and 13th layer. We set 20 pairs of source images and 10 guide

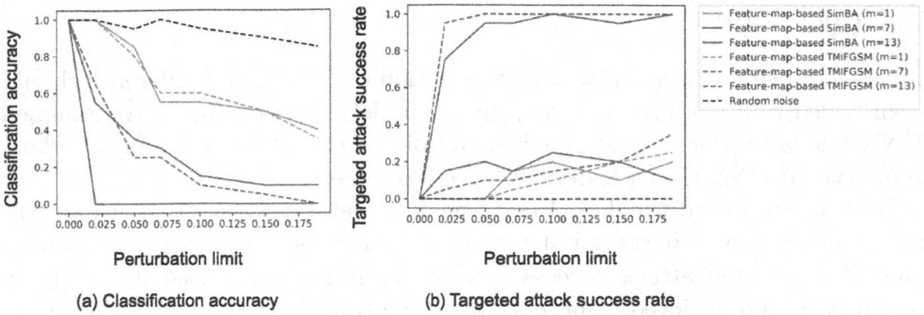

Fig. 18. (a) Classification accuracy and (b) success rate of targeted attack by SimBA with feature map, TMI-FGSM against feature extractor, and random noise.

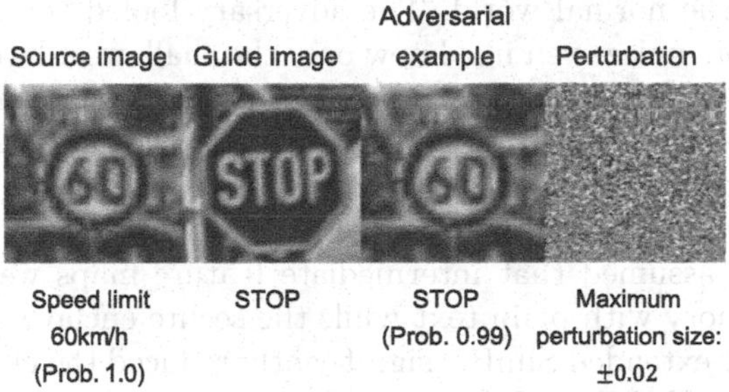

Fig. 19. Results of SimBA with feature map (m = 13) using 10 guide images.

images. We evaluated the success rate of the targeted attack and classification accuracy while increasing the perturbation limits from ±0.01 to ±0.2.

5.4 Experimental Results

Figure 18 shows the classification accuracy and the success rate of the targeted attack and by using intermediate feature maps from the feature extractor. The results of the TMI-FGSM against feature extractor and random noise attack, which adds uniformed random noise to input images, are also shown for comparison. A result of the SimBA with feature map (m = 13) is shown in Fig. 19.

As shown in Fig. 18(a), the SimBA with feature map significantly reduced the classification accuracy, similar to the TMI-FGSM against feature extractor. In (b), it also achieved a targeted attack success rate comparable to the TMI-FGSM against feature extractor. These results indicate that the gradient estimation-based model evasion attack with feature map is a threat to TEEs and it is necessary to encrypt feature maps in the normal world.

It requires additional execution time to encrypt and store the intermediate feature map in the normal world memory, but it is more important to prevent a gradient estimation-based model evasion attack with feature map.

6 Conclusion

In this work, we investigated which information of DNN model inference should be concealed from an adversary to prevent model evasion attacks. We assumed a DNN inference process performed in an isolated execution environment where the encrypted DNN model is decrypted and processed.

First, we improved the TMI-FGSM against feature extractor by using multiple guide images. Conventional techniques have used one guide image and achieved a targeted attack success rate of about 80%. We used five or more guide images and achieved a success rate of about 98% with 40 guide images.

Second, we performed the TMI-FGSM against feature extractor in an eNNclave scenario [13] and evaluated how many layers could be placed in the normal world. It was easier for an adversary to fool the model when more layers were executed in the normal world. The adversary fooled the model more efficiently than random noise even if it knew only the shallowest layer. These results demonstrate that an adversary can perform a gradient-based model extraction attack against feature extractor if even a part of the inference operations is calculated in the normal world.

Finally, we evaluated a gradient estimation-based model evasion attack with feature maps. We assumed that intermediate feature maps were stored in the normal world memory with plain text while the secure enclave switched the calculation layer. Our extended SimBA significantly reduced the classification accuracy, similar to the TMI-FGSM against the feature extractor. It also achieved a targeted attack success rate comparable to the TMI-FGSM. Additional execution time is required to encrypt and store the intermediate feature map in the normal world memory, but it is important to prevent a gradient estimation-based model evasion attack with feature maps.

Our findings demonstrate that DNN model parameters and intermediate feature maps should be concealed not only for protecting intellectual property but also for preventing model evasion attacks. To ensure safe and fast DNN inference, an isolated execution environment that allows accessing large memory space and DNN inference accelerators from a secure enclave is required.

Acknowledgments. This work was supported by JST-Mirai Program Grant Number JPMJMI19B6, Japan.

References

1. Bhagoji, A.N., He, W., Li, B., Song, D.: Practical black-box attacks on deep neural networks using efficient query mechanisms. In: Proceedings of the European Conference on Computer Vision (ECCV), September 2018
2. Deng, J., Dong, W., Socher, R., Li, L.J., Li, K., Fei-Fei, L.: ImageNet: a large-scale hierarchical image database, pp. 248–255. Institute of Electrical and Electronics Engineers (IEEE), March 2010
3. Dong, Y., et al.: Boosting adversarial attacks with momentum. In: Proceedings of the IEEE Computer Society Conference on Computer Vision and Pattern Recognition, pp. 9185–9193, October 2017

4. Goodfellow, I.J., Shlens, J., Szegedy, C.: Explaining and harnessing adversarial examples. In: 3rd International Conference on Learning Representations, ICLR, December 2015
5. Graepel, T., Lauter, K., Naehrig, M.: ML confidential: machine learning on encrypted data. In: Kwon, T., Lee, M.-K., Kwon, D. (eds.) ICISC 2012. LNCS, vol. 7839, pp. 1–21. Springer, Heidelberg (2013). https://doi.org/10.1007/978-3-642-37682-5_1
6. Hanzlik, L., et al.: MLCapsule: guarded offline deployment of machine learning as a service, August 2018
7. Huang, Q., Katsman, I., He, H., Gu, Z., Belongie, S., Lim, S.N.: Enhancing adversarial example transferability with an intermediate level attack. In: Proceedings of the IEEE International Conference on Computer Vision, pp. 4732–4741, July 2019
8. Inkawhich, N., Wen, W., Li, H.H., Chen, Y.: Feature space perturbations yield more transferable adversarial examples. In: Proceedings of the IEEE Computer Society Conference on Computer Vision and Pattern Recognition, vol. 2019-June, pp. 7059–7067. IEEE Computer Society, June 2019
9. Mohassel, P., Zhang, Y.: SecureML: a system for scalable privacy-preserving machine learning. In: Proceedings - IEEE Symposium on Security and Privacy, pp. 19–38. Institute of Electrical and Electronics Engineers Inc., June 2017
10. Narodytska, N., Kasiviswanathan, S.: Simple black-box adversarial attacks on deep neural networks. In: IEEE Computer Society Conference on Computer Vision and Pattern Recognition Workshops, vol. 2017-July, pp. 1310–1318, August 2017
11. Paszke, A., et al.: PyTorch: An Imperative Style, High-Performance Deep Learning Library. arXiv, December 2019
12. Sabour, S., Cao, Y., Faghri, F., Fleet, D.J.: Adversarial manipulation of deep representations. In: 4th International Conference on Learning Representations, ICLR 2016 - Conference Track Proceedings, November 2015
13. Schlögl, A., Böhme, R.: eNNclave: offline inference with model confidentiality. In: Proceedings of the 13th ACM Workshop on Artificial Intelligence and Security. ACM, New York (2020)
14. Senzaki, Y., Ohata, S., Matsuura, K.: Simple black-box adversarial examples generation with very few queries. IEICE Trans. Inf. Syst. **103**(2), 212–221 (2020)
15. Simonyan, K., Zisserman, A.: Very deep convolutional networks for large-scale image recognition. In: 3rd International Conference on Learning Representations, ICLR 2015 - Conference Track Proceedings, September 2015
16. Stallkamp, J., Schlipsing, M., Salmen, J., Igel, C.: Man vs. computer: benchmarking machine learning algorithms for traffic sign recognition. Neural Netw. **32**, 323–332 (2012)
17. Wang, B., et al.: With great training comes great vulnerability: practical attacks against transfer learning. In: USENIX, pp. 1281–1297 (2018)
18. Xie, P., Bilenko, M., Finley, T., Gilad-Bachrach, R., Lauter, K., Naehrig, M.: Crypto-Nets: Neural Networks over Encrypted Data, December 2014

On Reverse Engineering Neural Network Implementation on GPU

Łukasz Chmielewski[1,3](✉) and Léo Weissbart[1,2]

[1] Radboud University, Nijmegen, Nijmegen, The Netherlands
{lukaszc,l.weissbart}@cs.ru.nl
[2] Delft University of Technology, Delft, The Netherlands
[3] Riscure BV, Delft, The Netherlands

Abstract. In recent years machine learning has become increasingly mainstream across industries. Additionally, Graphical Processing Unit (GPU) accelerators are widely deployed in various neural network (NN) applications, including image recognition for autonomous vehicles and natural language processing, among others. Since training a powerful network requires expensive data collection and computing power, its design and parameters are often considered a secret intellectual property of their manufacturers. However, hardware accelerators can leak crucial information about the secret neural network designs through side-channels, like Electro-Magnetic (EM) emanations, power consumption, or timing.

We propose and evaluate non-invasive and passive reverse engineering methods to recover NN designs deployed on GPUs through EM side-channel analysis. We employ a well-known technique of simple EM analysis and timing analysis of NN layers execution. We consider commonly used NN architectures, namely Multilayer Perceptron and Convolutional Neural Networks. We show how to recover the number of layers and neurons as well as the types of activation functions. Our experimental results are obtained on a setup that is as close as possible to a real-world device in order to properly assess the applicability and extendability of our methods.

We analyze the NN execution of a PyTorch python framework implementation running on Nvidia Jetson Nano, a module computer embedding a Tegra X1 SoC that combines an ARM Cortex-A57 CPU and a 128-core GPU within a Maxwell architecture. Our results show the importance of side-channel protections for NN accelerators in real-world applications.

Keywords: Deep neural network · Side-channel analysis · Simple power analysis · Reverse engineering

1 Introduction

Deep learning is more and more deployed in many research and industry areas ranging from image processing and recognition [13], image recognition for autonomous vehicles [4], robotics [9], and natural language processing [27], medical applications [15], IoT speech recognition [26] to security [14,29]. This rapid

J. Zhou et al. (Eds.): ACNS 2021 Workshops, LNCS 12809, pp. 96–113, 2021.
https://doi.org/10.1007/978-3-030-81645-2_7

deployment is caused by the increased computational capabilities of computers and huge amounts of data available for machine learning. Additionally, it leads to more and more complex machine learning architectures.

In this paper, we focus on the analysis of Multilayer Perceptron (MLP) and Convolutional Neural Network (CNN) implemented using GPU accelerators, as they are the most commonly used feed-forward neural networks architectures.

Designing and finding parameters for neural networks has become an increasingly hard task since the NN architectures become more complex. From the industrial point of view, we can observe an increase in the number of intellectual property (IP) of NNs. Such IPs of commercial interest need to be kept secret. Moreover, in the medical context, the privacy aspects of NNs can also become a threat if revealed.

Additionally, EMVCo, an entity formed by MasterCard and Visa to manage specifications for payment systems, requires deep learning techniques for security evaluations [24]. Due to the above reasons, hackers might want to reverse neural networks to learn secret information.

There exist potentially easier ways to recover a network than using complex side-channels like EM or power consumption. For example, physical access to the device might be sufficient for an attacker to access the NN firmware and to reverse engineer it using binary analysis. As a countermeasure, those devices are equipped with standard protections like blocking binary access, blocking JTAG access, or code obfuscation. Furthermore, the IP vendors usually forbid users to access architectural side-channel information, such as memory and cache due to security and privacy concerns. Additionally, they implement countermeasures in software and hardware against logical attacks that would allow hackers to obtain run-time control on the device.

Therefore, for such protected implementations, side-channel attacks become viable for reverse engineering NNs. Side-channel analysis (SCA) has been widely studied for the last 20 years due to its capability to break otherwise secure algorithms and recover secret information. In 2019, Batina et al. [1] presented the first SCA attack to extract architecture and weights from a multilayer perceptron implemented on a microcontroller; this attack employed both timing and EM side-channels. This attack has shown that SCA is a serious threat to NNs.

However, there has been little work done on SCA against GPU-based neural networks[1]. To the best of our knowledge, there has been no power or EM side-channel attack presented that targets GPU-based neural networks, while GPU is the platform of choice to train and deploy neural networks.

In this work, we aim at evaluating the security of a setup that is as close to a real-world application as possible, and therefore, we target NNs running on GPU. Therefore, we target the Nvidia Jetson Nano, a module computer embedding a Tegra X1 SoC combining an ARM Cortex-A57 CPU and a 128-core GPU with Maxwell architecture. This hardware accelerator is relatively complex in

[1] The only SCA against GPU-based NN that we have found is presented in [28]. However, it works in a different context to ours and is based on software context-switching timing side-channel; see Subsect. 1.1 for details.

comparison to a simple microcontroller. In particular, our setup employs the PyTorch python framework running on the full Linux operating system (on the ARM CPU) to instruct the GPU accelerator to execute NN computations. This complexity poses several technical difficulties for our analysis due to a large amount of noise and misalignment. Because of these challenges, we limit our analysis to so-called simple EM analysis[2] and we recover numbers of layers and neurons as well as the types of activation function being executed. Our experiments show that all this secret information can be recovered using dozen of EM traces independent of inputs even when significant noise and misalignment are present when sufficient signal processing techniques are used.

Note that we need to analyze a GPU implementation as black-box since the low-level details of the implementation could not be public. Moreover, due to the parallel nature of GPUs, we cannot simply replicate existing attacks for other architectures, but adjust them adequately.

We leave recovering neuron weights and CNN hyperparameters using more complex side-channel attacks to be future work.

1.1 Related Works

Any computation running on a platform might result in physical leakages. Those leakages form a physical signature from the reaction time, power consumption, and EM emanations released while the device is manipulating data. Side-channel analysis (SCA) exploits those physical signatures to reveal secret information about the running program or processed data In its basic form, SCA was proposed to perform key recovery attacks on cryptographic implementations [10,11].

The application of SCA is not limited to the type of processing unit and can be applied to microcontrollers as well as other platforms. In [5,7,8,16], EM and power side-channel attacks are performed on GPU-based AES implementations.

In [19] SCA is used to break isolation between different applications concurrently using a GPU. Essentially this work identify different ways to measure leakage using software means from any shared component.

Side-channel attacks can be applied to extract the information of a neural network. Batina et al. [1] presented the first EM side-channel attack to extract the complete architecture and weights from an MLP network implemented on a CPU. Subsequently, Honggang Yu et al. [33] combined simple EM analysis with adversarial active learning to recover a large-scale Binarized Neural Network, which can be seen as a subset of CNNs, implemented on a field-programmable gate array (FPGA). In this attack, the recovery of the weights is not done through EM analysis, but using a margin-based adversarial learning method. This method can be seen as a cryptanalysis against NNs where weights are treated as an attacked secret key. Takatoi et al. [25] show how to use simple EM analysis to retrieve an activation function from a NN implemented on an Arduino Uno microcontroller. In [32], correlation power analysis is used to reveal neuron

[2] Simple EM analysis involves visually interpreting EM traces over time in order to recover the secret.

weights from the matrix multiplication implemented with systolic array units on an FPGA. Another relevant attack [30] uses power SCA together with machine learning classifier to reveal internal network architecture, including its detailed parameters, on an ARM Cortex embedded device. Maji et al. [17] demonstrated a timing attack combined with a simple power analysis of microcontroller-based NN to recover hyperparameters and the inputs of the network.

The only previous attack that targets GPU-based NN [28], to the best of our knowledge works in a different setting to ours; a model developer and an adversary share the same GPU when training a network and the adversary aims to break the isolation to learn the trained model. This attack is not applicable to an edge accelerator platform as the training phase is always performed in a controlled environment with more capable resources. This attack also relies on the presence of an adversary sharing GPU resources while our attack does not make such a requirement.

A recent survey of existing SCA methods for architecture extraction of neural networks implementations is presented in [2] and an overview of hardware attacks against NN is given in [31].

1.2 Contributions

In this paper, for the first time, to the best of our knowledge, we investigate using simple EM analysis to break side-channel security of NN (namely Multilayer Perceptron and Convolutional Neural Networks) running on a GPU. We present how to successfully recover the number of layers and neurons as well as the types of activation functions. Most importantly, our results show the importance of side-channel protections for NN accelerators in real-world applications.

We leave recovering neuron weights and CNN hyperparameters using more complex side-channel attacks, like DPA or template attack to be future work.

Our experimental results are obtained on the setup that is as close as possible to a real-world device setup in order to properly assess the applicability and extendability of our methods.

1.3 Organization of the Paper

Section 2 presents the necessary background on simple EM analysis, NNs, and the employed GPU architecture. Subsequently, our threat model is described in Sect. 3 and the target and NN implementation in Sect. 4. We present our reverse engineering methods and experimental results in Sect. 5. Finally, conclusions and future work are presented in Sect. 6.

2 Background

In this section we introduce the concepts of simple EM analysis (SEMA), Artificial Neural Network, and we describe a GPU Architecture that we analyze.

2.1 Simple EM Analysis

In the second half of the nineties, Paul Kocher et al. presented the first research publications about practical side-channel attacks [10,11]. They realized that the security of cryptographic algorithms does not only depend on the mathematical properties but also on implementation details, regardless of whether the implementation is hardware or software.

By monitoring side-channels of cryptographic implementations of DES and RSA using a low-cost oscilloscope, more specifically the power consumption [10] and the execution time [11], they were able to discover the side-channel leakages corresponding to the private key usage. As a result, they were able to recover the private key with little effort and low cost. The methods presented by Kocher et al. in [10] are called Simple Power Analysis (SPA) and Differential Power Analysis (DPA). SPA involves visually interpreting power consumption traces over time to recover the secret key[3]. Variations in power consumption occur particularly strongly as the device performs different operations. If the sequence of such operations depends on the key, then using a standard digital oscilloscope the attacker would learn information about the key. Additionally, the attacker might further use frequency filters and averaging to improve the signal quality.

DPA improves on SPA by employing a statistical analysis between intermediate values of cryptographic computations and the corresponding side-channel traces in order to recover the key.

In this paper we employ technique called Simple EM analysis (SEMA) that is equivalent to SPA but in the EM domain. For example, how to recognize different amount of layers in NN is shown in Fig. 7.

Template Attack [3] (TA) is another notable SCA technique that can be seen as an improved version of SPA. It combines statistical modeling with SPA and DPA and can achieve better accuracy than SPA. It consists of two phases, called *profiling* and *matching*. An attacker first creates a *"profile"* of a sensitive device, which is under their full control, and then *matches* this profile to measurements from the victim's device to quickly find the secret key.

We leave using aforementioned DPA and TA to recover neuron weights and CNN hypermarameters as future work.

2.2 Artificial Neural Network

Artificial Neural Network (ANN) is a category of computing systems that can exhibit generalization for a given task beyond the training data. A Neural Network (NN) is a network of many simple computing units (also called nodes) connected by communication channels to transmit a signal. The units transform numerical inputs together with local data (i.e., weights) to produce an output. During the so-called 'training process', weights and biases are adjusted to minimize a given loss function and stores the experimental knowledge about the training task.

A simple type of neural network is a perceptron (also called neuron). The perceptrons perform an inner product of the inputs in_i and weights w_i, plus

[3] In our case the secret key is the network architecture.

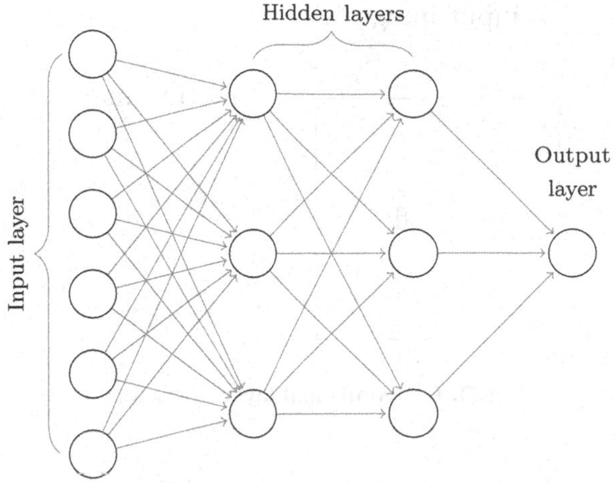

Fig. 1. Schematic of a multi-layer perceptron

a bias b through an activation function to compute its output. The activation function is usually a logistic or *tanh* function. Hence, the formula of an artificial neuron output is typically computed according to Eq. (1).

$$o = tanh(b + sum[w_i * x_i]) \tag{1}$$

A more advanced type of neural network is the Multi-layer Perceptron (MLP). An MLP is a neural network constituted of multiple perceptrons grouped in layers to form a directed graph. Each perceptron in a layer is fully connected with a given weight w for every node of the following layer. An MLP consists of at least three layers: one input layer, one output layer, and one hidden layer. An MLP is represented on Fig. 1 An MLP with more than one hidden layer is considered a deep learning architecture. To train the network, the backpropagation algorithm is used, which is a generalization of the least mean squares algorithm in the linear perceptron. Backpropagation is used by the gradient descent optimization algorithm to adjust the weight of neurons by calculating the gradient of the loss function [18]. After the training phase, only the forward loop is computed without backward propagation. This mode is called 'inference' and is the mode used when deploying a neural network.

More advanced deep neural network units involve convolution operation in place of the inner product of perceptrons. Neural networks with at least one layer of convolution units are called Convolutional Neural Networks (CNN). CNNs are commonly applied when analyzing visual imagery to take advantage of the hierarchical pattern in data and assemble patterns of increasing complexity using smaller and simpler patterns called filters. The convolutional layer consists of several filters (i.e., two-dimensional array of real values) used to detect a specific type of feature in the input. The operation consists in successive dot products of the filters with patches of the inputs of corresponding size. Because the filter

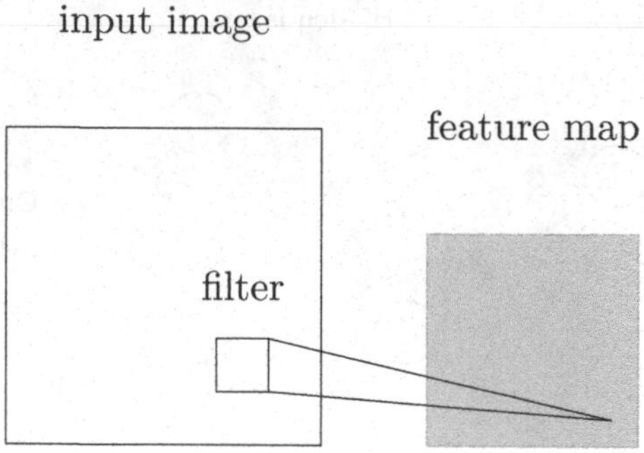

Fig. 2. Convolutional layer operation

size is smaller than the input size, the filters is shifted across the whole input area with overlapping to produce a feature map. This feature map is the layer's output. The output of one convolution operation with one filter is depicted in Fig. 2 Commonly, the filters are also called the weights of the convolutional layer. CNNs usually consist of successive Convolutional layers followed by an MLP structure to perform a classification task.

2.3 GPU Architecture

GPU is a specialized computer hardware designed to accelerate parallel computing for image processing. Deep learning algorithms can benefit from GPU high parallelization to boost their performances, especially when dealing with visual data. A GPU groups several GPU cores into a Streaming Multiprocessor (SM). The specific SM of Maxwell GPU architecture is shown in Fig. 3. All GPU cores within a SM can handle floating-point operations in a Single Instruction Multiple Data (SIMD) paradigm. This way, the exact same processing can be applied to a large volume of data to reach a higher throughput than for a CPU.

CUDA is the Software Development Kit (SDK) introduced by NVIDIA that gives direct access to the GPU's instruction set and facilitates general-purpose programming. From the programming perspective, a program that runs on a GPU is divided into parallel threads groups into wraps of 32 threads partitioned into blocks within grids executed on the SM [21]. When the number of blocks in a SM is less than the number of blocks assigned for the operation, the blocks are queued and scheduled to be executed at a later time. This method allows programs to be scalable for the hardware it is executed on and offers speed up for devices with more blocks per SM. Higher-level programming languages such as python frameworks relies on CUDA to call computation every low level function on GPU. We will see that it is possible to exploit this feature to perform side-channel a analysis of the size of data processed by the GPU.

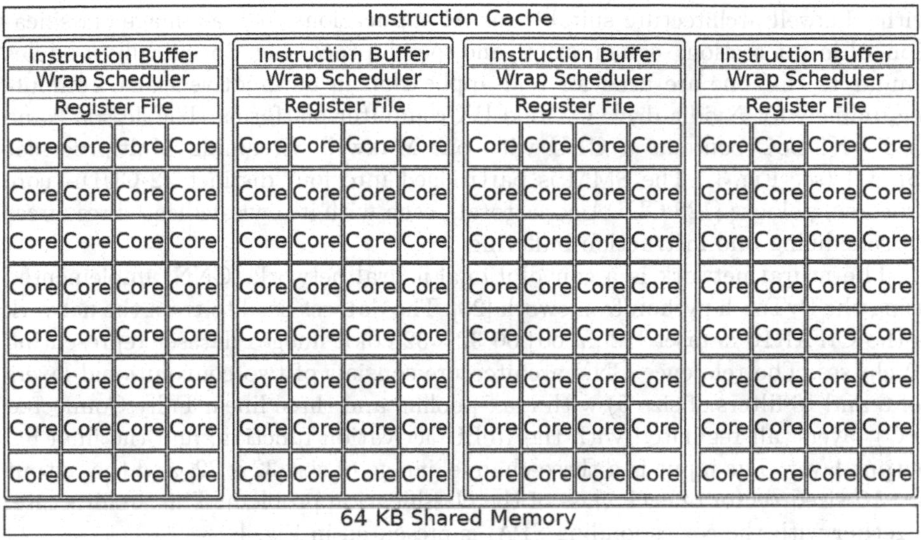

Fig. 3. Maxwell streaming multiprocessor architecture

3 Threat Model

The main goal of this attack is to reverse engineer the neural network architecture using only side-channel information. In this scenario, we consider an attacker with no insight of the inputs type, source or the implementation of the machine learning algorithm. Currently, to the best of our knowledge, there is no public implementation deploying side-channel countermeasure. We consider a passive and non-invasive attacker who can only acquire side-channel measurement while operating "normally" the target device and cannot control the flow of operation.

A suitable use case for this attack is considering an attacker who acquired a legal copy of the network in a black-box setting and aims to recover its internal details for IP theft. The attacker controls the inputs and performs side-channel measurement during the inference phase of the neural network. The goal is to reverse engineer the following information about the neural network architecture: number of layers, number of outputs, and activation functions in the network.

If successful, this attack can have severe monetary repercussions for companies investing significant resources to develop customized machine-learning models to create highly valuable IPs [22]. A successful attacker that is able to steal such models can offer similar services at much lower cost than the investing companies.

4 The Target and Network Implementation

The target is an Nvidia Jetson Nano [34], a module computer embedding a Tegra X1 SoC [35] combining an ARM Cortex-A57 CPU and a 128-core GPU with Maxwell architecture suitable for AI applications such as image classification, object detection, segmentation, and speech processing. Specifically, modules similar to this one are used for real application in automotive visual computing, namely for Nvidia drive CX and PX computer platforms. The Jetson Nano Tegra X1 SoC contains a GPU with one Maxwell Streaming Multiprocessor (SMM) (see Fig. 3). The SMM is partitioned into four distinct 32-CUDA core processing blocks (128 CUDA cores total), each with its own dedicated resources for scheduling and instruction buffering.

The neural network is a convolutional neural network (CNN) implemented using the PyTorch python framework [23]. The dataset used to train the network is the CIFAR10 dataset [12], a 60 000 32×32 color images dataset representing 10 classes. The reference CNN architecture consists of two convolutional layers (of 6 and 16 filters of size 5) with max-pooling and three linear Fully Connected (FC) layers, all regulated with the ReLU activation function, and the final FC output layer. The input is a three-channel image of size 32×32, and the output is a 10-sized vector of each class of the classification problem. This architecture, together with the corresponding SPA, is presented in Fig. 4.

To better measure the execution of the neural network, we use a power trigger. The Jetson Nano handles General Purpose Input/Outputs (GPIOs). We use one GPIO pin to implement a trigger around the forward loop of the neural network to be sure only to measure while the GPU is active. It is to be noticed that, the neural network is already trained and the gradient operation is disabled to prevent the backward loop from happening.

To record the EM traces we removed the heatsink of the target and placed a Riscure Low Sensitivity (LS) EM probe[4] above the main chip package. The best position of the probe is empirically chosen to maximize the leaking signal. We manually searched the position with a grid scanning above the chip for multiple locations and chose the most promising position based on visual inspection of the traces. This best location is presented in Fig. 5.

The oscilloscope in our experiment is the Teledyne Lecroy WaveRunner 8404M. We used it in two configurations, one for characterization with 5×10^9 samples/s and at most 32×10^6 samples and the second one for simple EM with 10^9 samples/s and at most 10^7. We used greater sampling rate in the first configuration because we performed frequency analysis and we needed to be able to record a signal up to the GPU maximum clock frequency, namely 900 MHz, in good quality; for simple EM we do not need that high accuracy. The oscilloscope has TCP/IP support for both controlling and downloading measurements, which helps to automatize the entire process.

We acquired and analyzed using Riscure's Inspector software package[5].

The goal of the neural network used in this paper is not meant for high efficiency or presenting a challenging classification task, but rather to show the methods and principles side-channel analysis can bring in to extract information from a neural network closed implementation.

---

4 https://www.riscure.com/uploads/2017/07/inspector_brochure.pdf.

5 https://www.riscure.com/security-tools/inspector-sca.

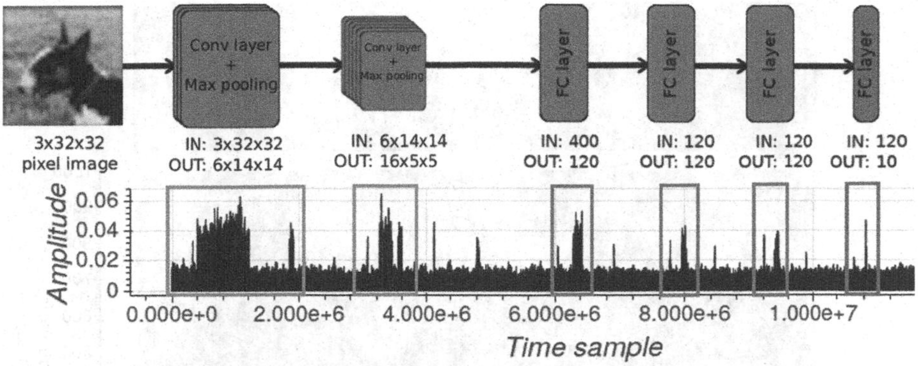

Fig. 4. SPA of CIFAR10 convolutional neural network

Fig. 5. Experimental setup: the EM probe location

5 Reverse Engineering

5.1 Characterization

In Fig. 4, the architecture of the neural network is showed next to an EM trace measured during its execution on the target. From the EM trace, we can observe that every different step of the forward loop of the NN is distinguishable. The two convolutional blocks are identifiable by a first activity corresponding to the convolutional operation followed by a smaller activity corresponding to the pooling operation. The layers of the MLP, namely, the FC layers, are also detectable by single peaks.

It is possible to verify whether the leakage is effectively coming from the GPU activity by observing the leakage in the frequency domain. Because the GPU maximum clock frequency is 900 MHz, the computation made on the device

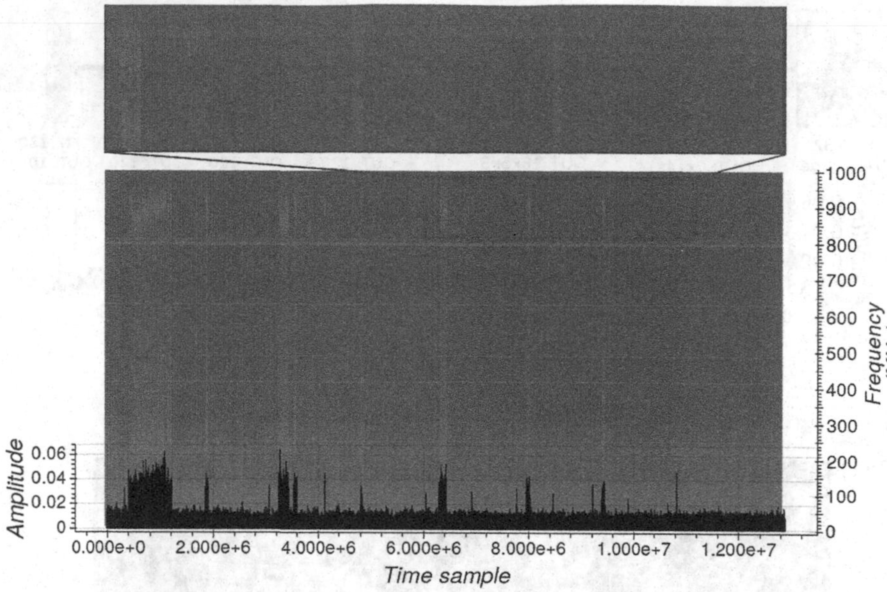

Fig. 6. A single EM trace (in the blue color at the bottom) and the corresponding spectrogram (middle) with the MLP activation zoomed-in (top)

will emit leakage in the same range of frequencies. In Fig. 6, we represented the absolute value of the leakage together with the spectrogram plot of the leakage. We can see that the detected leakage correspond to the frequency range of the GPU. It would be possible to continue the same analysis using this frequency signal, but in this paper, we will only focus on EM analysis in the time domain.

In the following analyses, we either use raw traces or apply an averaged window resampling method on the absolute value of the signal. The averaged window resampling reduces the number of features of the trace by averaging samples in a fixed-size window shifted without overlapping across all samples of the trace. This processing makes alignments on specific patterns faster and easier.

5.2 Reverse Engineering the Number of Layers

In this section we investigate how to recover the number of hidden layers in the MLP from the SCA during the inference phase.

Since the dataflow of a NN is such that layers are processed sequentially, the analysis of different number of fully connected layer is trivial from the EM traces. We measured three different implementations of a neural network, with a different number of fully connected layers and observe their leakage. From the reference neural network model, we change the number of fully connected layers from 4 to 6. The number of neurons in each of the additional layers is the same as the second fully connected layer from the reference model (i.e., 120 neurons).

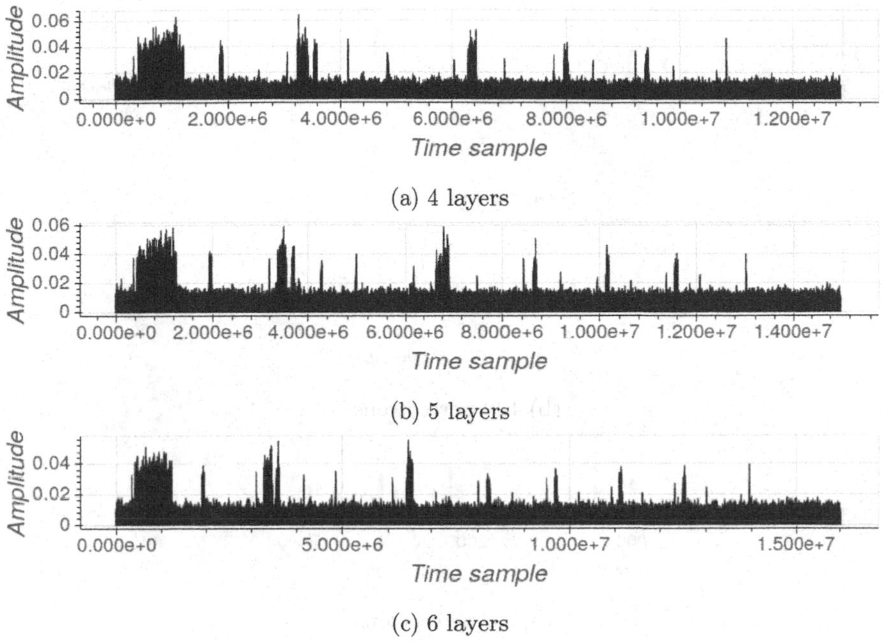

Fig. 7. Differences in the number of fully connected layers

The resulting EM measurements are represented in Fig. 7. From the three plots, the two first convolutional blocks and the fully connected layers are clearly identifiable. While the plots are aligned according to the first convolutional layer, the timing of the execution is not consistent. Many process interruptions occur during the computation, leading to misalignments in the traces. However, the additional layers do appear in the EM measurement and are easily identifiable.

5.3 Reverse Engineering the Number of Neurons

Now we investigate how to recover the number of neurons in a hidden MLP layer.

In a GPU implementation, every neuron operation is processed in parallel. However, the parallelization degree depends on the size of the inputs and number of neurons, as there is a limit on the number of floating-point operation that can be computed in parallel. For example, given N GPU threads, each capable of computing one floating-point operation per clock cycle, the GPU scheduler can compute N operations per clock cycle. If $n_{inputs} \times n_{neurons} > N$ then the number of neurons will partially leak, and if $n_{inputs} \geqslant N$ then the number of neurons will entirely leak as every neuron computation would require more than one cycle.

From the execution of the linear operation in the fully connected layers, it is possible to recover the number of perceptrons per layer using timing side-channel. In Fig. 8 different models are analyzed. Here, we control the number of

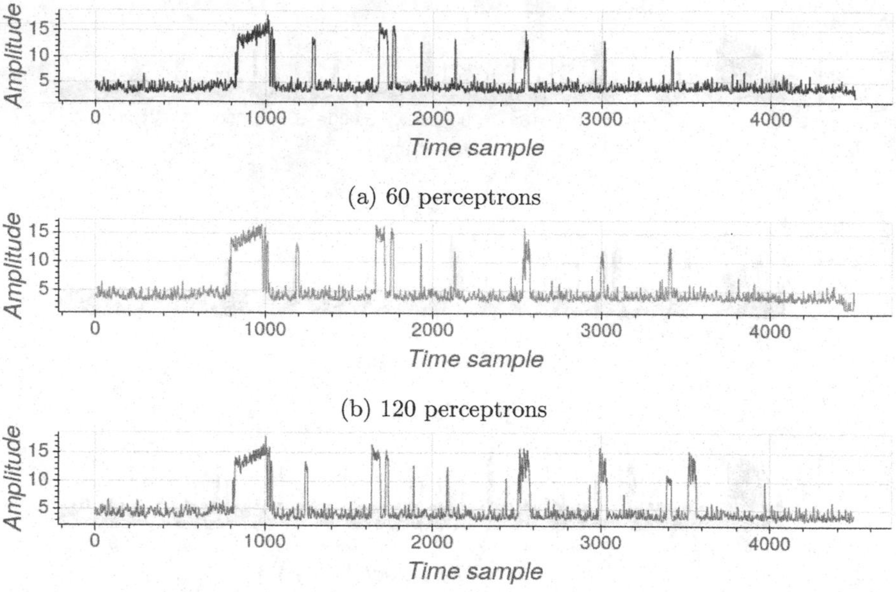

(a) 60 perceptrons

(b) 120 perceptrons

(c) 255 perceptrons

Fig. 8. Difference in number of perceptrons inside fully connected layers

neurons within the hidden layers. We can see that when the number of neurons in the layers increases, the execution time of each layer also increases.

Recovering the exact number of neurons in a layer would require to be capable to distinguish a single neuron difference. In Fig. 9, the timing of the first fully connected layer activity with an increasing number of perceptrons from 30 to 100 is represented. For every number of perceptron, we averaged fifty measurements and align the traces according to the desired pattern to measure the execution time of the specific layer. While the relation shows a linear behavior, the measurements noise and re-alignment, still make it difficult to distinguish a single perceptron change. However, approximate recovery is possible with a relatively low error margin.

5.4 Reverse Engineering the Type of Activation Function

Nonlinear functions are essential to approximate a linearly non-separable problem. The use of these functions also helps to reduce the number of network nodes. With the knowledge of the type of nonlinear function used in a layer, an attacker can deduce the behavior of the entire neural network using the input values.

We analyze the side-channel leakage from different commonly used activation functions, namely ReLU, Sigmoid, Tanh, and Softmax [6,20]. The activation function applied to the first convolutional layer of the network is changed in different measurements. We measured the EM leakage of the execution of the layer

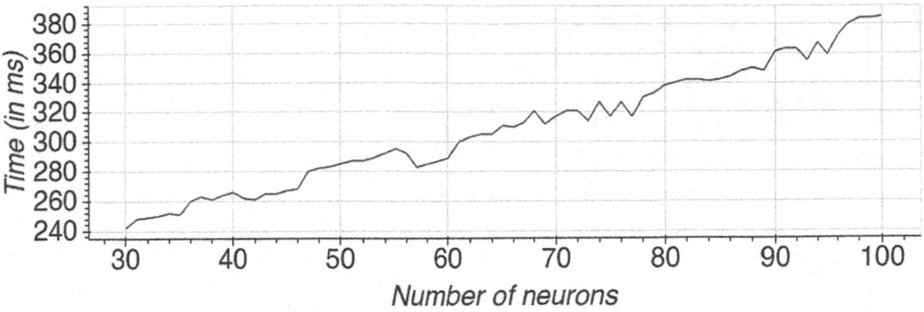

Fig. 9. Differences in the number of perceptrons (from 30 to 100 units)

Table 1. Statistical analysis on computation time (in μs).

Activation function	Mean	Maximum	Minimum
ReLU	33.5	34	33
Tanh	36.0	37	34
Sigmoid	43.3	46	41
Softmax	124.5	127	123

computation and the activation function for random input and is represented in Fig. 10. We identify the execution of the convolutional layer from 0 to 520 time samples and it is identical for all sub-figures. The execution of the activation function presents differences among all different activation functions. We can notice for example that the execution of the ReLU activation function is the shortest and that the Softmax function is the longest by far. The timing differences between ReLU, Tanh, and Sigmoid activation functions are smaller.

The computation time of the activation function does depend on the size of the input. Therefore, to identify the type of activation function, one should first recover the number of inputs. We measured fifty executions of the activation function after the first convolutional layer. The input of this activation function is of the size of the output of the convolutional layer before the pooling layer and is of size $6 \times 28 \times 28 = 4704$. All measurements are done on random data, and we draw a statistical analysis of the timing pattern for all types of activation functions considered in Table 1. It can be observed that each activation function stands out, and thus it is possible to recover trivially the type of activation function from a neural network implementation.

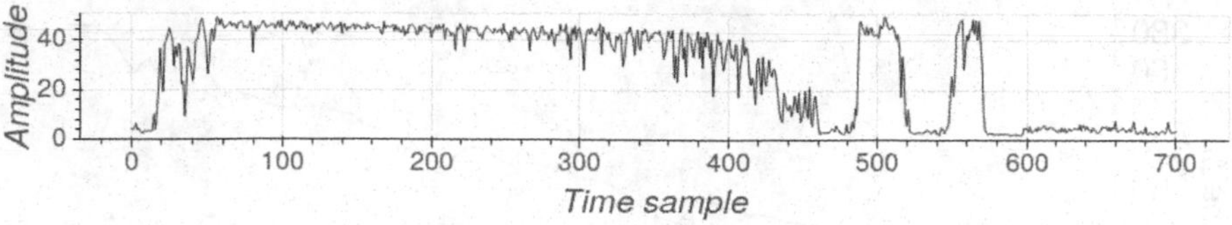

(a) ReLU

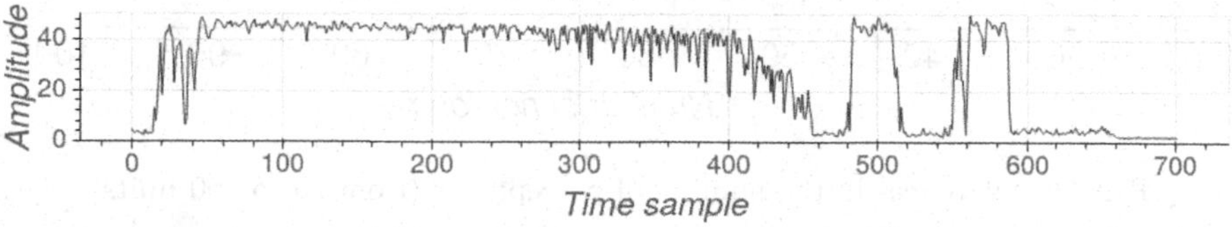

(b) Tanh

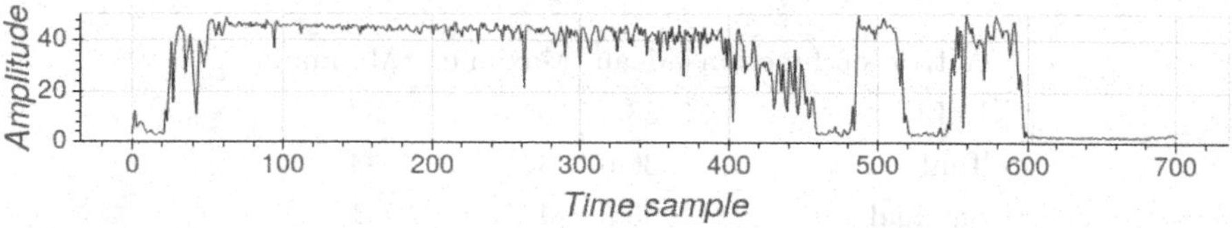

(c) Sigmoid

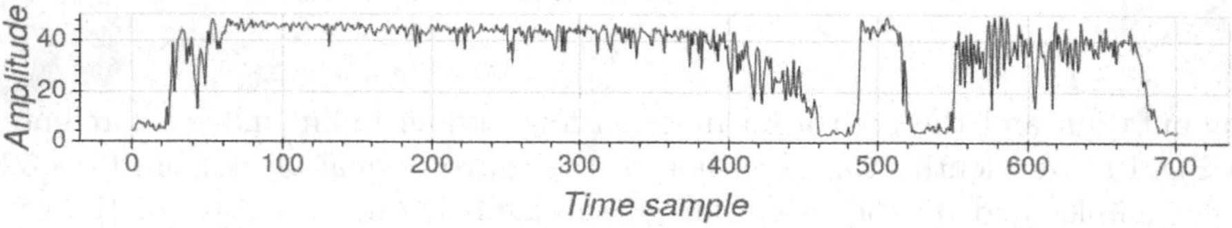

(d) Softmax

Fig. 10. Differences in the type of activation function applied on layer output

6 Conclusions and Future Work

Side-channel analysis have already been proven capable to reverse engineering a neural network implemented on a microcontroller architecture. While microcontrollers can be the hardware of choice for some small edge computing applications, GPU stays the most popular platform for deep learning. In this paper, we show the possibility to recover key parameters of a GPU implementation of a neural network. We can recover the number of layers and number of neurons per layer of a multi-layer perceptron with simple power analysis. We can also identify different types of activation functions with single power analysis for a given number of inputs. We can conclude that we have managed to recover all the secret information that can be achieved using only simple EM analysis.

For the reverse engineering of a complete neural network, the weights of all layers for both MLP and CNN networks and network hyperparameters for CNNs should be recovered too. We consider these tasks to be future work, but we envision that the weights can be recovered using correlation or differential power analysis on float vector multiplication similarly to [1]. However, the main challenges, besides noise and misalignment, would be the lack of information on how the multiplication is performed and the parallel aspect of GPU computation (i.e., multiple intermediate values might be computed at the same time). Recovery of CNN hyperparameters would be probably also a hard task and we suspect that it would require a template attack.

Acknowledgements. The authors would like to thank Carlos Castro, Louiza Papachristodoulou, and Yuriy Serdyuk from NavInfo for very informative discussions on using neural networks in the automotive context. Moreover, we would like to thank the anonymous reviewers for their insightful comments.

Łukasz Chmielewski is supported by European Commission through the ERC Starting Grant 805031 (EPOQUE) of P. Schwabe.

References

1. Batina, L., Bhasin, S., Jap, D., Picek, S.: CSI NN: reverse engineering of neural network architectures through electromagnetic side channel. In: 28th USENIX Security Symposium (USENIX Security 2019), pp. 515–532 (2019)
2. Chabanne, H., Danger, J.L., Guiga, L., Kühne, U.: Side channel attacks for architecture extraction of neural networks. CAAI Trans. Intell. Technol. **6**(1), 3–16 (2021)
3. Chari, S., Rao, J.R., Rohatgi, P.: Template attacks. In: Kaliski, B.S., Koç, K., Paar, C. (eds.) CHES 2002. LNCS, vol. 2523, pp. 13–28. Springer, Heidelberg (2003). https://doi.org/10.1007/3-540-36400-5_3
4. Fujiyoshi, H., Hirakawa, T., Yamashita, T.: Deep learning-based image recognition for autonomous driving. IATSS Res. **43**(4), 244–252 (2019)
5. Gao, Y., Zhou, Y., Cheng, W.: How Does Strict Parallelism Affect Security? A Case Study on the Side-Channel Attacks against GPU-based Bitsliced AES Implementation. IACR Cryptology ePrint Archive 2018/1080 (2018)
6. Haykin, S., Network, N.: A comprehensive foundation. Neural Netw. **2**(2004), 41 (2004)
7. Jiang, Z.H., Fei, Y., Kaeli, D.: A complete key recovery timing attack on a GPU. In: 2016 IEEE International Symposium on High Performance Computer Architecture (HPCA), pp. 394–405. IEEE (2016)
8. Jiang, Z.H., Fei, Y., Kaeli, D.: A novel side-channel timing attack on GPUs. In: Proceedings of the on Great Lakes Symposium on VLSI 2017, pp. 167–172 (2017)
9. Kober, J., Bagnell, J.A., Peters, J.: Reinforcement learning in robotics: a survey. Int. J. Rob. Res. **32**(11), 1238–1274 (2013). https://doi.org/10.1177/0278364913495721
10. Kocher, P., Jaffe, J., Jun, B.: Differential power analysis. In: Wiener, M. (ed.) CRYPTO 1999. LNCS, vol. 1666, pp. 388–397. Springer, Heidelberg (1999). https://doi.org/10.1007/3-540-48405-1_25
11. Kocher, P.C.: Timing attacks on implementations of Diffie-Hellman, RSA, DSS, and other systems. In: Koblitz, N. (ed.) CRYPTO 1996. LNCS, vol. 1109, pp. 104–113. Springer, Heidelberg (1996). https://doi.org/10.1007/3-540-68697-5_9
12. Krizhevsky, A.: Learning multiple layers of features from tiny images. Technical report, University of Toronto (2009)

13. Krizhevsky, A., Sutskever, I., Hinton, G.E.: ImageNet classification with deep convolutional neural networks. In: Pereira, F., Burges, C.J.C., Bottou, L., Weinberger, K.Q. (eds.) Advances in Neural Information Processing Systems 25, pp. 1097–1105. Curran Associates, Inc. (2012). http://papers.nips.cc/paper/4824-imagenet-classification-with-deep-convolutional-neural-networks.pdf
14. Kučera, M., Tsankov, P., Gehr, T., Guarnieri, M., Vechev, M.: Synthesis of probabilistic privacy enforcement. In: Proceedings of the 2017 ACM SIGSAC Conference on Computer and Communications Security, CCS 2017, pp. 391–408. Association for Computing Machinery, New York (2017). https://doi.org/10.1145/3133956.3134079
15. Lundervold, A.S., Lundervold, A.: An overview of deep learning in medical imaging focusing on MRI. Zeitschrift für Medizinische Physik **29**(2), 102–127 (2019)
16. Luo, C., Fei, Y., Luo, P., Mukherjee, S., Kaeli, D.: Side-channel power analysis of a GPU AES implementation. In: 2015 33rd IEEE International Conference on Computer Design (ICCD), pp. 281–288. IEEE (2015)
17. Maji, S., Banerjee, U., Chandrakasan, A.P.: Leaky nets: recovering embedded neural network models and inputs through simple power and timing side-channels - attacks and defenses. IEEE Internet Things J. 1 (2021). https://doi.org/10.1109/JIOT.2021.3061314
18. Mitchell, T.M., et al.: Machine Learning. McGraw-Hill, New York (1997)
19. Naghibijouybari, H., Neupane, A., Qian, Z., Ghazaleh, N.A.: Side channel attacks on GPUs. IEEE Trans. Dependable Secure Comput. (2019)
20. Nair, V., Hinton, G.E.: Rectified linear units improve restricted Boltzmann machines. In: ICML (2010)
21. Nickolls, J., Buck, I., Garland, M., Skadron, K.: Scalable parallel programming with CUDA: is CUDA the parallel programming model that application developers have been waiting for? Queue **6**(2), 40–53 (2008)
22. Papernot, N., McDaniel, P., Sinha, A., Wellman, M.P.: SoK: security and privacy in machine learning. In: 2018 IEEE European Symposium on Security and Privacy (EuroS P), pp. 399–414 (2018). https://doi.org/10.1109/EuroSP.2018.00035
23. Paszke, A., et al.: Pytorch: an imperative style, high-performance deep learning library. arXiv preprint arXiv:1912.01703 (2019)
24. Riscure: Automated Neural Network construction with Genetic Algorithm (blog post) (2018). https://www.riscure.com/blog/automated-neural-network-construction-genetic-algorithm
25. Takatoi, G., Sugawara, T., Sakiyama, K., Li, Y.: Simple electromagnetic analysis against activation functions of deep neural networks. In: Zhou, J., et al. (eds.) ACNS 2020. LNCS, vol. 12418, pp. 181–197. Springer, Cham (2020). https://doi.org/10.1007/978-3-030-61638-0_11
26. Tariq, Z., Shah, S.K., Lee, Y.: Speech emotion detection using IoT based deep learning for health care. In: Baru, C., et al. (eds.) 2019 IEEE International Conference on Big Data (Big Data), Los Angeles, CA, USA, 9–12 December 2019, pp. 4191–4196. IEEE (2019). https://doi.org/10.1109/BigData47090.2019.9005638
27. Teufl, P., Payer, U., Lackner, G.: From NLP (natural language processing) to MLP (machine language processing). In: Kotenko, I., Skormin, V. (eds.) MMM-ACNS 2010. LNCS, vol. 6258, pp. 256–269. Springer, Heidelberg (2010). https://doi.org/10.1007/978-3-642-14706-7_20
28. Wei, J., Zhang, Y., Zhou, Z., Li, Z., Al Faruque, M.A.: Leaky DNN: stealing deep-learning model secret with GPU context-switching side-channel. In: 2020 50th Annual IEEE/IFIP International Conference on Dependable Systems and Networks (DSN), pp. 125–137. IEEE (2020)

29. Wei, L., Luo, B., Li, Y., Liu, Y., Xu, Q.: I know what you see: power side-channel attack on convolutional neural network accelerators. In: Proceedings of the 34th Annual Computer Security Applications Conference, ACSAC 2018, pp. 393–406. Association for Computing Machinery, New York (2018). https://doi.org/10.1145/3274694.3274696
30. Xiang, Y., et al.: Open DNN box by power side-channel attack. IEEE Trans. Circuits Syst. II Express Briefs **67**(11), 2717–2721 (2020). https://doi.org/10.1109/TCSII.2020.2973007
31. Xu, Q., Arafin, M.T., Qu, G.: Security of neural networks from hardware perspective: a survey and beyond. In: Proceedings of the 26th Asia and South Pacific Design Automation Conference, ASPDAC 2021, pp. 449–454. Association for Computing Machinery, New York (2021). https://doi.org/10.1145/3394885.3431639
32. Yoshida, K., Kubota, T., Okura, S., Shiozaki, M., Fujino, T.: Model reverse-engineering attack using correlation power analysis against systolic array based neural network accelerator. In: 2020 IEEE International Symposium on Circuits and Systems (ISCAS), pp. 1–5 (2020). https://doi.org/10.1109/ISCAS45731.2020.9180580
33. Yu, H., Ma, H., Yang, K., Zhao, Y., Jin, Y.: DeepEM: deep neural networks model recovery through EM side-channel information leakage. In: 2020 IEEE International Symposium on Hardware Oriented Security and Trust (HOST), pp. 209–218. IEEE (2020)
34. NVIDIA Jetson Nano module Datasheet, April 2021. https://developer.nvidia.com/embedded/dlc/jetson-nano-system-module-datasheet
35. NVIDIA Tegra X1 White Paper, April 2021. http://international.download.nvidia.com/pdf/tegra/Tegra-X1-whitepaper-v1.0.pdf

On the Importance of Pooling Layer Tuning for Profiling Side-Channel Analysis

Lichao Wu(✉) and Guilherme Perin

Delft University of Technology, Delft, The Netherlands

Abstract. In recent years, the advent of deep neural networks opened new perspectives for security evaluations with side-channel analysis. Profiling attacks now benefit from capabilities offered by convolutional neural networks, such as dimensionality reduction and the inherent ability to reduce the trace desynchronization effects. These neural networks contain at least three types of layers: convolutional, pooling, and dense layers. Although the definition of pooling layers causes a large impact on neural network performance, a study on pooling hyperparameters effect on side-channel analysis is still not provided in the academic community. This paper provides extensive experimental results to demonstrate how pooling layer types and pooling stride and size affect the profiling attack performance with convolutional neural networks. Additionally, we demonstrate that pooling hyperparameters can be larger than usually used in related works and still keep good performance for profiling attacks on specific datasets.

Keywords: Side-channel analysis · Deep learning · Convolutional neural networks · Pooling

1 Introduction

The processing of confidential and secret information in embedded or electronic devices, in general, requires protection against different types of physical attacks. Encryption methods implement various algorithms to provide data protection for sensitive information, including cryptographic keys. An algorithm that proved to be mathematically secure is not necessarily implementation-secure. Side-channel analysis (SCA) is a class of non-invasive attacks where an adversary can record the unintended leakages, such as electromagnetic (EM) radiation [20] or power dissipation [9], and use those leakages to obtain secret information [14].

SCA can be divided into two categories based on the attack setting or security evaluation purpose (e.g., chip certification or security assessment). When an attacker can only access physical leakages captured on the target device, a non-profiled SCA, such as differential power analysis (DPA) [9], correlation power analysis (CPA) [2], and mutual information analysis (MIA) [5], could be used to retrieve the secret information. On the other hand, profiling SCA assumes an

J. Zhou et al. (Eds.): ACNS 2021 Workshops, LNCS 12809, pp. 114–132, 2021.
https://doi.org/10.1007/978-3-030-81645-2_8

adversary with full control of a clone device (i.e., by changing the key or installing malicious software) that is identical to the target device. On that device, the attacker can profile the side-channel leakages. This allows the adversary to learn statistics from leakages and build profiling models. The commonly used methods include template attack [4] and supervised machine learning-based attacks [3,8, 13,19].

Supervised machine learning-based attacks have drawn great attention within the SCA community in recent years due to their effectiveness in breaking targets and high applicability to different attack scenarios. Among different types of neural networks, convolutional neural networks (CNNs) are the most adopted method in coping with countermeasures due to their spatial invariance property [3,8], making these models appropriate to bypass countermeasures such as noise and side-channel trace desynchronization. While profiling models based on deep neural networks actively threaten the security of cryptographic devices in profiled settings, there are still severe limitations and unknowns.

Neural network hyperparameter selection is one of the biggest obstacles. Taking CNNs as an example, they usually consist of three types of layers (convolution layer, pooling layer, and dense layer), where each layer has at least two configurable hyperparameters. When an attacker tries to enhance the network capability by applying more layers, the hyperparameters' combinations increase exponentially. Although some researchers are trying to set general design rules [25,27] or applying neural architecture search to find the best-performing network automatically [21,26], the results are far from definitive. Indeed, the generality of such hyperparameter tuning methods is usually dataset-specific, but they demonstrate that deep neural networks are powerful methods that can be tailored to different datasets.

This paper focuses on the pooling layer of CNNs, which is, to the best of our knowledge, an analysis not done before. We experimentally investigate the influence of a pooling layer's hyperparameters variation on the attack performance. To achieve this, we use two models, one with a single pooling layer and the other with multiple pooling layers. The former is used to target an unprotected dataset; the latter is optimized for two datasets containing different AES implementations protected with masking countermeasure. Our results clearly show that the type of pooling layer should be selected based on the neural network depth and the number of input features. We also give guidelines on how to choose the hyperparameters in different cases. Finally, our results show that pooling hyperparameter tuning is important and can result in significantly different attack performance even when not considering other layers or hyperparameters.

2 Preliminaries

2.1 Notation

We use calligraphic letters $\mathcal{X}$ to represent sets. The upper-case letters (X) represent random variables and random vectors $\mathbf{X}$ over $\mathcal{X}$. The realizations of X and $\mathbf{X}$ are represented by lower-case letters x and $\mathbf{x}$, respectively.

A dataset $\mathbf{T}$ constitutes a collection of side-channel traces (measurements) $\mathbf{t}_i$ associated with an input value (plaintext or ciphertext) $\mathbf{d}_i$ and a key candidate $\mathbf{k}_i$ ($k \in \mathcal{K}$ where k^* is the correct key). As common in deep learning-based SCA, we divide the dataset into three parts: a profiling set of N traces, a validation set of V traces, and an attack set of Q traces. In terms of a deep learning-based profiling model, we denote the vector of learnable parameters with $\boldsymbol{\theta}$ and the set of hyperparameters defining the profiling model f with $\mathcal{H}$.

2.2 Deep-Learning Based Profiling Side-Channel Analysis

The goal of supervised machine learning is to learn a function f mapping an input to the output ($f : \mathcal{X} \rightarrow Y$)). To accomplish this, the function f uses examples of input-output pairs. In supervised learning for profiling SCA, the input-output pairs are represented by leakage traces and the corresponding intermediate data. The profiling stage is equivalent to the training phase in supervised learning, while the attack phase is equivalent to testing in supervised learning. Formally, the profiling SCA is executed in the following stages:

- Profiling stage: learn $\boldsymbol{\theta}'$ that minimizes the empirical risk represented by a loss function L on a profiling set of size N.
- Attack stage: predict the classes $y(x_1, k^*), \ldots, y(x_Q, k^*)$, where k^* represents the secret (unknown) key on the device under the attack.

By applying attack traces to the profiling models, probabilistic deep learning algorithms output a matrix of probabilities P of size $Q \times c$ (where c denotes the number of output classes). Each probability value denotes how likely a certain measurement should be classified into a specific class v (thus, $\mathbf{p}_{i,v}$ represents the probability that the class v is predicted). The class v is obtained from the key and input through a cryptographic function and a leakage model l. Every row of the matrix P is a vector of all class probabilities for a specific trace $\mathbf{x}_i$ ($\sum_v^c \mathbf{p}_{i,v} = 1, \forall i$). The probability $S(k)$ for any key byte candidate k is the maximum log-likelihood distinguisher:

$$S(k) = \sum_{i=1}^{Q} \log(\mathbf{p}_{i,v}). \tag{1}$$

As common in SCA, an adversary aims to obtain the secret key k^* with the minimum attack effort. To evaluate this effort, it is common to use a metric like guessing entropy (GE) [23] that represents the average position of k^* in a key guessing vector $\mathbf{g} = [g_1, g_2, \ldots, g_{|\mathcal{K}|}]$. Here, g_1 represents the most likely key candidate, while $g_{|\mathcal{K}|}$ represents the least likely key candidate. Note that this represents a significant difference from the machine learning settings where one would commonly consider validation accuracy as a metric of success.

2.3 Convolutional Neural Networks

Convolutional neural networks (CNNs) are widely used neural networks in many domains, including SCA. They commonly consist of three types of layers:

- **Convolutional layer**: this layer computes neurons' output connected to local regions in the input, each computing a dot product between their weights and a small region they are connected to in the input volume.
- **Pooling layer**: this layer aims at decreasing the number of extracted features by performing a down-sampling operation along the spatial dimensions. It is common to consider convolution and pooling layers to form a convolution block. Two main types of pooling layers are considered in this paper: *average-pooling* and *max-pooling*. Average-pooling layers perform the average of a pooling block concerning the *pooling size* (i.e., the number of elements covered with a single pooling operation). Max-pooling layers return the maximum element from a block concerning pooling size. Figure 1 illustrates the different types of pooling operations over a feature map (output of a convolution layer). As we see in this example, the selection of the pooling type can be crucial for the model performance, as each type of pooling returns different results. *Pooling stride* refers to the pooling step over the feature map.
- **Fully-connected layer**: the dense layers are normally applied after convolution layers and pooling layers. The goal of this layer is to compute either the hidden activations or the class scores.

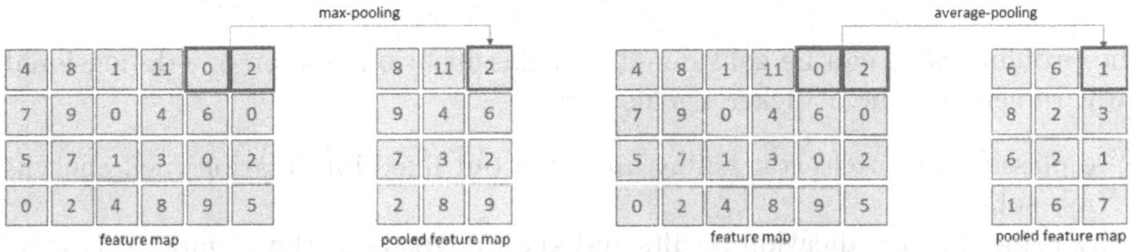

(a) Max-pooling operation with pooling size of 1x2 and pooling stride of 2.

(b) Average-pooling operation with pooling size of 1x2 and pooling stride of 2.

Fig. 1. A demonstration of max-pooling and average-pooling operations. The feature map is reduced from 4×6 to 4×3 after pooling.

2.4 Datasets

ChipWhisperer Dataset. The Chipwhisperer dataset is designed to evaluate various algorithms by providing a standard comparison base [15]. The dataset we consider contains 10 000 side-channel power traces measured by the ChipWhisperer CW308 target running an unprotected AES-128 implementation. Each trace contains 5 000 sample points (features). In our experiment, we use 7 500 traces for profiling and 2 000 traces for the validation. We use key byte two as the target secret data.

ASCAD Datasets. ASCAD datasets represent a common target for profiling SCA as they contain measurements protected with masking and settings with fixed or random keys [1]. The ASCAD dataset is the measurements from an 8-bit AVR microcontroller running a masked AES-128 implementation. Currently, there are two versions of this database: one that uses a fixed key for both profiling and attack dataset, and the other one with random keys in the profiling set. The datasets are available at https://github.com/ANSSI-FR/ASCAD.

The first dataset version has a fixed key, and it consists of 50 000 traces for profiling and 10 000 for the attack. From 50 000 traces in the profiling set, we use 45 000 traces for profiling and 5 000 for validation. Each trace has 700 features (preselected window corresponding to the processing of key byte 3, the first masked key byte). We denote this dataset as ASCAD_f.

The second version has random keys, with 200 000 traces for profiling and 100 000 for the attack. We use 45 000 traces for profiling and 5 000 traces from the attack set for validation (note that the attack set has a fixed but a different key from the profiling set). Each trace has 1 400 features (preselected window corresponding to the processing of key byte 3, the first masked key byte). We denote this dataset as ASCAD_r.

3 Related Works

The profiling SCA can be considered as a classification task on one-dimensional data. In general, the attacker's goals are:

- to classify the traces containing unknown but fixed information (i.e., encryption subkeys),
- by using the classification results and knowledge about the plaintexts/ciphertexts, retrieve the secret information.

From the information-theoretic point of view, template attack (TA) [4] represents the most powerful profiling SCA if the theoretical model and reality fully match. There, one uses the probability density function (PDF) as templates to perform the attack. In an ideal (but unrealistic) case where the attacker has an unlimited number of traces and the noise follows the Gaussian distribution, TA can reach its full attack capability [11].

In terms of machine learning-based profiling SCA, various approaches, such as random forest [10] and support vector machines [7] have been adopted first. More recently, multilayer perceptron (MLP) [6,18] and convolutional neural networks (CNN) [3,8,13] emerged as more powerful approaches.

Specifically, CNNs demonstrated to be capable of coping with various countermeasures due to their spatial invariance property [3,8]. Thus, they became one of the most powerful approaches for deep learning-based SCAs. However, a CNN optimized for one dataset is not necessarily applicable to other datasets, thus raising difficulties in implementing such attacks. To allow customization and optimization of CNN designs, Zaid et al. proposed a methodology to select hyperparameters related to the size of layers in CNNs [27]. This work is further improved by Wouters et al. [25] with the help of data standardization. In terms of neural architecture search, Bayesian optimization is adopted by Wu et al. to find optimal hyperparameters for MLP and CNNs [26]. Rijsdijk et al. used reinforcement learning to design CNNs that show strong attack performance with a small number of trainable parameters [22]. Several works consider tuning of specific CNN hyperparameters: Li et al. investigated the influence of weight initialization techniques [12] while Perin and Picek considered different optimizers [16].

4 Experimental Setup

In this section, we present our strategy to evaluate the performance of two types of commonly-used pooling layers: average-pooling and max-pooling. The analysis is conducted on three publicly available datasets described in Sect. 2.4. The default CNN models used to test the pooling layer are described in Table 1. Specifically, $CNN_{chipwhisperer}$ is used to attack the Chipwhisperer dataset. The ASCAD fixed key (ASCAD_f) and ASCAD random keys datasets (ASCAD_r) are profiled with CNN_{ascad} [1]. We consider only the HW leakage model as the conclusions drawn from the pooling layer with one leakage model can be easily extended to other leakage models. Also, considering the related work, the HW leakage model performs well for the considered datasets [22,26]. In terms of hyperparameters, we show the number of filters in the table for convolution layers. The convolution stride is set to 11 for both models following the network design from [1]. Pooling layers follow each convolution layer, and the pooling size and stride are set to two by default. For both models, *ReLU* is used as the activation function. The optimizer is *RMSProb* with a learning rate of 1e-5.

Table 1. CNN architectures used in the experiments.

Test models	Convolution layer	Pooling layer	Dense layer
$CNN_{chipwhisper}$	Conv(8)	avg(2, 2)	128 * 2
CNN_{ascad}	Conv(64, 128, 256, 512, 512)	avg(2, 2)*5	4 096 * 2

To evaluate the profiling attack performance, we consider three evaluation metrics:

- Guessing Entropy (*GE*): the averaged correct key rank after applying the maximum number of attack traces.
- T_{GE0}: the number of traces required to reach GE equal to zero.
- *ACC*: the classification accuracy on the validation traces.

GE aims at evaluating the key recovery capacity of trained neural networks by setting a limited number of attack traces. The second metric T_{GE0} is designed for cases that the models require few traces to retrieve the secret key. In this case, even if *GE* equals zero for different settings, we can better estimate the attack performance by evaluating the number of attack traces to reach it. For the *ACC* metric, although related works indicate a low correlation between validation accuracy and success of an attack [17], a higher validation accuracy could still mean a lower *GE* [21,26]. Therefore, the validation accuracy is also taken into consideration.

In the experimental results, we first investigate the influence of data standardization (by zeroing the mean and scaling to unit variance) on the attack performance for the ChipWhisperer dataset. Then, we perform extensive analysis towards the impact of two main configurable hyperparameters: pooling size and pooling stride, within a pooling layer with different evaluation metrics. Finally, we vary the pooling settings in different layers to understand the correlation between the pooling hyperparameter variation and layer depth.

5 Experimental Results

The experiments start with ChipWhisperer as this dataset is easily breakable even with a small CNN architecture. The required time to train a CNN model for this dataset is relatively low, and, therefore, we can tune the model's hyperparameter with smaller steps and a larger range. In terms of the evaluation aspects, with the $CNN_{chipwhisperer}$ specified in Table 1, we focus on tuning the pooling size and stride of the only available pooling layer. With such an analysis, we aim to understand the pooling hyperparameters' influence on the general performance of the model. Here, we experiment with both average-pooling and max-pooling methods by setting the range for pooling size and stride from 1 to 100 with a step of 1 and test all combinations (10 000 combinations in total). Besides, we investigate the link between the data standardization and the pooling layer's hyperparameters selection. As such, the experiments are performed with two versions of a dataset: original (no preprocessing) and standardized (forcing the amplitude ranges from −1 to 1).

CNN_{ascad} is used as the profiling model for standardized ASCAD_f and ASCAD_r. Compared with $CNN_{chipwhisperer}$, this model's complexity is increased to overcome the masking countermeasure. Note there are five pooling layers in the CNN_{ascad} model. When perturbing all pooling layers simultaneously, the variation range of the pooling layer is limited. Therefore, we only focus on varying the hyperparameters of the first and the last pooling layers. Due to the traces length differences, for ASCAD_f, we tune the pooling hyperparameters ranging from 1 to 20, while for ASCAD_r, we double this range (1 to 40). The step equals one for both datasets.

5.1 Case Study: The ChipWhisperer Dataset

The results for *GE* are shown in Fig. 2. Since *GE* remain zero for all pooling layer's hyperparameter combinations (pooling stride and pooling size) when attacking the standardized dataset, we only present the *GE* value for the original dataset. As mentioned, 2 000 traces are used for the validation. First, we can conclude that the data standardization increases the model's resilience towards the pooling layers' hyperparameter variation. As shown in Fig. 2, for both average- and max-pooling, the attack model is more sensitive to the pooling stride variation. Indeed, a larger pooling stride misses some critical features outputted by the previous convolution layer, finally causing degradation of the attack performance. However, we notice that there are several cases where a large pooling stride can achieve outstanding attack performance. Meanwhile, a large pooling stride can effectively reduce the number of outputted features, leading to a smaller model. This observation indicates the possibility of reducing the network size by using a large pooling stride and having a good understanding of the leakage measurements.

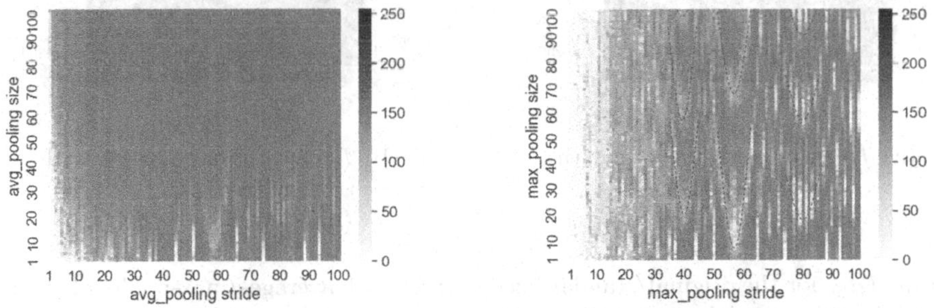

(a) *GE*: original dataset with average-pooling (min: 0; max: 150)

(b) *GE*: original dataset with max-pooling (min: 0; max: 151)

Fig. 2. *GE* for the original/standardized dataset with average-/max-pooling layer for the HW leakage model on ChipWhisperer.

Interestingly, when attacking the original dataset, the model equipped with the max-pooling layer performs better than the one with the average-pooling layer in general. Specifically, 97% of the average-pooling setting combinations lead to *GE* value larger than 50, while this value decreases to 85% when applying max-pooling. Additionally, when applying larger pooling size and pooling stride, max-pooling seems a better choice for a successful attack (*GE* converges or even decreases to zero). Simultaneously, we observe V-shaped patterns (e.g., at max-pooling stride: 57, 80) that occur periodically. The corresponding patterns are also marked by a red dashed line in Fig. 2b. A possible explanation could be that these (large) pooling hyperparameters accidentally cover the leakages appearing in specific locations. However, these critical features are most likely to be skipped, considering many unsuccessful setting combinations. This observation points out the importance of the leakage characterization: if an evaluator understands leakage positions (points of interest), he can confidently decrease the complexity of the attack model by increasing the stride of the pooling layer to a proper value. Similar conclusion is also drawn in [24].

Figure 3 provides results when evaluating the number of traces required to reach GE equal to zero (T_{GE0}). Since GE converges to zero with only a single trace with the standardized dataset, we only show the results attacking the original dataset in Fig. 3. Similar to the observation with the GE metric, the max-pooling layer seems more robust to the pooling size variation when the pooling stride is small.

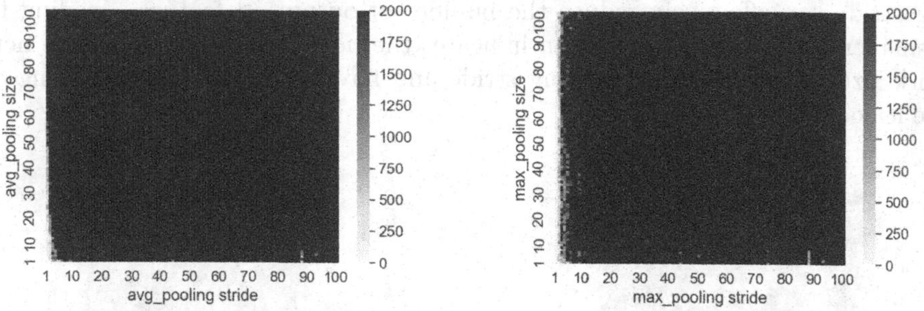

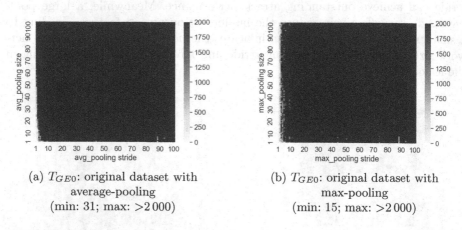

(a) T_{GE0}: original dataset with average-pooling (min: 31; max: >2 000)

(b) T_{GE0}: original dataset with max-pooling (min: 15; max: >2 000)

Fig. 3. T_{GE0} for the original/standardized dataset with average-/max-pooling layer for the HW leakage model on ChipWhisperer.

Finally, we analyze the attack performance with each hyperparameter combination with ACC. As shown in Fig. 4, aligned with the previous observation, attacks on the original dataset lead to low ACC, while for the standardized dataset, the accuracy is higher. When comparing the max-pooling and average-pooling layers, the former performs better, as it could lead to high ACC with more pooling setting combinations. Note that most of the ACC values in Figs. 4a and 4b are 0.263, which equals the number of traces labeled as the Hamming weight four (526) divided by the total number of validation traces (2 000). Thus, we conclude that the model is strongly influenced by the class imbalance problem [17] with the original dataset. Data standardization reduces the dominance of the feature in the biggest cluster and decrease the occurrence of overfitting.

Utilizing the observations for the Chipwhisperer dataset, we postulate that the dataset standardization increases the attack efficiency. Simultaneously, it dramatically increases the model's resilience towards the variation of the pooling layer's hyperparameters. Therefore, for the ASCAD datasets, we only attack the standardized versions of the datasets.

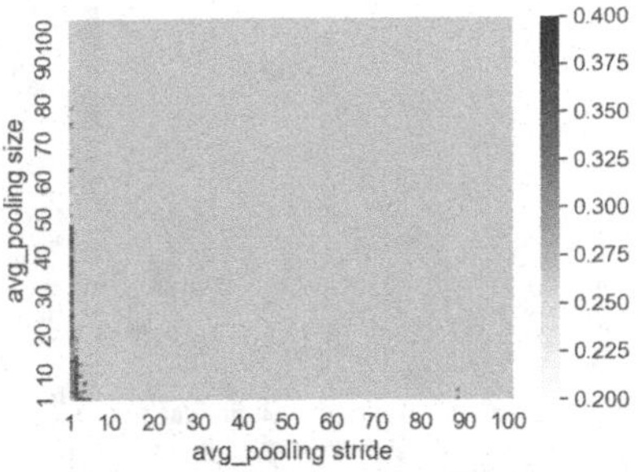

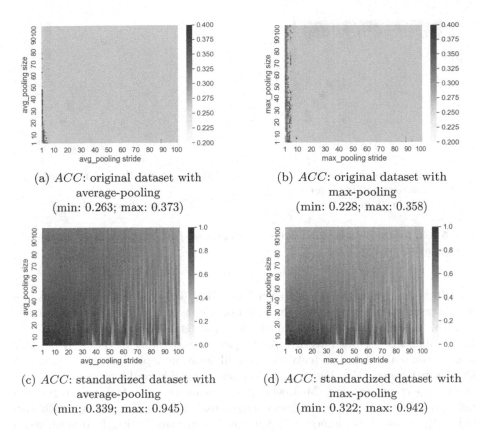

(a) ACC: original dataset with average-pooling (min: 0.263; max: 0.373)

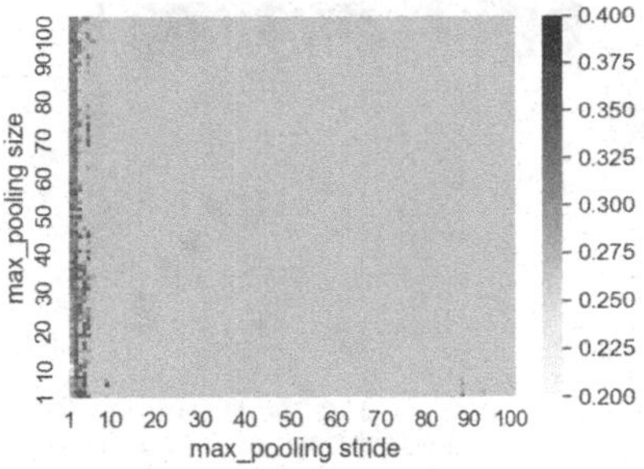

(b) ACC: original dataset with max-pooling (min: 0.228; max: 0.358)

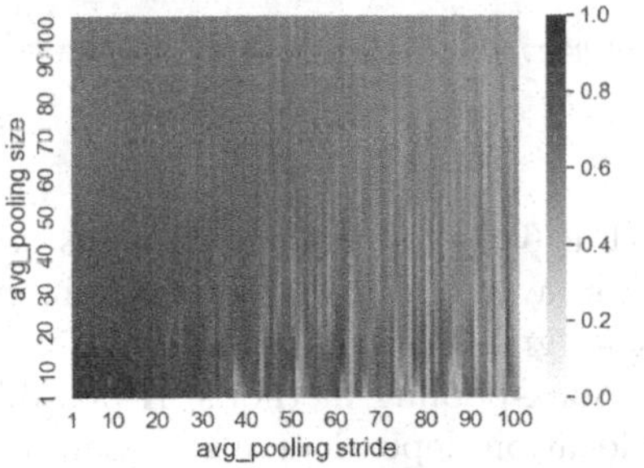

(c) ACC: standardized dataset with average-pooling (min: 0.339; max: 0.945)

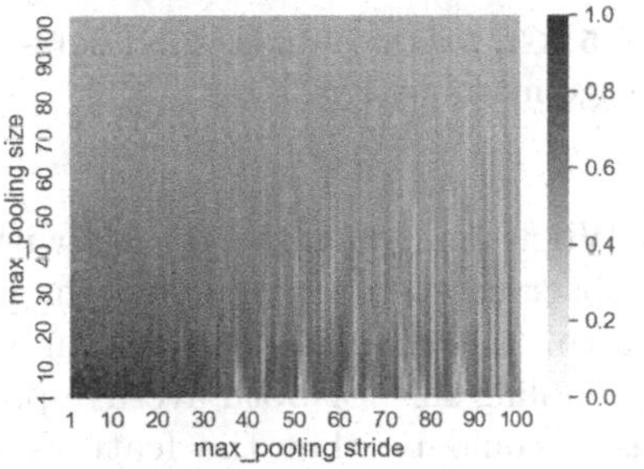

(d) ACC: standardized dataset with max-pooling (min: 0.322; max: 0.942)

Fig. 4. Accuracy for the original/standardized dataset with average-/max-pooling layer for the HW leakage model on ChipWhisperer.

5.2 ASCAD with a Fixed Key (ASCAD_f)

First, we evaluate the attack performance of each setting in combination with the GE metric. The results are shown in Fig. 5. Here, we omit the tuning results for the first pooling layer because of the constant GE value (zero) for all setting combinations. On the other hand, when tuning the last pooling layer, the average-pooling method provides inferior performance with a large pooling size. When going to a larger pooling stride, although not so obvious, the models applying both the average- and max-pooling layers method on the last layer have reduced attack performance. For the average-pooling method, a larger pooling size could lead to these critical features being 'averaged' by other less relevant features, thus degrading the attack performance. For the max-pooling method, the unique features can be picked up even with a larger pooling size. Interestingly, we see a 'slash line' on the right part of the figure for both pooling methods. One possible reason could be that with these pooling settings, the critical features are completely missed.

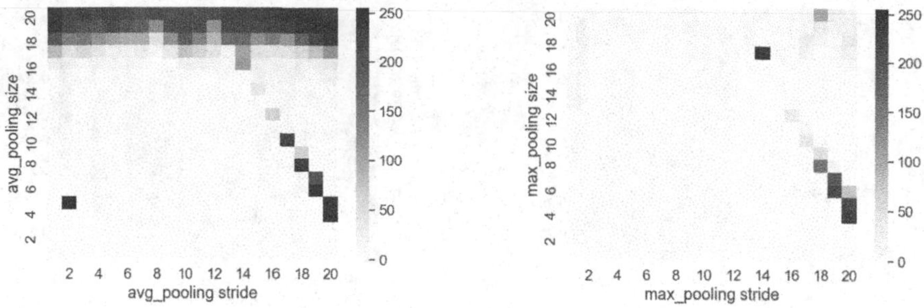

(a) GE: tuning the last average-pooling layer (min: 0; max: 248)

(b) GE: tuning the last max-pooling layer (min: 0; max: 248)

Fig. 5. GE for the standardized dataset with average-/max -pooling layer for the HW leakage model on ASCAD_f.

When analyzing the results with T_{GE0} (Fig. 6), some unique patterns can be observed even when tuning the first pooling layer. From Figs. 6a and 6b, we confirm that changing the pooling stride causes greater variation of T_{GE0} than the pooling size for both average-pooling and max-pooling methods. A possible reason could be that the features are still location-dependent after sampling by the first convolution layer. A smaller pooling stride could support capturing these important features. Meanwhile, comparing the results for average- and max-pooling, the latter method seems to enable more pooling settings with low-value T_{GE0}, which is aligned with the conclusion made in Fig. 5. Indeed, when counting the number of setting combinations that lead to T_{GE0} greater than 5 000, the values are 118 and 70 for the averaging-pooling and max-pooling method, respectively. Besides, when comparing Figs. 6a and 6c or Figs. 6b and 6d, the corresponding patterns seems to be rotated for 90 degrees. One explanation could be that the leakages in the deeper layers tend to distribute uniformly across the features. Thus, the selection of the pooling stride becomes less important than the pooling size.

Finally, we consider the ACC metric (Fig. 7). Interestingly, the ACC metric presents similar patterns as the other metrics but reversely. More specifically, the settings that reach better GE/T_{GE0} values are worse with ACC and vice versa. With this observation, we can conclude that overfitting is the cause of the degraded performance. Indeed, the HW leakage model forces the dataset to follow a binomial distribution. Thus, the overfitted model tends to output high probabilities for the middle classes (i.e., the HW class 4 and then HW classes 3 and 5) regardless of the input. On the other hand, the overfitting may also be triggered by the dataset property as the same key is used for both training and attack. Indeed, the model can easily "learn" the correct key instead of successfully exploiting leakages with this setting. Following this, although the model may have higher validation accuracy and lower loss, the model's classification

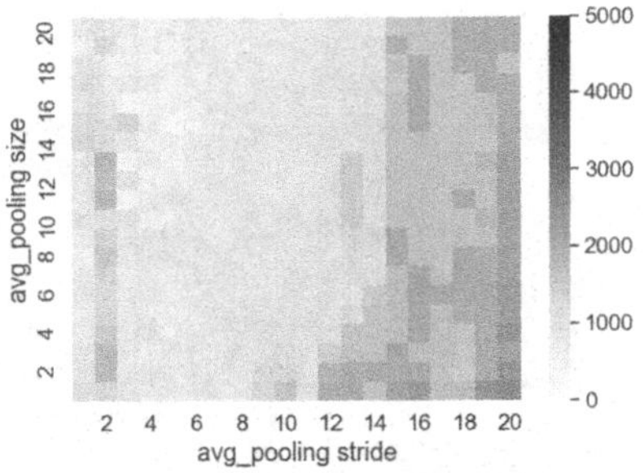

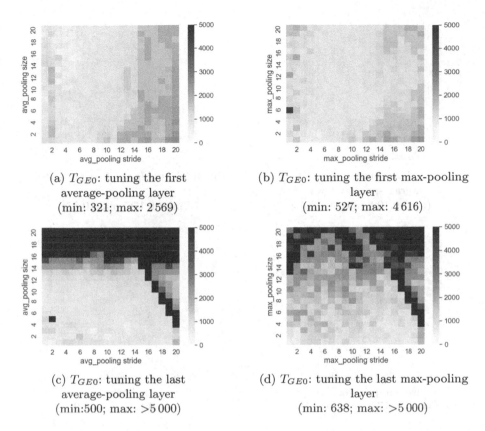

(a) T_{GE0}: tuning the first average-pooling layer (min: 321; max: 2 569)

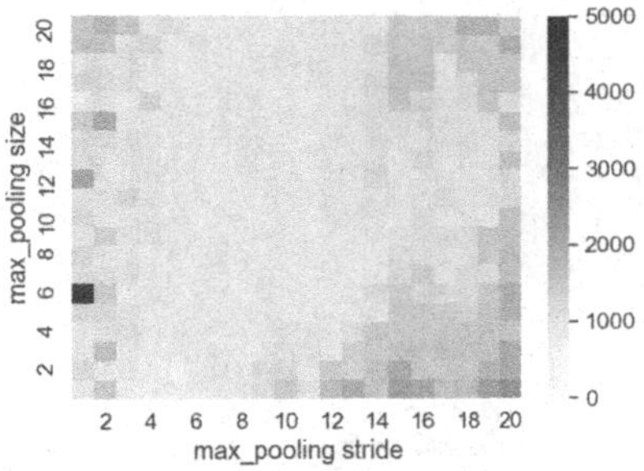

(b) T_{GE0}: tuning the first max-pooling layer (min: 527; max: 4 616)

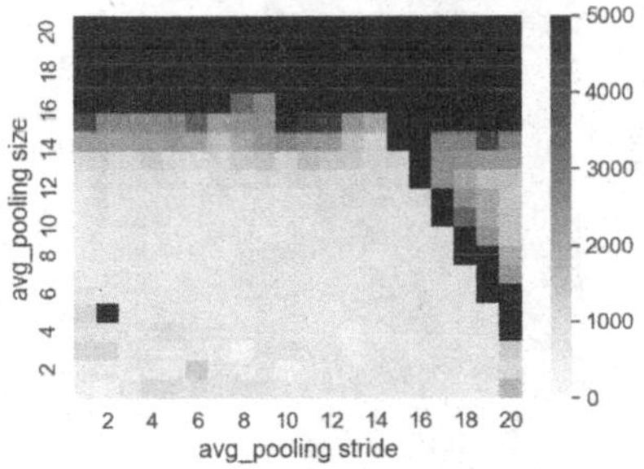

(c) T_{GE0}: tuning the last average-pooling layer (min:500; max: >5 000)

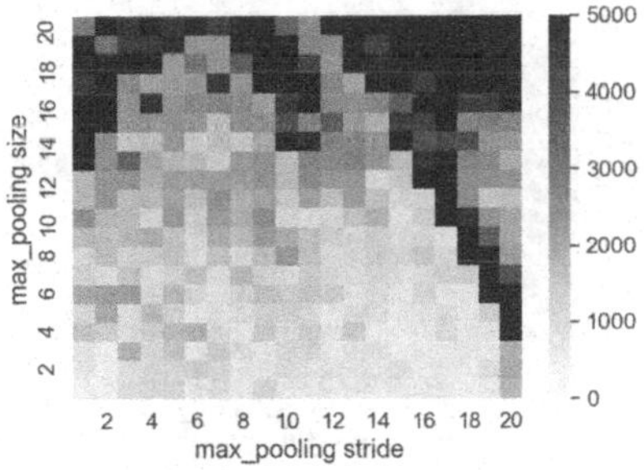

(d) T_{GE0}: tuning the last max-pooling layer (min: 638; max: >5 000)

Fig. 6. T_{GE0} for the standardized dataset with average-/max-pooling layer for the HW leakage model on ASCAD_f.

capability is degraded. Moreover, as can be seen from Figs. 7a, 7b, and 7c, overfitting is more easily triggered with larger pooling settings, which is equivalent to smaller network sizes. For the max-pooling in the last layer (Fig. 7d), a more uniform distribution of the *ACC* value can be seen, indicating its potential of reducing the network size while keeping good attack performance.

5.3 ASCAD with Random Keys (ASCAD_r)

Compared with the ASCAD_f dataset, the length of a trace in the ASCAD_r dataset is doubled (1 400 features). Since the same CNN model (CNN_{ASCAD}) is used as the profiling model, the number of features available at the output of the last convolution layer (input of the last pooling layer) is also doubled, providing additional range to tune the hyperparameter of the pooling layer. Aligned with the experiments for the ASCAD_f dataset, we tune both average- and max-pooling layer and analyze the results with different metrics.

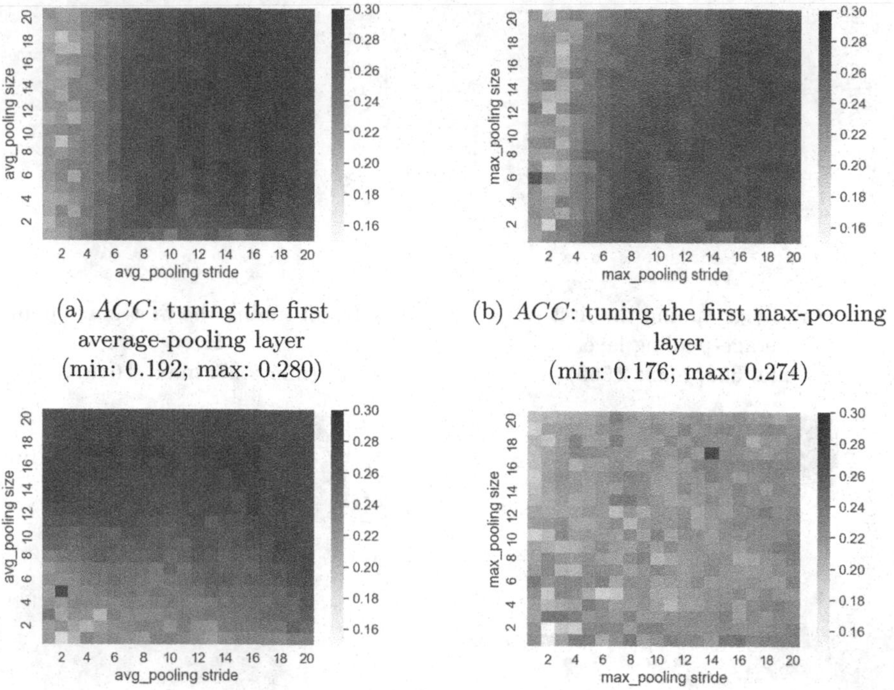

(a) *ACC*: tuning the first average-pooling layer (min: 0.192; max: 0.280)

(b) *ACC*: tuning the first max-pooling layer (min: 0.176; max: 0.274)

(c) *ACC*: tuning the last average-pooling layer (min: 0.177; max: 0.277)

(d) *ACC*: tuning the last max-pooling layer (min: 0.149; max: 0.270)

Fig. 7. *ACC* for the standardized dataset with average-/max-pooling layer for the HW leakage model on ASCAD_f.

First, we apply the *GE* metric and give results in Fig. 8. Interestingly, we again confirm the conclusion made for the ASCAD_f dataset: for the pooling layer in the shallower layers, pooling stride is essential in extracting and down-sampling the features, while the pooling size should be more carefully tuned in the deeper layers. Meanwhile, average-pooling performs better than max-pooling for most of the setting combinations. This tendency becomes more significant when investigating the first layer: for the max-pooling layer, 29% of the pooling setting combinations lead to *GE* value below 50 with 5 000 attack traces. When using the average-pooling layer, this value increases to 72%. Recall the observations for the ChipWhisperer dataset: an average-pooling layer is more suitable for the standardized dataset, while the max-pooling layer works better for the original (non-standardized dataset). Here, we reach the same conclusion from the results when attacking the ASCAD_r dataset.

Compared with the conclusions for ASCAD_f, it seems that more input features lead to a better performance of the average-pooling layer than max-pooling.

However, considering the different characteristics of the data, no definitive conclusions can be drawn.

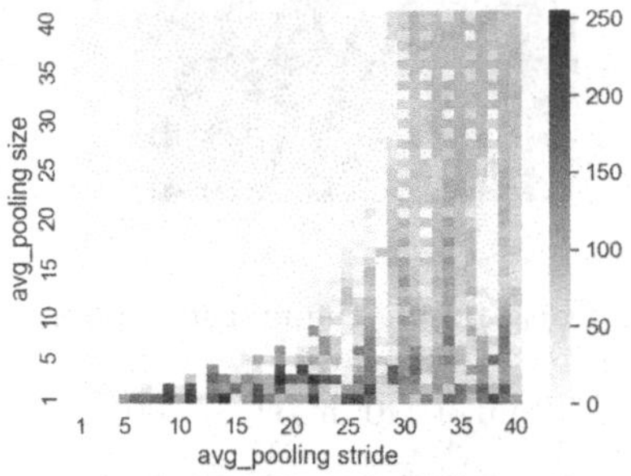

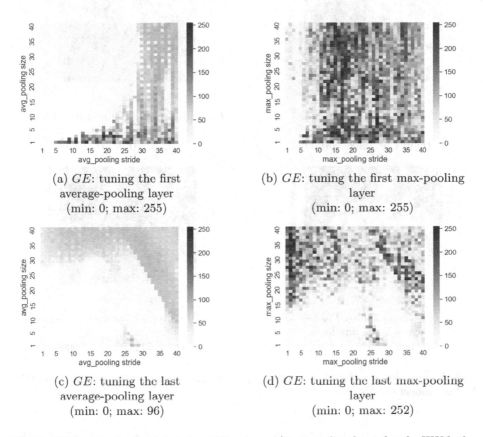

(a) GE: tuning the first average-pooling layer (min: 0; max: 255)

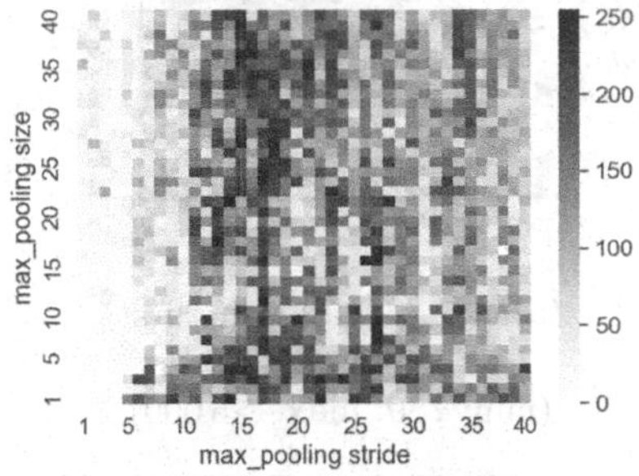

(b) GE: tuning the first max-pooling layer (min: 0; max: 255)

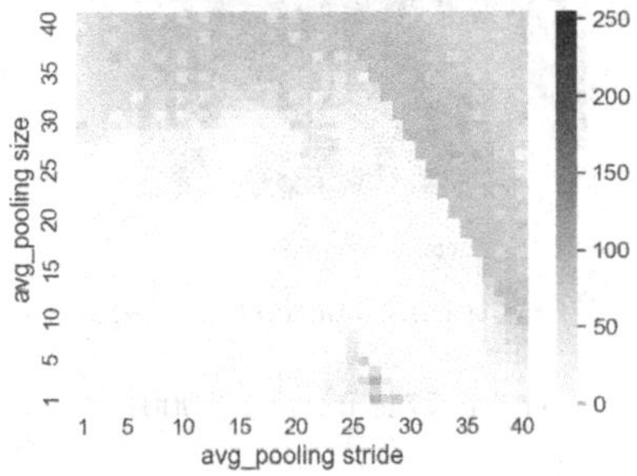

(c) GE: tuning the last average-pooling layer (min: 0; max: 96)

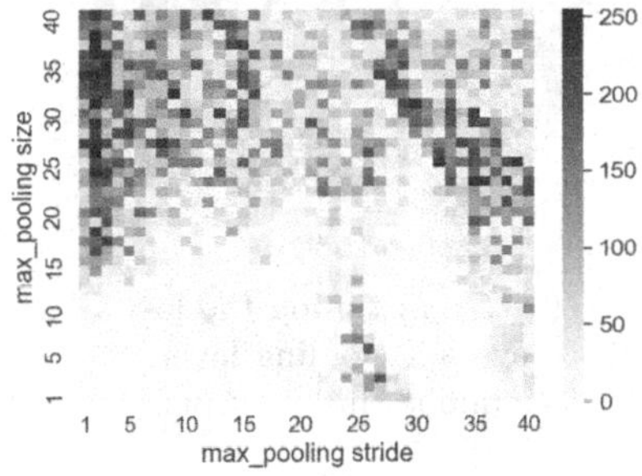

(d) GE: tuning the last max-pooling layer (min: 0; max: 252)

Fig. 8. GE for standardized dataset with average-/max-pooling layer for the HW leakage model on ASCAD_r.

The performance deviations of average- and max-pooling become more pronounced when considering T_{GE0} as depicted in Fig. 9. Specifically, from Fig. 9b, only 66 setting combinations (out of 1 600) required less than 2 000 attack traces to retrieve the correct key. When using the average-pooling as the first pooling layer, this value increases to 997. For the last pooling layer, the differences between the two pooling methods are reduced. Still, average-pooling has more tolerance (889 good settings) to the hyperparameter variation than max-pooling (414 good settings).

Finally, we analyze the attack results with the ACC metric (Fig. 10), which are similar to the one for ASCAD_f (see Fig. 10c). The model starts overfitting with a larger pooling stride and pooling size. Interestingly, this observation is more distinguishable for the average-pooling method. For the max-pooling layer

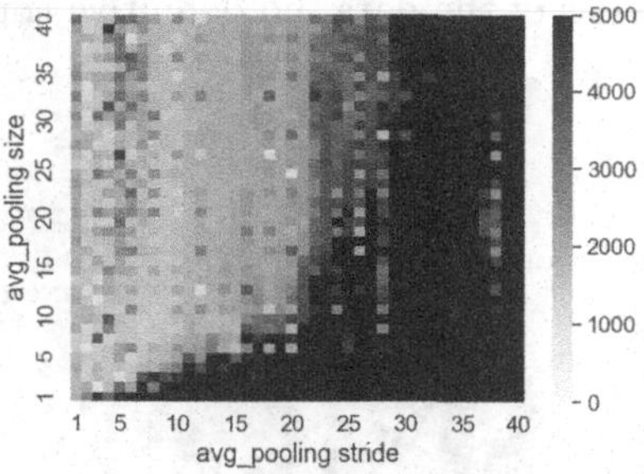

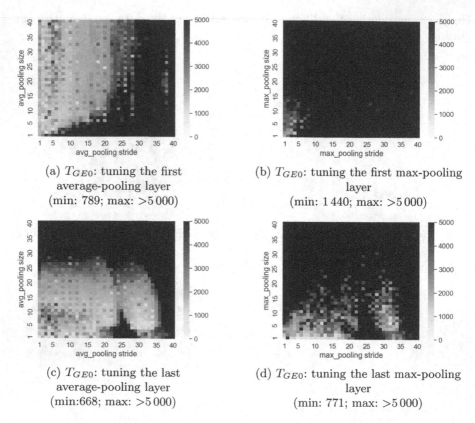

(a) T_{GE0}: tuning the first average-pooling layer (min: 789; max: >5 000)

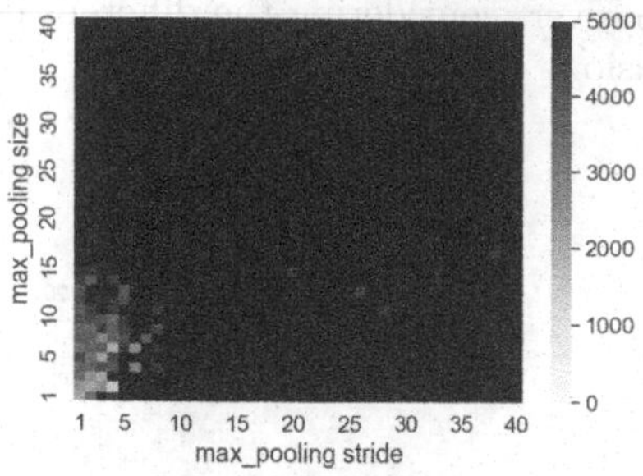

(b) T_{GE0}: tuning the first max-pooling layer (min: 1 440; max: >5 000)

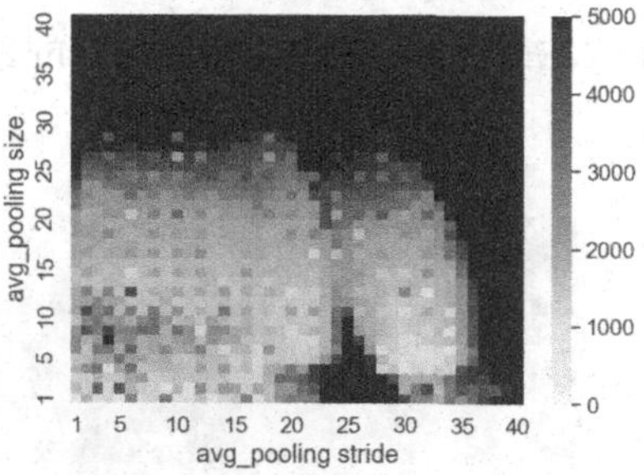

(c) T_{GE0}: tuning the last average-pooling layer (min:668; max: >5 000)

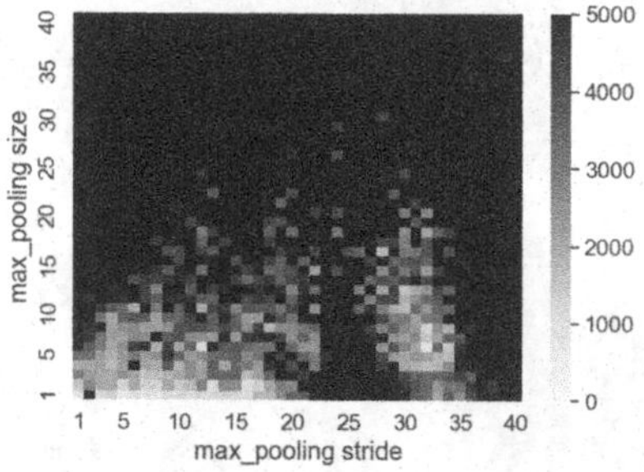

(d) T_{GE0}: tuning the last max-pooling layer (min: 771; max: >5 000)

Fig. 9. T_{GE0} for standardized dataset with average-/max-pooling layer for the HW leakage model on ASCAD_r.

(Figs. 10b and 10d), the *ACC* values distribute more uniformly, indicating the possibility of the trained model to be underfitting. Together with the observations from ASCAD_f with *ACC* metric: a model equipped with max-pooling layers may require more training effort, and additional training epochs may help enhance the attack performance.

5.4 General Observations and Suggestions

Based on experiments from previous sections, testing on three different datasets, we provide the following observations:

- Data standardization can be an effective tool to avoid the overfitting and improve the attack performance.
- When the input data has limited features, a pooling layer in the shallow part of the network is more sensitive to pooling stride variation. While in the deeper layer, the influence of pooling size becomes more significant.

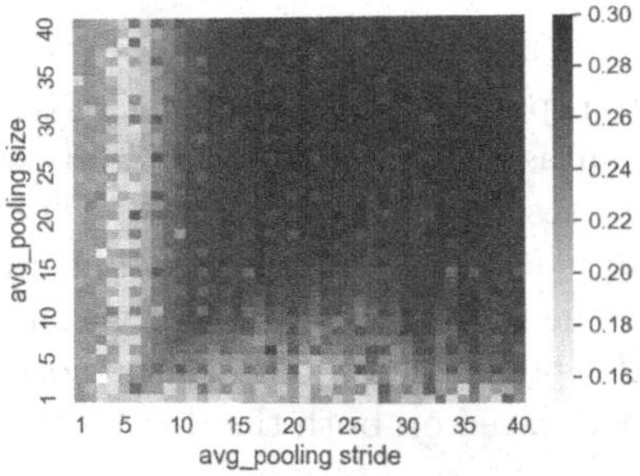

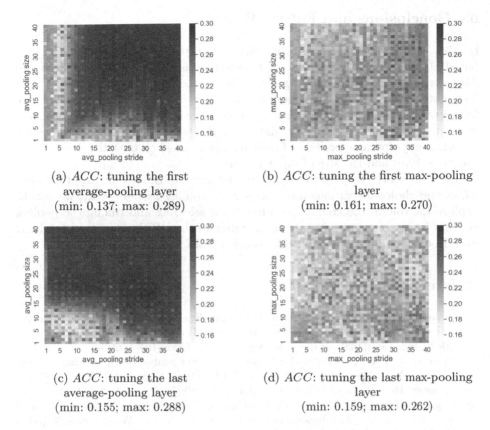

(a) *ACC*: tuning the first average-pooling layer (min: 0.137; max: 0.289)

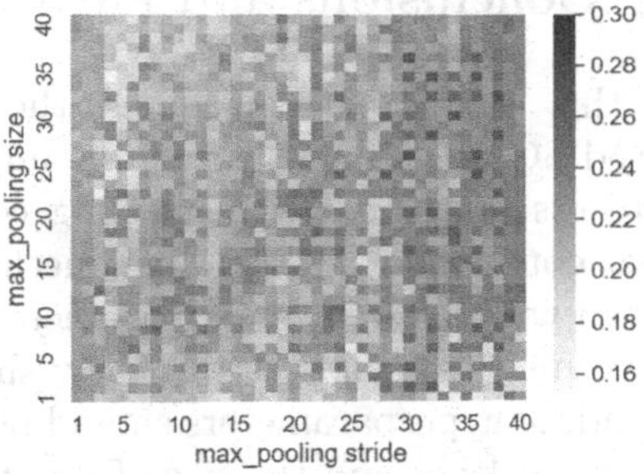

(b) *ACC*: tuning the first max-pooling layer (min: 0.161; max: 0.270)

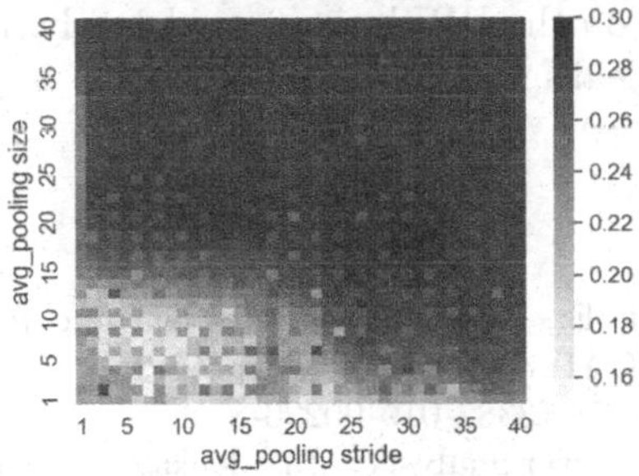

(c) *ACC*: tuning the last average-pooling layer (min: 0.155; max: 0.288)

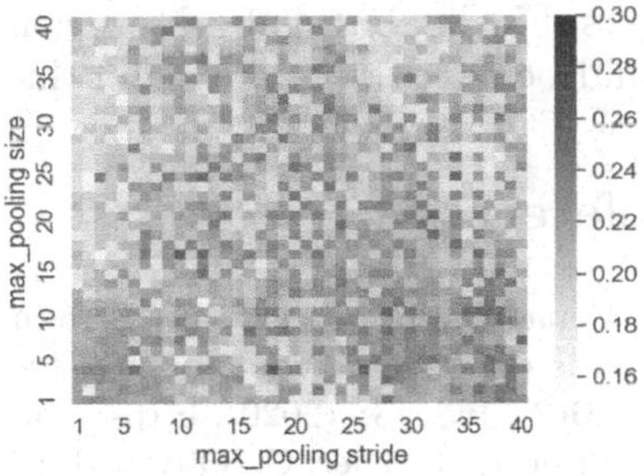

(d) *ACC*: tuning the last max-pooling layer (min: 0.159; max: 0.262)

Fig. 10. *ACC* for standardized dataset with average-/max-pooling layer for the HW leakage model on ASCAD_r.

Following these observations, we give the following suggestions regarding the pooling layer's hyperparameter selection:

- Applying data standardization can significantly increase the robustness of the model in terms of pooling layer's hyperparameter variation.
- Although in some cases the max-pooling layer slightly outperforms its counterpart, an average-pooling layer is more preferable as it can consistently give good attack performance.
- For the shallower pooling layers, smaller pooling strides are required to avoid omitting the important features. At the same time, the smaller pooling sizes are preferable for intermediate/deeper pooling layers.
- For the network size reduction, larger pooling sizes could be applied for the shallower pooling layers. The deeper pooling layers could be used with larger pooling strides.

6 Conclusions and Future Work

In this paper, we considered the effect of a pooling layer towards CNN-based SCA. We investigated one unprotected dataset (ChipWhisperer) and two datasets protected with masking countermeasures (ASCAD_f and ASCAD_r). Two commonly used pooling methods, average-pooling, and max-pooling are tested with different hyperparameter settings. The results are evaluated through three metrics. Our results clearly show that the pooling method and the corresponding hyperparameters should be determined based on both the depth of the (pooling) layer and the size of input features.

In future work, we plan to explore the influence of the pooling layer's hyperparameter choice for various input sizes and profiling models. Next, we aim to explore the role of the countermeasures when selecting and tuning the pooling layers. Finally, in this work, we concentrated on the HW leakage model only. It would be interesting to expand this to other leakage models.

References

1. Benadjila, R., Prouff, E., Strullu, R., Cagli, E., Dumas, C.: Deep learning for side-channel analysis and introduction to ASCAD database. J. Cryptograph. Eng. **10**(2), 163–188 (2020). https://doi.org/10.1007/s13389-019-00220-8
2. Brier, E., Clavier, C., Olivier, F.: Correlation power analysis with a leakage model. In: Joye, M., Quisquater, J.-J. (eds.) CHES 2004. LNCS, vol. 3156, pp. 16–29. Springer, Heidelberg (2004). https://doi.org/10.1007/978-3-540-28632-5_2
3. Cagli, E., Dumas, C., Prouff, E.: Convolutional neural networks with data augmentation against jitter-based countermeasures. In: Fischer, W., Homma, N. (eds.) CHES 2017. LNCS, vol. 10529, pp. 45–68. Springer, Cham (2017). https://doi.org/10.1007/978-3-319-66787-4_3
4. Chari, S., Rao, J.R., Rohatgi, P.: Template attacks. In: Kaliski, B.S., Koç, K., Paar, C. (eds.) CHES 2002. LNCS, vol. 2523, pp. 13–28. Springer, Heidelberg (2003). https://doi.org/10.1007/3-540-36400-5_3
5. Gierlichs, B., Batina, L., Tuyls, P., Preneel, B.: Mutual information analysis. In: Oswald, E., Rohatgi, P. (eds.) CHES 2008. LNCS, vol. 5154, pp. 426–442. Springer, Heidelberg (2008). https://doi.org/10.1007/978-3-540-85053-3_27
6. Gilmore, R., Hanley, N., O'Neill, M.: Neural network based attack on a masked implementation of AES. In: 2015 IEEE International Symposium on Hardware Oriented Security and Trust (HOST), pp. 106–111. IEEE (2015)
7. Heuser, A., Zohner, M.: Intelligent machine homicide. In: Schindler, W., Huss, S.A. (eds.) COSADE 2012. LNCS, vol. 7275, pp. 249–264. Springer, Heidelberg (2012). https://doi.org/10.1007/978-3-642-29912-4_18
8. Kim, J., Picek, S., Heuser, A., Bhasin, S., Hanjalic, A.: Make some noise. unleashing the power of convolutional neural networks for profiled side-channel analysis. IACR Trans. Cryptograph. Hardware Embedded Syst., 148–179 (2019)
9. Kocher, P., Jaffe, J., Jun, B.: Differential power analysis. In: Wiener, M. (ed.) CRYPTO 1999. LNCS, vol. 1666, pp. 388–397. Springer, Heidelberg (1999). https://doi.org/10.1007/3-540-48405-1_25

10. Lerman, L., Medeiros, S.F., Bontempi, G., Markowitch, O.: A machine learning approach against a masked AES. In: Francillon, A., Rohatgi, P. (eds.) CARDIS 2013. LNCS, vol. 8419, pp. 61–75. Springer, Cham (2014). https://doi.org/10.1007/978-3-319-08302-5_5
11. Lerman, L., Poussier, R., Bontempi, G., Markowitch, O., Standaert, F.-X.: Template attacks vs. machine learning revisited (and the curse of dimensionality in side-channel analysis). In: Mangard, S., Poschmann, A.Y. (eds.) COSADE 2014. LNCS, vol. 9064, pp. 20–33. Springer, Cham (2015). https://doi.org/10.1007/978-3-319-21476-4_2
12. Li, H., Krček, M., Perin, G.: A comparison of weight initializers in deep learning-based side-channel analysis. In: Zhou, J., et al. (eds.) ACNS 2020. LNCS, vol. 12418, pp. 126–143. Springer, Cham (2020). https://doi.org/10.1007/978-3-030-61638-0_8
13. Maghrebi, H., Portigliatti, T., Prouff, E.: Breaking cryptographic implementations using deep learning techniques. In: Carlet, C., Hasan, M.A., Saraswat, V. (eds.) SPACE 2016. LNCS, vol. 10076, pp. 3–26. Springer, Cham (2016). https://doi.org/10.1007/978-3-319-49445-6_1
14. Mangard, S., Oswald, E., Popp, T.: Power Analysis Attacks. Springer, Boston (2007). https://doi.org/10.1007/978-0-387-38162-6
15. O'Flynn, C., Chen, Z.D.: ChipWhisperer: an open-source platform for hardware embedded security research. In: Prouff, E. (ed.) COSADE 2014. LNCS, vol. 8622, pp. 243–260. Springer, Cham (2014). https://doi.org/10.1007/978-3-319-10175-0_17
16. Perin, G., Picek, S.: On the influence of optimizers in deep learning-based side-channel analysis. IACR Cryptology ePrint Archive 2020, 977 (2020). https://eprint.iacr.org/2020/977
17. Picek, S., Heuser, A., Jovic, A., Bhasin, S., Regazzoni, F.: The curse of class imbalance and conflicting metrics with machine learning for side-channel evaluations. IACR Trans. Cryptograph. Hardware Embedded Syst. **2019**(1), 209–237 (2018). https://doi.org/10.13154/tches.v2019.i1.209-237. https://tches.iacr.org/index.php/TCHES/article/view/7339
18. Picek, S., Heuser, A., Jovic, A., Bhasin, S., Regazzoni, F.: The curse of class imbalance and conflicting metrics with machine learning for side-channel evaluations. IACR Trans. Cryptograph. Hardware Embedded Syst. **2019**(1), 1–29 (2019)
19. Picek, S., Samiotis, I.P., Kim, J., Heuser, A., Bhasin, S., Legay, A.: On the performance of convolutional neural networks for side-channel analysis. In: Chattopadhyay, A., Rebeiro, C., Yarom, Y. (eds.) SPACE 2018. LNCS, vol. 11348, pp. 157–176. Springer, Cham (2018). https://doi.org/10.1007/978-3-030-05072-6_10
20. Quisquater, J.-J., Samyde, D.: ElectroMagnetic analysis (EMA): measures and counter-measures for smart cards. In: Attali, I., Jensen, T. (eds.) E-smart 2001. LNCS, vol. 2140, pp. 200–210. Springer, Heidelberg (2001). https://doi.org/10.1007/3-540-45418-7_17
21. Rijsdijk, J., Wu, L., Perin, G., Picek, S.: Reinforcement learning for hyperparameter tuning in deep learning-based side-channel analysis. Technical report, Cryptology ePrint Archive, Report 2021/071 (2021). https://eprint.iacr.org
22. Rijsdijk, J., Wu, L., Perin, G., Picek, S.: Reinforcement learning for hyperparameter tuning in deep learning-based side-channel analysis. Cryptology ePrint Archive, Report 2021/071 (2021). https://eprint.iacr.org/2021/071

23. Standaert, F.-X., Malkin, T.G., Yung, M.: A unified framework for the analysis of side-channel key recovery attacks. In: Joux, A. (ed.) EUROCRYPT 2009. LNCS, vol. 5479, pp. 443–461. Springer, Heidelberg (2009). https://doi.org/10.1007/978-3-642-01001-9_26
24. Tran, N.Q., Nguyen, H.Q.: Efficient CNN-based profiled side channel attacks. J. Comput. Sci. Cybern. **37**(1), 1–22 (2021)
25. Wouters, L., Arribas, V., Gierlichs, B., Preneel, B.: Revisiting a methodology for efficient CNN architectures in profiling attacks. IACR Trans. Cryptograph. Hardware Embedded Syst. **2020**(3), 147–168 (2020). https://doi.org/10.13154/tches.v2020.i3.147-168. https://tches.iacr.org/index.php/TCHES/article/view/8586
26. Wu, L., Perin, G., Picek, S.: I choose you: Automated hyperparameter tuning for deep learning-based side-channel analysis. Cryptology ePrint Archive, Report 2020/1293 (2020). https://eprint.iacr.org/2020/1293
27. Zaid, G., Bossuet, L., Habrard, A., Venelli, A.: Methodology for efficient CNN architectures in profiling attacks. IACR Trans. Cryptograph. Hardware Embedded Syst. **2020**(1), 1–36 (2019). https://doi.org/10.13154/tches.v2020.i1.1-36. https://tches.iacr.org/index.php/TCHES/article/view/8391

Towards Real-Time Deep Learning-Based Network Intrusion Detection on FPGA

Laurens Le Jeune[1,2(✉)], Toon Goedemé[2], and Nele Mentens[1,3]

[1] ES&S - imec-COSIC, ESAT, KU Leuven, Leuven, Belgium
{laurens.lejeune,nele.mentens}@kuleuven.be
[2] EAVISE - PSI, ESAT, KU Leuven, Leuven, Belgium
toon.goedeme@kuleuven.be
[3] LIACS, Leiden University, Leiden, The Netherlands

Abstract. Traditionally, network intrusion detection systems identify attacks based on signatures, rules, events or anomaly detection. More and more research investigates the application of deep learning techniques for this purpose. Deep learning significantly increases detection performance, and can abolish the need for expert knowledge-intensive feature extraction. The use of deep learning for network intrusion detection also has a major disadvantage, however, as it is not deployed yet in real-time implementations. In this paper, we propose two approaches that facilitate the transition towards functional real-time implementations: (1) the use of flow buckets to collect raw traffic-based features, and (2) the acceleration of neural network architectures for intrusion detection using the Xilinx FINN toolchain for FPGAs. We obtain promising results that show our flow bucket approach does not deteriorate detection performance when compared to traditional approaches, and we lay a foundation to further build on with respect to accelerating deep learning algorithms for network intrusion detection on FPGA.

Keywords: Network intrusion detection · Deep Learning · FPGA

1 Introduction

Ever since the introduction of AlexNet [13] in 2012, deep learning has gained increasing attention as its results significantly exceed those of traditional approaches. Besides applications in image processing and natural language processing, a wide range of other domains have since started employing deep learning as well. Also Network Intrusion Detection Systems (NIDSs), which up until that point were based on signatures or rules [22,23,25] as well as anomaly detection and other traditional machine learning techniques [10,28,32], have begun considering deep learning as a reliable approach for intrusion detection [2,33]. NIDSs aim at detecting intrusions in a network environment by inspecting incoming network traffic and either recognizing known attacks or observing deviations from what is considered to be normal traffic. And while (deep) learning-based

J. Zhou et al. (Eds.): ACNS 2021 Workshops, LNCS 12809, pp. 133–150, 2021.
https://doi.org/10.1007/978-3-030-81645-2_9

NIDSs have certainly improved over time, there still remain challenges. One major challenge is to be able to execute these new deep learning-based detection algorithms in real-time in network environments with ever increasing bandwidths. Most NIDSs in literature are currently CPU- or GPU-based and do therefore not have the capabilities of handling large network streams at a high throughput. Moreover, the features in publicly available datasets are typically pre-calculated offline, and it is not trivial to extract them online in real-time. In this paper, we examine these challenges, and aim to develop a deep learning-based NIDS with real-time throughput and feature extraction as well as high detection performance. Our contributions are the following:

- We propose an approach using *flow buckets* for real-time extraction of raw traffic-based features (Sect. 3);
- We examine the flow distribution of the CICIDS2017 and UNSW-NB15 datasets when using that approach (Sect. 5);
- We propose a method to relate model and network throughput for those flow bucket features (Sect. 4);
- We evaluate the performance of the resulting features in a deep learning model and compare to a baseline (Sect. 5);
- We train various quantized deep learning models to examine the effects on accuracy, and then deploy such a quantized model on a PYNQ-Z2 FPGA board using FINN [30] to examine the throughput (Sect. 5);

Before explaining these contributions, Sect. 2 gives an overview of related work.

2 Related Work

While the hardware acceleration of machine learning and deep learning algorithms is certainly increasingly relevant, the reported designs for network intrusion detection systems remain limited in number. This section considers work that has been done regarding the acceleration of machine learning algorithms on FPGAs, and provides insights regarding their performance and model sizes.

Das et al. [8] propose both a Feature Extraction Module (FEM) and a Principal Component Analysis (PCA) based anomaly detector. The FEM is able to collect connection-based as well as time-based features using feature sketches, with a reported throughput of 21.25 Gbps. Likewise, while the PCA achieves 99% attack detection with a 1.95% false alarm rate for the KDDCup1999 dataset, it also supports a 23.76 Gbps data throughput.

Ngo et al. [20] devise both a decision tree as well as a neural network trained on 6 features from the NSL-KDD dataset. The neural network consists of an input layer with the 6 input values, 2 hidden layers with 2 neurons and finally an output layer with 1 neuron. Both classifiers are implemented on a Xilinx Virtex-5 xc5vtx240t FPGA for a 100 MHz clock. They report a maximum throughput of 9.86 Gbps for both classifiers, but only for packets that contain 1500 bytes. The decision tree throughput drops to 7.42 Gbps for 64-byte packets, with the neural network only retaining 1.78 Gbps. While dropping some accuracy percentiles when compared to the same models on GPU, these hardware implementations feature a speedup of

11.6×. Expanding on this work in [19], the same authors provide a neural network with one hidden layer and 0–10 neurons in that layer as a building block for software defined network security. For this application, they report a maximum throughput of 5.12 Gbps if the hidden layer in the neural network is removed.

Ioannou et al. [11] train a three layer fully connected neural network with one hidden layer with 21 hidden neurons on the NSL-KDD dataset and accelerate it using a Xilinx Zynq Z-7020 FPGA. The authors indicate that the architecture supports over 10 Gbps, while they report an accuracy of 80.52%.

Murovič et al. [18] use a binarized neural network with 1 layer of 100 neurons to detect intrusions of the UNSW-NB15 dataset. They report an accuracy of 90.74%, with a latency of 19.62 ns.

Umuroglu et al. [29] propose *LogicNets* to map a quantized neural network to hardware building blocks that can be very efficiently accelerated on hardware. By representing neurons in a network as truth tables with a specific number of input and output bits, they are able to create scalable designs that allow for very high clock frequencies while maintaining a good performance. They report a supported clock frequency of 471 MHz with an accuracy of 91.30% for an architecture trained on the UNSW-NB15 dataset with 5 layers and $593 + 256 + 128 + 128$ neurons.

Maciel et al. [5] implement a reconfigurable architecture for K-means and K-modes intrusion detection on FPGA. They investigate the number of clock cycles and energy consumption for 5 iterations of the algorithm, when using a specific number of centroids and points. When compared to an Intel Xeon E5-2060, they require 91% fewer clock cycles and consume 99% less energy.

Even though these works are significant steps in the right direction, there is still a lot of room for improvement. While the proposed models vary in size, they are still quite small overall. As the 5-layer model of [29] appears to be the largest, real deep learning architectures are not available just yet. Furthermore, while the machine learning models are trained on (a subset of) pre-calculated features, the extraction of those features remains limited. Feature extraction modules serve to extract features to some extent, but do not support all features that are available in publicly available datasets. Finally, reporting the detection performance often remains limited to reporting an accuracy value, while previous work indicates this is not a good representation due to prevalent class imbalance [14]. This paper investigates both the application of deep learning for network intrusion detection, as well as the real-time extraction of generic features that are dataset independent.

3 Feature Extraction

Before any machine learning can be done, it is important to decide on what features to use. These features should represent all information that is required to allow the machine learning algorithm to make reliable predictions. Their representation can also determine what operations are required in the machine learning algorithm: Multidimensional matrices may require convolutions, while sequences might rely on recurrent structures. In this section, we will first discuss how and what features are traditionally used for network intrusion detection, after which we will discuss an alternative: raw traffic based features.

3.1 Traditional Features

Traditionally, network intrusion detection features are dataset dependent: They have been extracted during the inception or the analysis of a particular dataset. Some features can recur among multiple datasets, while others only concern one dataset. For example, both UNSW-NB15 [17] and CICIDS2017 [24] contain the source and destination IP (Internet Protocol) addresses, the TCP (Transmission Control Protocol)/UDP (User Datagram Protocol) ports and the traffic protocol. However, only UNSW-NB15 considers source and destination jitter, while CICIDS2017 includes the 8 TCP flags, among other things.

Typically, features represented in such a manner are numeric and/or symbolic and require some preprocessing before usage. The 41 features of KDDCup1999 [1] and NSL-KDD [26] contain 38 numeric values and 3 symbolic features, which are often represented with a vector containing 122 values[1] [4,7,9,16]. Of course, these features can also be used in other ways, for example by encoding them to pixel values [12] or reducing them in auto-encoders [3].

Although popular, these traditional features do not lend themselves easily for hardware acceleration for two reasons:

1. Extracting traditional features in real-time on hardware is not trivial, as many features require high-level interpretation and/or rely on network flow statistics. High-level features require additional design complexity and resource usage to be functional: Counting the number of HTTPS methods in UNSW-NB15 dataset for the *ct_flw_http_mthd* feature requires parsing incoming traffic to identify HTTPS traffic. Computing the standard deviation of the packet length in a network flow in CICIDS2017 requires keeping track of a flow until it is considered to be finished. This ties up resources and can result in significant detection delays for large flows. Feature extraction modules on FPGA, such as in [8] or [27], do not keep track of all features provided in different datasets, but rather concern smaller feature sets.
2. A machine learning model that is trained on one dataset cannot simply be used for a different dataset: Different (numbers of) features in a potentially different context require a new model for almost every dataset. This is not practical when designing models for real applications as opposed to synthetic datasets, as a model should be retrainable for use in various contexts.

Moreover, an additional argument against these traditional pre-calculated features, from a machine learning point of view, is that there is no guarantee that the provided features suffice to reliably model the circumstances, and that they do not contain unnecessary redundancy. In this paper we therefore investigate an alternative to traditional network intrusion detection: raw traffic-based features.

[1] The three features are one-hot encoded to 3, 11 and 70 values respectively.

3.2 Raw Traffic-Based Features

Raw traffic-based features, in contrast to traditional features, are based only on the raw network traffic that is being inspected by the NIDS. They can be extracted from this traffic by selecting a number of transmitted bytes and using those bytes directly as input for the machine learning model in one way or another. This abolishes the extensive resource usage to monitor traffic flows, and can be used in any situation: Independent of the situation, it is possible to train a model on extracted traffic bytes. In [31], two approaches to use raw traffic are investigated: HAST-I (HierArchical Spatial-Temporal features) considers the first i bytes of a traffic flow to create a large rectangle image. HAST-II extracts the first j bytes of the first k packets in a flow to create a sequence of smaller images. These images can then be processed in convolutional layers in a machine learning model. Similarly, in [33], the leading bytes of subsequent packets in a flow are concatenated to obtain a square image. These approaches report promising results, attaining state-of-the-art results on their evaluation datasets. Moreover, in [14], a comparison is made between the state-of-the-art results for traditional features and the use of raw traffic-based features in machine learning. The findings indicate that raw traffic-based features have the potential to match and even surpass traditional approaches. For real-time application however, the techniques considered in [14,31,33] are not sufficient, as they first sort the entire dataset before extracting features from the resulting flows. In a real-time scenario, it is not possible to wait until an entire dataset, or even a subset thereof, is available before features are extracted, as this would occupy too many memory resources and excessively delay detection. In the following section we will therefore present an approach to extract raw traffic-based features in real-time.

3.3 Our Proposed Approach: Flow Buckets

The research in [31] and [33] works on data that have been completely preprocessed before extracting the traffic bytes for machine learning. Concretely, this works on traffic that has been captured and sorted into complete flows. Traffic can be sorted into flows using flow identifiers (FID). A FID is a tuple comprising 5 values: The flow source and destination IP addresses, the source and destination TCP/UDP ports and the protocol number (6 for TCP or 17 for UDP). Raw traffic can be extract from packet capture files (PCAP), and the flows can be derived by using these FID values. Such an approach is however not representative of a real-time scenario with different flows in rapid succession, and where it might be necessary to keep track of various flows simultaneously. Once again, keeping track of too many flows for too long occupies too many memory resources and delays detection, so an alternative real-time solution is necessary. For this purpose, we will discuss *flow buckets* to keep track of l bytes from up to m packets for n separate flows concurrently.

A flow bucket represents a storage element that can store $l \times m$ bytes from one specific flow. Every flow packet adds l bytes to the bucket, causing it to fill up gradually. When the bucket is full, it produces one set of input features for

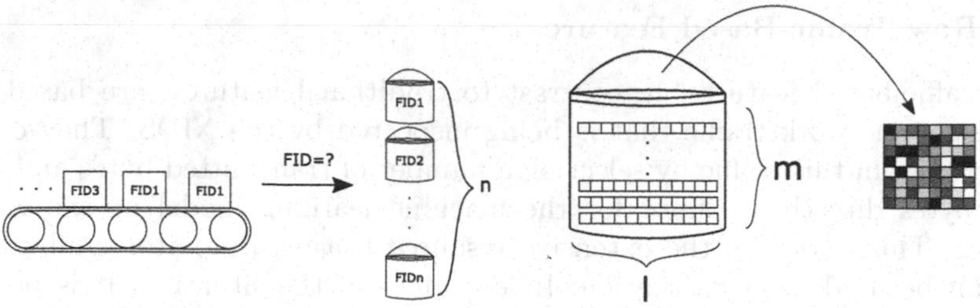

Fig. 1. (a) Packets are put into one of n buckets according to their FID. (b) Each bucket stores up to l packet bytes for up to m packets, and emptying a bucket produces input features for a machine learning model. Missing bytes are zero-padded.

the machine learning model, and it is emptied such that new bytes can be added, as shown in Fig. 1b.

Combining n separate buckets allows for the construction of a mechanism to process a packet stream in real-time, as demonstrated in Algorithm 1 and Fig. 1a. Each bucket can be identified with the FID of the flow it is currently keeping track of, and every flow consists of either a TCP or a UDP session. Whenever adding a packet to the buckets, it is first checked whether one of the current buckets is keeping track of the packet's FID. If this is not the case, either an empty bucket is filled, or the oldest bucket, that is the bucket that has gone the longest without new packets, is emptied to make place for the new FID. On the contrary, if there already is a bucket for the FID, the packet is added to that bucket instead. However, if this would cause the number of packets in the bucket to exceed m, the bucket should also be emptied first. Emptying a bucket simply implies taking l bytes of every packet in a bucket and using the bytes as input features for the machine leaning model. In the case that the number of packets in an emptied bucket is less than m, the missing packet bytes are padded with zeros to ensure the input features retain a fixed shape.

This principle is simpler to translate to hardware in comparison to traditional feature extraction, and by choosing a value for l, m and n, the total resource usage can be constrained. As only very limited processing is actually required, the flow bucket approach is very unlikely to form a bottleneck in any NIDS. We explore this approach further in the experiments in Sect. 5.

When comparing (l, m, n)-flow buckets against other approaches, such as HAST-II [31] or PCCN [33], there are common qualities as well as distinct differences: Flow buckets use a packet's leading bytes as features, and rely on the FID to distinguish between flows. Moreover, the resulting features can be used to construct images to use in a convolutional neural network. The most significant difference however is that unlike HAST-II or PCCN, flow buckets are suitable for extracting incoming network traffic at line speed. As PCCN or HAST-II are devised based on collected packet traces, they do not consider real-time extraction. In principle, the flow bucket approach can be used to extract features with

Algorithm 1: Processing a packet using flow buckets

```
input  : A packet stream PStream, where each packet is a sequence of bytes
output: Machine learning feature maps of size l × m
'Buckets' contains all buckets and their current FIDs;
Buckets ← InitializeBuckets(l, m, n);
for Packet in PStream do
    Extract the FID from the input packet;
    FID ← GetFlowID(P);
    if IsValidFlowID(FID) then
        if FID is in Buckets then
            AddPacket(Buckets, FID, Packet);
        else
            if IsEmptyBucket(Buckets) then
                AddNewBucket(Buckets, FID);
                AddPacket(Buckets, FID, Packet);
            else
                EmptyOldestBucket(Buckets);
                AddNewBucket(Buckets, FID);
                AddPacket(Buckets, FID, Packet);

Function AddPacket(Buckets, FID, Packet):
    if IsBucketFull(Buckets, FID) then
        EmptyBucket(Buckets, FID);
        AddNewBucket(Buckets, FID);
    FillBucket(Buckets, FID, Packet);
```

the same dimensions as PCCN or HAST-II features, and as such can serve as a tool to make these approaches suitable for real-time use.

3.4 Our Alternative Proposed Approach: Bidirectional Flow Buckets

It is possible to extend the flow bucket concept to bidirectional flows. Given flow F_1 with $FID_1 = (A, B, a, b, x)$ and its reverse flow F_2 with $FID_2 = (B, A, b, a, x)$, the bidirectional flow $F_{1,2}$ includes all packets from both F_1 and F_2. It is bidirectional because it considers all traffic in one connection, both the forward traffic (from host A at port a to host B at port b) and the reverse, backward traffic (from host B at port b to host A at port a). A and B are in this case IP addresses, while a and b are port numbers and x is the protocol number. It is possible to consider bidirectional flows instead of regular flows for the flow bucket approach. This implies, after calculating the FID of an input packet, the algorithm should not only check whether any of the buckets capture that flow, but also whether any of the buckets capture the reverse FID instead. If that is the case, the packet is considered a backward packet in that bidirectional flow, and is added to the bucket. If m and n would be infinitely large, and if for every forward flow its backward alternative would exist, using bidirectional flows would effectively halve the number of employed buckets as opposed to using regular flows. It might therefore be interesting to use bidirectional flows when trying to maximize the number of packets captured inside each bucket. Of course, in a real implementation, it is not feasible to achieve such large values for m or n. Our experiments in Sect. 5.1 show that realistic values already contribute to reducing the number of used buckets.

4 From Software to Hardware

There are various ways to map a software-based machine learning algorithm to an FPGA, such as using HLS4ML[2], Vitis AI[3] or FINN [6,30]. In this paper, we choose FINN for the acceleration of deep learning models, as it is open source and publicly available, and as it supports sufficient layers to synthesize an entire deep learning model. It works using a dataflow architecture, where each layer has its own compute engine and is implemented concurrently. FINN is suitable for high throughput applications, and allows for significant customization through its folding parameters that determine parallelization. The slowest layer will be the bottleneck in a pipelined architecture. In this section, we discuss the steps FINN takes to accelerate hardware, as well as how to interpret the reported results.

4.1 Accelerating a Model Using FINN

FINN requires a number of steps to turn a regular deep learning network into a dataflow architecture. Initially, the model needs to be quantized, for example using Quantization Aware Training (QAT) in Brevitas [21]. The resulting quantized model can then be processed using a set of transformations. First, streamlining transformations serve to remove floating point operations from the model, by shifting them around and aggregating them in multi-thresholding layers. This prepares the other layers to be then turned in HLS (High-Level Synthesis) layers, once all non-supported operations have been (re)moved. FINN can then synthesize these HLS layers into hardware using Xilinx Vivado, and this hardware can finally be deployed on an FPGA. In Sect. 5 we describe how we use FINN to accelerate a custom deep learning model.

4.2 Fps to Bandwidth

In FINN, the default reporting of model throughput uses the framerate r_f in *frames per second* or *fps*, which is common practice for image processing models. While this is a useful metric, it does not directly translate to a supported

[2] https://fastmachinelearning.org/hls4ml/.
[3] https://www.xilinx.com/products/design-tools/vitis/vitis-ai.html.

maximum network bandwidth. Nevertheless, as each emptied bucket in the flow bucket approach also corresponds with one input image for the subsequent algorithm, in our context, the r_f can also be defined as the number of *flows per second*, where each flow is one emptied bucket. When B is the number of traffic bytes in a dataset, and f is the total number of captured flows using the flow bucket method, $bpf = B \cdot 8/f$ is the average number of *bits per flow* that are transmitted in the dataset. This also includes non-flow bits such as Address Resolution Protocol (ARP) data. Consequently, it is also possible to find the relationship between the supported throughput r_f and the supported bitrate r_b in bits per second: $bpf = r_b/r_f$. This allows a FINN user to estimate what the supported bandwidth r_b would be, for a specific dataset with B, a specific flow bucket configuration with f and an accelerated model with r_f.

5 Experiments

In this section, we will describe the experiments we conducted for both the evaluation of flow buckets and the translation of machine learning models to hardware. All code is publicly available[4].

5.1 Flow Buckets

We have conducted a number of experiments to evaluate the impact of using flow buckets to extract features instead of using a completely preprocessed dataset. We consider buckets with $l = 96$ and $m = 5$, or concretely, buckets that can contain the leading 96 bytes of up to 5 packets with the same FID. Using these settings, one learning sample is a concatenation of 5 vectors of 96 elements, where each vector is separated from the other vectors with a FF-valued byte as described for Header-Payload features in [33]. Both the results in [33] as well as in [14] suggest this configuration is suitable to detect attacks. The resulting vector has a length of 484 bytes and can be reshaped into a 22×22 image. First we will consider the impact of m and the number of buckets, n, on the flow distribution, then we will inspect machine learning performance for these alternative features.

Flow Distribution. While maintaining l fixed at 96, different values for m and n will lead to different feature compositions for the machine learning model. First, we inspect the impact of n when m remains constant at a value of 5. We choose $m = 5$ to be able to generate features with the same shape as those in [33]. Increasing n leads to keeping track of more flows concurrently, which should in theory provide buckets with more opportunities to be filled up before being emptied to make space for a different flow. For this experiment, we use various values of n for the CICIDS2017 dataset. Figure 2a gives the flow distribution for this experiment. The flow distribution considers the percentage of all extracted flows (=emptied buckets) that consist of s packets, where s is a value between

[4] https://gitlab.com/EAVISE/real-time-dl-nids-on-fpga.

1 and m. Clearly, nearly 80% of all flows consist of only 1 packet, and nearly the entire other 20% comprise the 2-packet flows. Apparently, while there is space for 5 packets, the vast majority of buckets are already emptied when they contain 1 or 2 packets. One reason for this could be that, for the vast majority of the dataset, only flows with 1 or 2 packets exist. That however is very unlikely, as it would limit any communication to be finished with a maximum of 2 packets transmitted. Moreover, Fig. 2b considers a scenario with an infinitely large value for n in CICIDS2017. This can be achieved by sorting all packets in the dataset according to their FID first, and then by continuing filling buckets until all packets have been used for every FID separately. As there clearly are many flows with at least 5 packets, the results in Fig. 2a suggest that there are so many different concurrent flows in CICIDS2017 that it is nearly impossible to keep track of a flow long enough to consistently fill buckets. If we would keep on increasing n, more and more flows would contain 5 packets. However, as each bucket requires $m \cdot l = 96 \cdot 5 = 480$ bytes of storage, using $n = 10^4$ would already require 4.8 MB of on-chip memory, which is unrealistic for real-time acceleration on FPGA, especially if this memory might also be reserved for the machine learning model.

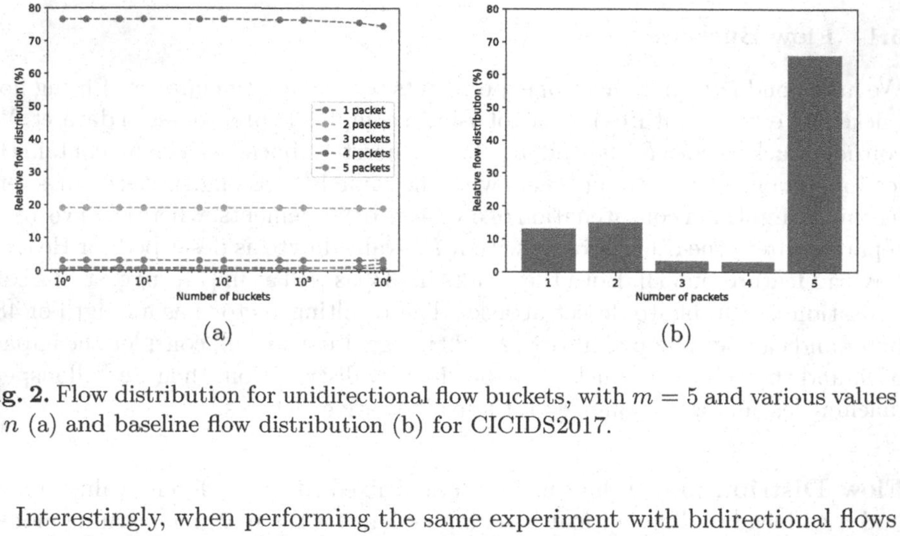

(a) (b)

Fig. 2. Flow distribution for unidirectional flow buckets, with $m = 5$ and various values of n (a) and baseline flow distribution (b) for CICIDS2017.

Interestingly, when performing the same experiment with bidirectional flows instead of unidirectional flows, the results are significantly different, as shown in Fig. 3a. While 1-packet and 2-packet flows still encompass about 65% of all flows, about 30% of all flows now comprise 5 packets. This indicates a significant portion of the traffic is bidirectional, and that it is a lot easier to keep track of bidirectional flows compared to unidirectional flows. As a result, the total number of extracted flows is considerably smaller for the bidirectional approach, as shown in Fig. 3b. For this approach more packets can be captured in the same bucket, which in turn results in fewer buckets being needed. In a real-time scenario,

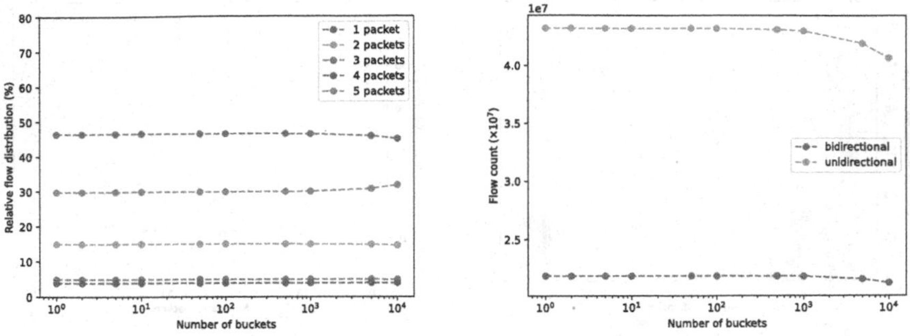

(a) (b)

Fig. 3. Flow distribution for bidirectional flow buckets (a) and flow counts for unidirectional and bidirectional flow buckets (b) with $m = 5$ and various values of n for CICIDS2017.

when compared to the unidirectional alternative, this would imply that for the same network traffic the overall architecture supports a higher throughput. It is also clear that realistic values for m and n already result in considerable improvements, which in turn implies that infinitely large values are not required.

For the bidirectional case, there can be merit in increasing m, as it is likely that deeper buckets will indeed be sufficiently utilized. Each 5-packet flow has the potential to be a larger total flow that is terminated due to the bucket being full. This is not the case for the unidirectional approach, where nearly all flows terminate at only 1 or 2 packets. Figure 4a gives the flow distribution for the bidirectional approach with $m = 10$ and $n = 100$, with Fig. 4b similarly giving the distribution for $m = 100$. As the bucket depth m increases, the portion of m-packet flows decreases, while other portions increase. This trend is most noticeable for the portion of 1-packet streams, that significantly increases from 54% to 62% as m goes from 10 to 100.

When repeating the first experiment for UNSW-NB15, the results in Fig. 5 show a behaviour similar to CICIDS2017. For unidirectional flows, most flows are captured with 2 or 4 packets, with only a few flows consisting of 5 packets. Once again, using bidirectional flows considerably decreases the total number of flows, which goes from about 7.5×10^7 unidirectional to about 5.3×10^7 bidirectional flows. This effect is also visible in Fig. 5b, as a significantly larger portion of the flows contains 5 packets. Both unidirectional and bidirectional cases also more clearly follow the expected behaviour compared to CICIDS2017 when increasing n, as being able to monitor more flows concurrently increases the relative portion of 5-packet flows, starting from about $n = 1000$. One reason for this can be found through the average number of packets per unique flow: CICIDS2017 contains 55,953,889 packets that belong to a flow, while UNSW-NB15 contains 187,072,760 packets. However, when counting the number of unique FIDs per day, and calculating the sum for every day for both datasets, CICIDS2017 has 2,649,163 unique FIDs and UNSW-NB15 has 3,996,364. On average, this means

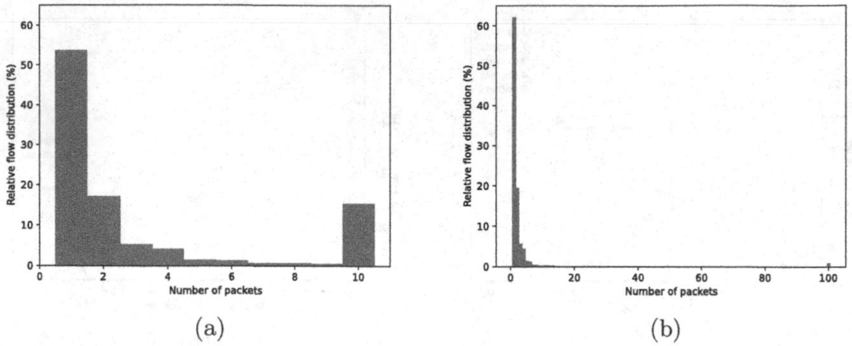

Fig. 4. Flow distribution for $m = 10$ (a) and $m = 100$ (b) bidirectional flow buckets with $n = 100$ for CICIDS2017.

that UNSW-NB15 has about 47 packets for each unique FID, while CICIDS2017 only has about 21. Therefore, on average more packets will belong to the same flow in UNSW-NB15, which in turn means it is easier to start completely filling up buckets while fewer buckets are available.

Machine Learning Performance. In order to measure the impact of using flow buckets, we first establish a baseline performance, obtained from training a machine learning model on raw traffic-based features from a dataset that has been completely sorted into flows. The employed model is a Convolutional Neural Network we name BaseCNN2D as presented in Fig. 6. Each convolutional layer is followed by one batch normalization layer (with $\epsilon = 10^{-5}$) and one ReLU activation layer. The 6×6 feature map is downsampled using max pooling, with the result being reformed to a 1024-sized vector. This vector, after one final batch normalization layer as well as a 50% dropout layer, is used as an input to a fully connected layer.

The model was trained for an initial learning rate of 0.001, which was divided by 10 if no improvement was shown during the last 10 epochs, for a total number of 100 epochs, with an SGD optimizer. We report our results using the accuracy Acc, the weighted average detection rate[5] DR_w, the weighted average F-measure F_w, as well as two metrics that are proposed in [14]: The detection score DS and the identification score IS. The DS is the F-measure of the binarized confusion matrix, where each detected attack that actually was an attack (even if it was another attack class) is considered a true positive. Equation 1 then gives the IS, which is the harmonic mean of the weighted average F-measure F_w and macro average F-measure F_M in a multiclass scenario. As the IS considers both minority and majority classes through respectively F_M and F_w, it assesses how well a model can identify specific attacks in a dataset.

[5] The DR is commonly used in intrusion detection literature to denote the recall.

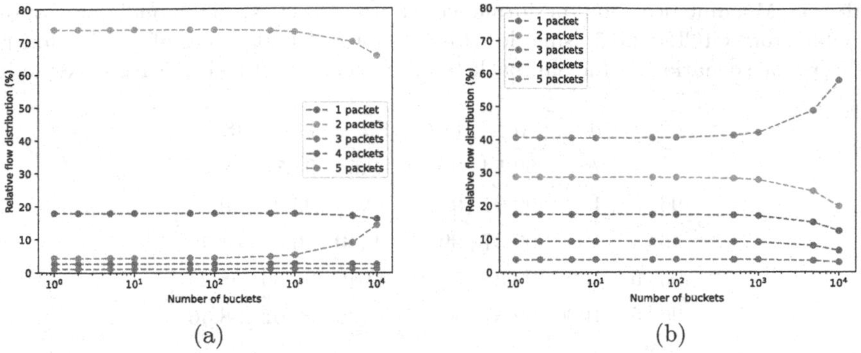

Fig. 5. Flow distribution for unidirectional (a) and bidirectional (b) flow buckets, with $m = 5$ and various values of n for UNSW-NB15.

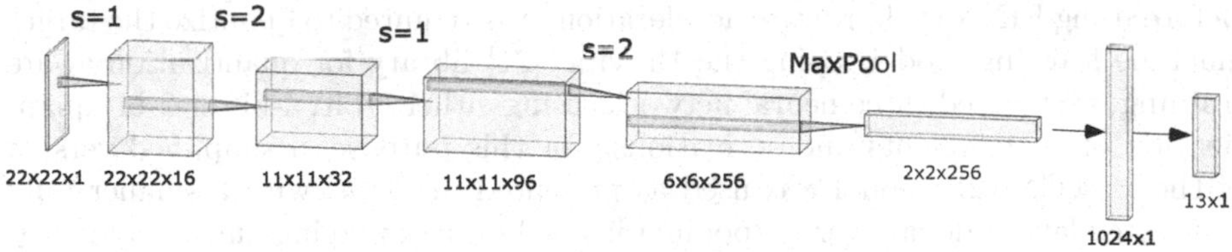

Fig. 6. The BaseCNN2D architecture that was used in the experiments, with s indicating the stride of a convolution layer while the feature map and fully connected layer sizes are provided below the graph. Visualized using [15].

$$IS = \frac{2 \cdot F_w \cdot F_M}{F_w + F_M} \tag{1}$$

For these training parameters and these metrics, the machine learning results are presented in Table 1.

To investigate the effect of using flow bucket feature extraction, we consider a unidirectional bucket configuration with $l = 96$, $m = 5$ and where n is either 1, 10, 100 or 1000. This configuration produces features that are in line with the features in [14, 33] and allows for assessing whether flow bucket features actually work for machine learning. As the results in Table 1 show, that is actually the case: For 10, 100 and 1000 buckets the results are only slightly lower than the baseline, without any indications that one is significantly worse than the other. This is to be expected, as Fig. 2a shows very little difference between the flow distributions of the selected values for n. Somewhat unexpectedly, the model for $n = 1$ achieves a near perfect classification, making only 1,263 errors for over 4 million test samples. This further underlines the potential that raw traffic-based features have for real-time deep learning based network intrusion detection.

Table 1. Machine learning performance of the BaseCNN2D model for datasets extracted from CICIDS2017 using flow buckets for different values of n. The first row considers the scenario in which all packets have been sorted before feature extraction.

l	m	n	Acc	DR_w	F_w	DS	IS
/	/	/	99.54	99.54	99.54	97.70	98.77
96	5	1	99.97	99.97	99.97	99.97	99.28
96	5	10	99.37	99.37	99.40	96.03	98.42
96	5	100	99.38	99.38	99.40	96.05	98.46
96	5	1000	99.37	99.37	99.39	96.02	98.46

5.2 Quantization

Before using FINN for hardware acceleration, it is required to quantize the target machine learning model. Using the Brevitas [21] library for quantization-aware training, we trained three neural networks using either 8-bit, 4-bit or 2-bit quantization of both weights and activations. For this purpose, a simplified version of the BaseCNN2D model was used as presented in Fig. 7, with a smaller fully connected layer, global average pooling instead of max pooling and without regularization after pooling. By training this network without quantization, and by then using the proposed quantization alternatives, we obtain the results presented in Table 2. All training is done using the CICIDS2017 dataset with raw traffic-based features extracted from presorted flows.

Table 2. Result of training the simplified BaseCNN2D model using 8-bit, 4-bit and 2-bit quantization, as well as baseline results without quantization.

Quantization	Acc	DR_w	F_w	DS	IS
None	99.52	99.52	99.52	97.59	98.58
8-bit	99.53	99.53	99.53	97.65	98.65
4-bit	99.49	99.49	99.49	97.46	98.36
2-bit	99.41	99.41	99.41	97.26	97.23

These results suggest that the 8-bit quantization has no negative impact on the model's performance. On the contrary, the 8-bit case appears to achieve better results than the baseline without any quantization. When the quantization is further extended to 4-bit, there are only minor drops in performance. And remarkably, even going down to 2-bit quantization, the results remain high. Because we want to limit the hardware footprint of our FPGA implementation as much as possible, we choose the 2-bit w2a2 model for hardware acceleration.

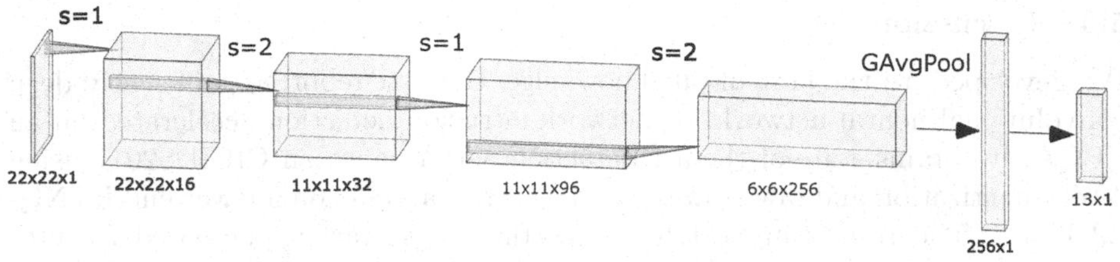

Fig. 7. The simplified BaseCNN2D architecture, used for quantization and hardware acceleration with s indicating the stride of a convolution layer while the feature map and fully connected layer sizes are provided below the graph. Visualized using [15].

Table 3. Resource utilization of the w2a2 quantized simplified BaseCNN2D model as accelerated on a PYNQ-Z2 board.

Resources	Utilization	Available	Utilization (%)
LUT	24,635	53,200	46.31%
LUTRAM	1,980	17,400	11,38%
FF	27,450	106,400	25,80%
BRAM	37.50	140	26.79%

5.3 FPGA Performance

We use the FINN workflow [6,30] to accelerate the trained and quantized model on FPGA. We first use a specific set of transformations in a specific order to turn the entire model into synthesizable hardware. Then, this hardware is synthesized using FINN in collaboration with Vivado 2020.1, resulting in a bitfile and Python code for the PYNQ-Z2 board with a Xilinx ZYNQ XC7Z020-1CLG400C FPGA. Using out-of-context synthesis for the accelerated model leads to the resource utilization depicted in Table 3. The included Python code reports a throughput of about 9635 images/second, or $r_f = 9635$ *fps* using a 100 MHz clock.

As $B = 50,557,729,836$ bytes for the CICIDS2017 dataset, we can calculate bpf for any flow bucket approach to estimate the supported bandwidth. For example for $(l, m, n) = (96, 5, 5)$, $f = 43,263,642$ flows, which in turn means bpf is about 9349 bits per flow. This means that for this architecture with $(96, 5, 5)$-buckets, the supported bitrate is $r_b = r_f \cdot bpf = 90.08$ Mbps.

The supported throughput for the flow buckets in hardware will depend on the network interface. Consider for example an implementation on a PYNQ-Z2 FPGA with a *Xilinx 1G/2.5G Ethernet Subsystem* and a physical ethernet interface supporting 1Gpbs. While internally the system may run faster, the total throughput will be constrained by the physical interface. For this example, the internal system could run with a 100 MHz clock and receive the ethernet packets in 32-bit blocks over an AXI Stream bus. In the absolute worst case, with the smallest possible 64-byte Ethernet packets, all featuring the same FID, it should take $max(l, 64)/4 \cdot m$ clock cycles to fill a bucket. For $(96, 5, n)$, that would be 120 clock cycles or $1.2 \cdot 10^6$ buckets per second.

5.4 Discussion

We developed, to the best of our knowledge, the first reported sufficiently deep convolutional neural network for network intrusion detection accelerated on an FPGA. It obtains state-of-the-art detection performance on CICIDS2017 using 2-bit quantization and raw traffic-based features, and fits on a lower-end PYNQ-Z2 board. The results in Sect. 5.1 show that these raw traffic-based features can be extracted in real-time using flow buckets without considerably adversely effecting detection performance. There is still room for improvement, as the throughput of the accelerated model should still be increased for real-time intrusion detection. We observe the following options to achieve this goal:

- There are still some computational bottlenecks in the network that can be solved in order to increase the speed. Currently the network is limited by the slowest layer.
- The current platform is relatively small resource-wise. Using a larger platform such as a Xilinx Alveo card would allow for more parallelization, which would in turn allows to speed up the computations in the layers.
- Further optimization of the machine learning model, through 1-bit quantization, pruning or other methods, reduces the functionality that needs to be translated to hardware.

We are confident that these optimizations will further improve the throughput towards real-time intrusion detection.

6 Conclusion and Future Work

In this paper, we set out to develop a deep learning-based NIDS with real-time throughput and feature extraction as well as high detection performance. We proposed the flow bucket approach to enable real-time raw traffic-based feature extraction. Analyzing the results of this approach for two recent and publicly available datasets, UNSW-NB15 and CICIDS2017, shows that using these features does not deteriorate learning performance, but rather allows for very high detection accuracy. Moreover, we also proposed a deep learning architecture that retains performance even when quantized towards 2-bit weights and activations. Finally, we have laid a foundation to further build upon with respect to accelerating our deep learning model in hardware. While the maximum bandwidth is currently still limited, there are clear possibilities to further improve throughput. For future work, we will aim at optimizing the hardware architecture to reach higher network traffic bandwidth. Moreover, we will further explore different ways in which raw-traffic based features can be used as input for machine learning models. E.g., for unidirectional flow buckets with $(l, m, n) = (96, 5, 5)$, the majority of the flows contains 1 or 2 packets. Using $m = 2$ significantly reduces input feature size, and thus model size, but might not impact the detection performance too drastically. Additional research concerning the applicability of bidirectional flows is also in order. Exploring all these options may finally lead to viable deep learning architectures for real-time NIDSs.

Acknowledgements. This work is supported by COllective Research NETworking (CORNET) and funded by VLAIO under grant number HBC.2018.0491. This work is also supported by CyberSecurity Research Flanders with reference number VR20192203.

References

1. KDD Cup 1999 Data. http://kdd.ics.uci.edu/databases/kddcup99/kddcup99.html
2. Abdulhammed, R., Musafer, H., Alessa, A., Faezipour, M., Abuzneid, A.: Features dimensionality reduction approaches for machine learning based network intrusion detection. Electronics **8**, 322 (2019)
3. Al-Qatf, M., Lasheng, Y., Al-Habib, M., Al-Sabahi, K.: Deep learning approach combining sparse autoencoder with SVM for network intrusion detection. IEEE Access **6**, 52843–52856 (2018)
4. Alrawashdeh, K., Purdy, C.: Toward an online anomaly intrusion detection system based on deep learning. In: 2016 15th IEEE ICMLA, pp. 195–200, December 2016
5. Andrade Maciel, L., Alcântara Souza, M., Cota de Freitas, H.: Reconfigurable FPGA-based K-means/K-modes architecture for network intrusion detection. IEEE TCAS-II **67**(8), 1459–1463 (2020)
6. Blott, M., et al.: FINN-R: an end-to-end deep-learning framework for fast exploration of quantized neural networks. ACM TRETS **11**(3), 1–23 (2018)
7. Chuan-long, Y., Yue-fei, Z., Jin-long, F., Xin-zheng, H.: A deep learning approach for intrusion detection using recurrent neural networks. IEEE Access **5**, 21954–21961 (2017)
8. Das, A., Nguyen, D., Zambreno, J., Memik, G., Choudhary, A.: An FPGA-based network intrusion detection architecture. IEEE Trans. Inf. Forensics Secur. **3**(1), 118–132 (2008)
9. Ding, Y., Zhai, Y.: Intrusion detection system for NSL-KDD dataset using convolutional neural networks. In: Proceedings of 2018 CSAI (CSAI 2018), pp. 81–85. ACM, New York (2018)
10. García-Teodoro, P., Díaz-Verdejo, J., Maciá-Fernández, G., Vázquez, E.: Anomaly-based network intrusion detection: techniques, systems and challenges. Comput. Secur. **28**(1), 18–28 (2009)
11. Ioannou, L., Fahmy, S.A.: Network intrusion detection using neural networks on FPGA SoCs. In: 2019 29th FPL, pp. 232–238, September 2019
12. Kim, T., Suh, S.C., Kim, H., Kim, J., Kim, J.: An encoding technique for CNN-based network anomaly detection. In: IEEE BigData, pp. 2960–2965, December 2018
13. Krizhevsky, A., Sutskever, I., Hinton, G.E.: ImageNet classification with deep convolutional neural networks. Adv. NIPS **25**, 1097–1105 (2012)
14. Le Jeune, L., Goedemé, T., Mentens, N.: Machine learning for misuse-based network intrusion detection: overview, unified evaluation and feature choice comparison framework. IEEE Access **9**, 63995–64015 (2021)
15. LeNail, A.: NN-SVG: publication-ready neural network architecture schematics. J. Open Source Softw. **4**(33), 747 (2019). https://doi.org/10.21105/joss.00747
16. Lopez-Martin, M., Carro, B., Sanchez-Esguevillas, A., Lloret, J.: Shallow neural network with kernel approximation for prediction problems in highly demanding data networks. Expert Syst. Appl. **124**, 196–208 (2019)

17. Moustafa, N., Slay, J.: UNSW-NB15: a comprehensive data set for network intrusion detection systems (UNSW-NB15 network data set). In: 2015 MilCIS, pp. 1–6, November 2015
18. Murovič, T., Trost, A.: Massively parallel combinational binary neural networks for edge processing. Elektrotehniski Vestnik/Electrotech. Rev. **86**, 47–53 (2019)
19. Ngo, D.M., Pham-Quoc, C., Thinh, T.N.: Heterogeneous hardware-based network intrusion detection system with multiple approaches for SDN. Mob. Netw. Appl. **25**(3), 1178–1192 (2020)
20. Ngo, D.-M., Tran-Thanh, B., Dang, T., Tran, T., Thinh, T.N., Pham-Quoc, C.: High-throughput machine learning approaches for network attacks detection on FPGA. In: Vinh, P.C., Rakib, A. (eds.) ICCASA/ICTCC -2019. LNICST, vol. 298, pp. 47–60. Springer, Cham (2019). https://doi.org/10.1007/978-3-030-34365-1_5
21. Pappalardo, A.: Xilinx/brevitas. https://doi.org/10.5281/zenodo.3333552
22. Paxson, V.: Bro: a system for detecting network intruders in real-time. Comput. Netw. **31**(23), 2435–2463 (1999)
23. Roesch, M.: Snort - lightweight intrusion detection for networks. In: 13th USENIX Conference on System Administration (LISA 1999), pp. 229–238. USENIX Association, USA (1999)
24. Sharafaldin, I., Habibi Lashkari, A., Ghorbani, A.: Toward generating a new intrusion detection dataset and intrusion traffic characterization. In: 4th ICISSP, Portugal, pp. 108–116 (2018)
25. Sommer, R., Paxson, V.: Enhancing byte-level network intrusion detection signatures with context. In: 10th ACM CCS (CCS 2003), pp. 262–271. ACM, New York (2003)
26. Tavallaee, M., Bagheri, E., Lu, W., Ghorbani, A.A.: A detailed analysis of the KDD CUP 99 data set. In: 2009 IEEE CISDA, pp. 1–6, July 2009
27. Tran, C., Vo, T.N., Thinh, T.N.: HA-IDS: a heterogeneous anomaly-based intrusion detection system. In: NAFOSTED NICS, vol. 2017, pp. 156–161 (2017)
28. Tsai, C.F., Hsu, Y.F., Lin, C.Y., Lin, W.Y.: Intrusion detection by machine learning: a review. Expert Syst. Appl. **36**(10), 11994–12000 (2009)
29. Umuroglu, Y., Akhauri, Y., Fraser, N.J., Blott, M.: LogicNets: co-designed neural networks and circuits for extreme-throughput applications. In: FPL, vol. 2020, pp. 291–297 (2020)
30. Umuroglu, Y., et al.: FINN: a framework for fast, scalable binarized neural network inference. In: Proceedings of the 2017 ACM/SIGDA FPGA, pp. 65–74. ACM (2017)
31. Wang, W., et al.: HAST-IDS: learning hierarchical spatial-temporal features using deep neural networks to improve intrusion detection. IEEE Access **6**, 1792–1806 (2018)
32. Zhang, J., Zulkernine, M., Haque, A.: Random-forests-based network intrusion detection systems. IEEE Trans. Syst. Man Cybern. Part C (Appl. Rev.) **38**(5), 649–659 (2008)
33. Zhang, Y., Chen, X., Guo, D., Song, M., Teng, Y., Wang, X.: PCCN: parallel cross convolutional neural network for abnormal network traffic flows detection in multi-class imbalanced network traffic flows. IEEE Access **7**, 119904–119916 (2019)

Towards Trained Model Confidentiality and Integrity Using Trusted Execution Environments

Tsunato Nakai[1,2(✉)], Daisuke Suzuki[1], and Takeshi Fujino[2]

[1] Mitsubishi Electric Corporation, Tokyo, Japan
Nakai.Tsunato@dy.MitsubishiElectric.co.jp
[2] Ritsumeikan University, Kyoto, Japan

Abstract. In the security of machine learning, it is important to protect the confidentiality and integrity of trained models. The leakage of the data in a trained model leads to not only the infringement of intellectual property but also various attacks such as adversarial example attacks. Recent works have proposed several methods using trusted execution environments (TEEs), which provide an isolated environment that cannot be manipulated by malicious software, to protect the trained models. However, the protection using TEEs generally does not work well by simply porting the program of a trained model to a TEE. There are mainly several reasons: the limitation of the memory size in TEEs prevents loading a large number of parameters into memory, which is particularly a characteristic of deep learning; the increase in runtime due to TEEs; and the threat of parameter manipulation (the integrity of the trained model). This paper proposes a novel method based on TEEs to protect the trained models, mainly for deep learning on embedded devices. The proposed method is characterized by memory saving, low runtime overhead, and detection of parameter manipulation. In the experiments, it is implemented and evaluated using Arm TrustZone and OP-TEE.

Keywords: Trained model protection · Trusted execution environment · Deep learning · Arm TrustZone · OP-TEE

1 Introduction

Machine learning, such as deep learning, has been widely used in various applications because of its technological breakthroughs. However, recent works indicate that a trained model is vulnerable to various attacks, which will compromise the security of the model itself and the application system. The trained model information, such as the architecture and parameters, can be regarded as the intellectual property of the model creators. Moreover, if the model information is revealed, it is easy to carry out adversarial example attacks [1] to cause misclassification by adding small perturbations to the input data of the model, and model inversion attacks [2] to steal the training data from the model, i.e., white-box attacks.

J. Zhou et al. (Eds.): ACNS 2021 Workshops, LNCS 12809, pp. 151–168, 2021.
https://doi.org/10.1007/978-3-030-81645-2_10

Therefore, stealing or illegally copying the model is one of the important issues in the security of machine learning. Machine learning implemented on embedded devices will especially face this issue due to reverse engineering when the devices are in the hands of attackers.

Several methods using trusted execution environments (TEEs) have been proposed for model protection recently [3]. TEEs provide an isolated environment for code execution that cannot be manipulated by malicious software running on the device, including the untrusted operating system (OS). Current various processors have a TEE mechanism such as Intel SGX, AMD SEV, and Arm TrustZone. TEEs have been mainly used for cryptographic applications, however, they have also been used for other critical applications with the increase in memory size of TEEs. Moreover, it has been proposed to execute machine learning applications using TEEs for model protection [4–10].

There are several problems with TEEs to protect trained models. In general, it does not work well to simply port the program of a trained model to a TEE. This paper focuses on three main problems as follows:

- **Lack of memory.** The memory size of TEEs is generally not enough for machine learning, especially deep learning. For example, the available memory size of TEEs is about a few MB in Arm TrustZone, depending on the hardware and OS [11,12]. However, the parameter size of typical deep learning is in the order of hundreds or tens of MB.
- **Runtime overhead.** To solve the lack of memory, existing works have proposed an approach where the loaded parameters to the memory and the execution of prediction are divided into each layer for memory saving [6,10]. This approach switches the execution environment for each layer. However, it increases the runtime due to frequent switching of execution environments.
- **Parameter manipulation.** A lot of existing works encrypt the trained model information for confidentiality, however do not consider the possibility of parameter manipulation, i.e., integrity [4–10]. An attacker can manipulate the parameters of a trained model, which can cause malfunctions and misrecognition in the application system.

This paper proposes a novel model protection method using TEE, mainly for deep learning on embedded devices. The proposed method presents a solution to three problems: lack of memory, runtime overhead, and parameter manipulation. The method saves memory to divide the loaded parameters and the execution of prediction into each layer or calculation unit, instead of loading all parameters into the memory, referring to existing works [6,10]. To reduce the number of times the execution environment is switched, the method uses the shared memory of TEEs to load the divided parameters and executes the decryption of the loaded parameters and the prediction in concurrent computing on TEEs. The method uses GCM (Galois/Counter Mode), the most widely used dedicated authenticated encryption mode, to achieve both the confidentiality and integrity of the parameters.

The experiments show the evaluation results of the proposed method in terms of measurable memory saving and runtime. The experiments are conducted on a Raspberry Pi 3 Model B with Arm TrustZone (for Cortex-A architecture) and

OP-TEE [13], which is an open-source TEE implementing the Arm TrustZone technology. The experimental results are compared with existing methods using three trained models (LeNet, VGG-7, and Darknet) implemented by Darknet [14], which is an open-source neural network framework.

The contributions of this work can be summarized as follows:

- The proposed method provides memory saving, low runtime overhead, and detection of parameter manipulation, for trained model protection using TEEs (Sect. 3). It is mainly for deep learning on embedded devices.
- The experiments show the effectiveness of the proposed method in terms of memory saving and runtime (Sect. 4). The runtime of the proposed method is about one-tens compared with existing works, however, it is a trade-off between the divided size of loaded parameters and the runtime overhead.
- The security technologies are discussed to build and support the model protection system applying the method (Sect. 5).

2 Problems

This section explains three main problems with TEEs to protect trained models, based on existing works. This paper focuses on Arm TrustZone for embedded devices. Related works are summarized in Sect. 6.

2.1 Lack of Memory

In Arm TrustZone, the available memory size of a TEE (called a secure world) is about a few MB, depending on the hardware and OS [11,12]. For example, in the case of Arm TrustZone and OP-TEE on the Raspberry Pi 3 Model B, the available memory size of the secure world is 7 MB [13]. One reason for this is that applications in the secure world need to fit into the on-chip memory. However, the parameter size of typical deep learning models is on the order of hundreds or tens of MB. There are lightweight models with the parameter sizes of a few MB, however, the matrix operations such as im2col require memory allocation several times larger than parameter size, when the convolutional operations are used. In addition, there could be the requirements to implement the program in the secure world as compactly as possible to eliminate potential vulnerabilities or avoid allocating as many resources as possible to applications executed only for specific purposes in the secure world.

2.2 Runtime Overhead

To solve the lack of memory, the approach of existing works increases the runtime of the deep learning applications [6,10]. The approach achieves memory saving by dividing the loaded parameters into each layer, however, the execution environment is switched for each layer. When frequently switching the execution environment, the runtime overhead is increased due to storing and restoring the state of a processor, i.e., context switch. In addition, the shortcomings of another approach present in the existing literature, where only several layers are implemented in the secure world [7,9], are discussed in Sect. 6.

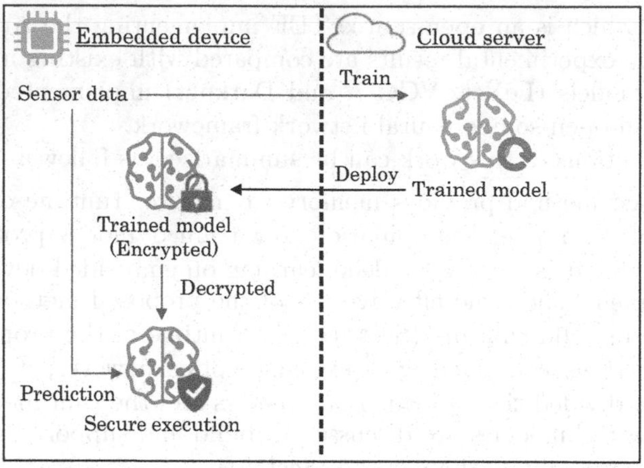

Fig. 1. Use case of the proposed method

2.3 Parameter Manipulation

A lot of existing works store the encrypted model information in storage for confidentiality, however do not consider the possibility of parameter manipulation [4–10]. In other words, although existing works keep the parameters secret, an attacker can manipulate them, which can cause malfunctions and misrecognition in the deep learning application system. For example, the application output can be fixed to a specific result due to the manipulated parameters. Although this threat cannot cause sophisticated malfunctions and misrecognition like adversarial example attacks, it is important to ensure the integrity of trained models.

3 Proposed Method

This section explains the proposed method using TEEs to protect trained models, based on the solutions of the problems in Sect. 2 and the use case. The basic idea is to divide the loaded parameters and execute GCM (decryption and detection of parameters manipulation) and prediction in concurrent computing.

3.1 Use Case

Figure 1 shows a use case of the proposed method. The use case describes that an embedded device executes a real-time or distributed prediction with deep learning on-site by using sensor data as input. A cloud server connected to the embedded device gathers the sensor data and generates a trained model. The generated model in the cloud server is fed back to the embedded device for making it smart.

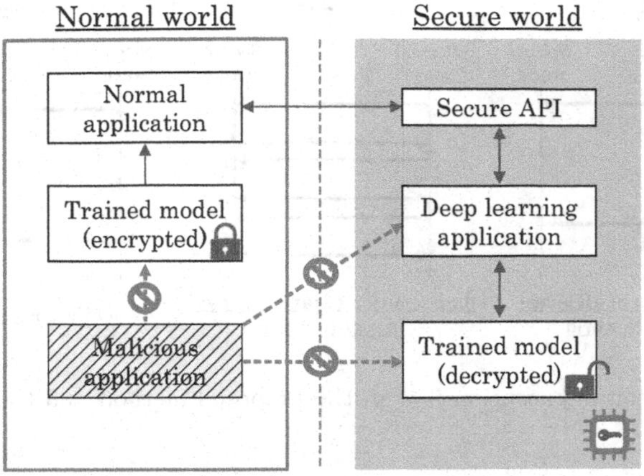

Fig. 2. Overview of trained model protection using TEEs

3.2 Threat Model

As shown in Fig. 1, the trained model can be regarded as a critical component and needs to be protected from theft or manipulation. The use case shows that the encrypted model delivered from the cloud server is securely decrypted and executed for prediction. This paper aims to protect against an attacker who may steal or manipulate the trained model with illegal memory access, etc. The proposed method uses TEEs to securely decrypt and execute trained models. Fault injection and side-channel attacks are out of scope.

Figure 2 shows an overview of trained model protection using a TEE. In this figure, the execution environment is separated between a normal world and a secure world using Arm TrustZone on an embedded device. Normal applications are executed in the normal world, and deep learning applications, which have the trained model information to be protected, are executed in the secure world. The normal applications can access the deep learning applications only through secure APIs, in other words, malicious applications or operations cannot freely access data in memory used on deep learning applications. The trained model is encrypted and stored in the storage of the normal world, and is decrypted in the secure world when it is called by the deep learning applications. The secret key for decryption is stored in a secure element accessible only from the secure world. Therefore, the trained model information cannot be revealed by malicious applications or operations.

3.3 Solutions

The solutions of the three problems in Sect. 2 are addressed as follows:

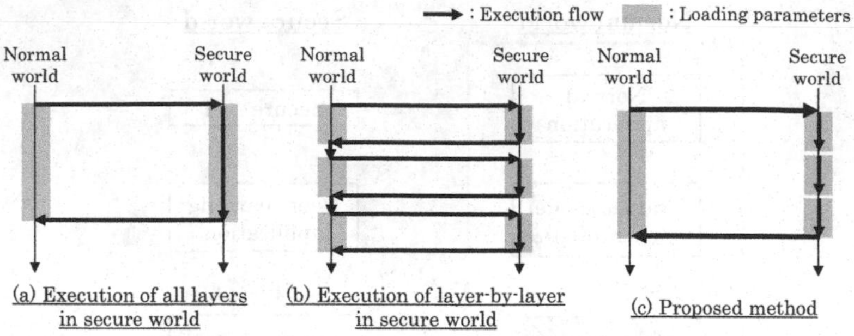

Fig. 3. Comparison of execution flow in the proposed method and the existing works

Memory Saving. The memory saving is achieved to divide the task composed of loading the parameters and executing prediction into each layer or computation unit such as matrix multiplication, instead of loading all parameters into the memory. It is based on the existing works [6,10]. In order to divide loading the parameters, it is necessary to decrypt the encrypted parameters according to the division unit (each layer or computation unit). The existing works encrypt the parameters layer-by-layer because they divide the loaded parameters into each layer for memory saving.

Low Runtime Overhead. The low runtime overhead is achieved to reduce the number of times switching the execution environment by using the shared memory of TEEs. The shared memory is a memory area accessible from both the secure and normal worlds to communicate data quickly and efficiently. Figure 3 shows a comparison of the execution flow in the proposed method and the existing works [4,6,10]. In this figure, the bold arrows indicate the execution flow, and the gray squares indicate loading the parameters to the memory. The execution of all layers in the secure world [4] can fall into the lack of memory due to loading a large number of parameters to the secure world. The execution of layer-by-layer in the secure world [6,10] saves the memory, however, it increases the runtime due to the switching overhead between the normal and secure worlds for each layer. The proposed method saves the memory by dividing the loaded parameters for each layer and reduces the number of times switching the execution environment by using the shared memory to load the divided parameters.

Detection of Parameter Manipulation. The detection of parameter manipulation is achieved by using GCM. The parameters are encrypted, and an authentication tag is produced to detect parameter manipulation. To execute the prediction, the parameters are decrypted, and then parameter manipulation is detected by verifying the authentication tag. The proposed method encrypts all parameters by GCM in advance. In prediction, the parameters can be obtained by stopping decryption for each division unit based on the counter value, since GCM

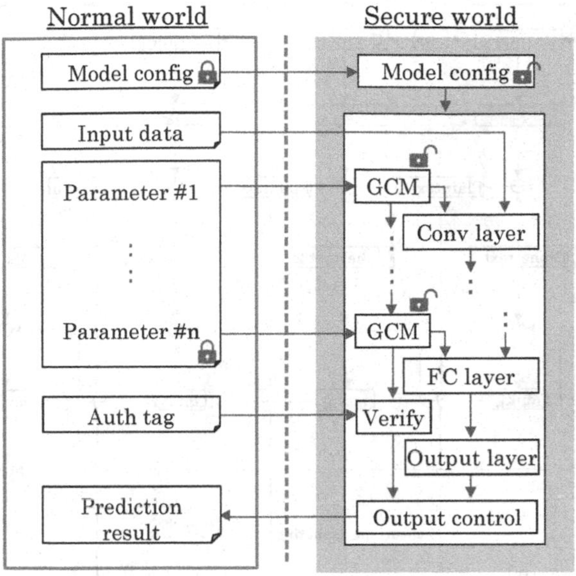

Fig. 4. Software architecture of the proposed method

encrypts them in counter mode. The decrypted parameters for each division unit can be deleted after the divided execution of prediction using them to save the memory for the next divided execution. This method reduces the runtime overhead for switching to the secure world because only the first pointer of the parameters stored in the shared memory is sent to the secure world. Note that the method needs to pad and encrypt the parameters according to the block size of a cipher used in GCM and the division unit so that the encrypted parameters can be decrypted according to the division unit.

3.4 Software Architecture

Figure 4 shows a software architecture of the proposed method. First, an encrypted model configuration is transferred to the secure world, and then it is decrypted and set in the secure world. The model configuration includes the model architecture such as the structure of a trained model and the parameter size. For example, it corresponds to a cfg file of Darknet framework [14]. Next, the pointers of input data, parameters, and an authentication tag in the shared memory are transferred to the secure world, and then the prediction is started. The proposed method executes GCM and prediction for a division unit in concurrent computing. The parameters of the division unit are decrypted, and a part of the authentication tag is calculated. The divided prediction is executed with the decrypted parameters. After the used parameters are removed from the memory in the secure world, the operations for the next division unit are

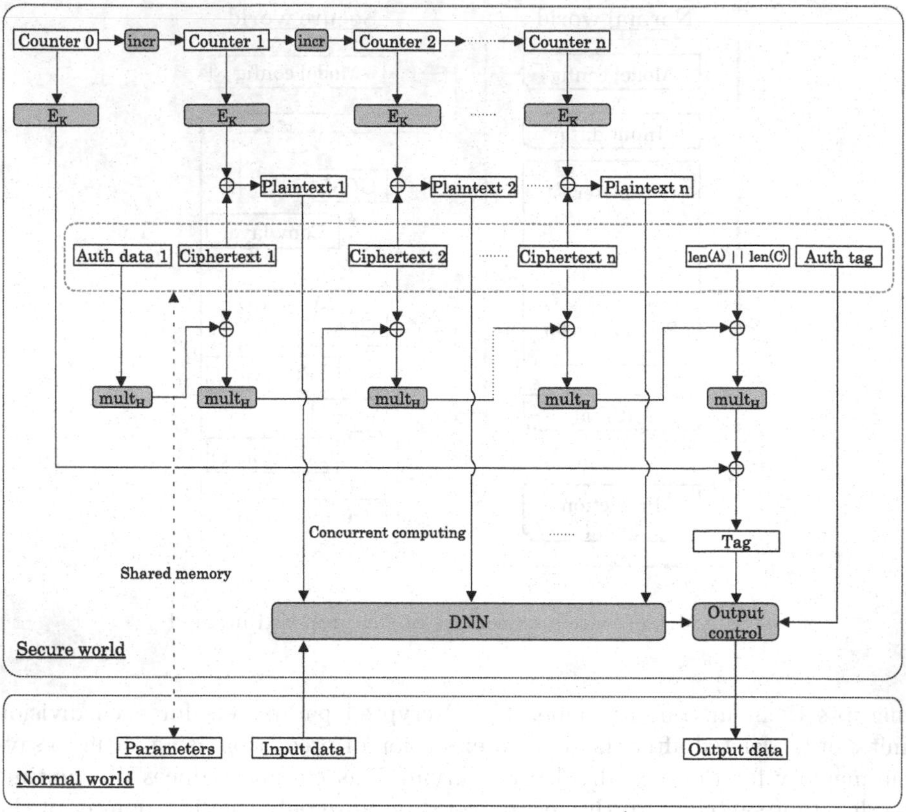

Fig. 5. Concurrent computing of prediction with deep learning and GCM decryption

executed in the same way. When an output layer is executed, the production of the authentication tag, which is partially executed for each division unit, is completed, so the parameter manipulation can be verified. Finally, the output of the prediction result to the normal world is controlled according to the verification result of the authentication tag. The proposed method enables to transfer of the encrypted input data to the secure world and decrypt it and execute prediction in the secure world, or to encrypt the prediction result in the secure world and transfer it to the normal world, depending on the use case.

Figure 5 shows the concurrent computing of prediction with deep learning and GCM decryption. The encrypted parameters (Ciphertext) are decrypted by GCM in the secure world, based on the counter value (Counter) according to each division unit. The decrypted parameters (Plaintext) are fed to the deep learning operation (DNN), and a part of the prediction is executed. Moreover, a part of the authentication tag (Tag) is calculated. These operations are executed for each division unit in concurrent computing. When the last parameters (Ciphertext n) are decrypted, the production of Tag is completed. Tag is compared

Table 1. Trained model information in the experiments

Trained model	Number of layers	Parameter size [kbyte]	Training dataset
LeNet	7	191.1	MNIST
VGG-7	7	274.5	Cifar10
Darknet(tiny)	16	3120.8	ImageNet

to the authentication tag associated with the ciphertext (Auth tag) to detect parameter manipulation. The prediction result (Output data) is transferred to the normal world after the verification with the authentication tag. When there is parameter manipulation, the prediction result should not be transferred to the normal world. A message of detecting parameter manipulation will be output.

4 Experiments and Evaluation

This section explains the experiments and evaluations of the proposed method. The method is evaluated in terms of memory saving and runtime overhead.

4.1 Experimental Setup

The experiments use a Raspberry Pi 3 Model B with Arm TrustZone (for Cortex-A architecture) and OP-TEE [13] to implement the proposed method. The available memory size of the secure world is 7 MB for a deep learning application in the experimental setup. In practice, the memory size left just for the loaded parameters would be less.

The experimental results are evaluated using three trained models. The models are implemented in C language using Darknet framework [14]. Table 1 summarizes the trained model information in the experiments. The three models are the LeNet model [15] for recognizing handwritten digit images in MNIST dataset [16], the VGG-7 model [17] for classifying object images in Cifar10 dataset [18], and the Darknet(tiny) model [14] for classifying object images in ImageNet dataset [19]. The parameter size of each model is 191.1 kbytes, 274.5 kbytes, and 3.1 MB, respectively.

The experimental results are compared using four execution methods based on the existing works. Figure 6 shows the compared execution methods in the experiments. The four methods are the execution of all layers in the normal world, which is no countermeasure, the execution of all layers in the secure world [4], the execution of layer-by-layer in the secure world [6, 10], and the proposed method.

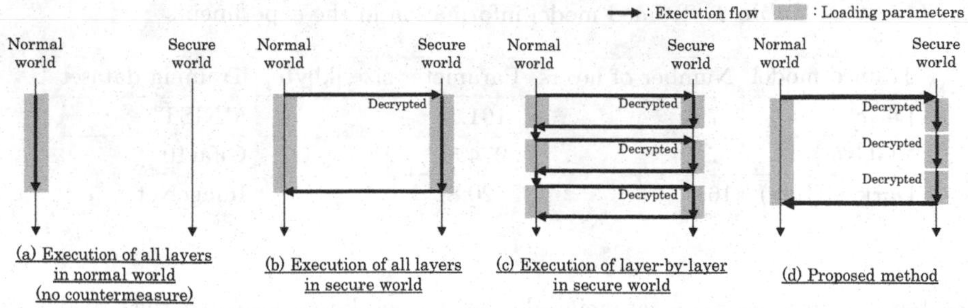

Fig. 6. Compared execution methods in the experiments

Table 2. Maximum size of loaded parameters and runtime among the methods

	All layers in normal world			All layers in secure world			Layer-by-layer in secure world			Proposed method		
	LeNet	VGG-7	Darknet	LeNet	VGG-7	Darknet	LeNet	VGG-7	Darknet	LeNet	VGG-7	Darknet
Max. size loaded param. of [kbytes]	191.1	274.5	3120.8	191.1	274.5	N/A	141.6	131.3	589.8	141.6	131.3	589.8
Runtime [*s*]												
Model setup	0.016	0.036	0.786	0.028	0.053	N/A	0.016	0.054	0.812	0.028	0.052	0.823
Prediction	0.016	0.178	0.941	0.026	0.206	N/A	3.073	5.803	29.906	0.229	0.499	1.411
Total	0.032	0.214	1.727	0.054	0.259	N/A	3.089	5.857	22.718	0.257	0.551	2.234

The experiments evaluate the proposed method in terms of the maximum size of loaded parameters, which is related to the memory saving, and the runtime, which is related to the overhead. The loaded parameters are encrypted in the cases of the three methods ((b)(c)(d) in Fig. 6) by using AES128-GCM of mbed TLS [20]. In other words, the methods include the decryption operation of the parameters. The execution of layer-by-layer in the secure world loads the parameter layer-by-layer. The division unit of the proposed method is also set layer-by-layer in the experiments. The runtime is measured separately for model setup and prediction.

4.2 Experimental Results

Table 2 shows the experimental results of the maximum size of loaded parameters and runtime among the four execution methods using the three trained models. The size of the loaded parameters is equal to the parameter size of the training model, in the case of the execution of all layers in the normal or secure world. The proposed method is compared with the other methods in Fig. 7 (the maximum size of loaded parameters) and Fig. 8 (the runtime). Note that the runtime in the experimental results is the average runtime of 10 samples, respectively.

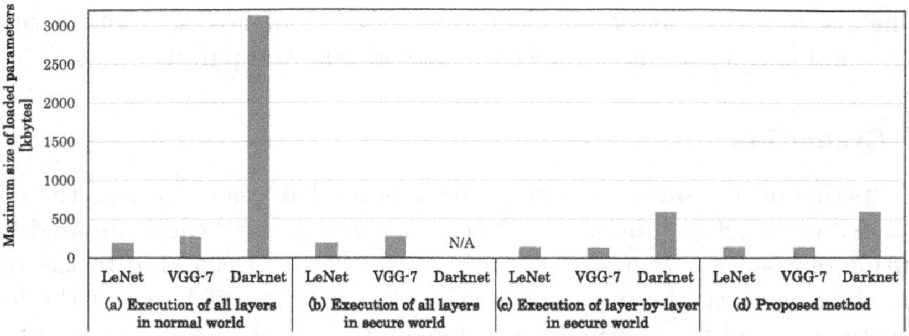

Fig. 7. Comparison of maximum size of loaded parameters among the methods

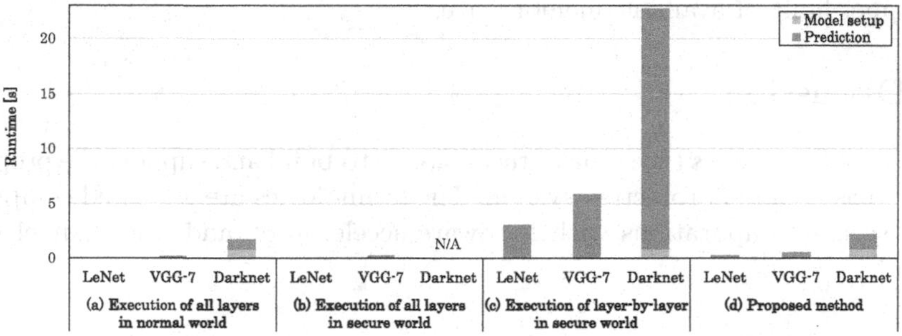

Fig. 8. Comparison of runtime among the methods

Maximum Size of Loaded Parameters. According to Fig. 7, the proposed method has the same results as the execution of layer-by-layer in the secure world. This is because the proposed method divides the loaded parameters layer-by-layer, the same as the exiting works [6,10]. Therefore, the maximum size of loaded parameters is equal to the parameter size of the layer with the largest size of the parameters in a trained model. Compared with the execution of all layers in the normal world, the proposed method cuts the size of loaded parameters by about one-fifth to one-half. It depends on the type of trained models because of the different parameter sizes in one layer. However, the Darknet model cannot be implemented by the execution of all layers in the secure world. This is due to the lack of memory in the secure world. The parameter size of the Darknet model is 3.1 MB to the available memory of 7 MB in the secure world. The available memory size left just for the loaded parameters is less than 7 MB.

Runtime. According to Fig. 8, the runtime of the proposed method is about one-tens compared with the runtime of layer-by-layer in the secure world [6,10]. Compared with the runtime of all layers in the normal world, the proposed method has a runtime overhead of about 2 to 10 times, depending on the type of trained models. Note that the execution of layer-by-layer and the proposed method have a disadvantage of the runtime because they require loading the parameters at every prediction. The execution of all layers in the normal or secure world can iteratively predict by only loading the parameters once.

4.3 Evaluation

The experimental results show that the proposed method reduces the size of the loaded parameters, and also reduces the runtime overhead compared to the execution of layer-by-layer in the secure world [6,10]. According to the results of the three models, the proposed method has a trade-off between the loaded parameter size and the runtime depending on the division unit. It is effective to set the division unit by considering the trade-off in the proposed method. For example, the division unit is set to the grouped multiple layers, depending on the upper limit of available memory size.

5 Discussion

This section discusses the security technologies to build and support the proposed method as a model protection system. The technologies are a trusted computing base, secure computations with hardware accelerators, and side-channel resistance.

5.1 Trusted Computing Base

It is necessary to guarantee the reliability of a platform applied to the proposed method including the TEE and OS, and the applications running on the platform. The proposed method protects trained model information and the execution of deep learning operations, however, the protection of the platform and application stored in storages goes beyond the proposed method. Therefore, it is necessary to verify the reliability of the platform and application by secure boot, trusted boot, or remote attestation. The verifications require security hardware such as secure memory as the root of trust (RoT). The proposed method also requires the RoT to protect a key used for GCM.

5.2 Secure Computations with Hardware Accelerators

In order to accelerate deep learning applications, hardware accelerators are used such as GPUs, FPGAs, or ASICs. This paper assumes that deep learning computations in the proposed method are executed on a CPU. When the proposed method outsources the deep learning computations to a hardware accelerator, it is necessary to consider the coordination between the TEE and the hardware accelerator. For example, the proposed method needs to control the access from the normal OS to the hardware accelerator, when the deep learning computations are executed with the hardware accelerator from the secure OS. In the NVIDIA Jetson embedded development board, the Google Trusty TEE [21] can be implemented as a TEE, however, there are no reports of secure deep learning computations with the TEE and the GPU acceleration [22].

5.3 Side-Channel Resistance

Even if trained model information is treated using TEEs, it has been reported that the information can be revealed by side-channel leaks such as memory access patterns, execution time, power consumption, or electromagnetic radiation. Tople et al. have reported that the prediction results of a deep learning application running on Intel SGX are leaked by the memory access patterns [23]. It is necessary to consider the countermeasure against side-channel leaks related to the trained model information in TEEs.

6 Related Works

This section introduces the related works pertaining to trained model protection. This paper splits up the related works into five groups: TEE-based schemes [4–10], homomorphic encryption schemes [24], multi-party computation schemes [25], watermark schemes [26], countermeasures against side-channel attacks [27]. This section provides an overview of each scheme; the TEE-based schemes are described in a separate subsection. Note that model extraction attacks [28], which extract trained model information from input/output data, are not covered in this paper because the attacks can not steal the model information itself. The attacks try to generate an alternative model with the equivalent property.

6.1 Model Protection Without TEEs

Homomorphic Encryption Schemes. The homomorphic encryption schemes execute deep learning computations while the input data is encrypted, and the prediction result is also encrypted [24]. Because the computation is executed while the data is encrypted, the computational cost is very high. Therefore, it is considered practical to apply the schemes to servers with high-performance computing resources. The schemes keep the input/output data secret, however, the trained model information itself such as the parameters is not protected basically. In addition, there are several limitations on the scale of the trained model and the type of activation function that can be applied depending on the homomorphic encryption algorithm.

Multi-party Computation Schemes. The multi-party computation schemes divide the input data and the trained model information among multiple parties (clients and servers) and communicate with them confidentially to execute deep learning computations [25]. In other words, the divided input/output data and trained model information are kept secret. The schemes have a lower computational cost than the homomorphic encryption schemes, however, the communication cost is high because the schemes require a lot of communications among the parties. Therefore, it is considered practical to apply the schemes to servers because the schemes need multiple trusted parties and online communication among parties.

Watermark Schemes. The watermark schemes embed watermark information into a trained model to detect unauthorized uses of the trained model [26]. The schemes are not countermeasures against the leaks of trained model information itself, however, the approach to detect whether the use of the trained models is unauthorized. To embed the watermark information into the trained model, several methods have been proposed to train a model for a specific output result according to input data [26]. There are several attacks against the schemes, to modify the stolen trained model by the techniques such as transfer learning or distillation to avoid the watermark. It is necessary for the schemes to evaluate the resistance to these attacks.

Countermeasures Against Side-Channel Attacks. The countermeasures against side-channel attacks have been proposed to prevent side-channel leaks of trained model information [27]. To prevent side-channel leaks depending on the parameters of a trained model, a countermeasure that adds random numbers to mask the computations with the parameters is proposed [27]. Since TEE-based schemes are countermeasures against software attacks in an isolated environment, a combination of both countermeasures is possible.

6.2 Model Protection with TEEs

Several technical reports describe using TEEs for model protection [29,30]. The existing works of TEE-based schemes have proposed several methods designed for cloud computing using Intel SGX [4–7]. Recently, several methods using Arm TrustZone have also been proposed for embedded devices [8–10]. This paper mainly focuses on embedded devices using Arm TrustZone. In Sect. 4, the proposed method is compared with the existing works related to Arm TrustZone for evaluation.

Intel SGX. Ohrimenko et al. propose a method to protect the execution of machine learning computations, including deep learning, by using Intel SGX for cloud computing [4]. The method decrypts encrypted input data in an isolated environment of Intel SGX, called an enclave, to generate a trained model. The trained model is output in encrypted form. The method also includes dummy memory accesses to prevent observing memory access patterns as side-channel leaks to reveal the trained model information by malicious software in the same cloud server. However, it cannot be applied to large-scale trained models due to the limitation of memory size in an enclave (128 MB).

Tramer et al. propose Slalom, which is a framework to verify the results of deep learning computations entrusted to an untrusted cloud server using Intel SGX on a trusted device [5]. Slalom entrusts the execution of linear computations, i.e., matrix multiplication with weights in deep learning, to an untrusted cloud server and verifies the results on an enclave of the trusted device using the Freivalds algorithm. The input data to the untrusted cloud server and the results from the server are kept secret by a stream cipher. Slalom can be applied to large-scale trained models, however, the trained model information such as the parameters is not protected.

Hanzlik et al. propose MLCapsule, which executes the commutations of each layer in deep learning on an enclave using Intel SGX [6]. MLCapsule can avoid the limitation of the memory size in the enclave because it divides the execution of deep learning computations layer-by-layer. Therefore, it can be applied to large-scale learned models. However, it has a runtime overhead because the execution environment is switched to execute layer-by-layer. In addition, the threat of differential attacks to reveal the parameters is pointed out because the intermediate data of each layer is outside the enclave [7]. The intermediate data is not encrypted.

Schlögl et al. propose eNNclave, which executes only computations of several layers in deep learning on an enclave and the other computations outside the enclave using Intel SGX [7]. The eNNclave divides the deep learning computations into two layers: the public layer is the computationally expensive first half of the layer, and the private layer is the second half of the layer, where features specific to the trained model. It mainly assumes transfer learning. The public layer is executed by hardware accelerators such as GPUs, while the private layer is executed by the enclave. It is debatable whether there are any problems in disclosing the parameters of the first half layer. It would not be secure that the first half layer is completely free of features specific to the trained model, and it depends on the trained model. In addition, it potentially becomes more vulnerable to other attacks such as adversarial example attacks. The model extraction attacks will only attack the latter layer, and the number of estimated parameters on the attack will be reduced. The attacks can easily extract the trained model information close to the original one.

Arm TrustZone. Bayerl et al. propose OMG, which protects the execution of deep learning computations using Arm TrustZone for embedded devices [8]. OMG utilizes the address space controller (TZASC) of the Arm TrustZone to create a temporary isolated environment (SANCTUARY) in a normal world to execute deep learning computations. Therefore, it can avoid the limitation of memory size in a secure world. However, the Arm Trusted Firmware and the OS need to be customized for OMG.

Mo et al. propose DarkneTZ, which executes each layer commutation of deep learning in the secure world [9]. DarkneTZ is similar to eNNclave, however, it selects the layers to execute in the secure world by calculating the privacy information of each layer against the model inversion attacks. It has the same issues as eNNclave. It is debatable whether there are any problems in disclosing the parameters of the several layers outside the secure world.

VanNostrand et al. propose a method that extends DarkneTZ and executes the commutations of each layer in deep learning on the secure world [10]. The method is similar to MLCapsule, and has the same issues. It has a runtime overhead because the execution environment is switched to execute layer-by-layer.

Table 3. Comparison of the proposed method and related works using TEEs

Method	Model parameter protection	Implementation	Lack of memory	Runtime overhead	Parameter manipulation
All layers in secure world [4]	Full layers	General TEE	✗	✓	✗
Layer-by-Layer in secure world [6,10]	Full layers	General TEE	✓	✗	✗
Partial layers in secure world [7,9]	Partial layers	General TEE	✓	✓	✗
Temporarily isolated environment [8]	Full layers	Specialized TEE	✓	✓	✗
Proposed method	Full layers	General TEE	✓	✓	✓

Note that the authors have not done the evaluation on devices yet, and the specific overhead is unknown in the paper.

Proposed Method. Table 3 summarizes the comparison of the proposed method and related works for model protection using TEEs in terms of three problems: lack of memory, runtime overhead, and parameter manipulation. The proposed method solves these problems by dividing the task composed of loading the parameters and executing GCM and prediction in concurrent computing. The execution of partial layers in a secure world [7,9] reduces the runtime overhead because of the execution of the other partial layers in a normal world. However, it requires attention to the threat such as model extraction attacks as well as parameter manipulation. The execution in a temporarily isolated environment [8] also requires the specific OS for the customized Arm Trusted Firmware.

7 Conclusion and Future Work

This paper proposes a model protection method using TEEs mainly to protect the deep learning models implemented in embedded devices. The porting the program of a trained model to a TEE simply does not work well, because of the limitation of the memory size in TEEs, the increase in runtime due to TEEs, and the threat of parameter manipulation. The features of the proposed method used to solve these problems are memory saving, a low runtime overhead, and the detection of parameter manipulation. The idea is to divide the loaded parameters and execute GCM and prediction in concurrent computing. In the experiments, the proposed method is compared with existing works using three types of trained models. The experimental results show that the proposed method reduces the memory size of the loaded parameters by about one-fifth to one-half, and also reduces the runtime overhead by about one-tens compared to the execution of layer-by-layer in the secure world [6,10]. The proposed method is effective by setting the division unit, considering the trade-off between the parameter size and the runtime. This paper discusses the security technologies to build and support the proposed method as a model protection system, such as a trusted computing base, secure computations with hardware accelerators, and side-channel resistance. The related works for model protection are summarized and compared with the proposed method.

In future work, the division unit of the proposed method will be expanded for the computation unit in a layer. In particular, the matrix multiplication of a convolutional layer such as im2col consumes a lot of memory. Therefore, it is necessary to save memory for the computations. The method will be also evaluated using the other types of trained models and the other authenticated encryption modes such as OCB (Offset Code Book) mode and on the other platforms. In particular, a recurrent neural network, which is different from the feed-forward neural networks featured in this paper, will be applied to the proposed method. Moreover, it will also be considered to use shared memory on the other platforms and cooperation with hardware accelerators.

Acknowledgments. This work was supported by JST-Mirai Program Grant Number JPMJMI19B6, Japan.

References

1. Szegedy, C., et al.: Intriguing properties of neural networks. arXiv:1312.6199 (2014)
2. Fredrikson, M., Jha, S., Ristenpart, T.: Model inversion attacks that exploit confidence information and basic countermeasures. In: Proceedings of the 22nd ACM SIGSAC Conference on Computer and Communications Security (CCS), pp. 1322–1333 (2015)
3. Isakov, M., Gadepally, V., Gettings, K., Kinsy, M.: Survey of attacks and defenses on edge-deployed neural networks. In: IEEE High Performance Extreme Computing Conference (HPEC), pp. 1–8 (2019)
4. Ohrimenko, O., et al.: Oblivious multi-party machine learning on trusted processors. In: Proceedings of the 25th USENIX Security Symposium, pp. 619–636 (2016)
5. Tramer, F., Boneh, D.: Slalom: fast, verifiable and private execution of neural networks in trusted hardware. In: International Conference on Learning Representations (ICML) (2019)
6. Hanzlik, L., et al.: MLCapsule: guarded offline deployment of machine learning as a service. arXiv:1808.00590 (2018)
7. Schlögl, A., Böhme, R.: eNNclave: offline inference with model confidentiality. In: Proceedings of the 13th ACM Workshop on Artificial Intelligence and Security (AISec), pp. 93–104 (2020)
8. Bayerl, S., et al.: Offline model guard: secure and private ML on mobile devices. In: Design, Automation & Test in Europe Conference & Exhibition (DATE), pp. 460–465 (2020)
9. Mo, F., et al.: DarkneTZ: towards model privacy at the edge using trusted execution environments. In: Proceedings of the 18th International Conference on Mobile Systems, Applications, and Services (MobiSys), pp. 161–174 (2020)
10. VanNostrand, P., Kyriazis, I., Cheng, M., Guo, T., Walls, R.: Confidential deep learning: executing proprietary models on untrusted devices. arXiv:1908.10730 (2019)
11. Amacher, J., Schiavoni, V.: On the performance of ARM TrustZone (practical experience report). In: IFIP International Conference on Distributed Applications and Interoperable Systems (DAIS), pp. 133–151 (2019)
12. Zhao, S., Zhang, Q., Qin, Y., Feng, W., Feng, D.: Minimal kernel: an operating system architecture for TEE to resist board level physical attacks. In: Proceedings of the 22nd International Symposium on Research in Attacks, Intrusions and Defenses (RAID) (2019)

13. Linaro OP-TEE. https://www.op-tee.org
14. Darknet: Open Source Neural Networks in C. https://pjreddie.com/darknet
15. LeCun, Y., Haffner, P., Bottou, L., Bengio, Y.: Object recognition with gradient-based learning. In: Shape, Contour and Grouping in Computer Vision. LNCS, vol. 1681, pp. 319–345. Springer, Heidelberg (1999). https://doi.org/10.1007/3-540-46805-6_19
16. LeCun, Y., Cortes, C.: MNIST handwritten digit database (2010)
17. Simonyan, K., Zisserman, A.: Very deep convolutional networks for large-scale image recognition. arXiv:1409.1556 (2014)
18. Krizhevsky, A.: Learning multiple layers of features from tiny images (2009)
19. Russakovsky, O., et al.: ImageNet large scale visual recognition challenge. Int. J. Comput. Vis. **115**(3), 211–252 (2015). https://doi.org/10.1007/s11263-015-0816-y
20. Mbed TLS. https://tls.mbed.org
21. Google Trusty TEE. https://source.android.google.cn/security/trusty
22. NVIDIA Jetson Linux Developer Guide 32.5 Release. https://docs.nvidia.com/jetson/l4t/index.html
23. Karan, G., Shruti, T., Shweta, S., Ranjita, B., Ramachandran, R.: Privado: practical and secure DNN inference with enclaves. arXiv:1810.00602 (2018)
24. Dowlin, N., Gilad-Bachrach, R., Laine, K., Lauter, K., Naehrig, M., Wernsing, J.: CryptoNets: applying neural networks to encrypted data with high throughput and accuracy. In: Proceedings of the 33rd International Conference on International Conference on Machine Learning (ICML), vol. 48, pp. 201–210 (2016)
25. Mohassel, P., Zhang, Y.: SecureML: a system for scalable privacy-preserving machine learning. In: IEEE Symposium on Security and Privacy (S&P), pp. 19–38 (2017)
26. Adi, Y., Baum, C., Cisse, M., Pinkas, B., Keshet, J.: Turning your weakness into a strength: watermarking deep neural networks by backdooring. In: Proceedings of the 27th USENIX Security Symposium, pp. 1615–1631 (2018)
27. Dubey, A., Cammarota, R., Aysu, A.: MaskedNet: the first hardware inference engine aiming power side-channel protection. arXiv:1910.13063 (2019)
28. Tramèr, F., Zhang, F., Juels, A., Reiter, M., Ristenpart, T.: Stealing machine learning models via prediction APIs. In: Proceedings of the 25th USENIX Conference on Security Symposium, pp. 601–618 (2016)
29. Huawei Technologies Co., Ltd.: Thinking ahead about AI security and privacy protection. In: Protecting Personal Data & Advancing Technology Capabilities (2019)
30. ETSI GR SAI 004: GROUP REPORT V1.1.1 Securing Artificial Intelligence (SAI); Problem Statement (2020)

AIoTS - Artificial Intelligence and Industrial IoT Security

Quantum Computing Threat Modelling on a Generic CPS Setup

Cher Chye Lee[1], Teik Guan Tan[1(✉)], Vishal Sharma[2], and Jianying Zhou[1]

[1] Singapore University of Technology and Design, Singapore, Singapore
teikguan_tan@mymail.sutd.edu.sg
[2] Queen's University Belfast, Belfast, NI, UK

Abstract. The threat of quantum computers is real and will require significant resources and time for classical systems and applications to prepare for the remedies against the threat. At the algorithm-level, the two most popular public-key cryptosystems, RSA and ECC, are vulnerable to quantum cryptanalysis using Shor's algorithm, while symmetric key and hash-based cryptosystems are weakened by Grover's algorithm. Less is understood at the implementation layer, where businesses, operations, and other considerations such as time, resources, know-how, and costs can affect the speed, safety, and availability of the applications under threat.

We carry out a landscape study of 20 better-known threat modelling methods and identify PASTA, when complemented with Attack Trees and STRIDE, as the most appropriate method to be used for evaluating quantum computing threats on existing systems. We then perform a PASTA threat modelling exercise on a generic Cyber-Physical System (CPS) to demonstrate its efficacy and report our findings. We also include mitigation strategies identified during the threat modelling exercise for CPS owners to adopt.

Keywords: Quantum computing · Threat modelling · Post-quantum cryptography · Cyber-physical systems

1 Introduction

Breakthroughs in quantum computing (QC) where the computational power of quantum computers exceed all possible classical computer systems are happening more regularly. In 2019, a team at Google demonstrated quantum supremacy by checking the validity of random samples [5] on their superconducting-based Sycamore 53-qubit quantum chip. More recently in 2020, a team in China also demonstrated quantum supremacy with Gaussian Boson sampling[44], this time using a photonics-based quantum setup. While these breakthroughs bring about potential advances in science and technology [31], it also threatens the security of classical computer systems. On a quantum computer, Shor's [35] algorithm can solve integer-factoring and discrete-logarithm problems in polynomial time which means that public key cryptosystems that are built on Rivest-Shamir-Adleman (RSA), Diffie-Hellman (DH), and Elliptic-Curve Cryptography (ECC)

J. Zhou et al. (Eds.): ACNS 2021 Workshops, LNCS 12809, pp. 171–190, 2021.
https://doi.org/10.1007/978-3-030-81645-2_11

algorithms are no longer secure, and can be crypt-analyzed easily. Another example is Grover's [14] algorithm, which on a quantum computer provides a quadratic speed-up in performing brute-force attacks against symmetric-key and hash-based cryptography. Applications that rely on cryptography to achieve confidentiality, integrity, authenticity and non-repudiation for their data, users and communication will need to use alternative mechanisms or have the security and trust eroded due to quantum computers. The National Institute of Standards and Technology (NIST) is currently running on a Post-Quantum Cryptography (PQC) contest [26] to standardize suitable quantum-resistant asymmetric key algorithms for key exchange and digital signatures and is expected to finalize the standard by 2024 [24].

The good news is that current quantum computers are not sufficiently powerful to run Shor's or Grover's algorithm on a large-enough scale. Shor's algorithm has been demonstrated up to a 7-qubit quantum computer [41] and none of the current-day noisy intermediate-state quantum computers (NISQ) [28] are fault-tolerant enough to beat classical computers at asymmetric key cryptanalysis. On the other hand, NIST mentions in 2016 [8] that by 2030 with a budget of $1 billion, a quantum computer could likely be built to break RSA-2048 keys. So how can organizations be sufficiently prepared to face the threat of quantum computers? The study by Arslan et al. [4] listed 4 areas that are all cryptography-specific. We intend to dive deeper and use threat modelling to find the answer.

The rationale to use threat modelling is logical. Organizations face circumstances and situations that can impact and cause harm to the organizations' own, other organizations' or even national assets, personnel, processes, mission, function, image or reputation. These circumstances or situations are potential violations of security are known as threats and are caused by threat sources [6]. Any environment where the system operates may have both known and unknown vulnerabilities or weaknesses and can be exploited by one or more threats causing a breach of the system's security processes or policy. As technology continually evolves (in the case of QC), new threats and even threat types emerge. NIST describes threat modelling as a risk assessment method that is used to model aspects of both offensive and defensive sides of a specific logical entity, which can be a system or an environment, an application or a host or even a piece of data or information [37]. Here, we have distinguished the difference between a threat, vulnerability and risk.

- *Threat.* The word "threat" has an extensive range of different meanings associated with it and it can be understood as people or person, event, weakness or vulnerability and in the context of cybersecurity, also as malware, criminal activity, and espionage. A threat can be described as an event or a development of events that are possible and harmful. Compared to danger which is more tangible and well-defined, a threat has a more uncertain evolution phase and has to be dealt with using risk management procedures. During the risk management process, threats are usually decomposed further to threat events and threat sources to give a more detailed picture of threats, their impact and

possible mitigation. In essence, a threat is an undesired event or something malicious that can happen to or through a system/product/service.
- *Vulnerability.* A vulnerability refers to any trust assumption that can be violated to exploit a system. It is a weakness in a system, process, individual, control, implementation, architecture or even organizational structure and external dependencies. These weaknesses can be exploited, and vulnerabilities revealed to provide attackers with the window of opportunity.
- *Risk.* A risk is uncertainty or insecurity affecting objectives. Risk causes a deviation from expected and can be positive, negative or both, although the word "risk" is often associated with being implicitly negative. A risk usually contains an evaluation of the likelihood and impact and it has a score based on these estimations [37]. In the case of Cyber-Physical system (CPS) and other critical infrastructure, there is an added safety risk to the human operators, system and environment that must be considered.

In this paper's context, the advent of quantum computers poses a *threat* to classical computing systems because adversaries can run Shor's algorithm [35] on quantum computers to exploit *vulnerabilities* in RSA/DH/ECC asymmetric key cryptography and, to a lesser extent, run Grover's algorithm [14] to carry out faster brute-force attacks on encrypted data, passwords, and hashes, thus rendering such cryptographic primitives inadequate to provide the necessary security primitives that the application requires. What is less known or unquantified is the potential extent of the threat and therefore the risks faced by present-day applications and data.

Highly operational systems such as CPS require to go through regular threat modelling exercises to update their design and/or processes to remain secure. But not all threat modelling methods (TMM) are suitable for evaluating and mitigating QC threats. Our paper attempts to complement the post-quantum cryptography (PQC) standardization efforts by NIST [24,26] by identifying an appropriate TMM that system owners can use in their preparation for the post-quantum computing era. Our contributions are:

- Performing a study of different threat modelling approaches and evaluating 20 TMMs to select PASTA, when complemented with Attack Trees and STRIDE, as the most appropriate TMM for evaluating QC threats for existing systems.
- Carrying out a threat modelling exercise using PASTA on a generic CPS set up to demonstrate its efficacy at evaluating QC threats, and providing the outputs of the exercise including mitigation strategies.

The rest of this paper is organized as follows. In Sect. 2, we perform a landscape study of different threat modelling approaches and methods to select an appropriate TMM for evaluating the QC threats. In Sect. 3, we carry out a threat modelling exercise using our selected method on a CPS setup to demonstrate its efficacy before concluding in Sect. 4.

2 Threat Modelling Landscape Study

Different threat modelling methodologies, frameworks, and tools have been developed. Some are more comprehensive than others; some have a higher abstraction level while some focus on one or a combination of a few domains with greater granularity. Different methods can be distinguished by the logical entity that is being modelled (data, software, system, service, product), the phase of the entity's lifecycle and the goal of the threat modelling. TMMs and tools can be consolidated with other methods and even risk management processes to create custom tools for special needs.

In selecting an appropriate TMM, it should be comprehensive enough to effectively communicate the relevant threats and risks to the management but should also have ample details for those responsible for mitigating the threat. Threat modelling is a continuous process against newer threats and matching it with the existing mitigation efforts. The key benefit from routine threat modelling is the precision of modelling results from the increased frequency in which newer data from the system is obtained, reviewed, and reported. We are mindful that as the evolving nature of QC still presents numerous facets of factors and considerations, it is unlikely to address all the QC threats by designing a perfect TMM. Instead, we start by identifying suitable threat modelling approaches that can be used, before narrowing them down to the most appropriate TMM for evaluating QC threats.

2.1 Threat Modelling Approaches

We describe the different (non-exclusive) approaches [36] and their suitability to analyzing the QC threat.

Asset-Centric Approach. An asset-oriented approach begins with the identification of critical assets and impacts or consequences towards them. Asset-centric modelling focuses on questions, such as what one's most valuable assets are and what can go wrong with them. A list of valuable assets is then cycled through, and each asset is considered one at a time. Threat scenarios that can have an impact on the asset are described and prioritized. Assets that have a supporting role or can be used as a secondary asset to harm primary assets should also be included [36]. In modelling for QC threats, we expect the effort to be large but the results to be comprehensive since the threat modelling exercise will cycle through each asset to evaluate the QC-specific vulnerability. **Relevance: High**.

Attacker-Centric or Threat-Centric Approach. In the attacker-centric approach, potential adversaries' intent, capabilities, resources, characteristics relationships and/or behaviour are consolidated as a type of threat model. Understanding what adversaries seek to achieve for their actions against a system, may give an organization more understanding and insight into the Tactics, Techniques, and Procedures (TTP) of these adversaries. Adversary behaviours can be organized using a cyber kill-chain model into a threat scenario or attack scenario. Threat sources and/or events are usually identified first, and threat scenarios and the developments of threats are described in more detail. Adversary characteristics and behaviours as well as intents and motivations are the key elements when identifying impacts [6]. Attacker-centric modelling focuses on questions, such as what the attacker wants and why as well as how attackers gain their objectives. In modelling for QC threats, this approach is efficient in narrowing down the scope as the QC threat posed by the cryptographic weakness is already known and the threat modelling effort can be targeted at identifying and mitigating negative outcomes. **Relevance: High**.

Software-Centric. Software-centric threat modelling is performed during the software design and development process to reduce vulnerabilities in the software [37]. Software-centric modelling focuses on questions, such as what the system is and how it works, as well as what can go wrong and how it can be used incorrectly or harmfully. Hence it is often requirements and vulnerability oriented. In software or system-centric modelling techniques, data flow diagrams are usually used to first model the system, data, and boundaries and then determine which threats are relevant to each component and trust boundary-crossing. In modelling for QC threats, this approach is useful mainly for developers since the vulnerabilities are well understood which allows the software to be designed and evaluated accurately. On the other hand, the unknown impact of QC threats may lead to a large number of overlapping threats being identified. **Relevance: Low**.

Data-Centric Approach. Data-centric threat modelling focuses on protecting types of data/ information within a system instead of hosts, operating systems or applications. The system and data of interest are identified and characterized and prioritised. The focus is on the characteristics of authorized locations for storing, transmitting, executing, inputting and outputting data within the system: data flows between authorized locations, security objectives and people and processes authorized to access the data [37]. In modelling for QC threats, this approach is efficient since a large proportion of the cryptographic implementation is meant for data protection. However, we are concerned that this focused approach may not be ideal for non-data-related considerations such as business-impact analysis. **Relevance: Medium**.

2.2 Risk Management

Risk management [40] is usually not a stand-alone threat modelling approach, but one that integrates risk considerations and processes into one or more of the approaches mentioned in Sect. 2.1. While it increases the overall effort in performing the threat modelling exercise, the outcome is a more comprehensive and complete picture, especially in threats where the resulting impact is not well defined or known. It also allows organizations to take on a more preventive posture when dealing with such threats. In modelling for QC threats, risk management extends the known QC threats into identified risk areas for application owners to calibrate and manage. It can help organizations assess, quantify and prioritize the various risk areas including business costs, probable losses, organizational preparedness, safety, etc., and embark on both technical and non-technical preventive and/or mitigation actions.

2.3 Threat Modelling Methods (TMM)

TMMs are used to create an abstraction of the system, profiles of potential attackers, including their goals and methods and producing a catalogue of potential threats that may arise. Some TMMs are typically used on their own while others are used in combination with others. We performed a landscape study that included a total of 20 different TMMs (see Table 1). The study includes all 12 TMMs studied by Shevchenko [33] and all 6 most popular TMMs listed by EC-Council [12].

In our study, we are looking for an asset-centric approach TMM that includes risk management techniques and can be complemented with a threat/data-centric approach to provide QC threat focus. This criterion is likely to yield the most appropriate TMM candidate for evaluating QC threats while balancing between completeness and efficiency.

2.4 Result of Study

PASTA [40], incorporating Attack Trees [32] and STRIDE [18], stands out as the TMM that is suitable for evaluating QC threats. The purpose of PASTA is to provide a process for simulating attacks to systems (even as a subset of just applications), analysing threats and mitigate the risks and impacts that these threats present to organizations. PASTA comprises a seven-stages process for modelling attacks and analysing threats to a particular system and environment. The objectives are curtailing risks and their associated impact on the organisation or business. Organisations or businesses can address the adequate level of countermeasures or risk mitigation measures to be deployed to mitigate the risk from threats and attacks by following this process. A description of the PASTA threat modelling method, along with Attack Trees and STRIDE, is found in Appendix A.

We chose PASTA over OCTAVE [7] due to the former's ability to incorporate attacker-centric and data-centric to its asset-centric approach. This allows the threat modelling exercise (see Sect. 3) to be more efficient in identifying and addressing the QC threats as compared to a generic threat modelling method. We chose PASTA over IDDIL/ATC [25] due to the former's availability of documentation and use-cases, and its ability to address risk at a strategic level.

Table 1. List of TMM studied on suitability for QC threat evaluation.

TMM	Approach	Risk	Pros	Cons	Suitability
ATT&CK [39]	Attacker		Indepth understanding of the adversary, useful for hunting new threats	Lacks focus on individual threats. Lacks operational impact analysis	No. Insufficient focus on QC threats
Attack trees[32]	Threat		Easy to use and can quickly map out threats	Does not consider business objectives and lacks operational impact analysis	Partial
CAPEC [27]	Attacker		Large searchable collection of known attack patterns	More suitable for penetration testing and less on understanding new threats	No. Much of QC threats and controls are still evolving
DREAD [20]	Attacker	✓	Relatively simple for a risk model	Incomplete risk modelling	Not considered. Deprecated
hTMM [21]	Attacker, Software	✓	Builds on SQUARE & Persona non Grata	Relatively new. Lacks documentation and use-cases	Not considered. Immature
IDDIL / ATC [25]	Asset, Data	✓	Comprehensive modelling methodology. Incorporates other TMMs	Lacking in available documentation as compared to other TMMs	Likely
Invincea [15]	Attacker		Process is made easier through gamification	Uses existing security products as controls	No. Much of QC threats and controls are still evolving
LINDDUN [10]	Data	✓	Strong focus on privacy threats	Lacking in available documentation as compared to other TMMs	Partial. Unclear if non-privacy related QC threats may be uncovered
NIST SP 800-154 [37]	Asset, Data		Easy to adopt	Highly dependent on collection of available references and known security controls	No. Much of QC threats and controls are still evolving
OCTAVE [7]	Asset	✓	Flexible methodology that incorporates security and operational risk considerations	Training and experience of team is important. Large effort needed	Likely
OWASP [42]	Attacker		Easy to adopt	Focused on threats on web-based platforms	No. Lacks non-web QC threats

(*continued*)

Table 1. (*continued*)

TMM	Approach	Risk	Pros	Cons	Suitability
PASTA [40]	Asset	✓	Comprehensive threat modelling at technical, operational, and business levels. Incorporates other TMMs	Large effort needed	Yes
Persona nonGrata [9]	Attacker		Easy to adopt	Lacks focus on individual threats. Lacks operational impact analysis	No. Insufficient focus on QC threats
Security Cards [11]	Attacker		Process is made easier through gamification	Inconsistent results as process relies on brainstorming	No. QC threats may not be well understood
SQUARE [22]	Software	✓	Proper security and risk considerations are built-in early	Mainly relevant during requirements and design phase	No. May not be suitable for existing systems
STRIDE [18]	Software, Data		Easy to learn and well-documented	Lacks analysis on different operational environments	Partial
Tara (Intel)[29]	Attacker		Easy to adopt by referencing Threat Agent Library	Highly dependent on completeness of library	No. Much of QC threats and controls are still evolving
TARA (Mitre) [43]	Asset, Threat	✓	Easy to adopt by scoring against known TTPs and CVS	Simplified risk modelling	Partial
Trike [30]	Asset	✓	Includes model for evaluating and prioritizing acceptable risk	Lacks documentation and use-cases	Not considered. Deprecated
VAST [3]	Attacker		Has an automated tool. Able to scale to large systems	Lacks open documentation	Not considered. Requires commercial license

3 QC Threat Modelling Exercise

We perform a threat modelling exercise using PASTA on a generic CPS set up as a walk-through on how QC threats can be identified, evaluated and mitigated.

3.1 Generic CPS Model

In [19], Lee described the CPS problem as the intersection between the cyber and physical problems and all three areas need to be examined and addressed separately. The environment we define in our model therefore comprises three parts, namely, physical environment, CPS and cyber IT, as shown in Fig. 1. The physical environment includes the external physical operations that control the inputs and manages the supply to the CPS. It includes several maintenance features that manage the external assets and the associated physical processes. The CPS layer is intermediate, and it involves the supervisory control system, the internal communication system which manages the sensors and controls the actuators. The operations of this layer are managed through command and control operations of the Programmable Logic Controller (PLCs) that use sensory data acquisition to take action based on the input as well as output from the sensors and actuators. Finally, the cyber IT environment involves parts supporting remote invocations and accessibility through the external communication network. This layer helps with the management of features of CPS allowing control over the cloud.

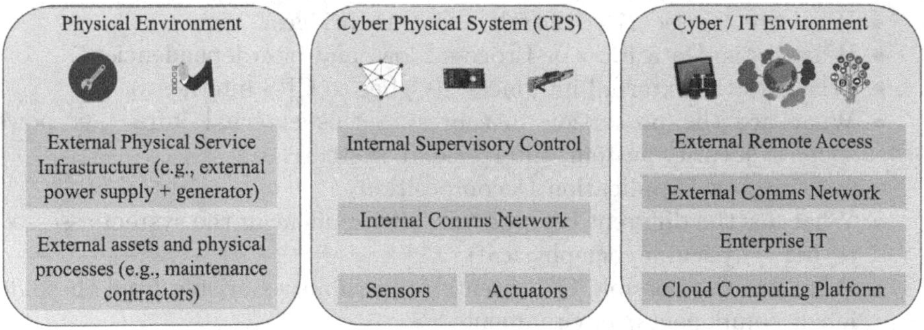

Fig. 1. An overview of a generic CPS model.

The security requirements for a CPS system extend beyond the traditional technical security requirements that govern a cyber IT system. The additional interface with the physical environment means that the security of the CPS system can impact the physical environment and vice versa. In NIST's "Guide to Industrial Control Systems (ICS) Security" [38], the health and safety of human lives as well as damage to the environment are identified security considerations that a CPS system, but not a cyber IT system, may face. Conversely, the CPS system is required to maintain its robustness and resilience [2] against possible events, such as weather hazards, acts of war, and power outage, that the physical environment may impact the safety and security of the CPS system.

In the rest of this section, we will only flesh out QC-related[1] threats and risks.

3.2 PASTA Stage 1 to 3

The first 3 PASTA stages require us to define the objectives, define the technical scope, and perform the decomposition of the system. The guiding questions we use at these stages are:

- Stage 1 - Define Objectives
  - What are the key business objectives?
  - What are the critical functions and assets that might be affected by a QC threat?
  - What are the system safety standards at risk?
  - How does the compromised system cause catastrophic or irreparable damages?
  - What are the risk tolerance levels concerning Confidentiality, Integrity, Availability and Authentication?
- Stage 2 - Define Technical Scope
  - What is the system architecture and the boundaries?
  - What are the security controls and draw bridges?
  - What is the Data Flow or Process Flow, and interdependencies?
  - What are the external interfaces? (Cyber to CPS interfaces)
  - What are the protection measures in this external infra (i.e. power sources, security system, enterprise IT system)?
- Stage 3 - System/Application Decomposition
  - What are the different components/environment in the system assessed? (cyber, physical, cyber-physical)
  - What are the possible QC threats/vulnerabilities arising from these different components/ environments?
  - Where are their entry points in a different environment?
  - Where are the "trusted environments/zones"?
  - What are the supply chain weakness in the system? (i.e. suppliers of a thumb drive, backup storage media, cloud enterprise system that needs transfer)

[1] For non-QC-related CPS threat modelling, the reader is invited to reference [1,13, 16,17].

Output. We reference a generic CPS model, as shown in Fig. 1. To evaluate QC threats, there are no changes to the boundaries of the technical environment and interdependencies between its infrastructure and application. Overall, the boundaries are depicted between the Physical environment, Cyber-Physical System (CPS) and the Cyber-IT environment. We next add on the objective that the critical systems and assets in the CPS can continue to operate safely and resiliently in the post-quantum era.

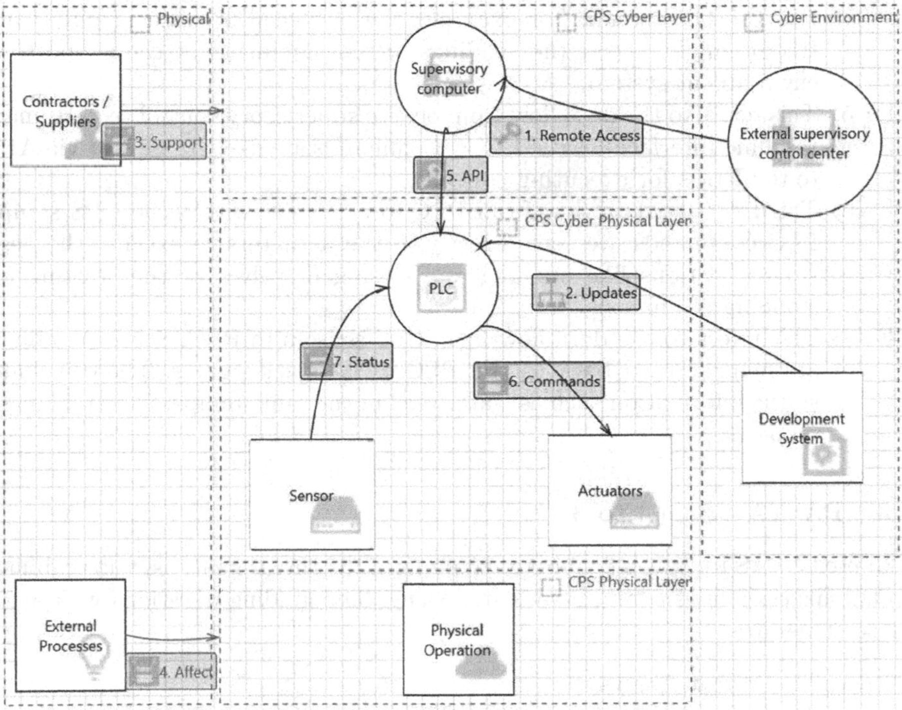

Fig. 2. Generic CPS setup with data flows identified.

We then divide the CPS boundary into the cyber layer, cyber-physical layer and physical layer, and identify seven major data flows (diagrammatically shown in Fig. 2) that could be affected by QC threats. These are:

DF#1: This refers to the data flow from an external supervisory control centre to the onsite supervisory control system via remote access. This allows a central body to remotely manage and monitor multiple CPS setups.

DF#2: This refers to the data flow from an external computing system (e.g. Enterprise IT or Cloud computing) via the external communication networks into the CPS setup. Updates and patches can be transmitted via this flow. Employees with access to the Enterprise IT or Cloud computing service might fall prey to social engineering and will in turn infect the CPS with transferred files, programs or malware.

DF#3: This refers to data flow from external assets and physical processes to the CPS setup. This can be in the form of external contractors conducting support and maintenance works on the CPS. For example, CPS patches handled by contractors via thumb drive, hard disk or vendor laptop will inevitably expose the CPS setup for exploits.

DF#4: This refers to data flow from external physical infrastructure providers into the CPS setup. For example, the electrical or water supply contractor might tweak the readings or measurements of the supporting environment system.

DF#5: This refers to the data flow from on-site supervisory control (e.g. Human Machine Interface) to the PLCs. Commands are likely to be sent via API to the PLCs for executing controls.

DF#6: This refers to data flow from PLC to actuators within the CPS setup. PLC commands are sent directly to the actuators to execute the designated actions like opening and closing of valves or the starting or stopping of pumps.

DF#7: This refers to the data flow from CPS sensors to PLC. Sensor readings are being routed back to the PLC as feedback signals. These include status information such as water level in the tank, temperature readings, or alerts.

3.3 PASTA Stage 4 to 6

The next 3 PASTA stages require us to perform the threat analysis, vulnerability and weakness analysis, and attack modelling. The guiding questions we use at these stages are:

- Stage 4 - Threat Analysis
  - What are the threats that the STRIDE model tells us?
  - How does the attack/hack take place? What are the probabilities of each of the attack vector?
  - What does the identified threats correlate with the severity and fix-ability of the threats from the available threat intelligence?
  - What is the analysed impact of these identified threats?
- Stage 5 - Vulnerability and Weakness Analysis
  - What are the available vulnerability and penetration testing reports?
  - Any recent audits or vulnerability scanning or penetration testing conducted?
  - Are there trends of certain vulnerabilities being exploited?
  - What are the false positives and false negatives trends?
  - What is the overall vulnerabilities score?
  - What is the security posture from vulnerabilities?

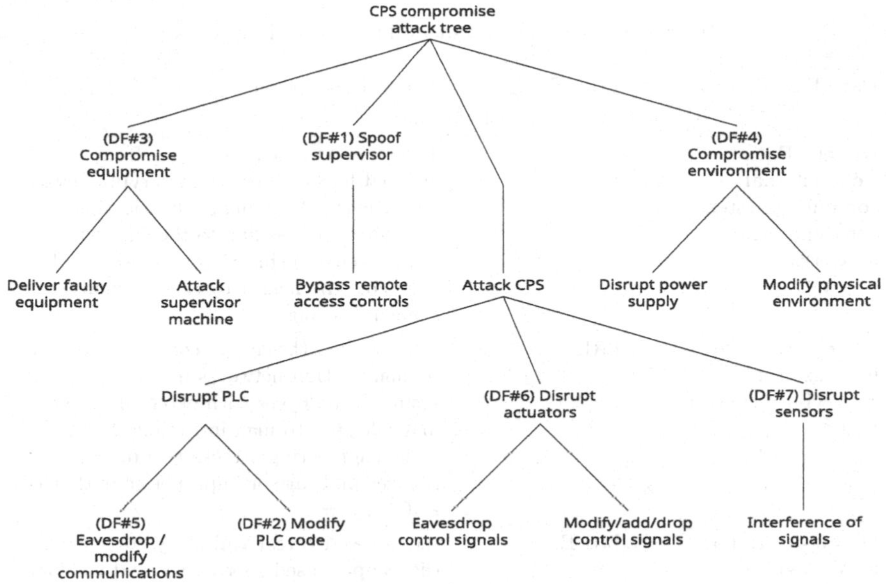

Fig. 3. Attack Tree for generic CPS setup when evaluating QC threats.

- Stage 6 - Attack Modelling
  - From the Attack Tree, for each application that uses public-key cryptography, how can Shor's algorithm be used to compromise the system? Can the algorithm be replaced with a PQC candidate algorithm [26]?
  - From the Attack Tree, for each application that uses symmetric key cryptography and hashing, how can Grover's algorithm be used to compromise the system? Can we increase the key size?
  - How are the vulnerabilities and attacks vector associated?
  - Are there attack vectors that have been made less effective with the vulnerabilities remediated?
  - Any vulnerabilities that could not be fixed?

Output. We use a combination of Attack Trees [32] (see Fig. 3) and STRIDE [18] to analyze the data flows to list out the threats in Table 2.

3.4 Stage 7 - Risk and Impact Analysis

This step requires the analysis of the business impact in both qualification and quantifiable terms. There is also a need to propose some countermeasures and residual risk mitigation measures. Lastly the need to identify and recommend some risk mitigation strategies for the system owners. The guiding questions we use at this stage are:

Table 2. STRIDE threat evaluation of data flows

Data Flow	STRIDE Property Affected	Threat Description
DF#1 - Data flow from external computing system and communication networks	STRI__	The assessed threat can come from external hackers performing cryptanalysis on the encryption and authentication for the remote access link to the supervisory control centre using Shor's algorithm. This will allow the hacker to view or modify the communications
DF#2 - Data flow from external supervisory control centre	STRI_E	The assessed threat can come via external communication networks into the CPS system. Employees with external access may fall prey to man-in-the-middle or social engineering attacks and in turn transfer malware or improper code that the PLC may use
DF#3 - Data flow from external environment controls	STRI_E	the assessed threat will likely come from the compromised contractors and vendors who turned against the CPS system owners. These contractors may be able to introduce exploits or malware that disrupt the internal CPS setup while supplying, maintaining and patching the CPS
DF#4 - Data flow from external physical infrastructure providers	ST____	Supply chain vendors can sabotage (deliberately or unintentionally) the electrical, water, temperature controls through the equipment they supply. The assessed threat is the vendor introducing errors in the parameters such as temperature, water, or even electrical level which affects the PLC's processing logic
DF#5 - Data flow from on-site supervisory control to PLC	ST_I__	The assessed threat is fake connections introduced by the malicious insider. Potentially, these staff, who turned rogue can view or modify the communications between the supervisory control system and the PLCs
DF#6 - Data flow from PLCs to actuators	ST_I__	The assessed threat is the malicious insider/staff who observe or modify the commands being sent to the actuator. This will potentially cause damage to the entire CPS such as overflow of water, or overheating or undercooling of equipment
DF#7 - Data flow from sensors to PLCs	ST_I__	The assessed threat is from a malicious insider who can view the sensor readings, deliberately tamper the sensor hardware or provide erroneous feedback to the programmable controller and supervisory control system

- What are the key business objectives and critical services that are affected?
- How else can the risk of safety be minimized? How resilient is the system to an unaddressed QC threat?
- What is the degraded mode of operations/ services?
- What mitigating / remediation measures are possible to counter the remaining threats?

Output. As the last step of PASTA, the broad mitigation strategies we identified for mitigating the threats brought about by QC are as follows:

1. *Strict Network Segregation.* Where algorithm replacement is not possible, this will ensure that the core CPS setup is separated from any external connectivity. This includes a clear delineation from Enterprise IT network and Cloud computing services. It will require that remote access to the supervisory control system to be terminated if the security measures cannot be strengthened to guard against QC threats. CPS should build an alert system to flag any illegitimate external connectivity or devices modification.
2. *Tight Supply Chain Controls.* Contractors and vendors will remain the weakest link in the entire ecosystem of the CPS. To prevent the unauthorised and unauthenticated actions by these contractors and vendors, there is a need for close monitoring and checks on the actions such as patching and system maintenance of the CPS setup.
3. *Internal Supervisory Controls and Monitoring.* To circumvent the malicious insider threat, procedural security clearance and monitoring need to be put in place. There must be a "check and balance" system to only allow authenticated actions by the staff and against any unsolicited actions.

4 Conclusion

In this work, we studied the different approaches for threat modelling to find the most appropriate TMM for evaluating QC threats. Although the cryptographic vulnerabilities exposed by QC on classical asymmetric and symmetric key cryptography is known, much of the potential impact from the threat of QC is still unknown and evolving. Hence, an asset-centric threat modelling approach with strong risk management, when complemented with a threat/data-centric approach to provide focus, is the criteria we used. We narrowed the field of 20 TMMs to find PASTA as the most appropriate TMM. We then carried out a threat modelling exercise using PASTA on a generic CPS setup to test its efficacy and showed the output of the threat modelling exercise. The effect of including risk management in the threat modelling exercise allows us to consider the possibility that some QC threats may not be completely addressable (due to constraints in time, resources, know-how, etc.) and hence adopt additional broad-based mitigation strategies.

Acknowledgement. This project is supported by the Ministry of Education, Singapore, under its MOE AcRF Tier 2 grant (MOE2018-T2-1-111).

Appendix A PASTA

PASTA, or Process for Attack Simulation and Threat Analysis, is developed by Tony UcedaVélez [40] in 2012 to merge business objectives and impact with technical requirements. It provides a hybrid risk and attacker (relying on Attack Trees, STRIDE and/or other methods) perspective to threat modelling and produces an output based on assets. PASTA focuses on understanding the effect on business and how to plan and implement effective countermeasures where the involvement of decision-makers and stakeholders are part of the process.

A.1 PASTA Threat Modelling Method

PASTA is first implemented at the system level, using high-level architecture. This initial round should allow for the effective definition of all inputs and outputs for each component of the system. Then, PASTA should be implemented recursively for each component. All findings from the high-level system architecture should be passed to the next level component as input. It is a seven-stage process where the objectives and scope are first defined, the system is described in its components, before the threat, vulnerability and risk analysis are done. The stages and activities within the stages are listed in Table 3.

A.2 Attack Trees Threat Modelling Method

Attack/threat trees was developed by Bruce Schneider [32] in 1999. It comprises diagrams depicting possible attacks on a system that spans out in a tree-like format, where the goal of an attack is akin to the root of the tree and the ways to achieve that goal are depicted as leaves of the tree, as seen in Fig. 4. Each separate tree represents a goal, and many aggregated trees form a "forest of attack trees. An attack tree can be formed for an exact use case or used together with existing and relevant attack trees to find threats. Each node of the attack tree is analysed on the issue that impacts the system, which is usually modelled with DFDs. Attack Trees is commonly used in combination with other TMMs.

In the Attack Tree example of a physical safe shown in Fig. 4, the goal of the attacker, i.e. an open safe, is first defined in the root node. The child nodes are then enumerated with the different actions or sub-goals that can lead to the goal, and their child nodes then list more detailed actions that may lead to the sub-goals. This process is repeated iteratively, and Attack Trees can be revisited after further studies or brainstorming sessions which can uncover other issues. Attack Trees require relatively less effort to model as it is a straightforward threat identification methodology. However, it does not consider factors like operating environment and operational/ business impact.

Table 3. 7 stages of the PASTA Threat Modelling Method [34,40]

PASTA stages	Threat Modelling Activities
#1-Define Objectives	Identify Business Objectives Identify Security & Compliance Requirements Business Impact Analysis
#2-Define Technical Scope	Capture the boundaries of the Technical Environment Capture Infrastructure | Application | Software Dependencies
#3-System/Application Decomposition	Identify Use Cases | Define App, Entry Points and Trust levels Identify Actors | Assets | Services | Roles | Data Sources Data Flow Diagramming (DFDs) | Trust Boundaries
#4-Threat Analysis	Probabilistic Attack Scenarios Analysis Regression Analysis on Security Events Threat Intelligence Correlation & Analytics
#5-Vulnerability & Weakness Analysis	Queries of Existing Vulnerabilities Reports & Issues Tracking Threats to Existing Vulnerability Mapping Using Threat Trees Design Flow Analysis Using Use & Abuse Cases Scorings | Enumerations
#6-Attack Modelling	Attack Surface Analysis Attack Tree Development | Attack Library Management Attack to Vulnerability & Exploit Analysis using Attack Trees (see Appendix A.2) and STRIDE (see Appendix A.3)
#7-Risk & Impact Analysis	Qualify & Quantify Business Impact Countermeasure Identification & Residual Risk Mitigation Measures Identify Risk Mitigation Strategies

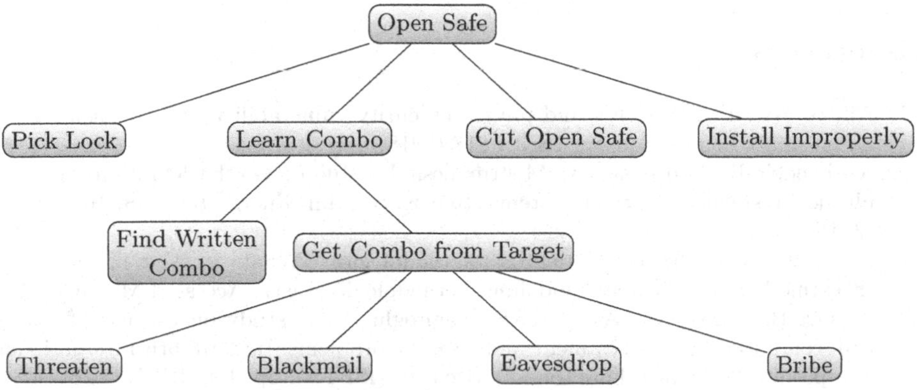

Fig. 4. Attack Tree example of a physical safe [32]

A.3 STRIDE Threat Modelling Method

STRIDE, short for "Spoofing, Tampering, Repudiation, Information Disclosure, Denial of Service and Elevation of Privilege", is a mnemonic that lists the six threats (described in Table 4) that can happen when a security property is violated. It is by far the most mature and well-understood TMM created by Loren Kohnfelder and Praerit Garg in 1999.

Table 4. STRIDE explained [36]

Threats	Property violated	Threat description
Spoofing	Authentication	Pretending to the something or someone other than yourself
Tampering	Integrity	Making changes to something that should not be modified
Repudiation	Non-repudiation	Claiming you did not do something, or were not responsible
Information Disclosure	Confidentiality	Providing information to someone not authorized to see it
Denial of Service	Availability	Preventing system to provide service by exhausting resources
Elevation of Privilege	Authorization	Allowing someone to do something they are not authorized to do

It starts by representing the system under evaluation using data flow diagrams (DFD) and identifying the entities, interfaces, boundaries and event flow. Using the DFD, every possible threat can then be enumerated and evaluated based on its vulnerability to the six properties of STRIDE. Microsoft has made available a STRIDE threat modelling tool available for download [23].

References

1. Ali, B., Awad, A.I.: Cyber and physical security vulnerability assessment for IoT-based smart homes. Sensors **18**(3), 817 (2018)
2. Arghandeh, R., Von Meier, A., Mehrmanesh, L., Mili, L.: On the definition of cyber-physical resilience in power systems. Renew. Sustain. Energy Rev. **58**, 1060–1069 (2016)
3. Arguwal, A.: Threat Modeling Methodologies: What is VAST? https://threatmodeler.com/threat-modeling-methodologies-vast/. Accessed March 2021
4. Arslan, B., Ulker, M., Akleylek, S., Sagiroglu, S.: A study on the use of quantum computers, risk assessment and security problems. In: 2018 6th International Symposium on Digital Forensic and Security (ISDFS), pp. 1–6. IEEE (2018)
5. Arute, F., et al.: Quantum supremacy using a programmable superconducting processor. Nature **574**(7779), 505–510 (2019)

6. Blank, R.M.: Guide for conducting risk assessments (2011)
7. Caralli, R.A., Stevens, J.F., Young, L.R., Wilson, W.R.: Introducing OCTAVE allegro: improving the information security risk assessment process. Technical report, Carnegie Mellon University, Pittsburgh, PA. Software Engineering Institute (2007)
8. Chen, L., et al.: NISTIR 8105 draft-report on post-quantum cryptography. Information Technology Laboratory Computer Security Resource Center (2016)
9. Cleland-Huang, J.: How well do you know your personae non gratae? IEEE Softw. **31**(4), 28–31 (2014)
10. Deng, M., Wuyts, K., Scandariato, R., Preneel, B., Joosen, W.: A privacy threat analysis framework: supporting the elicitation and fulfillment of privacy requirements. Requirements Eng. **16**(1), 3–32 (2011). https://doi.org/10.1007/s00766-010-0115-7
11. Denning, T., Friedman, B., Kohno, T.: The security cards: A security threat brainstorming toolkit. University of Washington (2013). http://securitycards.cs.washington.edu/
12. EC-Council: 6 of the most popular threat modelling methodologies (2020). https://blog.eccouncil.org/6-of-the-most-popular-threat-modeling-methodologies/. Accessed March 2021
13. Fernandez, E.B.: Threat modeling in cyber-physical systems. In: 2016 IEEE 14th International Conference on Dependable, Autonomic and Secure Computing, 14th International Conference on Pervasive Intelligence and Computing, 2nd International Conference on Big Data Intelligence and Computing and Cyber Science and Technology Congress (DASC/PiCom/DataCom/CyberSciTech), pp. 448–453. IEEE (2016)
14. Grover, L.K.: Quantum mechanics helps in searching for a needle in a haystack. Phys. Rev. Lett. **79**(2), 325 (1997)
15. invincea: Know Your Adversary: An Adversary Model for Mastering Cyber-Defense Strategies (2015). https://www.ten-inc.com/presentations/invincea1.pdf. Accessed March 2021
16. Islam, M.M., Lautenbach, A., Sandberg, C., Olovsson, T.: A risk assessment framework for automotive embedded systems. In: Proceedings of the 2nd ACM International Workshop on Cyber-Physical System Security, pp. 3–14 (2016)
17. Khan, R., McLaughlin, K., Laverty, D., Sezer, S.: Stride-based threat modeling for cyber-physical systems. In: 2017 IEEE PES Innovative Smart Grid Technologies Conference Europe (ISGT-Europe), pp. 1–6. IEEE (2017)
18. Kohnfelder, L., Garg, P.: The threats to our products (1999). https://adam.shostack.org/microsoft/The-Threats-To-Our-Products.docx. Accessed March 2021
19. Lee, E.A.: Cps foundations. In: Design Automation Conference, pp. 737–742. IEEE (2010)
20. Mackman, A., Dunner, M., Vasireddy, S., Escamilla, R., Murukan, A.: Improving web application security: threats and countermeasures. Microsoft, Redmond, WA (2003)
21. Mead, N.R., Shull, F., Vemuru, K., Villadsen, O.: A hybrid threat modeling method. Carnegie Mellon University-Software Engineering Institute-Technical Report-CMU/SEI-2018-TN-002 (2018)
22. Mead, N.R., Stehney, T.: Security quality requirements engineering (square) methodology. ACM SIGSOFT Softw. Eng. Notes **30**(4), 1–7 (2005)
23. Microsoft: Microsoft threat modeling tool 2016 (2016). https://www.microsoft.com/en-sg/download/details.aspx?id=49168. Accessed March 2021

24. Moody, D.: NIST PQC Standardization Update - Round 2 and Beyond (2020). https://csrc.nist.gov/CSRC/media/Presentations/pqc-update-round-2-and-beyond/images-media/pqcrypto-sept2020-moody.pdf. Accessed March 2021
25. Muckin, M., Fitch, S.C.: A threat-driven approach to cyber security: Methodologies, practices and tools to enable a functionally integrated cyber security organization (2017). https://www.lockheedmartin.com/content/dam/lockheed-martin/rms/documents/cyber/LM-White-Paper-Threat-Driven-Approach.pdf. Accessed March 2021
26. NIST: Post-Quantum Cryptography: Round 3 Submissions (2019). https://csrc.nist.gov/projects/post-quantum-cryptography/round-3-submissions. Accessed March 2021
27. numerous: Common Attack Pattern Enumeration and Classification (CAPEC). https://capec.mitre.org/. Accessed March 2021
28. Preskill, J.: Quantum computing in the NISQ era and beyond. Quantum **2**, 79 (2018)
29. Rosenquist, M.: Prioritizing information security risks with threat agent risk assessment. Intel Corporation White Paper (2009)
30. Saitta, P., Larcom, B., Eddington, M.: Trike v. 1 methodology document [draft] (2005). https://www.octotrike.org/papers/Trike_v1_Methodology_Document-draft.pdf. Accessed March 2021
31. Savage, N.: Google's Quantum Computer Achieves Chemistry Milestone (2020). https://www.scientificamerican.com/article/googles-quantum-computer-achieves-chemistry-milestone/. Accessed March 2021
32. Schneier, B.: Attack trees. Dr. Dobb's J. **24**(12), 21–29 (1999)
33. Shevchenko, N.: Threat Modeling: 12 Available Methods (2018). https://insights.sei.cmu.edu/sei_blog/2018/12/threat-modeling-12-available-methods.html. Accessed March 2021
34. Shevchenko, N., Chick, T.A., O'Riordan, P., Scanlon, T.P., Woody, C.: Threat modeling: a summary of available methods. Technical report, Carnegie Mellon University Software Engineering Institute Pittsburgh United ... (2018)
35. Shor, P.W.: Polynomial-time algorithms for prime factorization and discrete logarithms on a quantum computer. SIAM Rev. **41**(2), 303–332 (1999)
36. Shostack, A.: Threat Modeling: Designing for Security. Wiley, Hoboken (2014)
37. Souppaya, M., Scarfone, K.: Guide to data-centric system threat modeling. Technical report, National Institute of Standards and Technology (2016)
38. Stouffer, K., Falco, J., Scarfone, K.: Guide to industrial control systems (ICS) security. NIST Special Publication 800(82), 16 (2011)
39. Strom, B.E., Applebaum, A., Miller, D.P., Nickels, K.C., Pennington, A.G., Thomas, C.B.: MITRE ATT&CK: design and philosophy. Technical report (2018)
40. UcedaVélez, T.: Threat modeling w/pasta: risk centric threat modeling case studies. Technical report, Open Web Application Security Project (OWASP) (2017)
41. Vandersypen, L.M., Steffen, M., Breyta, G., Yannoni, C.S., Sherwood, M.H., Chuang, I.L.: Experimental realization of Shor's quantum factoring algorithm using nuclear magnetic resonance. Nature **414**(6866), 883–887 (2001)
42. Watson, C., Zaw, T.: OWASP automated threat handbook web applications. Technical report, OWASP (2018)
43. Wynn, J., et al.: Threat assessment & remediation analysis (TARA): methodology description version 1.0. Technical report, MITRE Corp., Bedford, MA (2011)
44. Zhong, H.S., et al.: Quantum computational advantage using photons. Science **370**, 1460–1463 (2020)

Cyber-Attack Case Studies on Dynamic Voltage Restorer in Smart Grid

Muhammad M. Roomi[1(✉)], Daisuke Mashima[1], Nandhakumar Kandasamy[2], and Partha P. Biswas[1]

[1] Illinois at Singapore Pte Ltd., Singapore, Singapore
{roomi.s,daisuke.m,partha.b}@adsc-create.edu.sg
[2] iTrust, Singapore University of Technology and Design, Singapore, Singapore
nandha001@e.ntu.edu.sg

Abstract. Distributed energy resources (DER) like solar panels, wind turbine, fuel cells, and batteries have revolutionized the traditional power grid by enhancing the resiliency, flexibility and efficiency of electricity services, and are increasingly integrated into the distribution system of power grids. In order to maintain stability in the distribution system, the Dynamic Voltage Restorer (DVR) is considered to be an efficient and cost-effective solution for the stable operation of DER. DER systems require continuous monitoring and control and thus require integration with Industrial IoT (IIoT) technology, which subsequently renders them susceptible to cyber-attacks. Like typical IoT settings, these resources often lack the capability for the implementation of state-of-the-art cyber security technologies (e.g., cryptographic protection), and consequently may be compromised by cyber-attackers affecting power grid operation. Furthermore, DVRs are geographically distributed and span over multiple management domains, which expands the potential attack surface. Once the attack is mounted against DVRs, the possible consequences include the damage of equipment and furthermore, in the worst case, power outage. Nevertheless, the significance and potential impacts of such attacks against DVRs on the power grid stability have not been extensively studied. In this paper, we explained the attacks targeting DVRs through a simulated study to highlight the necessity of cyber security measures in power grids.

Keywords: Smart grid · Distributed energy resources · Dynamic Voltage Restorer · Cyber-attack

1 Introduction

Power system is a critical infrastructure, and its physical and cyber vulnerabilities have to be addressed in order to avoid negative impact on power quality. Power quality refers to the ability of an electrical equipment to consume the energy supplied to it. Physical vulnerabilities can be caused by factors that affect the power quality. A disturbance in the power quality arises when there is

J. Zhou et al. (Eds.): ACNS 2021 Workshops, LNCS 12809, pp. 191–208, 2021.
https://doi.org/10.1007/978-3-030-81645-2_12

a deviation in the voltage or current waveforms from the ideal sine waveform [1]. These disturbances may occur due to the sudden change in load, failure of an equipment or faults due to external events. These incidents may happen at any of the transmission or distribution levels in power system. The major problems associated with the disturbance include voltage sag, voltage swell, voltage imbalance, voltage fluctuations, harmonic distortion, etc., and all these affect the stability of the system.

In order to enhance the controllability and stability of the transmission system, Flexible AC Transmission System (FACTS) is used [2]. FACTS generally comprises of power electronic and power system devices and is used in the high voltage side of the power network. A FACTS device utilizes inductive and capacitive elements to maximize the power transfer capability in the transmission system. The FACTS control devices can be classified based on the connection type in the system to achieve stability and maximum transfer capability. The types of FACTS controllers are: (1) Series Controllers, (2) Shunt Controllers, (3) Shunt-Series Controllers, and (4) Series-Series Controllers. The principle of operation for these types of devices is briefly provided herein:

- Series Controllers – this introduces voltage in series with the line by supplying/consuming reactive power (the sine wave of injected voltage must follow the sine wave of line voltage).
- Shunt Controllers – this introduces current in series with the line (the sine wave of current must follow the sine wave of line voltage).
- Shunt-Series Controllers – this introduces current and voltage through shunt and series controllers, respectively.
- Series-Series Controllers – combination of controllers to inject voltage in the line to provide series compensation.

Similar to the transmission system, the stability problem in the distribution system also needs to be addressed. There are two common solutions to alleviate the power quality problems in the distribution system. One solution is to ensure that the electrical equipment is less sensitive to disturbances and the other is to introduce additional power devices to counteract the disturbances [3]:

- Uninterruptible Power Supply (UPS) – provides backup power when the supply fails, or voltage drops to an unacceptable level.
- Dynamic Voltage Restorer (DVR) – corrects the voltage fluctuations and protects sensitive loads.
- Solid-State Transfer Switch (SSTS) – transfer the sensitive load from a faulty feeder to a healthy feeder.

These are the three common power devices that are considered as appropriate solutions to address the voltage swell, sag and fluctuations in the distribution system. Among these three, DVR is rated to be the most cost-effective solution [4]. Therefore, DVR has been increasingly implemented with information and communication technologies (ICT) in the distribution system. However, addressing only the physical vulnerabilities is insufficient for the modernized power grids.

Digital controllers and programmable logic controllers are increasingly utilized at both transmission-level and distribution-level power grid system to enable remote monitoring and automated control. This is particularly the case when distributed energy resources (DERs) are heavily integrated and their generation (or charging in case of battery storage system) status must be measured in real-time to maintain the stability of the grid [5]. Moreover, they are often communicating via public or wireless communication channels, which are prone to cyber-attacks. In particular, in order to manage increasingly-installed DERs, such as solar panels, wind turbines, and batteries, in the distribution system, dependency on ICT (information and communication technologies) used by the transmission and distribution level devices to communicate among themselves are prone to cyber-attacks [6]. Therefore, the need for addressing the cyber vulnerabilities arises.

Numerous cyber-attacks that compromised the security of the power system had been reported. Some notable targets of cyber-attacks were sewage control systems (Australia, 2000) [7], Devise-Besse nuclear power (U.S., 2003) [8], Natanz nuclear facility (Iran, 2010) [9], and energy distribution (Ukraine, 2015) [10]. The attacks primarily involved false data injection (FDI), data integrity attacks, attacks on automatic generation control loop, and coordinated switching [11,12]. These attacks targeted the communication between the control center, measurement unit, and field operation.

The indispensability of such studies is further reinforced by the recent trend of increased integration of DER with the distribution system. These devices are integrated with traditional grids through smart inverters, which provide the fault ride-through and VAR support to the resources. DER Energy management systems are employed to manage a set of DER systems via WAN/LAN [13,14]. An attack on DER might affect many devices and the impact depends on the size of the DER and the number of DERs connected in operation. National Electric Sector Cybersecurity Organization Resource (NESCOR) has enumerated many potential cyber security scenarios such as invalid command from DER supervisory control and data acquisition (SCADA), DER malfunction due to FDI, wireless connection exposing DER to adversary, and malware attacks [15]. With widespread adoption of DER, coordinated and targeted attacks on DER systems are highly possible. Targeted attacks may severely impact the operation of power grid and would lead to cascading blackouts [16,17]. Similarly, coordinated attacks may target multiple DERs and cause blackouts. Several research studies examining the relation between PV integration and grid stability [18–21] have been conducted.

Different research studies have been conducted to analyse the vulnerabilities of cyber-attacks on FACTS devices [22–24] in the transmission system. However, limited research has focused on the impact of cyber-attacks against devices in the distribution system. With the motive of contributing further insights into potential cyber-attacks on distribution system, this paper aims at examining the security of voltage compensation devices, namely DVRs, that are integrated with DER based power systems, and to our knowledge, no study has been conducted into the security of such devices. In order to fill this gap, this study focuses on the cyber-attacks targeting the compensation device (DVR) in the distribution system. Identification of the potential attack vector and the manipulation of the DVR output is the primary motivation of this study for demonstrating directions for future research.

The paper is structured as follows: Sect. 2 briefly explains the configuration, placement and applications of DVR. Section 3 discusses the cyber-aspects of the DVR. The simulation results of different case studies are present in Sect. 4. Finally, the conclusion is presented in Sect. 5.

2 Dynamic Voltage Restorer

Dynamic Voltage Restorer (DVR) is a voltage compensating device connected between the source and the load. The basic operation of a DVR is illustrated in Fig. 1. In Fig. 1, voltage disruptions in the utility is introduced. DVR remains in a dormant mode until it detects a change in the utility voltage. When voltage fluctuation is sensed, DVR activates and injects/absorbs the required voltage. Therefore, the load voltage does not get affected with the disturbance in the utility voltage. Numerous research studies discussed the methods for voltage injection (e.g., [25]). The methods of injecting voltage by the DVR is not the focus of this study. However, readers may refer to [26,27] for further insights into the DVR operation.

2.1 DVR Configuration

DVR requires a DC-link voltage for injecting the required voltage and restoring the supply voltage. This voltage is utilized by the voltage source converter [28–31] to generate the three-phase AC voltage. Subsequently, the switching harmonics in the generated AC voltage is removed by the filters, which is a combination

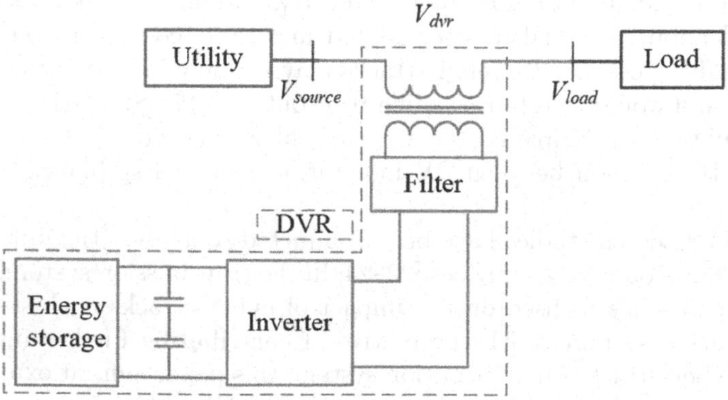

Fig. 1. Topology of DVR.

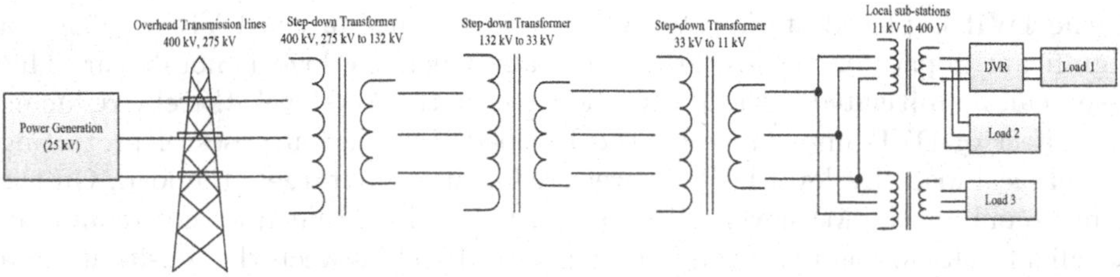

(a) Low-Voltage distribution

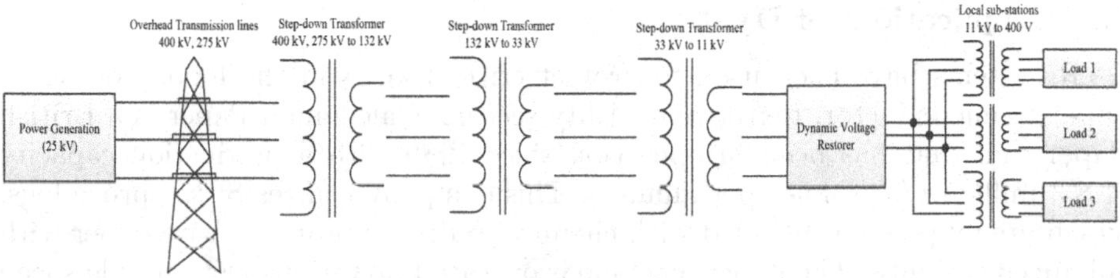

(b) Medium-Voltage distribution

Fig. 2. Location of DVR.

of inductors and capacitors. The voltage is then injected into the supply voltage through the injection transformer. The filters can be placed either on the primary or secondary side of the transformer. Furthermore, DVR includes bypass equipment for protection during disturbances. Therefore, the DVR provides protection to sensitive loads during voltage fluctuations and self-isolates during faults. The input to the DVR is either from an energy storage device or a rectifier. Some limitations of these inputs include, finite capacity of storage and the impracticality of remotely operating DVR with a rectifier. These issues can be addressed by integrating Distributed Generation (DG) with DVR. The wide range in the capacity of a DG (from a fraction of kW to a few MW) and the possibility of its remote placement makes DER an effective solution as input to DVR.

2.2 DVR Location

Unlike FACTS that is used in the transmission system, DVR is primarily implemented in the distribution system. Therefore, the DVR has to be placed either at a Medium Voltage (MV) distribution level or at a Low Voltage (LV) distribution level. In the LV-level, the DVR is placed near a critical load, thereby protecting only the critical load from disruptions. In the MV-level, DVR provides protection to a set of loads from disturbances. Figures 2a and 2b illustrate the placement of DVR in the LV- and MV-level, respectively. The placement of DVR at different voltage levels accrues varying advantages and disadvantages.

If the DVR is placed at the LV-level, the impedance in the DVR may have a significant impact on the LV load, especially when the load is non-linear. This issue can be mitigated if the DVR is located at the MV-level, thereby reducing the effect of DVR impedance on the LV load. For the purposes of protecting the critical load, LV-level DVR is preferred as it solely targets the load. On the other hand, at the MV-level, DVR may act on a load that does not require an excellent voltage quality. Therefore, it is a trade-off between the sensitivity of a single load and the level of protection required for the group of loads.

2.3 Applications of DVR

DVR systems have been used to protect critical loads in the food processing, paper, semiconductor, textile and utility sectors. Caledonian Paper is a British Paper mill that has been in operation since 1989 with a production capacity of 8.3 million t/a (tonnes per annum). This company utilizes Sitka spruce logs, which are pulped and blended with chemical pulp to produce a base paper with enhanced strength. The paper machine is operated by various DC variable speed drives. The paper producing machines are vulnerable to voltage fluctuations which may affect the precision of the production process. The interruptions in the machine operation due to voltage fluctuations may also affect other machines, such as coaters, super-calendars, and auxiliary equipment. Though the level of impact can vary, the interruption can result in huge losses. In order to address these problems, a fast reacting device such a DVR is implemented to avoid interruptions and to maintain the system stability. The case study can be found in [32]. Similarly, DVRs are used in utility sectors to protect sensitive loads. It is installed in 25 kV North American utility system to protect a 600 kVA sensitive load [33]. These are few examples where DVRs have been implemented in the industries/utilities, either at the LV-side or at the MV-side to mitigate the problems arising due to voltage fluctuations.

3 Cyber-Aspect of DVR

DVR plays a vital role in the distribution system. Therefore, the attacks that target this system are categorised as High Impact Low Frequency (HILF) events. The unique feature of DVR is the protection of sensitive loads and thereby, avoidance of any disruptions to the system. Therefore, the attacks targeting DVR would potentially cause widespread physical damage to the key components. In industries, this damage can lead to a chain of system failures, whereas, in utility sectors, this may cause catastrophic impact. Data-sheets of the DVR from few companies are available at [34,35]. The data-sheet implies that the status of the unit can be controlled remotely and various protocols can be included for establishing communication. Some of the software and hardware implementation procedures of DVR involve:

- The hardware control (measurement, control and regulation) is implemented through Digital Signal Processors (DSP). The software and the internal process can be accessed on-site through USB port.

- HMI access is provided via TCP/IP and it is not protected against unauthorized cyber-attacks. Therefore, the start/stop and the output of the DVR can be manipulated.
- Monitoring and remote functions can be obtained using HMI.

The aforementioned procedures for the control of DVR can be examined to determine the potential attack vector and associated scenarios. The attacks can differ based on the control aspect of DVR i.e., if the DVR is locally or remotely controlled. If the DVR is locally controlled, then the only choice of attack would be through USB. The software updates on DVR is carried out using an USB port and an adversary makes malicious software changes to the equipment software or firmware. Therefore, using a malware infected USB while updating the software is sufficient to cause serious damages to the system. This malware can cause single or multiple DVRs to ignore commands during voltage fluctuations. Several USB related incidents such as Stuxnet [36], Windows LNK family of Trojans [37], Dark Tequila [38], etc. are well known among cyber researchers. In addition, if the DVR is controlled remotely, there are chances for cyber-attacks to be mounted via network (e.g., manipulation of measurement data or commands transferred from/to DVR). By gaining access to the energy management system, the adversary can inject malicious data and cause DVR to respond inefficiently. The inefficient operation of DVR can lead to power outage due to protection trip (during injection of reactive power) or forcing the facility to purchase additional power from the grid (during reactive power absorption). The severity of attacks on the DVR primarily depends on the location of the DVR. If the DVR is located in LV side, as demonstrated in Fig. 2a, then only one load is affected. However, in cases depicted in Fig. 2b, where the DVR is connected in MV side, large number of loads/consumers will be affected.

4 Simulation Study on the Attacks Against DVR

In this section, the normal operation of the DVR is explained, followed by the description of potential scenarios of attacks caused due to the modification of the DVR output and the resulting voltage fluctuations that might be instigated upon the system. Similar to the block diagram depicted in Fig. 1, the model for this study is built within the modelling environment of MATLAB/Simulink.

4.1 Normal DVR Operation

DVR operates in two modes: dormant mode and active mode. The DVR is inactive (output is zero) when the voltage supply from the source is not disturbed, thereby remaining in dormant mode. If the supply voltage fluctuates due to any of the reasons mentioned earlier, the DVR activates. In active mode, the DVR supplies the voltage that is required to maintain a constant voltage at the load. The DVR senses the supply voltage at every instant in order to identify the fluctuations in the voltage. Though the DVR reacts to voltage sag and swell by injecting or consuming reactive power, respectively, most cases that have been reported in the power system are related to voltage sags. Therefore, DVRs are widely used to compensate the dips in voltage to protect the sensitive loads from debilitating interruptions. Figures 3 and 4 illustrate the DVR operation during dormant and active modes.

In the figures, the supply voltage is uninterrupted during the time period of 0 to 0.3 s. Hence, in this state, the DVR remains dormant (output 0V), as illustrated in the middle image in Figs. 3 and 4. At 0.3 s, an interruption to the source voltage occurs (a sag is introduced in Fig. 3 (top image) and a swell is introduced in Fig. 4 (top image)). If this voltage fluctuation is not corrected, the loads which are sensitive to voltage disturbances will be affected. These voltage fluctuations would cause significant damage to the sensitive equipment. These voltage fluctuations could be addressed by implementation of DVR. As seen in the middle images in Figs. 3 and 4, when the DVR senses a change in the source voltage, it switches from dormant mode to active mode. The main function of the DVR is to supply/consume reactive power in the system to counter voltage fluctuations. Therefore, DVR supplies reactive power (inject voltage) to the system during 0.3 to 0.6 s time period (Fig. 3) and absorbs power from the system during 0.3 to 0.6 s time period (Fig. 4). By provisioning the DVR, the load voltage is maintained at a constant magnitude irrespective of the voltage sag and swell from the source voltage. The constantly maintained load voltages during sag and swell conditions are depicted in the bottom images in Figs. 3 and 4.

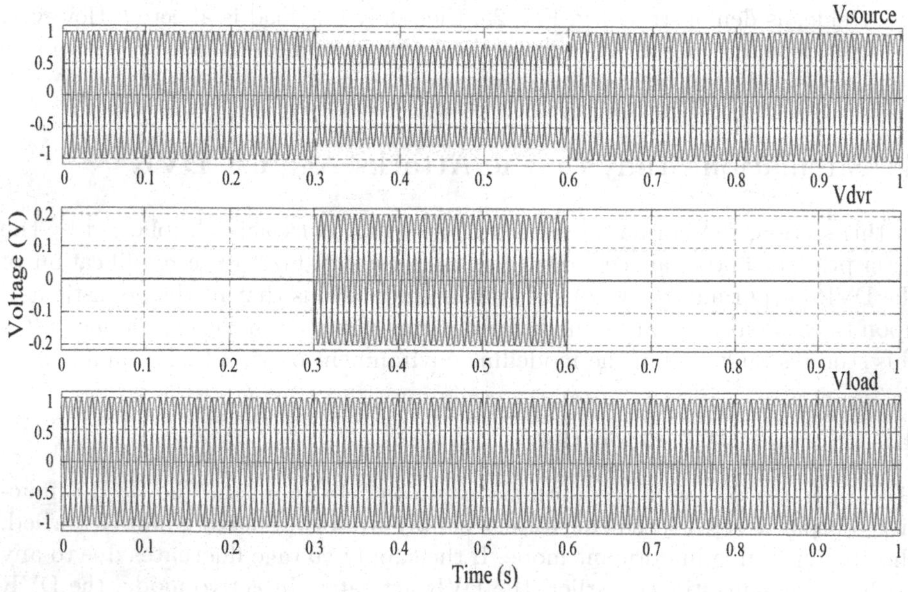

Fig. 3. Operation of DVR during voltage sag.

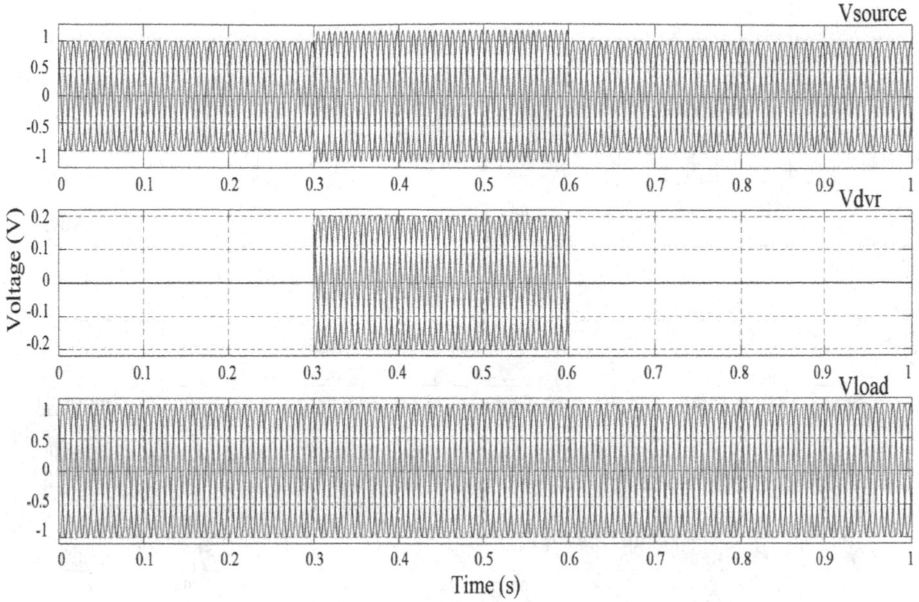

Fig. 4. Operation of DVR during voltage swell.

4.2 Cyber-Attacks Against DVR

If an adversary decides to interrupt the operation of the system, the communication between the sensors and the DVR controller could be targeted. This study assumes that the adversary has the data from the voltage sensors at every instance. These sensed voltage signals instruct the DVR to either activate or remain dormant. Therefore, an analysis on the various attacks to interrupt a system that an adversary can launch by manipulating the sensed data to DVR is described.

False Data Injection Attack. The adversary manipulates the sensed data to the controller to implement this attack. For instance, monitoring and control of smart grid systems are often done by using communication protocols like Modbus TCP traditionally and DNP3, IEC 60870-5-104, and IEC 61850 more recently, which do not have built-in security mechanisms for protecting the integrity and authenticity of communications [39,40]. Thus manipulation of payload and injection of bogus messages are highly feasible. The malicious data manipulation can be configured to induce two kinds of operation: (1) DVR is unresponsive for the entire period of compensation; and (2) Render DVR to be dormant after a short period of compensation. Subsequently, the load is subjected to voltage disturbances and can damage the sensitive load.

To demonstrate the first case, a sag is introduced in the system from time period 0.3 to 0.6 s as shown in Fig. 5. During this period, DVR has to inject

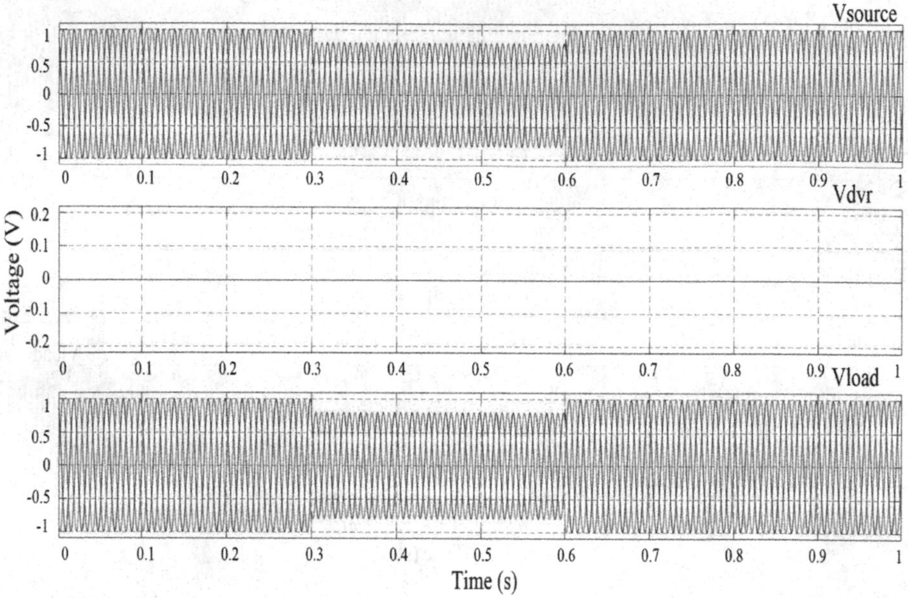

Fig. 5. FDI attack completely disabling DVR.

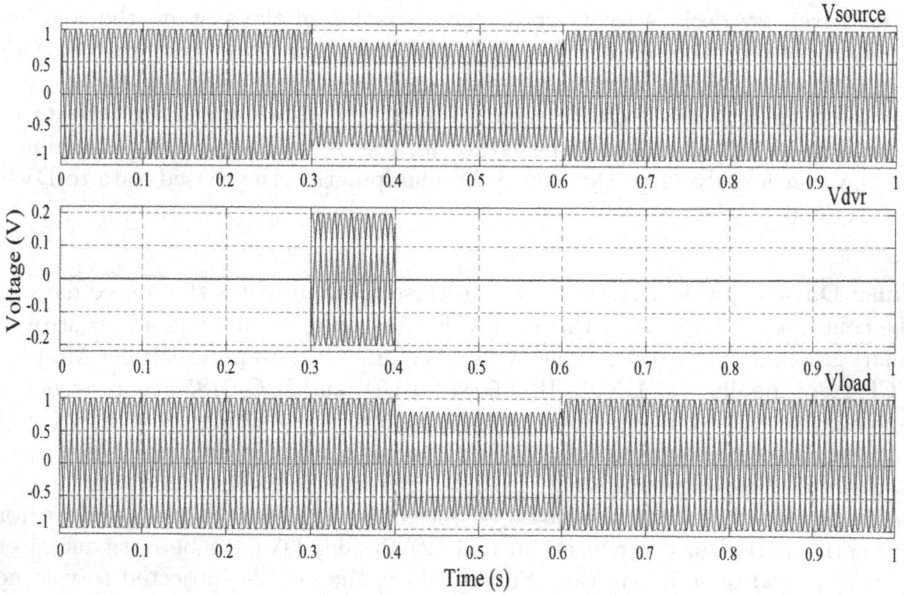

Fig. 6. FDI attack partially disabling DVR.

voltage, to ensure that the load voltage remains constant. However, under the assumption that the adversary has the sensed voltage signals, a false measurement is injected to the controller. Therefore, DVR does not recognize the voltage fluctuations and thus fails to compensate during the fluctuations. Similarly, in the second operation, the attack is introduced after few cycles of normal operation. As seen in Fig. 6, the source voltage is subjected to a voltage sag at 0.3 s and the DVR changes from dormant to active state from 0.3 to 0.4 s. During this time period the load voltage is maintained constant. After 0.4 s, the DVR suddenly becomes dormant and deny further support necessary to the load.

These interruptions can cause significant impact to the grid as the operator is unable to react and the attack was unforeseen. There exists a possibility in the first case that the control operator can manually turn 'on' the DVR noticing its unresponsiveness. However in the second case, the operator will be under the assumption that the DVR has turned 'on' at the right time to inject voltage and protect the sensitive load from interruptions. As the adversary succeeds delaying the attack, this attack would provide even shorter response time for the operator to manually turn 'on' the DVR or other devices like UPS. The outcomes of the two cases can be: (1) the attack damages few components in the system and would return to the usual operation mode when the mutable fluctuations recede. Over time, this attack leads to a massive black out/shut down; or (2) the attack damages the entire system, due to which the whole system will have to be shut down.

Another scenario caused by the manipulation of data is where the function of DVR is not required, yet it is forced to operate. DVR has to be active when the required set-point limit is reached. However, in this scenario, a configuration manipulation is performed by the adversary to affect the stability of the system. The adversary modifies the set-point data in the controller and triggers the turn 'on' signal in the DVR. This attack can be initiated by injecting false data into the communication between the DVR and the controller. As seen from Fig. 7 (V_{source}), the source voltage does not undergo any voltage fluctuations. Under this condition, the DVR is supposed to remain dormant. Due to the injected bad data, the DVR switches from dormant to active state during the 0.3 to 0.6 s time period. During this time period DVR injects additional voltage into the system, and consequently the magnitude of the load voltage increases.

A sudden increase in the voltage may damage the insulation and even destroy the equipment. Furthermore, increase in the voltage translates to additional reactive power in the system. If such an attack is reported in MV utility, then the reactive power injection would disrupt the stability of the distribution system.

Installation of Malicious Firmware via USB Drive. In this scenario, the adversary decides to replicate an attack similar to Stuxnet [36]. As the software upgrade of the DVR is performed using an USB drive, the adversary can install malicious firmware on the target DVR. Furthermore, as demonstrated by the recent SolarWinds attack [41], by compromising the supply chain, malicious firmware could be distributed broadly throughout the vendor's official update

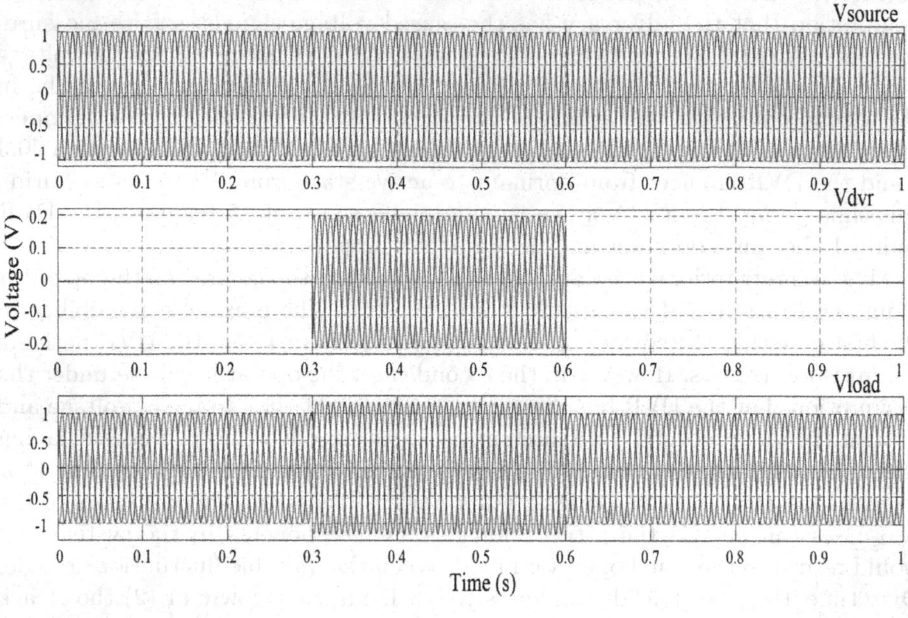

Fig. 7. FDI attack unnecessarily triggering DVR.

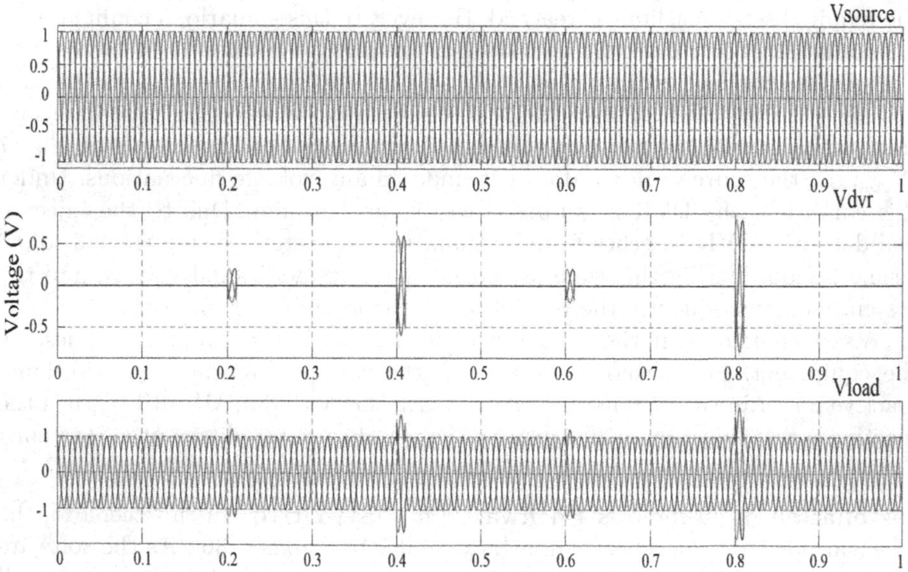

Fig. 8. Random control of DVR.

management system. Since relatively small number of vendors dominate the power system market, the consequences would be significant. Compared to the manipulation via networks that were discussed earlier, an attack of this type is more potent and it permits attackers more manipulation.

The targeted application can be an unmanned MV utility or high voltage industrial consumers. In the former case, where the DVR was turned 'on' to be active for a longer time period, manual shut down of the DVR by the operator may protect the system. However, in this case the malware activates the DVR randomly for short time periods. The protective relay or control operator may fail to intuit this variation, as this type of attack can sustain for a number of days given that the time period for manipulation is relatively short. The attack implementation is depicted in Fig. 8. The DVR is turned 'on' only for a short period and turned 'off' subsequently. Simultaneously, the voltage across the load continues to vary in sync with the DVR operation. The magnitude of the load voltage increases each time when the DVR is turned 'on'. If the DVR is used to protect a sensitive variable speed drive, this attack would change the rotational speed of the drives and affect the operation of the system. Subsequently, the affected drive and the connected equipment will be damaged.

Scaling Attack. In this scenario, the scaling attack on DVR is examined. Scaling attack involves the modification of the true measurements based on an attack parameter. The replication of the attack is done by interchanging the sag and swell action of DVR. In order to operate the DVR effectively, the voltage injected

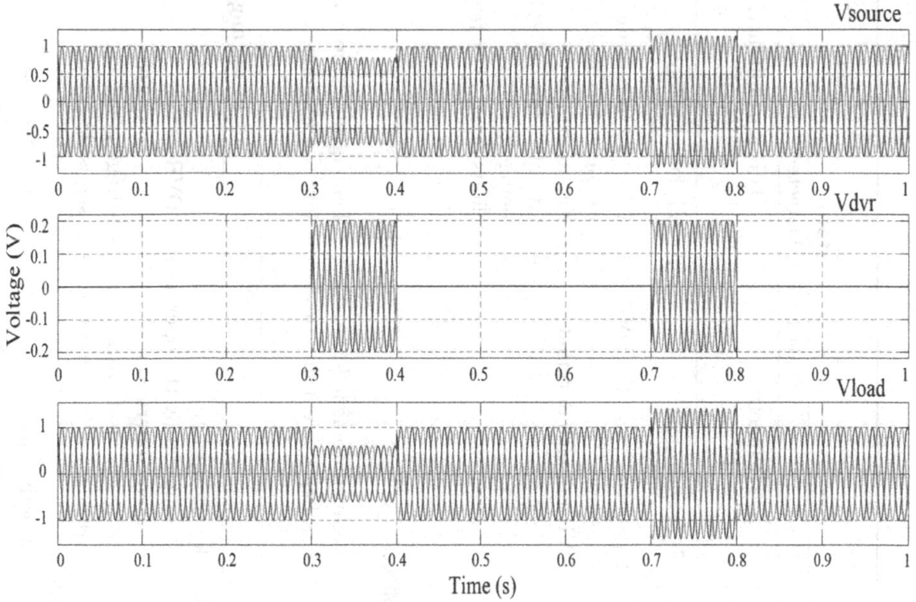

Fig. 9. Scaling attack.

Table 1. Overview of scenarios (expected operation and DVR manipulation).

Cyber vulnerabilities			
Active state		Dormant state	
Fluctuations Detected		No fluctuations	
DVR inactive (FDI)	DVR partially active (FDI)	DVR active (FDI)	DVR randomly active (USB)
Attack Description: – Signal to trigger the DVR is tampered – DVR remains dormant	Attack Description: – React to voltage fluctuation at the right time – Signal tampering is effective after few cycles of DVR being active – Shuts down after few cycles	Attack Description: – System operates normally – False data injected to trigger DVR – Sensitive loads receive high voltage than needed – Manual shutdown of DVR required	Attack Description: – System operates normally – DVR turned 'on' (not prolonged) – Random action of injecting voltage – Hard to sense the malfunction of DVR
Effect: – Single equipment failure or the whole system shut down	Effect: – Damages can be severe before the response time	Effect: – Delayed response damages the equipment	Effect: – Huge loss over a time
Phase angle manipulation (Scaling)			
Attack Description: – Manipulating the operation of DVR – Reverse operation – Voltage injected when excess voltage is detected – Voltage reduced when voltage sag is detected Effect: – Highly affects the stability of the system and destroys the equipment			

into the system has to be in phase with the source voltage. If the source voltage and the DVR voltage are in phase, the two signals are added to each other. Therefore, the load voltage is either the summation or difference in magnitudes of the source voltage and DVR voltage. Hence, the DVR voltage has to be injected carefully to effectively maximize the compensation. This logic can serve as a potential threat for the adversaries to exploit. The set-point measurements of DVR decide the sag and swell compensation. As such, the scaling attack can be implemented by modifying the phase angle data. In this case, when voltage fluctuations occur, the operator might get the false impression that the triggering of the DVR is to be expected. However, the modified scaling parameter sent by the adversary performs a reverse operation as explained below. For example, consider the source voltage in Fig. 9, where the voltage fluctuations are introduced as voltage sags from 0.3 to 0.4 s, and voltage swells from 0.7 to 0.8 s. Instead of injecting the voltage at 0.3 s, the DVR absorbs reactive power and this further reduces the magnitude of the load voltage. DVR supplies reactive power during the voltage swell at 0.7 s, which results in further increase in the magnitude of the load voltage. The exacerbated fluctuations in the load voltage can greatly affect the stability of the system. This may lead to domestic blackouts, power failure in transportation sectors, blow outs of expensive equipment in industries, etc. The overview of all the scenarios explained above is summarized in Table 1.

5 Conclusion

A discussion of cyber vulnerabilities in a voltage compensation device in the distribution system has been presented in this paper. DVRs are usually preferred for mitigating voltage fluctuations, and only the electrical perspective of this device has been previously researched. Furthermore, this device is commonly not protected against cyber-attacks. Therefore, this paper aims to present the different cyber security issues that are evident when DVR devices are integrated with power systems. The case studies presented herein describe the paradigms by which an adversary can compromise the stability of a system through a supporting device, which otherwise would have been operated only during emergencies. Based on the analysis, the impact on the system primarily depends on the location of the DVR.

Another point of concern is the incorporation of DVR into existing grids and the concomitant increases the vulnerabilities of the overall grid. The extension of Industrial Control System (ICS) for the control of DVRs requires thorough assessment to determine the vulnerable points of attack exploitable by adversaries. As smart and interdependent grids increase in size and complexity, the intended target of cyber-attacks can be any susceptible component of the grid.

Therefore, the potential vectors can originate at: the network level, during communication between components, the devices connected, and during remote or 3rd party access for supervisory purposes. According to the report by ICS-CERT, physical access control is one of the primary issues that can potentially arise with the DVR implementation in grids [42]. Therefore, the incorporation of any component to the grid infrastructure would require a thorough evaluation of the inherent susceptibility of the grid, as well as analysis of the impact of potential cyber-attacks on enhanced attack surface. The current work presents the simulation study using MATLAB/Simulink. A large scale cyber-attack study on the impact of the DVR in a realistic power grid model would be the focus of our future work.

Acknowledgment. This research is supported in part by the National Research Foundation and Singapore University of Technology and Design, Singapore under its National Satellite of Excellence in Design Science and Technology for Secure Critical Infrastructure Grant (NSoE_DeST-SCI2019-0005), and in part by the National Research Foundation, Prime Minister's Office, Singapore under its Campus for Research Excellence and Technological Enterprise (CREATE) programme.

References

1. Dugan, R.C., Mc Granaghan, M.F., Santoso, S., Beaty, H.W.: Electric power systems quality (2004)
2. Zhang, X.-P., Rehtanz, C., Pal, B.: Flexible AC Transmission Systems: Modelling and Control. Springer, Heidelberg (2012). https://doi.org/10.1007/3-540-30607-2
3. Ghosh, A., Ledwich, G.: Series compensation of power distribution system. In: Power Quality Enhancement Using Custom Power Devices. The Springer International Series in Engineering and Computer Science (Power Electronics and Power Systems). Springer, Boston (2002). https://doi.org/10.1007/978-1-4615-1153-3_9
4. Arun, A.: Innovative system solutions for power quality enhancement. ABB Rev. 4–11 (1999)
5. Ali, I., Hussain, S.S.: Control and management of distribution system with integrated DERs via IEC 61850 based communication. Eng. Sci. Technol. Int. J. **20**(3), 956–964 (2017)
6. Hussain, S.S., Ustun, T.S., Kalam, A.: A review of IEC 62351 security mechanisms for IEC 61850 message exchanges. IEEE Trans. Ind. Inform. **16**(9), 5643–5654 (2019)
7. Maroochy shire sewage spill. https://www.risidata.com/Database/Detail/maroochy-shire-sewage-spill
8. Poulsen, K.: Slammer worm crashed Ohio nuke plant network. https://www.securityfocus.com/news/6767
9. Kushner, D.: The real story of Stuxnet. https://spectrum.ieee.org/telecom/security/the-real-story-of-stuxnet
10. Cyber Autopsy Series: Ukrainian Power Grid Attack Makes History. https://www.globalsign.com/en/blog/cyber-autopsy-series-ukranian-power-grid-attack-makes-history
11. Wang, W., Lu, Z.: Cyber security in the smart grid: survey and challenges. Comput. Netw. **57**(5), 1344–1371 (2013)
12. Li, X., Liang, X., Lu, R., Shen, X., Lin, X., Zhu, H.: Securing smart grid: cyber attacks, countermeasures, and challenges. IEEE Commun. Mag. **50**(8), 38–45 (2012)
13. Qi, J., Hahn, A., Lu, X., Wang, J., Liu, C.-C.: Cybersecurity for distributed energy resources and smart inverters. IET Cyber-Phys. Syst. Theory Appl. **1**(1), 28–39 (2016)

14. Ali, I., Hussain, S.S.: Communication design for energy management automation in microgrid. IEEE Trans. Smart Grid **9**(3), 2055–2064 (2016)
15. NESCOR: Electric sector failure scenarios and impact analyses. https://smartgrid.epri.com/doc/NESCOR
16. Buldyrev, S.V., Parshani, R., Paul, G., Stanley, H.E., Havlin, S.: Catastrophic cascade of failures in interdependent networks. Nature **464**(7291), 1025–1028 (2010)
17. Qi, J., Ju, W., Sun, K.: Estimating the propagation of interdependent cascading outages with multi-type branching processes. IEEE Trans. Power Syst. **32**(2), 1212–1223 (2016)
18. Eftekharnejad, S., Vittal, V., Heydt, G.T., Keel, B., Loehr, J.: Small signal stability assessment of power systems with increased penetration of photovoltaic generation: a case study. IEEE Trans. Sustain. Energy **4**(4), 960–967 (2013)
19. Kawabe, K., Tanaka, K.: Impact of dynamic behavior of photovoltaic power generation systems on short-term voltage stability. IEEE Trans. Power Syst. **30**(6), 3416–3424 (2015)
20. Tamimi, B., Cañizares, C., Bhattacharya, K.: System stability impact of large-scale and distributed solar photovoltaic generation: the case of Ontario, Canada. IEEE Trans. Sustain. Energy **4**(3), 680–688 (2013)
21. Aleem, S.A., Hussain, S., Ustun, T.S.: A review of strategies to increase PV penetration level in smart grids. Energies **13**(3), 636 (2020)
22. Chen, B., Butler-Purry, K.L., Kundur, D.: Impact analysis of transient stability due to cyber attack on facts devices. In: 2013 North American Power Symposium (NAPS), pp. 1–6. IEEE (2013)
23. Phillips, L.R., et al.: Analysis of operations and cyber security policies for a system of cooperating flexible alternating current transmission system (facts) devices. Sandia National Laboratories, Tech. rep. (2005)
24. Liu, Y., Fan, R., Terzija, V.: Power system restoration: a literature review from 2006 to 2016. J. Mod. Power Syst. Clean Energy **4**(3), 332–341 (2016)
25. El-Gammal, M., Abou-Ghazala, A., El-Shennawy, T.: Fifteen years of the dynamic voltage restorer: a literature review. Aust. J. Electr. Electron. Eng. **8**(3), 279–287 (2011)
26. Roomi, M.M., Raj, P.H., Zhao, B.: Closed loop current control of dynamic voltage restorer for rectifier loads. In: 2020 IEEE International Conference on Power Electronics, Smart Grid and Renewable Energy (PESGRE2020), pp. 1–6 (2020)
27. Shafquat Ullah, K.M., Roomi, M.M., Tariq, M., Zhao, B.: A unity power factor rectifier based dynamic voltage restorer for microgrid applications. In: 2020 IEEE 17th India Council International Conference (INDICON), pp. 1–6 (2020)
28. Colak, I., Kabalci, E., Bayindir, R.: Review of multilevel voltage source inverter topologies and control schemes. Energy Convers. Manag. **52**(2), 1114–1128 (2011)
29. Roomi, M.M., Maswood, A.I., Tafti, H.D., Raj, P.H.: Reference disposition modulation method for non-ideal dual z-source neutral-point-clamped inverter. IET Power Electron. **10**(2), 222–231 (2017)
30. Roomi, M.: Analysis of an ideal dual-impedance network using reference disposition modulation. Electron. Lett. **53**(10), 668–670 (2017)
31. Roomi, M.M., Tariq, M., Zhao, B.: Analysis of cascaded z-source topology implementing dc-link voltage balancing. In: 2020 IEEE International Conference on Power Electronics, Drives and Energy Systems (PEDES), pp. 1–6 (2020)
32. Campbell, A., McHattie, R.: Backfilling the sinewave. A dynamic voltage restorer case study. Power Eng. J. **13**(3), 153–158 (1999)

33. Peel, M.K., Sundaram, A., Woodley, N.: Power quality protection using a platform-mounted SCD-demonstration project experience. In: 2000 IEEE Industrial and Commercial Power Systems Technical Conference. Conference Record (Cat. No.00CH37053), pp. 133–139 (2000)
34. Condensator-dominit. https://www.condensator-dominit.de/en/produkte/oskar/oskarr-600-kva/
35. Utility Systems Technologies, inc. https://ustpower.com/wp-content/uploads/SagFighter_Specification_Guide__03-03-17.pdf
36. Langner, R.: Stuxnet: dissecting a cyberwarfare weapon. IEEE Secur. Priv. **9**(3), 49–51 (2011)
37. Kaspersky treats. https://threats.kaspersky.com/en/threat/Trojan.WinLNK.Agent/
38. A. K. Lab. https://securelist.com/dark-tequila-anejo/87528/
39. Esiner, E., Mashima, D., Chen, B., Kalbarczyk, Z., Nicol, D.: F-pro: a fast and flexible provenance-aware message authentication scheme for smart grid. In: 2019 IEEE International Conference on Communications, Control, and Computing Technologies for Smart Grids (SmartGridComm), pp. 1–7. IEEE (2019)
40. Roomi, M.M., Biswas, P.P., Mashima, D., Fan, Y., Chang, E.-C.: False data injection cyber range of modernized substation system. In: 2020 IEEE International Conference on Communications, Control, and Computing Technologies for Smart Grids (SmartGridComm), pp. 1–7. IEEE (2020)
41. https://www.csoonline.com/article/3601508/solarwinds-supply-chain-attack-explained-why-organizations-were-not-prepared.html
42. https://www.us-cert.gov/sites/default/files/Annual_Reports/FY2016_Industrial_Control_Systems_Assessment_Summary_Report_S508C.pdf

Attacklets to Test Anomaly Detectors for Critical Infrastructure

Salimah Liyakkathali(✉), Gayathri Sugumar(✉), and Aditya Mathur(✉)

Singapore University of Technology and Design, Singapore, Singapore
gayathri_sugumar@alumni.sutd.edu.sg, aditya_mathur@sutd.edu.sg

Abstract. Critical Infrastructure (CI), such as electric power generation and water treatment plants, are susceptible to attacks that lead the underlying physical process to deviate from its expected behaviour. Such deviations create process anomalies that may result in undesirable consequences. Anomaly detectors are installed in CI to detect process anomalies quickly and reliably. In this work, *state and command mutation* (SCM) is studied as a means to test the effectiveness of anomaly detectors deployed in Critical Infrastructure. The methodology SCM is a framework to derive attacks through mutation. A reference attack that manipulates state and commands vectors of the plant is mutated to create several attacks, referred to as *attacklets*, using attack mutation operators (OPR). The method is applied to a functional water treatment plant testbed. Experiments show the value of SCM in assessing the effectiveness of ADUT.

Keywords: Anomaly detector · Cyber-physical systems · Cyber security · Attack model · Testing

1 Introduction

Cyber physical systems (CPS) which form the basis for critical infrastructure, are modern class of systems that closely integrate computing capabilities to control the physical components for safe, dependable and efficient operation [11,26]. CPSs are progressively adopted for a wide range of applications such as smart grids, water treatment systems, transport systems, health care, and so on. As CPSs are often used to provide key services to the society, their security is a key concern. Compromising a CPS especially in the context of critical infrastructure could have adverse effects on the human life and economy. Exploiting security vulnerabilities in CPS have impact on its availability, safety, integrity and dependability properties [7,23]. Under any circumstances, a CPS is required to perform functionalities during operation devoid of substantial degradation or failure in its performance and result. Cyber-security risks are widespread in today's world as new cyber incidents are reported frequently. As many as, one-third of the population of the United States is affected by the cyber-attacks [33]. Attacks such as stuxnet [9] and Ukraine Blackout [20] have increased the attention of academia, industry, and the government agencies to explore security in CPS.

J. Zhou et al. (Eds.): ACNS 2021 Workshops, LNCS 12809, pp. 209–227, 2021.
https://doi.org/10.1007/978-3-030-81645-2_13

The attacks on CPS is identified and located in a timely manner, the overall system can be protected from damage and failure to a certain degree. Hence, the anomaly detectors play a crucial role in protecting the CPS and maintaining its safety and performance. Anomaly detectors have been largely studied and experimented in recent times. Anomaly Detector Under Test (ADUT) are deployed in critical infrastructure to raise alerts when the underlying plant deviates from its expected behaviour. Statistical models [16] and machine learning techniques [29,34] are some of the non-parametric mechanisms that monitor the measurements and control signals to detect the presence of attacks. Other mechanisms using data-mining techniques such as clustering [4], support-vector machines, are also explored in [4,19,37]. In the research work [8], spatio-temporal correlations between sensors are used as lightweight solutions to detect attacks in the system. In [2,30], invariant based anomaly detection techniques are studied where invariants are derived based on the process dynamics of the CPS.

Errors in ADUT may occur especially in a complex network of components and nexus of conditions that govern the operation of the plant leading to complex invariants. Two types of errors are considered in this study: incorrectly coded and missing invariants or rules. Although invariants can be derived both manually and through automation, errors exist when invariants are missed or programmed incorrectly. These challenges can be addressed by effectively testing the ADUT in place. There exists several work on design of ADUT, but systematic methodology to test them is missing. To develop a reliable ADUT, it has to be tested against variety of existing and unknown attacks to validate if the desired reliability of ADUT is achieved prior to deployment.

Problem Statement: Let C denote a cyber physical system for which anomaly detectors A, B and C are designed. The anomaly detectors ADUT monitor the plant dynamics and operational data to detect the process anomalies. The anomaly detectors could be of various types depending on the design and monitoring parameters. An ADUT could be based on machine learning or design-centric anomaly detectors. The research problem that this work aims to address is to demonstrate the process of comparing heterogeneous anomaly detectors using the method SCM [31].

Contributions: In this work, the following contributions are made. (a) The anomaly detector testing method referred as SCM is implemented on an operational water treatment plant. (b) Attack launcher which launches the attack generated by SCM. (c) The implemented method is then used to test three different anomaly detectors on an operational plant.

Organisation: The remainder of the paper is organised as follows. An introduction to mutation analysis is in Sect. 2. The proposed methodology is detailed in Sect. 3. The Sect. 4 describes the modelling of attacks through the purposed methodology. A case study on a water treatment tested is presented in Sect. 5. The experimentation and the results are discussed in Sect. 7. Section 9 offers conclusions from this study.

2 Mutation Analysis: Background

Mutation testing or analysis, is performed to design and evaluate test suites of computer programs [10, 36]. For an implementation under test (IUT), it is required to test the expected behaviour as well as its behaviour under unexpected inputs. Mutation analysis is a widely researched, extensive, and systematic approach with a broad applicability [18]. The analysis is performed using a set of well-defined mutation operators. The process of mutation testing is described below to create a proper context for further application to attack mutation SCM.

2.1 Process

Given a set of requirements R for program P, a test suite T is designed and its adequacy is assessed against the program P and its mutants $\mathcal{M}$. Improving the adequacy of a partially adequate test, by adding new tests to T, leads to the detection of errors in P with high probability. During this process, mutants of P are created using a pre-defined set of mutation operators. The operator set includes those to mutate program elements such as boolean and arithmetic operators, variables, and constants. P and its set of mutants $\mathcal{M} = \{\mathcal{M}_1, \mathcal{M}_2, ...\mathcal{M}_n\}$, are executed against tests in T. Let $\mathcal{P}(t)$ and $\mathcal{M}(t)$ denote, respectively, the outcome of executing program $\mathcal{P}$ and mutant $\mathcal{M}$ against a test input t. Mutation analysis is performed, as below, on the outcome of each execution.

- $\mathcal{P}(t) = \mathcal{M}(t)\ \forall t \in T$, implies that either $\mathcal{P}$ and $\mathcal{M}$ are equivalent, or T is inadequate.
- $\mathcal{P}(t) \neq \mathcal{M}(t)$, for any $t \in T$, implies that the mutant is distinguished from its parent program P.

Mutation Score (MS) of test suite T is computed as the following.

$$\text{MS} = \frac{\text{Number of distinguished mutants}}{\text{Number of non-equivalent mutants}}.$$

In the context of program correctness, a test set with a higher value of MS is considered superior to that with a lower score. "Equivalence" above refers to the case when there does not exist any test case that would distinguish the output of the program under test against that of the mutant.

2.2 Operators

Researchers have extensively designed and experimented with mutation operators for many programming languages. The operators are intended to mimic commonly occurring programming errors such as using $>$ instead of $\geq$, or using an incorrect variable, or initialising a variable 0 instead of 1, etc. Some of the traditional mutation operators include statement deletion, logical operator replacement, and arithmetic operator replacement. Essentially mutants are created as $O : \mathcal{P} \Rightarrow \mathcal{M}$, where $\mathcal{M}$ is a finite set of mutants, $\mathcal{O}$ is a mutation operator and $\mathcal{P}$ is the program.

3 Attack Mutation

In this section, mutation based approach for generating attacks for CPS is defined. The approach consists of a set of operators that when applied, transform data and commands exchanged in the system. The operator set is designed to model a variety of attacks that have been observed in real plants, as well as those that might have never been observed or reported in the literature. The hypothesis that formed the basis of program mutation analysis is redefined in SCM in [31]. The analysis of the hypothesis is not presented in this work.

3.1 Purpose

Similar to conventional mutation analysis, the purpose for SCM is described as follows. Given the requirement $\mathcal{R}$ for the ADUT $\mathcal{AD}$, which is to detect the anomalies, the attack set $\mathcal{A}$ is used to evaluate the effectiveness of anomaly detector. To effectively verify, we use SCM to create variants of attack models. The question is that "Is $\mathcal{AD}$ effective to detect attacks $\mathcal{A}$?". The parameter detection score (DS) is introduced to evaluate $\mathcal{AD}$ effectiveness against $\mathcal{A}$ as follows where $|D_a|$ is the number of attacks detected, $|G_a|$ is the number attacks launched.

$$DS = \frac{|D_a|}{|G_a|} \tag{1}$$

3.2 Operators

The operator categories to mutate attack models are presented briefly here. The mutation operators are broadly classified into biased and command categories.

State/Biased. State mutation is applied on the sensor measurements in the CPS. The sensor data is manipulated by applying state mutation operator, creating manipulated state vectors during the plant operation. These mutation operators are further split based on their function: set, add and bit-shift operators. The operators for biased mutation is tabulated in Table 1, classified according to their function. The add mutation category is broadly defined that it also represents other arithmetic operators as well. The state mutation is described as follows where s is an instance of state variable and s' is the manipulated measurement.

$$f(s) \rightarrow s' \tag{2}$$

Command. Mutation on control signals from controller to actuator is defined under command mutation. Commands supported by actuators are valid commands while commands that are not part of control signal handled by actuators are invalid commands. There are two mutations on commands i.e. valid command set (VCS) and invalid command set (iVCS). For instance, the commands processed by motorised valve are Open (2), Close (1) and if the command is mutated to value 99, it is an invalid command to the valve. The commands generated through iVCS such as LZFuzz [27], where the bit pattern of a command is altered to generate an invalid command, could be detected and ignored by the hardware embedded in an actuator. Yet, they are still explored in this work to test if the actuators are capable of discarding such commands. The command mutation is defined as follows where c and c' are different commands. c' is either valid or invalid command and c is the actual command sent by controller to actuator.

$$f(c) \rightarrow c' \tag{3}$$

Table 1. Attack mutation operators

Tag	Operator	Description
ASD	Add Static Delta δ	Adds/subtracts a static value to state measurements
ALD	Add Limits Delta δ	Adds/subtracts δ to state measurements
ARD	Add Random Delta δ	Adds/subtracts a random value to state measurements
STZ	Set to Zero	Set state measurement to zero
STO	Set to One	Set state measurement to one
STS	Set to Static	Set state measurement to a static (not changing) value
STR	Set to Random	Set state measurement to a random value
BSL	Bit Shift Left	State measurement is bit-shifted to the left by one bit
BSR	Bit Shift Right	State measurement is bit-shifted to the right by one bit
VCS	Valid Command Set	Command to an actuator is mutated to another valid command
iVCS	Invalid Command Set	Command to an actuator is mutated to an invalid command

4 Modelling Attacks

A critical infrastructure is a complex system consisting of an CPS that monitors and controls a physical process. The sensors in the plant measure the state of the physical process and send the data to the controller in the CPS. In turn the controller computes control commands and send these to appropriate actuators such as pumps, generators, and valves. The following captures a state space model of a CPS.

$$\mathcal{P} : \begin{cases} x_{k+1} = Ax_k + Bu_k \\ y_k = Cx_k \end{cases} \tag{4}$$

where $x_k = [x_1\ x_2\ ...\ x_n]^T$ represent the plant state at sampling instance k. The measurements from sensor at instant k is given by $y_k = [y_1\ y_2\ ...\ y_p]^T$. The input vector represents the control signal to the system given by $u_k = [u_1\ u_2\ ...\ u_r]^T$ and A, B and C are proportionality matrices. The attacks are performed on the sensor measurements sent to the controller. These attacks represent the integrity attacks where manipulated sensor measurements are sent to the controller. The attacks affect the state vector and output vector of a system, which in turn can eventually move the system to unsafe state.

Let $s_i(k)$ denote a measurement from sensor i at instant k, and q denote the number of sensors in the system such that $q \in \mathbb{N}$. These measurements may not directly indicate the state of system, but the state of system can be monitored from the measurements.

Then $\forall i,\ k,\ s_i(k) \in \mathbb{S}_i$ where $\mathbb{S}_i = [s_i^{min},\ s_i^{max}]$. s_i^{min} and s_i^{max} define the range of sensor measurement of s_i. Note that, $\forall i \in q,\ \mathbb{S}_i \in \mathbb{S}$ and $\mathbb{S} = [\mathbb{S}_1\ \mathbb{S}_2\ ...\ \mathbb{S}_q]^T$.

Let $c_j(k)$ be a command to actuator j at instant k, for $p \in \mathbb{N}$, p denoting the number of actuators in the system which control the physical process. Actuators are physical components which take action upon reception of command or signal from the controller. For example, a valve travels to open state to allow flow of water in a water distribution system when the PLC command to open is received. Therefore $\forall j,\ k,\ c_j(k) \in \mathbb{G}_j$ where $\mathbb{G}_j = [c_1^j\ c_2^j\ ...\ c_m^j]$. $\mathbb{G}_j$ indicate the set of possible valid commands to actuator j. It is defined that $\forall j \in p,\ \mathbb{G}_j \in \mathbb{G}$ and $\mathbb{G} = [\mathbb{G}_1\ \mathbb{G}_2\ ...\ \mathbb{G}_p]^T$.

4.1 Modelling State/Biased Attacks

An integrity attack on sensor measurements from sensor is performed by manipulating the real sensing data to false data and send to controller. Let $s_i(k)$ be the original measurement from the sensor i and $\hat{s}_i(k)$ be the false data injected by the malicious actor. The attack period is defined as the duration in which attack is launched and denoted by k_a. The notation k denotes the instance of time with $k \in [0\ K]$.

$$s_i(k) : \begin{cases} \hat{s}_i(k) : k \in k_a \\ s_i(k) : otherwise \end{cases} \tag{5}$$

With the intention to develop a systematic attack strategies, the following mutation based operators are designed. There are three categories of operators; set, add and bit-shift types which are discussed below. The notation δ represents the bias parameter used to launch the integrity attacks.

Set Operator in Attack Model. With the mutation operator *Set*, the false data used to manipulate the sensor measurement is set to a static value δ_s and δ_s varies based on the state mutation operator.

$$s_i(k) : \begin{cases} \delta_s : k \in k_a \\ s_i(k) : otherwise \end{cases} \tag{6}$$

Add Operator in Attack Model. The mutation based attack model template includes the *Add* operator, where additive attacks are developed. δ_a is the parameter to manipulate the sensor measurements.

$$s_i(k) : \begin{cases} s_i(k) + \delta_a : k \in k_a \\ s_i(k) : otherwise \end{cases} \tag{7}$$

The *Add* operator is further classified to three types. Add static delta adds a static value of δ_a to sensor measurements. Depending on the δ_a value, the operator can be either added or subtracted from the measurement. In Add limits delta, the δ_a is choose as a value out of range from the possible measurement data. Though this attack model is relatively easy to detect with fault-tolerant algorithm in place, it is still a valid attack scenario given that attacker does not have knowledge on the system. The Add random delta operator models the attack model where the measurements are added or subtracted by a random value of δ_a.

Bit-Shift Operator in Attack Model. The Bit-shift operator essentially modifies the measurements based on shifting operators. There are two categories of this operator namely bit-shift right and left. δ_b notates the number of bits to shift during the attack interval.
Bit-shift right (BSR):

$$s_i(k) : \begin{cases} s_i(k) \gg \delta_b : k \in k_a \\ s_i(k) : otherwise \end{cases} \tag{8}$$

Bit-shift Left (BSL):

$$s_i(k) : \begin{cases} s_i(k) \ll \delta_b : k \in k_a \\ s_i(k) : otherwise \end{cases} \tag{9}$$

4.2 Modelling Attacks on Actuator Commands

The attacks on commands from controller to actuator are designed based on the attack mutation operators. The command to actuator can be mutated to either a valid command or invalid command. The well-formed commands are grouped to valid command set (VCS), while ill-formed commands to Invalid command set (iVCS). Let $c_j(k)$ be the command from the controller to actuator j at instance k and $\hat{c}_j(k)$ be the manipulated command. With $\hat{c}_j(k)$ belong to either iVCS or VCS; during the attack period,

$$\hat{c}_j(k) : \begin{cases} c_j(k) : k \in k_a \\ c_j(k) : otherwise \end{cases} \tag{10}$$

Algorithm 1. Attack Model by Mutation for STR

procedure MUT_ATTACK($mutOpt, vector, t_a$)
  if $mutOpt \neq$ STR **then**
    return
  end if
  $t \leftarrow CurrentTime$
  while $t \leq t_a$ **do** ▷ During the attack interval
    Choose $\delta_r \in [vector^{min}, vector^{max}]$
    $vector \leftarrow \delta_r$
    $t \leftarrow CurrentTime$
  end while ▷ End of attack interval
end procedure

The mutation operators used in this work mutate the sensor values and actuator states [31]. Mutation algorithm for set to random (STR) operator is given in Algorithm 1. *mutOpt* denotes the mutation operator to mutate the measurements; in this case *mutOpt* is STR. The state vector to mutate is given be $vector$ while t_a gives the attack interval.

5 Case Study: Water Treatment Plant

The SCM method is studied on an operational water treatment plant, namely the secure water treatment testbed (SWaT) [32]. SWaT consists of six stages each performing distinct operations. Each stage consists of PLC which collects measurements from sensors and controls the actuators in the respective stage. The operators performed in each stage is water storage & supply, chemical dosing, ultra-filtration (UF), de-chlorination, reverse osmosis (RO) and backwash. A detailed description of functions carried our in each stage is available in [32].

5.1 Set to Zero (STZ)

This attack was performed on LIT101 in stage-1, which measures the current level of water in Tank T101 of stage-1 (supply & storage). A valve MV101 is present at the inlet of T101 to fill when the water level in tank is less than LowLow (LL) threshold. Similarly, when the water level is more than HighHigh (HH) set point, the inflow of water should be stopped by closing the valve to avoid over-flow of water. The flow indicator FIT101 measures the rate of flow of water through inlet valve MV101. The attack considered in this case-study using STZ is presented in Fig. 1. The setting of the performed attack is the level of water at 857 mm, High (H) set point and MV101 is closed as there is sufficient water in T101 and FIT101 is 0 m^3/hr indicating that there is no inflow to T101. The attack operator Set to zero (STZ) is performed on LIT101. At t = 5460 s, the LIT101 is manipulated to be 0 mm (LL set point). The MV101 is turned OPEN by PLC by receiving the spoofed level readings. Hence, there is flow of water to tank and flow meter readings show around 4 m^3/hr flow rate of water. This attack is continued until t = 5794 s. The observed LIT101 was 1084 mm which was higher than HH threshold (1000 mm) eventually causing over-flow of water in T101.

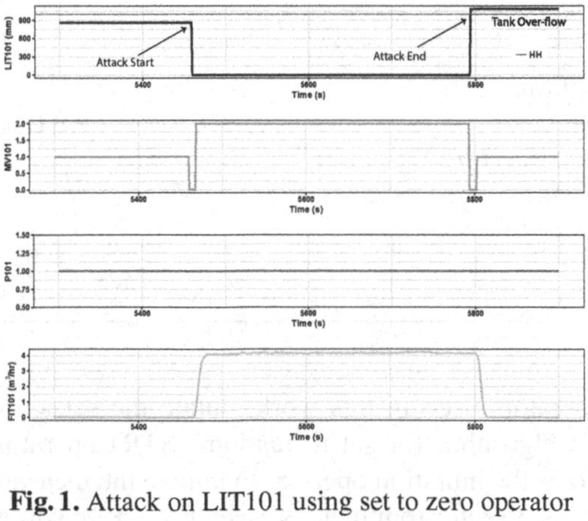

Fig. 1. Attack on LIT101 using set to zero operator

5.2 Set to Static (STS)

This attack was performed on LIT301 in stage-3, which measures the current level of water in Tank T301. This stage performs the ultra-filtration process which supplies the filtered water to subsequent RO processing stage. The mutation operator used in this study is set to static and the δ was chosen as 1000 to showcase the impact of this attack on the stability of system. Similar to LIT101, there are set point to LIT301 as well, such as LL = 250 mm, HH = 1200 mm. The water from T301 is sent to subsequent stage through Pump P301 and its corresponding outflow rate is indicated through flow sensor FIT301. When the water is less ($\leq$ LL), the outflow has to cut-off to avoid underflow conditions. Initially the water in Tank T301 was low and so pump P301 is turned Off and there is no outflow of water. When the attack is launched at instance time = 6265 s, the LIT301 is assigned to $\delta = 1000$. Since the LIT301 is high, the water outflow is started by turning ON the pump P101. This was reflected in the increase in flow readings from FIT301 which was approximately 2.01 m^3/hr. This was continued and observed that flow readings was started to fall down and indicating the pump running dry. This was because the water level in T301 was below LL, but the spoofed data was sent to PLC that it was high. As observed in Fig. 2, the attack was stopped at $t = 6455$ s, when the actual LIT301 was observed to be 181 mm, which is below the LL set point making the tank underflow and the pump P301 run dry.

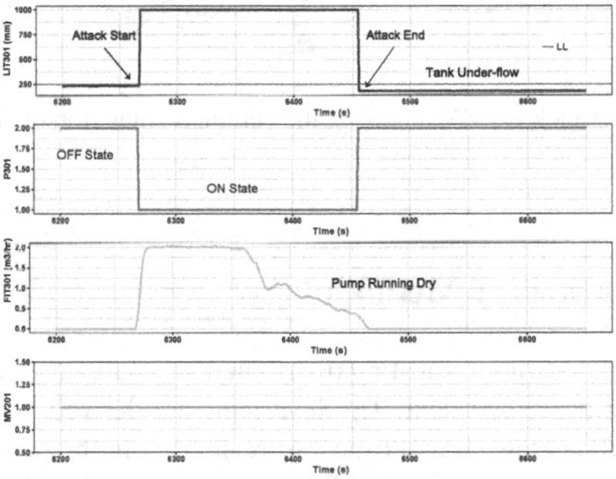

Fig. 2. Attack on LIT301 using the set to static operator.

5.3 Valid Command Set Operator

The attack on the actuator MV303 in stage-3 is performed using VCS mutation operator. Valve MV303 is placed at Ultra-filtration stage, whose function is to drain the backwash water through UF membrane. Only during UF backwash process, the valve is turned OPEN and remains CLOSE otherwise. The attack was performed during the normal UF, where the flow of water is through Pump P301 to UF membrane and then passes through MV302 to the subsequent stage storage tank LIT401 for the de-chlorination process. The attack performed on MV303 is shown in Fig. 3 switches the state of valve from CLOSE to OPEN at t = 35 s. The water is pumped normally from T301 but it is drained through MV303 before reaching T401 in stage-4. As seen that during the attack, the flow meter FIT301 indicating the outflow from T301 is high around 2.17 m^3/hr and correspondingly LIT301 also shows decrease of water level. But the reflection of this scenario in stage-4 is not effected i.e., the water level shown by LIT401 remains unchanged during attack duration. The attack is continued till t = 770 s. During this attack period, the average water flow is 2.172 m^3/hr and for the attack of 735 s, an approximate quantity of 443.45 mm of water is wasted by draining.

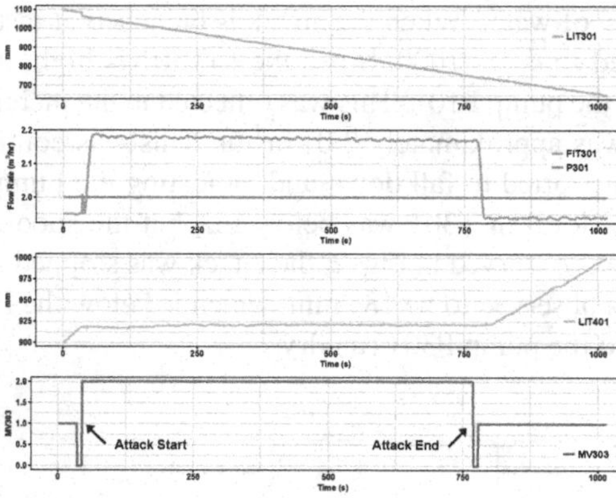

Fig. 3. Attack on MV303 using the command mutation operator.

6 SCM to Test ADUT: A Methodology

SCM is a generic methodology for testing distributed anomaly detectors. The framework as shown in Fig. 4 is described next. The invariants are derived based on plant design which monitor the plant state in real time and raise alert in the presence of anomalies. The derived invariants are coded as PLC logic or place in SCADA systems. In order to generate attacklets i.e. attack mutants, the reference attacks and mutation operators are used. The mutant generator creates an attacklet for every mutation operator on the reference attack. The attacklets are launched on the system to study if the anomaly detector finds the presence of attack. Then the attack detection analysis is performed to compute the detection score for the anomaly detector with respect to the attacklets generated. If the detection score is of satisfactory range, then the process is terminated. Else, the process is repeated by updating the invariants based on attack detection analysis.

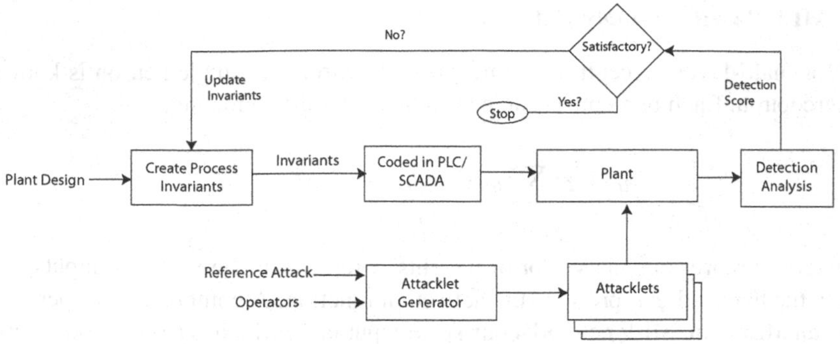

Fig. 4. Steps in testing a distributed anomaly detector (ADUT) using attack mutation SCM. The detection score (DS) indicates the effectiveness of ADUT in detecting anomalies created by reference attacks and attacklets.

6.1 GARX Anomaly Detector

ARX is a Auto-regressive models with eXogenous input. It is a design-centric approach to build invariants for a time dependant system. Given a multivariate time series dataset from the operational plant, ARX technique creates invariants by using a combination of search techniques and machine learning techniques. GARX is a simplified model from ARX. The streamlined regression form used in GARX is as follows.

$$F(\theta) = 1 - \sqrt{[\frac{\sum_{t=1}^{N} |y(t) - \hat{y}(t|\theta)|^2}{\sum_{t=1}^{N} |y(t) - \bar{y}|^2}]} \tag{11}$$

In one step, the use of a single delay for each exogenous variable x to predict the change in the endogenous variable y can be done. The fitness function $F(\theta)$ is used to find and sort the generated invariants in descending order, where $y(t)$ is the observed value, $\bar{y}$ is the mean of the observed values $y(t)$, and $\hat{y}(t|\theta)$ is the estimated value. The value of the fitness function is between zero and one. A high value indicates that the invariant model fits well with the observed data.

6.2 GARX Implementation in SWaT

In SWaT, the GARX algorithm decides whether if there is a change from the measured sample. If the change is detected, the sum of the value is added to a sum variable, $\mathcal{Z}_k^+$ where $\mathcal{Z}_k^+ \in \mathcal{R}^+$. The cumulative sum of $\mathcal{Z}_k^+$ is stored in $\mathcal{S}_{k+1}$. If $\mathcal{S}_{k+1}$ is bigger, the array index 1 is set to 1 because the threshold is exceeded and $\mathcal{S}_k$ is reset to 0. Otherwise, the array index 1 is set to 0. GARX determines if strategy c out of d ones occurred where $c < d$ and c, $d > 0$. For example, 7 out of 9 strategy means if number of one exceeded 6 out of 9 readings, an alarm is raised. With GARX model of SWaT built, the constructed model is used as an anomaly detector for the system. In order to utilise the model, an error threshold profile is developed for anomaly detector.

6.3 MLP Based Anomaly Detector

MLP or multi-layer perceptron is a network of neurons. A single neuron is known as the perceptron. Each perceptron can be calculated by the following:

$$y = \varphi(\sum_{i=1}^{n} w_i x_i + b) = \varphi(w^T x + b) \tag{12}$$

where **w** represents the vector of weights, **x** represents the vector of inputs, b represents the bias and φ represents the activation function. A combination of perceptron forms an MLP. The MLP network consists of input layer which is a set of source nodes, hidden layers which is a set of computation nodes and output layer.

MLP learn to model the correlation between the input and output nodes. The training consists of fine-tuning the parameters, weights and bias. In back-propagation, it adjusts the weights and biases according to the error which can be calculated by the root mean squared error or by other means. The network goes through the forward pass and the backward pass until it reaches convergences.

MLP Implementation in SWaT: In SWaT, it is designed to monitor and detect real-time anomalies on water level sensors [24]. It uses a unsupervised approach for the identification of anomalies. As values of these state variables are time-dependent during the entire operation of SWaT, it treats the measurements as a time series prediction problem the temporal dependencies to effectively capture for prediction. The MLP model predicts future values by treating it as a time series prediction problem. In the training phase, using the normal operation of the plant, several parameters such as the number of hidden units, hidden layers, learning rate, momentum, weight decay, look back were fine-tuned to obtain minimal prediction error. Further, window-based CUSUM approach is integrated with MLP to detect abnormal deviation between the actual and predicted values. Overall, as values of these state variables are time-dependent during the entire operation of SWaT, MLP treats the measurements as a time series prediction problem the temporal dependencies to effectively capture for prediction.

6.4 DAD Anomaly Detector

Distributed anomaly detector (DAD) is an invariant based anomaly detector [1,3]. Invariants are conditions that remain true during the normal operation of the plant. Invariants are derived based on the physics of the plant and are represented as conditions on state variables from single or multiple state variables of the plant. For instance, an invariant that monitors the state of MV101 and its influence on FIT101 is condition based on state variables from stage-1 of SWaT. An example of invariant comprising of state variables from multiple stages is as follows. When MV201 is open, the level of water in stage-3 tank T301 is increasing provided there is no outflow of water in T301. The invariants are placed in controllers (PLC) which monitors the dynamics of the state variables; and raises an alert when any of the invariant does not hold.

DAD Implementation in SWaT: The invariants are implemented across the six stages of SWaT and are coded in the corresponding PLCs. Each PLCs consists of invariants that monitor the sensors, actuators and plant components in that stage and also its neighbouring stages. The invariants which focus on single stage are grouped single-stage invariants and neighbouring stages are grouped as multi-stage invariants. Examples of single-stage invaraints include an invariant which monitors the inflow of water to tank T101 along with the valve MV101 which controls the inflow of water i.e. When water in tank is high, inflow should be turned closed. An example of multi-stage invariant is when water in stage-3 tank T301 is high, the inflow of the tank is controlled by P101 and MV201. The invariant monitoring the status of T301 (LIT301), P101 and MV201 is a multi-stage invariant.

The DAD anomaly detector is implemented in SWaT as part of PLC and SCADA logic. The modules validate the invariants against the plant dynamics and if any of the invariants do not hold, an alarm is triggered. The alarms provide information on invariants ID which did not hold. These information provide insights to operator/engineer to locate the anomaly in the plant.

6.5 Reference Attacks Selection

The reference attacks are selected based on their coverage and impact on the system. Each reference attack caused different anomaly or damage to the system and selected reference attacks manipulated multiple components across different stages of SWaT. Also, the attacks are included to affect various processes such as filling, chemical dosing, backwash, emptying and so on. Based on the above mentioned criteria, the attacks that covered wide range of components and with different impacts are designed as reference attacks. A total of 15 reference attacks are designed and are presented in Table 2. The reference attack are independently developed from the system and the attacklets created eventually add to the library of attacks generated.

7 Experiments

This section describes the experimentation settings and the results obtained. As the invariants are loaded in the controller, the attacks derived are launched in the system. All experiments were conducted safely in operational testbed. Implementation of attacklets testing can also be tested on a simulation system or on a digital twin if researchers do not have the access to such testbeds. Reference attacks are designed to create process anomalies in the system. Each reference attack is then mutated to create attack variants. The reference attacks along with attack variants also referred as attack mutants are launched in the system to test if the anomaly detector i.e. invariants are able to detect the presence of the attacks in the system.

7.1 Attack Launcher

The attacks are launched in the plant through three techniques which are described next.

Table 2. Reference attacks and impacted sensors and actuators

ID	Impact	Targeted sensors and actuators
R1*	Overflow tank T101	MV101, P101, LIT101
R2*	Underflow tank T301	MV201, P301, LIT301
R3*†	Disturb UF operation	P301, LIT301
R4*†	Affect chemical dosing	P203
R5‡	Chatter Motorised Valve	MV201
R6*†	Drain permeate water	MV303
R7*†	Overflow tank stage-1 through stage-6	P601
R8*†	Underflow UF feed water tank	MV201, P301
R9*	P101 running dry	MV101, P101, LIT101
R10†	Alter feed water FIT	FIT101
R11*	Turning off UV	P401, UV401
R12*	Flipping level switch	LS202, LS203
R13*†	Spoof pH meter	AIT202
R14*†	Spoof DPIT301 value	DPIT301
R15†	Change Duty of RO pump	P501, P502

* Attacks launched using A6L0 tool
† SCADA manipulation-based attack
‡ Pycomm based attack

Table 3. Result: Experimental evaluation of anomaly detectors

ID	Impact	Attacks	DAD	MLP	GARX
R1	Overflow tank T101	14	12	6	2
R2	Underflow tank T301	13	13	11	11
R3	Disturb UF operation	12	10	0	11
R4	Affect chemical dosing	4	3	0	0
R5	Chatter Motorised Valve	2	1	0	0
R6	Drain permeate water	4	0	0	0
R7	Overflow tank stage-1 through stage-6	4	0	0	0
R8	Underflow UF feed water tank	14	14	0	10
R9	P101 running dry	14	13	1	8
R10	Alter feed water FIT	12	10	0	10
R11	Turning off UV	4	2	0	0
R12	Flipping level switch	4	2	0	0
R13	Spoof pH meter	9	3	0	0
R14	Spoof DPIT301 value	10	0	0	0
R15	Change Duty of RO pump	7	3	0	0

- *A6_L0 tool-based attacks:* The A6_L0 tool is an attack tool that launches attack at layer 0 network in SWaT testbed. With this tool, the instrument component of SWaT is controlled. The attacks generated are launched as on-the-path attacks between the Remote Input Output (RIO) Module through the communication protocol ENIP. The tool changes the command/values that is sent to the actuators and as well as the command/values that is going back to the PLCs.
- *Pycomm based attacks:* The Pycomm library is used for communicating to the PLCs. This library contains a classification of modules that is meant for PLC communication. Attacks launched using this library are in the form of simulation mode (for sensors) and manual mode (for actuators). When an attack is launched, the instrument(s) is first set to simulation/manual mode and then the values/commands are manipulated.
- *SCADA Manipulation based attacks:* Similar to Pycomm-based attacks, the attacks launched are in the form of simulation mode (for sensors) and manual mode (for actuators). This attack is carried out by changing the commands/values directly via the engineering workstation.

7.2 ADUT Reference Attacks

The study is performed with 15 reference attacks as presented in Table 2. For instance, the attack R_6 to drain permeate water is presented in Sect. 5.3 which mutates the command sent to the motorised valve MV303 from the stage-3 PLC. Similarly, the attack R_1 which overflows tank T101 by manipulating components LIT101, MV101 and P101 in stage-1 of SWaT. The attack turns off the outlet pump P101 and simultaneously opens the inlet valve MV101. The controller is deceived by manipulating the level sensor of tank 101 by setting it to safe range. Through this sequence, the goal to overflow the tank is achieved.

7.3 ADUT Effectiveness Evaluation

The reference attacks designed are mutated to create attacklets. The mutation operators are applied to each reference attacks to generate attacklets. Table 3 presents the number of attacks created for each reference attack. The number of attacks include the reference attack and the number of attacklets created for the reference attack. For reference attack R_1 which targets components LIT101, MV101 and P101, a total of 14 attacklets are created. All created attacklets along with reference attack are launched on the system to check if the ADUT detects the presence of attacks. For R_1, 12 attacks were detected by DAD, 6 by MLP and 2 by GARX and the detection score computed are 0.85, 0.43 and 0.14 respectively. This process is performed for all 15 reference attacks. Totally 123 attacks were created for 15 reference attacks. A total of 86 attacks were detected with overall detection score being 70% detected by DAD, 18 attacks were detected with overall detection score being 15% detected by MLP and 52 attacks were detected with overall detection score being 42% detected by DAD.

On analysis, it is found that a number of undetected attacks were due to their stealthy nature. The attacks manipulate the sensor measurement to a value closer to the normal value of the corresponding sensor. These kinds of attacks were not be able to detected by these mechanism especially by MLP. For GARX, it only detects specific attacks like continuous increasing the values of LIT. Hence, attacks that does not trigger these conditions were not detected. When a change is detected in GARX, the value is set to the sum variable that is added cumulatively. Hence, majority of the attacks did not surpass the threshold. The attacks that were not detected by DAD were due to the lack of invariants or conditions that were not designed for. Hence this methodology helped to identify missing invariants.

In addition, some of the mutants were not an attack itself as it corresponds to the actual plant process. For example, in R4 a total of 4 attacks were launched. The attacks were done on P203 which is a HCl dosing pump. The mutations were set value of the pump to 1, 0, −99 and 15. The actual state of the pump of the pump is 1 which indicated the pump is ON. Hence, this attacklet used will not be considered as a deviation in the plant process. Interestingly, when values -99 and 15 were send to the pump, the status of the pump turned OFF. Both GARX and MLP detected attack based on the change in water level. Attacks R4, R11, R12 and R13 which corresponded the chemical aspect and the quality of the water were not be detected. In R11, the attacklets changed the value of the UV reading, and in R12, the attacklets changed the level switch which is responsible for HCl and in R13, the attacklets changed the value of AIT202 which is the pH meter. All defense mechanism, failed to detect attacks on pressure sensor. In R14, the attacklets changed the values of the DPIT301. None of the anomaly detected raised alarm. These defense mechanism were on-going research and has been improved since the experiments were carried out.

8 Related Work

Attack models represents the sequence of actions to compromise a system and lead the system to unsafe state. Generally, attack models are used to find weaknesses or vulnerabilities in the design or implementation of the system. The analysis of system behavior under attacks will lead to research on defense and mitigation techniques to protect system. Information systems have well defined attack models such as Doleve-Yao [12] where that adversary has unlimited computation power and capabilities. In [28], researchers extended the Doleve-Yao model to make it suitable for CPS. They modelled the physical layer as abstract interaction to reason with the security of the physical layer in CPS. Timed Intruder Models based from Dolev-Yao intruder model for verification of cyber-physical security protocol was discussed [25]. This model takes into consideration of the physical properties of the system. Graphical techniques to derive attacks include attack trees [6]. The attack trees are created with root being the goal of the attacker and the branches describe the steps to successfully achieve the attack goal. These techniques may help to create attack models for cyber part of the CPS but not for the physical system. Records of cyber physical attacks are present in [14,22]. In [15], threat models for chemical reactor plant is introduced to launch attacks such as integrity attacks. In [5], attack templates were used to launch attacks on Automatic Generation Control(AGC) in power system. False data injection attack models were used in [21] to launch attacks in electric power grids. Aspect-oriented Modeling (AOM) [35] is used to model attacks. AOM technique is explored to model attacks as aspect of system, execution and evaluating system under attack. In [17], implementation of attack graphs using the architecture analysis and design language are shown. The architecture analysis and design language are used to determine information such as the system design, links, weaknesses, resources, potential attack instances, and their conditions. In [13], a hybrid graph (both the physical and cyber components) to model CPS attacks in smart grid. The hybrid graph model provided insight into potential attack vectors.

9 Conclusion

A methodology based on mutation to generate attacks for cyber-physical systems is experimentally studied in this work. The methodology mutates the states and commands in the plant thereby creating process anomalies. It is applied on an operational water treatment plant to test the effectiveness of three anomaly detectors based on DAD, GARX and MLP. A set of reference attacks were designed for the proposed framework and they are mutated using the mutation operators for CPS to create attacklets. The attacklets are launched using the attack launcher tool to create process anomalies in the testbed. The experimental results proved the applicability of the proposed approach on a functional plant and its effectiveness in testing anomaly detectors.

Acknowledgements. This research/project is supported by the National Research Foundation, Singapore, and Cyber Security Agency of Singapore under its Award No.: NRF2018NCR-NSOE005-0001. Any opinions, findings and conclusions or recommendations expressed in this material are those of the author(s) and do not reflect the views of National Research Foundation and Singapore Cyber Security Agency of Singapore.

References

1. Adepu, S., Mathur, A.: Distributed attack detection in a water treatment plant: method and case study. IEEE Trans. Dependable Secure Comput. (2017, under review)
2. Adepu, S., Mathur, A.: Distributed detection of single-stage multipoint cyber attacks in a water treatment plant. In: Proceedings of the 11th ACM Asia Conference on Computer and Communications Security (2016, in Press)
3. Adepu, S., Mathur, A.: Using process invariants to detect cyber attacks on a water treatment system. In: Hoepman, J.-H., Katzenbeisser, S. (eds.) SEC 2016. IAICT, vol. 471, pp. 91–104. Springer, Cham (2016). https://doi.org/10.1007/978-3-319-33630-5_7
4. Almalawi, A., Fahad, A., Tari, Z., Alamri, A., AlGhamdi, R., Zomaya, A.Y.: An efficient data-driven clustering technique to detect attacks in scada systems. IEEE Trans. Inf. Forensics Secur. **11**(5), 893–906 (2016)
5. Ashok, A., Wang, P., Brown, M., Govindarasu, M.: Experimental evaluation of cyber attacks on automatic generation control using a CPS security testbed. In: 2015 IEEE Power & Energy Society General Meeting, pp. 1–5. IEEE (2015)
6. Byres, E., Franz, M., Miller, D.: The use of attack trees in assessing vulnerabilities in SCADA systems. In: International Infrastructure Survivability Workshop IISW 2004, Lisbon, December 2004
7. Cardenas, A.A., Amin, S., Sastry, S.: Secure control: towards survivable cyber-physical systems. System **1**(a2), a3 (2008)

8. Chen, P.Y., Yang, S., McCann, J.A., Lin, J., Yang, X.: Detection of false data injection attacks in smart-grid systems. IEEE Commun. Mag. **53**(2), 206–213 (2015)
9. Chen, T.M.: Stuxnet, the real start of cyber warfare [editor's note]. IEEE Network **24**(6), 23 (2010)
10. Demillo, R., Lipton, R., Sayward, F.: Hints on test data selection help for the practicing programmer. Computer **11**(4), 34–41 (1978)
11. Denker, G., Dutt, N., Mehrotra, S., Stehr, M.-O., Talcott, C., Venkatasubramanian, N.: Resilient dependable cyber-physical systems: a middleware perspective. J. Internet Serv. Appl. **3**(1), 41–49 (2012). https://doi.org/10.1007/s13174-011-0057-4
12. Dolev, D., Yao, A.: On the security of public key protocols. IEEE Trans. Inf. Theory **29**(2), 198–208 (1983)
13. Hawrylak, P.J., Haney, M., Papa, M., Hale, J.: Using hybrid attack graphs to model cyber-physical attacks in the smart grid. In: 2012 5th International Symposium on Resilient Control Systems, pp. 161–164. IEEE (2012)
14. He, H., Yan, J.: Cyber-physical attacks and defences in the smart grid: a survey. IET Cyber-Phys. Syst. Theory Appl. **1**(1), 13–27 (2016)
15. Huang, Y.L., C'ardenas, A.A., Amin, S., Lin, Z.S., Tsai, H.Y., Sastry, S.: Understanding the physical and economic consequences of attacks on control systems. Int. J. Crit. Infrastruct. Prot. **2**(3), 73–83 (2009)
16. Hurley, N., Cheng, Z., Zhang, M.: Statistical attack detection. In: Proceedings of the third ACM Conference on Recommender Systems, pp. 149–156. ACM (2009)
17. Ibrahim, M., Al-Hindawi, Q., Elhafiz, R., Alsheikh, A., Alquq, O.: Attack graph implementation and visualization for cyber physical systems. Processes **8**(1), 12 (2020)
18. Jia, Y., Harman, M.: An analysis and survey of the development of mutation testing. IEEE Trans. Software Eng. **37**(5), 649–678 (2011)
19. Kuang, F., Xu, W., Zhang, S.: A novel hybrid KPCA and SVM with GA model for intrusion detection. Appl. Soft Comput. **18**, 178–184 (2014)
20. Lipovsky, R.: New wave of cyberattacks against Ukrainian power industry, January 2016. https://www.welivesecurity.com/2016/01/20/new-wave-attacks-ukrainian-power-industry/
21. Liu, Y., Ning, P., Reiter, M.: False data injection attacks against state estimation in electric power grids. In: Proceedings of the 16th ACM Conference on Computer and Communications Security, pp. 21–32 (2009)
22. Loukas, G.: Cyber-Physical Attacks: A Growing Invisible Threat. Butterworth-Heinemann, Oxford (2015)
23. Miclea, L., Sanislav, T.: About dependability in cyber-physical systems. In: 2011 9th East-West Design & Test Symposium (EWDTS), pp. 17–21. IEEE (2011)
24. MR, G.R., Somu, N., Mathur, A.: A multilayer perceptron model for anomaly detection in water treatment plants. Int. J. Crit. Infrastruct. Prot. **31**, 100393 (2020)
25. Nigam, V., Talcott, C., Aires Urquiza, A.: Towards the automated verification of cyber-physical security protocols: bounding the number of timed intruders. In: Askoxylakis, I., Ioannidis, S., Katsikas, S., Meadows, C. (eds.) ESORICS 2016. LNCS, vol. 9879, pp. 450–470. Springer, Cham (2016). https://doi.org/10.1007/978-3-319-45741-3_23
26. Poovendran, R.: Cyber-physical systems: close encounters between two parallel worlds [point of view]. Proc. IEEE **98**(8), 1363–1366 (2010)
27. Rice, M., Guernsey, D., Shenoi, S.: Using deception to shield cyberspace sensors. In: Butts, J., Shenoi, S. (eds.) ICCIP 2011. IAICT, vol. 367, pp. 3–18. Springer, Heidelberg (2011). https://doi.org/10.1007/978-3-642-24864-1_1
28. Rocchetto, M., Tippenhauer, N.O.: CPDY extending the Dolev-Yao attacker with physical-layer interactions. In: Proceedings of the International Conference on Formal Engineering Methods (ICFEM) (2016)

29. Shon, T., Moon, J.: A hybrid machine learning approach to network anomaly detection. Inf. Sci. **177**(18), 3799–3821 (2007)
30. Sugumar, G., Mathur, A.: Testing the effectiveness of attack detection mechanisms in industrial control systems. In: 2017 IEEE International Conference on Software Quality, Reliability and Security Companion (QRS-C), pp. 138–145, July 2017
31. Sugumar, G., Mathur, A.: A method for testing distributed anomaly detectors. Int. J. Crit. Infrastruct. Prot. **27**, 100324 (2019). https://doi.org/10.1016/j.ijcip.2019.100324
32. SWaT Secure Water Treatment Testbed (2015). https://itrust.sutd.edu.sg/itrust-labs-home/itrust-labs_swat
33. Wallace, G.: Target and Neiman Marcus hacks: the latest. CNN Money (2014)
34. Wang, J., Tu, W., Hui, L.C., Yiu, S., Wang, E.K.: Detecting time synchronization attacks in cyber-physical systems with machine learning techniques. In: 2017 IEEE 37th International Conference on Distributed Computing Systems (ICDCS), pp. 2246–2251. IEEE (2017)
35. Wasicek, A., Derler, P., Lee, E.A.: Aspect-oriented modeling of attacks in automotive cyber-physical systems. In: 2014 51st ACMEDACIEEE Design Automation Conference (DAC), pp. 1–6. IEEE (2014)
36. Wong, E.: On mutation analyis. Ph.D. thesis, Purdue University (1993)
37. Ye, Y., Li, T., Adjeroh, D., Iyengar, S.S.: A survey on malware detection using data mining techniques. ACM Comput. Surv. (CSUR) **50**(3), 41 (2017)

CIMSS - Critical Infrastructure and Manufacturing System Security

WiP: Distributed Intrusion Detection System for TCP/IP-Based Connections in Industrial Environments Using Self-organizing Maps

Aleksei Kharitonov(✉) and Axel Zimmermann

Aalen University, Beethovenstr. 1, 73430 Aalen, Germany
{aleksei.kharitonov,axel.zimmermann}@hs-aalen.de

Abstract. Digitization of the industry comes along with improvements for modern production, because the processes can be influenced, monitored and coordinated. A digitized facility needs the possibility of communication between distributed nodes, e.g. to react to events or to provide useful information to adjust the production process. However, processes of communication can be misused by attackers. Security holes in different information systems can be found by third parties and exploited. Thus, growing data exchange needs growing security of communication. Modern intrusion detection systems (IDS) often do not fulfill the requirements of industrial systems, because they either neglect safety aspects or are not failure resistant or interrupt the data flow. The aim of this paper is to propose improvements regarding all those issues. In this paper, an online intrusion detection system architecture for industrial Ethernet is being researched on an industrial line testbed. In the current work, the requirements for intrusion detection in an industrial environment are analyzed and a hardware architecture to carry out online intrusion detection for Ethernet-based connections using a passive sniffer approach is proposed. The data is being processed in-place in a microcontroller. For the developed platform an intrusion detection algorithm using self-organizing map algorithm was implemented. The model has to be trained with normal vectors in a semi-supervised way. A prototype of the proposed architecture is evaluated on an industrial line testbed (cyber-physical factory) using TCP/IP/Ethernet header analysis. The proposed IDS, which is based on two microcontrollers, monitors an Ethernet 100-BaseTX cable and was able to detect TCP port scans, remote denial-of-service exploits and ARP cache poisoning which targeted the programmable logic controller in an industrial testbed. The proposed architecture can be used for online intrusion detection under speed restrictions.

Keywords: Self-organizing maps · Intrusion detection · Industrial network security · Critical infrastructure protection

J. Zhou et al. (Eds.): ACNS 2021 Workshops, LNCS 12809, pp. 231–251, 2021.
https://doi.org/10.1007/978-3-030-81645-2_14

1 Introduction

Motivation. An automated production process is advantageous in different fields of industry, like manufacturing, power generation and food or pharmaceutical industry, because the production parameters can be controlled automatically, fast, easily and, if necessary, remotely. Any kind of automation requires to maintain control of the production lines, i.e. the possibility to check and change production parameters, e.g. speed of a motor, temperature in a tank or air pressure. In a company working with automated production, the industrial control system (ICS) is one of the essential parts, because it enables to monitor and adjust industrial processes. A secure and reliable functioning of the ICS is desired. The ICS consists of one or more control system units connected to field devices, namely actuators and sensors. The functions of the ICS include data acquisition, supervisory control and coordination of the production process. Electrical, mechanical, chemical and other types of components can be incorporated for detection and control purposes, depending on the respective industrial needs [33]. The production parameters are collected via measurement devices, converted into a digital form and usually integrated into a supervisory control and data acquisition (SCADA) system. These data are transported between sensors, actuators and control units through communication channels. Thus, the data play a crucial role in industrial processes, and their control is based on the data. As a consequence, the security of data of control systems is a core part regarding the security of the industry.

Security vulnerabilities can arise in many areas. Due to growing variety of field devices and their specific interfaces, a systematization of the data exchange was inevitable, which means the creation of standardized industrial communication protocols. But at that time, most of the industrial communication protocols didn't consider data security aspects. Nowadays it is still possible to damage an industrial facility remotely. In 2010, the Stuxnet attack has shown that it is feasible to damage physical objects via cyber attacks even in trusted environments [21]. Even an air-gap between the industrial and office networks didn't protect the centrifugal machine. In 2014, attackers infiltrated a German steel facility using spear phishing attack and got access down to the production network [30]. The attack led to outage of control components and a steel mill damage afterwards.

To prevent intruders and to minimize risks, an intrusion detection system as a first stage of prevention is needed, which can be adjusted to specific industrial requirements. In Sect. 2 those requirements are discussed. Algorithms for anomaly based detection have been taken into consideration, namely Self-Organizing Maps (SOM), Artificial Neural Networks (ANN), Transductive Support-Vector Machines (TSVM) and Local Outlier Factor (LOF) [7,19,27,42]. SOM are known for their ability to structure data by creating a map that represents the data pattern [19]. Because of a relatively small latency, small memory footprint and the ability to implement semi-supervised training, SOM was the algorithm of choice for the implementation. SOM have been successfully applied for intrusion detection purposes [1,6,15,26,32,43,44].

Basic Classification of IDS. A possible way to protect against cyberattacks is to analyze data continuously and trigger an alarm at an early stage of the attack. The alarm is caused by the anomalous behavior of data of the production system. Such tools are known as Intrusion Detection Systems (IDS). The IDS analyses for example data like logs, network traffic, security reports, etc., and warns automatically about possible threats that are present in the system. The taxonomy of IDS is a highly researched topic [4,8,22,28]. There are two main types of IDS: a misuse-based, which is also called signature-based or rule-based, and an anomaly-based approach. The misuse-based detection technique involves comparison of a monitored object to an attack database. Thereby it helps to detect already known attacks with high reliability and few false alarms, i.e. this approach usually exhibits a high true positive and low false positive rate. But the preformed database restricts the detection of novel attacks. The anomaly-based IDS type builds a normal behavior model of a system based on the data that are produced under normal working conditions. A deviation of the tested object from the learned model is identified as anomaly. The advantage of this method is its ability to detect zero-day attacks, i.e. new attacks. The disadvantage of this method is a possible high number of false alarms (high false positive rate). Most of the times, it is not possible to build a complete normal model of the monitored objects, because it would be necessary to collect all variations of data that are correct and normal. To make advantage of both types of IDS, a sometimes separately classified combination of these techniques (hybrid) is used.

Another categorization of IDS refers to where it is located: on the network side monitoring traffic or on the host side monitoring software and processes. Depending on its application, the IDS is classified as network-based or host-based. It would be beneficial to obtain the data on the host side, where the data is properly interpreted and can be easily analyzed, in contrast to laborious analysis of non-dissected data on the network interface [39]. But because the focus of this paper lies on industrial networks, where it is not possible to implement a host-based IDS for all kind of field devices that are to be monitored in the factory (see Sect. 2, paragraph functional requirements), a network-based approach is chosen instead as the only meaningful way to detect attacks on sensors and actuators.

The IDS can also be categorized by the data processing mode. The data that is analyzed by the IDS can be processed in continuous mode or in batch mode. Furthermore, the IDS can be characterized by the way of data processing, which is done either in-place or in a centralized way. Not only the processing, but also the collection of the data can be carried out at the edge device or centralized.

Previous Research About IDS for Industrial Environments. An architecture of distributed IDS for ICS was proposed by Cruz et al. [11]. The data acquisition takes place using a passive tap that sends data to a shadow security unit, which reports security events to the security management platform. An input/output (IO) channel operation which monitors on the physical layer is briefly described. It is questionable to directly connect to the analog wires using an analog-digital converter device. This setup could affect the field level of the actuators or sensors leading to undefined behavior. Another approach for intrusion detection using hierarchical monitoring inside the industrial environment is proposed by Ghaeini et al. [13]. The data acquisition occurs in-place using a bridge device. The bridge device should meet the requirements of industrial networks and be able to guarantee the real-time requirements of the network communication. An anomaly-based IDS based on semi-supervised learning using a multi-agent approach is proposed by Clotet et al. [9]. To detect intrusions by monitoring of control parameters and building of an autoregression model is proposed by Hadžiosmanović et al. [14]. This approach was evaluated on two real-life water treatment plants. It continuously tracks updated values of the process variables to detect and counteract against process control attacks. Another semantic security approach is proposed by Lin et al. [23]. It was evaluated on the IEEE 30-bus system and includes steps such as monitoring of control commands, collecting measurements, checking integrity of network packets followed by intrusion detection.

Previous Research About Anomaly Detection Using SOM. Hormann et al. have researched the applicability of SOM in industrial environments [16]. The feature extraction of this technique is dependent on the tool Wireshark[1]. Some features were indexed to an integer and some feature values were left as is. A normalization of the features is applied as well. More research is needed concerning the real-time and speed performance. Furthermore, to provide an IDS that is retrofit ready would also be important. In the current paper, we try to address those aspects.

Zanero et al. have researched the possibility to analyze the packet payload using a two-tier architecture with SOM [45]. A survey on different modifications of the SOM algorithm for intrusion detection is described by Qu et al. [31].

Previous Research About Hardware-Accelerated IDS. A common way to detect anomalies in the traffic is deep packet inspection using a rule-based method. Hardware-accelerated IDS usually use rule-based methods. The task of the hardware in this case is to accelerate specific computations that must be executed quickly. The following examples give a short insight in research about hardware IDS. Methods that inspect high speed TCP data could be implemented via FPGA as it has been done by Schuehler et al. [36]. Another rule-based approach that uses FPGA for acceleration of string matching in intrusion detection problems is proposed by Hutchings et al. [17]. A mechanism of a network-based IDS for detection of Man-In-The-Middle (MitM) attacks has been proposed for example by Belenguer and Calafate [5]. In their research a low-cost hardware is proposed that analyzes ARP traffic and helps to detect or prevent MitM attacks. An approach to speed up in-depth traffic analysis via partitioning that divides the overall network traffic into subsets of smaller size is proposed by Kruegel et al. [20]. In this paper the IDS is proven to be effective, but the aspect of costs for implementing such a system is not discussed. An intrusion detection system based on artificial neural networks that uses network data acquisition based on

[1] https://wireshark.org/.

Ethernet hub is discussed by Linda et al. [24]. However, in general the use of active taps in industrial environments is discouraged, due to the influence of the tap on the communication itself. A failure in the tap system can lead to a failure in the control system. A retrofitting of the IDS with hub based data acquisition is not always possible. This results from the fact that some industrial devices are not designed to work on the physical layer, but instead operate on the data link layer, where the extraneous MAC addresses would not occur due to routing at the switch side. Also, the shutdown of the hub ceases the communication. Thus, some important safety requirements and cost optimization have not been considered in previous proposals.

Contributions

- New and simple hardware design, which takes into consideration the strict industrial requirements and is applicable to detect anomalies in industrial Ethernet in real time and is retrofit ready
- Proposed anomaly detection algorithm allows to detect malicious packets based on Ethernet/IP/TCP header information
- Online network-based anomaly detection on the edge, e.g. on the network cable of a device, is possible under speed restrictions

The remainder of this paper is organized as follows. In Sect. 2 requirements for IDS in industrial environments are analyzed. In Sect. 3 a semi-supervised anomaly detection algorithm based on self-organizing maps is described. Section 4 describes materials and methods used in the paper. In Sects. 5 and 6 a hardware IDS module and IDS network are presented. In Sect. 7 the evaluation results of the detection algorithm running on real hardware are discussed. Finally, we conclude the paper in Sects. 8 and 9.

2 Requirements for IDS in Industrial Environments

Functional Requirements. In industrial environments a quick reaction to anomalous behavior is necessary, because a cyberattack on a factory is able to endanger human safety or cause great economical damage. To achieve a quick reaction to cyberattacks, *real-time* intrusion detection is needed, i.e. the IDS must react as quickly as possible to suspicious behavior in the data. This fact determines that the data should be processed *continuously* instead of working with batches. As said before, it is impossible to implement a host-based IDS for all types of sensors and actuators in even a small industrial environment due to the variety of their architectures, software resources, their embedded nature and therefore, lack of modifiability. For a host-based approach it would be necessary to modify the firmware of each sensor and actuator. As a consequence, the source of the audit data (i.e. the data that should be monitored) must be the network traffic going to and from the monitored device. In other words, the IDS must be *network-based.* The IDS can be designed active, i.e. it can prevent or mitigate the attacks according to the IDS's decision, which turns the IDS into an intrusion prevention system (IPS). However, as experience shows, the anomaly based detection methods tend to have nonzero false alarm rates [37]. That fact hinders the application of anomaly based IDS as an IPS, because it can disrupt an adequate data flow. Thus, the IDS must not disturb the natural traffic and cannot be authorized to block data packets by itself. This means that the interruption of the signal, which can be the result of power dependent tapping, is to be avoided. Therefore, the IDS has to be *transparent with respect to the transmission medium*. The IDS should notify an overlaying authority about the malicious activity instead of taking action itself. Because the attacks in an industrial network can be caused at the field level of the ICS, it is meaningful to capture and process the data in a distributed manner near to the monitored device.

To summarize, the functional requirements of the industrial IDS are:

- real-time operation
- continuous working mode
- network-based
- transparent with respect to the transmission medium

Requirements for IDS Hardware. For online intrusion detection, online data acquisition is unavoidable. Derived from the functional requirements, the data for purposes of processing and analysis in IDS should be captured transparently from the view of the transmission medium. In this paper, the communication in the network will be limited to wired connections and especially to industrial Ethernet. In general, the application of a network hub for wired networks can be used to capture data, where the data is broadcasted to all participants and filtered later at the Media Access Control (MAC) level by every network participant. This approach produces a computational overhead for the industrial network devices if more than two appliances are connected to the hub. But thereby, the requirement for IDS not to interfere with the natural traffic in the industrial environment would be violated, because the natural communication flow is changed. Moreover, the data that moves through the network hub will suffer additional delay due to hub processing delay, which is undesired, because of real-time requirements for industrial networks [38]. An important property of the data capture is its *transparency for the data* going over the medium. This is the reason why in this case it is impossible to use network hubs for more than two network participants. Because it is meaningful to *capture and process traffic in place* to reduce latency, it is necessary to have a unit that is able to read and interpret data on the physical layer. For industrial Ethernet this function can be implemented via an Ethernet physical layer chip (PHY) and a data processing unit (PSU) with a proper interfacing between them [3]. To run IDS algorithms, a computational hardware is needed. This can be a separate processor or the same PSU which is used for the data processing unit. Because of the non-interference requirement, the emerging alarm messages can not be sent over the same industrial network, which would create unnatural additional data for the equipment. As an appropriate solution a separate physical network can be built, where the

IDS can communicate with superior authorities without influence on the data flow of the monitored data stream. A disadvantage of this method is an increasing maintenance overhead and, hence, additional costs. But the IDS by itself should not be able to influence the industrial network. Because switches are store and forward devices, they can potentially introduce nondeterministic latency to the forwarded packets. Another important requirement for the hardware is *reasonable costs*. It is uneconomical to implement a high-end processor for intrusion detection. Thus, an embedded solution could be preferred. To summarize, the important parameters to consider about the hardware are the following:

- transparent at the physical layer
- online data acquisition and processing
- low-cost

Requirements for IDS Software. The following requirements for the intrusion detection algorithm should be fulfilled:

- Fast. Maximal data throughput over time, i.e. low latency. Minimal time for processing of one vector.
- Low and static size memory footprint. Use of minimal memory resources with constant size to fit in the embedded processor's RAM.
- High classification power, e.g. high area under the curve of receiver operating characteristics (ROC AUC).
- Be able to be trained in a semi-supervised way [40].

The relevant aspects for comparison of the algorithms are shown in Table 1. All of the compared algorithms are able to be trained in a semi-supervised way.

Table 1. Estimated algorithm comparison

Algorithm	Latency	Memory footprint
ANN	High [25]	Low
TSVM	Medium [10]	High [29]
LOF	Low [2]	High [35]
SOM	Low [34]	Low

Transductive support-vector machines (TSVM) and Local Outlier Factor (LOF) algorithms need a big amount of memory [7,42]. Before the training one must save all of the training vectors. The training is done in a batch manner afterwards. The computational complexity of artificial neural networks (ANN) is high, because a single neuron is connected to all neighbored neurons in the next layer and the activation function is calculated in each neuron. This also increases the latency. The suitability of the SOM algorithm results from a low latency due to only one layer of nodes, its low memory requirements and good results from other researchers concerning the ROC AUC. Although the classification power of the SOM algorithm may be lower in comparison to the other techniques, its ability to be used in online intrusion detection sounded promising. There are variants and modifications of the SOM algorithm, such as Hierarchical SOM (HSOM) and growing hierarchical SOM (GHSOM). But their memory footprint is not static, therefore they are not considered in this work. One of the crucial parameters for choice of an algorithm was the latency. The algorithm of choice was the self-organizing map algorithm.

3 SOM Based Anomaly Detection Algorithm

Self-organizing maps are used to map high-dimensional feature vectors onto a low dimensional map, most of the time onto a two dimensional one, that preserves the neighboring proximity for similar vectors. In comparison to error-correction algorithms, SOM uses competition learning, where the winning node gets the highest activation and the neighboring nodes are activated proportional to a neighboring activation function [19]. A simplified overview of a 3×5 SOM architecture is represented on Fig. 1. Every node contains a weight vector which has the same dimension as the input vectors.

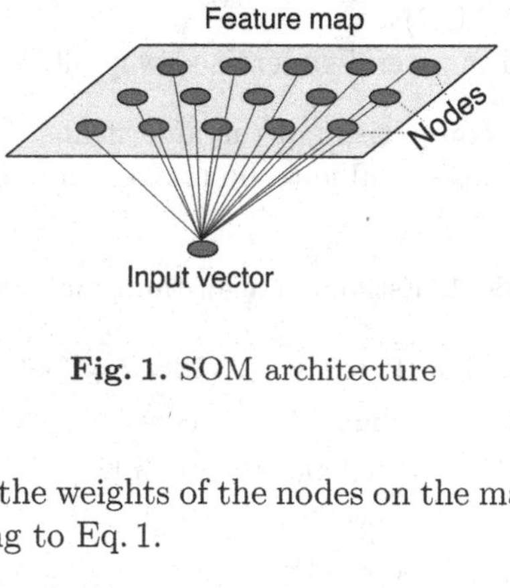

Fig. 1. SOM architecture

During the training the weights of the nodes on the map are updated towards the input data according to Eq. 1.

$$w_i\left(t+1\right) = w_i\left(t\right) + \alpha\left(t\right) \cdot h_{ci}\left(t\right) \cdot \left(x\left(t\right) - w_i\left(t\right)\right) \tag{1}$$

In which w_i is the weight vector, t is the iteration number, α is the learning rate, h_{ci} is the neighborhood function, which is usually used as a Gaussian function returning a value between $[0, 1]$, and x is the input vector. It was observed that the decay speed of the neighborhood function had an influence on the map topology defect, where the trained map tangles [41]. To avoid this defect, a decay of the function was found via trial and error. An exponential decay function was used, see Eq. 2.

$$h_{ci} = e^{-\frac{d}{2\sigma^2(t)}} \tag{2}$$

Where d is a distance between the input vector and the neuron for which the neighborhood function is calculated, $a(t)$ is the map area exponentially decreasing over time by time constant τ, so that $\sigma(t) = re^{-\frac{t}{\tau}}$ applies, where t is the iteration number, $r = \arg\max\{\text{size\_x}, \text{size\_y}\}$ is the maximal map width in 2D space. A very high value of τ will lead to a long convergence, i.e. training time, whereas a too small value may lead to map entanglement, as mentioned before. In retrospect of our observations, the value of τ should be considered to be chosen in the way that τ will be bigger than the mean period of the rarest periodical packet times 5. This assumption is derived from the reasoning that the map model would converge after 5τ iterations.

Weight vectors and input vectors have the same dimensions. After the training, all input vectors can be mapped to a best matching unit (BMU) found using Eq. 3.

$$c = \arg\min_i (d) \tag{3}$$

In which $d(x, w_j) = \|x - w_j\|$ is the distance between an input vector x and a weight vector w_j. The relevant parameter to determine whether a vector is an anomaly or not is the distance threshold for the distance d. If the calculated distance d for a given vector exceeds threshold

$$d > d_{max}, \tag{4}$$

then an alarm is generated. This threshold can be set in various ways, for example, by calculating the maximum distance that can occur for normal vectors and set the threshold to this value. The second way is to calculate the threshold value as a moving average for a large number of normal packets. The third way is to set the value manually by first analyzing the distances to normal vectors with some sigma addition to eliminate possible unwanted false alarms. The third way implies the risk of incorrect classification of anomalous vectors that could be specially created by the attacker to disguise them as normal packets.

Comparison with Other Works. A similar approach for anomaly detection was proposed by Hormann et al. [16]. The main difference to the present work is that Hormann et al. calculated the threshold with some pre-defined percentile tolerance. In our case, no percentile tolerance was needed to achieve good results. Furthermore, the features in that work are derived using the Wireshark tool, while string values were uniquely indexed and those indexes were used as features in feature vectors. This method is therefore dependent on the application of the tool Wireshark. In our case, TCP packets are used directly to build feature vectors. Another approach using self-organizing maps is proposed by Zanero et al. [45]. A two stage learning technique is proposed. In the first stage, network packets are being clustered and in the second stage, anomaly detection using time correlation of multiple packets is carried out. This approach is computationally heavy, even today, because of high algorithmical complexity, and therefore not considered to be implemented in microcontrollers.

4 Materials and Methods

4.1 Materials

The information about the software and hardware which was developed in this paper is structured as follows. The anomaly detection algorithm has been described in Sect. 3. A simplified model of the implemented software is depicted on Fig. 2. The hardware for the prototype was build in accordance with the architecture proposed in Sect. 5.

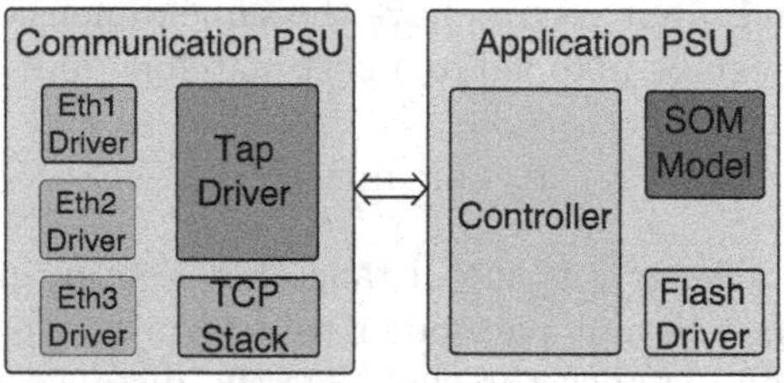

Fig. 2. Software view of the IDS module. The communication processing unit (PSU) handles the drivers and the TCP stack. The tap driver extracts Ethernet frames from the bridge and pushes them into the application PSU. The controller handles the application logic, feature extraction, self-organizing map training and interacts with the IDS manager. Trained models are saved in the non-volatile flash memory.

4.2 Methods

The following methods for feature extraction, training and test of the IDS have been applied. An industrial testbed, i.e. the cyber-physical factory, was used to train and evaluate the IDS. The testbed consists of seven different production modules, which carry out specific operations, e.g. in our case these are drilling, turning, heating, feed parts, storaging, optical inspection and forwading to packaging with an automated guided vehicle [12]. All the modules are connected in a single network. The entire testbed has to be secured, even if it is considered to be located in a trusted network. In our case, only one module was used for the IDS evaluation.

Feature Extraction. The packets used for the training set are based on TCP protocol. Feature vectors for training are derived from each TCP packet, see Table 2. Each feature was normalized to the range $[0, 1]$ by $\hat{f} = \frac{f}{2^s - 1}$, where f represents the feature value, $\hat{f}$ is the normalized value, s is the size of the feature in bits. The size of the feature is calculated by dividing the size of the feature object in bytes by the number of features that are derived from it.

Because there are different lengths of the data fields inside the TCP packet, this can cause smaller features having superior influence on the model. Such a dominance of smaller features is due to a bigger difference in a change of the least significant bit and thus a higher distance to the BMU. Thereby, fields that have a bigger possible value range, like MAC-address that exhibit a size of 6 bytes, are divided into independent byte-features. This allows for bigger quantization steps. E.g. after normalization of a one-byte feature the precision should be in the order of 10^{-3}, for a two-byte feature in the order of 10^{-5}, while the precision of the math for a 6-byte number should lie in the order of 10^{-15}. For numeric fields, like packet length or TCP port number, the whole value was normalized. E.g. for the TCP port number 102 the normalized value has to be calculated via $\frac{102}{2^{16}-1}$.

Table 2. Chosen features for TCP protocol.

Feature object	Size/Bytes	Number of derived features from object
Source MAC	6	6
Destination MAC	6	6
IPv4 length	2	1
Source IPv4	4	4
Destination IPv4	4	4
Source TCP port	2	1
Destination TCP port	2	1

Training. The command to start or stop the training process is sent from the IDS manager over the isolated network. The required map size is embedded in this command. After the IDS module receives the start command, a SOM model with randomly initialized weights with the defined size is created. From each TCP packet going over the tap a feature vector is derived, see Sect. 4.2. The model of the SOM is then updated in accordance with Eq. 1. Training of the normal model is done during the normal operation of the production line. At first, the IDS module was trained online during operation with data from the PLC of the industrial line testbed until no packets were detected as anomaly within two minutes. I.e. training was carried out until the true negative rate reached 100%. This means if there didn't occur any false positive alarms in two minutes, the SOM counted for being trained. To determine the time needed to wait until training can be considered as done, the longest time period of packet occurence between participants was taken with a fivefold margin.

Test. After training, the IDS module is set to the monitoring state. During this phase, all TCP packets are tested in accordance to Eq. 4. If a packet is classified as anomaly, a message including packet information is sent to the IDS manager.

5 IDS Module Architecture for Industrial Ethernet Networks

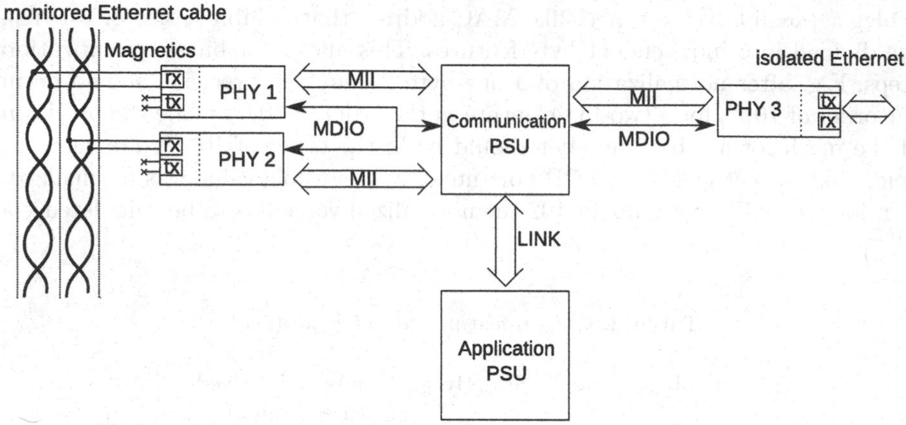

Fig. 3. IDS module hardware view

On Fig. 3 a concept of the system view is represented. The most used data transmission rate for industrial Ethernet is 100 Mbps based on 100Base-TX standard. This standard defines the full-duplex transmission mode over two wire pairs, where one pair is used for each direction. The monitored Ethernet cable is represented as two twisted pairs. For capturing and processing of the data, two PHY chips are used for each direction. The transmit interfaces (tx) of the PHYs are not connected, because the data should be captured only and the communication should not be interfered by the data acquisition units, as it is described in the requirements for the data capture in Sect. 2. The increasing capacity of Ethernet networks requires other capture techniques that may have higher complexity. The tap will not be passive anymore and will have the drawback that the capture of data will not be transparent with respect to the transmission medium. This will interfere with the network communication and even add security risks to the system, because the sniffer itself can become an attack platform. Thus, its application is questionable and should be researched in future works. From the view of the physical layer, the data is routed over the media-independent interface (MII), which is interconnected to the PSU. A single communication processor should be able to serve three MIIs, two MDIOs and be able to communicate to the application PSU with sufficient speed with respect to real-time captured data. This requires highly parallel code execution for the PSU. Therefore, XMOS xCORE-200 microcontroller chips were chosen. Those were assumed to meet the software and hardware requirements during the IDS module design. In the data PSU a software MAC is implemented, which allows to process the captured data from the wire pairs. A third MII is connected to a separate PHY chip to facilitate communication to a separate Ethernet port, e.g. to send an alarm message or to configure the IDS. The tap-PHYs share the same Management Data Input/Output (MDIO) interface from the data PSU to enable the change of data rates or of the duplex modes. The communication PHY uses its own MDIO interface separated from the monitored Ethernet cable, which allows different data rates and duplex from the tap side. To relieve the computation load of the data PSU, a separate application PSU based on XMOS xCORE-200 chip is connected via XMOS xCONNECT 2-wire link. This step enables a data transmission rate of 160 Mbps[2] and should be able to handle 80% of the throughput of Fast Ethernet. This speed was sufficient for the given industrial factory testbed as discussed in Sect. 7. The maximum throughput could be further enhanced via using a 5-wire link.

6 IDS Network Architecture

An example of a network architecture monitored via an IDS is depicted on Fig. 4. The manufacturing execution systems (MES), which is connected to the industrial network, sends commands to the PLCs. For each sensor or PLC for monitoring, it is necessary to install an IDS module. Each module is located between the switch and the monitored device. The IDS is transparent to them both, i.e. it does not modify the communication. Configuration and communication with the IDS takes place via a separate alarm network that is completely isolated from the factory network. Even if the unlikely event happens that the alarm network fails or is compromised, it has no effect on the industrial network.

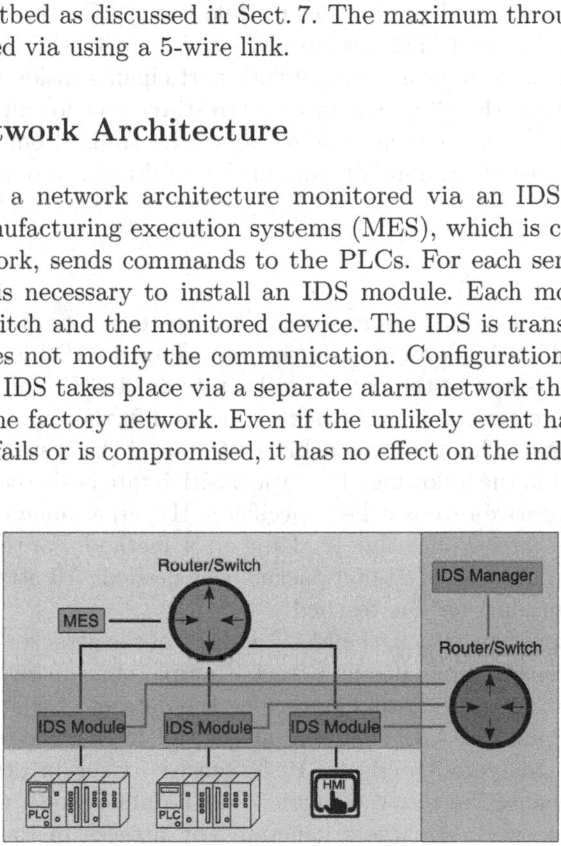

Fig. 4. IDS network

IDS modules are connected in an own subnet. Direct communication from the security specialist's PC to an IDS module has disadvantages, such as:

- A possible overload of the module if several users want to configure an IDS module,
- Resource consumption increases with multiple connections.

[2] https://www.xmos.com/download/xCONNECT-Architecture(1.0).pdf.

Therefore, the communication to the individual IDS modules was implemented via client-server architecture. The IDS modules connect to a manager who takes over control, configures and monitors the individual modules. Example commands are: start training on IDS No. 1, turn on the detection mode on IDS No. 2 and 3, load a pre-trained model, etc. The distribution of the IDS modules accross a cyber-physical factory is advantageous, because the communication patterns are simpler and, therefore, the concomitant data processing and detection of the malicious activities are computationally lighter than for a merged model of all network participants inside the factory. The intrusion detection occurs inside the IDS modules. The testbed production modules are PLC, energy sensor, touch panel and a working part that may be wired directly to the PLC over Input-Output (IO) wires. Because all the network participants inside the module are communicating with the PLC, the most interesting asset for an attacker is the PLC. Thereby, we narrowed the monitoring of the traffic from the whole production module down to the monitoring of the production module's PLC.

7 Results

Test of the IDS: Detection Performance. The detection rate of tested vectors is depicted on Table 3. A good classification regarding the IDS is achieved, when the true positive as well as the true negative rate are 100%. This means that all attack vectors were recognized as attack vectors and furthermore all normal data classified as normal. This goal was achieved for all of the tested attacks, as it's further explained in the following. The true positive rate is also called sensitivity, while the true negative rate is called specificity. Hyperparameter tuning such as learning rate was carried out using trial and error method. For the used learning rate $\alpha = 0.05$, an amount of 21,000 packets was needed. All attacks focused on the PLC of the production line testbed.

In the ARP spoofing attack, the MAC address of the attacker's laptop wasn't changed. This scenario simulates an attack example of an intruder that doesn't know the network infrastructure. Concerning the dataset of 30,000 packets that are produced during the ARP spoofing attack, all of them were recognized as attack vectors. This corresponds to 100% sensitivity, or in other words true positive rate. Because the test was carried out in online mode, the IDS will see normal packets as well as packets generated by attacks in the order of their appearance. During the test, all of the normal packets were recognized correctly as normal. That corresponds to 100% specificity.

The dataset for the TCP port scan attack consists of 30,000 attack vectors. Those vectors were produced by an attacker laptop with unchanged MAC address. All of the malicious packets were classified correctly as anomaly. All of the normal data were classified correctly, too. This corresponds to 100% sensitivity and 100% specificity.

The dataset for remote denial-of-service exploit on the PLC of a production module consists of 300 packets produced by an attacker laptop with unchanged MAC address. All of the attack vectors were classified correctly as anomaly. All normal packets were recognized as true negatives. This corresponds to 100% sensitivity and 100% specificity. The scope of the intended exploit attack was to represent a sabotage of the cyber-physical factory. There are different kinds of exploit attacks. In case that a change of communication pattern occurs, the proposed IDS should be able to detect the attack.

Table 3. Detection rate for normal vectors and four tested attacks.

Description	Detection rate
Normal traffic (true negative rate)	100%
ARP spoofing	100%
TCP port scan	100%
PLC specific exploit traffic	100%
PLC specific exploit traffic + manipulated MAC address	100%

The dataset for remote denial-of-service exploit on the PLC of a production module with changed MAC address of the attacker's laptop consists of 300 packets. In order to minimize the distance between the vectors produced by the attack packets and the trained packets, the attacker would want to imitate the victim's IP and MAC address with just one single bit difference. A possible problem for the IDS is the loss of accuracy in mathematical operations in floating point data types, especially for microcontrollers that use fixed size floating point data types. When using fixed size floating point data types, it is necessary to ensure that the precision of the data type for weights is greater than the precision when normalizing a single feature. For example, part of the information is lost if a feature with a length of 6 bytes is normalized via mathematical operations that use floating point data type with 4 bytes size. In such a case, a change of the least significant bit (LSB) in the feature will not be sensed in the normalized value after the normalization. This means that the calculated distance of a malicious vector could lie under the alarm threshold value.

To set the threshold value, the following three modes can be used. The first mode is called peak mode calculation. The corresponding formula for the threshold is $q = \arg\max_k \|x_k - w_k\|$, where k is the number of vectors. The distance of vectors to their BMUs is calculated and the maximum value is used as the alarm threshold. For all normal packets, the distance to the best matching units was 0. This can occur in case training vectors have little variance and are distributed in a very deterministic way. For the current dataset, a SOM with a size of 10×10 nodes could learn all the vectors.

The second mode is the moving average threshold calculation. Here the corresponding formula is $q_{i+1} = q_i + \frac{\|x-w_j\|}{(i+1)}$, in which q_{i+1} is the threshold value for the current iteration $i+1$, $\|x - w_j\|$ is the distance for a given vector x to the

BMU that has a weight vector w_j. For the used map with a learning factor of $\alpha = 0.05$ and with a size of 10×10 nodes, the mean calculated threshold value was 0.0551.

The third mode is the manual mode. The manual mode for setting the threshold value can be useful for alarm threshold fine tuning. Vectors with a manipulated LSB of one MAC address byte exhibit the smallest possible variation in comparison to a normal vector. Therefore, for a dataset that contains vectors with a manipulated LSB of one MAC address byte, the manual mode is the method of choice to set the alarm threshold. A small margin should be added to the distance peak value to avoid false alarms. In our case the maximal distance to the best matching unit was not higher than $q = 0.0008$, while the distance to the vectors generated via manipulating LSB of a byte in the MAC address has shown a Euclidean distance of $q_{arp} = 0.0011$. This means the threshold should be set no smaller than $q = 0.0008$, but no higher than $q_{arp} = 0.0011$. In case the threshold would be set smaller than $q = 0.0008$, the false positive rate will increase. In case the threshold would be set higher than $q = 0.0011$, the false negative rate will increase. The manual mode could be advantageous in comparison to the peak mode, because the security expert can set the alarm threshold in the best way to avoid false negatives or false positives. To carry out the ARP cache poisoning attack, one needs to have deep knowledge of the infrastructure, such as used TCP ports, IP and MAC addresses, and the communication paths, i.e. who establishes connections with whom. The requirement to gather all this data before the attack complicates the success of the attack to be carried out undetected. Concerning the classification performance of the proposed IDS, the ROC AUC for the researched attacks was 1.0, which means perfect classification of all tested vectors.

Speed Performance and Latency. The results of the speed performance measurements are depicted on Fig. 5a. From the graph one can see that in the detection mode the IDS performs about twice as fast as during the training phase. With increasing number of nodes on the map, the processing speed S and can be represented with the approximate function $S(x) = 62.0191x^{-0.8131}$ for the training curve and with $S(x) = 92.8045x^{-0.6743}$ for the testing curve, where x is the number of nodes in the map. The relative average errors of the approximation functions are not higher than 10.8%. In the experiment, only the SOM with size of 10×10 was used. The attained speed without packet drop was 1.4 Mbps during the training and 4.05 Mbps during the testing (i.e. detection) phase. These speeds could be seen as low in comparison to the maximal 100Base-Tx standard, but were enough to handle all the traffic of a PLC in the testbed in real time. The latency measurements are presented on Fig. 5b, i.e. the time needed for processing a single packet in the IDS module. For the used size of the SOM, the average training latency was 3.733 ms and the average testing latency was 1.215 ms. To achieve full real-time detection, the latency should not exceed several microseconds to comply with 100Base-TX standard. To fulfill this requirement, a special hardware implementation might be necessary.

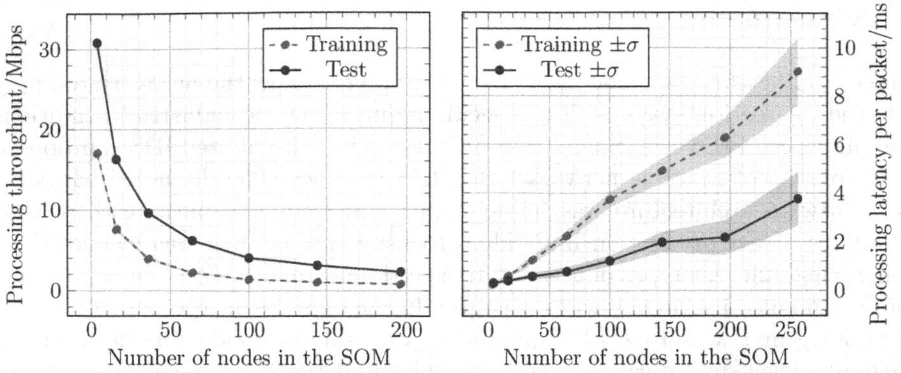

(a) Throughput performance (b) Latency per packet

Fig. 5. Throughput and latency measurements for the IDS moduleThroughput and latency measurements for the IDS module

8 Discussion with Respect to Critical Infrastructure (CI)

The proposed IDS covers some security issues concerning CI by early alert of the security team. This means that the proposed IDS can be used to detect a cyber attack at the early stage and, therefore, avoid bigger damage. The setup of the proposed IDS has a small reaction time on attacks inside the CI because of the in-place data evaluation, which is followed by the anomaly detection algorithm. The proposed IDS is designed for TCP-based communication. For other industrial communication protocols a different feature extraction algorithm is needed, but the anomaly detection algorithm can stay the same. Retrofitting of the proposed IDS to already existing industrial facilities is possible. In this case, there is no need of software or protocol changes concerning the already existing communication processes inside the CI. The semi-supervised method reduces the rule creation efforts and increases the chances to detect zero-day attacks. As it is impossible to detect and defend against advanced persistent threats (APT) with one technique alone, a multitude of detection techniques is needed. Because the proposed IDS is network based, it aims to detect activities of an attacker during weaponization and command & control inside a cyber-physical factory [18]. Therefore, the proposed IDS can be part of a defense mechanism against APT.

An in-place intrusion prevention system using modified architecture of our intrusion detection system can be seen as a future research area. Instead of alerting and waiting for the reaction of the security experts, an in-place blocking of the malicious behavior could reduce or prevent possible damage inside the CI.

9 Conclusion

The emerging threats in the industrial environment show the necessity to apply intrusion detection systems. The specific requirements of industrial conditions demand special IDS implementation. In this work, a distributed IDS is proposed that consists of multiple network-based IDS modules. The discussed hardware and software architecture was implemented and evaluated on a testbed, that simulates a real production line. The proposed IDS module was evaluated by generating different types of attacks. Its speed performance for training and test modes and also its latency was measured. In the experiment the size of the self-organizing map was 10×10. The module was able to handle the data stream without packet drop during the training at around 1.4 Mbps and around 4 Mbps during the detection mode. The proposed architecture of the IDS module hardware and the SOM based intrusion detection algorithm have shown applicability for intrusion detection in an industrial network. An inference speed of 4 Mbps doesn't comply with a 100Base-TX standard, but was enough for the experiment on the testbed. To increase the training and inference throughput, a more powerful processor has to be used, or a specialized processor with hardware accelerated functions can be developed. The proposed system was able to detect port scans and exploit attacks with 100% accuracy. It also should be able to detect novel attacks based on Enthernet/IP/TCP and to alarm at their early stage. To reduce risks and increase the detection ratings, a rule-based stateful engine should be used in parallel with an anomaly based engine to hinder attacks. There are possibilities for improvement of the proposed IDS. No semantical security monitoring has been implemented in the IDS. This means, in the case of undistorted communication patterns, a modification of control variables may remain undetected. For that kind of scenarios, protocol dependent feature selection/extraction and other detection algorithms may be required.

Author Contributions. A.K. conceived the project, performed the laboratory work and experiments, designed and implemented the software, also worked on the hardware design, and wrote the manuscript. Estimated percentage of contribution is 80%. A.Z. supervised the laboratory work and project, developed and implemented the hardware platform. Estimated percentage of contribution is 20%.

References

1. Albayrak, S., Scheel, C., Milosevic, D., Muller, A.: Combining self-organizing map algorithms for robust and scalable intrusion detection. In: International Conference on Computational Intelligence for Modelling, Control and Automation and International Conference on Intelligent Agents, Web Technologies and Internet Commerce (CIMCA-IAWTIC'06), vol. 2, pp. 123–130, November 2005. https://doi.org/10.1109/CIMCA.2005.1631456
2. Alghushairy, O., Alsini, R., Soule, T., Ma, X.: A review of local outlier factor algorithms for outlier detection in big data streams. Big Data Cogn. Comput. **5**(1) (2021). https://doi.org/10.3390/bdcc5010001

3. Arregoces, M., Portolani, M.: Data Center Fundamentals. Cisco Press, Indianapolis (2003)
4. Axelsson, S.: Intrusion detection systems: a survey and taxonomy. Technical report (2000). http://www1.cs.columbia.edu/~locasto/projects/candidacy/papers/axelsson00intrusion.pdf. Accessed 20 Mar 2021
5. Belenguer, J., Calafate, C.T.: A low-cost embedded ids to monitor and prevent man-in-the-middle attacks on wired LAN environments. In: The International Conference on Emerging Security Information, Systems, and Technologies (SECUREWARE 2007), pp. 122–127, October 2007. https://doi.org/10.1109/SECUREWARE.2007.4385321
6. Bolzoni, D., Etalle, S., Hartel, P.H., Zambon, E.: POSEIDON: a 2-tier anomaly-based network intrusion detection system. In: Fourth IEEE International Workshop on Information Assurance (IWIA 2006), pp. 144–156. IEEE Computer Society (2006). https://doi.org/10.1109/IWIA.2006.18
7. Breunig, M.M., Kriegel, H.P., Ng, R.T., Sander, J.: LOF: identifying density-based local outliers. In: Proceedings of the 2000 ACM SIGMOD International Conference on Management of Data, SIGMOD 2000, pp. 93–104. Association for Computing Machinery, New York (2000). https://doi.org/10.1145/342009.335388
8. Buczak, A.L., Guven, E.: A survey of data mining and machine learning methods for cyber security intrusion detection. IEEE Commun. Surv. Tutor. **18**(2), 1153–1176 (2016). https://doi.org/10.1109/COMST.2015.2494502
9. Clotet, X., Moyano, J., León, G.: A real-time anomaly-based ids for cyber-attack detection at the industrial process level of critical infrastructures. Int. J. Crit. Infrastruct. Prot. **23**, 11–20 (2018). https://doi.org/10.1016/j.ijcip.2018.08.002. http://www.sciencedirect.com/science/article/pii/S1874548217300884
10. Collobert, R., Sinz, F., Weston, J., Bottou, L.: Large scale transductive SVMs. J. Mach. Learn. Res. **7**, 1687–1712 (2006)
11. Cruz, T., et al.: A distributed ids for industrial control systems. Int. J. Cyber Warfare Terrorism (IJCWT) (2014). https://doi.org/10.4018/ijcwt.2014040101. https://www.igi-global.com/article/a-distributed-ids-for-industrial-control-systems/123509
12. Festo: CP factory - the cyber-physical factory (2019). www.festo-didactic.com/int-en/learning-systems/learning-factories,cim-fms-systems/cp-factory/cp-factory-the-cyber-physical-factory.htm. Accessed 20 Mar 2021
13. Ghaeini, H.R., Tippenhauer, N.O.: Hamids: hierarchical monitoring intrusion detection system for industrial control systems. In: Proceedings of the 2nd ACM Workshop on Cyber-Physical Systems Security and Privacy, CPS-SPC 2016, pp. 103–111. Association for Computing Machinery, New York (2016). https://doi.org/10.1145/2994487.2994492
14. Hadžiosmanović, D., Sommer, R., Zambon, E., Hartel, P.H.: Through the eye of the PLC: semantic security monitoring for industrial processes. In: Proceedings of the 30th Annual Computer Security Applications Conference, ACSAC 2014, pp. 126–135. Association for Computing Machinery, New York (2014). https://doi.org/10.1145/2664243.2664277
15. Hoglund, A.J., Hatonen, K., Sorvari, A.S.: A computer host-based user anomaly detection system using the self-organizing map. In: Proceedings of the IEEE-INNS-ENNS International Joint Conference on Neural Networks. IJCNN 2000. Neural Computing: New Challenges and Perspectives for the New Millennium, vol. 5, pp. 411–416, July 2000. https://doi.org/10.1109/IJCNN.2000.861504

16. Hormann, R., Fischer, E.: Detecting anomalies by using self-organizing maps in industrial environments. In: Proceedings of the 5th International Conference on Information Systems Security and Privacy - Volume 1: ICISSP, pp. 336–344. INSTICC, SciTePress (2019). https://doi.org/10.5220/0007364803360344
17. Hutchings, B.L., Franklin, R., Carver, D.: Assisting network intrusion detection with reconfigurable hardware. In: Proceedings. 10th Annual IEEE Symposium on Field-Programmable Custom Computing Machines, pp. 111–120, April 2002. https://doi.org/10.1109/FPGA.2002.1106666
18. Hutchins, E.M., Cloppert, M.J., Amin, R.M., et al.: Intelligence-driven computer network defense informed by analysis of adversary campaigns and intrusion kill chains. Lead. Issues Inf. Warfare Secur. Res. **1**(1), 80 (2011)
19. Kohonen, T.: Self-organized formation of topologically correct feature maps. Biol. Cybern. **43**(1), 59–69 (1982). https://doi.org/10.1007/bf00337288
20. Kruegel, C., Valeur, F., Vigna, G., Kemmerer, R.: Stateful intrusion detection for high-speed networks. In: Proceedings 2002 IEEE Symposium on Security and Privacy, pp. 285–293, May 2002. https://doi.org/10.1109/SECPRI.2002.1004378
21. Langner, R.: Stuxnet: dissecting a cyberwarfare weapon. IEEE Secur. Priv. **9**(3), 49–51 (2011). https://doi.org/10.1109/msp.2011.67
22. Liao, H.J., Richard Lin, C.H., Lin, Y.C., Tung, K.Y.: Review: intrusion detection system: a comprehensive review. J. Netw. Comput. Appl. **36**(1), 16–24 (2013). https://doi.org/10.1016/j.jnca.2012.09.004
23. Lin, H., Slagell, A., Kalbarczyk, Z., Sauer, P.W., Iyer, R.K.: Semantic security analysis of SCADA networks to detect malicious control commands in power grids. In: Proceedings of the First ACM Workshop on Smart Energy Grid Security, SEGS 2013, pp. 29–34. Association for Computing Machinery, New York (2013). https://doi.org/10.1145/2516930.2516947
24. Linda, O., Vollmer, T., Manic, M.: Neural network based intrusion detection system for critical infrastructures. In: 2009 International Joint Conference on Neural Networks, pp. 1827–1834, June 2009. https://doi.org/10.1109/IJCNN.2009.5178592
25. Livni, R., Shalev-Shwartz, S., Shamir, O.: On the computational efficiency of training neural networks. In: Ghahramani, Z., Welling, M., Cortes, C., Lawrence, N., Weinberger, K.Q. (eds.) Advances in Neural Information Processing Systems, vol. 27. Curran Associates, Inc. (2014). https://proceedings.neurips.cc/paper/2014/file/3a0772443a0739141292a5429b952fe6-Paper.pdf
26. Lotfi Shahreza, M., Moazzami, D., Moshiri, B., Delavar, M.: Anomaly detection using a self-organizing map and particle swarm optimization. Sci. Iran. **18**(6), 1460–1468 (2011). https://doi.org/10.1016/j.scient.2011.08.025
27. McCulloch, W.S., Pitts, W.: A logical calculus of the ideas immanent in nervous activity. Bull. Math. Biophys. **5**(4), 115–133 (1943)
28. Mitchell, R., Chen, I.R.: A survey of intrusion detection techniques for cyber-physical systems. ACM Comput. Surv. **46**(4) (2014). https://doi.org/10.1145/2542049
29. Montague, P., Kim, J.: An efficient semi-supervised SVM for anomaly detection. In: 2017 International Joint Conference on Neural Networks (IJCNN), pp. 2843–2850 (2017). https://doi.org/10.1109/IJCNN.2017.7966207
30. MultiMedia LLC: German steel mill cyber attack (2014). https://ics.sans.org/media/ICS-CPPE-case-Study-2-German-Steelworks_Facility.pdf. Accessed 20 Mar 2021
31. Qu, X., et al.: A survey on the development of self-organizing maps for unsupervised intrusion detection. Mob. Netw. Appl. **26**(2), 808–829 (2019). https://doi.org/10.1007/s11036-019-01353-0

32. Rhodes, B., Mahaffey, J., Cannady, J.: Multiple self-organizing maps for intrusion detection. In: Proceedings of the 23rd National Information Systems Security Conference, pp. 16–19 (2000)
33. Ross, R.S.: Assessing security and privacy controls in federal information systems and organizations (2014). https://doi.org/10.6028/nist.sp.800-53ar4
34. Roussinov, D.G., Chen, H.: A scalable self-organizing map algorithm for textual classification: a neural network approach to thesaurus generation. In: Communication Cognition and Artificial Intelligence, Spring, vol. 15, pp. 81–112 (1998)
35. Salehi, M., Leckie, C., Bezdek, J.C., Vaithianathan, T., Zhang, X.: Fast memory efficient local outlier detection in data streams. IEEE Trans. Knowl. Data Eng. **28**(12), 3246–3260 (2016). https://doi.org/10.1109/TKDE.2016.2597833
36. Schuehler, D.V., Moscola, J., Lockwood, J.: Architecture for a hardware based, TCP/IP content scanning system [intrusion detection system applications]. In: Proceedings of 11th Symposium on High Performance Interconnects, pp. 89–94, August 2003. https://doi.org/10.1109/CONECT.2003.1231483
37. Sellappan, D., Srinivasan, R.: Performance comparison for intrusion detection system using neural network with KDD dataset. ICTACT J. Soft Comput. **4**, 743–752 (2014). https://doi.org/10.21917/ijsc.2014.0106
38. Skeie, T., Johannessen, S., Holmeide, O.: Timeliness of real-time IP communication in switched industrial ethernet networks. IEEE Trans. Industr. Inf. **2**(1), 25–39 (2006). https://doi.org/10.1109/TII.2006.869934
39. Spafford, E.H., Zamboni, D.: Data collection mechanisms for intrusion detection systems. Technical report, Center for Education and Research in Information Assurance and Security, CERIAS (2000)
40. Thomas, P.: Review of "semi-supervised learning" by O. Chapelle, B. SchöLkopf, and A. Zien, Eds. London, UK, MIT Press, 2006. IEEE Trans. Neural Netw. **20**(3), 542 (2009). https://doi.org/10.1109/TNN.2009.2015974
41. Valova, I., Georgiev, G., Gueorguieva, N., Olson, J.: Initialization issues in self-organizing maps. Procedia Comput. Sci. **20**, 52–57 (2013). https://doi.org/10.1016/j.procs.2013.09.238. https://www.sciencedirect.com/science/article/pii/S1877050913010387
42. Vapnik, V.N.: Statistical Learning Theory. Wiley-Interscience, New York (1998)
43. Zanero, S.: Analyzing TCP traffic patterns using self organizing maps. In: Roli, F., Vitulano, S. (eds.) ICIAP 2005. LNCS, vol. 3617, pp. 83–90. Springer, Heidelberg (2005). https://doi.org/10.1007/11553595_10
44. Zanero, S.: Improving self organizing map performance for network intrusion detection. In: SDM 2005 Workshop on Clustering High Dimensional Data and Its Applications (2005)
45. Zanero, S., Savaresi, S.M.: Unsupervised learning techniques for an intrusion detection system. In: Proceedings of the 2004 ACM Symposium on Applied Computing, SAC 2004, pp. 412–419. Association for Computing Machinery, New York (2004). https://doi.org/10.1145/967900.967988

Demand Manipulation Attack Resilient Privacy Aware Smart Grid Using PUFs and Blockchain

Soumyadyuti Ghosh[1(✉)], Urbi Chatterjee[2], Durba Chatterjee[1], Rumia Masburah[1], Debdeep Mukhopadhyay[1], and Soumyajit Dey[1]

[1] Indian Institute of Technology Kharagpur, Kharagpur, India
{soumyadyuti.ghosh,durba,rumiamasburah}@iitkgp.ac.in
{debdeep,soumya}@cse.iitkgp.ac.in

[2] Indian Institute of Technology Kanpur, Kanpur, India
urbic@cse.iitk.ac.in

Abstract. In recent years, the transitioning of conventional power grid system into the smart grid infrastructure has made the power distribution network more susceptible towards faults and physical attacks. In this context, we discuss recently proposed Manipulation-of-Demand via IoT attack, False Data Injection Attacks and Electric Fault Attacks. These attacks directly or indirectly can lead to localized blackout, falsified load forecasting, imbalance in demand-response system, generator tripping, frequency instability and loss of equipment etc. To *detect* and trace back to the source of such attacks, in this paper we inspect the potential of the promising permissioned blockchain technology which is designed for digital transaction, but has been extended to authenticate and assure integrity of real power consumption information in a seem-less manner. This information can be picked up from the smart meters, however the trusted gathering and recording of the information is imperative for end-to-end security. In this work, we bind the smart meter readings to the underlying hardware by enabling the properties of *Physically Unclonable Functions* (PUFs) which works as a hardware fingerprint of the device. The proposed PUF based power profile verification scheme would further *prevent* the system from the injection of any false data by an illegitimate smart meter. The novelty of the proposed work is to blend these two technologies in developing a robust and privacy-aware framework which detects and prevents the above mentioned security vulnerabilities and can be easily integrated with the smart grid infrastructure. Finally an end-to-end demonstration of the attack has been presented using MATLAB and Power World simulator whereas the proposed framework has been prototyped using commercial off-the-shelf products such as Raspberry Pi and Artix 7 FPGA along with an in-house blockchain simulator and a privacy-preserving detection scheme.

We would like to thank Swarnajayanti fellowship funded by DST, India, Information Security Education Awareness Project funded by DIT India, and Cyber Security Research in CPS funded by TCG Foundation, India for partially funding our research.

J. Zhou et al. (Eds.): ACNS 2021 Workshops, LNCS 12809, pp. 252–275, 2021.
https://doi.org/10.1007/978-3-030-81645-2_15

Keywords: MadIoT attacks · Electric fault attack · False data injection attack · Physically unclonable functions · Blockchain · Privacy

1 Introduction

The rapid changes in consumer participation, urge for improved reliability and efficiency and incorporation of renewable energy sources have made the modernisation of power grid imperative and accelerated. On one hand, smart grid systems have become increasingly sophisticated in terms of efficiency, while on the other hand, increased sophistication has opened up avenues for new security threats. In this work, we mainly focus on recently proposed three important categories of attacks that can pose a serious challenge for grids. These attacks are illustrated as follows:

1. **MadIoT Attacks:** Rapid growth of Internet-of-Things (IoT) devices and their integration with electrical appliances have opened up a new dimension for attackers to affect the transmission as well as cyber plane of the grid with a multitude of penetration techniques. A large-scale compromise of such devices against Mirai Botnet [16] can lead to a Distributed Denial of Service (DDoS) attack. The impact of such DDoS attacks can be accentuated beyond network infrastructures and can cause localised or complete blackout in the grid if not handled carefully. Subsequently, Dabrowski et al. [11] explored the possibility of compromising IoT devices to disrupt the normal operation of the power grid. A novel attack called Manipulation-of-Demand via IoT (MadIoT) [24] has been proposed where an attacker can collude with thousands of high-energy electrical appliances through IoT devices. Such an attack can disrupt the black start process which may further provoke a significant drop/rise in frequency of grid leading to cascading faults and increase in operational costs. To handle such grid disruption, there are some power system protection mechanisms [15] present in the framework such as automatic disconnection of generators, under frequency load shedding, over current protection, over/under voltage protection etc. However, such attacks can still lead to partition of a bulk power system and even to localised blackout. *Additionally, these protection mechanisms cannot lead to the source of such Botnet attacks.*
2. **Electric Fault Attacks:** Similarly, adversary can physically initiate electric fault attacks (EFA) [22] in the transmission line to introduce cascading line failures. The failure in one network eventuates in the disruption of another network, which subsequently perturbs the former network. Set-Valued Observers (SVOs) have been used for distributed fault detection systems in the literature. This technique has been utilised for both centralized detection systems as well as fully decentralized systems [23] where various detector nodes are distributed over the network and share a subset of measurements. Several machine learning (ML) and deep learning (DL) based schemes [20] have been proposed to provide reasonable accuracy for detecting electric faults. *However, such schemes work with original voltage/current*

consumption signals, thus violating the privacy of the consumers. Keeping this in mind, we address the issue of developing a detection mechanism for EFA which does not compromise user privacy.

3. **False Data Injection Attacks:** Load forecasting [3] is one of the most important processes that involves an in-depth analysis of smart meter measurements and is prone to false data injection attacks (FDIA) [18]. In such attacks, it is assumed that adversary can access information regarding system setup and skillfully modify smart meter data to stealthily inject errors without being noticed by existing detection algorithms. Though several works have been proposed in literature [25,27] to detect such bad measurements in the control system, *no mechanism has been suggested so far to prevent such data from entering the system.* Hence, we build up a verification framework for smart meters to detect falsified power profile information before it gets inserted in the cyber plane by the adversary.

1.1 Motivation

Physically Unclonable Functions (PUFs) have been proposed as a promising unconventional cryptographic primitive for certificate-less identity based authentication [8,9]. A silicon PUF is an input-output mapping $\gamma : \{0,1\}^n \rightarrow \{0,1\}^m$, where the m-bit *response* words are unambiguously identified by both the n-bit input *challenge* words, and the unclonable, unpredictable (but repeatable) instance-specific system behaviour. Simultaneously, Blockchains offer a natural technology to combine various entities under a single infrastructure to provide *trust, accountability, immutability, integrity, transparency* and *provenance* to the information. On the other hand, the Hashed Database is mainly centralized and controlled by an authorized entity. Any modification or deletion will need authorized permission, and internal malicious actors can alter the database content which leads to transparency and trust issues. But in Blockchain, any changes in one of the blocks will result in the updation of the previously associated blocks. Unlike databases, this added security feature engrossed within Blockchain makes them extremely useful to resist repudiation attacks. Subsequently, timestamps are created to ensure that each transaction can be traced and verified by the participating nodes. All of those ensures trust, accountability, and transparency to the system, which the Hashed Database fails to achieve. In the state-of-the-art literature, Blockchain has been used in smart grid application for key management [26], energy trading [19], grid monitoring [13], trustworthy data aggregation [14], group signature and covert channel authorization [12] etc. However, to the best of our knowledge, no previous work has been proposed using this technology as a possible countermeasure against demand manipulation based attacks. All the three attacks discussed above targets the same endgame, which is, to introduce falsified, malicious data and subsequently cause disruption by destabilizing the grid infrastructure; eventually leading to partial or total failure of the grid functionalities. The novelty of the proposed work is to detect such sources of any active/passive tampering of the critical data for the smart grid operations irrespective of their nature or mode of attack implementation. *Thus it is effective against a powerful attacker who may be employing a combination of these different classes of attacks possible in a power system.* This is one of the major contributions of the proposed work. The advantage of blending PUF and Blockchain technology together in order to detect the source of EFA, MADIoT attacks and prevent FDIA are mentioned as follows.

- MADIoT attacks compromise the high-energy electrical appliances remotely through IoT devices in such a way that the consumers may not be aware of appliances' power fluctuation. Blockchain technology can provide a grid functionality to keep track of these immutable power profiles generated at the user end. Our Blockchain based framework is able to trace back the source of such attacks whenever any user appliance is compromised. It also flags such attacks to the user accordingly.
- Adversary can cause EFA leading to cascading line failures in the grid. Various security measures such as overcurrent, overvoltage and undervoltage protection relays try to prevent the occurrence of such attacks by generating a breaker trip signal that cuts the transmission lines in the network leading to controlled load-shedding. Blockchain can provide the infrastructure to identify these broken links between different entities and subsequently initiate a rerouting process to find alternate paths to transmit electricity.
- However, FDIA can hamper such Blockchain functionalities by providing falsified data leading to erroneous load forecasting. To prevent physical data tampering and provide an efficient authentication mechanism, PUFs can be embedded in smart meters to bind actual power readings to the devices and maintain the integrity of the power profiles. PUF provides hardware root of trust and any data tampering would lead to unsuccessful authentication, rejection of the power profile by the other smart grid components.

Public key infrastructure (PKI) can also be used to resist FDIA. However, it will not guarantee key freshness. Hence, in the case of exponential growth in the number of smart meters, the key management will have a large overhead. Additionally, if the adversary has physical access to the meters and a strong protection mechanism is not deployed to secure the key, then the secret of PKI can be compromised. Table 1 provides the security assessment of different protection schemes on the smart grid against the above mentioned three attacks with/without having PUFs and Blockchain based countermeasures in place.

Table 1. Security assessment of different protection schemes in smart grid.

Security scheme	Vulnerable to MADIoT?	Vulnerable to EFA?	Vulnerable to FDIA?
Grid without security	Yes	Yes	Yes
Grid with secret key stored in smart meters	Yes	Yes	No
Grid with PUF, without Blockchain	Yes	Yes	No
Grid with Blockchain, without PUF	No	No	Yes
Grid with PUF and Blockchain	No	No	No

1.2 Our Contribution

Hence, to summarize our work, our contributions in the paper are as follows:

- First, we demonstrate the MADIoT, EFA and FDI attacks and explain their impact on the smart grid system.
- Next, we propose a lightweight countermeasure against FDIA by integrating PUF based power profile verification process with the smart meter.
- We also propose a strategic solution to integrate blockchain network with Non intrusive Load Monitoring (NILM) process of the smart grid to trace back to the physical attack and electrical fault source. The process *does not compromise the privacy* of individual legitimate consumers.
- Finally a prototype of the proposed scheme has been implemented to demonstrate our solution.

The rest of the paper is organised as follows. Section 2 describes a recently proposed PUF based authenticated key exchange protocol [7] that has been referred in our power profile verification scheme. In Sect. 3, we demonstrate MadIoT attacks, EFAs and FDIAs. In Sect. 4, we describe our proposed scheme and present the experimental results in Sect. 5. We conclude our work in Sect. 6.

2 Background: A PUF Based Authenticated Key Exchange Protocol

Here, we first discuss the traditional PUF based authentication scheme. It involves two parties, a prover and a verifier and proceeds as mentioned below:

1. *Enrolment Phase:* We consider that every prover has an embedded PUF instance. In this phase, the PUF instance of a device is characterized based on a set of randomly selected challenges and the responses are stored by the verifier in a Challenge-Response Pair Database (CRPDB) along with the identity of the prover. It is assumed that the enrolment phase is executed in a secure and trusted environment outside the reach of the adversary. Hence we assume that no data access or tampering attack can be launched in this phase.
2. *Authentication Phase:* This phase is assumed to be executed in an untrusted environment. Here the prover first sends its identity to the verifier. The verifier randomly chooses an entry from CRPDB with respect to that identity and sends the challenge to the prover. The prover characterizes the PUF instance by applying the challenge. It then collects the response and sends it to the verifier. If the collected response and the stored response are same, the prover is authenticated by the verifier.

But the naive authentication protocol can be vulnerable to model building attacks on PUFs, limited authentication and replay attacks. Very recently, Boyapally *et al.* have proposed an PUF based authenticated key exchange protocol [7] for smart meter. We have referred to this protocol as it is best suited for our proposed power profile verification scheme. Hence, in this section, we briefly explain the working principle of the authentication protocol. The protocol consists of three parties, utility server which acts as a trusted third party (TTP), the data concentrator unit (DCU) and the meter. The protocol executes in four phases as mentioned below:

Setup Phase: It is assumed that IBE is an identity-based encryption scheme and SKE is a symmetric-key encryption scheme. $\mathcal{H} : \{0,1\}^* \longrightarrow \{0,1\}^\lambda$ and $\mathcal{H}' : \{0,1\}^* \longrightarrow \mathbb{G}$ be two collision-resistant hash functions where λ is the security parameter and $\mathbb{G}$ be a group of prime order q. CG sets up its private/public key pair using IBE scheme as: $(msk, mpk) \xleftarrow{R} IBE.SetUp$.

Enrollment Phase. In this phase, the credential for the meter is generated by characterising the embedded PUF instance for challenge $\mathcal{C}$ and collecting the response $\mathcal{R}$. The secret key sk_A is generated by applying $\mathcal{R}$ to $\mathcal{H}$. Next the credentials for the DCU sk_{id} is generated by using the $IBE.KeyGen$ applying the msk and the DCU's identity id as input. The DCU then stores sk_{id} in its non-volatile memory (NVM). Finally associations between (id, sk_A) and $(sk_{id}, \mathcal{C}, A)$ are created using $\mathcal{H}$ as $\alpha_1 = \mathcal{H}(sk_A||id)$ and $\alpha_2 = \mathcal{H}(sk_{id}||\mathcal{C}||A)$. These two entities are encrypted with respective secret keys of meter A and DCU id using the encryption scheme of SKE and IBE. The encrypted association data $\sigma_1 = \mathsf{SKE.Encrypt}(sk_A, \alpha_2)$ and $\sigma_2 = \mathsf{IBE.Encrypt}(sk_{id}, \alpha_1)$ along with the challenge are stored in the utility server as σ. The control flow of the enrolment phase has been illustrated in Fig. 2.

Mutual Authentication. For each authentication request from the meter, the DCU responds with σ and a nonce value. The node then characterises its embedded PUF instance with $\mathcal{C}$ and generates the response $\mathcal{R}$ and re-generates sk_A and α_1 as described in enrollment phase. Further it decrypts σ_1 to retrieve α_2'. α_2' ideally should be equal to α_2. Similarly, teh DCU also decrypts σ_2 to retrieve α_1' using its secret key sk_{id}. It also generates α_2 by hashing sk_{id}, $\mathcal{C}$ and A. Next the meter and the DCU generate: $\beta_1 = \mathcal{H}(\alpha_1||\alpha_2'||\mathsf{nonce})$, $\beta_2 = \mathcal{H}(\alpha_1||\alpha_2'||(\mathsf{nonce}+1))$, $\gamma_1 = \mathcal{H}(\alpha_1'||\alpha_2||\mathsf{nonce})$, $\gamma_2 = \mathcal{H}(\alpha_1'||\alpha_2||(\mathsf{nonce}+1))$.

Session Key Exchange. Finally, the meter and the DCU randomly choose x and y from $\mathbb{Z}_q$ respectively. They next exchange $\mathcal{H}'(\alpha_1||\alpha_2)^x$ and $\mathcal{H}'(\alpha_1||\alpha_2)^y$. The final session key is: $K = \mathcal{H}(\mathcal{H}'(\alpha_1||\alpha_2)^{xy}||(nonce+2))$. If $\beta_1 == \gamma_1$ and $\beta_2 == \gamma_2$, then both parties successfully authenticate each other.

Now, to execute this protocol the smart meter needs to have an embedded PUF hardware and the capability of computing a hash function and a symmetric key algorithm (that uses K for encryption of the power profile). The major advantages of using this protocol are as follows:

1. **Resistance Against FDIA:** As every power profile is accepted by the DCU only after successfully authenticating the smart meter and as any modification/tampering over the communication channel via through Man-in-The-Middle (MiTM) attack can be detected by the hash function (i.e. $Hash(P||K)$), the proposed scheme is resistant against FDIAs.

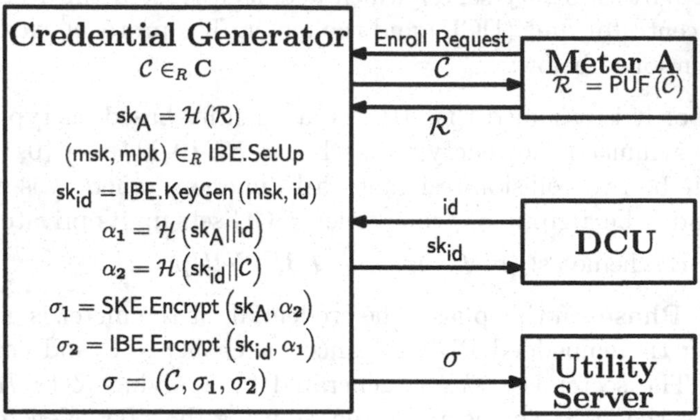

Fig. 1. Enrolment phase [7]

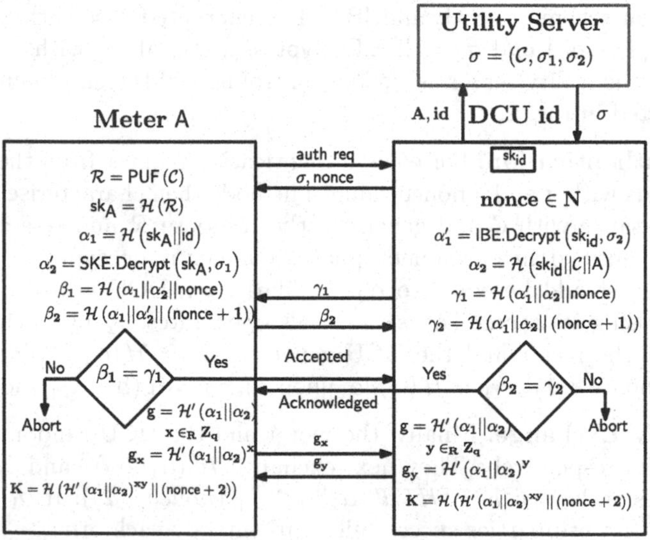

Fig. 2. Authentication and key exchange phase [7]

2. **Unlimited Authentication:** The protocol is designed in such a way that a single association data can be repeatedly used for multiple authentication sessions. Any modification in the association data would result in failed authentication. Hence, no power profile would be accepted by the DCU.
3. **Resistance Against Replay Attacks:** The protocol uses nonce values to resist against replay attacks.
4. **Resistance Against Model-Building Attacks:** As no PUF response is exposed in plain text, the scheme is resistant against model building attacks.

3 Consolidating Attack Surfaces on Smart Grid

The main objective of this work is to develop an attack source detection methodology for demand manipulation attacks and address some key concerns for each of these attack classes. Hence, for completeness purpose and to fully realise the effectiveness of the countermeasure, we have recreated our own setup to replicate the attack scenarios.

3.1 MADIoT Demonstration

Smart grid demand-response management systems continuously strive to minimize the imbalance of power consumed and power generated, ramping up or ramping down the power generation based on real-time demand. Here, we show how power demand can be manipulated through IoT devices to disrupt the frequency of the grid [24]. We run our demonstration in a Power World simulator using Western System Coordinating Council (WSCC) 9-bus model (refer to Fig. 3) as described in the MADIoT attack [24]. This grid model consists of 9 buses, 9 lines having a total of 315 MW initial demand. The generators present at buses 2 and 3 are buses with inertia, whereas the generator at bus 1

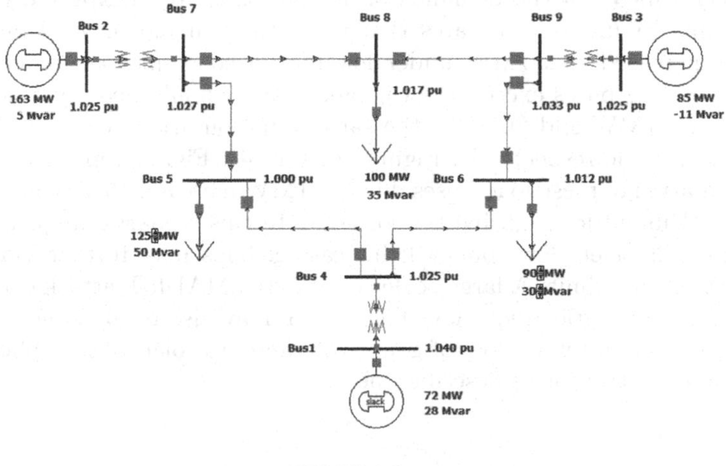

Fig. 3. WSCC 9-bus system

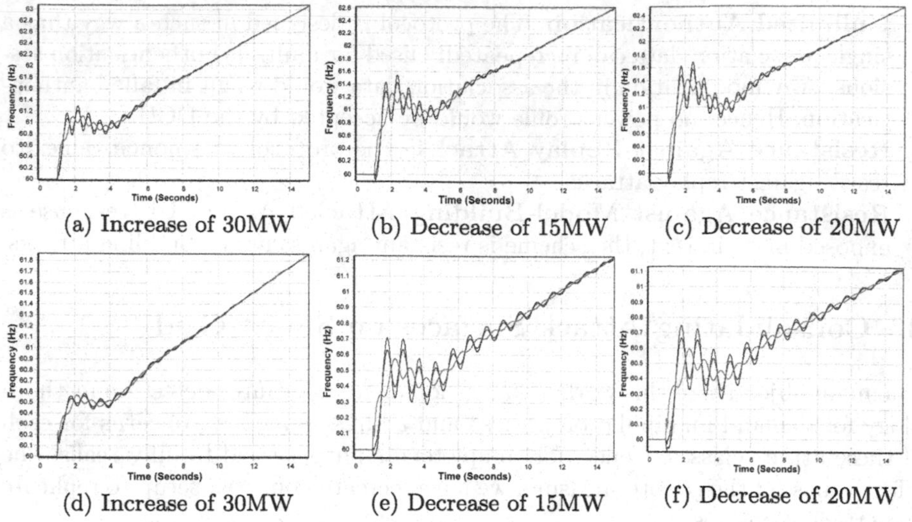

(a) Increase of 30MW (b) Decrease of 15MW (c) Decrease of 20MW

(d) Increase of 30MW (e) Decrease of 15MW (f) Decrease of 20MW

Fig. 4. Frequency deviations in load bus 5(blue), 6(red) and 8(green) of the generators due to unpredicted demand alteration in all the loads for low Inertia (5 s) constant (a, b, c) and high Inertia (15 s) constant (d, e, f) (Color figure online)

has no inertia, but it can alter its overall generation for making the power flow feasible. The bus numbers 5, 6 and 8 are the load buses of the corresponding model. The nominal frequency of the system 60 Hz and it is assumed that the frequency should be within 58.2 and 61.3 Hz approximately for normal operation of the grid. We know that frequency of the system is directly proportional to the difference between supply and demand generated. So any deviation in demand causes fluctuation in the grid frequency. Figure 4 shows the frequency disturbances of the load buses under low (5 s) and high (15 s) inertia constants of the generators when the demands of all the loads are unexpectedly alerted at same time. Figure 4a illustrates that when the demand on load buses 5, 6 and 8 are increased by 30 MW under low inertia constant, the frequencies in the corresponding buses exceed the tolerable limit. Simultaneously, if loads are decreased by 15 MW and 20 MW, the same situation arises again as shown in Fig. 4b and Fig. 4c respectively. Figure 4d, Fig. 4e, Fig. 4f represents the frequency alteration of these load buses due to 30 MW increase, 15 MW and 20 MW decrease of demand for high inertia constant. In this scenario, frequency deviation is comparatively low, but still increasing. This may further violate the frequency tolerance limit. A large-scale coordinated MADIoT attack can lead to further deviation of grid frequency. This attack may also result in activation of generator protection relays, loss of generators and grid blackout. Implication of such unwanted activation is described next.

3.2 Electric Fault Attack Demonstration

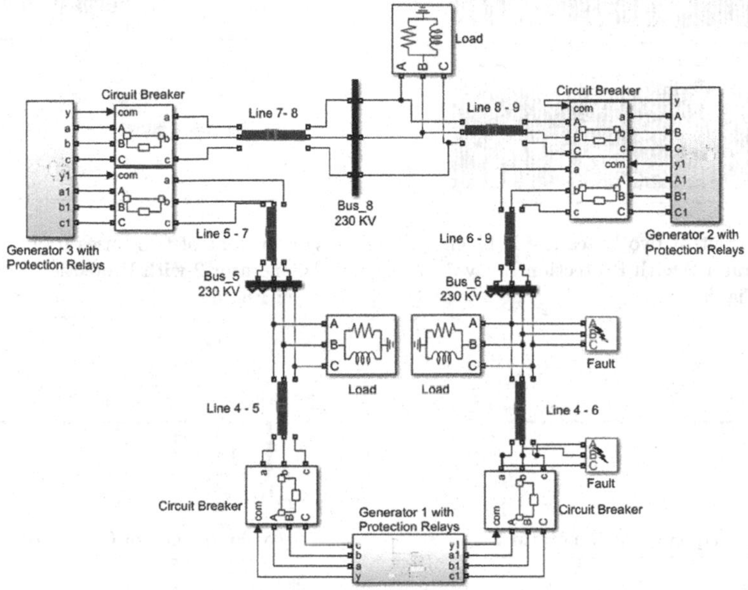

Fig. 5. An IEEE 9-bus model augmented with fault injection.

In this demonstration, we show how electrical faults may cause a localized blackout of a system by disconnecting faulty transmission lines from the grid. The attack setup as shown in Fig. 5, consists of an IEEE 9-Bus power system model with three generators, nine buses, circuit breakers, transmission lines, three loads and three protection relay modules along with multiple faults. The "Generator 2 with Protection Relays" block consists of a generator with overcurrent, overvoltage and undervoltage protection systems to check whether the current and voltage of a bus are maintained within predefined threshold values. A circuit breaker trip signal is generated if the corresponding voltage and current values violate any of these predefined thresholds. We simulate our model using Simulink in Matlab. Fig. 6 shows the current through two of the buses and the frequency of both generator 1 and generator 2 under normal condition. On the other hand, Fig. 7 shows the behaviour of the corresponding buses and generators when the fault is induced after one second. Due to the fault, the current through one of the buses starts increasing resulting into a frequency disturbance. This leads to destabilization of the speed of generators which may permanently damage the generators. As a countermeasure, the overcurrent relay module generates an undesired breaker trigger that cuts the line 6–9 and line 4–6 in the circuit resulted in a load-shedding, as shown in Fig. 5a by using the red colour.

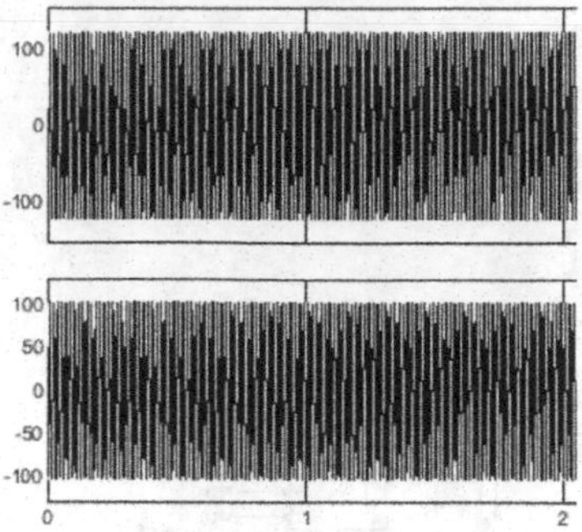

(a) Current of two buses inside block "Generator 2 with Protection Relays" as of Fig. 5

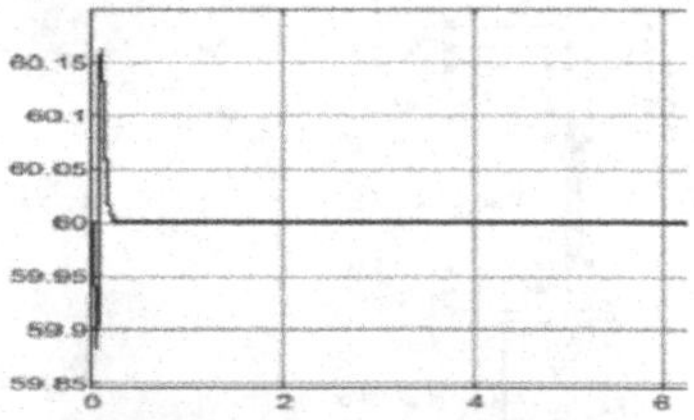

(b) Frequency of Generator 2

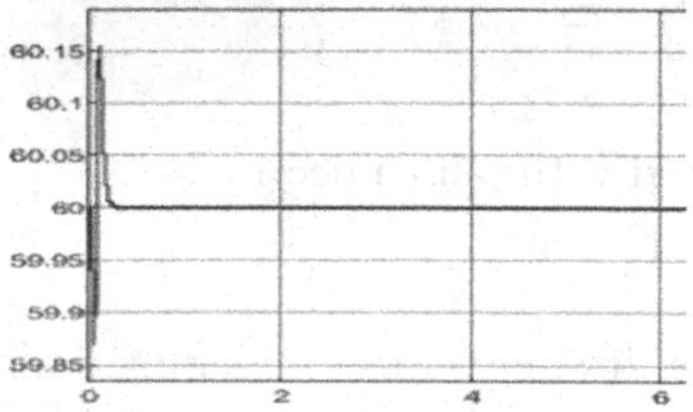

(c) Frequency of Generator 1

Fig. 6. Signals under normal operation

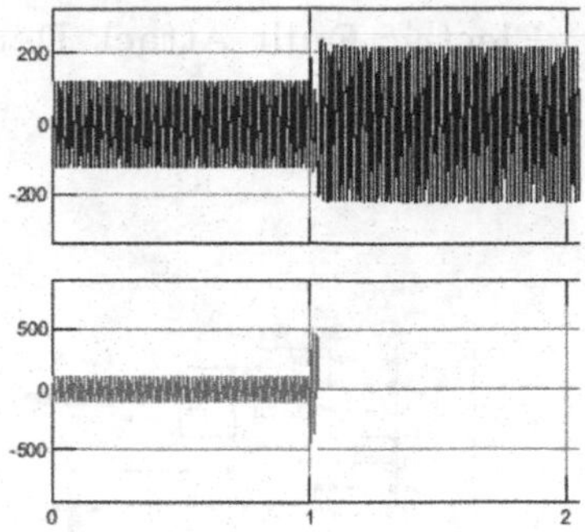

(a) Current of two buses inside block "Generator 2 with Protection Relays" as of Fig. 5

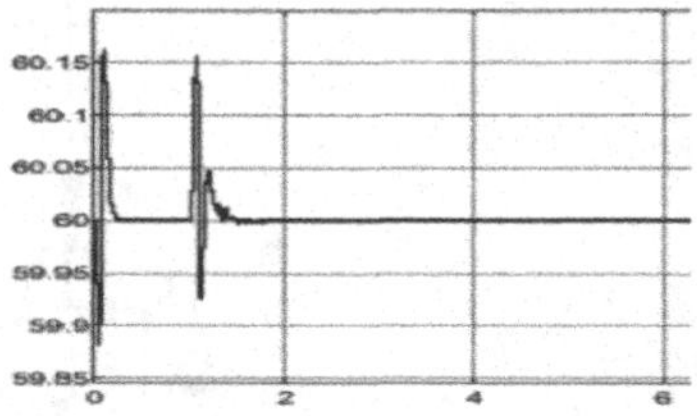

(b) Frequency of Generator 2

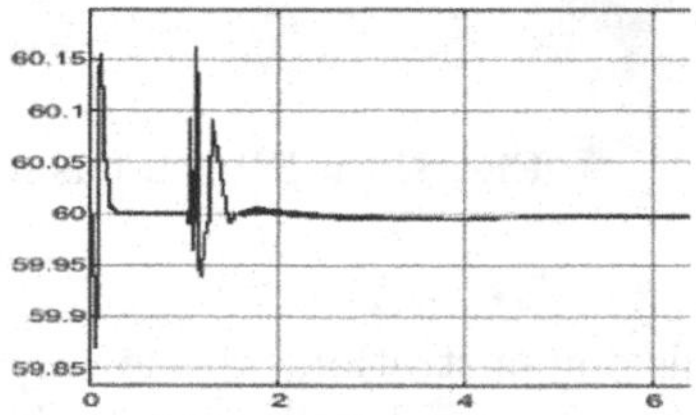

(c) Frequency of Generator 1

Fig. 7. Signals after fault is induced

3.3 False Data Injection Attack via Smart Meters

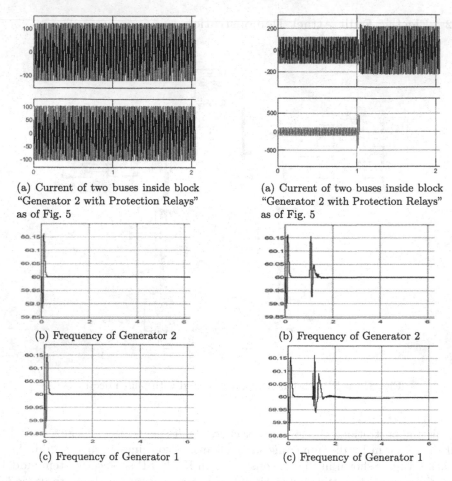

The load forecasting process generates pertinent information about the tentative power consumption of the loads in immediate future. It collects the smart meter readings of a set of loads for a time period and predicts the estimated demand for the same. Incorrect load forecasting can lead to frequency destabilization of the system as the rate of frequency change is proportional to the power imbalance between the demand and generation [21]. In our demonstration, we have used freely available aggregated time series data for all the consumers (sampling frequency 15 min) from Elia electric grid [1] and used support vector machine (SVM) based ML tool [6] to forecast the power demand one month ahead of time. As shown in Fig. 8, the x-axis denotes the date of the month and the y-axis denotes the predicted powers in kilowatts. Now the cyan colored line denotes the actual consumption of the loads, whereas the black line is the predicted value for the month that almost matches with the original data. Now, we insert false data in the time series for 1, 15, 30 and 45 at different time slots respectively and execute the same prediction model. As shown in the figure, the misprediction increases with the increase of false data injected in the system. In the next section, we discuss our novel robust and privacy-aware framework which detects and prevents all of the three security vulnerabilities and can be easily integrated with the infrastructure.

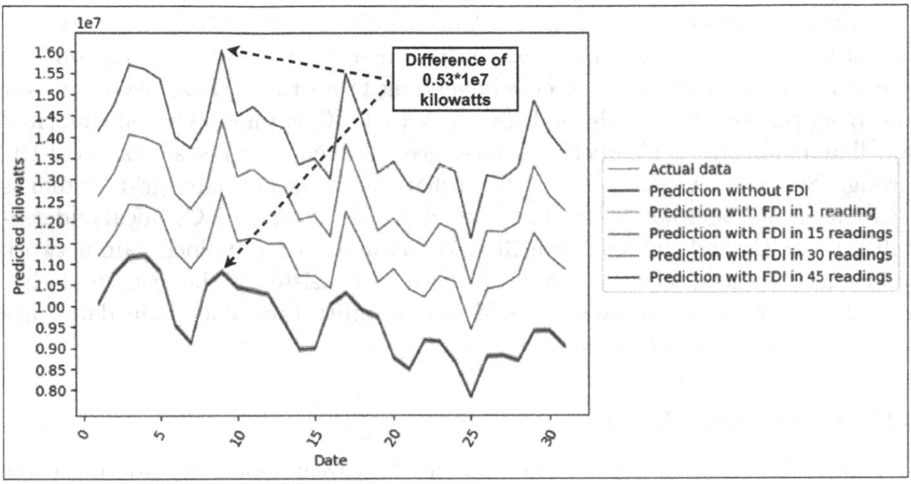

Fig. 8. False data injection attack against load forecasting.

4 Proposed Architecture of the Smart Grid System

In this section, we describe how the PUF enabled smart meter component guarantees that only legitimate users can log data in the system, whereas the attack source tracing procedure with blockchain fabric can detect if a legitimate user poses any malice in the system.

4.1 System Model

The setting assumed here is that the components of the grid are divided into two planes: a) Transmission Plane, b) Data Plane. Both the planes are monitored and managed by a supervisory control and data acquisition (SCADA) system which provides various grid functionalities by maintaining power and information flow between the grid entities. The information from the power system passes through the Remote Terminal Units (RTUs) which is a fundamental part of SCADA, to the Load Dispatch Centre (LDC). LDC also plays a crucial role in the reliable and efficient operation of the grid infrastructure. It is mainly responsible for the real-time grid monitoring, operation and control of the system. The transmission plane consists of generation, transmission, distribution networks and the consumers. It connects the communication between the power generation module, substations and consumers within a vast geographical region. This plane controls the power lines that are responsible for supplying the electricity to the household as per the demand request. Local substations regulate the power distribution between generation systems and the loads along with sending operational data to SCADA systems. The data plane maintains the information flow between the smart meters and the trusted utility server. Smart meters periodically collect consumers' energy profiles before sending the reading streams to the utility through Data Concentrator Units (DCUs). SCADA consists of a collection of these information from meters distributed throughout the area through RTUs, before selectively sending them to the LDC. While power flow from power systems through SCADA to LDC is unidirectional, information flow maintains a bidirectional interface between power systems and LDC through SCADA. A permissioned blockchain network of smart grid system is constructed by the power generation modules, substations, LDCs (local and centralized), DCUs and the trusted utility. We assume that the blockchain network maintains the basic security properties such as consistency (i.e. each node has the same view of the blockchain) and immutability (i.e. blockchain data once committed cannot be changed).

4.2 Adversarial Model

As discussed earlier in Sect. 3, we assume the threat model considering three potential scenarios through which the grid can be compromised. First, the attacker has physical access to the appliances or can control those appliances from a remote location. The attacker can manipulate the demand of these appliances, which can lead to disrupting the grid frequency as a result of the supply and demand imbalance. Secondly, we assume that the attacker can introduce electric fault attacks into the system, which can result in a disconnection of the transmission lines for preventing generation tripping. Moreover, in the last scenario, we assume the attacker with network access can perform eavesdropping, false data injection and replay attack to insert falsified power profile information in the smart metering setup which may further cause inaccurate load forecasting in the grid. Also, from a privacy aspect, we consider the grid nodes to be honest but curious entities, who want to gain the power consumption information of individual consumers to sell it to the marketing companies or obtain additional information about consumers' daily life patterns.

4.3 Working Flow of the Blockchain Network

The blockchain network consisting of the power generation modules, substations, DCU(s) and LDC(s) and a trusted utility server, is entrusted with the role of logging the events of the smart grid. The blockchain allows grid functionalities such as link break scenario between a generator and substation, change of utility request from consumers, or sending power consumption data of a consumer to be transparent and accessible to all participants of the blockchain network.

The above-mentioned functionalities of the grid operations are realized with the help of a grid topology encoded in the form of a graph and updated during every transaction. For instance, if an electrical link is broken between a generator module and a substation, the graph is updated by removing the corresponding edge to reflect the change and the generator informs the other members of the network by posting a new transaction. The PUF enabled smart meters, being resource thrifty, are not a part of the blockchain network. After a consumer's successful authentication of his/her PUF embedded in the smart meter to the DCU, the power profile is communicated to the same. The power profile of the consumer is sent to the DCU by the respective smart meter after its PUF instance is authenticated by the DCU. DCU then stores the data in Inter Planetary File System (IPFS) [2] and adds hashed value of the data (denoted by *IPFS Hash*) in a blockchain transaction (refer to Sect. 4.4 for details). The various transactions in our blockchain network are given as follows:

- **InitialTemplateTxn** creates the genesis block and shares initial grid topology with all the nodes in the blockchain network. It is posted by the utility server and consists of a template file which is used to generate the graph. All the blockchain nodes fetch the template file to build the initial grid view.
- **LinkDownTxn** is posted by a node to inform other nodes about link breaks down in the grid. As shown in Fig. 10, all the current transmission links are provided to the node, before it reports a particular breakdown. The nodes in the network, on receiving this transaction, update their local graph to reflect the changes in the grid.
- **LinkUpTxn** informs about restoration of a broken link and is posted by the same node which has posted **LinkDownTxn** previously after the link is again available.
- **DownReroutingTxn** initiates the rerouting process after a link breakdown to identify an alternate path to deliver electricity.
- **ChangeUtilityTxn** is posted by a substation informing the other nodes in the network regarding the change in utility of a consumer.
- **ConsumptionTxn** posts the power profile of a consumer. It consists of the Consumer Id and the IPFS hash of the power profile.
- **RegisterTxn** logs the registration data of a consumer with a substation.
- **CredGenTxn** shares the association data $(\mathcal{C}, \sigma_1, \sigma_2)$ (refer to Sect. 2) of a PUF enabled smart meter and a DCU binding the root-of-trust of smart meter with blockchain permanently and immutably.
- **AuthStatusTxn** broadcasts the status after authentication and key-exchange between a smart meter and a DCU.
- **NotifyLDCTxn** is posted by a generator which notifies the LDC whenever the frequency difference becomes more than the tolerance threshold τ. It consists of the ID of the generator and the timestamp when the disturbance has happened.
- **TraceSubstationsTxn** is posted by the LDC to trace the substations that need to initiate the backtracking process to identify the source of the frequency disruption. It consists of the identity of LDC, the list of substations needed to be triggered and timestamp of the attack.

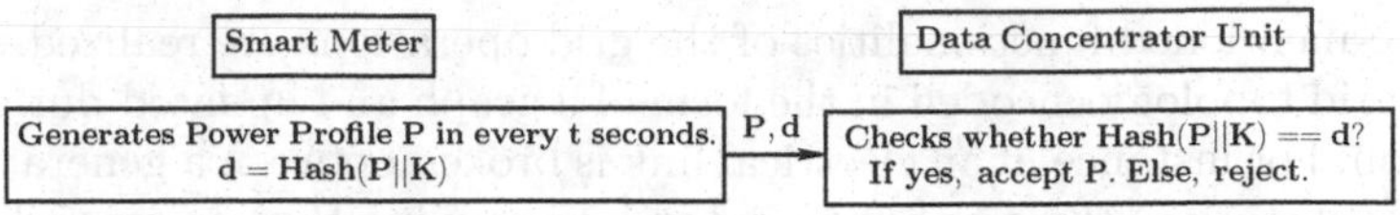

Fig. 9. Power profile verification protocol

4.4 Proposed Power Profile Verification Process

Here, we first map the PUF based authentication and key exchange protocol explained in Sect. 2 in our use case. We consider the utility server as a *TTP*. If there is a demand to install a smart meter in a household, an association between the smart meter and DCU is made by utility server in a secure and trusted environment. Hence, DCU is analogous to the *Server* as shown in Fig. 1 and Fig. 2 (refer to Sect. 2) and assumed to have a secret key stored in its NVM. The smart meter is enabled with an embedded PUF instance. The utility server stores the authentication credentials between the smart meter-DCU pair in the IPFS and adds a **CredGenTxn** in the blockchain to log this event. This is considered as the *enrolment phase.* For every sampling period, the smart meter and DCU generates a session key K by following the *authentication and key exchange protocol* and a **AuthStatusTxn** is posted by the DCU in case the PUF instance of the smart meter is successfully authenticated by the DCU. As this procedure is not part of the main contributions of the paper and can be followed from [7], we are not going into further details. Rather, we concentrate on the power profile verification procedure. For every new sampling period, the smart meter generates the power profile. It is to be noted that the power profile can not be encrypted with the session key as it is not possible to aggregate encrypted data collected from multiple smart meters at the DCU side. Moreover, encryption of such condensed data also might incur considerable execution time. Hence, a privacy preservation metering scheme is applied to it to camouflage the usage pattern of the household (refer to Sect. 5 for details). Now, we denote the privacy preserved power signature as P (refer to Fig. 9) for a sampling period of t seconds. It then calculates a hash of P appended with session key K, i.e., $d = Hash(P||K)$ and sends (P, d) to the DCU. As the DCU has also calculated the session key K, it can immediately verify the authenticity of the source of P. If the hash value matches, it saves the power profile in IPFS and posts **ConsumptionTxn** along with the smart meter ID. The aggregated power profile from multiple sources is then sent to utility server for further analysis. Now, for every sampling period, a new session key is used to generate the hash value. Hence, the freshness of the session is maintained and replay attack is resisted. Moreover, if the adversary wants to inject or modify the actual power profile, she would fail to calculate a valid hash value corresponding to the modified data as she has no knowledge about the session key K. Hence, simple verification procedure as proposed in this work can resist illegitimate and unauthenticated access, whereas the tracing algorithm can detect the sources of any physical disturbance induced by legitimate consumers through EFA or MadIoT attack.

4.5 Proposed Tracing Algorithm for Attack Source Detection

In this section, we propose the approach to detect the source of physical attack when an adversary compromises thousands of electric appliances and creates a power surge in the grid. As mentioned in Sect. 4, the software component in an LDC processes collects smart metering data to maintain the security and stability of the system in real-time. However, since the number of components that need to be monitored is vast, sophisticated digital processing of the data is required. In this context, we propose our detection algorithm to identify compromised consumers in the grid infrastructure as described in Algorithm 1 without

---

Algorithm 1. Algorithm for Detection of Attack Source

Inputs: V_G : Set of Generator nodes; V_S : Set of Substation nodes;
V_C : Set of Consumer nodes; Grid Network G;
Blockchain Ledger $T = \{t_1, \cdot, t_i, \cdot, t_n\}$; ▷ t_i is the tth block in the ledger;
Frequency Tolerance Threshold τ; Ideal Frequency f^*;
Appliance Disturbance Threshold ϕ;
Output: A set of consumers $Consumer\_Id$, set of broken links $Broken\_Links$;
Initialize: $flag \leftarrow false$, $Consumer\_Id \leftarrow \{\emptyset\}$, $Broken\_Links \leftarrow \{\emptyset\}$;

for all $v_i \in V_G$ **do**
  if $|f_{v_i}^{TS} - f^*| > \tau$ **then**
    Consumer_Id$_{v_i}$ ← NotifyLDC(v_i, TS);
    $flag \leftarrow true$;
  Consumer_Id ← Consumer_Id ∪ Consumer_Id$_{v_i}$;
if $flag = true$ **then** $Broken\_Links \leftarrow$ isLinkBroken(T, V_G, V_S, V_C, G);
return $\langle Consumer\_Id, Broken\_Links \rangle$;

function isLinkBroken(T, V_G, V_S, V_C, G)
  for $t_i \in T$ **do**
    if $t_i.type =$ "$linkdown$" & $t_i.timestamp \geq TS$ **then**
      $Broken\_Links \leftarrow Broken\_Link \cup t_i.link$;
  return $Broken\_Links$;

function NotifyLDC(v_i, TS)
  $C\_id \leftarrow \{\}$;
  V_S^* is set of substations in TraceSubstationsTxn t_i where $t_i.timestamp \geq TS$.
  for all $v_s \in V_S^*$ **do**
    $C\_id_{v_s} \leftarrow \{\}$;
    V_C^* is the set of all consumers under v_s.
    for all $v_c \in V_C^*$ **do**
      $C\_id_{v_s} \leftarrow C\_id_{v_s} \cup$ TriggerNILM(v_c, TS);
    $C\_id \leftarrow C\_id \cup C\_id_{v_s}$;
  return C_id ;

function TriggerNILM(v_c, TS)
  $flag \leftarrow false$;
  $P_{ideal} \leftarrow getAveragePowerProfile(v_c, TS)$;
    ▷ Returns average power profile of v_c till last date
  $P_{current} \leftarrow getPowerProfile(v_c, TS)$; ▷ Power profile of v_c at TS
  $flag \leftarrow$ Compare(v_c, P_{ideal}, $P_{current}$);
  if flag **then return** v_c;

function Compare(v_c, P_{ideal}, $P_{current}$)
  for all $a_c \in v_c$ **do**
    $P_{ideal}(a_c) \leftarrow NILM(P_{ideal})$;
    $P_{current}(a_c) \leftarrow NILM(P_{current})$;
    if $Distance(P_{ideal}(a_c), P_{current}(a_c)) \geq \phi$ **then return** $true$;

---

compromising user privacy. In our scheme, we assume that a privacy preserving smart metering algorithm is executing in every meter ensuring privacy aware data streaming. The state LDCs (located in state capitals) are usually connected to multiple area/sub LDCs, which are individually connected to major substations and power generation stations. If there is a significant change in the frequency of any generator, the LDC gets notified. As mentioned in Algorithm 1, it continuously looks for deviation in the frequency of a particular generator v_i (denoted as $f_{v_i}^{TS}$) at timestamp TS from the ideal frequency (denoted as f^*) by a tolerable limit τ, as shown in line 5. For an unwanted scenario, the generator v_i notifies the associated LDC about the disturbance (line 6). It also adds a **NotifyLDCTxn** in the blockchain to log this event. The LDC immediately triggers the corresponding substations under generator v_i through **TraceSubstationsTxn** to check the consumers under its jurisdiction for any unexpected demand alteration. Every substation v_s is individually configured to identify the compromised consumer by executing $TriggerNILM$ function (Lines 26–31). For every consumer v_c, the $TriggerNILM$ function collects the average power profile of v_c. The average value is calculated using the power data until before the abnormality is suspected at the timestamp TS (line 28). This estimated power profile P_{ideal} is then compared with the current power profile $P_{current}$ of the consumer (line 29). The P_{ideal} and $P_{current}$ are then disaggregated by the NILM algorithm to find power profile for each appliance a_c (lines 34–35). The algorithm then uses a *Distance* function, *t-test* to find any difference between the means of these two power profiles. If the t-value resulted from the test is higher than the appliance disturbance threshold ϕ, then the algorithm considers the consumer v_c to be compromised. If the correlation metric is considered to find the linear relationship between these power profiles, the appliance disturbance threshold ϕ has to be defined/set by the authority himself, whereas the *t-test* provides an expected value from the *t-Distribution Table* w.r.t. a certain confidence level to compare with the resulted t-value. Hence in our case, the *t-test* is preferred over correlation. Algorithm 1 compares the ideal profile against the current power profile of the system to identify any unexpected demand manipulation. In both cases, the profiles are privacy preserved. As a result, the disaggregated profiles of the appliances generated by the NILM tool are different from the original profile. Hence, the proposed scheme ensures the attack source detection without hampering the consumer privacy. The major crux of the MADIoT attacks is that it compromises the appliances through IoT devices in such a frequency that the consumers are not aware of such power fluctuations. Profiling of customers' overall usage information does not provide the usage patterns of individual appliances. However, NILM and t-test can detect such disruptions, but to make the users convinced that the attack has actually been launched in their household, we need to keep track of the power profiles generated at the user end. Blockchain provides the ability to the substations and the users to trace back to the attack source and compromised appliances. Additionally, the frequency deviation can also be caused by electric faults in the transmission lines. Along with triggering the NILM functionality in the substations, the LDC also calls for $IsLinkBroken$ function (Lines 11–15) to check whether there is any link that has been brought down recently. The $IsLinkBroken$ function traverses in the

ID	BUS	ID	BUS
0	('Gen1', 'Sub1')	10	('Sub2', 'Consumer5')
1	('Gen1', 'Sub2')	11	('Sub2', 'Consumer6')
2	('Gen2', 'Sub2')	12	('Sub2', 'Consumer7')
3	('Gen3', 'Sub2')	13	('Sub3', 'Consumer8')
4	('Gen3', 'Sub4')	14	('Sub3', 'Consumer9')
5	('Gen4', 'Sub3')	15	('Sub3', 'Consumer10')
6	('Sub1', 'Consumer1')	16	('Sub4', 'Consumer11')
7	('Sub1', 'Consumer2')	17	('Sub4', 'Consumer12')
8	('Sub1', 'Consumer3')	18	('Sub4', 'Consumer13')
9	('Sub2', 'Consumer4')	19	('Sub4', 'Consumer14')

Fig. 10. Transmission links in the grid

Fig. 11. PUF enabled smart meter

blockchain and retrieves all **LinkDownTxn** transactions whose timestamp is same or more than TS and returns the links which are down. If there is any such fault, it triggers **DownReroutingTxn** transaction to deliver the power supply through an alternative link.

5 Experimental Setup and Results

In this section, we describe our experimental setup comprising of PUF enabled smart meter, blockchain network and the attack source detection procedure.

5.1 Experimental Setup for PUF and Blockchain Prototype

To realise the proposed scheme, we have made a PUF enabled smart meter prototype using Raspberry Pi, a non-invasive split core current transformer (SCT-013-030) and a Digilent Nexys 4 FPGA board, as shown in Fig. 11. In any metering setup, current flowing through the meter to load is monitored using a current sensor. Current measured by the sensor is captured by Raspberry Pi and sent to blockchain node (utility server). We choose a 5-4 Double Arbiter PUF [10], and deploy it on Digilent Nexys-4 board containing Xilinx Artix-7 FPGA. Raspberry Pi communicates with the PUF instance over USB to send challenges and receive the corresponding response. Now, the blockchain framework (refer to Sect. 4.3) is implemented in Golang and Python. Each blockchain node is enabled with a REST API built using Gorilla MUX that is used to post transactions to the blockchain, along with providing the ability to view the blockchain data in a web browser. Creation of point-to-point (P2P) network and handling the P2P connections are implemented using go-libp2p library. The web-server returns the chain of transactions in JSON format for simplicity. File sharing in the blockchain is enabled by IPFS. In order to share a file, the node posting the transaction adds the IPFS hash of the file to be shared in the transaction block. The transactions used in the blockchain and their corresponding actions are explained in Sect. 4.3. The JSON structures for Blockchain transactions **InitialTemplateTxn**, **LinkDownTxn** are provided in Fig. 12. As mentioned in Sect. 4.1, the functionalities of utility server, LDC, DCU and substation are executed using machine equipped with a Quadcore Intel i5-4570 @3.20 GHz CPU. The authentication and key-exchange protocol (refer to Sect. 2) is implemented in C

```
{
  "Index": 0,
  "Timestamp": "2020-07-17 21:26:34.686624149 +0530 IST m=+0.651107272",
  "TxnType": 0,
  "TxnPayload": "",
  "Comment": "Genesis Block",
  "Proposer": "/ip4/192.168.43.201/tcp/5000/ipfs/QmV92Dz4ns3jsnnYGevFa3GsEfS7uCq
  "PrevHash": "BIG-BANG!",
  "ThisHash": "56040237765a4334e734b4b132d0571efdaf7cc25a1ac15bc0b1eacda5931a31"
}
```


(a)


```
{
  "Index": 3,
  "Timestamp": "2020-07-17 21:35:18.603977222 +0530 IST m=+58.360716793",
  "TxnType": 4,
  "TxnPayload": {
    "Link": "('Gen1', 'Sub1')",
    "Time": "Fri Jul 17 21:35:18 2020",
    "Sender": "Gen1",
    "Command": "link_break"
  },
  "Comment": "Link Down Transaction (Type 4)",
  "Proposer": "/ip4/192.168.43.201/tcp/5000/ipfs/QmeczHmSf6CHTozXNicrjhMGeX4nqw3i
  "PrevHash": "762aaac8c79f7846b5cc07e87a300f6a410c768246681d38d97a321564c98887",
  "ThisHash": "ff32bbfb53bf07ed9534c337d8467de13ab479ca2966c728792002ee36cbd2c0"
}
```


(b)

Fig. 12. JSON structures of Blockchain transactions (a) InitialTemplateTxn, (b) LinkDownTxn

language. The IBE scheme used in the protocol is implemented using Pairing-Based Cryptography (PBC) library, which provides APIs to securely instantiate all bilinear pairing-related operations on the Barreto-Naehrig family of elliptic curves with embedding degree 12 and a security level of 160 bits of finite field. The SKE scheme is realised using AES-128, hash function $\mathcal{H}$ using SHA-256 and hash function $\mathcal{H}'$ using the `element_from_hash` API of PBC library. The AES-128 and SHA-256 are implemented using Libgcrypt and executed in Raspberry Pi which replicates the meter setup in our proposed work. The smart meter requires very less memory footprint of 89.8 kB in order to store the executable of the software. The time taken to generate the association data binding a smart meter and a substation is 0.124 s, whereas the end-to-end authentication and key exchange protocol also incurs 0.885 s. Besides, setting up the initial grid topology and posting the transaction takes 0.124 s and events such as link breakdown or rerouting take around 0.009 s.

5.2 Results for Attack Source Detection Methodology

To realise the attack source detection methodology as proposed in Sect. 4.5, we use the REDD data set [17] provided by Kolter and Johnson. For our experiment, we consider the building number 3 of the REDD dataset with sampling period of 15 minutes. Next, we implement a privacy preserved smart metering scheme that hides the usage patterns by providing differential privacy guarantees for the appliances [4]. Here, the smart meters transmit masked measurements by adding noise generated by a distribution model. The maximum allowed error

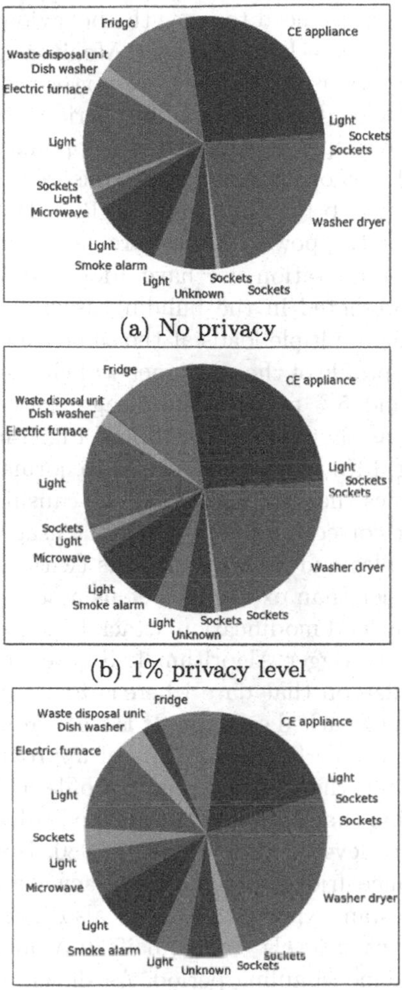

(a) No privacy

(b) 1% privacy level

(c) 5% privacy level

Fig. 13. NILM disaggregation of normal profile.

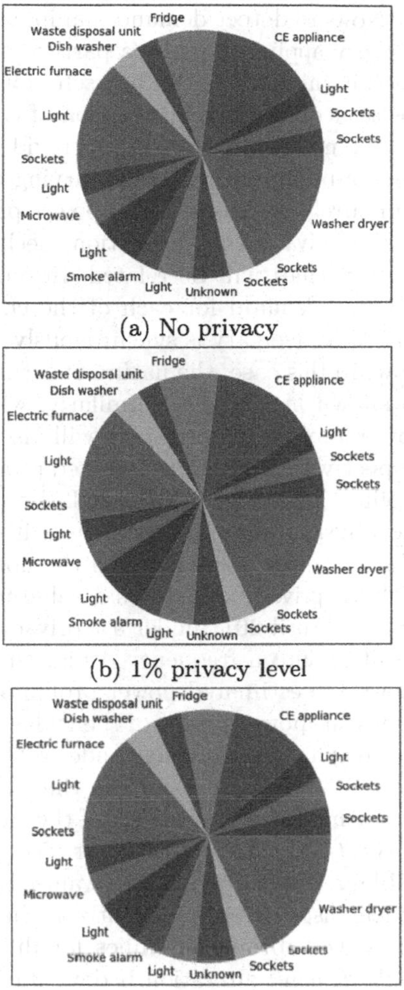

(a) No privacy

(b) 1% privacy level

(c) 5% privacy level

Fig. 14. NILM disaggregation of attacked profile

between the original and the masked power consumption over a billing period is bounded by a desired percentage, denoted by privacy level ϵ. Based on this, the variance of the normal distribution is calculated in such a way that the probability of obtaining the error within the desired value ϵ is very high, for e.g. 98%. If Laplace distribution model is used for the privacy, the magnitude of the Laplacian noise is determined by the scale parameter of the original distribution which can be calculated using the obtained variance and the total number of measurements. With the increasing value of ϵ, the privacy of resulting stream w.r.t the original power profile increases.

Now, to detect demand manipulation attack, we need to trace the behaviour of every appliance under a particular consumer. Non-Intrusive Load Monitoring Toolkit (nilmtk) [5] can be useful for this purpose as it disaggregates power profile to acquire the consumption of each appliance during a sampling period. As shown in Fig. 13a, NILM tool provides the correct split-up of individual appliance consumption, whereas with varying privacy levels of 1% and 5%, the misprediction surely increases in the power profiles (refer to Fig. 13b and Fig. 13c). But as the privacy transformation mechanism for the power profiles are same, all three profiles will be related. In our attack preparation, we have added 30 W of extra demand for each of the channels presented in the building assuming that the adversary is synchronously controlling multiple loads at the same time. Now, in this case, the nature of actual power profile of the consumer will change as shown in Fig. 14a. Similarly, with 1% and 5% privacy, the disaggregated power profiles under attack will also change as shown in Fig. 14b and Fig. 14c respectively. But as the attacked profiles (Fig. 14(a–c)) are not related to normal profiles (Fig. 13(a–c)), the NILM tool identifies the appliances that are causing the physical disturbance, though it does not correctly predict the exact usage. When we run *t*-test between the normal profiles and attacked profiles (with or without privacy), it shows a value much higher than expected. Let us assume, on 23rd April 2011 under 5% privacy level the load modification attack happens resulting into a frequency deviation which will trigger Algorithm 1. Figure 14a shows the estimated power profile of the fridge on that date whereas Fig. 14b shows the power profile of the fridge under the attacked scenario. It is clear from the graph that the magnitude of the power profile has got a shift of approximately 30 W. Hence, we run the *t*-test between the received power profile and the estimated power profile of the fridge during that period. The expected value in the *t-Distribution Table* for 95% confidence level is around 1.960–1.980. But Table 2 shows calculated *t*-value for appliance fridge under 5% privacy level which displays a significantly higher value than expected. Table 2 also illustrates the obtained *t*-values for different privacy levels (0%–5%) if 30 W and 20 W demand alteration is done during the same sampling period. As shown in Table 2, all the resulted *t*-values are very much higher compared to the expected

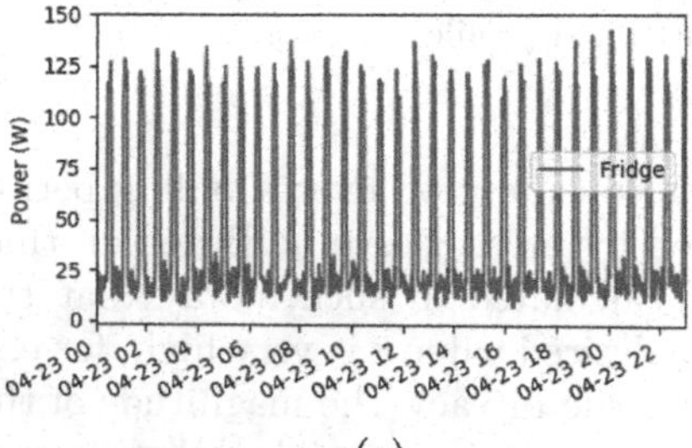

(a)

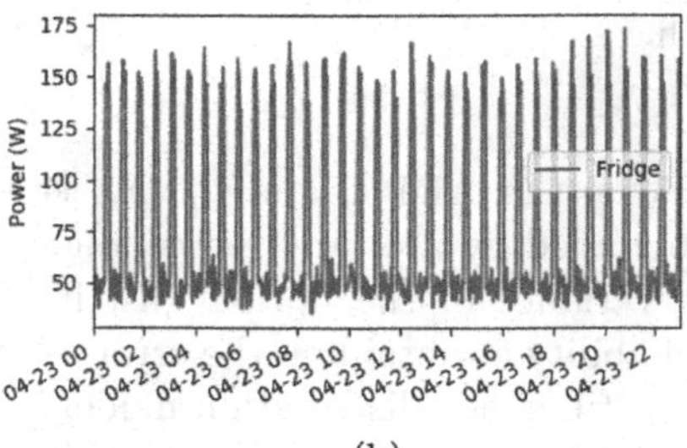

(b)

Fig. 15. Disaggregated power profile of fridge with 5% privacy on 23rd April,2011 (a) in estimated scenario (b) after demand manipulation

Table 2. *t*-test result between the fridge's original and attacked power profile for different privacy levels due to 30 W and 20 W demand alteration in every channel.

Privacy level (ϵ)		No privacy	1% privacy	2% privacy	3% privacy	4% privacy	5% privacy
t-value	20 W increase	6.04991	6.07545	6.11155	6.01353	5.81902	5.90373
	30 W increase	9.07487	9.11317	9.16732	9.02029	8.72853	8.85561

value. Hence, we can consider the appliance fridge to be compromised for all the privacy levels. Also, it reveals that the privacy level of the metering infrastructure does not significantly affect the outcome of our scheme (Table 2).

The time taken to generate the fraction of energy consumption of each appliance for each of the buildings present in the REDD dataset using the NILM tool is 2.15851 s on average which is significantly lower than the given sampling period (15 min). After obtaining the corresponding power profiles, it takes 0.001912 s on average to validate the credibility of each appliance.

6 Conclusion

In this paper we have demonstrated three demand manipulation attacks that can inflict undesired load-shedding. We have proposed a PUF based power profile verification and attack source detection methodology without compromising differential privacy guarantees. We have also addressed issues related to transparency and accountability in smart grid operations using a blockchain network and prototyped an end-to-end security solution. In the future, we would like to perform rigorous analysis of existing cyber-security issues in the communication protocols such as Modbus, DNP3 and IEC 61850. These protocols lack mature security mechanisms and can slow down overall throughput of the grid. We are also exploring lightweight blockchain consensus protocol specifically designed for smart grid applications in order to improve scalability of the proposed scheme.

References

1. Elia Group Grid Data. http://www.elia.be/en/grid-data
2. Inter Planetary File System (November 2019). https://ipfs.io/
3. Ali, S., Mansoor, H., Arshad, N., Khan, I.: Short term load forecasting using smart meter data. In: Proceedings of the Tenth ACM International Conference on Future Energy Systems, pp. 419–421 (2019)
4. Barbosa, P., Brito, A., Almeida, H.: A technique to provide differential privacy for appliance usage in smart metering. Inf. Sci. **370**, 355–367 (2016)
5. Batra, N., et al.: NILMTK: an open source toolkit for non-intrusive load monitoring. In: Proceedings of the 5th International Conference on Future Energy Systems, pp. 265–276 (2014)
6. Benning, L.: Load-Forecasting. https://github.com/lbenning/Load-Forecasting
7. Boyapally, H., et al.: Safe is the new smart: PUF-based authentication for load modification-resistant smart meters. IEEE Trans. Dependable Secur. Comput. 1–1 (2020)

8. Chatterjee, U., et al.: Building PUF based authentication and key exchange protocol for IoT without explicit CRPs in verifier database. IEEE Trans. Dependable Secur. Comput. **16**(3), 424–437 (2019)
9. Chatterjee, U., et al.: PUFSSL: an OpenSSL extension for PUF based authentication. In: 23rd IEEE International Conference on Digital Signal Processing, DSP 2018 (2018)
10. Chatterjee, U., Sahoo, D.P., Mukhopadhyay, D., Chakraborty, R.S.: Trustworthy proofs for sensor data using FPGA based physically unclonable functions. In: 2018 Design, Automation & Test in Europe Conference & Exhibition, DATE 2018 (2018)
11. Dabrowski, A., Ullrich, J., Weippl, E.R.: Grid shock: coordinated load-changing attacks on power grids: the non-smart power grid is vulnerable to cyber attacks as well. In: Proceedings of the 33rd Annual Computer Security Applications Conference, pp. 303–314 (2017)
12. Gai, K., Wu, Y., Zhu, L., Xu, L., Zhang, Y.: Permissioned blockchain and edge computing empowered privacy-preserving smart grid networks. IEEE Internet Things J. **6**(5), 7992–8004 (2019)
13. Gao, J., et al.: GridMonitoring: secured sovereign blockchain based monitoring on smart grid. IEEE Access **6**, 9917–9925 (2018)
14. Guan, Z., et al.: Privacy-preserving and efficient aggregation based on blockchain for power grid communications in smart communities. IEEE Commun. Mag. **56**, 82–88 (2018)
15. Huang, B., Cárdenas, A.A., Baldick, R.: Not everything is dark and gloomy: power grid protections against IoT demand attacks. In: Heninger, N., Traynor, P. (eds.) 28th USENIX Security Symposium, USENIX Security (2019)
16. Kolias, C., Kambourakis, G., Stavrou, A., Voas, J.: DDoS in the IoT: Mirai and other botnets. Computer **50**(7), 80–84 (2017)
17. Kolter, J.Z., Johnson, M.J.: REDD: a public dataset for energy disaggregation research. In: Workshop on Data Mining Applications in Sustainability (SIGKDD), San Diego, CA, vol. 25, pp. 59–62 (2011)
18. Liu, Y., Ning, P., Reiter, M.K.: False data injection attacks against state estimation in electric power grids. In: Proceedings of the 16th ACM Conference on Computer and Communications Security, CCS 2009, pp. 21–32 (2009)
19. Lombardi, F., Aniello, L., De Angelis, S., Margheri, A., Sassone, V.: A blockchain-based infrastructure for reliable and cost-effective IoT-aided smart grids. Living Internet Things: Cybersecur. IoT **2018**, 1–6 (2018)
20. Mohammadi, F., Nazri, G.A., Saif, M.: A fast fault detection and identification approach in power distribution systems. In: 2019 International Conference on Power Generation Systems and Renewable Energy Technologies. IEEE (2019)
21. Nourizadeh, S., Yari, V., Ranjbar, A.M.: Frequency monitoring and control during power system restoration based on wide area measurement system. Math. Probl. Eng. **2011**, 9 (2011)
22. Ruj, S., Pal, A.: Analyzing cascading failures in smart grids under random and targeted attacks. In: 2014 IEEE 28th International Conference on Advanced Information Networking and Applications. pp. 226–233 (2014)
23. Silvestre, D., Hespanha, J.P., Silvestre, C.: Fault detection for cyber physical systems: smart grid case. In: 23rd International Symposium on Mathematical Theory of Networks and Systems (MTNS), pp. 475–481. IEEE (2018)
24. Soltan, S., Mittal, P., Poor, H.V.: BlackIoT: IoT botnet of high wattage devices can disrupt the power grid. In: Enck, W., Felt, A.P. (eds.) 27th USENIX Security Symposium, USENIX Security, August 15–17, 2018, pp. 15–32 (2018)

25. Wang, H., et al.: Deep learning-based interval state estimation of AC smart grids against sparse cyber attacks. IEEE Trans. Ind. Inform. **14**(11), 4766–4778 (2018)
26. Zhang, H., Wang, J., Ding, Y.: Blockchain-based decentralized and secure keyless signature scheme for smart grid. Energy **180**, 955–967 (2019)
27. Zhao, J., Zhang, G., La Scala, M., Dong, Z.Y., Chen, C., Wang, J.: Short-term state forecasting-aided method for detection of smart grid general false data injection attacks. IEEE Trans. Smart Grid **8**(4), 1580–1590 (2017)

Cloud S&P - Cloud Security and Privacy

BFV, CKKS, TFHE: Which One is the Best for a Secure Neural Network Evaluation in the Cloud?

Pierre-Emmanuel Clet(✉), Oana Stan, and Martin Zuber

CEA LIST, Université Paris-Saclay, 91120 Palaiseau, France
{pierre-emmanuel.clet,oana.stan,martin.zuber}@cea.fr

Abstract. We provide clear and concise guidelines for the use of three of the most popular homomorphic cryptosystems: BFV, CKKS and TFHE. Because they are unified under the Chimera framework and it is now possible to switch a ciphertext from one cryptosystem to another, such a comparison is essential to better understand which cryptosystem to use in which use-case or for which part of a secure computation on the cloud. We do this by comparing the application of the three cryptosystems to the evaluation phase of standard feed-forward neural networks tested on the MNIST (http://yann.lecun.com/exdb/mnist/) database. We tested their application in the case where both the query and the neural network model are encrypted and in the case when only the query is encrypted. We evaluated the results obtained using the three homomorphic schemes in terms of precision, memory usage and execution time for a minimal security of 128 bits.

Keywords: FHE · Cloud · Neural Networks · TFHE · BFV · CKKS · Chimera

1 Introduction

In this paper, we address the general problem commonly known as the *secure cloud computation problem*, associated with multiple real-world scenarios. More precisely, we target the private remote evaluation of a neural network by means of homomorphic encryption techniques. In a cloud computation application, a *user* with private data wishes to use a service provided by the cloud or a distant *server*. This cloud or server owns a complex algorithm and offers to run the user's data through that algorithm. "Naive" (in terms of security) options to solve this problem include the user sending its data in clear form for a distant computation or the server publishing its algorithm. Both options are acceptable in the case where data confidentiality is not an issue for the user or in the case where the server does not mind publishing its algorithm and the user has the computational power to run it.

J. Zhou et al. (Eds.): ACNS 2021 Workshops, LNCS 12809, pp. 279–300, 2021.
https://doi.org/10.1007/978-3-030-81645-2_16

However, there are a number of real-world applications that cannot make use of these naive options for a host of reasons. One can think of medical applications (distant diagnosis tools for patients or large epidemiological studies), biometric authentication for access control, DNA-matching for crime-solving, and the list goes on. These kinds of applications are being increasingly regulated regarding data confidentiality for service users in Europe and around the world, which explains a growing interest in the production of secure alternatives to existing algorithms. Even when regulations are weak or do not exist, providing the same service as a competitor but with security guarantees on top can give an edge to companies in the context of evermore confidentiality-conscious populations worldwide.

One of the hottest topics at the moment and one that raises major privacy issues is the use of remote Machine Learning (ML) applications and in particular of Neural Networks (NN). It is thus natural that in this paper we choose to focus on the matter of *secure cloud neural network evaluation*. While there are a host of machine learning algorithms worthy of an evaluation in an cloud setting, neural networks have, by far, the best accuracy performances among them on a wide range of applications (e.g. image classification, voice recognition, etc.). However, since many machine learning algorithms present similarities in the mathematical structure on which they are built, finding efficient ways to ensure the secure evaluation of a NN can be further translated without major effort to use on other ML algorithms. Neural networks (by that we mean feed-forward neural networks), in their simplest form, consist of a number of layers of computations. Each of the layers is composed of a multiplication of the input vector from the last layer with a weight matrix determined during the training phase. Then, at every neuron, an activation function is applied, usually a non-linear function such as a sigmoid. While a considerable number of optimizations and tweaks can be added, these two operations for every layer describe a simple, generic, feed-forward neural network.

We aim to show and compare the different ways that a secure, cloud neural network evaluation can be addressed using Fully Homomorphic Encryption (FHE). Since its theoretical breakthrough a little over 10 years ago [20,21], FHE has made great leaps forward in terms of efficiency. While a general purpose FHE remains elusive as a practical application, several works [6,18] have already showed that homomorphic cryptosystems can be adapted very efficiently to produce secure alternatives to specific existing algorithms. Secure FHE applications to machine learning algorithms in general - and neural networks in particular - have been the focus of an increasing amount of work in the community in the last few years.

Several efficient FHE cryptosystems have been proposed in the literature and there exists a theoretical framework [5] unifying three of the most popular ones - BFV [7,19], CKKS [11] and TFHE [13,14,16]. Therefore, one can now jump from one cryptosystem to another in the middle of a computation. This begs the question: which one is more appropriate and for which purpose when doing FHE-computation?

Let us now emphasize the purpose of this paper and our main contributions.

Contribution. This work aims to provide guidelines about which FHE scheme - between BFV, CKKS and TFHE - to use in the context of the secure evaluation of a neural network in the cloud and to identify their tradeoffs for this particular application. This is part of a benchmarking effort for the FHE schemes meant to provide a comparison study for a unique, simple, yet representative application - the inference step for a neural network - under the same baseline, same machine, same characteristics of the neural network, and similar security parameters.

The structure of the neural network (NN) employed here is a basic one, with two fully connected layers followed by an activation function. The main issue with computing inference in the homomorphic domain for the neural network model is the non linear nature of the usual activation functions (*e.g. ReLu*, *sigmoid*, etc.). As such, we decided to take advantage of the different computational models offered by the three schemes, by implementing two variants of this model, one using the *square* as activation function and the other one using the *sign* as activation. TFHE seems a more appropriate choice to perform computation over Boolean circuits (bitwise) and to apply the bootstrapping which can be easily seen as a sign function. BFV is adapted for modular arithmetic and CKKS is meant for floating point arithmetic so it is rather simple to implement a square activation function. As such, we implemented the first variant (with the square activation) on the three cryptosystems and we implemented the variant with the sign only in TFHE. Moreover, for each network, we evaluate not only the inference over an encrypted instance using a clear model but also the case where both the instance to classify and the model are encrypted. Of course, BFV and CKKS could be also used to encrypt bitwise and therefore execute over Boolean circuits and have an implementation for the sign variant. However, even for our small NN, this would lead to a prohibitive choice of parameters in terms of computational times and memory usage.

Let us also note that the purpose of this paper is not to implement the neural network with the best prediction accuracy since this requires a more careful design of the NN model and more fine-tuned activation functions in the homomorphic domain. For some relevant work on the private evaluation of a neural network with homomorphic encryption, please refer to Sect. 2.3. Our objective is to take a basic neural network and to compare its implementation using three of the most popular homomorphic cryptosystems nowadays. Of course, we are not expecting a clear "winner" between the homomorphic schemes but rather to have a more concrete insight on the possibilities offered by each scheme and which cryptosystem to use for the different parts of computation of a neural network. This first step can help in the design of more efficient neural network implementations in the homomorphic domain, by exploiting the strengths of each scheme and switching to (and from) another if needed, thanks to Chimera [5]. Let us also note that even if the structure of the neural network is quite basic, the building blocks are representative and even necessary for the construction of more complex neural networks.

Beside the numerical experimental results (in terms of execution times and memory requirements), our paper also gives insightful details on the computational model we used for each cryptosystem, the particularities of each scheme (*i.e.* possible use of packing for BFV and CKKS, use of the bootstrapping as a sign function, etc.), the way to set up the different parameters and to control the noise (which is particularly important for BFV and CKKS schemes).

Paper Organization. Next section (Sect. 2) presents a quick view of the different cryptographic tools for performing secure computation and then focuses on the application of the homomorphic encryption to the field of machine learning and in particular of the neural networks. This section also gives a view of the previous work on the comparison of various homomorphic schemes. The necessary background for the comprehension of our approach is given in Sect. 3. Our approach for the design of the neural network and the implementation of its variants in the homomorphic domain using the three cryptosystems is detailed in Sect. 4. Section 5 gives the experimental results in terms of the evaluation accuracy, memory consumption and execution times as well as our personal feedback following these experiments. Last section consists in a conclusion and some perspectives worth further investigating.

2 Related Work

2.1 Secure Machine Learning on a Cloud

In the realm of cryptography, most work done on the matter of secure cloud machine learning uses either Multi-Party Computation (MPC) techniques or Homomorphic Encryption (HE). These two methods address similar use-cases, achieving different properties: MPC protocols require a few rounds of interactions between the server and the user. This renders the computation time for the server lower than in the HE case. This time/bandwidth trade-off is the main difference between these two approaches at the moment.

Most machine learning algorithms have a *linear* phase in which a scalar product or a simple difference operation is applied to the data. In a second phase, the *non-linear* phase, a more complex function is applied in order to extract some information from the data. These two phases can then be iterated a number of times. In the neural network example, the linear phase would correspond to the weight matrix multiplication (a set of scalar products) and the analysis phase to the application of the activation function. The main (strictly in terms of number of publications) way to achieve security for cloud machine learning is to use some kind of Additive Homomorphic Encryption (AHE) for the *linear* phase of the computation and then use MPC techniques to compute the more complex *non-linear* phase.

Our work provides a comparison between several homomorphic schemes when applied to machine learning problems. Therefore, we will not mention any of the MPC solutions and only mention here the prior works that use homomorphic encryption *exclusively.*

2.2 HE-Based Secure Cloud Machine Learning

While there are HE-based secure applications for other machine learning applications, we will focus on Neural Networks (NN). Indeed, most secure machine learning papers nowadays do so because neural networks - especially Convolutional Neural Networks (CNNs) - have been shown to have the best performances on a wide range of classification problems. Figure 1 presents an exclusively HE solution to the cloud NN problem. It is not the only possible such protocol however. In the solution presented in Fig. 1, the user has the secret key and the computation is made on the server with a clear machine learning algorithm and an encrypted query. The opposite - whereby the server sends an encrypted NN to the user for computation - is also possible. In terms of homomorphic computations, these two protocols are basically equivalent. Another protocol would have both the query and the neural network be encrypted and the computation be made on by a third party. This can be useful when neither the NN owner, nor the user has the will or the resources to run the computation themselves. This third protocol would require an additional security assumption: the absence of collusion between the third party and the owner of the secret key.

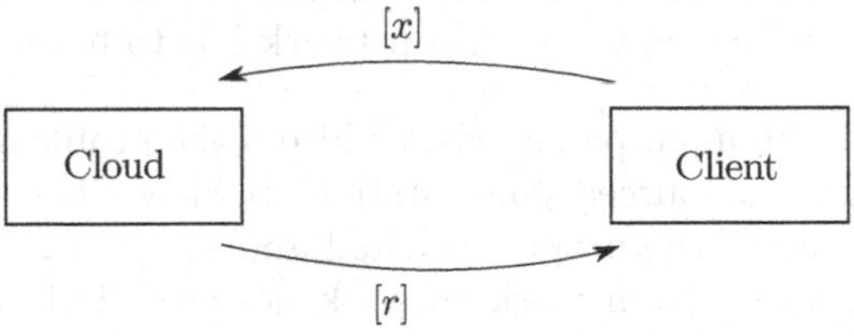

Fig. 1. A general possible protocol for FHE usage in a confidentiality-preserving cloud machine learning scenario on a cloud. We use brackets ([·]) to indicate that data is encrypted. A "query" x is sent encrypted by a client to a remote cloud hosting a machine learning algorithm. The algorithm is run over that encrypted input and the result r is sent back to the user for decryption.

2.3 Prior Work on the HE-Based Evaluation of Neural Networks

Please note, we do not aim to compare ourselves and our FHE constructions directly to other existing works. Rather, we built our homomorphic neural networks in order to compare several FHE schemes and their use over a single application. Therefore any existing work mentioned in this section is only presented to help the reader better understand the nuances and choices in the FHE neural networks presented in Sect. 4.

For this purpose, we define 3 other properties that prior papers on the subject may have (on top of the type of encryption scheme that they use).

- We mentioned that an *activation function* is a complex function used in any neural network. The most used ones are the sigmoid ($\theta(x) = (1 + e^{-x})^{-1}$), the rectified linear function (ReLu) ($\theta(x) = \max(0, x)$) and the softmax function (see [26]). It is hard to produce an exact alternative to some existing activation functions in the homomorphic domain. Therefore, some works choose to replace that function with a sign function and others with a polynomial function. It is possible to produce an exact homomorphic activation function

when using homomorphic binary gates over data encoded in a binary format. This, however, produces considerably slower constructions.
- HE can be *Full* (as in FHE) or *Levelled* (as in LHE). In an FHE construction, the parameters used during the encryption process do not depend on the depth of the computation (the number of layers in the case of a NN). This can be useful when the user (who encrypts her data) does not know the nature of the Neural Network that will evaluate it (for instance if she is not allowed to know to ensure the security of the NN). However, in the case where the computation depth is known to the user, an LHE construction can be used.
- The neural networks used in the literature for secure evaluation are all very different and the activation function is not the only aspect of them that changes from one work to another. *The number of layers in the neural network* is a good indication of its complexity and when constructing a secure evaluation, one has to trade classification rate with time performance when choosing how many layers the neural network has to have.

Table 1 presents the main papers that address the problem of an exclusively homomorphic secure outsourced computation. It shows how they address the problem differently using the properties cited above.

Not everything varies from work to work however. It is worth mentioning that all of the works cited here test their NN evaluation on the MNIST database [23] (although comparisons on the CIFAR-10 database are also made in some cases [22]). All of them present the case where only one side uses encryption (either the query or the NN model is encrypted). Additionally, although they all use some kind of packing, it is hard to describe here how that packing technique varies from paper to paper.

Table 1. Table presenting the different papers published on the subject of HE-based secure outsourced NN evaluation. Notably, [26] is mainly about the training of a NN, but the choices they had to make resemble closely those found in a work centered on the evaluation problem. [10] use several different exponents for their polynomial approximation of the activation function.

Paper	Encryption scheme	Activation	Full/Levelled	Number of layers
[18]	YASHE	x^2	Levelled	5
[9]	BFV	x^2	Levelled	11
[10]	BGV	x^l	Levelled	9 and 24
[6]	TFHE	sign	Full	3
[26]	BGV-TFHE	ReLu and softmax	Full	3

2.4 Prior Work on Comparing and Benchmarking Homomorphic Cryptosystems

The Homomorphic Encryption Security Standard [3], published in 2018, presents most homomorphic cryptosystems. It does not address the matter of their use in any specific applicative context but rather provide an extensive review of their security. It is worth mentioning that while [26] choose BGV-TFHE for their final implementation, they compare it with the Chimera alternative using BFV-TFHE. [28] is an unpublished review of several homomorphic encryption schemes (BFV, TFHE, BGV) archived in 2018. It does not delve into parameters or specific applications and rather presents the general properties of each cryptosystem. Other past works either compare BFV with YASHE scheme [24], BGV with BFV [17] and the libraries HELib, SEAL and FV-NFLib [2]. Thus, to the best of our knowledge, there are no approaches for comparing BFV, CKKS and TFHE and none in the context of the evaluation of a neural network.

3 Background

In this section, we will summarize the main points the reader needs to be familiar with in order to grasp all the notions used in this paper.

3.1 Neural Networks

We will only consider here the most simple neural networks which are composed of a succession of layers densely connected. To be more precise, a layer is composed of neurons which compute the dot product between a vector of weights and the input vector coming from the preceding layer, to which it adds a bias. It then computes an activation function on the output. The inputs given to the network form a special layer called input layer which only provides those values to the next layer. The last layer is called the output layer as it outputs the result of the network. Any layer which is neither the output layer or the input layer is called a hidden layer. For an illustration of a neural network see Fig. 2 in Sect. 4. We can naturally group the weights vector in a matrix and the biases in a vector which allows us to compute the layer with one product between the weights matrix and the input and one addition with the vector of biases followed with an element-wise activation.

This combination of a scalar product (linear phase of the computation) and an activation function (non-linear) is - as mentioned in Sect. 2.1 - a staple of machine learning algorithms. Any LHE or FHE-based secure machine learning algorithm will thus have to make the choices that we present for our neural network in this paper. This makes our findings relevant both for other possible machine learning applications and for larger neural networks in a cloud setting.

3.2 Homomorphic Encryption

A cryptosystem is said to be homomorphic if we can compute operations directly on encrypted data without needing the secret key. We used two particular types of homomorphic encryption:

- **Levelled Homomorphic Encryption (LHE):** For any sequence of operations, there exists a set of parameters for the scheme that allows its computation in the encrypted domain. The SEAL framework which we used to use the cryptosystems BFV and CKKS works in LHE mode.
- **Fully Homomorphic Encryption (FHE):** There exists a set of parameters for the scheme that allows the computation of any sequence of operations in the encrypted domain. The TFHE library which we used for the cryptosystem TFHE works in FHE mode.

For each of the considered cryptosystems, a noise appears in the decryption that grows with each operation. The parameters chosen for the plaintext and the ciphertext spaces dictate the number of operations we can do before the noise becomes too high (resulting in a failed decryption) but no set of parameters allow for unlimited amount of operations. That is why we need a *bootstrapping* operation in order to deal with this noise if we wish to make a fully homomorphic scheme. Indeed, for a given ciphertext, bootstrapping allows us to create a new ciphertext encrypting the same message with a noise small enough to compute new operations, by executing the decryption circuit in the homomorphic domain. The idea given by Gentry can be found in [21]. Let us note that even if, in theory, the bootstrapping is possible for BFV and CKKS cryptosystems, in practice this still remains a very costly operation and this is the reason why these two cryptosystems are almost always used in the levelled mode. Meanwhile, TFHE was designed with the idea to have a fast bootstrapping procedure (<13ms) and thus it is meant to be executed in fully homomorphic mode.

3.3 Quick Overview of the Cryptosystems

Let us recall here some common characteristics of the three cryptosystems we consider: BFV [19], CKKS [11], and TFHE [13].

They are composed of:

- A plaintext space which is the set of all the possible messages we can encrypt. This set depends on some parameters such as a polynomial degree parameter. For more information on these parameters, refer to the papers cited above.
- A ciphertext space which is the set of all the possible encrypted messages. It also depends on some parameters such as a polynomial degree parameter.
- Key generating functions which can create random secret and public keys.
- A randomized encryption function which can encrypt any message from the plaintext space thanks to the public key.
- A decryption function which can decrypt any ciphertext from the ciphertext space using the secret key.

Thus, one can encrypt a message into a ciphertext using a public key, and only the holder of the secret key will be able to decrypt and get access to the message. On a theoretical level, these three cryptosystems are extremely similar, and the Chimera framework [5] allows to switch between any of them.

3.4 Details About the Cryptosystems

We will now get into a more detailed explanation of each cryptosystem.

BFV: The plaintext space is $\mathbb{Z}_p[X]/(X^N+1)$ where the plaintext modulus p is an integer and the polynomial degree N is a power of 2. Let q be the ciphertext modulus. The cryptosystem is composed of the following algorithms:

- **Secret Key generation:** The secret key s is a sample from a random distribution over a subspace of $\mathbb{Z}_p[X]/(X^N+1)$.
- **Public key generation:** Given an element a sampled from a uniform distribution over $\mathbb{Z}_q[X]/(X^N+1)$ and an element e sampled from an error distribution (usually Gaussian) over $\mathbb{Z}_q[X]/(X^N+1)$, the public key is computed as $pk = ([-(a.s+e)]_q, a) = (p_0, p_1)$.
- **Encryption:** Let $\mu \in \mathbb{Z}_p[X]/(X^N+1)$ be a message. Let u, e_1 and e_2 be small errors. We can encrypt the message as $c = ([p_0.u + e_1 + \Delta.\mu]_q, [p_1.u + e_2]_q) = (c_0, c_1)$.
- **Decryption:** We can then retrieve the messages thanks to the following function: $[\lfloor \frac{p.[c_0+c_1.s]_q}{q} \rceil]_p$. The noise must be lower than $\Delta/2$ for this operation to work properly.

CKKS: Let L, q_0, Δ and k be integers. We write $q_l = \Delta^l.q_0$ for any l integer in $[0, L]$. We say that the level of a ciphertext is l if it is sampled from $\mathbb{Z}_{q_l}[X]/(X^N+1)$. The cryptosystem is composed of the following algorithms:

- **Secret key generation:** The secret key s is a sample from a random distribution over $\mathbb{Z}_3[X]/(X^N+1)$.
- **Public key generation:** Given an element a sampled from a uniform distribution over $\mathbb{Z}_{q_L}[X]/(X^N+1)$, and an element e sampled from an error distribution over $\mathbb{Z}_{q_L}[X]/(X^N+1)$, the public key is computed as $pk = ([-a.s+e]_{q_L}, a) = (p_0, p_1)$.
- **Encryption:** Let v be sampled from a distribution over $\mathbb{Z}_3[X]/(X^N+1)$. Let e_0 and e_1 be small errors. Then the message μ is encrypted as $c = [(v.pk_0, v.pk_1) + (\mu + e_0, e_1)]_{q_L} = (c_0, c_1)$.
- **Decryption:** We can retrieve the message from a level l ciphertext thanks to the function $\mu = [c_0 + c_1.s]_{q_l}$. Note that with this cryptosystem, the level of a ciphertext goes down each time a multiplication is computed.

TFHE: This cryptosystem has three kinds of ciphertexts which are called respectively TLWE ciphertexts, TRLWE ciphertexts, and TRGSW ciphertexts. We work here with TLWE ciphertexts and the other two are only used internally for bootstrapping. Let n be an integer. The cryptosystem is composed of the following algorithms:

- **Secret key generation:** The secret key s is a sample from a random distribution over $\mathbb{T}^n$.
- **Public key generation:** Given an element a sampled from a uniform distribution over $\mathbb{T}^n$, and an element e sampled from an error distribution over $\mathbb{T}$, the public key is computed as $pk = (a, [a.s + e]) = (p_0, p_1)$.
- **Encryption:** Let v be sampled from a distribution over $\mathbb{T}$. Let e_0 and e_1 be small errors. Then the message μ is encrypted as $c = (v.p_0+e_0, \mu+v.p_1+e_1) = (c_0, c_1)$.
- **Decryption:** We can retrieve the message from a ciphertext thanks to the function $\mu = [c_1 - c_0.s]$. The rounding part depends on the discretization of the Torus chosen in the implementation.

3.5 Batching

The cryptosystems BFV and CKKS allow us to use a technique called batching. It allows us to put a vector of plaintexts called a batch inside one ciphertext and the operations done between ciphertexts correspond to element-wise operations between these batches. In addition to that, it is possible to use rotation to move between the slots (elements) of a same ciphertext. Thus, it allows us to make Single Input Multiple Data (SIMD) types of operation and make our neural network work faster. For more information on batching, refer to [29] and [11].

Let us also note that this batching technique uses the ring isomorphism to preserve the structure of the finite ring defining the message space. Meanwhile the theoretical packing method proposed in [12] is quite different and refers to the mapping of N scalar TLWE messages into a single TRLWE message.

In order to efficiently compute products between matrices and vectors, we used the same technique as described in the article [9]. By putting multiple lines or column of a matrix into one batch while batching a vector in an adapted way, we can compute their product with one multiplication and a few rotations and additions.

3.6 Notations

Here are some useful notations related to the parameters of each cryptosystem.

- For ciphertexts on polynomial ring, N will denote the polynomial degree of the cyclotomic polynomial used as a quotient.
- Ciphertexts on non-polynomial ring will be vectors of $\mathbb{T}^n \times \mathbb{T}$ where $\mathbb{T}$ is the torus.
- If ciphertexts are vectors of polynomials, the size of the vector will be $k + 1$.
- We will use *stdev* for the standard deviation whether it is the one used for the key switch (*ks_stdev*), the one for the bootstrapping algorithm (*bk_stdev*), or the maximum allowed (*max_stdev*).
- *bk_Bgbit* is the base for the approximate gadget decomposition in the TRGSW encryption scheme in TFHE. Along with *bk_l*, it defines the precision of the TRGSW encryption.
- *ks_length* and *ks_basebit* are parameters for the keyswitch used in the bootstrapping.

4 Homomorphic Encryption for Neural Networks

The goal of this paper is to make a comparison of the cryptosystems BFV, CKKS, and TFHE for the conception of neural networks using available implementations and without major modifications on the current libraries. We used SEAL [27] for BFV and CKKS and TFHE [15] library for TFHE. Indeed these cryptosystems are so similar that, if and when needed, one can switch between them, thanks to Chimera. But each of them has its own specificities. CKKS makes approximate arithmetic, BFV works with integers, and TFHE is intended for a bitwise encryption. Now the question is to find when each should be used in the context of a neural network evaluation.

4.1 Overview of the Neural Networks

In this subsection, we describe the structure of the neural networks we used for training in the clear domain. Note that in order to evaluate them in the homomorphic domain, some changes may be needed such as scaling and rounding steps in order to adapt to each cryptosystem. These changes are detailed in the Sects. 4.2 and 4.3.

The goal of our simple neural network is to classify an image from the well known MNIST database [23], the "Hello world!" equivalent for machine learning. This database contains 70000 images of hand-written digits from 0 to 9, composed of a training set of 60000 images and a test set of 10000 images. Thus our neural network's last layer has 10 neurons (one for each digit). Besides, since each image contains $28 \times 28 = 784$ pixels, our neural network takes 784 features as inputs. In order to keep our neural networks simple, we decided to put only one hidden layer, with 128 neurons. As explained in Sect. 3.1, this choice of a simple neural network does not affect the wide range of our findings on other cloud machine learning applications.

In order to highlight the pros and cons of the different cryptosystems in the Subsects. 4.2 and 4.3, we made two different networks based on the structure described above. The first neural network use the square function as an activation for both layer and will be called the *square network*. Figure 2 shows the structure of this network. The second network use the sign function as first activation and the sigmoid function ($\theta(x) = (1 + e^{-x})^{-1}$) as second activation and will be called the *sign network*.

For a given input, we consider the decision of our network to be the index of the maximum value in the output vector. The neural networks were then trained with Tensorflow [1] and reached 96.34% of precision for the square network, and 82.53% for the sign network. Note that our goal in this paper is not to design high precision networks, but rather to compare three cryptosystems on a certain task.

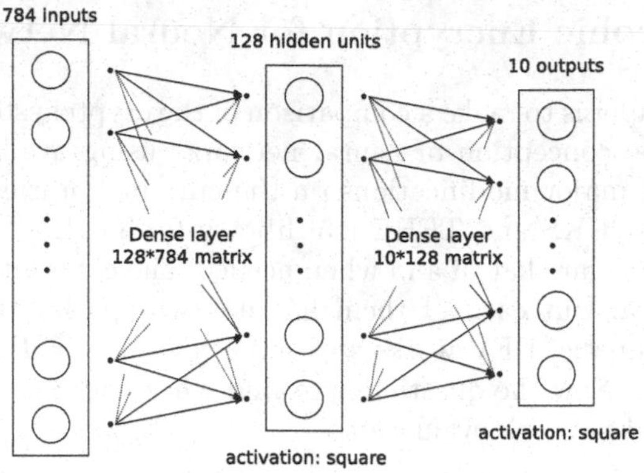

Fig. 2. Structure of our network

4.2 Homomorphic Square Network

Here we will discuss the challenges we had to address in order to make the square networks work in the homomorphic domain.

SEAL: Since SEAL is a LHE implementation of BFV and CKKS, a good set of parameters has to be used in order to compute the network. Note that parameters allowing more operations will also make each operations slower.

BFV: The network trained with Tensorflow is a standard network with floats as weights. Since BFV's batching in SEAL is built to encrypt integers, we rescaled and rounded the weights before encrypting them. This rescaling operation is possible without changing the classification result thanks to the network only using polynomial functions. Furthermore, a number with a value too high cannot be decrypted properly because of the modulus used for the ciphertexts and plaintexts. Because of that, the rescaling is limited and a loss of accuracy could occur because of the rounding operation. We set on a rescaling that allowed us to keep 8 bits of precision for the weights.

The square network was implemented in two modes with BFV:

- **BFVnn-c:** The input features are encrypted but the weights of the neural network are clear.
- **BFVnn-e:** The input features and the weights are encrypted.

CKKS: The cryptosystem CKKS is built to batch arbitrary numbers. Thanks to that, it could be used in a straightforward manner. However, since it intrinsically does approximate arithmetic, a loss of precision could also occur. Same as CKKS, two modes are implemented for the square network:

- **CKKSnn-c:**The inputs are encrypted but the weights of the neural network are clear.
- **CKKSnn-e:** The inputs and the weights are encrypted.

TFHE: The library TFHE is a FHE implementation of the cryptosystem TFHE. However, the bootstrapping is intended for a bitwise encryption of messages. It led us to encrypt values bit-by-bit. We then encoded our neural network as a Boolean circuit. Since the computation time would depend on the number of bits used for each value, we used a rescale-and-round technique like with BFV in order to keep the smallest amount of bit of precision at each step without loosing too much precision. Here too, we rescaled the values in order to get 8 bits of precision for the weights. Once again, two modes are implemented for the square network:

- **TFHEnn-c:** The inputs are encrypted but the weights of the neural network are clear.
- **TFHEnn-e:** The inputs and the weights are encrypted.

4.3 Homomorphic Sign Network

It is possible to avoid using TFHE in a bitwise fashion if the structure of the network allows it. The sign network shows an example where TFHE can be used for modular arithmetic without resorting to bitwise encryption. In addition, it shows an example of operation available with TFHE but not with SEAL.

SEAL: The sign function can only be calculated by either encrypting messages bit-by-bit or by implementing a bootstrapping function similar to the one in TFHE. The first choice is not reasonable as the number of bitwise operations needed to make the whole network would lead to parameters so high it would be practically impossible to use. The second case would defeat the point of being in LHE mode. Because of that, we recommend the use of TFHE in order to use the sign function and we tested only the square network with SEAL.

TFHE: When the messages encrypted are not limited to bits, the bootstrapping algorithm actually computes an encryption of the sign of the messages. This allowed us to avoid encrypting messages bit by bit for this network since the bootstrapping function actually compute the activation function. However, only logic operations are allowed between ciphertexts, leading us to have only one mode:

- **TFHEsign:** The input features are encrypted but the weights are clear.

4.4 Parameters

This section summarize the parameters we choose for each cryptosystem.

BFV: In order to make safe parameters, the SEAL implementation of BFV require that we give the polynomial degree N and the number of bits needed to write the plaintext modulus p. If the plaintext modulus is lower than the end result of the network, the result is decrypted wrongly. Since this cryptosystem works with integers, we chose the lowest value of the plaintext modulus allowing for the decryption to be right. This value is encoded using 50 bits. The number of operations depends on the ciphertext modulus and the plaintext modulus. As a first approximation, we consider that we can apply as many additions as needed and $\frac{q}{p}$ multiplications where q is the ciphertext modulus. Knowing that the polynomial degree N follows approximately the formula $N = 1024 * \log_2(q)/27$ and must be a power of 2, we settled in our case with $N = 16384$. We then used the build in function to get safe parameters according to N and the number of bits of p. This leads SEAL to use a ciphertext modulus using 390 bits. According to Albrecht's lwe-estimator [4], the security is of 146 bits which is more than high enough for most applications.

CKKS: In order to make safe parameters, the SEAL implementation of CKKS require that we give the polynomial degree N and a list which represents the number of bits of all the primes in the decomposition of the ciphertext modulus. This list must have two more values than the number of multiplications to be made. A generally good strategy to choose them is to have the first values at 60 bits as it will give the most precision, the last value also at 60 bits as it must be at least as big as the other values, and choose every other values close to each other. The list chosen was $\{60, 40, 40, 40, 40, 60\}$ which means that the ciphertext's modulus is a number using 280 bits. The sum of the values in the list must stay lower to a bound depending on the polynomial degree N. Same as with BFV, we chose a polynomial degree of $N = 16384$, as it was the smallest value that allowed the list above. With the lwe-estimator, we find a security of 279 bits.

TFHE: We used the default parameters for a security of 128 bits which can be separated in three categories:

- **Main parameters:** $N = 1024$, $n = 630$, $k = 1$, $ks\_stdev = 2 * 10^{-15}$, $bk\_stdev = 2 * 10^{-25}$, $max\_stdev = 0.012467$.
- **Bootstrapping parameters:** $bk\_l = 3$, $bk\_Bgbit = 7$.
- **Keyswitch parameters:** $ks\_length = 8$, $ks\_basebit = 2$.

The set of parameters chosen also have implications over the speed of each operations. For example, the time needed for an homomorphic addition increases linearly with N while the time needed for an homomorphic multiplication increase quadratically with N. For more details on the meaning of each parameter, read the paper [13]. Note that since TFHE is used in FHE mode, this set of parameters stays good no matter the multiplicative depth of the network.

5 Results

In this section, we will interpret the results we obtained in our experiment. The calculus were made using an Intel Core i7-6600U CPU @ 2.60 GHz. Let us also precise that we used the version 3.5.4 of SEAL and the version 1.1 of TFHE.

5.1 Precision

Two factors may lead to a discrepancy between the precision of the neural network in the clear domain and the neural network in the encrypted domain. The first one is the discretization of each value which leads to small errors propagating through the network. The more precise the discretization is, the bigger the parameters are, leading to more time consuming operations. The second factor comes from the noise in the ciphertext. A bigger noise leads to better security at the cost of making errors when deciphering. Rather than focusing on the precision of the neural networks, we will focus on this variation in precision occurring from calculating in the homomorphic domain.

BFVnn-c and BFVnn-e: The cryptosystem BFV makes exact calculus, but since it works on integers, we had to make some rounding errors. Thus, the precision depends on how much we rounded each value. Since the end result must stay low enough to be decrypted properly, we cannot take too many bits of precision at the beginning. Because of this trade off between precision and the end result size, we decided to scale the values of the input instances and the weights so that they can be stocked on 8 bits. For both BFVnn-c and BFVnn-e we lost only 0.01 percentage points of precision which means that the computation in the clear domain only has one more good guess on 10000 samples.

CKKSnn-c and CKKSnn-e: This cryptosystem is meant to make approximate calculations and we expected that as long as the maximum value of the output is far enough from the other values, then the ciphered network should output the same values. This assumption comes from the fact that our network is actually a low degree polynomial function. In practice, the precision of both CKKSnn-c and CKKSnn-e were the same as the one in clear at 96.34%.

TFHEnn-c and TFHEnn-e: We used the same scaling as with BFV so that each input instance and each weight is stocked on 8 bits, resulting in the same loss of 0.01 percentage points of precision. In this case, the scaling was chosen in order to make a trade between the precision and the time of computation.

TFHEsign: For the network using the sign activation function, the precision went from 82, 53% for the clear network to 82, 70% for the ciphered network. The big change in precision comes from the fact that the sign function is not continuous, thus a rounding on the weights can lead to big changes on the result. Thus one should be careful of the use of discontinuous function when using approximations.

5.2 Memory

The memory used depends on multiple parameters such as the number of ciphertexts and the parameters used for the cryptosystem. Through the Table 2 we show the memory requirements by homomorphic scheme for each of the neural network. For the case we only encrypt the input features (the networks denoted "nn-c"), one can ignore the line corresponding to the size of weights.

Table 2. Memory usage

	BFVnn-e	BFVnn-c	CKKSnn-e	CKKSnn-c
Keys	609 Mbytes		274 Mbytes	
Weights	31.5 Mbytes		37.5 Mbytes	
MNIST sample	12.5 Mbytes		9.3 Mbytes	
	TFHEnn-e	THFEnn-c	TFHEsign	
Keys	146 Mbytes		146 Mbytes	
Weights	1.5 Gbytes		245 Mbytes	
MNIST sample	6 Mbytes		2 Mbytes	

As we can see, even though BFV and CKKS are both working in a pretty close way, a big difference appear in the memory usage. This is caused by parameters chosen through SEAL which, in our case, lead the ciphertext modulo to be twice as big with BFV than with CKKS. It has as consequence that each ciphertext and key takes about twice as much memory with BFV. Besides, the batching with BFV has twice as many slots as CKKS's batching for a given polynomial degree N which leads us to have similar memory usage for the weights.

As far as TFHE is concerned, the parameters used are a lot smaller which leads each ciphertext and key to take less memory than the other two. These small parameters can be used because we use bootstrapping. The counterpart is that we have no batching available, so we need a lot of ciphertexts, most notably for the weights, leading to big memory usage when encrypting them. Note that we are considering here the bitwise use of TFHE, which means that many more ciphertexts are used. When encrypting bit-by-bit, a huge loss of space occur as seen in the Table 2. So it should be avoided when possible. Even though one encrypted sample is a lot smaller using TFHE than using BFV or CKKS, the opposite is seen when encrypting the weights. This shows how effective batching is with BFV and CKKS.

5.3 Time

Here, in Table 3 we show the time results (in seconds) we obtained by cryptosystem and by type of network.

We can see that when using TFHE, the preparation step and the encryption step are extremely fast thanks to the small parameters used for the cryptosystem. On the other hand, the evaluation of the network is pretty slow. This is actually due to the fact that the bootstrapping operation is a very slow operation compared to an homomorphic addition or multiplication. Indeed, the network takes approximately 2.4 s computing the bootstrapping operations in the network and only 0.1 s to compute the rest. In bitwise mode, the number of bootstrapping gets extremely high. Indeed, each multiplications and additions between integers need to be computed, each of them requiring multiple bootstrapping operations. The Table 4 gives more detail about the amount of operations.

Table 3. Time usage

	BFVnn-c	BFVnn-e	CKKSnn-c	CKKSnn-e
KeyGen	4.5 s		1.96 s	
Features encryption	0.16 s		0.29 s	
Weights encryption	-	0.24 s	-	0.35 s
Network evaluation	0.97 s	2.16 s	0.24 s	0.56 s
	TFHEnn-c	TFHEnn-e	TFHEsign	
KeyGen	0.16 s			
Features Encryption	0.08 s		0.001 s	
Weights encryption	-	16 s	-	
Network evaluation	3 days	>3 days	2.5 s	

The big speed difference between BFV and CKKS comes from the difference in parameters. Indeed, in our case, the parameters make the BFV ciphertexts about twice as big as the CKKS ciphertexts making each operation slower in the BFV case. This highlights the importance of optimizing the parameters before starting the calculus. We can also note that with every cryptosystem used, the evaluation of the network where the weights are in clear is much faster than its encrypted version. Indeed, BFVnn-c is two times faster than BFVnn-e, and the same difference occur between CKKSnn-c and CKKSnn-e. Since that difference in speed is quite big, one should only encrypt the weights if necessary for their use case.

For a better understanding of the time usages, Table 4 presents the number of operations in each case. Note that the number of multiplications is the number of multiplications between ciphertexts.

Table 4. Number of homomorphic operations

	BFVnn-c	BFVnn-e	CKKSnn-c	CKKSnn-e
Additions	21		26	
Multiplications	2	10	2	16
	TFHEnn-c	TFHEnn-e	TFHEsign	
Bootstrappings	15000000	25000000	138	

In order to understand the number of homomorphic operations, let's first calculate the number of operations for the clear network:

- The first fully connected layer consists of $784 * 128 = 100352$ multiplications and $783 * 128 = 100224$ additions between messages followed by the activation function consisting of either 128 sign functions or 128 multiplications for the square function.

- The second fully connected layer consists of $128 * 10 = 1280$ multiplications and $127 * 10 = 1270$ additions between integers followed by the activation function consisting of either 10 sign functions or 10 multiplications.

For the algorithms using batching, one homomorphic operation computes as many operations between integers as there are slots in a batch. The number of operations is different between the two cryptosystems BFV and CCKS since the number of slots in a batch for BFV is equal to the polynomial degree N while it is equal to $N/2$ for CKKS.

On the opposite, the bitwise algorithm needs multiple operations to make one addition or multiplication.

In the case of TFHE, we only counted the number of bootstrapping operations since it is by far the most time consuming part. For TFHEsign, bootstrappings are only used to compute the activation functions. The homomorphic networks TFHEnn-c and TFHEnn-e use bootstrapping operations to compute each binary gate in the network which leads to the approximate values given in the Table 4.

5.4 Guidelines Summary

In this section, based on this experience and the obtained results, we will provide some guidelines on how and when we would use each cryptosystem. Note that in order to handle the TFHE library properly it is recommended to acquire knowledge about the cryptosystem as the library does not come with any kind of user manual. Conversely, the SEAL library comes with detailed information on how to handle it.

First, however, a note on the results that we present in Sects. 5.2 and 5.3. We chose to use fixed parameters for all of our experimental results and one could conceivably want to implement their own secure cloud-based machine learning algorithm using a different set of parameters. In that context, what should be their choice of cryptosystem?

We go into some details in this paper about the scalability of our results with regard to the parameters, and depending on the cryptosystem. The parameters that could be set to be the same in each implementation are indeed the same (neural network size, polynomial size N). The rest of the parameters (p, q, bootstrapping parameters, ...) are set to ensure, in each case, the most efficient computation with a message space big enough to accommodate our input values.

SEAL-BFV: This cryptosystem allows for exact calculus of polynomials using the LHE implementation of SEAL. Since high parameters would make each operation slower, the ideal case is for the polynomial function to be of small degree. In addition to that, the structure of the function should allow the use of batching, which can lead to tremendous improvement in speed and memory usage. Note that if your function is not over integers, some operations such as rounding will be unavoidable as seen in our square network. Our square network is an example of such a function where SEAL's implementation of BFV fares well.

SEAL-CKKS: If an approximate result of a low degree polynomial function over floats is enough and that function allows for a good use of batching, SEAL's CKKS will be your best option. Indeed, this cryptosystem can make calculus over real and even complex numbers, as opposed to BFV which works over integers. However, in the light of the recent attack from [25], one should carefully choose the setting in which to use CKKS (where the result of decryption is kept private) and favor the implementations proposing mitigation strategies such as the ones from Palisade[1] and HElib[2] libraries. In the case of our square network, we would recommend this cryptosystem.

TFHE: This cryptosystem shines when bitwise operations are used. It should be used when simple polynomial functions are not sufficient for your purpose. On top of that, TFHE is the only cryptosystem with which one can build a *fully* homomorphic scheme. In the case of an encrypted query to a remote NN on a server, this means that no information is leaked about the size of the NN to the user through the parameters. FHE can also be useful when the parameters need to be created when the depth of the network is not yet known or when it is liable to change.

It can also be used for modular arithmetic when some function derived from the sign function are needed. Note that the sign function allows to compute the maximum and minimum functions which can lead to a wide variety of use. As an example, our sign network can only be evaluated using TFHE.

6 Conclusion

The approach presented in this paper consists in the evaluation and comparison of three of the most currently used homomorphic cryptosystems (BFV, CKKS and TFHE) for the private evaluation of a neural network on the cloud, on the classical MNIST dataset. We implemented the case where both the model and the instance to be predicted are encrypted and sent on the cloud for computation. We also implemented the case where only the instance is encrypted and sent on the cloud for a computation with a clear model. For this, we used both the SEAL and the TFHE library. The structure of the neural network is a rather simple one since we are not focusing on the model accuracy per se. Instead, we evaluated the results obtained using the three homomorphic schemes (under the same machine) in terms of precision (loss of accuracy), memory usage and execution time for a minimal security of 128 bits. Even though BFV and CKKS seem to obtain better evaluation times than TFHE, the latter one offers a lower memory usage and higher flexibility depending on the protocol used. We also gave some insights in the computational model we used, on how we set up the parameters for each one and a personal feedback of the usage to be made for these three cryptosystems. We argue that this is important not only to have a better idea about the strengths and the weaknesses of each scheme but also to be

1 Palisade: https://palisade-crypto.org/.
2 HElib: https://github.com/homenc/HElib.

able to mix them (thanks to the unified framework Chimera) for more efficient homomorphic-based applications.

There are several interesting perspectives for the current work. First, we feel that there is the need of updated benchmarks and guidelines for the FHE current landscape. As such, a research line that it is worth investigating is how the three cryptosystems targeted here also compare with BGV [8], another popular homomorphic cryptosystem, available in HElib open-source library. In the same effort for benchmarking and quest of efficiency, it would be interested to have an up-to-date review of the various options for the hardware acceleration. Second, on the direction of the application of homomorphic encryption to neural networks, even if this is a topic of increasing interest in these last years, there is still a lot of progress to be made. To obtain better accuracy scores, there is a need of homomorphic activation functions which better approximate those performing on clear networks. Moreover, to obtain better efficiency, one could use different homomorphic encryption schemes for the various parts of the computation and switch between them when needed.

References

1. Abadi, M., et al.: TensorFlow: Large-scale machine learning on heterogeneous systems (2015). https://www.tensorflow.org/, software available from tensorflow.org
2. Aguilar Melchor, C., Kilijian, M.O., Lefebvre, C., Ricosset, T.: A comparison of the homomorphic encryption libraries helib, seal and fv-nfllib. In: Innovative Security Solutions for Information Technology and Communications, pp. 425–442 (2019)
3. Albrecht, M., et al.: Homomorphic encryption security standard. Technical report, HomomorphicEncryption.org, Toronto, Canada, November 2018
4. Albrecht, M.R., Player, R., Scott, S.: On the concrete hardness of Learning with Errors. J. Math. Cryptol. **9**, 169–203 (2015). https://bitbucket.org/malb/lwe-estimator/src/master/
5. Boura, C., Gama, N., Georgieva, M., Jetchev, D.: Chimera: combining ring-lwe-based fully homomorphic encryption schemes. J. Math. Cryptol. **14**(1), 316–338 (2020). https://doi.org/10.1515/jmc-2019-0026
6. Bourse, F., Minelli, M., Minihold, M., Paillier, P.: Fast homomorphic evaluation of deep discretized neural networks. In: Shacham, H., Boldyreva, A. (eds.) CRYPTO 2018. LNCS, vol. 10993, pp. 483–512. Springer, Cham (2018). https://doi.org/10.1007/978-3-319-96878-0_17
7. Brakerski, Z.: Fully homomorphic encryption without modulus switching from classical GapSVP. In: Safavi-Naini, R., Canetti, R. (eds.) CRYPTO 2012. LNCS, vol. 7417, pp. 868–886. Springer, Heidelberg (2012). https://doi.org/10.1007/978-3-642-32009-5_50
8. Brakerski, Z., Gentry, C., Vaikuntanathan, V.: (Leveled) fully homomorphic encryption without bootstrapping. In: Electronic Colloquium on Computational Complexity (ECCC), vol. 18, p. 111, January 2011. https://doi.org/10.1145/2090236.2090262
9. Brutzkus, A., Oren Elisha, O., Gilad-Bachrach, R.: Low latency privacy preserving inference. In: Proceedings of the 36th International Conference on MachineLearning, Long Beach, California, PMLR 97 (2019)

10. Chabanne, H., de Wargny, A., Milgram, J., Morel, C., Prouff, E.: Privacy-preserving classification on deep neural network. IACR Cryptology ePrint Archive, p. 35 (2017)
11. Cheon, J., Kim, A., Kim, M., Song, Y.: Homomorphic encryption for arithmetic of approximate numbers. In: International Conference on the Theory and Application of Cryptology and Information Security, pp. 409–437, November 2017
12. Chillotti, I., Gama, N., Georgieva, M., Izabachène, M.: Faster packed homomorphic operations and efficient circuit bootstrapping for TFHE, pp. 377–408, November 2017
13. Chillotti, I., Gama, N., Georgieva, M., Izabachène, M.: Faster fully homomorphic encryption: bootstrapping in less than 0.1 seconds. In: Cheon, J.H., Takagi, T. (eds.) ASIACRYPT 2016. LNCS, vol. 10031, pp. 3–33. Springer, Heidelberg (2016). https://doi.org/10.1007/978-3-662-53887-6_1
14. Chillotti, I., Gama, N., Georgieva, M., Izabachène, M.: Faster packed homomorphic operations and efficient circuit bootstrapping for TFHE. In: ASIACRYPT (2017)
15. Chillotti, I., Gama, N., Georgieva, M., Izabachène, M.: TFHE: fast fully homomorphic encryption library, August 2016. https://tfhe.github.io/tfhe/
16. Chillotti, I., Gama, N., Georgieva, M., Izabachène, M.: TFHE: fast fully homomorphic encryption over the torus. J. Cryptol. **33**(1), 34–91 (2019). https://doi.org/10.1007/s00145-019-09319-x
17. Costache, A., Laine, K., Player, R.: Evaluating the effectiveness of heuristic worst-case noise analysis in FHE. Cryptology ePrint Archive, Report 2019/493 (2019). https://eprint.iacr.org/2019/493
18. Dowlin, N., Gilad-Bachrach, R., Laine, K., Lauter, K., Naehrig, M., Wernsing, J.: Cryptonets: applying neural networks to encrypted data with high throughput and accuracy. In: Proceedings of the 33rd International Conference on International Conference on Machine Learning - Volume 48. ICML'16, pp. 201–210 (2016)
19. Fan, J., Vercauteren, F.: Somewhat practical fully homomorphic encryption (2012). https://eprint.iacr.org/2012/144.pdf
20. Gentry, C.: A Fully Homomorphic Encryption Scheme. Ph.D. thesis, Stanford, CA, USA (2009)
21. Gentry, C.: Fully homomorphic encryption using ideal lattices. In: Proceedings of the Forty-first Annual ACM Symposium on Theory of Computing, STOC 2009, New York, NY, USA, pp. 169–178, ACM (2009). https://doi.org/10.1145/1536414.1536440
22. Krizhevsky, A.: Learning Multiple Layers of Features from Tiny Images. University of Toronto (2012)
23. Lecun, Y., Bottou, L., Bengio, Y., Haffner, P.: Gradient-based learning applied to document recognition. Proc. IEEE **86**(11), 2278–2324 (1998). https://doi.org/10.1109/5.726791
24. Lepoint, T., Naehrig, M.: A comparison of the homomorphic encryption schemes FV and YASHE. In: Pointcheval, D., Vergnaud, D. (eds.) AFRICACRYPT 2014. LNCS, vol. 8469, pp. 318–335. Springer, Cham (2014). https://doi.org/10.1007/978-3-319-06734-6_20
25. Li, B., Micciancio, D.: On the security of homomorphic encryption on approximate numbers. Cryptology ePrint Archive, Report 2020/1533 (2020). https://eprint.iacr.org/2020/1533
26. Lou, Q., Feng, B., Fox, G., Jiang, L.: Glyph: fast and accurately training deep neural networks on encrypted data (2019)
27. Microsoft: SEAL. https://github.com/Microsoft/SEAL

28. Sathya, S.S., Vepakomma, P., Raskar, R., Ramachandra, R., Bhattacharya, S.: A review of homomorphic encryption libraries for secure computation (2018)
29. Smart, N., Vercauteren, F.: Fully Homomorphic SIMD Operations (2011). https://eprint.iacr.org/2011/133.pdf

Memory Deduplication as a Protective Factor in Virtualized Systems

Abdullah Albalawi, Vassilios Vassilakis(✉), and Radu Calinescu

Department of Computer Science, University of York, York, UK
vv573@york.ac.uk

Abstract. We introduce a method for protection against a side-channel attack made possible by the use of a cloud-computing feature called *memory deduplication*. Memory deduplication improves the efficiency with which physical memory is used by the virtual machines (VMs) running on the same server by keeping in memory only one copy of the libraries and other software used by multiple VMs. However, this allows an attacker's VM to find out the memory locations (and thus the operations) used by a victim's VM, as these locations are cached and can be accessed faster than memory locations not used by the victim. To perform the attack, the malicious VM needs to execute an abnormal sequence of cache flushes, and our new method detects this by monitoring memory locations associated with sensitive (e.g., encryption) operations and using logistic regression to identify the abnormal cached operations. Furthermore, by using its own cache flushing, our method disrupts the side channel, making it more difficult for the attacker to acquire useful information. The experiments we ran using the KVM hypervisor and Ubuntu 18.04 LTS VMs on both Debian 10 and CentOS physical servers show that our method can detect attacks with 99% accuracy, and can feed fake information to an attacker with between 2–8% CPU overheads.

Keywords: Side-channel attacks · Memory deduplication · Flush+reload · Flush+flush

1 Introduction

Cloud computing is an important technology that greatly reduces costs and increases operations and economic efficiencies [1] through the use of shared computing resources provided with lightweight administrative procedures [2]. However, the multi-tenancy model and the sharing of virtualized resources in cloud computing have also introduced new security vulnerabilities [3,4]. An important such vulnerability arises when a malicious user exploits the cloud allocation techniques or virtual machine (VM) placement policies to co-locate their VM on the same physical server as a target victim VM. This then allows the malicious user to perform co-resident side-channel attacks leading to confidentiality violations [5] such as obtaining cryptographic keys used on the victim's VM [6].

J. Zhou et al. (Eds.): ACNS 2021 Workshops, LNCS 12809, pp. 301–317, 2021.
https://doi.org/10.1007/978-3-030-81645-2_17

In this paper, we focus on a specific type of side-channel attack, which is enabled by the use of a cloud-computing virtualisation feature called *memory deduplication*. Memory deduplication is a method of reducing memory usage by keeping in the memory of the server only one copy of the data and code used by multiple VMs. An attacker can use deduplication to access the physical addresses of the shared memory area, followed by cache flush operations on any addresses of interest. Subsequently, any memory locations used by the victim VM are brought back into the cache, and can be identified by the attacker since the time to retrieve them is much shorter than the retrieval time for memory locations that were not used by the victim. Determining the memory locations accessed by the victim VM in this way can reveal sensitive information about the victim [7–10].

Although several methods for mitigating this type of side-channel attack have been proposed [11–17], these methods have significant drawbacks. First, they require the execution of code on the host (i.e., the physical machine), which is not something that the victim (i.e., the user of the VM) can typically do. Additionally, they do not provide any preventative protection for the victim VM. In particular, any false-negatives allow the malicious VM to perform the attack undetected.

We address these limitations of current mitigation solutions by introducing a new method that protects against memory-deduplication side attacks from within the victim's VM. Our method monitors sensitive data addresses, and renders attacks ineffective by providing the malicious VM with fake results during attack attempts, even in the (rare) instances when these attacks are not detected (due to false negatives). To this end, the method uses memory deduplication itself to get readings of the monitored functions of an executable program and then analyzes the readings using logistic regression. The proposed method can be used inside the VM to be protected from cache attacks, with no changes to the virtualization platforms. The main contributions of our paper are:

1. We present a method for protection against memory-deduplication side-channel attacks by using memory deduplication and logistic regression from within the victim VM.
2. We introduce the design and implementation of the method.
3. We evaluate the method in multiple scenarios, in terms of attack detection accuracy and performance characteristics.

The remainder of this paper is organized as follows. Section 2 provides the required background. In Sect. 3, we explain and analyze the problem. Section 4 describes the proposed protection method. Section 5 provides an overview of the experiments we carried out using the new method. In Sect. 6, we discuss the evaluation of the implemented method. Section 7 compares our method to related work. Finally, Sect. 8 provides a brief conclusion and suggestions for future work.

2 Background

2.1 Memory Deduplication

Memory deduplication is a feature that increases memory utilization on physical servers running multiple VMS by allowing the data used by several VMs to be shared between these VMs. The redundant copies of the data are removed from the memory. Memory deduplication was introduced around the mid-1990s, and it has been implemented in virtual platforms recently [18]. For example, Red Hat proposed the KSM technique to implement memory deduplication in the Linux kernel. KSM has merged into the Linux kernel since version 2.6.32 in 2009 [19]. This feature is supported and offered in almost all the hypervisors, for instance, VMWare ESX and Linux KVM [20]. This feature's central concept is that if there are many identical pages in the content over multiple VMs, the hypervisor removes all copies while keeping only one shared copy between them. While memory deduplication increases memory efficiency, it has a significant influence on virtualized systems security. Accessing the same data or the same library, especially the shared cryptographic libraries, can be potentially manipulated to leak confidential data of the victim VM's encryptions processes. Thus, memory deduplication can be exploited by attackers for obtaining sensitive information regarding encryption processes. The exploit of the memory deduplication is accomplished when the attacker's VMs prime or flush the cached data and give the victim's VM some time to access or reload any of these data to be cached again. Hence, the accessed cache data leaks information regarding the victim's activities [7,20].

Several kinds of memory deduplication mechanisms are implemented by popular hypervisors, such as the Kernel Based-Virtual Machine (KVM) hypervisor. KVM is a hypervisor software applied on the Linux kernel, which employs the Kernel Samepage Merging (KSM) technique. KSM explores or scans all VMs in the virtualized environment looking for all pages that have the same content, and if it finds pages with the same content, they are then deduplicated and shared [21].

In virtualized systems that support the memory deduplication feature, pages may be data, libraries, or executable files shared between two VMs. One of these devices may be a malicious VM. In this case, the malicious VM is able to discover the victim's behavior. The attacker must load an executable file or a page into the memory and then wait for pages with the same content to be scanned, deduplicated, and shared with the victim's VM, which has the same page. Then the attacker can recognize the victim VM's actions and operations by writing on the shared page. If it takes longer, this means that the page has been shared and ready to launch the attack on the victim's VM using this shared page, resulting in sensitive information disclosure [20].

2.2 Memory-Deduplication Cache Attacks

In this work, we focus on cache attacks that target the shared cache memory between users in virtualized systems, where the attacker analyzes the timing information gained from retrieving data from the cache or from the main memory [6]. When the CPU looks for data, it can be found in the main memory or in the cache. If the data is recovered from the cache, the retrieval time or amount of CPU cycles is low. However, suppose the data is not cached in memory. In that case, it must be recovered from the main memory, ensuring a relatively larger amount of time and CPU cycles would be taken to recover it. Then the recovered data will temporarily remain in the cache memory to improve the system performance if the data is retrieved next time. Consequently, the attack process depends on exploiting the time difference between recovering data either from cache or the main memory; in other words, the time difference between cache hits and cache misses [7].

The attackers take advantage of timing information to launch attacks on the victim's VM using the cache hits and cache misses to measure the CPU cycles or the time to recover the cache memory's targeted addresses. In this attack, the attacker can break the isolation between VMs, uncover the victim's actions, obtain information about cryptographic operations, and then break the encryption key.

The attackers can obtain sensitive information from encryption processes using timing information extracted from the shared cache memory. This may lead to breaking encryption systems, e.g., by using timing information in the TableLookUp implementation of AES. For making the encryption process easy and fast in AES, the T-Table implementation was designed in addition to the XORing process (TableLookUp operation). However, the T-table entries will be stored in the cache memory when used in encryption processes, which leads to ease of breaking the encryption key using timing information [7,22].

Three main ways to exploit cache memory and extract sensitive data are given below [14,23]:

- Prime + Probe: In this method, the attacker's VM loads the cache lines with its data. Next, it gives the victim some time to perform some encryption operations. After that, the previously loaded data retrieval time is measured by the attacker's VM. As a result, the attacker will know what data has been removed from the cache memory and, thus, recognize the cache lines used in the victim's encryption operations. This technique does not require shared libraries or page deduplication.
- Flush + Reload: The attacker's VM first flushes the required memory lines out of the cache. After that, it gives the victim time to perform some encryption operations. Next, the attacker reloads the evicted lines and measures their access time. Thus, the attacker can identify if the victim's encryption process has recovered the cache lines, using the timing information. This technique relies on shared libraries and memory deduplication.
- Flush + Flush: In this approach, the attacker's VM first flushes the required memory lines out of the cache. After that, it gives the victim time to perform some encryption operations. Next, the attacker's VM flushes again the previous memory lines and measures the flush instructions' execution time,

bypassing direct cache accesses. The attacker can use this type of attack to break a cryptographic key. This technique relies on shared libraries and memory deduplication.

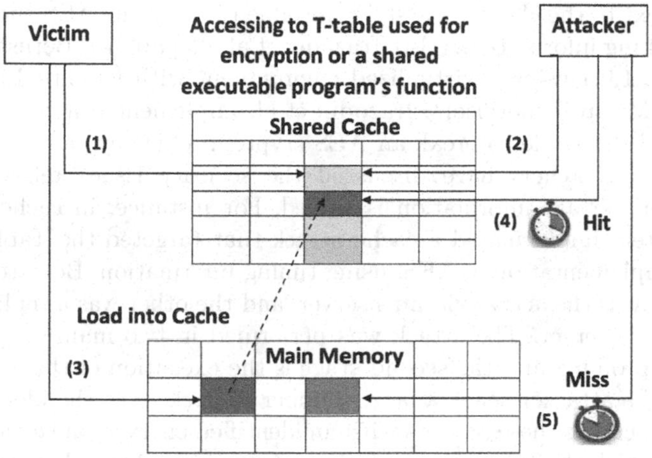

Fig. 1. Cache side-channel attack

The attacker takes several steps to execute cache side-channel attacks, taking advantage of shared resources and memory deduplication, as shown in Fig. 1. The attack is carried out with the following steps: (1) In the beginning, the victim can use the shared program that contains a number of sensitive operations and functions that are loaded into the shared cache by simply entering one of them and executing one of the functions. (2) The attacker evicts these physical addresses from the cache memory by using the flush command (*clflush*) to ensure that the addresses will be retrieved from the main memory if requested next time, as a trap for the victim to find out the data retrieved and stored in the cache memory, if the victim used one of these addresses. (3) The victim may use one or more of the sensitive program's functions, and as soon as the victim uses one of them, it will be restored to the cache memory. That means that the victim has actually fallen into the trap set by the attacker. (4) The attacker retrieves all the addresses that have been flushed while keeping track of how long it takes to retrieve each of these addresses using Time Stamp Counter (*rdtsc*). (5) The attacker analyzes the results. If the retrieval time for any of the physical addresses is longer than the specified threshold, this means that none of them was used. However, if the retrieval time for any of them was less than the threshold, this means that it was used in the sensitive operations.

Data leakage is the result of sharing the same physical machine. Prior studies have shown the possibility and practicality of cache side-channel attacks in cloud computing. For instance, in the case of a cross-VM attack on AES implementations, Irazoqui et al. [7] found that the attack exploits Tthe ransparent Page

Sharing used in virtualization environments. Suzaki et al. [19] employed memory deduplication to detect processes running on the target VM. Bernstein's attack is a cache attack that is implemented in a client-server-based environment that is non-virtualized [24]. Bernstein used a client to send UDP packets to request encryption from the server, and then the server sends back the encrypted text to the client. Bernstein was able to crack the AES encryption key using the timing information. Also, Irazoqui et al. [25] applied Bernstein's attack on OpenSSL 1.0.1 using a virtualized environment with Ubuntu 12.04 running XEN and VMware hypervisors. Irazoqui et al. implemented a cross-VM attack scenario, and were able to break an AES cryptographic key.

Multiple researchers have discussed the security issues related to cache attacks when certain information is leaked. For instance, in cache attacks on AES, Bernstein implemented a cache attack that targeted the TableLookup of OpenSSL implementation of AES, using timing information. Bernstein used two servers. One was the actual victim's server, and the other was a replica identical to the victim's server. The attack was performed in two main stages: the first stage is the profiling and the second stage is the execution of the attack. In the first stage, the attacker sends a large number of packets to the identical server. The server encrypts these packets with an identified encryption key and provides the attacker with the encryption's timing information. After that, in the second stage, a similar operation is executed again, but in this stage targeted the actual server itself using a private encryption key. Next, the timing profiles from these two stages are correlated to indicate the most likely value to be the encryption key used for the encryption process [24,26,27].

Yarom et al. presented the cache attack based on Flush + Reload technique to extract a secret encryption key from the GnuPG 1.4.13 implementation of RSA. The result of their cache attack was the breaking of the encryption key from an ECDSA (Elliptic Curve Digital Signature Algorithm) [8,28]. Gullasch et al. [29] applied a cache timing attack on the OpenSSL 0.9.8n using Linux kernel 2.6.23. The attack was executed using the Flush + Reload technique to find out the memory accesses' timing information. The key was broken with a few encryption attempts during the attack. Also, Irazoqui et al. [7] implemented a cache attack with different scenarios on AES by using the Flush + Reload attack to gain the AES cryptographic key in a virtualized environment. The attack needed to enable memory deduplication in VMware ESXI 5.5.0 with several Ubuntu 12.04 64-bit guest OSs.

3 Problem Definition

Due to cloud computing relying on multi-tenancy or a shared system that permits numerous users to access and share computing power on a shared physical machine, attackers can exploit the co-residency feature in a multi-tenant environment to extract sensitive information using side-channel attacks. This kind of attack exploits the shared hardware resources as a covert channel for collecting vital information to break the isolation between VMs. Our proposed method intends to improve security controls that preserve a shared environment's benefits while reducing co-resident attack risks.

The paper concentrates on flush-based attacks that exploit the memory deduplication feature. Memory deduplication removes multiple memory copies, and it also allows sharing of pages among multiple VMs over the virtualized systems to save memory. It occurs if a set of processes or VMs run identical executable programs or identical libraries [7]. This optimization technique is beneficial, especially in virtualized environments where multiple VMs share computing resources.

Although the memory deduplication method reduces memory footprint and enables additional VMs to run on a physical machine, it also gives attackers the ability to discover shared memory addresses, leading to isolation breaches and cache vulnerabilities in side-channel attacks. While VMs that share a single host cannot change or destroy the cache data because of the COW protection, the attackers can exploit access ability to shared memory addresses to obtain informations about the activities of other VMs, hence gaining information about the victim's behavior.

The security vulnerabilities associated with memory deduplication, which have been proven in many academic studies [7,8,10,19] and cloud computing security communities, highlight the need to address these concerns by stopping and disabling this feature [30]. However, we should not remove this feature and its many benefits in the shared environment. Instead, we should adequately address the defect and convert it into strengths that help provide the required protection and allow the detection of suspicious behavior. This paper presents a new method for detecting such side-channels attacks and related suspicious behavior *and* for making an attack more difficult for malicious users aiming to exploit the memory deduplication feature.

4 Protection Method

This section explains our proposed protection method. Consider two VMs in a virtualised environment that supports memory/page deduplication. One of the VMs is the attacker and the other is the attack target (victim). Both VMs are located on the same physical host and share the LLC and some files (e.g., libraries and executable files). The memory deduplication mechanism removes redundant copies of these files, so that only a single version of each shared file is retained.

As illustrated in Fig. 2, users can access the shared memory addresses and are able to conduct flush-based side-channel attacks. Attacker's actions when executing the flush-based attack are as follows. The attacker identifies the desired memory pages that are to be monitored over a certain period of time and flushes them out of the cache, using the *clflush* instruction (flushing may need to be repeated multiple times to ensure the attack's success). The aim is that the flushed pages are recovered from the main memory when these pages are requested by the victim. Next, the attacker reloads the desired pages and measures the access

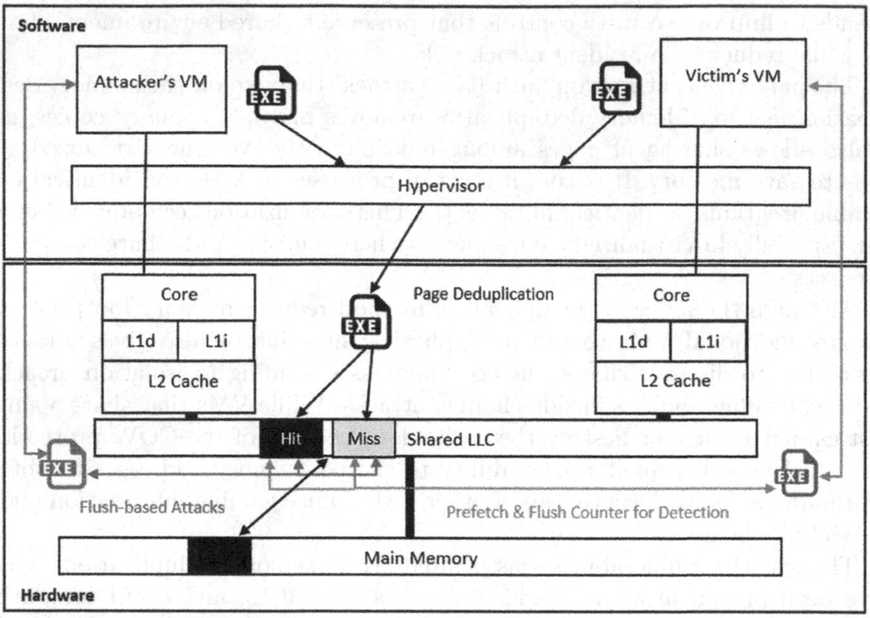

Fig. 2. Flush-based attacks exploiting shared LLC.

time (using the *rdtsc* instruction) to determine whether or not the victim has requested those pages.

The protection method involves the following steps.

- Receives the addresses of the executable program's functions to be monitored and protected from the flush-based cache attacks.
- Retrieves the monitored functions into the cache memory.
- Measures the time taken to retrieve each function over each specified period of time. As a result, the functions will be pre-fetched and the flush instructions will be discovered. The measurement is carried out using the *rdtsc* instructions that provide a high-resolution time stamp counter [31]. It uses the *mfence* instructions as well.
- Sets a sample for each function so that the retrieval time is measured frequently. It is then measured against the threshold of the system to detect if flush instructions have been performed on the functions.

The aforementioned method can detect attacks based on a flush instructions, including the Flush+Flush attack. It requires no memory access and thus produces no cache misses. However, the cache hits are significantly decreased because of the continuous cache flushes, comparing to any other cache attack [31]. The protection mechanism runs parallel to the execution of sensitive operations in another terminal. It can run on a VM to monitor the sensitive program's physical addresses obtained by the debugging tool. Debugging process may be complicated for the user unless the sensitive program's physical addresses are identified and entered automatically. The attacker may notice that the protection mechanism is running because the attacker continuously records the same results.

5 Experimental Results

We performed experiments on the KVM hypervisor that runs KSM as a memory-saving deduplication feature. We created two VMs running a Linux operating system; one VM acting as a victim and the other acting as an attacker. We used QEMU-KVM hypervisor on a Debian 10 (buster) host with Intel Core i5-4200M CPU, 12 GiB memory, and Ubuntu's guest VMs 18.04.4 LTS. We also used QEMU-KVM hypervisor on a CentOS Linux 8 host with Intel Core i5-5300U CPU, 8 GiB memory, and Ubuntu guest VMs 18.04.4 LTS. We created the shared virtualized environment using the hypervisor's default settings. We assumed that the victim's and the attacker's VMs were pinned to different processor cores, which means the LLC was shared between them. Thus, the other levels of cache were not shared among the VMs. The method intends to provide data about the shared executable program using a side-channel carried between two VMs within the shared LLC.

In both VMs, we installed and ran the same executable program, shared using KSM. We checked the number of pages that have been shared between VMs. We found the addresses of the application's functions using debugging tools such as GDB to be used as inputs in our proposed detection program. After that, we created a covert channel between VMs to monitor the attacker behavior. We used a Mastik Framework [10,32], which has several libraries to use and recreate many important functions such as $map\_offset(), fr\_monitor(), and\ fr\_probe()$.

We developed a C program implementing Algorithm 1, which counts the number of flushes that happen to the shared executable program; flushes for each function are counted. This indicates the instability status of the cache memory due to the presence of a large number of flushes that occur in a short interval of time (e.g., 5 s). Figure 3 shows the results from a series of experiments that we carried out to evaluate the feasibility of our method.

The protection mechanism performs a series of functions. First, using the $map\_offset()$ function to load the executable program into memory as a Read-Only file means none of the users can modify the file to be shared between users. However, once the user modifies the file, the KSM will create a separate copy of the modified file only for the user who made the modification and will stop the deduplication of the file. After that, the user inputs the addresses of the functions that are needed to be monitored. It then initially measures the time it takes to retrieve data from these addresses, and thus we ensure that all addresses have been placed in the cache memory. In addition, the approach will be ready to measure any flush instructions that occur to addresses that cause successive cache misses; their impact will be clear at the measurement time. We can then measure the actual time to retrieve data from addresses. Before that, we determine the system's threshold to differentiate between retrieving data from

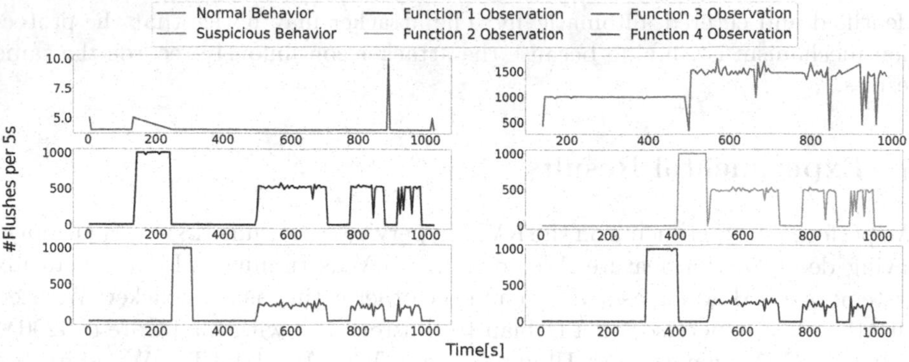

Fig. 3. Number of flushes per 5 s for different attack scenarios: no attack (top left), attack on all four functions of a software application (top right), attack on one of the functions of the application at a time (second and third row). (Color figure online)

the cache memory comparing with retrieving data from the main memory. If the retrieving time is greater than the system's threshold, this means that the addresses have just been flushed out of the cache. After that, we measure the time that the CPU takes to measure the time of retrieving data, showing that the cache memory is unstable and exposed to flush operations and thus an attack on the cache memory. To be more precise, we create a sample loop so that we can measure the retrieving time for each address several times. The frequency can be changed according to the system.

We recorded the results for Debian 10 and CentOS 8 in different cases. First, we recorded the results in a normal case without any attack on the cache memory. Secondly, we recorded the results when the attack was on only one function in the shared executable program. Finally, we recorded the results in the case of an attack on all functions in the shared executable program. The relationship between the attack state (red line) and the normal state (green line) has been clarified using the plot charts shown in Fig. 3. The plot charts show a big difference between an attack and no attack, thus a big difference in the stability of the cache memory in a short period.

In Fig. 3, the results are recorded during all the scenarios mentioned above. In the first plot, the results are represented for all addresses that were monitored in the absence of an attack. It is also considered a stable case for a longer period compared to the results of other cases. As for the second chart, it represents the suspicious state of all the sensitive functions addresses, in cases of attacks on them all. It shows a high rise in flush commands on the addresses, indicating the attack status. As for the following charts, they show the cases of the attack on an address for one function only, as they show instances of instability for different periods due to the presence of the flush commands, indicating the attack on the specific function in each chart.

Algorithm 1. Flush Counter in a Given Interval of Time

```
Input: App.elf, F_Add1, F_Add2....F_Addn
Output: Number of flush operations in a given time interval
Read-Only Mmap App.elf into Memory Offset = 0;
for i = F_Add1 to F_Addn do
    Initial Access Time Measurement, Prefetching to Cache
    FlushCounter[ i ] = 0;
end for
while true do
    T1 = Start Clock ();
    Pause for 5 seconds
    for Iteration = 1 to Total No of Measurements do
        for i ← F_Add1 to F_Addn do
            Time = Access Time Measurement(i);
            if Time > Access Threshold then
                FlushCounter[ i ] ++;
            end if
        end for
    end for
    T2 = Stop Clock();
    Time_Elapsed = T2 − T1 // time in microseconds
end while
```

6 Evaluation and Comparison to Other Solutions

In this section, we evaluate and compare our protection method to the existing methods. Previous works have been based on the performance counter provided by Linux and Intel, such as Intel PCM (Performance Counter Monitor), Intel CMT (Cache Monitoring Technology), and Linux perf. Most previous studies have used these tools inside the host machine to monitor counters affected by an attack. However, if they are used inside a VM then there will be limitations; the guest VM needs authorization from the host to use the hardware performance counters, and not all provided counters are supported for use in a VM[33–35], which makes it difficult to detect an attack using these tools inside a VM in order to provide it with self-protection.

To validate our approach, we ran it on different operating systems (Debian 10 and CentOS 8) in different scenarios for the virtualized platform. We used the Mastik framework to recreate the attack. The attacker flushes the functions of the shared executable program and the sharing was achieved by the data deduplication feature. The scenarios were as follows.

- *No-Attack Scenario:* The attacker conducts no cache attack on the side channel, nor is there any sign of suspicious behavior. The results were almost consistent with only one flush for all functions and for both operating systems used in the experiment, indicating no attack on shared re-sources.
- *One-Function-Attack Scenario:* The attacker executes the flush-based cache attack on a shared executable program to attack only one function. The attacker specifies the function address to execute repeated flush instructions on this address. We recorded a very high number of flush instructions. The results were similar for both operating systems used.
- *Multiple-Functions-Attack Scenario:* In this scenario, the attacker performs the side-channel attack on a shared executable program to attack multiple

functions. In both Debian 10 and CentOS 8, we recorded a different number of flush instructions, and the results were clear enough to indicate an attack on all functions. We produced plot charts that better illustrate the results of the experiment's scenarios, as shown in Fig. 3.

Based on the obtained results, we were able to identify suspicious behavior in using the shared executable program, which indicates the attack status. Also, the VM provided self-protection by knowing the impact of the attack on shared resources. The attack's effect on the system was identified, which was the cache state's instability for a long time and a huge increase in the number of flushes, which meant that there was a significant difference in the case of an attack and no attack.

Like in the experiments shown in Fig. 3, we evaluated the proposed approach in several scenarios: no attack, attacks on only one function of an application, and attacks on all four functions from our application. In the no attack case, the results were almost constant at one flush per time period (i.e., per 5—s) for all functions within the application, making it proof of non-attack. In the case of attacking one function, the results show a high number of flush instructions. For the attack on multiple functions, the results (shown in Fig. 4) differed between the operating systems we used in our experiments. In Debian 10, we recorded very large numbers of flushes (Figs. 4a), while for CentOS 8 (Figs. 4a) we had to increase the number of iterations of the for loop from lines 9–16 in Algorithm 1 in order to observe the increased number of flushes caused by the attack. The explanation for the fewer flushes when several functions are under attack is that the attack is distributed across the multiple functions, with fewer flushes of individual memory locations occurring within a given period of time. With this calibration, we distinguished between the no attack and attack cases easily for both operating systems.

Although the results recorded in the case of attacking multiple functions in CentOS 8 showed fewer flush instructions than the results in Debian 10, the difference between it and the non-attack case was obvious and significant, and we could easily distinguish between them, as shown in Fig. 4b. We could also specify a threshold to help increase the accuracy of the results or even increase the number of iterations. For example, if we set the threshold at 12 flushes, all the attack cases could be detected, as was proven in the experiment results. Suppose we set 12 flushes as a threshold to indicate suspicious behaviors. In such a case, the attack will always be detected because, for all experiments, the recorded results would be more than 12 flushes for all attack cases. That makes the proposed approach effective in helping to detect an attack.

The results were also recorded in CSV format to be used as a dataset in machine learning algorithms. We created a logistic regression model to support attack detection. We also analyzed the results and measured the accuracy of our detection mechanism. As shown in Table 1, our method achieved a mean accuracy of 99% in these experiments. Table 1 also shows a comparison of the proposed attack detection method to the methods introduced in previous studies. While the CPU usage of our solution (2–8%) is above that of some of the

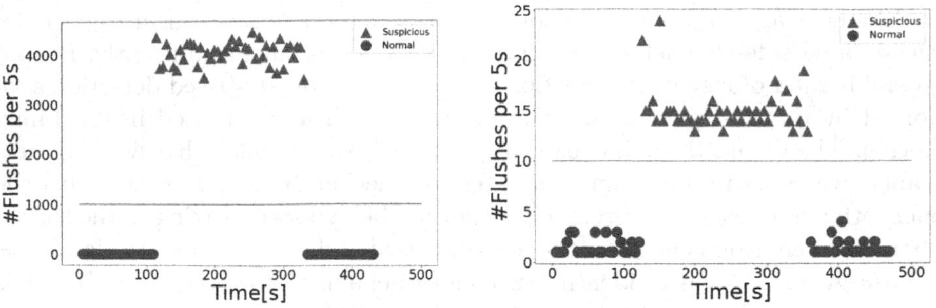

(a) Suspicious behavior in Debian 10 (b) Suspicious behavior in CentOS 8

Fig. 4. Number of flushes per 5 s for attacks on multiple functions (the horizontal axis shows the time in seconds). Different thresholds (1000 flushes for Debian 10, and 10 for CentOS 8) were used to distinguish between normal behaviour (shown as green circles) and suspicious behaviour (shown as red triangles). (Color figure online)

existing approaches, this additional overhead comes with the major advantage that our solution can be deployed and run within the VM requiring protection. Furthermore, this overhead only occurs while our approach is activated during periods when the protected VM performs sensitive operations, which is typically infrequent. In contrast, the other approaches need to be active at all times, since finding out when the victim's VM performs sensitive operations and requires protection is difficult to know.

7 Related Work

There have been numerous prior works focussing on the detection and prevention of cache side-channel attacks. This section reviews some of these works and identifies their limitations, which urged us to focus on these limitations and take them into consideration in our work.

Table 1. Comparison to other approaches

Method	Tool	CPU usage (%)	Detection rate	
			Accuracy (%)	F-score
Zhang et al. [14,16]	Linux perf	5%	–	0.85
Chiappetta et al. [12]	Linux perf	0.6%	–	0.93
Mohammad-Mahdi et al. [11]	Intel CMT	2%	–	0.67
Jonghyeon Cho et al. [13]	Intel PCM	0.9%	97%	–
Gulmezoglu et al. [14]	Intel PCM	18%	99%	0.99
Mushtaq et al. [15]	Intel CMT	4%	99%	–
Our Method	Memory Deduplication	2–8%	99%	0.99

Zhang et al. [16] presented CloudRadar, a detection mechanism to decrease cache-based side-channel attacks threats in cloud systems significantly. It used a combination of signature detection method and anomaly-based detection supported by the hardware performance counter such as *perf* used in the Linux Kernel. The CloudRadar has used a group of VMs to collect hardware performance events and send them to a detection mechanism synchronized with the encryption operations to detect any abnormal behaviors occurring in the shared virtualized environment. The CloudRadar used a database to store signatures for use in comparison to identify suspicious behavior. However, CloudRadar is unable to recognize attacks that exhibit only small changes from existing attacks.

Chiappetta et al. [12] introduced several detection mechanisms that can detect Flush + Reload attacks in real-time. The detection mechanisms relied on hardware performance events counter. Two of these mechanisms relied on machine-learning techniques. The proposed mechanisms were able to detect the attack and fulfilled the essential purpose. Nevertheless, all of the proposed methods are limited in terms of implementation. They only detect one cache timing attack, which means they need to expand their scope to include more than one cache attack. Mohammad-Mahdi et al. [11] introduced a detection mechanism utilizing Intel Cache Monitoring Technology (Intel CMT) for collecting hardware events. This detection mechanism relied on the Gaussian anomaly detection algorithm. This detection mechanism produced accurate results, but only in specific situations, and it was negatively affected if there was noise [15].

Another study that used a machine learning algorithm for monitoring users behaviors and detecting cache side-channel attacks was that of Cho et al. [13], who proposed a machine learning technique for cache side-channel attack detection by monitoring five kinds of performance counters provided by Intel Performance Counter Monitor (Intel PCM), classifying the attacks according to performance counter output in realtime. It provides some accurate attack detection. However, it has some limitations that can change the attack detection results and make it challenging to adopt. It requires some modifications to the Intel PCM tool. Furthermore, Cho et al. addressed that the method assumed that the attacker's VM must have privileged access mode to the resources; this may cause a security issue that leads to manipulating the hardware performance counter's data.

Gulmezoglu et al. [14] proposed FortuneTeller, which is a method for detecting multiple cache attacks using the Intel PCM and Unsupervised Deep Learning. FortuneTeller models benign execution performance and anticipates how the performance is supposed to be in real-time, detecting any unpredicted performance in real-time. The detection mechanism requires much-complicated computation and much training data for unsupervised deep learning models [13].

Wang et al. [17] proposed SCARF, which is a real-time side-channel attack detection mechanism based on machine learning algorithms. The detection mechanism collects hardware performance events to monitor VMs' behaviors in several scenarios, including attack cases, no attack, and training the models to detect malicious activities according to the hardware events output. Mushtaq et al. [15]

used Intel CMT (Intel Cache Monitoring Technology) for monitoring several hardware events. Then analyzing these events using a set of machine learning models to indicate the suspicious results lead to malicious behavior detection. It provides accurate results, but it is inadequate at detecting some cache side-channel attacks, such as Flush+Flush Attack.

Another mechanism, called HomeAlone, is an approach that can use the second level of cache to detect co-residency, which is considered a security threat. In HomeAlone, the basic idea is for the tenant to coordinate its VMs (called friendly VMs) to pause their operation for a period of time in a selected cache area. During the next quiet time, the tenant then tests the cache utilization and checks that there is no unwanted operation or any behavior that indicates an adversary's VM existence, thus detecting undesired co-residency. However, it only focuses on a specific cache level while an attack could be conducted using other levels of cache [36,37].

In summary, some of these approaches are not comprehensive for a sufficient number of cache attacks. Also, some are not attractive because they require fundamental changes in the infrastructure of the environment. Moreover, some of them do not give consistent results in certain circumstances. In our work, we focus on detecting at least several of the major cache attacks to extract accurate detection results for these attacks with acceptable system performance.

8 Conclusion and Future Work

We proposed a flush-based attack detection mechanism that works inside the protected VM without additional requirements to provide readings of a shared executable program's performance between VMs. The experimental results indicate that method works with a mean accuracy of 99% if a suitable threshold is set to determine the attack status. The new method helps VMs to detect an attack by knowing the attack readings, thus providing self-protection for the VM. This differs from previous solutions, which need to run in the host machine.

In future work, we will run additional experiments to further evaluate the effectiveness of our method in a broader range of scenarios. In addition, we will explore the possibility to use machine learning to create a runtime mechanism for attack detection by exploiting the readings obtained by the solution provided in this paper. To this end, the readings obtained by the current method will be recorded, and then analyzed to identify suspicious behavior, thus providing the opportunity to respond to attacks timely.

References

1. Takabi, H., Joshi, J.B., Ahn, G.-J.: Security and privacy challenges in cloud computing environments. IEEE Secur. Privacy **8**(6), 24–31 (2010)
2. Garrison, G., Kim, S., Wakefield, R.L.: Success factors for deploying cloud computing. Commun. ACM **55**(9), 62–68 (2012)

3. Hussain, S.A., Fatima, M., Saeed, A., Raza, I., Shahzad, R.K.: Multilevel classification of security concerns in cloud computing. Appl. Comput. Inform. **13**(1), 57–65 (2017)
4. Kuyoro, S., Ibikunle, F., Awodele, O.: Cloud computing security issues and challenges. Int. J. Comput. Networks (IJCN) **3**(5), 247–255 (2011)
5. Saxena, S., Sanyal, G., Srivastava, S., Amin, R.: Preventing from cross-vm side-channel attack using new replacement method. Wireless Pers. Commun. **97**(3), 4827–4854 (2017)
6. Anwar, S., et al.: Cross-VM cache-based side channel attacks and proposed prevention mechanisms: a survey. J. Network Comput. Appl. **93**, 259–279 (2017)
7. Irazoqui, G., Inci, M.S., Eisenbarth, T., Sunar, B.: Wait a minute! a fast, cross-vm attack on AES. In: International Workshop on Recent Advances in Intrusion Detection, pp. 299–319 (2014)
8. Yarom, Y., Falkner, K.: Flush+ reload: a high resolution, low noise, l3 cache side-channel attack. In: 23rd {USENIX} Security Symposium ({USENIX} Security 14), pp. 719–732 (2014)
9. Hornby, T.: Side-channel attacks on everyday applications: distinguishing inputs with flush+reload. BlackHat USA (2016)
10. Philippe-Jankovic, D., Zia, T.A.: Breaking VM isolation-an in-depth look into the cross VM flush reload cache timing attack. Int. J. Comput. Sci. Network Secur. (IJCSNS) **17**(2), 181 (2017)
11. Bazm, M.-M., Sautereau, T., Lacoste, M., Sudholt, M., Menaud, J.-M.: Cache-based side-channel attacks detection through intel cache monitoring technology and hardware performance counters. In: 3rd International Conference on Fog and Mobile Edge Computing (FMEC), pp. 7–12 (2018)
12. Chiappetta, M., Savas, E., Yilmaz, C.: Real time detection of cache-based side-channel attacks using hardware performance counters. Appl. Soft Comput. **49**, 1162–1174 (2016)
13. Cho, J., Kim, T., Kim, S., Im, M., Kim, T., Shin, Y.: Real-time detection for cache side channel attack using performance counter monitor. Appl. Sci. **10**(3), 984 (2020)
14. Gulmezoglu, B., Moghimi, A., Eisenbarth, T., Sunar, B.: Fortuneteller: predicting microarchitectural attacks via unsupervised deep learning. arXiv preprint arXiv:1907.03651 (2019)
15. Mushtaq, M., Akram, A., Bhatti, M.K., Rais, R.N.B., Lapotre, V., Gogniat, G.: Run-time detection of prime+ probe side-channel attack on AES encryption algorithm. In: Global Information Infrastructure and Networking Symposium (GIIS), pp. 1–5 (2018)
16. Zhang, T., Zhang, Y., Lee, R.B.: Cloudradar: a real-time side-channel attack detection system in clouds. In: International Symposium on Research in Attacks, Intrusions, and Defenses, pp. 118–140 (2016)
17. Wang, H., Sayadi, H., Rafatirad, S., Sasan, A., Homayoun, H.: Scarf: detecting side-channel attacks at real-time using low-level hardware features. In: IEEE 26th International Symposium on On-Line Testing and Robust System Design (IOLTS), pp. 1–6 (2020)
18. Xia, W., et al.: A comprehensive study of the past, present, and future of data deduplication. Proc. IEEE **104**(9), 1681–1710 (2016)
19. Suzaki, K., Iijima,K., Yagi, T., Artho, C.: Memory deduplication as a threat to the guest OS. In: 4th European Workshop on System Security, p. 1 (2011)

20. Xiao, J., Xu, Z., Huang, H., Wang, H.: Security implications of memory deduplication in a virtualized environment. In: 43rd Annual IEEE/IFIP International Conference on Dependable Systems and Networks (DSN), pp. 1–12 (2013)
21. Lindemann, J., Fischer, M.: A memory-deduplication side-channel attack to detect applications in co-resident virtual machines. In: 33rd Annual ACM Symposium on Applied Computing, pp. 183–192 (2018)
22. Yan, L., Guo, Y., Chen, X., Mei, H.: A study on power side channels on mobile devices. In: 7th Asia-Pacific Symposium on Internetware, pp. 30–38 (2015)
23. Briongos, S., Irazoqui, G., Malagón, P., Eisenbarth, T.: Cacheshield: detecting cache attacks through self-observation. In: 8th ACM Conference on Data and Application Security and Privacy, pp. 224–235 (2018)
24. Bernstein, D.J.: Cache-timing attacks on AES (2005)
25. Irazoqui, G., Inci, M.S., Eisenbarth, T., Sunar, B.: Fine grain cross-VM attacks on Xen and VMware. In: IEEE 4th International Conference on Big Data and Cloud Computing, pp. 737–744 (2014)
26. Jayasinghe, D., Fernando, J., Herath, R., Ragel, R.: Remote cache timing attack on advanced encryption standard and countermeasures. In: 5th International Conference on Information and Automation for Sustainability, pp. 177–182 (2010)
27. Atici, A.C., Yilmaz, C., Savaş, E.: Cache-timing attacks without a profiling phase. Turkish J. Electr. Eng. Comput. Sci. **26**(4), 1953–1966 (2018)
28. Yarom, Y., Benger, N.: Recovering OpenSSL ECDSA nonces using the Flush+Reload cache side-channel attack. IACR Cryptology ePrint Archive, vol. 2014, p. 140 (2014)
29. Gullasch, D., Bangerter, E., Krenn, S.: Cache games-bringing access-based cache attacks on AES to practice. In: IEEE Symposium on Security and Privacy, pp. 490–505 (2011)
30. Base, V.K.: Security considerations and disallowing inter-virtual machine transparent page sharing, VMware Knowledge Base, vol. 2080735 (2014)
31. Gruss, D., Maurice, C., Wagner, K., Mangard, S.: Flush+ flush: a fast and stealthy cache attack. In: International Conference on Detection of Intrusions and Malware, and Vulnerability Assessment, pp. 279–299 (2016)
32. Yarom, Y.: Mastik: a micro-architectural side-channel toolkit. https://cs.adelaide.edu.au/~yval/Mastik/
33. Intel: Virtual targets. https://software.intel.com/content/www/us/en/develop/documentation/vtune-help/top/set-up-analysis-target/on-virtual-machine.html
34. Du, J., Sehrawat, N., Zwaenepoel, W.: Performance profiling of virtual machines. In: 7th ACM SIGPLAN/SIGOPS International Conference on Virtual Execution Environments, pp. 3–14 (2011)
35. Hat, R.: 2.2. Virtual Performance Monitoring Unit (vPMU) Red Hat Enterprise Linux 7. https://access.redhat.com/documentation/en-us/red_hat_enterprise_linux/7/html/virtualization_tuning_and_optimization_guide/sect-virtualization_tuning_optimization_guide-monitoring_tools-vpmu
36. Zhang, Y., Juels, A., Oprea, A., Reiter, M.K.: Homealone: co-residency detection in the cloud via side-channel analysis. In: IEEE Symposium on Security and Privacy, pp. 313–328 (2011)
37. Xiao, Z., Xiao, Y.: Security and privacy in cloud computing. IEEE Commun. Surv. Tutor. **15**(2), 843–859 (2012)

SCI -Secure Cryptographic Implementation

A (Bit)slice of Rainbow

Florian Caullery(✉)

Hensoldt Cyber, Taufkirchen, Germany
florian.caullery@hensoldt-cyber.de

Abstract. We explore the performance impact of *bitslicing* on implementations of the NIST PQC Round 3 Finalist Digital Signature Algorithms: Rainbow. We show that for the Ia parameters set, when not using special or vector instructions, our bitsliced implementation signs 40% faster and verifies 50% faster than the submission implementation while remaining constant time. We argue that using this technique, when combined with vector instructions might lead to substantial speed-up as well.

Keywords: Rainbow · Post-quantum cryptography · Digital Signature Algorithms · Multivariate quadratic cryptography

1 Introduction

Rainbow is NIST PQC Round 3 [8] Finalist for the Digital Signature Algorithms based on multivariate quadratic polynomials. Rainbow is a declination of the Unbalanced Oil and Vinegar signature scheme with two layers. Its security is based on the hardness of inverting a map $\mathcal{P}: \mathbb{F}_{2^q}^n \to \mathbb{F}_{2^q}^m$ with

$$\mathcal{P}(x_1, \ldots, x_n) = (p_1(x_1, \ldots, x_n), \ldots, p_m(x_1, \ldots, x_n)),$$

where the p_i's are random homogeneous quadratic polynomials (i.e. $p_i(x_1, \ldots, x_n) = \sum_{j=1,k=1}^{j=n,k=n} p_{i,j,k} x_j x_k$).

This map constitutes the Public Key and is obtained from a Private Key $(\mathcal{S}, \mathcal{F}, \mathcal{T})$ where $\mathcal{S}: \mathbb{F}_{2^q}^m \to \mathbb{F}_{2^q}^m$ and $\mathcal{T}: \mathbb{F}_{2^q}^n \to \mathbb{F}_{2^q}^n$ are random isomorphisms and $\mathcal{F}: \mathbb{F}_{2^q}^n \to \mathbb{F}_{2^q}^m$ is a map such that

$$\mathcal{F}(x_1, \ldots, x_n) = (f_1(x_1, \ldots, x_n), \ldots, f_m(x_1, \ldots, x_n)),$$

where $f_i(x_1, \ldots, x_n) = \sum_{j=1,k=1}^{j=v_1,k=v_1+o_1} f_{i,j,k} x_j x_k$ for $i = 0, \ldots, v_1$ and $f_i(x_1, \ldots, x_n) = \sum_{j=1,k=1}^{j=v_1+o_1,k=n} f_{i,j,k} x_j x_k$ for $i = v_1 + 1, \ldots, m$, where $0 < v_1, o_1 < n/2$ are defined by the parameters set. Note here that the special form of $\mathcal{F}$ is such that it is easy to find a pre-image of a given element by this mapping. More details about it are shown in Sect. 5. The linear transformations $\mathcal{S}$ and $\mathcal{T}$ are acting as masks.

As the reader can already guess from here, the performance of Rainbow heavily depends on the latency of the underlying finite field operations. This fact

J. Zhou et al. (Eds.): ACNS 2021 Workshops, LNCS 12809, pp. 321–331, 2021.
https://doi.org/10.1007/978-3-030-81645-2_18

is pointed out by the authors of the scheme in the submission documentation [5] as well as by subsequent works, e.g. [6]. In the latter, the use of the AES dedicated instruction sets GF-NI and in particular the VGF2P8MULB instruction allows a speed-up of up to almost 5 times in the signature operation. However, this work suffers from two drawbacks: the full speed-up comes at the expense of changing the representation of the finite field from the original submission, and the GF-NI instruction set is only available to machines where the AVX512 instructions are present. This confines this improvement to high-end modern computers or servers. In this work, we show that we can improve the current implementation by changing the finite field multiplication technique[1]. To this end, we describe the strategy we adopted to implement Rainbow Classic Ia using only standard C99 functions and explicitly forbidding compiler the use of vector instructions.

At the time of submission of the paper, the NIST implementation package was the only optimized dedicated implementation available. We refer to the recent similar work of [4] which proposes an implementation of Rainbow on a Cortex-M4 and points out to the same conclusion that bitsliced implementation are the most suitable when vector instructions are not available. We also show evidences that adapting our implementation technique to AVX2 instructions might lead to an important speed-up.

We first present the scheme and the parameters set we target as well as the submission implementation choices in Sect. 2. Sections 3 to 5 will detail our strategy and display the algorithms we have implemented. We will summarize the performance impacts in Sect. 6 and propose future potential improvement over the current work in Sect. 7.

2 Preliminaries

We refer the readers who are not familiar with Rainbow to the submission package [5] for a full description of the scheme and all proposed parameters set. We focus on the variant Classic Ia of which we recall the parameters in Table 1 as well as the core algorithms in their optimized form (i.e. as described in [5, Section 3.1]) in Algorithms 1 to 3. At a high-level, the secret key generation consists of m homogeneous quadratic polynomials $f_i \in \mathbb{F}_{2^q}[x_1, \ldots, x_n]$ for which it is easy to find a pre-image of $(a_1, \ldots, a_m) \in \mathbb{F}_{2^q}^m$ by the mapping $\mathcal{F} : (x_1, \ldots, x_n) \to (f_1(x_1, \ldots, x_n), \ldots, f_m(x_1, \ldots, x_n))$, and two linear masks $\mathcal{T}, \mathcal{S}$. The public key is the composition of the three mappings $\mathcal{S} \circ \mathcal{F} \circ \mathcal{T}$. To be a bit more precise, $\mathcal{F}$ is made of two layers of polynomials. The first layer consists of o_1 homogeneous quadratic polynomials in $x_1, x_2, ..., x_{v_1+o_1}$ where all terms are depending on $x_1, x_2, \ldots, x_{v_1}$. That is

$$\forall i \in \{1, 2, \ldots, o_1\}, f_i = \sum_{\substack{j=1,2,\ldots,v_1 \\ k=1,2,\ldots,v_1+o_1}} f_{i,j,k} x_j x_k.$$

[1] The code can be found at https://github.com/FlorianF89/pqc_rainbow_signature.

The second layer consists of o_2 homogeneous quadratic polynomials in $x_1, x_2, ..., x_m$ where all terms are depending on $x_1, x_2, \ldots, x_{v_1+o_1}$. That is

$$\forall i \in \{1, 2, \ldots, o_1\}, f_i = \sum_{\substack{j=1,2,\ldots,v_1+o_1 \\ k=1,2,\ldots,m}} f_{i,j,k} x_j x_k.$$

Given a vector $\mathbf{y} = (\mathbf{y_1}, \ldots, \mathbf{y_m}) \in \mathbb{F}_{2^q}^m$, finding $z = (z_1, \ldots, z_n) \in \mathbb{F}_{2^q}^n$ such that $\mathcal{F}(z) = y$ is done by the following steps:

1. Select randomly $\mathbf{z_1}, \ldots, \mathbf{z_{v_1}}$,
2. Because of the particular form of the polynomials f_i in the first layer, the equation system $(f_i(\mathbf{z_1}, \ldots, \mathbf{z_{v_1}}, z_{v_1+1}, \ldots, z_{v_1+o_1}) = \mathbf{y_i})_{i=1,2,\ldots,o_1}$ is now a linear system of o_1 equations in o_1 unknown. Assuming it has at least a solution we denote one solution by $\mathbf{z_{v_1+1}}, \ldots, \mathbf{z_{v_1+o_1}}$. If no solution is found then we go back to step 1.
3. Similarly, duc to the form of the polynomials f_i in the second layer, the equation system $(f_i(\mathbf{z_1}, \ldots, \mathbf{z_{v_1+o_1}}, z_{v_1+o_1+1}, \ldots, z_n) = \mathbf{y_i})_{i=o_1+1,\ldots,m}$ is now a linear system of o_1 equations in o_2 unknown. A solution to this equation will yield a pre-image of $\mathbf{y}$ by $\mathcal{F}$. If no solution is found then we go back to step 1.

The signature algorithm simply hashes a message into a random element $(a_1, \ldots, a_m) \in \mathbb{F}_{2^q}$ and publishes one of its pre-image by the public key using the fact that $\mathcal{F}$ is easily invertible. The verification is a simple evaluation of the given pre-image by the public key. Note that throughout the paper, the step size change for all loop variablcs defaults to 1.

Table 1. Rainbow classic Ia parameters.

$\mathbb{F}$	v_1	o_1	o_2	$n(= v_1 + o_1 + o_2)$	$m(= o_1 + o_2)$
$\mathbb{F}_{2^4}$	36	32	32	96	64

The Submission Implementation

The submission implementation is detailed in Sect. 4 and 5 of the documentation [5]. In order to keep the field operation constant time, it adopts a tower representation of $\mathbb{F}_{2^4}$. An element of $\mathbb{F}_{2^4}$ is stored on 4 bits and a 32bits (resp. 64bits) register stores 8 (resp. 16) elements. The field multiplication is achieved via a Karatsuba method implemented via various shifts and masks in the reference implementation and via vectorized look-up table in the AVX2 optimization, notably based on the PSHUFB instruction. The multiplication is conducted in parallel, i.e., all elements in the first operand register are multiplied by the corresponding elements in the second operand register.

Algorithm 1: Rainbow Classic key generation

input : Parameters (v_1, o_1, o_2)
output : The secret key $\mathsf{sk} = (\mathcal{S}, \mathcal{F}, \mathcal{T})$ and the public key $\mathsf{pk} = (\mathcal{P})$

$\mathcal{S}' \leftarrow_{\$} \mathcal{M}_{o_1}(\mathbb{F}_{2^q})$

$\mathcal{S} = \begin{pmatrix} I_{o_1} & \mathcal{S}' \\ 0 & I_{o_1} \end{pmatrix}$

$\mathcal{T}_1, \mathcal{T}_2, \mathcal{T}_3 \leftarrow_{\$} \mathcal{M}_{o_1}(\mathbb{F}_{2^q})$

$\mathcal{T} = \begin{pmatrix} I_{o_1} & \mathcal{T}_1 & \mathcal{T}_2 \\ 0 & I_{o_1} & \mathcal{T}_3 \\ 0 & 0 & I_{o_1} \end{pmatrix}$

for $i = 1, \ldots, o_1$ **do**
  for $j = 1, \ldots, o_1$ **do**
    for $k = 1, \ldots, n$ **do**
      $f_{i,k,j} \leftarrow_{\$} \mathbb{F}_{2^4}$

for $i = o_1, \ldots, m$ **do**
  for $j = 1, \ldots, m$ **do**
    for $k = 1, \ldots, n$ **do**
      $f_{i,k,j} \leftarrow_{\$} \mathbb{F}_{2^4}$

$\mathcal{F} = (f_1, \ldots, f_m)$
$\mathcal{P} = \mathcal{S} \circ \mathcal{F} \circ \mathcal{T}$
return sk, pk

The tower representation of the field is the following:

$$\mathbb{F}_{2^2} = \mathbb{F}_2[Y]/(Y^2 + Y + 1)$$
$$\mathbb{F}_{2^4} = \mathbb{F}_{2^2}[X]/(X^2 + X + Y).$$

From the source code (file gf16_u64, function `gf16v_mul_u64_u64`), a multiplication of 16 elements by 16 other elements is performed by 51 logical operations, which, in amortized costs, is 3.18 logical operations (i.e. shift, OR, XOR, AND) per multiplication of 2 elements for the non-AVX code. This is obviously not the number of instructions in the compiled code but already gives an idea of the multiplication cost.

3 Bitslicing the Field Operations

Bitslicing is a widespread technique for constant-time implementation of symmetric cryptography tracing back to Biham's paper [2]. Up to now, it has not seen application to asymmetric cryptography since this technique does not scale well when the size of underlying fields is too large. However, Rainbow is based on binary field extensions of size comparable to those used to define S-Box components of symmetric ciphers.

Algorithm 2: Rainbow Classic sign

input : message $\mathcal{M}$, hash function $H : \{0,1\}^\star \rightarrow \{0,1\}^h$
output : signature $(r, (y_1, \ldots, y_n) \in (\{0,1\}^h, \mathbb{F}_{2^q}^n)$
repeat
  $r \leftarrow_\$ \{0,1\}^h$
  $(a_1, \ldots, a_m) \in \mathbb{F}_{2^4}^m = \mathcal{S}^{-1}(H(\mathcal{M}||r))$
  if $\exists(x_1, \ldots, x_n)$ *s.t.* $\mathcal{F}(x_1, \ldots, x_n) = (a_1, \ldots, a_m)$ **then**
    pre_image_found = True
    return $(r, \mathcal{T}^{-1}(x_1, \ldots, x_n))$
until *pre_image_found* = *True*;

Algorithm 3: Rainbow classic Ia verify

input : signature $(r, (y_1, \ldots, y_n) \in (\{0,1\}^h, \mathbb{F}_{2^4}^n)$ and pk.
output : True or False
return $\mathcal{P}(y_1, \ldots, y_n) == H(\mathcal{M}||r)$

In this section, we show that it is possible to achieve an amortized cost of 0.59 logical operations per multiplication of 2 elements by adopting a bitsliced representation without vector instructions. In the chosen representation of $\mathbb{F}_{2^4} = \mathbb{F}_{2^2}[X]/(X^2 + X + Y), \mathbb{F}_{2^2} = \mathbb{F}_2[Y]/(Y^2 + Y + 1)$, an element $a \in \mathbb{F}_{2^4}$ is a polynomial in X and Y written

$$a = a_{0,0} + a_{0,1}Y + a_{1,0}X + a_{1,1}YX, a_{i,j} \in \mathbb{F}_2,$$

With this representation, the result of the multiplication $c = a \times b \in \mathbb{F}_{2^4}$ is

$$\begin{aligned}
c_{0,0} =& a_{0,0}b_{0,0} + a_{0,1}b_{0,1} + a_{1,1}b_{1,0} + a_{1,0}b_{1,1} + a_{1,1}b_{1,1} \\
c_{0,1} =& a_{0,1}b_{0,0} + a_{0,0}b_{0,1} + a_{0,1}b_{0,1} + a_{1,0}b_{1,0} + a_{1,1}b_{1,0} + a_{1,0}b_{1,1} \\
c_{1,0} =& a_{1,0}b_{0,0} + a_{0,0}b_{1,0} + a_{1,1}b_{0,1} + a_{1,0}b_{1,0} + a_{0,1}b_{1,1} + a_{1,1}b_{1,1} \\
c_{1,1} =& a_{1,1}b_{0,0} + a_{1,0}b_{0,1} + a_{0,1}b_{1,0} + a_{1,1}b_{0,1} + + a_{1,1}b_{1,0} + a_{0,0}b_{1,1} + a_{0,1}b_{1,1} \\
& + a_{1,0}b_{1,1} + a_{1,1}b_{1,1}
\end{aligned}$$

where the product is implemented with an AND and the addition is a XOR. We propose to encode 64 elements of $\mathbb{F}_{2^4}$ over four 64-bit words, each word storing one of the terms of 64 polynomials, and use the above equations to obtain the products of 64 elements by 64 others. The representation is graphically shown in Fig. 1. Each bitsliced representation is represented in C by a list of four 64-bit words. The multiplication algorithm implementation is shown in the C code snippet 1.1. Note that this implementation is naturally constant time.

```

typedef uint64_t bitsliced_gf16_t [4]

void bitsliced_multiplication(bitsliced_gf16_t a_times_b ,
    const bitsliced_gf16_t a, const bitsliced_gf16_t b) {
```

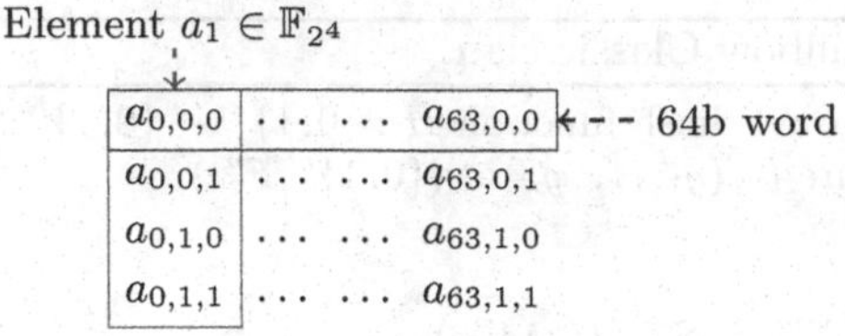

Fig. 1. Bitsliced representation of 64 elements of $\mathbb{F}_{2^4}$

```
    a_times_b[0] = (a[0] & b[0])
                 ^ (a[1] & b[1])
                 ^ (a[2] & b[3])
                 ^ (a[3] & (b[2] ^ b[3]));

    a_times_b[1] = (a[0] & b[1])
                 ^ (a[1] & (b[0] ^ b[1]))
                 ^ (a[2] & (b[2] ^ b[3]))
                 ^ (a[3] & b[2]);

    a_times_b[2] = (a[0] & b[2])
                 ^ (a[1] & b[3])
                 ^ (a[2] & (b[0] ^ b[2]))
                 ^ (a[3] & (b[1] ^ b[3]));

    a_times_b[3] = (a[0] & b[3])
                 ^ (a[1] & (b[2] ^ b[3]))
                 ^ (a[2] & (b[1] ^ b[3]))
                 ^ (a[3] & (b[0] ^ b[1] ^ b[2] ^ b[3]));
}
```

Listing 1.1. Bitsliced multiplication of elements of $\mathbb{F}_{2^4}$

Other important field operations such as squaring and inversion are implemented in a similar fashion and reach an amortized cost of respectively 1/16 and 0.45 logical operations per element. The addition is a trivial componentwise XOR.

4 Matrix Arithmetic

In the Ia parameters set, we deal with matrices of size 32 by 32 or 36 by 36 with elements in $\mathbb{F}_{2^4}$. The two main operations are multiplication and Gaussian elimination. For the Gaussian elimination, we chose a slightly different approach than the one in [1] and [3] (which is also the one adopted by the Rainbow reference implementation). Instead of adding multiple of lines to other, we take advantage of the fact that lines of our matrices fit entirely in a single bitsliced representation. We use the following conditional line swap inspired by the value swap without intermediate value of [7]:

```c
//cond has to be -1 (i.e. TRUE) or 0 (i.e. FALSE)
#define COND_SWAP(a, b, cond) (((a) ^= ((b) & cond)), \
                ((b) ^= ((a) & cond)), \
                ((a) ^= ((b) & cond)))
```

Listing 1.2. Conditional uint64_t swap

The condition is set by checking, for the i-th step of the Gaussian elimination, if the i-th element of the i-th line is 0 and scanning one by one the i-th elements of the remaining lines. Once one suitable replacement line is found, the condition is set to 0. If at the end of the procedure, the condition is still set, then we return an error as it means that the matrix cannot be put into triangular form. We summarize the procedure in Algorithm 4.

Algorithm 4: Rainbow classic Ia verify

```
input  : A 0 < m ≤ 64 lines matrix A whose lines are represented by
         bitsliced_gf16_t
output : A in triangular form
for i = 0,...,m do
    cond ← 0 - is_zero(A_{i,i}) // cond is -1 if A_{i,i} is 0, 0 otherwise, as
        required in COND_SWAP
    for j = i+1,...,m do
        cond1 ← cond & (-1 + is_zero(A_{j,i}))
        // If cond is -1 and A_{j,i} is 1, cond1 will be -1 and the swap
            will occur
        COND_SWAP(A_i, A_j, cond1)
        cond ← cond ∧ cond1
        // If we have found a suitable line for swapping, we no longer
            need to swap the lines and cond is set to 0
    if cond == -1 then
        return FAIL // Did not find a suitable line to swap, all the
            column is 0
return SUCCESS
```

Matrix multiplication is conducted without particular optimization. Simply note that that we did not take advantage of the fact that we could actually conduct two matrix multiplications in parallel when multiplying matrices of size $k \times 32$ by matrices of size 32×32. This could lead to further speed-up but would make the code more intricate.

The last optimization we applied to the matrix multiplication is on the 32 by 32 matrices transposition. Instead of transposing four 32 by 32 binary matrices, each one of them containing one component of each element, we copy the elements in a 64 by 64 binary matrix which we transpose. Following [9], transposing a 32 by 32 binary matrix can be done in 1639 instructions while a 64 by 64 binary matrix is transposed in 3886 instructions. Hence, we save almost

60% of operations, taking into account the preparation of the 64 by 64 matrix. The procedure is depicted graphically in Fig. 2. For the sake of keeping notations more simple, for $A \in \mathcal{M}_{32}(\mathbb{F}_{2^4})$, we call $A.c$ the constant term of all elements $a \in A$ ordered by column number, $A.Y$, $A.X$ and $A.YX$ their term in Y, X and YX respectively.

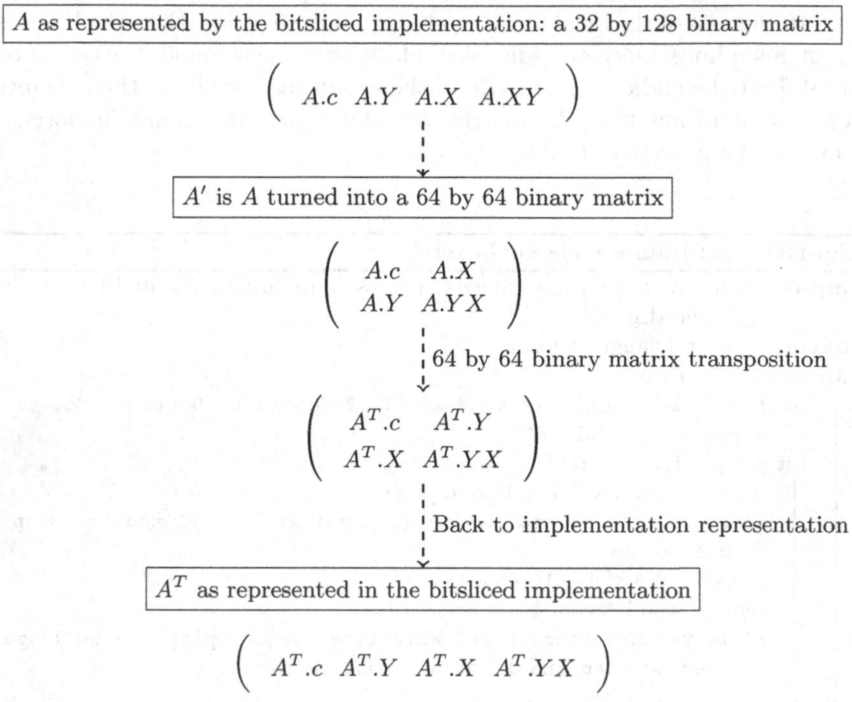

Fig. 2. Transposition of 32 by 32 matrix with elements in $\mathbb{F}_{2^4}$.

5 Operations on Quadratic Polynomials

For the set of parameters Ia, we have to deal with exactly 64 quadratic homogeneous polynomials with coefficients in $\mathbb{F}_{2^4}$. This is ideal since we are using 64-bit registers. If we write $f_i = \sum_{j=1,k=1}^{n} f_{i,j,k} x_j x_k, \quad i = 1, \ldots, 64$, we can use one bitsliced representation to store the coefficients $f_{i,j,k}$ of all the 64 polynomials. Unfortunately, this representation renders the key generation and the signing operation slower. On top of this, it does not scale well for other parameter sets. Hence, we switch to a representation where we use bitsliced elements to represent the coefficients of one polynomial. The coefficients of the polynomials are stored following the matrix representation given in Sect. 3 of the submission documentation [5], each line of the matrices being represented by bitsliced elements. The polynomial evaluation is done by performing $X^t.F_i.X$ where F_i is the matrix representation of the polynomial f_i and X is the column vector containing the values $x_0, \dots, x_{n-1}$. This constitutes the core of the `Verify` procedure.

For the inversion of the central map, which is the main operation in the signature algorithm, our goal is to find a pre-image $\mathbf{y} = y_1, \dots, y_n \in \mathbb{F}_{2^4}^n$ of $z = (z_1, \dots, z_m) \in \mathbb{F}_{2^4}^m$ by $\mathcal{F}$ The first step is to generate 32 random elements $y_1, \dots, y_{32} \in \mathbb{F}_{2^4}$ and evaluate the polynomials of the first layer in those variables (setting the others to 0). The second step is to solve the following linear system:

$$\begin{pmatrix} \sum_{j=1}^{32} f_{1,j,33} y_j & \cdots & \sum_{j=1}^{32} f_{1,j,64} y_j \\ \vdots & & \vdots \\ \sum_{j=1}^{32} f_{32,j,33} y_j & \cdots & \sum_{j=1}^{32} f_{32,j,64} y_j \end{pmatrix} \cdot \begin{pmatrix} y_{32} \\ \vdots \\ y_{64} \end{pmatrix} = \begin{pmatrix} z_1 - f_1(y_1, \dots, y_{32}) \\ \vdots \\ z_{32} - f_{32}(y_1, \dots, y_{32}) \end{pmatrix}.$$

Because the polynomials of the first layers are of the form $f_i(x_1, \dots, x_n) = \sum_{j=1,k=1}^{j=32,k=64} f_{i,j,k} x_j x_k$, $i = 1, \dots, 32$, we now have $f_i(y_1, \dots, y_{64}) = z_i$ for $i = 1, \dots, 32$ (provided that the system has a solution). We conduct the same operation for the polynomials of the second layer with the difference that we are now solving is

$$\begin{pmatrix} \sum_{j=1}^{64} f_{33,j,65} y_j & \cdots & \sum_{j=1}^{64} f_{33,j,96} y_j \\ \vdots & & \vdots \\ \sum_{j=1}^{64} f_{64,j,65} y_j & \cdots & \sum_{j=1}^{64} f_{64,j,96} y_j \end{pmatrix} \cdot \begin{pmatrix} y_{65} \\ \vdots \\ y_{96} \end{pmatrix} = \begin{pmatrix} z_{33} - f_{33}(y_1, \dots, y_{64}) \\ \vdots \\ z_{64} - f_{64}(y_1, \dots, y_{64}) \end{pmatrix}.$$

Now, because the polynomials of the second layers are of the form $f_i(x_1, \dots, x_n) = \sum_{j=1,k=1}^{j=64,k=96} f_{i,j,k} x_j x_k$, $i = 33, \dots, 64$, we now have $f_i(y_1, \dots, y_{96}) = z_i$ for $i = 33, \dots, 64$ (provided that the system has a solution). We hence found a pre-image $\mathbf{y}$ of $\mathbf{z}$ by $\mathcal{F}$. These operation rely solely on matrix multiplication and our Gaussian algorithm (see Sect. 4).

The last operation we need to describe is the variable substitution. Indeed, the transformation $\mathcal{T}$ is nothing more than replacing variables of the polynomials by a linear combination of variables. In this, we follow the matrix approach given in Sect. 3 of the submission documentation [5]. Note that it is where we take advantage of the matrix transposition described in Sect. 4.

6 Performance Summary

This section measures the performance of our implementation on a HP Elitebook 840 G7 with an Intel®Core™i7-10510U processor and 16 GB of RAM running Ubuntu 20.04, the code has been compiled with the flag -Ofast and -fno-tree-vectorize (for both the reference and our implementation) to make sure that the compiler did not use any vectorized instructions. We compare only core functions and not the other functions like the random number generation and writing to files[2]. (Table 2) displays the performance of our implementation against the ones of the submission package. The results are the average of 100,000 runs.

Table 2. Rainbow classic Ia performance in clock cycle per operation.

Operation	Reference impl	Our impl	Improvement
Multiplication (cost/element)	0,4596	0,2998	53%
Derive public key from private key	39,861,081	34,216,191	16.5%
Sign	487,498	352,111	38%
Verify	280,131	189,593	48%

Our bitsliced multiplication is around 50% faster than the one in reference implementation which translates into a 15% improvement for key generation, 40% for signing and 50% faster for verifying than the reference implementation. The 50% speed-up of the multiplication does not translate directly into a 50% speed-up in all operations certainly because the bitsliced representation involves a bit more data movement. Also, we do not perform any matrix multiplication in parallel (this especially impacts the key generation).

7 Conclusion and Future Research

We showed that the bitsliced representation of elements can bring a speed-up to the Rainbow Classic Ia Digital Signature Algorithm, even without conducting extensive optimizations of the code (e.g. not performing parallel matrix multiplication). A natural research track for the future is to use vector instructions set combined with the bitsliced implementation and to check this improvement scale for other parameter sets. A quick experiment showed that bitsliced multiplication using AVX2 instructions is four times faster than the method based on PBSHUFFLE used in the Rainbow submission package. And this is counting the AVX load and stores which are known to be slow instructions. Hence, a fully dedicated AVX implementation which avoids at maximum this kind of movement is needed to take the most out of the AVX2 instructions and certainly allows further improvement. It will be worth to compare these improvements to the ones of [6]. In future works, we can also address the other variants of Rainbow (e.g. Rainbow Cyclic mode).

References

1. Bernstein, D.J., Chou, T., Schwabe, P.: McBits: fast constant-time code-based cryptography. In: Bertoni, G., Coron, J.-S. (eds.) CHES 2013. LNCS, vol. 8086, pp. 250–272. Springer, Heidelberg (2013). https://doi.org/10.1007/978-3-642-40349-1_15

[2] Note that, as we change the representation of internal element, there might be a slight overhead with switching back to a serialized representation but it would be simply a matter of interleaving bits.

2. Biham, E.: A fast new des implementation in software. In: Biham, E. (ed.) Fast Software Encryption, pp. 260–272. Springer, Berlin Heidelberg, Berlin, Heidelberg (1997)
3. Chou, T.: Mcbits revisited: toward a fast constant-time code-based kem. J. Cryptographic Eng. **8**(2), 95–107 (2018)
4. Chou, T., Kannwischer, M.J., Yang, B.Y.: Rainbow on cortex-m4. Cryptology ePrint Archive, Report 2021/532 (2021). https://eprint.iacr.org/2021/532
5. Ding, J., Chen, M.S., Petzoldt, A., Schmidt, D., Yang, B.Y.: Rainbow, The 2nd Round Proposal (2018). https://csrc.nist.gov/CSRC/media/Projects/Post-Quantum-Cryptography/documents/round-2/submissions/Rainbow-Round2.zip
6. Drucker, N., Gueron, S.: Speed up over the rainbow. Cryptology ePrint Archive, Report 2020/408 (2020). https://eprint.iacr.org/2020/408
7. Eron Anderson, S.: Bit twiddling hacks. https://graphics.stanford.edu/~seander/bithacks.html. Accessed 3 May 2019
8. NIST: Post-Quantum Cryptography Call for Proposals. https://csrc.nist.gov/Projects/Post-Quantum-Cryptography/Post-Quantum-Cryptography-Standardization/Call-for-Proposals (2018). Accessed 01 Jan 2020
9. Warren, H.S.: Hacker's Delight. Addison-Wesley Longman Publishing Co., Inc, USA (2002)

Cryptanalysis of a Lattice-Based Group Signature with Verifier-Local Revocation Achieving Full Security

Yanhua Zhang[1(✉)], Ximeng Liu[2], Yupu Hu[3], Qikun Zhang[1], and Huiwen Jia[4]

[1] Zhengzhou University of Light Industry, Zhengzhou 450001, China
yhzhang@email.zzuli.edu.cn
[2] Fuzhou University, Fuzhou 350108, China
[3] Xidian University, Xi'an 710071, China
yphu@mail.xidian.edu.cn
[4] Guangzhou University, Guangzhou 510006, China
hwjia@gzhu.edu.cn

Abstract. For all existing non-fully dynamic (i.e., only supporting membership revocation and no member's enrollment is involved) lattice-based group signature schemes with verifier-local revocation (VLR-GS), only selfless-anonymity (SA) is achieved, which is strictly weaker than the de facto standard anonymity notion, full-anonymity (FA), where the adversary is allowed to corrupt all members. At ICICS 2018, Perera and Koshiba delivered a new VLR-GS scheme and claimed that it is the first lattice-based construction achieving full security (i.e., FA and full-traceability). In this paper, we demonstrate that their construction does not achieve the claimed FA security by presenting an attack, and only SA security is achieved, the same as the first lattice-based VLR-GS scheme introduced by Langlois et al. at PKC 2014.

Keywords: Group signature · Lattice-based cryptography · Verifier-local revocation · Selfless-anonymity · Full-anonymity

1 Introduction

Supporting for membership revocation (i.e., disabling the signing ability of some misbehaving members or honest members who voluntarily leave) is a desirable functionality of many multi-member digital signature systems. Moreover, the revocation not affecting the remaining valid members is also a non-trivial problem. For group signatures (GS) [7] with membership revocation, the verifier-local revocation (VLR) mechanism seems to be the most flexible choice (compared with re-initialized whole system or accumulators) when considering certain large

J. Zhou et al. (Eds.): ACNS 2021 Workshops, LNCS 12809, pp. 332–345, 2021.
https://doi.org/10.1007/978-3-030-81645-2_19

group, because it only requires verifiers to download up-to-date revocation information for signature verification, and signers have no involvement. In particular, the VLR mechanism is more practical and suitable for mobile environments where signers (i.e., members) are often off-line (in addition, the number of verifiers is much less than that of signers) or computationally weak devices are pervasively adopted (e.g., smart cards).

LATTICE-BASED GS-VLR. As for GS with verifier-local revocation (VLR-GS), this concept was formalized by Boneh and Shacham [5] at CCS 2004, and subsequently investigated and extended in [4,6,12,16,17]. However, all of these constructions are operating in the bilinear map setting, and vulnerable to be resistance against quantum computers for a future post-quantum cryptography era. And as the old saying goes, not putting all your eggs in one basket, thus it is encouraging to consider some alternative instantiations, post-quantum constructions, e.g., based on lattice-based cryptosystem.

Lattice-based VLR-GS scheme was first introduced by Langlois et al. [11] at PKC 2014, and thus, the first such quantum-resistant scheme supporting of membership revocation. Subsequently several improved schemes achieving different levels of efficiency and security notions were proposed [8,13,18,20–24]. But almost of them (i.e., all non-fully dynamic constructions that only support of membership revocation and no member's enrollment) can only achieve selfless-anonymity (SA), which is strictly weaker than the de facto standard anonymity notion, full-anonymity (FA), where the adversary is allowed to corrupt all group members. At SCN 2018, Ishida et al. [10] gave an affirmative answer to the problem whether a fully anonymous VLR-GS scheme even exists and proposed the basic framework building on ideas from creative works of Bellare et al. [3]. However, no any specific cryptographic scheme was given by Ishida et al., and we do not know how to adopt algorithms over lattices to substitute all the operations efficiently and safely, and we cannot simply follow the steps of [10] to design a lattice-based fully anonymous GS-VLR scheme. Therefore, we have to tailor a new construction so that it can rely on some new and creatively techniques for lattice-based cryptography.

For a conventional lattice-based VLR-GS, an additional argument called revocation list (RL) is provided for signature verification, which contains a list of revocation tokens (RT) for the revoked members. Once some member is revoked (by adding his RT to RL, no matter for the misbehaving member or a voluntary one), the issued signatures after the member's revocation cannot be accepted by signature verification algorithm any more. More specifically, the member's RT can be used to detect the signatures issued by the corresponding member (although the real identity information may not be disclosed), thus any verifier can check whether or not the given signature is issued by some revoked member with RT in RL. Furthermore, anyone (including group manager, verifiers and even adversary) owning all members' RTs (i.e., the corresponding relationship between the member's real identity and his RT) can determine the member's identity by successively executing signature verification algorithm which returns Invalid. Thus, in the anonymity definition of a conventional lattice-based VLR-GS, the RTs of two distinct members id_0 and id_1 selected by an adversary cannot be given. To eliminate a need for a trusted revocation authority and not disclosure the real identity of revoked members, the RT is directly dependent on member signing secret-key (e.g., the modular multiplication of a public matrix and part of signing secret-key vector). Therefore, the signing secret-keys of the two selected members for challenge also cannot be provided to adversary. Thus, the SA security was introduced by Boneh and Shacham [5], which ensures the anonymity of a signature only against an adversary not possessing the signing secret-keys of the challenged ones.

As it was asserted by Ishida et al. [10], a VLR-GS scheme with the above design structure (i.e., RT is directly and exactly dependent on signing secret-key) can *never* achieve the FA security, and we have to look for other way to construct, or even from scratch. Encouragingly, Perera and Koshiba [19] recently delivered a new VLR-GS scheme and claimed that it is the first lattice-based construction achieving full security (i.e., FA and full-traceability) at ICICS 2018. The main contents of their new construction almost entirely follow the first lattice-based VLR-GS scheme introduced by Langlois et al. [11] at PKC 2014 and the full and corrected version [13] in 2018 (i.e., RT is still directly and exactly dependent on group member signing secret-key). The unique and central work of [19] is that a group manager additionally owns a signing secret-key (independent from group members signing secret-keys) with which to sign each RT before adding it to RL. In the signature verification phase, besides checking whether or not signature is valid and the signer's token is included in RL, a third step to check whether or not the RTs in RL are signed validly by group manager is also needed. That is exactly based on the third step operation, Perera and Koshiba [19] concluded that in the anonymity model, their new construction allows to provide all members' signing secret-keys to adversary, and thus, the FA security is achieved and the first fully secure lattice-based VLR-GS scheme is constructed successfully.

Our results and techniques. In this paper, we demonstrate that the scheme of Perera and Koshiba [19] does not achieve the claimed FA security by presenting an attack, and only achieves the SA security as defined in the first lattice-based VLR-GS scheme introduced by Langlois et al. [11] at PKC 2014. Next, we briefly sketch our techniques (for details, see Sect. 4).

Technically, the new construction of Perera and Koshiba [19] is first built from Langlois et al.'s two schemes [11,13], in which the design of RTs is a direct modular multiplication of public matrix and the first part of signing secret-key vector, which brings two benefits: to eliminate the need for some trusted revocation authority and not disclosure the real identity of revoked members, to some extent, protecting anonymity for revoked members, specially the voluntary ones who intentionally leave the group. In [19], RT should be signed by a trustworthy authority before it is added to RL. Recall that one motivation of Langlois et al. [11,13] to design the special structure of RTs is to eliminates the need for the trusted revocation authority, thus from this point of view, the re-introduction of a trusted revocation authority (although in [19], group manager can play this role) seems contradict the spirt of simplified and secure construction for a practical cryptosystem. To say the least, even if group manager takes the responsibility of signing the RTs, there is another serious problem in the construction of [19], precisely, a misunderstanding of adversary's ability in the anonymity model.

Normally, when we define an adversary, we usually give it a stronger ability, within reason, and cannot required adversary to follow all prescribed procedures set by the scheme designer strictly. That is to say, the stronger the adversary is, the more secure scheme is. In the anonymity model of Perera and Koshiba [19], the adversary is required to strictly execute all the steps as those in verification algorithm of their specific designed scheme, namely, the adversary must check whether or not the RTs of two distinct members $\mathsf{id}_0 \neq \mathsf{id}_1$ selected by himself have been signed validly by group manager, and because the adversary does not know group manager's signing secret-key, moreover, he is not allowed to query the signatures on RTs for the two challenge identities. Given a valid message-signature pair, the adversary can not determine the real identity between id_0 and id_1 effectively (i.e., with a non-negligible probability larger than 1/2). While we show a contrarian view that the adversary will not strictly follow all prescribed procedures one by one as described by Perera and Koshiba [19], and the third step operation can be skipped and ignored completely, and only to implement the operations of the first two verification steps, which is exactly our attack, and since the adversary owns both signing secret-keys (further, owing both RTs) for the challenge members id_0 and id_1, the adversary can determine the real identity from the given message-signature pair with the probability 1 (may be negligibly close to 1). Therefore, the above analysis definitely demonstrates that Perera and Koshiba [19] cannot achieve their claimed FA security (in fact, only enjoys the SA security), and to construct a fully anonymous lattice-based VLR-GS remains an open problem. The detailed attack description is given latter in Sect. 4.

ORGANIZATION. After establishing some preliminaries (e.g., the syntax and security model of VLR-GS and the background on lattices) in Sect. 2. Section 3 turns to review the first fully anonymous lattice-based VLR-GS scheme proposed by Perera and Koshiba at ICICS 2018. In Sect. 4, we give a detailed attack to show that their anonymity model is unreasonable, and the adversary can break the FA security efficiently. In the final section, we conclude our whole paper.

2 Preliminaries

NOTATIONS. All vectors are in the column form and denoted in bold-faced, lower-case letters (e.g., $\mathbf{a}$, $\mathbf{b}$), and matrices are denoted in bold-faced, upper-case letters (e.g., $\mathbf{A}$, $\mathbf{B}$). We use $h \xleftarrow{\$} \mathcal{S}$ to denote that the variable h is uniformly sampled from a finite set $\mathcal{S}$. $\|\cdot\|$ ($\|\cdot\|_\infty$) is used to denote the Euclidean norm ℓ_2 (the infinity norm ℓ_∞) of a vector. The standard notations $\mathcal{O}$ and ω are used to classify the growth of functions, without specification, $\log e$ denotes the logarithm of e with base 2, and PPT stands for "probabilistic polynomial-time".

2.1 VLR-GS

In this subsection, we first recall the syntax and security model of a conventional VLR-GS, which was formalized by Boneh and Shacham [5], and further studied in [8,11,13,16,17,21–24].

Definition 1. *A* VLR-GS *scheme consists of three following algorithms:*

KeyGen$(1^n, N)$*: A* PPT *algorithm takes as input the security parameter n and the group size N (i.e., N is the maximum number of members), and it outputs the group public-key* Gpk*, a set of members' signing secret-keys* $\mathsf{Gsk} = (\mathsf{gsk}_0, \mathsf{gsk}_1, \cdots, \mathsf{gsk}_{N-1})$*, a set of members'* RT*s,* $\mathsf{Grt} = (\mathsf{grt}_0, \mathsf{grt}_1, \cdots, \mathsf{grt}_{N-1})$*, where* gsk_i *(and* grt_i*) denotes signing secret-key (and* RT*) for member* id *with index* $i \in \{0, 1, \cdots, N-1\}$.

Sign$(\mathsf{Gpk}, \mathsf{gsk}_i, \mathsf{m})$*: A* PPT *algorithm takes as input* Gpk*, a signing secret-key* gsk_i *for* id *with an index i, a message* $\mathsf{m} \in \{0,1\}^*$*, and it outputs a signature* σ.

Verify$(\mathsf{Gpk}, \mathsf{RL}, \sigma, \mathsf{m})$*: A deterministic algorithm takes as input* Gpk*, a set of* RT*s,* $\mathsf{RL} \subseteq \mathsf{Grt}$ *and a signature* σ *on a message* $\mathsf{m} \in \{0,1\}^*$*, and it returns either* Invalid *or* Valid*. The* Valid *indicates that* σ *is a valid signature on* m *and the real signer (i.e., a member) has not been revoked.*

Remark: Any valid VLR-GS scheme, as introduced by Boneh and Shacham [5], enjoys an *implicit-tracing* algorithm: given (m, σ), the party owning Grt (i.e., the corresponding relationship between the member's identity and his RT) can determine the signer (i.e., the member) of σ by successively executing algorithm $\mathsf{Verify}(\mathsf{Gpk}, \mathsf{RL} = \{\mathsf{grt}_i\}, \sigma, \mathsf{m})$ for $i = 0, 1, \cdots$ and outputting the first index $i^* \in \{0, 1, \cdots, N-1\}$ for which Verify returns Invalid.

A conventional VLR-GS scheme should satisfy the following three properties: correctness, selfless-anonymity and traceability.

Definition 2. *A* VLR-GS *scheme is* correct *if for all* $(\mathsf{Gpk}, \mathsf{Gsk}, \mathsf{Grt}) \leftarrow \mathsf{KeyGen}$*, any member* $i \in \{0, 1, \cdots, N-1\}$*, all* $\mathsf{gsk}_i \subseteq \mathsf{Gsk}$*, all* $\mathsf{RL} \subseteq \mathsf{Grt}$ *and* $\mathsf{m} \in \{0,1\}^*$*, we have that* $\mathsf{Verify}(\mathsf{Gpk}, \mathsf{RL}, \mathsf{Sign}(\mathsf{Gpk}, \mathsf{gsk}_i, \mathsf{m}), \mathsf{m}) = \mathsf{Valid} \Leftrightarrow \mathsf{grt}_i \notin \mathsf{RL}$.

Definition 3. *A* VLR-GS *scheme is* SA-anonymous *if no* PPT *adversary has a non-negligible advantage* $\mathsf{Adv}_{\mathcal{A}}^{\mathsf{Self\text{-}anon}}$ *in the following game (between a challenger* $\mathcal{C}$ *and an adversary* $\mathcal{A}$*).*

a. Initialization: $\mathcal{C}$ *obtains* $(\mathsf{Gpk}, \mathsf{Gsk}, \mathsf{Grt}) \leftarrow \mathsf{KeyGen}$ *and provides Gpk to* $\mathcal{A}$ *(not including* Gsk*).*

b. Query phase: *Before outputting two challenge identities (for group members),* $\mathcal{A}$ *adaptively makes a polynomially bounded number of queries:*

- Signing*: Request for a signature on* $\mathsf{m} \in \{0,1\}^*$ *for* id *with index i,* $\mathcal{C}$ *returns* $\sigma \leftarrow \mathsf{Sign}(\mathsf{Gpk}, \mathsf{gsk}_i, \mathsf{m})$.
- Corrupting*: Request for a signing secret-key for* id *with i,* $\mathcal{C}$ *returns* gsk_i.
- Revoking*: Request for a revocation token* RT *for* id *with i,* $\mathcal{C}$ *returns* grt_i.

c. Challenge: *$\mathcal{A}$ outputs a message* $\mathsf{m}^* \in \{0,1\}^*$, *two distinct members* id_0 *and* id_1, *with indices* i_0 *and* i_1, *respectively.* $\mathcal{A}$ *did not make corrupting query or revoking query at either member, i.e., the signing secret-keys of* id_0 *and* id_1 *cannot be corrupted, and* id_0 *and* id_1 *have not been revoked.* $\mathcal{C}$ *chooses a bit* $b \xleftarrow{\$} \{0,1\}$, *and returns* $\sigma^* \leftarrow \mathsf{Sign}(\mathsf{Gpk}, \mathsf{gsk}_{i_b}, \mathsf{m}^*)$ *as a challenge on* m^*.

d. Restricted query: *After obtaining a challenge signature* σ^*, $\mathcal{A}$ *can still make queries as before, but with the following restrictions: it is not allowed to make corrupting query and revoking query for* id_0 *or* id_1.

e. Guessing: $\mathcal{A}$ *outputs a bit* $b^* \in \{0,1\}$, *and wins if* $b^* = b$.

The advantage of $\mathcal{A}$ in the above Selfless-anonymity game is defined as

$$\mathsf{Adv}_{\mathcal{A}}^{\mathsf{Self\text{-}anon}} = |\Pr[b^* = b] - 1/2|.$$

Definition 4. *A* VLR-GS *scheme is* traceable *if no* PPT *adversary has a non-negligible advantage* $\mathsf{Adv}_{\mathcal{A}}^{\mathsf{Trace}}$ *in the following game.*

a. Initialization: $\mathcal{C}$ *obtains* $(\mathsf{Gpk}, \mathsf{Gsk}, \mathsf{Grt}) \leftarrow \mathsf{KeyGen}$ *and provides* $(\mathsf{Gpk}, \mathsf{Grt})$ *to* $\mathcal{A}$. *It also defines a initial corruption set* $\mathsf{Corr} = \varnothing$.

b. Query phase: *Before outputting a valid forgery,* $\mathcal{A}$ *adaptively makes a polynomially bounded number of queries:*

- Signing*: Request for a signature on* $\mathsf{m} \in \{0,1\}^*$ *for* id *with index* i, $\mathcal{C}$ *returns* $\sigma \leftarrow \mathsf{Sign}(\mathsf{Gpk}, \mathsf{gsk}_i, \mathsf{m})$.
- Corrupting*: Request for a signing secret-key for* id *with an index* i, $\mathcal{C}$ *returns* gsk_i *and sets* $\mathsf{Corr} = \mathsf{Corr} \cup (\mathsf{id}, i)$.

c. Forgery: $\mathcal{A}$ *outputs a message-signature pair* (m^*, σ^*), *a set of members' revocation tokens* $\mathsf{RL}^* \subseteq \mathsf{Grt}$. $\mathcal{A}$ *wins the game if:*

- $\mathsf{Verify}(\mathsf{Gpk}, \mathsf{RL}^*, \sigma^*, \mathsf{m}^*) = \mathsf{Valid}$.
- *The implicit-tracing algorithm fails, or traces to a member outside of the coalition* $\mathsf{Corr} \backslash \mathsf{RL}^*$ *(Because* σ^* *cannot be traced to a member* $i^* \in (\mathsf{Corr} \cap \mathsf{RL}^*)$, *thus* $\mathsf{Corr} \backslash \mathsf{RL}^*$ *can also be modified to* Corr*).*
- σ^* *is non-trivial, i.e.,* $\mathcal{A}$ *has not obtained* σ^* *by making a query on* m^*.

The advantage of $\mathcal{A}$ in the above Traceability game is defined as its probability in wining as $\mathsf{SuccPT}_{\mathcal{A}}$, and denoted by $\mathsf{Adv}_{\mathcal{A}}^{\mathsf{Trace}} = \mathsf{SuccPT}_{\mathcal{A}}$.

2.2 Cryptographic Tools from Lattices

In this subsection, we recall some useful cryptographic tools (for our cryptanalysis) from lattices.

Definition 5. *For integers* n, m, $q \geq 2$, *a random matrix* $\mathbf{A} \in \mathbb{Z}_q^{n \times m}$, *the* m*-dimensional* q*-ary orthogonal lattice* $\Lambda_q^{\perp}(\mathbf{A})$ *is defined as:*

$$\Lambda_q^{\perp}(\mathbf{A}) = \{\mathbf{e} \in \mathbb{Z}^m \mid \mathbf{A} \cdot \mathbf{e} = \mathbf{0} \bmod q\}.$$

For $s > 0$, Gaussian function on $\mathbb{R}^m$ with center $\mathbf{c}$ is defined as:

$$\forall \mathbf{e} \in \mathbb{R}^m,\ \rho_{s,\mathbf{c}}(\mathbf{e}) = \exp(-\pi\|\mathbf{e}-\mathbf{c}\|^2/s^2).$$

For $\mathbf{c} \in \mathbb{R}^m$, discrete Gaussian distribution over Λ is defined as:

$$\forall \mathbf{e} \in \mathbb{Z}^m,\ \mathcal{D}_{\Lambda,s,\mathbf{c}} = \rho_{s,\mathbf{c}}(\mathbf{e})/\textstyle\sum_{\mathbf{e}\in\Lambda}\rho_{s,\mathbf{c}}(\mathbf{e}),$$

where $\mathcal{D}_{\Lambda,s,\mathbf{c}}$ is denoted as $\mathcal{D}_{\Lambda,s}$ if $\mathbf{c} = \mathbf{0}$.

Lemma 1 ([9]). *For integers n, $q \geq 2$, $m \geq 2n\log q$, let a positive real number $s \geq \omega(\sqrt{\log m})$, the following properties are satisfied:*

1. *For all but a $2q^{-n}$ fraction of all $\mathbf{A} \in \mathbb{Z}_q^{n\times m}$, and $\mathbf{e} \xleftarrow{\$} \mathcal{D}_{\mathbb{Z}^m,s}$, the distribution of $\mathbf{A}\cdot\mathbf{e} \bmod q$ is statistical close to uniform distribution over $\mathbb{Z}_q^n$.*
2. *For $\mathbf{e} \xleftarrow{\$} \mathcal{D}_{\mathbb{Z}^m,s}$ and $\beta = \lceil s\cdot\log m\rceil$, $\Pr[\|\mathbf{e}\|_\infty \leq \beta]$ is overwhelming.*
3. *The min-entropy of $\mathcal{D}_{\mathbb{Z}^m,s}$ is at least $m-1$ (i.e., for any $\mathbf{e} \in \mathcal{D}_{\mathbb{Z}^m,s}$, we have $\mathcal{D}_{\mathbb{Z}^m,s}(\mathbf{e}) \leq 2^{1-m}$).*

We recall two PPT algorithms from previous works. The TrapGen algorithm is adopted to obtain a statistically close to uniform $\mathbf{A} \in \mathbb{Z}_q^{n\times m}$ together with a trapdoor (with a low *Gram-Schmidt* norm) for q-ary $\Lambda_q^\perp(\mathbf{A})$; The SamplePre algorithm is adopted to return some short Gaussian vectors over $\Lambda_q^{\mathbf{u}}(\mathbf{A})$, a coset of $\Lambda_q^\perp(\mathbf{A})$.

Lemma 2 ([1,2,15]). *Let $n \geq 1$, $q \geq 2$, and $m = 2n\lceil\log q\rceil$, there exists a* PPT *algorithm* TrapGen(q,n,m) *outputting $\mathbf{A} \in \mathbb{Z}_q^{n\times m}$ and $\mathbf{R_A}$, such that $\mathbf{A}$ is statistically close to a uniform matrix in $\mathbb{Z}_q^{n\times m}$ and $\mathbf{R_A}$ is a trapdoor for orthogonal lattice $\Lambda_q^\perp(\mathbf{A})$.*

Lemma 3 ([9,15]). *Let $n \geq 1$, $q \geq 2$, and $m = 2n\lceil\log q\rceil$, given $\mathbf{A} \in \mathbb{Z}_q^{n\times m}$, a trapdoor $\mathbf{R_A}$ for $\Lambda_q^\perp(\mathbf{A})$, a Gaussian parameter $s = \omega(\sqrt{n\log q\log n})$, $\mathbf{u} \in \mathbb{Z}_q^n$, there exists a* PPT *algorithm* SamplePre$(\mathbf{A},\mathbf{R_A},\mathbf{u},s)$ *returning a short Gaussian vector $\mathbf{e} \in \Lambda_q^{\mathbf{u}}(\mathbf{A})$ sampled from a distribution statistically close to $\mathcal{D}_{\Lambda_q^{\mathbf{u}}(\mathbf{A}),s}$, where $\Lambda_q^{\mathbf{u}}(\mathbf{A})$ is a coset of $\Lambda_q^\perp(\mathbf{A})$.*

We review two well-known *average-case* lattices problems, the short integer solution (SIS) problem and learning with errors (LWE) problem, together with their hardness results.

Definition 6. *The $\mathsf{SIS}^\infty_{n,m,q,\beta}$ problem is defined as follows: given a uniformly random $\mathbf{A} \in \mathbb{Z}_q^{n\times m}$, a real $\beta > 0$, to output a vector $\mathbf{e} \in \mathbb{Z}^m$ such that $\mathbf{A}\cdot\mathbf{e} = \mathbf{0} \bmod q$ and $0 < \|\mathbf{e}\|_\infty \leq \beta$.*

The ISIS problem is a variant of SIS, *additionally given a random syndrome $\mathbf{u} \in \mathbb{Z}_q^n$. The $\mathsf{ISIS}^\infty_{n,m,q,\beta}$ problem is asked to return a vector $\mathbf{e} \in \mathbb{Z}^m$ such that $\mathbf{A}\cdot\mathbf{e} = \mathbf{u} \bmod q$, and $\|\mathbf{e}\|_\infty \leq \beta$. For both problems, they are as hard as certain* worst-case *problems, such as the shortest independent vectors problem (*SIVP*).*

Lemma 4 ([9,14]). *For* m, $\beta = poly(n)$, *and* $q > \beta \cdot \widetilde{O}(\sqrt{n})$, *the* average-case $\mathsf{SIS}^{\infty}_{n,m,q,\beta}$ *and* $\mathsf{ISIS}^{\infty}_{n,m,q,\beta}$ *problems are at least as hard as the* $\mathsf{SIVP}_{\beta \cdot \widetilde{O}(n)}$ *problem in the worst-case.*

Definition 7. *The* $\mathsf{LWE}_{n,q,\chi}$ *problem is defined as follows: given a random vector* $\mathbf{s} \xleftarrow{\$} \mathbb{Z}_q^n$, *a probability distribution* χ *over* $\mathbb{Z}$, *let* $\mathcal{A}_{\mathbf{s},\chi}$ *be a distribution obtained by sampling* $\mathbf{A} \in \mathbb{Z}_q^{n \times m}$, $\mathbf{e} \xleftarrow{\$} \chi^m$, *and output* $(\mathbf{A}, \mathbf{A}^\top \mathbf{s} + \mathbf{e})$, *and make distinguish between* $\mathcal{A}_{\mathbf{s},\chi}$ *and uniform distribution* $\mathcal{U} \xleftarrow{\$} \mathbb{Z}_q^{n \times m} \times \mathbb{Z}_q^m$.

Let $\beta \geq \sqrt{n} \cdot \omega(\log n)$, *for a prime power* q, *given a* β*-bounded distribution* χ, *the* $\mathsf{LWE}_{n,q,\chi}$ *problem is as least as hard as* $\mathsf{SIVP}_{\widetilde{O}(nq/\beta)}$.

3 Perera and Koshiba's VLR-GS Scheme

In this section, we review Perera and Koshiba's fully secure (i.e., achieving FA and full-traceability) lattice-based VLR-GS [19]. Before that, we introduce the FA security, an extended notion of SA security, also defined by Ishida et al. [10].

3.1 The Full-Anonymity Model

The precise definition of FA security for VLR-GS scheme is as follows.

Definition 8. *A* VLR-GS *scheme is* FA-anonymous *if no* PPT *adversary has a non-negligible advantage* $\mathsf{Adv}_{\mathcal{A}}^{\mathsf{Full\text{-}anon}}$ *in the following game (between a challenger* $\mathcal{C}$ *and an adversary* $\mathcal{A}$*).*

a. Initialization: $\mathcal{C}$ *obtains* (Gpk, Gsk, Grt) $\leftarrow$ KeyGen *and provides* (Gpk, Gsk) *to* $\mathcal{A}$, *thus using* Gsk, $\mathcal{A}$ *can sign any message by himself.*

b. Query phase: *Before outputting two challenge identities,* $\mathcal{A}$ *adaptively makes a polynomially bounded number of* revoking query: *request for a revocation token* RT *for* id *with index* i, $\mathcal{C}$ *returns* grt_i.

c. Challenge: $\mathcal{A}$ *outputs a message* $\mathsf{m}^* \in \{0,1\}^*$, *two distinct members* id_0 *and* id_1, *with indexes* i_0 *and* i_1, *respectively.* $\mathcal{A}$ *did not make revoking query at either member, i.e.,* id_0 *and* id_1 *have not been revoked.* $\mathcal{C}$ *chooses a bit* $b \xleftarrow{\$} \{0,1\}$, *and returns* $\sigma^* \leftarrow \mathsf{Sign}(\mathsf{Gpk}, \mathsf{gsk}_{i_b}, \mathsf{m}^*)$ *as a challenge on* m^* *by* id_b.

d. Restricted query: *After obtaining a challenge signature* σ^*, $\mathcal{A}$ *can still make queries as before, but with a following restriction: it is not allowed to make revoking query for* id_0 *or* id_1.

e. Guessing: $\mathcal{A}$ *outputs a bit* $b^* \in \{0,1\}$, *and wins if* $b^* = b$.

The advantage of $\mathcal{A}$ in the above Full-anonymity game is defined as

$$\mathsf{Adv}_{\mathcal{A}}^{\mathsf{Full\text{-}anon}} = |\Pr[b^* = b] - 1/2|.$$

3.2 The VLR-GS Scheme

The description of Perera and Koshiba's lattice-based VLR-GS scheme [19] is as follows. First, we define a function Bin to denote the binary representation of a member's identity index, i.e., the member id $= \mathsf{Bin}(i) = (d_1, d_2, \cdots, d_\ell) \in \{0,1\}^\ell$ for $i \in \{0, 1, \cdots, N-1\}$, where $N = 2^\ell$ is the group size.

$-\mathsf{KeyGen}(1^n, N)$: On input a security parameter n, and the group size $N = 2^\ell = poly(n)$. The dimension $m = 2n\lceil \log q \rceil$, a prime modulus $q = \omega(n^2 \log n)$, a Gaussian parameter $s = \omega(\sqrt{n \log q \log n})$, the norm bound $\beta = \lceil s \cdot \log m \rceil$, and the number of protocol repetitions $\kappa = \omega(\log n)$. This algorithm works as follows:

1. Run $\mathsf{TrapGen}(q, n, m)$ to generate $\mathbf{A}_0 \in \mathbb{Z}_q^{n\times m}$, and a trapdoor $\mathbf{R}_{\mathbf{A}_0}$.
2. Sample 2ℓ matrices $\mathbf{A}_j^b \xleftarrow{\$} \mathbb{Z}_q^{n\times m}$ for all $b \in \{0,1\}$, $j \in \{1, 2, \cdots, \ell\}$, and a vector $\mathbf{u} \xleftarrow{\$} \mathbb{Z}_q^n$. Then define $\mathbf{A} = [\mathbf{A}_0|\mathbf{A}_1^0|\mathbf{A}_1^1|\cdots|\mathbf{A}_\ell^0|\mathbf{A}_\ell^1] \in \mathbb{Z}_q^{n\times(2\ell+1)m}$.
3. Run $\mathsf{TrapGen}(q, n, m)$ to generate $\mathbf{B}_0 \in \mathbb{Z}_q^{n\times m}$, and a trapdoor $\mathbf{R}_{\mathbf{B}_0}$.
4. For id with $i \in \{0, 1, \cdots, N-1\}$, let id $= \mathsf{Bin}(i) = (d_1, d_2, \cdots, d_\ell) \in \{0,1\}^\ell$, and do the followings:
   4.1. Sample $\mathbf{e}_1^{d_1}, \mathbf{e}_2^{d_2}, \cdots, \mathbf{e}_\ell^{d_\ell} \xleftarrow{\$} \mathcal{D}_{\mathbb{Z}^m, s}$, and set $\mathbf{z} = \sum_{j=1}^{\ell} \mathbf{A}_j^{d_j} \cdot \mathbf{e}_j^{d_j} \bmod q$.
   4.2. Run $\mathsf{SamplePre}(\mathbf{A}_0, \mathbf{R}_{\mathbf{A}_0}, \mathbf{u} - \mathbf{z}, s)$ to obtain $\mathbf{e}_0 \in \mathbb{Z}^m$.
   4.3. Let $\mathbf{e}_1^{1-d_1}, \mathbf{e}_2^{1-d_2}, \cdots, \mathbf{e}_\ell^{1-d_\ell}$ be $\mathbf{0}^m$, define $\mathbf{e}_{\mathsf{id}}^i = (\mathbf{e}_0, \mathbf{e}_1^0, \mathbf{e}_1^1, \cdots, \mathbf{e}_\ell^0, \mathbf{e}_\ell^1) \in \mathbb{Z}^{(2\ell+1)m}$. If $\|\mathbf{e}_{\mathsf{id}}^i\|_\infty > \beta$, repeat steps 4.1 and 4.2.
   4.4. Let id's signing secret-key be $\mathsf{gsk}_i = \mathbf{e}_{\mathsf{id}}^i \in \mathbb{Z}^{(2\ell+1)m}$, and its revocation token be $\mathsf{grt}_i = \mathbf{A}_0 \cdot \mathbf{e}_0 \bmod q \in \mathbb{Z}_q^n$.
5. Output group public-key $\mathsf{Gpk} = (\mathbf{A}, \mathbf{u})$, the manager's secret-key $\mathsf{Gmsk} = \mathbf{R}_{\mathbf{B}_0}$ and public-key $\mathsf{Gmpk} = \mathbf{B}_0$, the members' signing secret-keys $\mathsf{Gsk} = (\mathsf{gsk}_0, \mathsf{gsk}_1, \cdots, \mathsf{gsk}_{N-1})$ and tokens $\mathsf{Grt} = (\mathsf{grt}_0, \mathsf{grt}_1, \cdots, \mathsf{grt}_{N-1})$.

$-\mathsf{Sign}(\mathsf{Gpk}, \mathsf{gsk}_i, \mathsf{m})$: Let $\mathcal{H} : \{0,1\}^* \to \{1,2,3\}^{\kappa=\omega(\log n)}$ and $\mathcal{G} : \{0,1\}^* \to \mathbb{Z}_q^{n\times m}$ be two hash functions, modeled as random oracles. On input Gpk and a message $\mathsf{m} \in \{0,1\}^*$, the member id with signing secret-key $\mathsf{gsk}_i = \mathbf{e}_{\mathsf{id}}^i$ first generates a key-pair $(\mathsf{ovk}, \mathsf{osk}) \leftarrow \mathsf{OGen}$ for a one-time signature $\mathcal{OTS} = (\mathsf{OGen}, \mathsf{OSig}, \mathsf{OVer})$ and specifies the following steps:

1. Sample $\mathbf{v} \xleftarrow{\$} \{0,1\}^n$, and let $\mathbf{B} = \mathcal{G}(\mathbf{A}, \mathbf{u}, \mathsf{m}, \mathbf{v}) \in \mathbb{Z}_q^{n\times m}$.
2. Sample $\mathbf{e} \xleftarrow{\$} \chi^m$ (a β-bounded distribution as in Definition 7), and define a vector $\mathbf{b} = \mathbf{B}^\top \cdot \mathsf{grt}_i + \mathbf{e} = (\mathbf{B}^\top \cdot \mathbf{A}_0) \cdot \mathbf{e}_0 + \mathbf{e} \bmod q \in \mathbb{Z}_q^m$.
3. Generate an efficient ZKP protocol that the signer id with index i is indeed a member who owns a valid signing secret-key and has signed $\mathsf{m} \in \{0,1\}^*$, and its token is correctly embedded in $\mathbf{b}$ designed as above. These are achieved by repeating κ times the Stern-type interactive protocol as constructed in [19] with the tuple $(\mathbf{A}, \mathbf{u}, \mathbf{B}, \mathbf{b})$ and the witnesses $(\mathsf{id}, \mathsf{gsk}_i, \mathbf{e})$, then making it non-interactive via the *Fiat-Shamir* heuristic as a triple, $\Pi = (\{\mathsf{CMT}^{(r)}\}_{r=1}^{\kappa}, \mathsf{CH}, \{\mathsf{RSP}^{(r)}\}_{r=1}^{\kappa})$, where challenges

$$\mathsf{CH} = \{\mathsf{CH}^{(r)}\}_{r=1}^{\kappa} = \mathcal{H}(\mathsf{m}, \mathbf{A}, \mathbf{u}, \mathbf{B}, \mathbf{b}, \{\mathsf{CMT}^{(r)}\}_{r=1}^{\kappa}) \in \{1,2,3\}^\kappa.$$

4. Compute a one-time signature $sig = \mathsf{OSig}(\mathsf{osk}, \Pi)$.
5. Output the signature $\sigma = (\mathsf{ovk}, \mathsf{m}, \Pi, \mathbf{v}, \mathbf{b}, sig)$.

–$\mathsf{Verify}(\mathsf{Gpk}, \mathsf{RL}, \mathsf{m}, \sigma)$: On input Gpk, a signature σ on message $\mathsf{m} \in \{0,1\}^*$, and a set of revocation tokens $\mathsf{RL} = \{\{\mathbf{u}_{i'}\}_{i' \le N-1}\} \subseteq \mathsf{Grt}$, the verifier specifies the following steps:

1. Parse $\sigma = (\mathsf{ovk}, \mathsf{m}, \Pi, \mathbf{v}, \mathbf{b}, sig)$.
2. If $\mathsf{Over}(\mathsf{ovk}, \Pi, sig) = 0$, then return Invalid.
3. Compute $\mathbf{B} = \mathcal{G}(\mathbf{A}, \mathbf{u}, \mathsf{m}, \mathbf{v}) \in \mathbb{Z}_q^{n\times m}$.
4. If $\mathsf{CH} = \{\mathsf{CH}^{(1)}, \mathsf{CH}^{(2)}, \cdots, \mathsf{CH}^{(\kappa)}\} \neq \mathcal{H}(\mathsf{m}, \mathbf{A}, \mathbf{u}, \mathbf{B}, \mathbf{b}, \{\mathsf{CMT}^{(r)}\}_{r=1}^{\kappa})$, then return Invalid.
5. For $r = 1$ to κ, run the verification steps of the protocol as in [19] to check the validity of $\mathsf{RSP}^{(r)}$ *w.r.t* $\mathsf{CMT}^{(r)}$ and $\mathsf{CH}^{(r)}$. If any of these conditions does not hold, then return Invalid.
6. For each $\mathbf{u}_{i'} \in \mathsf{RL}$, do the followings:
   6.1. Parse the token $\mathbf{u}_{i'} = (\mathsf{grt}_{i'}, \sigma_{rt_{i'}})$.
   6.2. If $\mathsf{Verify}(\mathsf{Gmpk}, \mathsf{grt}_{i'}, \sigma_{rt_{i'}}) = 0$, then return Invalid.
   6.3. Compute $\mathbf{e}_{i'} = \mathbf{b} - \mathbf{B}^\top \cdot \mathsf{grt}_{i'} \bmod q$. If there exists an index $i' \le N-1$ such that $\|\mathbf{e}_{i'}\|_\infty \le \beta$, then return Invalid.
7. Return Valid.

–$\mathsf{Revoke}(\mathsf{Gpk}, \mathsf{Gmsk}, \mathsf{grt}_i, \mathsf{RL})$: On input Gpk, Gmsk, a revoked member's token grt_i and the latest revocation list RL', the manager specifies the following steps:

1. Computer a signature $\sigma_{rt_i} = \mathsf{Sign}(\mathsf{Gmsk}, \mathsf{grt}_i)$.
2. Return a new revocation list $\mathsf{RL} = \mathsf{RL}' \cup (\mathsf{grt}_i, \sigma_{rt_i})$.

4 Our Attack

By our analysis carefully, technically, the VLR-GS scheme of Perera and Koshiba [19] is built from Langlois et al.'s first lattice-based VLR-GS scheme [11] at PKC 2014 and a full and corrected version [13] in 2018, and the main contents almost entirely follow these two constructions (in particular, the RT of a member id with an identity index i is directly and exactly dependent on his signing secret-key, i.e., $\mathsf{grt}_i = \mathbf{A}_0 \cdot \mathbf{e}_0 \bmod q \in \mathbb{Z}_q^n$).

The unique and central work of [19] is that the manager additionally enjoys a key-pair (Gmsk, Gmpk), with which a revocation algorithm Revoke is added to sign grt_i before adding the revoked member id with index i to RL. In verification algorithm Verify, besides checking whether or not the signature σ is valid and the signer's revocation token is included in RL, a third step to check whether the RTs in RL are signed validly by manager is also needed. That is exactly based on the third step operation (for our view, this is a trivial building block and invalid for improving the anonymity), Perera and Koshiba [19] claimed that the FA security for their new lattice-based VLR-GS construction is achieved, because it allows to provide all members' signing secret-keys to adversary in the FA security model (defined in Sect. 3.1), and thus, they took it for granted that the first fully secure lattice-based VLR-GS scheme is constructed successfully. As we have discussed in Introduction, when defining an adversary, we usually give it stronger ability, within reason, and the stronger the adversary is, the more secure scheme is. The adversary may adopt all he owns and all he can use to try to attack, and it is impossible to require the adversary to carry out attacks strictly following all prescribed procedures set by the scheme designer. That is to say, in the FA security model of [19], the adversary may not strictly execute all the steps one by one as those in Verify of the specific construction. Based on this basic fact, we describe an attack for the FA security of [19].

Description of Our Attack. The description of our attack is as follows.

1. Once $\mathcal{A}$ receives $\mathsf{Gpk} = (\mathbf{A}, \mathbf{B}_0, \mathbf{u})$, $\mathsf{Gsk} = (\mathsf{gsk}_0, \cdots, \mathsf{gsk}_{N-1})$, where $\mathsf{gsk}_i = \mathbf{e}^i_{\mathsf{id}} = (\mathbf{e}_0, \mathbf{e}^0_1, \mathbf{e}^1_1, \cdots, \mathbf{e}^0_\ell, \mathbf{e}^1_\ell) \in \mathbb{Z}^{(2\ell+1)m}$, $i \in \{0, 1, \cdots, N-1\}$. $\mathcal{A}$ computes $\mathsf{grt}_i = \mathbf{A}_0 \cdot \mathbf{e}_0 \bmod q$ as the revocation token for member id (with an index i).
2. At the challenge phase, $\mathcal{A}$ submits a message $\mathsf{m}^* \in \{0,1\}^*$, two target members id_0, $\mathsf{id}_1 (\neq \mathsf{id}_0)$, with indexes i_0, $i_1 (\neq i_0)$, respectively. Before and after that, $\mathcal{A}$ should not make a revoking query at either member. Then, $\mathcal{C}$ returns the challenge signature $\sigma^*_{i_b} = (\mathsf{ovk}^*, \mathsf{m}^*, \Pi^*, \mathbf{v}^*, \mathbf{b}^*_{i_b}, sig^*)$ such that

$$\mathbf{v}^* \in \{0,1\}^n,\ \mathbf{e} \in \chi^m,\ \mathbf{B} = \mathcal{G}(\mathbf{A}, \mathbf{u}, \mathsf{m}^*, \mathbf{v}^*),\ \mathbf{b}^*_{i_b} = \mathbf{B}^\top \cdot \mathsf{grt}_{i_b} + \mathbf{e} \bmod q,$$
$$\Pi^* = (\{\mathsf{CMT}^{(r)}\}_{r=1}^{\kappa}, \{\mathsf{CH}^{(r)}\}_{r=1}^{\kappa} = \mathcal{H}(\mathsf{m}^*, \mathbf{A}, \mathbf{u}, \mathbf{B}, \mathbf{b}^*_{i_b}, \{\mathsf{CMT}^{(r)}\}_{r=1}^{\kappa}), \{\mathsf{RSP}^{(r)}\}_{r=1}^{\kappa}),$$
$$\mathcal{OTS} = (\mathsf{OGen}, \mathsf{OSig}, \mathsf{OVer}),\ (\mathsf{ovk}^*, \mathsf{osk}^*) \leftarrow \mathsf{OGen},\ sig^* = \mathsf{OSig}(\mathsf{osk}^*, \Pi^*),$$

   where b is a random bit chosen by $\mathcal{C}$.
3. Once receiving $\sigma^*_{i_b} = (\mathsf{ovk}^*, \mathsf{m}^*, \Pi^*, \mathbf{v}^*, \mathbf{b}^*_{i_b}, sig^*)$, $\mathcal{A}$ does as follows:
   3.1. Check $\mathsf{OVer}(\mathsf{ovk}^*, \Pi^*, sig^*) \stackrel{?}{=} 0$, if not, output $\perp$ and abort.
   3.2. Compute $\mathbf{B} = \mathcal{G}(\mathbf{A}, \mathbf{u}, \mathsf{m}^*, \mathbf{v}^*) \in \mathbb{Z}_q^{n\times m}$.
   3.3. Check $\{\mathsf{CH}^{(1)}, \cdots, \mathsf{CH}^{(\kappa)}\} \stackrel{?}{\neq} \mathcal{H}(\mathsf{m}^*, \mathbf{A}, \mathbf{u}, \mathbf{B}, \mathbf{b}^*_{i_b}, \{\mathsf{CMT}^{(r)}\}_{r=1}^{\kappa})$, if not, output $\perp$ and abort.
   3.4. For $r = 1$ to κ, run the verification steps of the protocol as in [19] to check the validity of $\mathsf{RSP}^{(r)}$ *w.r.t.* $\mathsf{CMT}^{(r)}$ and $\mathsf{CH}^{(r)}$. If any of the conditions does not hold, then output $\perp$ and abort.
   3.5. For grt_{i_0} and grt_{i_1}, compute $\mathbf{e}_{i_0} = \mathbf{b}^*_{i_b} - \mathbf{B}^\top \cdot \mathsf{grt}_{i_0} \bmod q$, $\mathbf{e}_{i_1} = \mathbf{b}^*_{i_b} - \mathbf{B}^\top \cdot \mathsf{grt}_{i_1} \bmod q$, respectively. If $\|\mathbf{e}_{i_0}\|_\infty \leq \beta$, return i_0; if $\|\mathbf{e}_{i_1}\|_\infty \leq \beta$, return i_1; otherwise, output $\perp$ and abort.

Correctness of Our Attack. The correctness of our attack algorithm is straightforward. First, the steps 3.1–3.4 are same as those in [19]. Second, although we do not provide the tokens with the manager's signatures, i.e., $(\mathsf{grt}_{i_0}, \sigma_{rt_0})$ and $(\mathsf{grt}_{i_1}, \sigma_{rt_1})$, we exactly own $(\mathsf{grt}_{i_0}, \mathsf{grt}_{i_1})$ and if $\sigma^*_{i_b}$ is generated honestly from $i_b \in \{i_0, i_1\}$ (simultaneously, satisfying all previous checks), the step 3.5 can be carried out correctly and efficiently, which means there must be an index i_0 or i_1 is returned, thus the real signer (i.e., member) is traced, and so our attack algorithm outputs the correct answer with probability 1. We note that our attack algorithm succeeds regardless of whether grt_{i_0} (or grt_{i_1}) has been signed by the manager or not.

5 Conclusion

In this paper, we presented an attack on a lattice-based group signature with verifier-local revocation, proposed by Perera and Koshiba [19] at ICICS 2018, and drew a negative conclusion on their construction for the full-anonymity. In particular, to construct an efficient lattice-based fully anonymous group signature scheme with verifier-local revocation still remains an open problem.

Acknowledgments. The authors would like to thank the anonymous reviewers of ACNS-SCI 2021 for their helpful comments, and this research is supported by the National Natural Science Foundation of China (No. 61802075), Guangxi key Laboratory of Cryptography and Information Security (Grant No. GCIS201907), the Natural Science Foundation of Henan Province (Grant No. 202300410508) and the Key Foundation of Science and Technology Development of Henan Province (No. 202102210356).

References

1. Ajtai, M.: Generating hard instances of lattice problems (extended abstract). In: STOC, pp. 99–108. ACM (1996). https://doi.org/10.1145/237814.237838
2. Alwen, J., Peikert, C.: Generating shorter bases for hard random lattices. Theor. Comput. Syst. **48**(3), 535–553 (2011). https://doi.org/10.1007/s00224-010-9278-3
3. Bellare, M., Micciancio, D., Warinschi, B.: Foundations of group signatures: formal definitions, simplified requirements, and a construction based on general assumptions. In: Biham, E. (ed.) EUROCRYPT 2003. LNCS, vol. 2656, pp. 614–629. Springer, Heidelberg (2003). https://doi.org/10.1007/3-540-39200-9_38
4. Bichsel, P., Camenisch, J., Neven, G., Smart, N.P., Warinschi, B.: Get shorty via group signatures without encryption. In: Garay, J.A., De Prisco, R. (eds.) SCN 2010. LNCS, vol. 6280, pp. 381–398. Springer, Heidelberg (2010). https://doi.org/10.1007/978-3-642-15317-4_24
5. Boneh, D., Shacham, H.: Group signatures with verifier-local revocation. In: CCS, pp. 168–177. ACM (2004). https://doi.org/10.1145/1030083.1030106
6. Bringer, J., Patey, A.: VLR group signatures: how to achieve both backward unlinkability and efficient revocation checks. In: Pierangela, S. (eds.) SECRYPT 2012, pp. 215–220 (2012). https://doi.org/10.1007/3-540-46416-6_22
7. Chaum, D., van Heyst, E.: Group signatures. In: Davies, D.W. (ed.) EUROCRYPT 1991. LNCS, vol. 547, pp. 257–265. Springer, Heidelberg (1991). https://doi.org/10.1007/3-540-46416-6_22
8. Gao, W., Hu, Y., Zhang, Y., et al.: Lattice-based group signature with verifier-local revocation. J. Shanghai JiaoTong Univ. (Sci.) **22**(3), 313–321 (2017). https://doi.org/10.1007/12204-017-1837-1

9. Gentry, C., Peikert, C., Vaikuntanathan, V.: Trapdoor for hard lattices and new cryptographic constructions. In: STOC, pp. 197–206. ACM (2008). https://doi.org/10.1145/1374376.1374407
10. Ishida, A., Sakai, Y., Emura, K., Hanaoka, G., Tanaka, K.: Fully anonymous group signature with verifier-local revocation. In: Catalano, D., De Prisco, R. (eds.) SCN 2018. LNCS, vol. 11035, pp. 23–42. Springer, Cham (2018). https://doi.org/10.1007/978-3-319-98113-0_2
11. Langlois, A., Ling, S., Nguyen, K., Wang, H.: Lattice-based group signature scheme with verifier-local revocation. In: Krawczyk, H. (ed.) PKC 2014. LNCS, vol. 8383, pp. 345–361. Springer, Heidelberg (2014). https://doi.org/10.1007/978-3-642-54631-0_20
12. Libert, B., Vergnaud, D.: Group signatures with verifier-local revocation and backward unlinkability in the standard model. In: Garay, J.A., Miyaji, A., Otsuka, A. (eds.) CANS 2009. LNCS, vol. 5888, pp. 498–517. Springer, Heidelberg (2009). https://doi.org/10.1007/978-3-642-10433-6_34
13. Ling, S., Nguyen, K., Langlois, A., et al.: A lattice-based group signature scheme with verifier-local revocation. Theor. Comput. Sci. **730**, 1–20 (2018). https://doi.org/10.1016/j.tcs.2018.03.027
14. Micciancio, D., Peikert, C.: Hardness of SIS and LWE with small parameters. In: Canetti, R., Garay, J.A. (eds.) CRYPTO 2013. LNCS, vol. 8042, pp. 21–39. Springer, Heidelberg (2013). https://doi.org/10.1007/978-3-642-40041-4_2
15. Micciancio, D., Peikert, C.: Trapdoors for lattices: simpler, tighter, faster, smaller. In: Pointcheval, D., Johansson, T. (eds.) EUROCRYPT 2012. LNCS, vol. 7237, pp. 700–718. Springer, Heidelberg (2012). https://doi.org/10.1007/978-3-642-29011-4_41
16. Nakanishi, T., Funabiki, N.: Verifier-local revocation group signature schemes with backward unlinkability from bilinear maps. In: Roy, B. (ed.) ASIACRYPT 2005. LNCS, vol. 3788, pp. 533–548. Springer, Heidelberg (2005). https://doi.org/10.1007/11593447_29
17. Nakanishi, T., Funabiki, N.: A short verifier-local revocation group signature scheme with backward unlinkability. In: Yoshiura, H., Sakurai, K., Rannenberg, K., Murayama, Y., Kawamura, S. (eds.) IWSEC 2006. LNCS, vol. 4266, pp. 17–32. Springer, Heidelberg (2006). https://doi.org/10.1007/11908739_2
18. Perera, M.N.S., Koshiba, T.: Achieving almost-full security for lattice-based fully dynamic group signatures with verifier-local revocation. In: Su, C., Kikuchi, H. (eds.) ISPEC 2018. LNCS, vol. 11125, pp. 229–247. Springer, Cham (2018). https://doi.org/10.1007/978-3-319-99807-7_14
19. Perera, M.N.S., Koshiba, T.: Achieving full security for lattice-based group signatures with verifier-local revocation. In: Naccache, D., et al. (eds.) ICICS 2018. LNCS, vol. 11149, pp. 287–302. Springer, Cham (2018). https://doi.org/10.1007/978-3-030-01950-1_17
20. Perera, M.N.S., Koshiba, T.: Achieving strong security and verifier-local revocation for dynamic group signatures from lattice assumptions. In: Katsikas, S.K., Alcaraz, C. (eds.) STM 2018. LNCS, vol. 11091, pp. 3–19. Springer, Cham (2018). https://doi.org/10.1007/978-3-030-01141-3_1
21. Zhang, Y., Hu, Y., Gao, W., et al.: Simpler efficient group signature scheme with verifier-local revocation from lattices. KSII Trans. Internet Inf. Syst. **10**(1), 414–430 (2016). https://doi.org/10.3837/tiis.2016.01.024

22. Zhang, Y., Hu, Y., Zhang, Q., Jia, H.: On new zero-knowledge proofs for lattice-based group signatures with verifier-local revocation. In: Lin, Z., Papamanthou, C., Polychronakis, M. (eds.) ISC 2019. LNCS, vol. 11723, pp. 190–208. Springer, Cham (2019). https://doi.org/10.1007/978-3-030-30215-3_10
23. Zhang, Y., Liu, X., Hu, Y., Zhang, Q., Jia, H.: Lattice-based group signatures with verifier-local revocation: achieving shorter key-sizes and explicit traceability with ease. In: Mu, Y., Deng, R.H., Huang, X. (eds.) CANS 2019. LNCS, vol. 11829, pp. 120–140. Springer, Cham (2019). https://doi.org/10.1007/978-3-030-31578-8_7
24. Zhang, Y., Liu, X., Yin, Y., Zhang, Q., Jia, H.: On new zero-knowledge proofs for fully anonymous lattice-based group signature scheme with verifier-local revocation. In: Zhou, J., et al. (eds.) ACNS 2020. LNCS, vol. 12418, pp. 381–399. Springer, Cham (2020). https://doi.org/10.1007/978-3-030-61638-0_21

An Efficient Proactive Secret Sharing Scheme for Cloud Storage

Shuihai Zhang[1], Jingfu Wang[1], Yan Zhang[1], Bei Pei[2], and Chunli Lyu[1(✉)]

[1] College of Information and Electrical Engineering, China Agricultural University, Beijing, China
lvcl@cau.edu.cn

[2] The 3rd Research Institute of the Ministry of Public Security, Shanghai, China

Abstract. Aiming at the security problems of cloud storage industry, this paper proposes an efficient proactive secret sharing (PSS) scheme for cloud storage. The scheme divides the secret of large amount of data into multi-secrets, and uses secret sharing to make multi-secrets meet the security of the (k, n) threshold scheme. The scheme periodically updates and verifies the shadow shares held by cloud service providers. In this way, an adversary can recover the secret if and only if it captures at least k shares during a period of update rather than any time. The scheme only calculates a few of multi-secrets at a time, which reduces the computational cost of the system. The scheme takes into account the long-term security issues and processing performance of the system, which can effectively protect the confidentiality and integrity of data, and can also be used to prove the integrity of remote data. Compared with the previous PSS scheme, the scheme has higher execution efficiency, less interaction between shareholders, and lower requirements for communication channels, which can better to meet the needs of cloud storage in the current era.

Keywords: Proactive secret sharing · Threshold cryptography · Cloud storage · Proactive safety · Data integrity verification

1 Introduction

In today's era, more and more people choose to store their data on the cloud server. Cloud servers are generally third-party hosted virtual servers, rather than their own private servers for users. People who need data storage hosting services can purchase or lease storage space from third-party platforms to meet their data storage needs. However, with more and more service providers joining the cloud storage industry, the accompanying information security issues such as data confidentiality, data isolation, application security, user privacy, copyright risks, etc. have to be taken seriously. Among these security issues, one of the most concerned is the data confidentiality issue.

This work was supported by the Key Laboratory of Information and Network Securi-ty, Ministry of Public Security, the Third Research Institute of the Ministry of Public Security(C19605).

J. Zhou et al. (Eds.): ACNS 2021 Workshops, LNCS 12809, pp. 346–357, 2021.
https://doi.org/10.1007/978-3-030-81645-2_20

For individual users, they hope to store photos, files and correspondence records in the cloud server safely and completely. For enterprise users, they may hand over a large number of important industry data to the cloud server for hosting. These data may involve important industry secrets, which will have disastrous consequences once leaked [1]. Therefore, ensuring the confidentiality and integrity of data in third-party platform servers is the key to the development of the cloud storage industry. It also has been a research hot-spot in both industry and academia in recent years.

1.1 Related Works about Secret Sharing

Secret sharing (SS) technology is one of the important branches of modern cryptography. Its emergence is to solve the problem of high risk and poor intrusion tolerance caused by excessive concentration of secrets. And it is also one of the important means to protect information security and secret. The basic idea of SS is to split the secret in an appropriate way. Each share of the split is managed by different shareholders. A shareholder can't recover the secret, and only a certain number of shareholders work together to recover the secret.

The SS scheme was first proposed by Shamir [2] and Blakley [3] independently on different occasions in 1979, namely (k, n) threshold scheme. There exist two types of entities: one dealer and some shareholders. In addition, n is the total number of shareholders involved in storage, and k is the minimum number of shareholders that can recover the secret. When k or more shareholders pool their shares together to execute the secret reconstruction algorithm, the secrets can be recovered. However, up to $k - 1$ shareholders can't reconstruct the secret.

Shamir's (k, n) threshold scheme is based on Lagrange interpolation method, while Blakley's (k, n) threshold scheme is based on the characteristics of multidimensional space points. Shamir and Blakley threshold schemes are linear. In 1982, Mignotte [4] first proposed a (k, n) SS scheme based on the Chinese Remainder Theorem (CRT), but this scheme is not perfect. Shareholders who are less than the threshold are able to narrow the secret into a small range. Asmuth and Bloom [5] proposed a new CRT-based PSS scheme on this basis, which made up for the deficiencies in this field.

However, the above (k, n) threshold SS scheme is based on the honesty of secret dealer and shareholders. In the process of practical using, there may be fraud of entities. The types of fraud can be divided into external attacks and internal fraud. External attack refers to the members outside the scheme disguised as shareholder to deceive secrets; Internal fraud includes a shareholder providing false share for secret recovery, which leads to the system can't recover the correct secret [6]. It also includes dealers cheating at the initial stage of secret distribution and distributing false secrets to shareholders.

In order to solve the above problem, Chor [7] first proposed the concept of verifiable secret sharing (VSS) in 1985. In this scheme, in the process of secret sharing, the secret share is verified through multiple interactions between dealer and shareholders. However, due to the excessive number of interactions, this scheme has high requirements for the load of communication channels, and can only solve whether the secret dealer is honest, which can't verify the honesty of shareholders. In 1987, Feldman [8] proposed the first VSS scheme that requires no trusted agency and is non-interactive based on the solubility of discrete logarithms. But this scheme is proven to be the security risk in the presence of malicious adversaries. Since then, Pederson [9] proposed another unconditionally VSS scheme on this basis in 1991. Kamer Kaya et al. [10] proposed a VSS scheme based on CRT. This scheme can solve the problem of cheating between secret dealer and shareholders, but the technical means adopted in this scheme lead to a large amount of computation required for verification.

1.2 Related Works about Proactive Secret Sharing

Another more typical case in the development of SS is the long-term security threat. Since some confidential data is stored on servers for decades or even a hundred years, long-term system running may give the adversary enough time to break through k or more shareholders one by one, and ultimately crisis the confidential data. The concept of proactive security was first proposed by Ostrovsky and Yung [11] in 1991. Subsequently, Herzberg et al. [12] first proposed the concept of proactive secret sharing in 1995. In a PSS scheme, secret shares are periodically renewed (without changing the secret) in such a way that information gained by adversary in one time period is useless for attacking the secret after the shares are renewed.

In the past twenty years, a large number of PSS schemes for different problems and execution environments have been proposed. For example, Feng and Guo et al. [13] proposed the first complete proactive multi-secret sharing scheme (PMSS) based on Xu [14], in which multi-secrets can be shared in a secret sharing process, and shareholders can be regularly updated their shares without changing the secret. Zhou L et al. [15] proposed a PSS scheme used in asynchronous communication model. In this scheme, there is no fixed limit on message delivery delay and processor execution speed. The scheme also can against attacks that PSS scheme can't withstand in some synchronous systems. Schultz and Liskov [16] proposed the concept of mobile proactive secret sharing (MPSS). MPSS provides mobility: The group of nodes holding the shares of the secret can change at each resharing. Since the advent of quantum computers may cause the failure of existing security protocols, that is, they cannot resist quantum attacks, Qin and Dai [17] proposed a proactive quantum secret sharing (PQSS) scheme in 2015, which can effectively resist mobile adversarys while resisting quantum attacks.

1.3 Contribution

In this paper, we present an efficient PSS scheme for cloud storage, aiming to protect the information stored by cloud service providers. The scheme divides the secret of large amount of data into multi-secrets, and uses secret sharing to make multi-secrets meet the security of the (k, n) threshold scheme. The scheme periodically updates and verifies the shadow shares held by cloud service providers. In this way, an adversary can recover the secret if and only if it captures at least k shares during a period of update rather than any time. The scheme only calculates a few of multi-secrets at a time, which reduces the computational cost of the system. The scheme takes into account the long-term security issues and processing performance of the system, which can effectively protect the confidentiality and integrity of data, and can also be used to prove the integrity of remote data.

2 Preliminaries

2.1 Shamir (*k*, *n*) Threshold Scheme

The SS scheme proposed by Shamir is based on Lagrange interpolation formula. The basic idea is the polynomial of $k - 1$ needs k points to be defined. Its descriptions are as follows.

1) Initialization stage: Let q be a prime number, $s \in Z_q$ be the secret to be shared, n the number of participants (or shareholders), and k the constructability threshold. The dealer D of the secret randomly chooses n different non-zero elements $x_1, x_2, \ldots, x_n$ from $GF(q)$ to identify the shareholder U_r $(r = 1, 2, \ldots, n)$.
2) Secret distribution stage: The dealer D of the secret chooses a random polynomial $f(x)$ of degree $k - 1$ over Z_q subject to the condition $f(0) = s$.

$$f(x) = \mathrm{s} + \sum\nolimits_{i=1}^{k-1} a_i * x^i \bmod q$$

The dealer D generates secret shares s_r for all participants U_r:

$$s_r = f(x_r) = a_0 + \sum\nolimits_{i=1}^{k-1} a_i * x_r^i \bmod q(\mathrm{r} = 1, 2, \ldots, \mathrm{n})$$

3) Secret reconstruction stage: Any k shareholders $\{U_1, U_2, \ldots, U_t\}$ provide their shares and use polynomial interpolation to compute secret s.

$$\mathrm{s} = f(0) = \sum\nolimits_{i=1}^{k} f(x_i) \prod_{v=1, v \neq i}^{k} \frac{x_v}{x_v - x_i} \bmod q$$

In general, the SS scheme has a certain fault tolerance. Even if several participants are corrupted, as long as the number of normal participants is within the corresponding range, the secret information still can be reconstructed. From a mathematical point of view, SS is a process of splitting and restoring a mathematical object at different time points. From this perspective, the key of SS scheme is how to design better secret splitting and restoring methods.

2.2 Periodic Share Renewal

The core of PSS is the periodic updating of secret shares. The PSS scheme first decomposes the secret data into n secret shares according to the secret sharing method, and then shareholders regularly update their shares. As long as the number of corrupted servers within one time period doesn't exceed the threshold k, corrupted servers can be restored in the update phase and the secure system environment can be reconstructed.

Since Herzberg proposed the concept of PSS in 1995, proactive security has received extensive attention. The difficulty in the design of PSS scheme is how to renew the share: To improve the system flexibility and reduce the time complexity of the algorithm as much as possible without changing the secret. Most of the update protocols of active secret sharing schemes are designed and improved according to Herzberg's update scheme. Share update protocol is as follows.

Every server U_r randomly selects $k-1$ elements δ_i $(i = 1, 2, \ldots, k-1)$ in $GF(p)$ to constituting polynomial $f_r(x)$:

$$f_r(x) = \sum\nolimits_{i=1}^{k-1} \delta_i * x^i \bmod p$$

For all shareholders U_j, U_r sends $u_{rj} = f_r(j)$ secretly to U_j. In addition, U_r calculates $u_{rr} = f_r(r)$ and stores it secretly locally.

After all shareholders have completed the above operations, U_r calculates its new share $s_r^{(t)} = s_r^{(t-1)} + u_{1r} + u_{2r} + \cdots + u_{nr}$ $(mod\ p)$, and destroys all variables generated at this stage except for the new share $s_r^{(t)}$ (The upper right corner represents period t).

Herzberg updating scheme uses the additive characteristic of Lagrange polynomial $f'(x) = f(x) + \delta(x)$. Because of $f'(0) = f(0) + \delta(0) = f(0) + 0$, shares renewal will not cause the original secret to change.

3 PSS Scheme for Cloud Storage

3.1 Models and Related Definitions

The Roles Involved in the Scheme. Secret distributor D: D participates in the share renewal of the scheme, including setting various parameters and dividing secret.

Trusted third party A: A participates in the share renewal of the scheme, and regularly generates update coefficients. A can't obtain any information about the secret.

Verifiers $B_1, B_2, \ldots, B_l$: $B_1, B_2, \ldots, B_l$ participate in the share verification work of the scheme, regularly verify whether the share is correct. Verifiers can't obtain any information about the secret.

Cloud service provider $U_r (1 \leq r \leq n)$: It represents shareholders of the scheme.

The Models of the Scheme. Time period model: The scheme has two time periods, namely the period T_1 for performing share update and the period T_2 for performing share verification.

Service and communication model: In order to reduce communication consumption, the cloud service provider U_r participating in sharing doesn't communicate directly with each other. The communication service is conducted with trusted third party A as a relay.

Adversary model: The adversary can monitor any information transmitted over the communication channel, and can also send its own information. Adversary have limited computing power and can't invade the underlying cryptography primitives. The adversary can corrupt cloud service providers at any moment during a time period. If a server is corrupted, it is controlled by the adversary before the adversary is found and cleared.

The adversary's performance in the system is achieved by interacting with other shareholders by the role it controls. The controlled role may not be executed according to the agreement, and maliciously destroy the agreement. It may also perform protocol actions, but secretly spy on protocol execution. For the former controlled participant, this scheme can detect abnormal behaviors in the execution process, so as to clear adversary and restore the server to normal state by restarting the server. For the latter controlled participant, as long as the number of service providers attacked in a time period T_1 is less than k, the adversary cannot obtain any information about secret S.

3.2 Secret Data's Sharing and Recovery

Protocol of Initialization

1) The secret distributor D divides the secret data S into m blocks, and the size of each block is x *bit*. Every block is a multi-secret $s^t (1 \leq t \leq m)$. If s^m is less than x *bit*, 0 *bit* is added until x bit is satisfied. The size of x depends on the specific situation of the system.
2) Putting a special public secret s^0 in the multi-secret, and the content is disclosed in the system. s^0 will be updated together with other multi-secrets.
3) D chooses a large prime number p: $p > n > k$, $p > \forall s^t (0 \leq t \leq m)$. n number of cloud storage providers participating in storage, k is the minimum number of service providers required to restore S.
4) D randomly selects n different non-zero elements $x_1, x_2, \ldots, x_n$ from the finite field $GF(p)$ to identify each cloud storage provider $U_r (1 \leq r \leq n)$.
5) D public U_r and its corresponding x_r.

Protocol of Secret Sharing

1) D takes multi-secret $s^t (0 \leq t \leq m)$ as the secret to be distributed, and randomly selects $k - 1$ elements $a_i (i = 1, 2, \ldots, k - 1)$ in $GF(p)$ to constitute polynomial $f(x)$.

$$f(x) = s^t + \sum\nolimits_{i=1}^{k-1} a_i * x^i \bmod p \tag{1}$$

2) D uses the polynomial $f(x)$ and the x_r corresponding to the cloud service provider U_r to generate the corresponding shadow secret share s_r^t for U_r.

$$s_r^t = f(x_r) = s^t + \sum\nolimits_{i=1}^{k-1} a_i * x_r^i \bmod p (\mathrm{r} = 1, 2, \ldots, \mathrm{n}) \tag{2}$$

3) D sends the generated s_r^t to the corresponding U_r safely, and destroys all the coefficients a_i generated in the process.
4) Repeating the above-mentioned secret distribution process for each multi-secret $s^t (0 \leq t \leq m)$.

Protocol of Secret Recovery

1) Randomly select k normal operating cloud service providers $\{U_1, U_2, \ldots, U_k\}$.
2) According to their secret shares s_r^t and x_r, using the Lagrange interpolation polynomial to recover the multi-secret s^t.

$$s^t = \sum\nolimits_{i=1}^{k} s_i^t \prod\nolimits_{v=1, v \neq i}^{k} \frac{x_v}{x_v - x_i} \bmod p \tag{3}$$

The above-mentioned secret data's sharing and recovery scheme meets the security requirements of the (k, n) threshold scheme. Shareholders more than or equal to k can recover the secret. And Shareholders less than k can't infer any information about secret.

3.3 Secret Share Update

The administrator sets a time period T_1. Every time period T_1, the following secret share update is performed for all cloud service providers.

Protocol of Generating Update Shares

1) The trusted third party A uses 0 as the secret for Shamir SS. A randomly selects $k-1$ elements $a_i (i = 1, 2, \ldots, k-1)$ in $GF(p)$ to constitute polynomial $f(x)$.
2) A generates its corresponding secret update share g_r for each service provider $U_r (1 \leq r \leq n)$.
3) A sends the calculated g_r to the corresponding U_r safely.
4) Repeat steps 1–3 x times. After completion, the cloud service provider $U_r (1 \leq r \leq n)$ has the update share of $g_r^1, g_r^2, \ldots, g_r^x$.
5) A deletes all random coefficients a_i generated in this process.

Protocol of Generating Update Sequence. Every cloud service provider $U_r (1 \leq r \leq n)$ has two pairs of public and private keys. One set of public and private keys is used for encryption, and another is used for digital signatures. The two pairs of public keys are disclosed in the group, and the two pairs of private keys are secretly held by the service provider U_r. The setting symbol $ENC_j(x)$ indicates that the public key of the service provider U_j is used to encrypt the data x. $SIG_j(x)$ indicates that the service provider U_j digitally signs the data x. $Hash(x)$ represents the hash value of data x.

1) Every cloud service provider U_r randomly generates k_r of x *bit* in local.
2) U_r generates a message VSS_r and sends it together with the digital signature $SIG_r(VSS_r)$ to the trusted third party A.

$$VSS_r = \{ENC_1(k_r), ENC_2(k_r), \cdots, ENC_n(k_r), time, Hash(k_r)\} \tag{4}$$

3) The trusted third party A acts as a relay and forwards the message and digital signature to cloud service providers other than U_r.
4) The cloud service provider U_j verifies the signature after receiving VSS_r then uses U_j's own private key to decrypt $ENC_j(k_r)$ to get k_r, and verifies it with $Hash(k_r)$. If they correspond, it means U_r in a normal state. If U_j finds that $Hash(k_r)$ does not corresponding to k_r, U_j will initiate a signature accusation against U_r to A.
5) If A receives the signature accusation against U_r, A informs the accused party U_r to perform steps 1–4 and notifies the system administrator.
6) If step 5 doesn't hold, U_r calculates the update sequence $K^1 = \sum_{i=1}^{n} k_i$ locally.
7) U_r generates $K^2, K^3, \ldots, K^m$ through K^1 and the stream key generation algorithm.

Protocol of the Update Share Verification. There are l verifiers B in the scheme, and their numbers are $B_1, B_2, \ldots, B_l$. At this time, verifiers send a verification update share request to cloud service providers. Every cloud service provider U_r performs the following operations.

1) Every cloud service provider U_r establishes a set G in local. Elements in G are composed of subscript positions with all bits of 1 in the shared random sequence K^1(for example, if the sequence is 0110, the elements stored in the set G are 2 and 3).
2) U_r updates the share s_r^0 it holds.

$$s_r^{0\prime} = s_r^0 + \sum_j g_r^j (j \in G) \tag{4}$$

3) U_r sends the updated shares $s_r^{0\prime}$ and $SIG_r(s_r^{0\prime})$ to verifiers $B_1, B_2, \ldots, B_l$.
4) $B_1, B_2, \ldots, B_l$ verify whether $s_r^{0\prime}$ and $SIG_r(s_r^{0\prime})$ are consistent, and then perform secret recovery on the n shares $s_r^{0\prime}$ to verify whether s^0 can be recovered.
5) If all verifiers can successfully recover the special secret s^0, verifiers announce that the update process is correct, and inform U_r to delete G and old share s_r^0.
6) If step 6 doesn't hold, verifiers notify the system administrator. The system re-executes protocol of generating update shares and protocol of generating update sequence.

Protocol of the Share Update

1) U_r creates a set G for any shadow share $s_r^t (1 \le t \le m)$. Elements in G are composed of subscript positions with all bits of 1 in the shared random sequence $K^t (1 \le t \le m)$.
2) U_r updates the share s_r^t it holds. $s_r^{t}\text{'} = s_r^t + \sum_j g_r^j (j \in G)$.
3) U_r deletes old share s_r^t and the corresponding G and K^t.
4) This process is repeated until all m shares of U_r are updated.

3.4 Verification of Shadow Shares

In order to periodically verify the integrity of the distributed storage of multi-secrets, verifiers $B_1, B_2, \ldots, B_l$ perform the following scheme every time period T_2 to verify whether the shares are correct.

Protocol of the Secret Integrity Verification

1) Verifiers $B_1, B_2, \ldots, B_l$ randomly select a verification sequence $V \subset S$ from the secret S. The length of the verification sequence V needs to be statistically guaranteed to ensure that the error rate of the secret S is below 1%.
2) $B_1, B_2, \ldots, B_l$ send a share verification notice to cloud storage service providers.
3) Every cloud service provider U_r performs $M_r = \sum s_r^t (t \in V)$.
4) U_r sends M_r and $SIG_r(M_r)$ to verifiers $B_1, B_2, \ldots, B_l$.
5) $B_1, B_2, \ldots, B_l$ receive the set $M_r = \{M_1, \ M_2, \ \ldots, \ M_n\}$ and verify whether the signature is correct.
6) $B_1, B_2, \ldots, B_l$ randomly select k of them for secret recovery. $B_1, B_2, \ldots, B_l$ combine them several times and verify whether combination results are equal.
7) If combination results are not equal, verifiers notify the system administrator.

4 Project Analysis

4.1 Feasibility Analysis of the Scheme

This paper proposes an efficient PSS scheme for cloud storage. The feasibility analysis are as follows.

The traditional SS algorithm based on finite field has high computational cost when the data amount is large, so it is not suitable for processing large data. However, in this paper, according to splitting the larger secret data S, participants calculate a few of multi-secrets at a time, thereby reducing the cost of computing for sharing and recovery.

In addition, the communication cost of the traditional PSS scheme is relatively high. In this paper, shareholders don't communicate directly. Though the trusted third party A and verifiers $B_1, B_2, \ldots, B_l$ to complete the update and verification of the scheme, reducing the communication cost of the scheme.

In the aspect of integrity verification, verifiers $B_1, B_2, \ldots, B_l$ put forward the integrity verification request for cloud storage providers by a probabilistic sampling method. The integrity of secret data can be verified only by calculating, restoring and comparing part of the share information. Its feasibility and correctness are described in detail in [18].

4.2 Security Analysis of the Scheme

In this scheme, the information available to the adversary includes public information (threshold and total number of cloud providers) and secret information (secret share and two pairs of public and private keys of the service provider) when the service provider is corrupted. In addition, with regard to the behavior of adversary, the corrupted server may not perform protocol actions and maliciously destroy the protocol. It may also perform protocol actions, but secretly spy on protocol execution. In this section we prove that the scheme has the following three properties.

Theorem 1. *In a time period T_1, when the number of service providers are corrupted is less than k, the adversary can't destroy secret S or obtain any information about secret S.*

Proof. Suppose that the adversary can read or change the share stored in the corrupted cloud service provider U_r. Due to the limitation of secret sharing (k, n) threshold scheme, in a time period T_1, if the number of service providers attacked by the adversary maliciously is less than k, the adversary can't learn any information about secret S.

Theorem 2. *In a time period T_1, if trusted third party A is corrupted by the adversary, the adversary can't destroy secret S or obtain any information about secret S.*

Proof. If the controlled trusted third party A wants to destroy the execution of the protocol, there are the following means: Constructing a random polynomial $f(x)$ of $a_0 \neq 0$ at the stage of executing protocol of generating update shares; In protocol of generating update sequence, VSS_r and $SIG_r(VSS_r)$ sent by one or more service providers are tampered with. For the first possibility, protocol of the update share verification will find the exception, so that the exception of A can be found. For the second possibility, since A can't obtain the private key used by the service provider U_r for signature, it cannot produce $SIG_r(VSS_r)$ that matches the tampered VSS_r. Therefore, in step 4 of Protocol of generating update sequence, by verifying the signature of VSS_r, the adversary will also be cleared due to exposure.

Theorem 3. *In a time period T_1, the number of verifiers is corrupted is less than l, the adversary can't destroy secret S or obtain any information about secret S.*

Proof. If the controlled verifier B wants to destroy the execution of the protocol, there are the following means: in protocol of the update share verification and protocol of the secret integrity verification, the verifier B sends the wrong verification results; After receiving the share set to be verified, the secret record share is extrapolated to some secret S after enough time. For the first possibility, the scheme designs multiple verifiers B. In a time period T_2, as long as the adversary fails to break all verifiers B, the system can't be misled with the wrong share of the verification results. For the second possibility, some random sub-fragments (without secret information, similar to multi-secret) can be inserted into the original secret . It is required that the verification sequence generated by at each verification must contain a random sub-fragment, and each random sub-fragment can only be used once.

However, when an adversary breaks the trusted third party and one or more cloud service providers at the same time, the security of the share update may be affected to a certain extent. We can use a hardware-based trusted execution environment to defend it. In recent years, hardware security technologies with processor security as the core have competed in development. A wide range of mainstream technologies include virtualization technologies such as Intel VT and AMD SVM technologies, and trusted computing technologies (TPM) based on trusted platform modules such as Intel TXT, etc. In 2013, Intel launched software guard extensions (SGX), which aims to make hardware security mandatory. It doesn't depend on the security status of firmware and software. SGX allows the application to define a secure code and data area, which can maintain its confidentiality. Even if an adversary can physically control the platform and directly attack the memory, it also can be effectively defended.

4.3 Summary of the Scheme Advantages

The advantages of this paper are summarized as follows:

1) By splitting the secret data , only one or more multi-secrets are calculated each time, which reduces the computational overhead of the system;
2) By setting up trusted third party and verifiers , the communication interaction cost between cloud storage service providers is reduced while meeting the system security;
3) Meeting long-term security needs;
4) Support long-term data integrity verification;
5) Suitable for storing large-scale confidential data.

5 Conclusions

An efficient proactive secret sharing scheme for the cloud storage proposed in this paper. The scheme divides the secret of large amount of data into multi-secrets, and uses secret sharing to make multi-secrets meet the security of the threshold scheme. The scheme periodically updates and verifies the shadow shares held by cloud service providers. In this way, an adversary can recover the secret if and only if it captures at least shares during a period of update rather than any time. The scheme only calculates a few of multi-secrets at a time, which reduces the computational cost of the system. The scheme takes into account the long-term security issues and processing performance of the system, which can effectively protect the confidentiality and integrity of data, and can also be used to prove the integrity of remote data.

References

1. Ateniese, G., et al.: Remote data checking using provable data possession. ACM Trans. Inf. Syst. Secur. (TISSEC) **14**, 1–34 (2011)
2. Shamir, A.: How to share a secret. Commun. ACM **22**, 612–613 (1979)
3. Blakley, G.R.: Safeguarding cryptographic keys. In: International Workshop on Managing Requirements Knowledge, vol. 313. IEEE Computer Society (1979)
4. Mignotte, M.: How to share a secret. In: Beth, Thomas (ed.) EUROCRYPT 1982. LNCS, vol. 149, pp. 371–375. Springer, Heidelberg (1983). https://doi.org/10.1007/3-540-39466-4_27
5. Asmuth, C., Bloom, J.: A modular approach to key safeguarding. IEEE Trans. Inf. Theor. (1983)
6. Harn, L., Fuyou, M., Chang, C.C.: Verifiable secret sharing based on the Chinese remainder theorem. Secur. Commun. Netw. **7**, 950–957 (2014)

7. Chor, B., Goldwasser, S., Micali, S., Awerbuch, B.: Verifiable secret sharing and achieving simultaneous broadcast. In: Proceedings of the 26th Symposium on Foundations of Computer Science, pp. 335–344 (1985)
8. Feldman, P.: A practical scheme for non-interactive verifiable secret sharing, pp. 427–438. IEEE (1987)
9. Pedersen, T.P.: Non-interactive and information-theoretic secure verifiable secret sharing. In: Feigenbaum, J. (ed.) Annual International Cryptology Conference, pp. 129–140. Springer, Heidelberg (1991). https://doi.org/10.1007/3-540-46766-1_9
10. Kaya, K., Selçuk, A.A.: A verifiable secret sharing scheme based on the chinese remainder theorem. In: Chowdhury, D.R., Rijmen, V., Das, A. (eds.) International Conference on Cryptology in India, pp. 414–425. Springer, Heidelberg (2008). https://doi.org/10.1007/978-3-540-89754-5_32
11. Ostrovsky, R., Yung, M.: How to withstand mobile virus attacks. In: Proceedings of the Tenth Annual ACM Symposium on Principles of Distributed Computing, pp. 51–59 (1991)
12. Herzberg, A., Jarecki, S., Krawczyk, H., Yung, M.: Proactive secret sharing or: how to cope with perpetual leakage. In: Coppersmith, D. (ed.) CRYPTO 1995. LNCS, vol. 963, pp. 339–352. Springer, Heidelberg (1995). https://doi.org/10.1007/3-540-44750-4_27
13. Feng, B., Guo, C., Li, M., Wang, Z.: A novel proactive multi-secret sharing scheme. IJ Netw. Secur. **17**, 123–128 (2015)
14. Zou, H., Jiandong, Y.U.: Multilevel threshold multi-secret sharing scheme with proactive security: multilevel threshold multi-secret sharing scheme with proactive security. J. Comput. Appl. **29**, 2218–2219 (2009)
15. Zhou, L., Schneider, F.B., Van Renesse, R.: APSS: Proactive secret sharing in asynchronous systems. ACM Trans. Inf. Syst. Secur. (TISSEC) **8**, 259–286 (2005)
16. Schultz, D., Liskov, B., Liskov, M.: MPSS: mobile proactive secret sharing. ACM Trans. Inf. Syst. Secur. (TISSEC) **13**, 1–32 (2010)
17. Qin, H., Dai, Y.: Proactive quantum secret sharing. Quantum Inf. Process. **14**(11), 4237–4244 (2015). https://doi.org/10.1007/s11128-015-1106-x
18. Chen, S.S., Donoho, D.L., Saunders, M.A.: Atomic decomposition by basis pursuit. SIAM REV **43**, 129–159 (2001)
19. Fan, Y., Lin, X., Tan, G., Zhang, Y., Dong, W., Lei, J.: One secure data integrity verification scheme for cloud storage. Futur. Gener. Comput. Syst. **96**, 376–385 (2019)
20. Shacham, H., Waters, B.: Compact proofs of retrievability. In: Pieprzyk, J. (ed.) International Conference on the Theory and Application of Cryptology and Information Security, pp. 90–107. Springer, Heidelberg (2008). https://doi.org/10.1007/978-3-540-89255-7_7
21. Harn, L., Hsu, C., Xia, Z., Zhou, J.: How to share secret efficiently over networks. Secur. Commun. Netw. **2017** (2017)
22. Harn, L., Xia, Z., Hsu, C., Liu, Y.: Secret sharing with secure secret reconstruction. Inform. Sci. **519**, 1–8 (2020)
23. Dehkordi, M.H., Mashhadi, S., Oraei, H.: A proactive multi stage secret sharing scheme for any given access structure. Wireless Pers. Commun. **104**, 491–503 (2019)
24. Maram, S.K.D., et al.: CHURP: dynamic-committee proactive secret sharing. In: Proceedings of the 2019 ACM SIGSAC Conference on Computer and Communications Security, pp. 2369–2386 (2019)
25. Qiu, S., Wang, D., Xu, G., Kumari, S.: Practical and provably secure three-factor authentication protocol based on extended chaotic-maps for mobile lightweight devices. IEEE T Depend. Secur. (2020)
26. Wang, D., Wang, P.: Two birds with one stone: two-factor authentication with security beyond conventional bound. IEEE Trans. Depend. Secur. Comput. **1** (2016)

PoliCT: Flexible Policy in Certificate Transparency Enabling Lightweight Self-monitor

Aozhuo Sun[1,2,3], Bingyu Li[4], Huiqing Wan[1,2,3], and Qiongxiao Wang[1,2,3(✉)]

[1] State Key Laboratory of Information Security, Institute of Information Engineering, Chinese Academy of Sciences, Beijing 100093, China
{sunaozhuo,wanhuiqing,wangqiongxiao}@iie.ac.cn

[2] Data Assurance and Communications Security Center, Chinese Academy of Sciences, Beijing 100093, China

[3] School of Cyber Security, University of Chinese Academy of Sciences, Beijing 100049, China

[4] School of Cyber Science and Technology, Beihang University, Beijing 100191, China
libingyu@buaa.edu.cn

Abstract. Certificate Transparency (CT) is proposed to detect maliciously or mistakenly issued certificates by recording all certificates in publicly-visible logs. CT assumes that any individual can undertake the role of a CT monitor which fetches all the certificates in the logs and discovers suspicious ones from them. However, studies in recent years shows that ordinary individuals have to pay an unbearable price to operate a monitor by themselves, which makes the originally distributed trust be concentrated on several third-party monitors. Unfortunately, some researches indicate that problems of timeliness, security, and reliability exist in third-party monitors. In this paper, we propose the PoliCT, a flexible and customizable certificate transparency management solution where domain owners can designate how their certificates should be submitted and validated. It enables domain owners (*a*) to release their CT policies to monitor a few logs purposefully, thereby greatly reducing monitoring costs; (*b*) to demand more SCTs to increase the transparency of their certificates. After that, we discuss the design of a reliable lightweight self-monitor in detail. Expectably, the actual data collection and the theoretical analysis of the prototype system show that PoliCT enables a common individual to maintain its CT policies with negligible overhead, and significantly improves the performance of monitoring service.

Keywords: PKI · Certificate transparency · Monitor · Fraudulent certificate

This work was supported in part by the National Natural Science Foundation of China under Grant 62002011, in part by the National Key Research and Development Program of China under Grant 2018YFB0804600, and in part by the Open Project of State Key Laboratory of Information Security, Institute of Information Engineering, Chinese Academy of Sciences, under Grant 2020-ZD-05.

J. Zhou et al. (Eds.): ACNS 2021 Workshops, LNCS 12809, pp. 358–377, 2021.
https://doi.org/10.1007/978-3-030-81645-2_21

1 Introduction

Public key infrastructure (PKI) has been maturely applied to network identity authentication. Its effectiveness is based on the absolute trust in the certification authorities (CAs). However, lots of researches [2,9,16,22,34,43,65] have disclosed that some CAs have issued fraudulent TLS certificates now and then, which greatly reduces the security and credibility of PKI. Worse still, certificates bind a public cryptographic key to a domain name, and if a CA maliciously or mistakenly issues a fraudulent certificate for a social or financial website, this can lead to users' privacy leakage and even significant property loss. In order to detect fraudulent certificates and strengthen the supervision of CAs, Google proposed the Certificate Transparency (CT) framework [28,37] in 2013.

Compared with the traditional PKI, log server, auditor and monitor are introduced into CT framework. *Log server* provides publicly-auditable, append-only logs to record all issued certificates. The logs are publicly auditable so that it is possible for anyone to verify the correctness of each log and to monitor when new certificates are added to the logs [37]. *Monitor* watches for that if there are suspicious certificates existing in logs. Additionally, users can query or discover the certificate of interest through the monitor. *Auditor* supervises the correct operation of the log server to ensure that all submitted certificates are recorded in logs and are publicly visible.

CT has become the most widely used trust enhancement scheme of PKI. A research [58] shows that 63.2% of HTTPS links support CT on February 1, 2018, and this proportion is still rising. Specifically, the four browers with the highest market share, including Chrome [23], Apple Platform [4], Mozilla Firefox [44], Microsoft Edge, all support CT directly or in the form of plug-ins. As of January 20, 2021, there has been 103 log servers [27] in total in the world with more than 4.2 billion certificates [28]. A large number of well-known organizations currently also provide a monitor and/or an auditor service, namely Censys [61], Cert Spotter [49], crt.sh [8], CT-Observatory [12], Entrust [17], Facebook Monitor [18], Google Monitor [26], Hardenize [31], Report URI [50], etc.

The security of CT is not affected by a single point failure in a certain component. Any error in any component can be discovered by the audit mechanism or eliminated by the distributed design. The original design of CT is that any individual can run its own monitor. However, a recent study [40] shows that it is costly and impractical for ordinary domain owners to act as CT monitors by themselves. Therefore, a more practical solution is to rely on third-party monitors maintaining a complete copy of all the certificates recorded in the public logs, which centralizes the trust that should be dispersed. But according to the survey [38,40], the third-party monitors have defects in reliability, security and timeliness. For example, monitors sometimes cannot return complete certificates for all queries, and some of them even use insecure communication connections. Therefore, the current status of centralized trust in CT is a serious shortcoming especially for those who cannot operate the CT monitor by themselves.

As of October 2018, there were over 2.87 billion certificates in 88 public log servers and the daily growth of the certificate entries was 6 M at that time. This means that a monitor has to fetch and process 30 GB of data per day at least, which is a huge consumption of network bandwidth and storage. And the growth rate of certificates in logs still continues to accelerate, because of (*a*) the popularity of CT; (*b*) the lifetime of SSL/TLS certificates being no longer than 13 months (397 days) [46]; and (*c*) the success of Let's Encrypt [1]. From January 20 to 25, 2021, the average daily increase in the number of certificates in logs is 11 million [26], nearly twice as that of 2018. In addition, the idea of CT in the future may be applied in more fields, such as the Internet of Things (IOT) which has a larger number of certificates, making it more expensive to operate a monitor.

For another, both Google [23] and Apple [4] discuss their respective CT policies. They have different policies for certificates with different lifetimes. The longer the lifetime of a certificate is, the more SCTs from distinct logs are required. It can be seen that it is necessary to formulate unique policies for different security requirements. However, domain owners have little control over how their certificates are submitted and verified. They cannot specify any criteria of their own that the SCTs of their certificates must fulfill. If a domain owner can designate how browsers verify the SCTs of its certificate, then it can monitor the CT logs in a targeted manner, and even the number of SCTs can be requested to increase to enhance the security and transparency of the certificate.

As a result, a flexible and customizable certificate transparency management scheme is highly advantageous. This paper proposes a scheme called PoliCT, which allows domain owners to independently control the CT verification policy (CVP). Moreover, this scheme makes it cost-effective to run a self-monitor, because domain owners only need to monitor a small amount of logs which are specified in the CVP. We also discuss the specific format of CVP and how it should be submitted, distributed, and revoked.

Besides, we design a lightweight self-monitor based on CVP which can be operated by an ordinary domain owner. This self-monitor consumes very few resources, because it (*a*) only needs to monitor a small number of logs to ensure monitoring integrity; and (*b*) only stores a small amount of certificates interested.

Finally, we conducted a theoretical evaluation of PoliCT. The analysis shows that the scheme can help individuals run the self-monitor at less overhead. In addition, any single point of failure will not affect its correct operation. What's more, we actually tracked the data in the logs from January 20 to 25, 2021, and analyzed the monitoring cost produced by our scheme, finding that PoliCT can reduce the cost by tens of thousands of times at most. In conclusion, our scheme is lightweight, secure and workable.

In summary, the contributions of this paper are as follows: (*a*) we design a CT component with customizable policies for domain owners, which allows them to independently control the verification policy of SCTs in certificates according to their security and performance requirements; (*b*) we design a lightweight self-monitor scheme, with small network, storage, and computing consumption, which can be run locally by any individual.

The rest of this paper is organized as follows. Section 2 introduces the CT framework. We illustrate the design idea of PoliCT in Sect. 3, and describe the specific design of a lightweight self-monitor in Sect. 4, followed by a theoretical evaluation in Sect. 5. We discuss the related work in Sect. 6 and conclude the paper in Sect. 7.

2 Certificate Transparency

The CT framework [28,37], proposed by Google, works for a wider ecosystem, Web Public Key Infrastructure, which incorporates everything necessary to issue and verify certificates used for TLS on the web. More importantly, CT can record all the certificates issued by CAs in publicly-auditable and append-only logs and provide a signed certificate timestamp (SCT) for every certificate submitted to the logs, indicating that the certificate has been logged. Meanwhile, any party can monitor the logs to see if there are any suspicious or fraudulent certificates existing. Comparing to the traditional PKI system, CT mainly introduces three new components, including *log server*, *monitor* and *auditor*, as shown in Fig. 1. And all the components in CT can work together to ensure the correct behaviors of each other, especially the CAs and log servers.

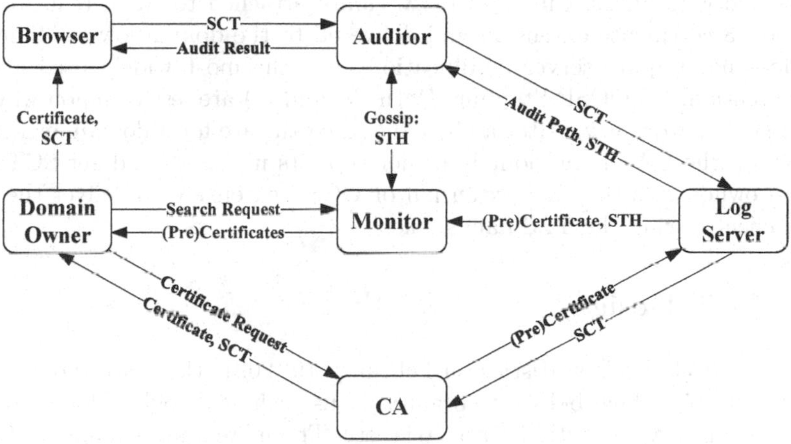

Fig. 1. The framework of certificate transparency

Log Server. A log server is to record all the CA-issued certificates in a publicly-auditable and append-only log. Anyone can submit a certificate to a log and get an SCT from the log as a promise that the certificate has been submitted to it. Since the logs are distributed and independent, any party of interest can query them to see which CAs have issued which certificates, when, and for which domains. Besides, because the logs is append-only, which is achieved by recording the certificates in a Merkle hash tree and signing the root node by the log server periodically, called the signed tree head (STH), they are verifiable by the monitors.

Monitor. Monitors are publicly run servers to watch for that if there are certificates mistakenly or maliciously issued by CAs in the logs. A monitor usually keeps a complete copy of records in each log it supervises, decodes and checks certificates of interest. Although anyone can run a monitor according to the original design of CT, it is common that some monitors are run by large-scale companies or organizations, such as Google, banks or governments. Other monitors may be run as subscription services for domain owners and certificate authorities. An individual with sufficient skills and capabilities can also run his own monitor.

Auditor. Auditors are used to ensure whether the log servers works normally. Specifically, they compare two STHs of the logs to confirm that the logs are append-only and validate the audit path to make sure every SCT has a corresponding record in the logs. Generally, auditors can act as a standalone service, or an additional function of a monitor or an integral component of a TLS client.

As for the delivery of SCTs, there are three methods provided at present [37]. (a) X.509v3 certificate extension. In this method, upon receiving a certificate request for a domain owner, CA checks the request and creates a pre-certificate, which contains all the information a final certificate does but has a poison extension so that user agents won't accept it. Then, the CA submits the pre-certificate to logs and gets SCTs. Finally, the SCTs are attached to the certificate using an X.509v3 certificate extension and delivered to the domain owner. Since this way does not require server modification, it is the most widely used one. (b) TLS extension. (c) OCSP Stapling. Both (b) and (c) are less common ways and have a similar workflow. After a CA issues a certificate for a domain owner(e.g., a website), the CA or the domain owner submits it to logs and get SCTs. The domain owner uses the TLS extension or OCSP extension to deliver the SCTs to the client during the TLS handshake.

3 PoliCT Design

According to Google's statistics on February 19, 2021, there are a total of 103 known logs [27], which belong to organizations such as Google, Cloudflare, DigiCert, Let's Encrypt, Sectigo, TrustAsia, etc. There are a large number of duplicated certificates in public logs, since each certificate is required to be submitted to multiple logs [4,24,40]. From January 20 to 25, 2021, the average amount of certificates issued per day is nearly 4.64 M [7], while the amount of increase in certificate items in logs is nearly 11 M [26]. Due to the randomness in submitting to logs, monitors have to supervise numerous logs and download massive certificates, avoiding omission for fraudulent certificates. This places an unacceptable burden on ordinary individuals who want to act as a CT monitor.

In addition, both Google [23] and Apple [4] discussed their CT policies respectively. Google requires that there are at least 2 SCTs in a certificate and the one is from a Google-operated log and the other is from a Non-Google-operated log. While Apple's policy requires at least 2 SCTs issued from a CT log – once-approved or currently approved at the time of check. In addition, they also have different policies for certificates with different lifetimes. The longer the lifetime of a certificate is, the more SCTs from distinct logs are required. The different CT policies of various organizations bring several security risks to the management and monitoring of certificates. For example, a certificate that provides two SCTs issued by Non-Google-operated logs from different organizations can be trusted by the Apple platform, but it will be missed by Entrust, a third-party monitor that only monitors the Google-operated logs in our ongoing research. It turns out that it is necessary for CT to adapt to multiple customizable policies to meet diverse security and monitoring requirements.

In consideration of the above two aspects, we design a scheme in which the CT policy can be customized according to the domain owner's need. A domain owner can require its certificates to provide more SCTs to improve security, and it can also demand that its certificates must provide an SCT from a specific log to reduce monitoring costs. For this we customize a new data structure, called *CT verification policy* (CVP), which is used to designate the browser's verification policy for SCTs. Next, we mainly design how the domain owner distributes, revokes and submits the CVP. And the specific data structure is also defined.

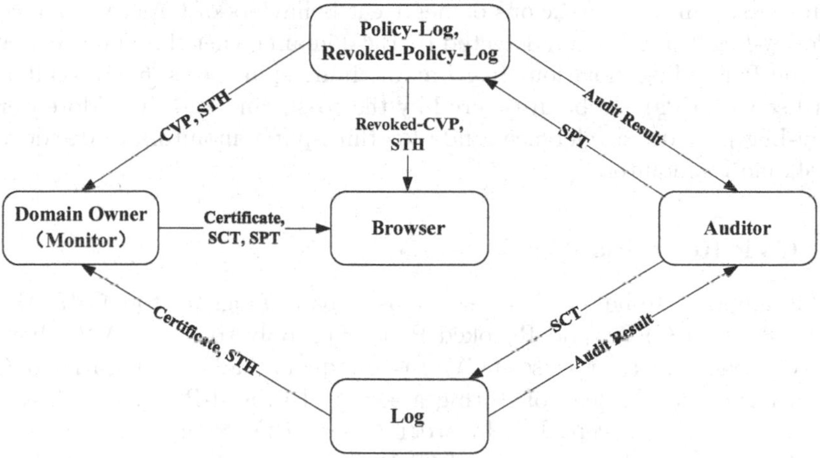

Fig. 2. Overview of how to distribute and revoke CVPs

Challenge. Like certificate distribution, CVP also faces various problems and challenges in the delivery process. In addition, it also faces the attack of malicious forging fraudulent CVP by the attacker, so it is necessary to establish a CVP revocation and verification mechanism, and overcome various defects and challenges in the existing certificate revocation mechanism, such as privacy leakage, inefficiency and so on [10,15,41,52]. Finally, in addition to ensuring security and availability, the design of the scheme also needs to consider time delay, false negatives/positives, error recoverability, and deployability.

3.1 CVP Distribution

In order to store CVPs auditably, we design a new public log called Policy-Log, as shown in Fig. 2. The Policy-Log uses a Merkle hash tree to ensure that the data cannot be tampered with and is convenient for effective auditing. When a valid CVP is submitted to the Policy-Log, Policy-Log must immediately returns a Signed Policy Timestamp (SPT). The SPT is the promise to incorporate the CVP in the Merkle tree within the MMD. And SPTs can be embedded in a TLS extension or an X.509v3 certificate extension to be distributed to the browser. Since the design of Policy-Log and SPT are similar to that of CT log and SCT [37] respectively, the Policy-Log can piggyback on CT's existing gossip-audit security mode.

The CVP is designed to be defined only by the domain owner, and it can be submitted by the domain owner itself or by CAs on behalf of the domain owner. Therefore, Policy-Log maintains a list of trusted CAs and only accepts CVPs signed by a valid domain certificate or a trusted CA certificate. For example, a CVP on domain "example.com" needs to be signed by a certificate of "example.com" (or a trusted CA certificate) before it can be accepted. This effectively prevents the logs from being flooded with fraudulent or invalid CVPs.

In our scheme, the malicious or negligent behaviors of CAs can be recorded by Policy-Log/CT Logs and detected by the domain owner through the monitor. And the Policy-Log violations (e.g., maintaining split-views [6,47], omitting to record some CVPs) can be discovered by the gossip and auditing. Moreover, the Policy-Log provides a reference guide for third-party monitors to decide which logs should be monitored.

3.2 CVP Revocation

CVP is supposed to be revocable, so we use a pair of logs to store CVPs, Policy-Log to store all CVPs, and Revoked-Policy-Log only to store CVPs that have been revoked. Since the release of CVPs is infrequent, and the revocation of CVPs is even rarer, the overhead of storing a copy of Revoked-Policy-Log directly on the browser side is acceptable. In order to save the storage space as much as possible, the detailed information of CVPs is not stored in the Revoked-Policy-Log, but only the fingerprint is stored. And Revoked-Policy-Log is designed to be sharded annually like some CT logs (e.g., the log server "Google Argon 2021" only accepts certificates that are valid until 2021 [63]), which prevents the size of Revoked-Policy-Log from increasing all the time.

When a domain owner detects a fraudulent CVP, or wants to update a CVP, the present CVP need to be revoked. The domain owner initiates a revocation request to Policy-Log, specifies the CVP to be revoked, and signs the request with a valid domain certificate. After receiving the request, Policy-Log verifies (a) the validity of the signature; (b) whether the CVP really exists. If the verification is successful, Policy-Log submits the fingerprint of the CVP to Revoked-Policy-Log. Revoked-Policy-Log merges it into the Merkle tree within the MMD.

For a browser, when it receives a certificate, it verifies (1) the validity of the certificate (chain); (2) the validity of the SCTs one by one; (2) the signature and revocation of the SPT, and (3) whether the SCTs provided complies with the SPT. A certificate that is successfully verified is accepted by the browser.

3.3 CVP Submission

This scheme requires mandatory SPT validation for all certificates. If the SPT validation is not compulsory, which means a certificate without SPT can still be trusted, an attacker can completely ignore this scheme. As a result, this section designs two ways to submit CVP, as shown in Fig. 3: (*a*) submitted by domain owner; and (*b*) submitted by CA.

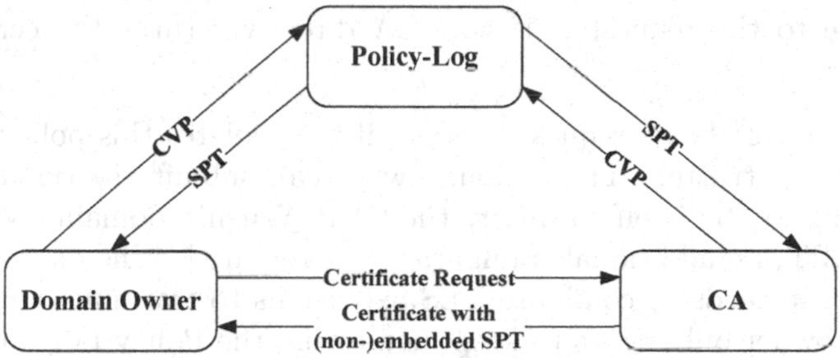

Fig. 3. Overview of CVP submission

Submitted by Domain Owner. A domain owner can submit a CVP to Policy-Log to create its policy. The specific process is as follows:

1) The domain owner customizes a CVP;
2) The domain owner encodes and signs the CVP in a standard format;
3) The domain owner submits the CVP to Policy-Log, and obtains an SPT;
4) The domain owner submits certificates to the corresponding logs according to the CVP;

Submitted by CA. We can't expect all domain owners to submit CVPs to the Policy-Logs in accordance with our scheme. Therefore, it is necessary for CAs to check/submit a CVP for each issued certificate. CAs should store a copy of Policy-Log and Revoked-Policy-Log locally, aiming to search CVPs of requesters. During the certificate request process, CA first confirms the CVP of the domain requested. If there is a valid CVP, CA will issue a certificate and submit it to the corresponding logs according to the CVP; if not, CA will demand the requester to formulate a CVP, and then issue the certificate. Finally, CA returns a certificate with an SPT embedded or not. Since there is a pre-certificate design in CT, it is convenient to embed an SPT. For example, when a requester wants to apply for a certificate of "a.b.c.example.com" :

1) CA asks the requester for an SPT;
2) If the requester provides a valid SPT, go to step 6. Otherwise, CA queries the valid CVP of "a.b.c.example.com", and if it fails, the same query for "b.c.example.com", the "c.example.com", etc. until reaching the eTLD [45] or a match is found. When more than one is found, the newest one is selected;
3) If any CVP is found, go to step 6. Otherwise, CA initiates a selection: (*a*) General CVP (two SCTs, one is from a Google-operated log, the other is from a Non-Google-operated log); (*d*) Customized CVP (the requester determines the number of SCTs and the policy of each SCT);
4) CA encodes and signs it in a standard format;
5) CA submits the CVP to Policy-Log, and obtains an SPT;
6) CA submits the certificate to the corresponding logs according to the CVP;
7) CA asks the requester about whether to embed SPT into the certificate;
8) If it is embedded, CA embeds the SPT into the certificate and returns the certificate to the requester; if not, CA directly returns the certificate and SPT;

During the certificate request process, if CA violates this policy, the certificate will not be trusted. The domain owner can submit the certificate to the corresponding log by itself to satisfy the CVP. When a domain owner uses the embedded SPT, no additional configuration is required. When a non-embedded SPT is used, it needs to configure TLS extensions to transmit the SPT. Then, the domain owner only needs to keep monitoring the Policy-Log and a few logs specified, and once a fraudulent certificate/SPV is found, it will take revocation or other measures to deal with this problem.

3.4 Data Format

CVP. The CVP mainly includes the domain name to be protected and specific policies, which consist of the expected number of SCTs and the specific restrictions. The remaining basic information is used to help update the CVP format, limit its validity period, and protect its integrity. The structure of CVP is as follows:

```
struct {
    Version               cvp_version;
    uint64                not_before;
    uint64                not_after;
    list<Domain>          domain_list;
    int                   sct_quantity;
    list<Policy>          policy_list(sct_quantity);
    HashAlgorithm         hash_algorithm;
    SignatureAlgorithm    saignature_algorithm;
    SignatureValue        signature_value;
} CTVerificationPolicy
```

Domain is the domain name to which the CVP restricts. It can be with or without wildcards. If it does not contain wildcards, the CVP demands any certificate to bind to (*a*) the domain name; or (*b*) the parent domain with wildcard.

If it has a wildcard, the CVP demands any certificate to bind to (*a*) the domain name; (*b*) the parent domain with wildcard; or (*c*) any subdomain name with wildcard or not. ***domain_list*** is a series of ***Domain***, which allows one CVP to restrict multiple domains.

sct_quantity is the number of SCTs in the certificate required by the domain owner. ***Policy*** is a restriction on SCT, which has three types: (*a*) "All", means all logs; (*b*) one or more *Log Names* separated by ';', indicating that the SCT should belong to one of these logs; (*c*) one or more *Log Names* separated by ';' after a '^', indicating that the SCT cannot belong to any of these logs. The ***Log Name*** can be (*a*) the name of a specific log, such as "Google Rocketeer", "Cloudflare Nimbus 2020"; (*b*) a log name with a wildcard instead of the specific year such as "Google Xenon*" which represents "Google Xenon" logs of all years including "Google Xenon 2018", "Google Xenon 2019", "Google Xenon 2020", etc.; or (*c*) an organization name with a wildcard, such as "DigiCert*" which represents all DigiCert-operated logs.

SPT. The SPT mainly refers to the structural design of SCT [37], replacing (pre)certificate with CVP, which makes it compatible with existing audit mechanisms. The structure of SPT is as follows:

```
struct {
    Version                  spt_version;
    LogID                    id;
    uint64                   timestamp;
    CVP                      cvp;
    HashAlgorithm            hash_algorithm;
    SignatureAlgorithm       saignature_algorithm;
    SignatureValue           signature_value;
} SignedPolicyTimestamp
```

4 Light-Weight Self-monitor

In the CT with customizable policies, domain owners can greatly reduce the cost of monitoring work through CVP. In this section, we discuss how to run a lightweight self-monitor in detail.

There is currently no standard specifying how to build a CT monitor. Therefore, we investigate the standard document [37], third-party monitors service and source code of crt.sh and Cert Spotter [11,55], and summarize the necessary steps for building CT monitors, as shown in Fig. 4: (1) select a set of logs based on CT policy or requirements and fetch certificates from them; (2) parse certificates and extract the domainNames, referring to all items related to domain name in the certificate, including CN and dNSNames; (3) match certificates according to the domains input/preset.

Based on the above approach, we design a lightweight self-monitor from the following three improvement points: (1) obtaining complete data from as few

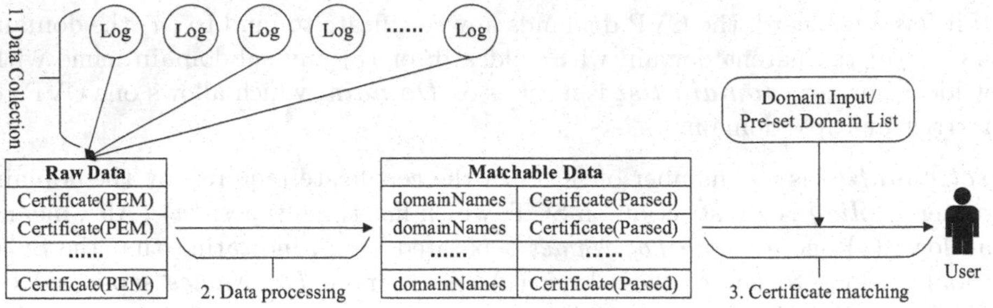

Fig. 4. The workflow of a CT self-monitor

logs as possible; (2) processing data with the simple and error-free method; and (3) matching certificates with preset domains, and only storing the matched certificates.

The purpose of monitoring is to discover certificates interested. Meanwhile, we define a certificate interested (or related certificate) to refer to any certificate that binds the domain interested (or related domain), including (*a*) the domain (i.e., "sub.example.com"); (*b*) any subdomain with wildcard or not (i.e., "a.sub.example.com", "*.sub.example.com", etc.); and (*c*) the wildcard domain of its parent domain (i.e., "*.example.com").

4.1 Targeted Monitoring

The domain owner can use the CVP to designate the browser's verification policy for its related certificate, which means that the certificates must be submitted to certain specific logs before it can be trusted. Therefore, as long as the domain owner monitors the logs designated in a targeted manner, it can find all the fraudulent certificates interested. For example, an owner of "example.com" defines a CVP with *policy_list* as {"Google*", "Sectigo Sabre; DigiCert Nessie"}, which means that the related certificate of "example.com" must provide two SCTs, one from Google-operated logs and the other from "Sectigo Sabre" or "DigiCert Nessie". Therefore, it only needs to monitor "Sectigo Sabre" and "DigiCert Nessie".

4.2 Lazy Parsing

The public log is flooded with a large number of nonconformant certificates, because the coding standards of the certificates are complex and hard-to-follow. Most parsers cannot parse all certificates correctly. For example, due to the extremely strict standards conformance, any substandard content can possibly lead to the failure of parsing certificate by Go's parser. In addition, the parser from Google's Certificate Transparency library [25] which treats several of the most common encoding errors as warnings, can still fail to parse some certificates.

Fortunately, Cert Sportter considered this problem and they designed the *Lazy Parsing* [54]. The Lazy Parsing parses different parts of the certificate separately, so that an error in one part of the certificate does not affect the ability to parse the rest of the certificate. In actual situations, the Lazy Parsing performs very well. Therefore, we design to use the lazy parsing to parse certificates. A certificate consists of many information of varying importance. The most important information for a monitor is the domainNames, which tells us who may be interested in the certificate. Therefore, the Lazy Parsing we use only parses the part of domainNames. When a certificate of interest is discovered, the rest part of it can be parsed or not. Of course, the method of parsing the certificates is not limited to this, and the operator of the self-monitor can define its own parser.

4.3 Subscription Service

There are two kinds of working modes of the monitor: search mode and subscription mode. In search mode, when a domain (or a fingerprint) is input, the monitor searches and returns the result, so the complete copy of logs have to be stored locally; while in subscription mode, the monitor will prompt the user when it discovers a matched certificate with a preset domain list, which makes it unnecessary to store all the certificates. Now that millions of certificates are issued every day, we select a subscription service to reduces the huge overhead brought by storing a complete copy.

Specifically, the user presets a list of domains which will be monitored. Then, for some specific logs, the monitor periodically (1) fetches the current STH; (2) verifies the signature of current STH; (3) fetches all certificates in the Merkle tree corresponding to the STH; (4) extracts the domainNames from each certificate; (5) determines whether any domainName extracted is a domain interested; (6) adds the processed certificates (including the interested and uninterested certificates) to a temporary list; (7) confirms that the Merkle tree made from the list produces the same hash as that in the STH, to ensure that no certificates are missed.

5 Theoretical Evaluation

5.1 Feasibility Analysis

The PoliCT is designed to be secure, reliable and workable. Specifically, this scheme decentralizes the current centralized trust in several third-party monitors. Moreover, if there is an error in the added Policy-Log, its error will be discovered by the auditor.

In addition, our scheme enables ordinary individuals to run a self-monitor, and its performance requirements are diminutive. A domain owner uses the CVP to designate the browser's verification policy for SCTs, and continuously monitor the Policy-Log and logs specified.

Further, if an attacker wants to avoid the monitoring of the domain owner, it means that the SCTs provided to the browser do not meet the CVP, and the certificate will not be trusted. If the attacker can provide SCTs that comply with the CVP, then the fraudulent certificate must appear in logs specified by the domain owner, so it will inevitably be discovered. The attacker may also create a fraudulent CVP to make SCTs meet requirements and avoid surveillance, which can still be discovered by the domain owner who monitors Policy-Log. What's more, the malicious or negligent behavior of CAs can also be discovered just like an attacker. Even if CA does not issue the certificate in accordance with our standards, the domain owner can still submit the CVP/certificate to Policy-Log/CT logs to make the certificate trusted. Therefore, it does not affect the use of a valid certificate.

5.2 Reduced Monitoring Costs

We tracked the changes in the number of certificates in each log from January 20 to 25, 2021 through Cert Spotter Stats [56]. There are currently 46 logs included in Chrome, and a total of 33 logs are usable after excluding 12 retired logs and 1 read-only log. We conduct statistics on the 33 logs and find that their growth rates vary greatly. The smallest average daily growth rate is only 2 ("DigiCert Nessie 2023"), and the largest is 3,483,672 ("Google Xenon 2021"). These 33 logs belong to 6 organizations, namely "Google", "Cloudflare", "DigiCert", "Sectigo", "Lets Encrypt", "TrustAsia". Among them, the 2020 and 2021 logs of "TrustAsia" have retired, so our subsequent discussion does not include its logs. From the operator's point of view, "Google" has the fastest growth rate of 7,146,919 per day; "Sectigo" has the slowest growth rate of 494,042 per day. If we merge logs sliced in different years, there are 13 logs in total. From the logs' point of view, "Google Xenon" has the fastest growth rate of 3,797,446; "Google Pilot" has the slowest rate of 171 (Table 1).

Table 1. Daily growth of usable logs included in Chrome

Operator	Log name	Growth	
		Log	Operator
Google	Google Argon (2020–2023)	3,315,423	7,146,919
	Google Xenon (2020–2023)	3,797,446	
	Google Icarus	209	
	Google Pilot	171	
	Google Rocketeer	16,813	
	Google Skydiver	16,857	
Cloudflare	Cloudflare Nimbus (2020–2023)	818,929	818,929
DigiCert	DigiCert	2,193	1,181,434
	DigiCert Yeti (2020–2023)	852,481	
	DigiCert Nessie (2020–2023)	326,760	
Sectigo	Sectigo Sabre	22,593	494,042
	Sectigo Mammoth	471,449	
Let's Encrypt	Let's Encrypt Oak (2020–2023)	1,145,225	1,145,225

It can be seen that the growth rate of logs is very unbalanced. In the current CT framework, domain owners need to monitor all logs with a daily growth of about 11 million. In our scheme, the domain owner can only monitor the most unpopular logs (e.g., "Google Pilot", "Google Icarus"), and only need to download a few hundred certificates per day, which reduces the number of downloaded certificates by tens of thousands of times in the best cases. What's more, in the general case, the domain owner selects one or a group of less popular logs for monitoring. For example, assuming that the domain owner requires its certificates to be recorded in a Sectigo-operated log, then it only needs to download about 0.5 M certificates per day, which reduces the number of download certificates by about 22 times. Besides, the domain owner may not impose any restrictions on the record of its certificates, so all logs need to be monitored in the worst case. We calculate, based on the average size of the certificate, 5.93 KB [40], the demand for downloads, storage, and minimum bandwidth with or without PoliCT, see Table 2 for details.

Table 2. The overhead of monitoring the certificates

	w/o PoliCT	w/ PoliCT		
		Best case	General case	Worst case
Downloads	61 GB	1 MB	2.8 GB	61 GB
Storage	61 GB	–	–	–
Minimum bandwidth	6 Mbps	0.1 Kbps	0.27 Mbps	6 Mbps

–: It indicates that the storage depends on the number of related certificates of the monitored domains, usually on the order of KB/MB, which is negligible compared to keeping copies of entire logs (e.g., 61 GB).
Minimum Bandwidth = $Downloads \div (24\,h \times 60\,min \times 60\,s)$: The minimum network bandwidth required to complete the download within 24 h.

In addition, PoliCT may prompt domain owners to submit certificates to unpopular logs, making the growth of 13 logs balanced. In this case, the monitoring cost of the domain owner can be reduced by 13 times and the cost can be further reduced when more logs are applied.

5.3 Additional Overhead

This scheme generates additional overhead for storage, network transmission and verification time, but they are all acceptable.

As for storage, CA needs to store a queryable copy of Policy-Log and Revoked-Policy-Log. Since a CVP (*a*) corresponds to many certificates; (*b*) does not change for a long time; and (*c*) is defined as a unified standard format, storing locally will not consume too much storage and computing resources. Moreover, CAs in the same organization can share it. The browser only needs to store the Revoked-Policy-Log, which is designed for the smallest storage and is sliced annually. Besides, the release of CVPs is infrequent, and the revoked CVP is even rarer. Therefore, the storage overhead is also acceptable.

In terms of network transmission, only an SPT is added to the communication between the domain owner and the browser. According to the data format we designed, an SPT is about 0.5 KB in size. This level of overhead is negligible.

With regard to verification time, the browser requires an additional signature verification calculation, local revocation query and checks whether the SCT complies with the SPT when verifying the certificate. These calculations are local, and the added verification time in the network environment is negligible.

In general, all additional overhead are acceptable. Moreover, the implementation of our scheme is flexible, which means it is compatible with other CVP delivery and revocation methods.

5.4 Comparison with Other Solutions

The current schemes used to manage certificate policies or CT policies include CAA [30], DANE [33], Elaphurus [42], Expect-CT [57] and PoliCert [60]. Not all of these schemes can be extended for CT management, since they may have insufficiencies such as ignoring malicious CAs, false negatives/positives, additional communication/storage overhead, difficulty in recovering from errors, etc. Similar to PoliCert, PoliCT combines CT features, introduces policies, supports user-defined and revoked policies, to achieve CT policy security management and trust security enhancement.

Besides, Dahlberg et al. [14] proposed a scheme to reduce the cost of monitoring. Although we focus on the same point, we adopt a completely different method: Dahlberg tries to make the STH returned by logs as small as possible, while we let users monitor as few logs as possible. In addition, the trust in Dahlberg's design is still concentrated in LWM API. And they assume that it is error-free in any stage of building Authenticated Dictionarys (ADs), which is obviously unreliable. However, our scheme truly achieves the decentralization of trust.

6 Related Work

TLS/HTTPS Ecosystem. The certificates recorded in CT logs help us understand the TLS/HTTPS ecosystem. VanderSloot et al. [62] used the data obtained from active scanning and CT to map the complete view of the certificates in the wild. Gasser et al. [21] investigated the actual violation of certificate issuance standards, and Cui et al. [13] analyzed the properties of fraudulent certificates in the wild. Similarly, Kumar et al. [36] analyzed the specific reasons for the certificate errors through the data in Censys. Fasllija et al. [19] realized a phishing websites detection scheme based on machine learning by analyzing the domain names in CT logs.

CT Ecosystem. Some researchers investigated the ecosystem of CT. Amann et al. [3] completed a large-scale research of the TLS/HTTPS trust enhancement scheme, including CT, HPKP, CAA, DANE and etc. Gustafsson et al. [29] focused on investigating the certificates recorded in 11 public CT logs and their usage in TLS/HTTPS. Nykvist et al. [48] investigated the support of Alexa Top-1M websites for CT, the way they deliver SCTs, and the consumption of different ways. In addition, there were also some studies that focused on the defects of CT. Scheitle et al. [53] discussed the issue of domain information leakage caused by public logs by analyzing server-side deployment. Analogously, Roberts et al. [51] analyzed a variety of information types of users and enterprises that were leaked by public logs. Korzhitskii et al. [35] investigated the root CA accepted by CT logs and revealed some problems caused by log mismanagement. Li et al. [39] explored the security of CT framework in practice and discovered potential exploitable security vulnerabilities in various components. Stark et al. [58] comprehensively researched the compliance, user experience and potential risks of adoption CT in the network.

Monitor in CT. There are also some researches on the security and efficiency of CT monitors. B. Li et al. [40] analyzed in detail the cost of operating a monitor in the wild, and exposed the unreliability of third-party monitors. Then, they [38] explored the TLS/HTTPS configurations of third-party monitors, and discovered insecure communication connections. Dahlberg et al. [14] designed a verifiable light-weight monitoring solution for CT logs.

CT Variations. The idea of transparency has been extended to various fields. PoliCert [60] records certificates and the issuance policy separately in public logs to improve the security of the certificates. PKISN [59] records all certificates and revocations in public logs in chronological order, which makes it possible to revoke a CA certificate while maintaining the validity of the leaf certificates. Software transparency [32] requires developers to submit software update packages, including all source code and metadata, to the public logs. Ticket transparency [5] applies the idea of transparency to single sign on. It records all the tickets used for login to audit the misbehaviors of the identity providers. Ferretti et al. [20] extended CT to the Internet of Things to implement public audits of misbehaviors of intermediate services. Wang et al. [64] propose a scheme in which the domain owner publishes the CA-signed certificates and its revocation status information as a transaction to the blockchain to balance the absolute authority of CAs.

7 Conclusion

This paper proposes a flexible and customizable certificate transparency management, PoliCT, which allows domain owners to customize the CVP to specify how its certificates should be verified. In addition, we define and illustrate what items are included in a CVP, and make detailed instructions on how to distribute, submit, and revoke the CVPs. What's more, we design a reliable lightweight self-monitor based on PoliCT, which has the following three characteristics (*a*) targeted monitoring of a few logs; (*b*) simple and error-free parsing; and (*c*) minimal storage. Then, we theoretically evaluate our scheme and conclude that it is secure and workable. Additionally, we tracked the growth of records in CT logs, analyzed the data, and concluded that our solution can save tens of thousands of times at most in monitoring costs.

References

1. Aas, J., et al.: Let's encrypt: an automated certificate authority to encrypt the entire web. In: Proceedings of the 2019 ACM SIGSAC Conference on Computer and Communications Security, pp. 2473–2487 (2019)
2. Adkins, H.: An update on attempted man-in-the-middle attacks. Website (2011). https://security.googleblog.com/2011/08/update-on-attempted-man-in-middle.html
3. Amann, J., Gasser, O., Scheitle, Q., Brent, L., Carle, G., Holz, R.: Mission accomplished? Https security after diginotar. In: Proceedings of the 2017 Internet Measurement Conference, pp. 325–340 (2017)
4. Apple Inc.: Apple's certificate transparency policy. Website (2021). https://support.apple.com/en-us/HT205280
5. Chu, D., Lin, J., Li, F., Zhang, X., Wang, Q., Liu, G.: Ticket transparency: accountable single sign-on with privacy-preserving public logs. In: Chen, S., Choo, K.-K.R., Fu, X., Lou, W., Mohaisen, A. (eds.) SecureComm 2019. LNICST, vol. 304, pp. 511–531. Springer, Cham (2019). https://doi.org/10.1007/978-3-030-37228-6_25
6. Chuat, L., Szalachowski, P., Perrig, A., Laurie, B., Messeri, E.: Efficient gossip protocols for verifying the consistency of certificate logs. In: 2015 IEEE Conference on Communications and Network Security (CNS), pp. 415–423. IEEE (2015)
7. Cloudflare Inc.: Explore the certificate transparency ecosystem. Website (2021). https://ct.cloudflare.com/
8. Comodo CA Limited: crt.sh: Certificate search. Website (2021). https://crt.sh
9. Comodo Group Inc.: Comodo report of incident. Website (2011). https://www.comodo.com/Comodo-Fraud-Incident-2011-03-23.html
10. Cooper, D., et al.: Internet x. 509 public key infrastructure certificate and certificate revocation list (CRL) profile. RFC **5280**, 1–151 (2008)
11. crt.sh Inc.: Certificate Transparency log monitor of crt.sh. Website (2021). https://github.com/crtsh
12. CT Observatory: Website. https://www.ct-observatory.org/
13. Cui, M., Cao, Z., Xiong, G.: How is the forged certificates in the wild: practice on large-scale SSL usage measurement and analysis. In: Shi, Y., et al. (eds.) ICCS 2018. LNCS, vol. 10862, pp. 654–667. Springer, Cham (2018). https://doi.org/10.1007/978-3-319-93713-7_62
14. Dahlberg, R., Pulls, T.: Verifiable light-weight monitoring for certificate transparency logs. In: Gruschka, N. (ed.) NordSec 2018. LNCS, vol. 11252, pp. 171–183. Springer, Cham (2018). https://doi.org/10.1007/978-3-030-03638-6_11
15. Eastlake, D., et al.: Transport layer security (TLS) extensions: extension definitions. Technical Report, RFC 6066, January 2011
16. Eckersley, P.: A Syrian man-in-the-middle attack against Facebook. Website (2011). https://www.eff.org/deeplinks/2011/05/syrian-man-middle-against-facebook

17. Entrust Inc.: Certificate transparency search tool. Website (2021). https://www.entrust.com/ct-search/
18. Facebook Inc.: Facebook: certificate transparency monitoring. Website (2021). https://developers.facebook.com/tools/ct/search/
19. Fasllija, E., Enişer, H.F., Prünster, B.: Phish-hook: detecting phishing certificates using certificate transparency logs. In: Chen, S., Choo, K.-K.R., Fu, X., Lou, W., Mohaisen, A. (eds.) SecureComm 2019. LNICST, vol. 305, pp. 320–334. Springer, Cham (2019). https://doi.org/10.1007/978-3-030-37231-6_18
20. Ferretti, L., Longo, F., Colajanni, M., Merlino, G., Tapas, N.: Authorization transparency for accountable access to IoT services. In: 2019 IEEE International Congress on Internet of Things (ICIOT), pp. 91–99. IEEE (2019)
21. Gasser, O., Hof, B., Helm, M., Korczynski, M., Holz, R., Carle, G.: In log we trust: revealing poor security practices with certificate transparency logs and internet measurements. In: Beverly, R., Smaragdakis, G., Feldmann, A. (eds.) PAM 2018. LNCS, vol. 10771, pp. 173–185. Springer, Cham (2018). https://doi.org/10.1007/978-3-319-76481-8_13
22. GlobalSign: Security incident report. Website (2011). https://www.globalsign.com/resources/globalsign-security-incident-report.pdf
23. Google Inc.: Certificate transparency in Chrome. Website (2018). https://chromium.googlesource.com/chromium/src/+/master/net/docs/certificate-transparency.md
24. Google Inc.: Certificate transparency in Chrome policy. Website (2018). https://github.com/chromium/ct-policy/blob/master/ct_policy.md
25. Google Inc.: certificate-transparency-go. Website (2021). https://github.com/google/certificate-transparency-go
26. Google Inc.: Google: HTTPS encryption on the web. Website (2021). https://transparencyreport.google.com/https/certificates
27. Google Inc.: The list of all known and announced CT logs. Website (2021)
28. Google Inc.: Working together to detect maliciously or mistakenly issued certificates. Website (2021)
29. Gustafsson, J., Overier, G., Arlitt, M., Carlsson, N.: A first look at the CT landscape: certificate transparency logs in practice. In: Kaafar, M.A., Uhlig, S., Amann, J. (eds.) PAM 2017. LNCS, vol. 10176, pp. 87–99. Springer, Cham (2017). https://doi.org/10.1007/978-3-319-54328-4_7
30. Hallam-Baker, P., Stradling, R., Laurie, B.: DNS certification authority authorization (CAA) resource record. Internet Eng. Task Force **6844** (2013)
31. Hardenize Limited: Hardenize: meet the new standard for web site network and security configuration monitoring. Website (2021). https://www.hardenize.com/
32. Hof, B., Carle, G.: Software distribution transparency and auditability. arXiv ePrint arXiv:1711.07278 (2017)
33. Hoffman, P., Schlyter, J.: The DNS-based authentication of named entities (DANE) transport layer security (TLS) protocol: TLSA. Technical Report, RFC 6698, August 2012
34. Inc, V.D.S.I.: DigiNotar reports security incident (2011). https://www.vasco.com/about-vasco/press/2011/news_diginotar_reports_security_incident.html
35. Korzhitskii, N., Carlsson, N.: Characterizing the root landscape of certificate transparency logs. In: 2020 IFIP Networking Conference (Networking), pp. 190–198. IEEE (2020)
36. Kumar, D., et al.: Tracking certificate misissuance in the wild. In: 2018 IEEE Symposium on Security and Privacy (SP), pp. 785–798. IEEE (2018)

37. Laurie, B., Langley, A., et al.: RFC6962: Certificate Transparency (2013)
38. Li, B., Chu, D., Lin, J., Cai, Q., Wang, C., Meng, L.: The weakest link of certificate transparency: exploring the TLS/HTTPS configurations of third-party monitors. In: 2019 18th IEEE International Conference On Trust, Security And Privacy In Computing And Communications/13th IEEE International Conference On Big Data Science And Engineering (TrustCom/BigDataSE), pp. 216–223. IEEE (2019)
39. Li, B., Li, F., Ma, Z., Wu, Q.: Exploring the security of certificate transparency in the wild. In: Zhou, J., et al. (eds.) ACNS 2020. LNCS, vol. 12418, pp. 453–470. Springer, Cham (2020). https://doi.org/10.1007/978-3-030-61638-0_25
40. Li, B., et al.: Certificate transparency in the wild: exploring the reliability of monitors. In: Proceedings of the 2019 ACM SIGSAC Conference on Computer and Communications Security, pp. 2505–2520 (2019)
41. Li, B., Lin, J., Wang, Q., Wang, Z., Jing, J.: Locally-centralized certificate validation and its application in desktop virtualization systems. IEEE Trans. Inf. Forensics Secur. **16**, 1380–1395 (2020)
42. Li, B., Wang, W., Meng, L., Lin, J., Liu, X., Wang, C.: Elaphurus: ensemble defense against fraudulent certificates in TLS. In: Liu, Z., Yung, M. (eds.) Inscrypt 2019. LNCS, vol. 12020, pp. 246–259. Springer, Cham (2020). https://doi.org/10.1007/978-3-030-42921-8_14
43. Morton, B.: More google fraudulent certificates. Website (2014). https://www.entrust.com/google-fraudulent-certificates/
44. Mozilla: Certificate transparency checker. Website (2019). https://addons.mozilla.org/en-US/firefox/addon/certificate-transparency/
45. Mozilla Inc.: Public suffix list. Website (2021). https://publicsuffix.org/list/public_suffix_list.datl
46. Nohe, P.: Maximum SSL/TLS certificate validity is now one year. Website (2020). https://www.globalsign.com/en/blog/maximum-ssltls-certificate-validity-now-one-year
47. Nordberg, L., Gillmor, D.K., et al.: IETF Internet-Draft - Gossiping in CT. Website (2018). https://datatracker.ietf.org/doc/html/draft-ietf-trans-gossip-05
48. Nykvist, C., Sjöström, L., Gustafsson, J., Carlsson, N.: Server-side adoption of certificate transparency. In: Beverly, R., Smaragdakis, G., Feldmann, A. (eds.) PAM 2018. LNCS, vol. 10771, pp. 186–199. Springer, Cham (2018). https://doi.org/10.1007/978-3-319-76481-8_14
49. Opsmate Inc.: SSLMate: cert spotter. Website (2021). https://sslmate.com/certspotter/
50. Report URI Inc.: Report URI. Website (2021). https://report-uri.com/account/
51. Roberts, R., Levin, D.: When certificate transparency is too transparent: analyzing information leakage in https domain names. In: Proceedings of the 18th ACM Workshop on Privacy in the Electronic Society, pp. 87–92 (2019)
52. Santesson, S., Myers, M., Ankney, R., Malpani, A., Galperin, S., Adams, C.: X. 509 internet public key infrastructure online certificate status protocol-OCSP. RFC 6960, pp. 1–41 (2013)
53. Scheitle, Q., et al.: The rise of certificate transparency and its implications on the internet ecosystem. In: Proceedings of the Internet Measurement Conference, vol. 2018, pp. 343–349 (2018)
54. SSLMate Inc.: How cert spotter parses 255 million certificates. Website (2017). https://sslmate.com/blog/post/how_certspotter_parses_255_million_certificates
55. SSLMate Inc.: Certificate transparency log monitor of SSLMate. Website (2020). https://github.com/SSLMate/certspotter

56. SSLMate Inc.: Cert spotter stats. Website (2021). https://sslmate.com/certspotter/stats
57. Stark, E.: IETF draft - Expect-CT extension for HTTP. Website (2018). https://tools.ietf.org/id/draft-ietf-httpbis-expect-ct-03.html
58. Stark, E., Sleevi, R., et al.: Does certificate transparency break the web? Measuring adoption and error rate. In: 2019 IEEE Symposium on Security and Privacy (SP), pp. 211–226. IEEE (2019)
59. Szalachowski, P., Chuat, L., Perrig, A.: PKI safety net (PKISN): addressing the too-big-to-be-revoked problem of the TLS ecosystem. In: 2016 IEEE European Symposium on Security and Privacy (EuroS&P), pp. 407–422. IEEE (2016)
60. Szalachowski, P., Matsumoto, S., Perrig, A.: PoliCert: secure and flexible TLS certificate management. In: Proceedings of the 2014 ACM SIGSAC Conference on Computer and Communications Security, pp. 406–417 (2014)
61. University of Michigan: Censys. Website (2021). https://censys.io/
62. VanderSloot, B., Amann, J., Bernhard, M., Durumeric, Z., Bailey, M., Halderman, J.A.: Towards a complete view of the certificate ecosystem. In: Proceedings of the 2016 Internet Measurement Conference, pp. 543–549 (2016)
63. Vincent Lynch: Mscaling CT logs: temporal sharding. Website (2018). https://www.digicert.com/dc/blog/scaling-certificate-transparency-logs-temporal-sharding/
64. Wang, Z., Lin, J., Cai, Q., Wang, Q., Zha, D., Jing, J.: Blockchain-based certificate transparency and revocation transparency. IEEE Trans. Dependable Secure Comput. (2020)
65. Wilson, K.: Distrusting new CNNIC certificates. Website (2015). https://blog.mozilla.org/security/2015/04/02/distrusting-new-cnnic-certificates/

Aggregate Signature with Traceability of Devices Dynamically Generating Invalid Signatures

Ryu Ishii[1(✉)], Kyosuke Yamashita[2,3], Yusuke Sakai[2], Takahiro Matsuda[2], Tadanori Teruya[2], Goichiro Hanaoka[2], Kanta Matsuura[1], and Tsutomu Matsumoto[2,4]

[1] The University of Tokyo, Tokyo, Japan
{ryuishii,kanta}@iis.u-tokyo.ac.jp

[2] National Institute of Advanced Industrial Science and Technology, Tokyo, Japan
{yusuke.sakai,t-matsuda,tadanori.teruya, hanaoka-goichiro,matsumoto.tsutomu}@aist.go.jp

[3] Kyoto University, Kyoto, Japan
yamashita.kyousuke.75w@st.kyoto-u.ac.jp,

[4] Yokohama National University, Yokohama, Japan

Abstract. Aggregate signature schemes enable us to aggregate multiple signatures into a single short signature. One of its typical applications is sensor networks, where a large number of users and devices measure their environments, create signatures to ensure the integrity of the measurements, and transmit their signed data. However, if an invalid signature is mixed into aggregation, the aggregate signature becomes invalid, thus if an aggregate signature is invalid, it is necessary to identify the invalid signature. Furthermore, we need to deal with a situation where an invalid sensor generates invalid signatures probabilistically. In this paper, we introduce a model of aggregate signature schemes with interactive tracing functionality that captures such a situation, and define its functional and security requirements and propose aggregate signature schemes that can identify all rogue sensors. More concretely, based on the idea of Dynamic Traitor Tracing, we can trace rogue sensors dynamically and incrementally, and eventually identify all rogue sensors of generating invalid signatures even if the rogue sensors adaptively collude. In addition, the efficiency of our proposed method is also sufficiently practical.

Keywords: Sensor networks · Aggregate signature · Aggregate signature with tracing functionality · Dynamic traitor tracing

1 Introduction

Aggregate signature schemes allow multiple signatures to be aggregated into a short signature. In information systems with a large number of signed data,

J. Zhou et al. (Eds.): ACNS 2021 Workshops, LNCS 12809, pp. 378–396, 2021.
https://doi.org/10.1007/978-3-030-81645-2_22

aggregate signature schemes enable us to aggregate the signatures on the communication channel into a single short signature, thus significantly reduce the communication cost. As observed in [AGH10,Mak20], one example of such information systems is a sensor network where a large number of users and devices measure their environments and generate signatures to ensure the integrity of the measurements and transmit their signed data. However, if invalid signatures are produced due to a failure or a replacement of a sensor, an aggregate signature becomes invalid. If such a case, it is necessary to identify (and repair/exclude) a sensor that generated an invalid signature. At this point, if we know that there is only one such sensor, and that it always issues an invalid signature, it is trivial to identify the sensor. In practice, however, it is conceivable that multiple sensors that have failed or been replaced work in conjunction with each other to probabilistically generate invalid/valid signatures. In this paper, we propose an aggregate signature scheme that can identify all rogue sensors even in such a case. More concretely, based on the idea of Dynamic Traitor Tracing [FT99], we can trace rogue sensors dynamically and incrementally, and finally identify all rogue sensors that generate invalid signatures.

Problem Setting. When we consider a sensor network in which a large number of devices send signed data periodically, it is natural to assume that the devices that generate invalid signatures may change from time to time due to failures. However, in previous works, the signature set to be aggregated is assumed to be constant during tracing, and there has been no method that can capture the situation where the devices generating invalid signatures could change from time to time. In this paper, we consider the situation where many users/devices send signed data periodically, an adversarial user/device set (that may generate invalid signatures) consists of multiple devices, and the user/device that generates the invalid signature could change dynamically from time to time. However, we assume that, when an aggregate signature is generated, at least one of the attackers sends an invalid signature.

Hartung et al. [HKK+16] proposed fault-tolerant aggregate signatures that allow a verifier to trace a certain number of invalid signatures. At first glance, it might seem that [HKK+16] can be used in our setting, but this is not the case. When [HKK+16] is used in the above setting, we need to assume that either (i) all rogue sensors always produce invalid signatures, or (ii) all signatures are temporarily stored before aggregation. Note that an adversary that captures the first condition does not meet our setting. Thus, the setting described above cannot be solved by a naive application of the method in [HKK+16].

Our Contribution. In this paper, we introduce *aggregate signature schemes with interactive tracing functionality* (ASIT scheme for short) that captures our problem setting, and define its functional and security requirements. In addition, we propose a generic construction of an ASIT scheme that combines an ordinary aggregate signature scheme and a dynamic traitor tracing (DTT) scheme [FT99]. A DTT is a method to trace adversaries who commit piracy in a contents distribution service. Since the definition in the original paper [FT99] is not so easy to work with, we also give a formalization of the syntax and security notions for DTT that is suitable and convenient for our purpose.

Our security definitions of ASIT scheme take into account all the situations of our problem setting mentioned earlier. Namely, it is possible to trace an adaptive collusion of rogue sensors. This situation was not captured in the previous work [HKK+16]. As an additional feature, the efficiency of our scheme is also sufficiently practical. For example, when $d = 10$ rogue sensors are mixed among $n = 100000$ sensors, each of which sends signed data every minute, they can always be traced within $R = d\log_2(n) + d \approx 176$ minutes. Furthermore, since our generic construction can be instantiated with any aggregate signature scheme and DTT, many different instantiations of an ASIT scheme can be obtained.

Basic Idea of the Proposed Method. In the proposed ASIT scheme, we assume that a user/device periodically sends signed data to an aggregator. The aggregator generates an aggregate signature based on the feedback received from the verifier in the previous round for the signed data periodically sent by the user/device. The verifier, which has an internal state, verifies the aggregate signature from the aggregator, runs a tracing algorithm, updates the internal state and outputs a feedback and a set of excluded users/devices. This feedback is sent to the aggregator. These processes are repeated to finally find out all the users/devices that generated invalid signatures. The tracing algorithm of the proposed ASIT scheme is based on the tracing algorithm of the underlying DTT.

We consider two types of attacks on an ASIT scheme: a forgery of (aggregate) signatures and a generation of invalid signatures. The security notions against these attacks are EUF-CMA security and R-identifiability respectively, where the latter notion intuitively ensures that the set of users/devices that generated invalid signatures will be eventually identified within R rounds of interaction between the aggregator and the verifier. The security notion that guarantees that legitimate users/devices are not mistakenly traced is called correctness. The proposed method satisfies all of these security notions. For the formal definitions, see Sect. 4.

Related Work. The first aggregate signature scheme was proposed by Boneh et al. [BGLS03], which is in the random oracle model and uses bilinear maps. Hohenberger et al. [HSW13] gave an aggregate signature scheme using multilinear maps in the standard model. These schemes can aggregate individual signatures as well as already aggregate signatures in any order. There are other types of aggregate signature schemes. One is sequentially aggregate signature, first proposed by Lysyanskaya et al. [LMRS04] in the random oracle model. Since then, a number of schemes have been proposed both in the random oracle model [LMRS04, Nev08, GLOW12] and in the standard model [LOS+06, LLY15]. Another type is aggregate signature with synchronized aggregation, first proposed by Gentry and Ramzan [GR06] (in the identity-based setting) in the random oracle model. Again, since then, several constructions have been proposed both in the random oracle model [GR06, AGH10] and the standard model [AGH10].

Hartung et al. [HKK+16] proposed fault-tolerant aggregate signatures that allow a verifier to trace a certain number of invalid signatures using a cover-free family. Sato et al. [SS19, SSM20, SS20] proposed an aggregate message authentication code and an aggregate signature scheme with interactive tracing functionality using adaptive group tests.

Outline. In Sect. 2, we define basic notation and review standard aggregate signature schemes. In Sect. 3, we review and formulate DTT. In Sect. 4, we define the functional and security requirements of ASIT scheme that captures the problem setting of this study. In Sect. 5, we give a generic construction of an ASIT scheme combining a standard aggregate signature scheme and a DTT, and prove its security. Finally, in Sect. 6, we compare the efficiency of the proposed scheme with existing aggregate signature schemes.

2 Preliminaries

2.1 Notation

Throughout this paper, we let $\lambda \in \mathbb{N}$ be a security parameter, $n \in \mathbb{N}$ be the number of users, $[n] := \{1, \ldots, n\}$, ϵ be an empty string, $\emptyset$ be an empty set, $\mathrm{poly}(\cdot)$ be a polynomial function, $\mathrm{negl}(\cdot)$ be a negligible function, and $\mathcal{M} = \mathcal{M}(\lambda)$ be a message space. We say an algorithm is probabilistic polynomial time (PPT) if it is a probabilistic algorithm and its running time is polynomial in λ. We denote a subroutine func of an algorithm X by $X.\mathsf{func}$.

Let U be a set. We say P is a partition of the set U if P satisfies the followings: $P = (S_1, \ldots, S_p)$ where $p \in [|U|]$, $S_1, \ldots, S_p \in 2^U \setminus \{\emptyset\}$, $\bigcup_{i \in [p]} S_i = U$, and for every $i \neq j$ $(i, j \in [p])$, it holds that $S_i \cap S_j = \emptyset$. We denote by $|P| = p$.

2.2 Aggregate Signature Schemes

Here we review the syntax, correctness, and security definitions of aggregate signature schemes. We focus on an aggregate signature scheme which aggregates only one message and signature pair per one verification key[1].

Definition 1 (Aggregate Signature). *An aggregate signature scheme consists of the five PPT algorithms* $(\mathsf{KeyGen}, \mathsf{Sign}, \mathsf{Verify}, \mathsf{Agg}, \mathsf{AggVerify})$ *that work as follows:*

$\mathsf{KeyGen}(1^\lambda) \to (\mathsf{pk}, \mathsf{sk})$: KeyGen *is the key generation algorithm that takes a security parameter* 1^λ *as input, and outputs a public/secret key pair* $(\mathsf{pk}, \mathsf{sk})$.

$\mathsf{Sign}(\mathsf{sk}, m) \to \sigma$: Sign *is the signing algorithm that takes a secret key* sk *and a message* $m \in \mathcal{M}$ *as input, and outputs a signature* σ.

[1] In general, aggregate signature schemes can aggregate multiple signatures even if they are generated under the same key, but for simplicity, we do not introduce such version in this paper.

$\mathsf{Verify}(\mathsf{pk}, m, \sigma) \to 1/0$: Verify *is the verification algorithm for non-aggregate signatures: It that takes a public key* pk, *a message* m, *and a signature* σ *as input, and outputs 1 (valid) or 0 (invalid).*

$\mathsf{Agg}(\{(\mathsf{pk}_i, m_i, \sigma_i)\}_i) \to \tau$: Agg *is the aggregation algorithm that takes a set of triplets of a public key, a message and a signature* $\{(\mathsf{pk}_i, m_i, \sigma_i)\}_i$ *as input, and outputs an aggregate signature* τ.

$\mathsf{AggVerify}(\{(\mathsf{pk}_i, m_i)\}_i, \tau) \to 1/0$: $\mathsf{AggVerify}$ *is the verification algorithm for aggregate signatures: It takes a set of pairs of a public key and a message* $\{(\mathsf{pk}_i, m_i)\}_i$ *and an aggregate signature* τ *as input, and outputs 1 (valid) or 0 (invalid).*

Definition 2 (Correctness). *An aggregate signature scheme* $\Sigma_{\mathrm{AS}} = (\mathsf{KeyGen}, \mathsf{Sign}, \mathsf{Verify}, \mathsf{Agg}, \mathsf{AggVerify})$ *satisfies correctness if for any* $\lambda \in \mathbb{N}$, *any* $n = \mathrm{poly}(\lambda)$, *and any* $m_1, \ldots, m_n \in \mathcal{M}$, *it holds that*

$$\Pr\left[1 \leftarrow \mathsf{AggVerify}(\{(\mathsf{pk}_i, m_i)\}_{i \in [n]}, \tau) \;\middle|\; \begin{array}{l} \forall i \in [n],\ (\mathsf{pk}_i, \mathsf{sk}_i) \leftarrow \mathsf{KeyGen}(1^\lambda), \\ \text{and } \sigma_i \leftarrow \mathsf{Sign}(\mathsf{sk}_i, m_i); \\ \tau \leftarrow \mathsf{Agg}(\{(\mathsf{pk}_i, m_i, \sigma_i)\}_{i \in [n]}) \end{array}\right] = 1.$$

For security, we consider EUF-CMA (Existential UnForgeability against Chosen Message Attacks) security in the model where all generated key pairs are generated honestly (honest-key model).

Definition 3 (EUF-CMA security). *An aggregate signature scheme* $\Sigma_{\mathrm{AS}} = (\mathsf{KeyGen}, \mathsf{Sign}, \mathsf{Verify}, \mathsf{Agg}, \mathsf{AggVerify})$ *satisfies EUF-CMA security if for any* $\lambda \in \mathbb{N}$, *any* $n = \mathrm{poly}(\lambda)$ *and any PPT adversary* $\mathcal{A}$, *it holds that* $\Pr\left[\mathsf{ExpAS}^{EUF\text{-}CMA}_{\Sigma_{\mathrm{AS}},\mathcal{A}}(\lambda, n) = 1\right] = \mathrm{negl}(\lambda)$ *where* $\mathsf{ExpAS}^{EUF\text{-}CMA}_{\Sigma_{\mathrm{AS}},\mathcal{A}}(\lambda, n)$ *is the following experiment:*

$\mathsf{ExpAS}^{EUF\text{-}CMA}_{\Sigma_{\mathrm{AS}},\mathcal{A}}(\lambda, n)$

$\forall i \in [n],\ (\mathsf{pk}_i, \mathsf{sk}_i) \leftarrow \Sigma_{\mathrm{AS}}.\mathsf{KeyGen}(1^\lambda)$; $Q := \emptyset$; $(\{m_i\}_{i \in S}, \tau, S) \leftarrow \mathcal{A}^{\Sigma_{\mathrm{AS}}.\mathsf{Sign}(\mathsf{sk}_1, \cdot)}(\mathsf{pk}_1, \{(\mathsf{pk}_i, \mathsf{sk}_i)\}_{i \in [n] \setminus \{1\}})$	Output 1 if $S \subseteq [n]$, $1 \in S$, $m_1 \notin Q$ and : $\Sigma_{\mathrm{AS}}.\mathsf{AggVerify}(\{(\mathsf{pk}_i, m_i)_{i \in S}, \tau\}) = 1$, else output 0

where when $\mathcal{A}$ *makes a query* $m \in \mathcal{M}$ *to the signing oracle* $\Sigma_{\mathrm{AS}}.\mathsf{Sign}(\mathsf{sk}_1, \cdot)$, *it computes* $\sigma \leftarrow \Sigma_{\mathrm{AS}}.\mathsf{Sign}(\mathsf{sk}_1, m)$, *sends* σ *to* $\mathcal{A}$, *and sets* $Q \leftarrow Q \cup \{m\}$.

Note that in the experiment, the user index 1 is used as a challenger user whose secret key is unknown to an adversary, and the remaining keys $(\mathsf{pk}_i, \mathsf{sk}_i)_{i \in [n] \setminus \{1\}}$ are directly given to $\mathcal{A}$. Thus, the signing oracle is provided only for the index 1.

3 Dynamic Traitor Tracing

A Dynamic Traitor Tracing (DTT) [FT99] is a method for tracing piracy by having a distributor of a video or another distribution service that delivers a variant of the content with a (generally) different digital watermark for each user. The distributor adaptively generates new watermarks when it finds a pirate version, repeats this process until it traces all of the pirates, and when the distributor finally identifies a pirate, it excludes the pirate from the user set.

In this section, we give our own formalization of DTT that is suitable and convenient for our purpose, based on the treatment in [FT99]. For DTT, we define the following two security requirements: *R-identifiability*, which ensures that the distributor can identify all pirates with R or fewer deliveries, and *completeness*, which ensures that the distributor does not exclude legitimate users. After defining the syntax of DTT in Sect. 3.1, we define these two security notions in Sect. 3.2. Finally, we present two concrete schemes proposed by Fiat and Tassa [FT99] in Sect. 3.3.

3.1 Syntax

We define the syntax of a DTT as follows.

Definition 4 (Dynamic Traitor Tracing). *A dynamic traitor tracing (DTT) scheme consists of the two PPT algorithms* (Initialize, Trace) *that work as follows:*

Initialize$(1^\lambda, 1^n) \rightarrow (\alpha, P)$: Initialize *is the initialization algorithm that takes the security parameter 1^λ and the number of users 1^n (in the unary form) as input, and outputs an internal state α and a partition P of the user set $[n]$.*

Trace$(\alpha, i) \rightarrow (\alpha', P', V)$: Trace *is the tracing algorithm that takes an internal state α and an index i as input, and outputs the new internal state α' and set partition P' for the next round, and a traced pirate set V.*

This syntax captures the following usage scenario: First, the distributor executes Initialize to generate the initial partition $P = (S_1, \ldots, S_p)$ (for some p) of the user set $[n]$ (and initial internal state α), generates different watermarks for each element S_i in the partition P, and sends each user a watermarked content that corresponds to a subset S_i in P to which the user belongs.[2] Note that each subset S_i in the partition P is uniquely indexed. The collusion of pirate users chooses one of the watermarked contents sent by the distributor, and delivers it as a pirated version. The distributor identifies which watermark is embedded to the pirated version, and executes Trace based on the index of the pirate version and the distributor's internal state to determine the new partition for the next round. If a subset in the partition consists of only a single user (in other words, the distributor identifies a pirate), then Trace excludes the pirate. These procedures are repeated to exclude all pirates.

3.2 Security Requirements

Here, we formally define security requirements of DTT. In our model, we assume that an adversary declares a set C (where $|C| \leq d$) of pirates at first. Therefore,

[2] The mechanism for watermarking contents is detached from the syntax and beyond the scope of this primitive, which is the same treatment as in [FT99].

we consider DTTs that only excludes the pirates in this set. Furthermore, we assume that a pirate rebroadcasts the content that it receives. In other words, we do not consider the case where a pirate eavesdrops other user's content and rebroadcasts it. We remark that the same restrictions were implicitly put in [FT99]. We leave a definition of DTTs in the model where the set of traitors dynamically changes as an interesting future work.

As mentioned earlier, we define two security notions for DTT: *R-identifiability*, which ensures that a distributor can identify all the pirates within R (or less) rounds, and *completeness*, which ensures that a distributor does not trace legitimate users as pirates. These are defined using the following experiment $\mathsf{ExpDTT}_{\Sigma_{\mathrm{DTT}},\mathcal{A}}(\lambda, n)$ in which a stateful adversary $\mathcal{A}$ is executed.

$$\frac{\mathsf{ExpDTT}_{\Sigma_{\mathrm{DTT}},\mathcal{A}}(\lambda, n)}{\begin{array}{c}(\alpha_1, P_1) \leftarrow \Sigma_{\mathrm{DTT}}.\mathsf{Initialize}(1^\lambda, 1^n);\\ C \leftarrow \mathcal{A}(\alpha_1, P_1); t := 1; W := \emptyset; \text{run } \mathcal{A}^{O_T(\cdot)}(\alpha_1, P_1)\end{array} : \text{Output } (W, C)}$$

where $\mathcal{A}$ may adaptively make multiple queries i_t to the tracing oracle O_T. However, $\mathcal{A}$'s t-th O_T query i_t must satisfy $i_t \in [|P_t|]$ and $S_{i_t,t} \cap C \neq \emptyset$, where α_t is the internal state and $P_t = (S_{1,t}, \ldots, S_{p_t,t})$ (for some natural number p_t) denotes the partition after $\mathcal{A}$'s $(t-1)$-th O_T query is answered. Given the t-th O_T query i_t from $\mathcal{A}$, O_T runs $(\alpha_{t+1}, P_{t+1}, V_t) \leftarrow \Sigma_{\mathrm{DTT}}.\mathsf{Trace}(\alpha_t, i_t)$, and returns $(\alpha_{t+1}, P_{t+1}, V_t)$ to $\mathcal{A}$. Then, O_T updates $W \leftarrow W \cup V_t$ and $t \leftarrow t+1$. We remark that W in the output of the experiment is that at the point $\mathcal{A}$ halts.

Definition 5 (R-Identifiability). *A DTT Σ_{DTT} satisfies R-identifiability if for any $\lambda \in \mathbb{N}$, any $n = \mathrm{poly}(\lambda)$, and any PPT adversary $\mathcal{A}$, it holds that*

$$\Pr\left[C \not\subseteq W \,\middle|\, (W, C) \leftarrow \mathsf{ExpDTT}_{\Sigma_{\mathrm{DTT}},\mathcal{A}}(\lambda, n) \wedge t \geq R\right] = \mathrm{negl}(\lambda).$$

where t is the value of the counter when $\mathcal{A}$ stops.

Definition 6 (Completeness). *A DTT Σ_{DTT} satisfies completeness if for any $\lambda \in \mathbb{N}$, any $n = \mathrm{poly}(\lambda)$, and any PPT adversary $\mathcal{A}$, it holds that*

$$\Pr\left[([n] \setminus C) \cap W \neq \emptyset \,\middle|\, (W, C) \leftarrow \mathsf{ExpDTT}_{\Sigma_{\mathrm{DTT}},\mathcal{A}}(\lambda, n)\right] = \mathrm{negl}(\lambda).$$

3.3 Instantiations

Fiat and Tassa [FT99] proposed three concrete DTT. Here, we present the second scheme (FT-2) and the third scheme (FT-3) of [FT99], which are binary search-based methods. The DTT FT-2 and FT-3 are described in Fig. 1. For these schemes, Fiat and Tassa [FT99] showed the following theorems.

Theorem 1. *Let n be the number of users and d be the number of pirates. Then,* FT-2 *excludes all of the pirates within $d \log_2 n + d$ rounds. Furthermore,* FT-2 *uses at most $2d + 1$ variants in each round.*

Theorem 2. *Let n be the number of users and d be the number of pirates. Then,* FT-3 *excludes all of the pirates within $2 \cdot 3^d d \log_2 n + d$ rounds. Furthermore,* FT-3 *uses at most $d + 1$ variants in each round.*

FT-2:

Initialize$(1^\lambda, 1^n)$:
  $I := [n]$; $P_1 := (I)$; $\alpha_1 := P_1$
  return (α_1, P_1)

Trace(α_t, i) :
  $P := \alpha_t$; $p := (|P| - 1)/2$; $V := \emptyset$
  parse $(Q_j)_{j \in [|P|]} \leftarrow P$
  if $Q_i = I$ **then**
    $(L_{p+1}, R_{p+1}) \leftarrow$ Halve(I); $I \leftarrow \emptyset$
    $P \leftarrow P \cup (\{L_{p+1}\} \cup \{R_{p+1}\})$
    $p \leftarrow p + 1$
  else if $\exists j \in [p] : Q_i = L_j$ **then**
★ $I \leftarrow I \cup R_j$
★   **if** $|L_j| = 1$ **then**
★ $V \leftarrow L_j$; $p \leftarrow p - 1$
★ $P \leftarrow P \setminus (\{L_j\} \cup \{R_j\})$
★   **else** $(L_j, R_j) \leftarrow$ Halve(L_j)
  else if $\exists j \in [p] : Q_i = R_j$ **then**
    Execute the lines marked with ★ with switching L_j and R_j.
  $P_{t+1} := P$; $\alpha_{t+1} := P$; $V_t := V$
  return $(\alpha_{t+1}, P_{t+1}, V_t)$

Halve(I) :
  $A :=$ the first $\lfloor |I|/2 \rfloor$ elements of I
  $B := I \setminus A$
  return (A, B)

FT-3:

Initialize$(1^\lambda, 1^n)$:
  $I := [n]$; $P_1 := (I)$; $S_1 := P_1$; $\alpha_1 := (P_1, S_1)$
  return (α_1, P_1)

Trace(α_t, i) :
  parse $(P, S) \leftarrow \alpha_t$; $p = (|S| - 1)/2$; $V := \emptyset$
  parse $(Q_j)_{j \in [|P|]} \leftarrow P$; $k := |P| - 1$
  if $k = 2p$ or ($k < 2p$ and $i \in [k]$) **then**
    if $Q_i = I$
      $(L_{p+1}, R_{p+1}) \leftarrow$ Halve(I); $I \leftarrow \emptyset$
      $S \leftarrow S \cup (\{L_{p+1}\} \cup \{R_{p+1}\})$; $p \leftarrow p + 1$
      if $p > k$ **then** $k \leftarrow k + 1$
    else if $\exists j \in [p] : Q_i = L_j$ **then**
★ $I \leftarrow I \cup R_j$
★   **if** $|L_j| = 1$ **then**
★ $V \leftarrow L_j$; $S \leftarrow S \setminus (\{L_j\} \cup \{R_j\})$
★ $p \leftarrow p - 1$; $k \leftarrow k - 1$
★   **else** $(L_j, R_j) \leftarrow$ Halve(L_j)
    else if $\exists j \in [p] : Q_i = R_j$ **then**
      Execute the lines marked with ★ with switching L_j and R_j.
  else if $t = \sum_{k'=0}^{k} \binom{2p+1}{k'}$ **then**
    $k \leftarrow k + 1$
  for $i := 1$ to k **do**
    if $i \le p$ **then** $T_i := \{L_i, R_i\}$
    else $T_i := S \setminus (\{Q_j\}_{j \in [i-1]})$
    $Q'_i :=$ a randomly selected set from T_i
  $Q'_{k+1} := [n] \setminus \bigcup_{i \in [k]} Q'_i$
  $P_{t+1} := (Q'_i)_{i \in [k+1]}$; $S_{t+1} := S$
  $\alpha_{t+1} := (P, S)$; $V_t := V$
  return $(\alpha_{t+1}, P_{t+1}, V_t)$

Fig. 1. The descriptions of the DTT by Fiat and Tassa [FT99]: FT-2 (left-top), FT-3 (right), and the subalgorithm Halve used in both of the schemes (left-bottom).

We now show that FT-2 and FT-3 satisfy the security notions formalized in this paper, namely R-identifiability and completeness, with an appropriate choice of R for each scheme.

Lemma 1. FT-2 *satisfies both* $(d \log_2 n + d)$*-identifiability and completeness.*

Proof. Due to Theorem 1 and the assumption that at least one pirate does piracy in each round, $(d \log_2 n + d)$-identifiability is trivial if completeness is satisfied. Thus, we only prove completeness. It is sufficient to prove that FT-2 never excludes a valid user. Let L_i and R_i be singleton sets that appear during the execution of FT-2 (i.e., $|L_i| = |R_i| = 1$). Since we are assuming that a pirate does not rebroadcast other user's content, the users in the sets are excluded if and only if the corresponding variants are detected by the distributor. (Note that if they never rebroadcast the content anymore, we regard them as valid users.) Therefore, FT-2 never excludes a valid user, which guarantees completeness. □

Lemma 2. FT-3 *satisfies both* $(2{\cdot}3^d d \log_2 n{+}d)$*-identifiability and completeness.*

We skip the proof of Lemma 2, since it is almost the same as the proof of Lemma 1 and due to the space limitation.

4 Aggregate Signature with Interactive Tracing Functionality

In this section, we give formal definitions for aggregate signature schemes with interactive tracing functionality (ASIT scheme). We define the syntax of ASIT scheme and the correctness of subalgorithms in Sect. 4.1. We then define the security and functionality requirements for ASIT scheme in Sect. 4.2, which include EUF-CMA security (in the honest-key model), R-identifiability, and correctness.

4.1 Syntax

Definition 7 (ASIT). *An ASIT scheme consists of the six PPT algorithms* (KeyGen, Sign, Agg, Verify, PartVerify, Trace) *that work as follows:*

$\mathsf{KeyGen}(1^\lambda) \rightarrow (\mathsf{pk}, \mathsf{sk})$: KeyGen *is the key generation algorithm that takes a security parameter* 1^λ *as input, and outputs a public/secret key pair* $(\mathsf{pk}, \mathsf{sk})$.

$\mathsf{Sign}(\mathsf{sk}, m) \rightarrow \sigma$: Sign *is the signing algorithm that takes a secret key* sk *and a message* $m \in \mathcal{M}$ *as input, and outputs a signature* σ.

$\mathsf{Verify}(\mathsf{pk}, m, \sigma) \rightarrow 1/0$: Verify *is the verification algorithm (for a non-aggregated signature) that takes a public key* pk*, a message* m*, and a signature* σ *as input, and outputs either 1 (valid) or 0 (invalid).*

$\mathsf{Agg}(f, \{(\mathsf{pk}_i, m_i, \sigma_i)\}_i) \rightarrow \tau$: Agg *is the aggregation algorithm: It takes as input a feedback* f *(from the previous round) and a set of triplets of a public key, a message and a signature* $\{(\mathsf{pk}_i, m_i, \sigma_i)\}_i$*. Then, it outputs an aggregate signature* τ.

$\mathsf{PartVerify}(\beta, \{(\mathsf{pk}_i, m_i)\}_i, \tau, j) \rightarrow 1/0$: PartVerify *is the "partial verification" algorithm that is used for defining EUF-CMA security. It takes as input an internal state* β*, a set of tuples of a public key and a message* $\{(\mathsf{pk}_i, m_i)\}_i$*, an aggregate signature* τ*, and a user index* j*. Then, it outputs either 1 (indicating that* τ *is valid with respect to the user index* j*) or 0 (indicating that* τ *is invalid with respect to the user index* j*).*

$\mathsf{Trace}(\beta, \{(\mathsf{pk}_i, m_i)\}_i, \tau) \rightarrow (\beta', f, V)$: Trace *is the tracing algorithm: It takes as input an internal state* β*, a set of tuples of a public key and a message* $\{(\mathsf{pk}_i, m_i)\}_i$*, and an aggregate signature* τ*. It then outputs the new internal state* β' *(for the next round), a feedback* f*, and a traced user set* V *(which could be empty). It is required that a feedback* f *and a traced user set* V *can be uniquely retrieved from an internal state* β.

$\mathsf{ExpASIT}^{\mathrm{Trace}}_{\Sigma_{\mathrm{ASIT}}}(\lambda, n, \{m_i\}_{i\in[n]})$:	$\mathsf{ExpASIT}^{\mathrm{PartVrf}}_{\Sigma_{\mathrm{ASIT}}}(\lambda, n, \beta, j, \{m_i\}_{i\in[n]})$:

for $i := 1$ to n **do**
  $(\mathsf{pk}_i, \mathsf{sk}_i) \leftarrow \Sigma_{\mathrm{ASIT}}.\mathsf{KeyGen}(1^\lambda)$
$t := 1$; $V_1 := \epsilon$; $\beta_1 := \epsilon$; $f_0 := \epsilon$
while true
  for $i := 1$ to n **do**
    $\sigma_{i,t} \leftarrow \Sigma_{\mathrm{ASIT}}.\mathsf{Sign}(\mathsf{sk}_i, m_{i,t})$
  $\tau_t \leftarrow$
    $\Sigma_{\mathrm{ASIT}}.\mathsf{Agg}(f_{t-1}, \{(\mathsf{pk}_i, m_{i,t}, \sigma_{i,t})\}_{i\in[n]})$
  $(\beta_{t+1}, f_t, V_t) \leftarrow$
      $\Sigma_{\mathrm{ASIT}}.\mathsf{Trace}(\beta_t, \{(\mathsf{pk}_i, m_{i,t})\}_{i\in[n]}, \tau_t)$
  $t \leftarrow t+1$
	for $i := 1$ to n **do**
	  $(\mathsf{pk}_i, \mathsf{sk}_i) \leftarrow \Sigma_{\mathrm{ASIT}}.\mathsf{KeyGen}(1^\lambda)$
	  $\sigma_i \leftarrow \Sigma_{\mathrm{ASIT}}.\mathsf{Sign}(\mathsf{sk}_i, m_i)$
	Let f be the feedback and V be the set of traced users that are determined by β
	$\tau \leftarrow \Sigma_{\mathrm{ASIT}}.\mathsf{Agg}(f, \{(\mathsf{pk}_i, m_i, \sigma_i)\}_{i\in[n]\setminus V})$
	$v \leftarrow$
	  $\Sigma_{\mathrm{ASIT}}.\mathsf{PartVerify}(\beta, \{(\mathsf{pk}_i, m_i)\}_{i\in[n]\setminus V}, \tau, j)$
	return v

Fig. 2. The experiments used for defining the correctness of an ASIT scheme.

This syntax captures the following usage scenario: First, all signers execute KeyGen. Next, each signer periodically runs Sign, and sends signed data to the aggregator. The aggregator executes Agg on the signed data periodically received from the signers, based on the feedback received from the verifier in the previous round. The verifier executes Trace on the aggregate signature received from the aggregator, updates the internal state, and outputs the feedback and the traced user set V. (Note that V is the set of users providing an invalid signature that the verifier identifies and thus the users in V are excluded from the user set used in the aggregation from the next round.) This feedback is sent to the aggregator.

Readers may wonder that the above definition lacks the verification algorithm AggVerify for an aggregate signature. However, we implicitly assume that Trace works as the verification algorithm. That is, if Trace outputs $V \neq \emptyset$, it implies that the given aggregate signature τ is invalid. We remark that PartVerify is an algorithm that is used only to define EUF-CMA security.

Definition 8 (Correctness of Trace). *Let Σ_{ASIT} be an ASIT scheme. The algorithm $\Sigma_{\mathrm{ASIT}}.\mathsf{Trace}$ satisfies correctness if for any $\lambda \in \mathbb{N}$, any $n = \mathrm{poly}(\lambda)$, any $t \in \mathbb{N}$, and any $m_1, \ldots, m_n \in \mathcal{M}$, it holds that $\Pr[V_t = \emptyset] = 1$ where V_t is the value in the experiment $\mathsf{ExpASIT}^{\mathrm{Trace}}_{\Sigma_{\mathrm{ASIT}}}(\lambda, n, \{m_i\}_{i\in[n]})$ described in Fig. 2.*

Definition 9 (Correctness of PartVerify). *Let Σ_{ASIT} be an ASIT scheme. The algorithm $\Sigma_{\mathrm{ASIT}}.\mathsf{PartVerify}$ satisfies correctness if for any $\lambda \in \mathbb{N}$, any $n = \mathrm{poly}(\lambda)$, any possible form of internal state β, any $j \in [n]$, and any $m_1, \ldots, m_n \in \mathcal{M}$, it holds that $\Pr[v = 1] = 1$ where v is an output of the experiment $\mathsf{ExpASIT}^{\mathrm{PartVrf}}_{\Sigma_{\mathrm{ASIT}}}(\lambda, n, \beta, j, \{m_i\}_{i\in[n]})$ described in Fig. 2.*

4.2 Security Notions

We define three security properties: EUF-CMA security, R-identifiability, which means that the verifier traces all attackers within R executions, and correctness, which means that the verifier does not trace legitimate users.

EUF-CMA Security. We define EUF-CMA security for an ASIT scheme. A potential adversary in this security notion includes all signers apart from an honest one and an aggregator. Note that we regard the aggregator as a potential adversary as in the same manner as in ordinary aggregate signature schemes.

Definition 10. *An ASIT scheme Σ_{ASIT} satisfies EUF-CMA security if for any $\lambda \in \mathbb{N}$, any $n = \mathrm{poly}(\lambda)$, and any PPT adversary $\mathcal{A}$, it holds that* $\Pr[\mathsf{ExpASIT}^{\mathrm{EUF\text{-}CMA}}_{\Sigma_{\mathrm{ASIT}},\mathcal{A}}(\lambda, n) = 1] = \mathrm{negl}(\lambda)$ *where* $\mathsf{ExpASIT}^{\mathrm{EUF\text{-}CMA}}_{\Sigma_{\mathrm{ASIT}},\mathcal{A}}$ *is the following experiment.*

$\mathsf{ExpASIT}^{\mathrm{EUF\text{-}CMA}}_{\Sigma_{\mathrm{ASIT}},\mathcal{A}}(\lambda, n)$

$\forall i \in [n], (\mathsf{pk}_i, \mathsf{sk}_i) \leftarrow \Sigma_{\mathrm{ASIT}}.\mathsf{KeyGen}(1^\lambda);$

$t := 1; Q := \emptyset; W_1 := \emptyset;$: Output 0 when $\mathcal{A}$ halts

run $\mathcal{A}^{O_S(\cdot), O_V(\cdot)}(\mathsf{pk}_1, \{(\mathsf{pk}_i, \mathsf{sk}_i)\}_{i \in [n] \setminus \{1\}})$

where $\mathcal{A}$ can halt at an arbitrary point, $\mathcal{A}$ is allowed to make arbitrarily polynomial many queries to the signing oracle O_S and the verification oracle O_V, which work as follows:

- O_S**:** *Given a query $m \in \mathcal{M}$, O_S runs $\sigma \leftarrow \Sigma_{\mathrm{ASIT}}.\mathsf{Sign}(\mathsf{sk}_1, m)$, returns σ to $\mathcal{A}$, and updates $Q \leftarrow Q \cup \{m\}$.*
- O_V**:** *Given a set of pairs of an index and a message and an aggregate signature $(\{(i, m_{i,t})\}_{i \in I_t}, \tau_t)$, O_V outputs 1 (indicating that $\mathcal{A}$ wins) and terminates the experiment if it holds that $\Sigma_{\mathrm{ASIT}}.\mathsf{PartVerify}(\beta_t, \{(\mathsf{pk}_i, m_{i,t})\}_{i \in I_t}, \tau_t, 1) = 1$, $1 \notin W_t$, and $m_{1,t} \notin Q$. Otherwise, O_V executes $(\beta_{t+1}, f_t, V_t) \leftarrow \Sigma_{\mathrm{ASIT}}.\mathsf{Trace}(\beta_t, \{(\mathsf{pk}_i, m_{i,t})\}_{i \in I_t}, \tau_t)$, returns (f_t, V_t) to $\mathcal{A}$, and updates $W_t = W_t \cup V_t$ and $t \leftarrow t + 1$.*

Note that the user index 1 is treated as the challenge user, and an adversary is given the secret keys for the remaining users with index 2 to n, and thus the signing oracle is necessary only for the user index 1. Note also that the experiment can output 1 only if $\mathcal{A}$ makes an O_V-query that contains a forged signature with respect to the user index 1 (judged using the algorithm PartVerify).

***R*-Identifiability and Correctness.** Similar to DTT, we define R-identifiability and correctness of Σ_{ASIT}. A potential adversary in these security notions is a set of users $C \subseteq [n]$ that may generate invalid signatures. Thus, an aggregator and the verifier behave honestly. These security notions are defined based on the following experiment $\mathsf{ExpASIT}^{\mathrm{trace}}_{\Sigma_{\mathrm{ASIT}},\mathcal{A}}(\lambda, n)$ in which a stateful adversary $\mathcal{A}$ is executed:

$\mathsf{ExpASIT}_{\Sigma_{\mathrm{ASIT}},\mathcal{A}}(\lambda, n)$

$\forall i \in [n], (\mathsf{pk}_i, \mathsf{sk}_i) \leftarrow \Sigma_{\mathrm{ASIT}}.\mathsf{KeyGen}(1^\lambda);$

$C \leftarrow \mathcal{A}(\{(\mathsf{pk}_i, \mathsf{sk}_i)\}_{i \in [n]});$

$t := 1; r := 0; W_1 := \emptyset; \beta_1 := \epsilon;$

$f_0 := \epsilon; I_1 := [n]; J_1 := C;$

run $\mathcal{A}^{O_T(\cdot)}(\{(\mathsf{pk}_i, \mathsf{sk}_i)\}_{i \in [n]})$

: Output $(W := \bigcup_{t'=1}^{t} V_{t'}, C, r)$ when $\mathcal{A}$ halts

where $\mathcal{A}$ can halt at an arbitrary point, and $\mathcal{A}$ is allowed to make arbitrarily (polynomially) many queries to the tracing oracle O_T. Let $W_t := \bigcup_{t'=1}^{t} V_t$, $I_t := [n] \backslash W_t$, and $J_t := C \setminus W_t$. Given a query $(\{m_{i,t}\}_{i \in I_t}, \{(m_{j,t}, \sigma_{j,t})\}_{j \in J_t})$ from $\mathcal{A}$, O_T operates as follows:

1. If there exists $j \in J_t$ such that $\Sigma_{\mathrm{ASIT}}.\mathsf{Verify}(\mathsf{pk}_j, m_{j,t}, \sigma_{j,t}) = 0$, then set $r \leftarrow r + 1$.
2. For every $i \in I_t$, compute $\sigma_{i,t} \leftarrow \Sigma_{\mathrm{ASIT}}.\mathsf{Sign}(\mathsf{sk}_i, m_{i,t})$.
3. Compute $\tau_t \leftarrow \Sigma_{\mathrm{ASIT}}.\mathsf{Agg}(f_{t-1}, \{(\mathsf{pk}_i, m_{i,t}, \sigma_{i,t})\}_{i \in I_t \cup J_t})$.
4. Compute $(\beta_{t+1}, f_t, V_t) \leftarrow \Sigma_{\mathrm{ASIT}}.\mathsf{Trace}(\beta_t, \{(\mathsf{pk}_i, m_{i,t})\}_{i \in I_t \cup J_t}, \tau_t)$.
5. Return (f_t, V_t) to $\mathcal{A}$ and set $t \leftarrow t + 1$.

We define R-identifiability and correctness of an ASIT scheme as follows.

Definition 11 (R-Identifiability). *An ASIT scheme Σ_{ASIT} satisfies R-identifiability if for any $\lambda \in \mathbb{N}$, any $n = \mathrm{poly}(\lambda)$, and any PPT adversary $\mathcal{A}$, we have*

$$\Pr[(C \not\subseteq W) \mid (W, C, r) \leftarrow \mathsf{ExpASIT}_{\Sigma_{\mathrm{ASIT}}, \mathcal{A}}(\lambda, n) \wedge (r \geq R)] = \mathrm{negl}(\lambda).$$

Definition 12 (Correctness). *An ASIT scheme Σ_{ASIT} satisfies correctness if $\Sigma_{\mathrm{ASIT}}.\mathsf{Trace}$ and $\Sigma_{\mathrm{ASIT}}.\mathsf{PartVerify}$ satisfy correctnesses respectively, and for any $\lambda \in \mathbb{N}$, any $n = \mathrm{poly}(\lambda)$, and any PPT adversary $\mathcal{A}$, we have*

$$\Pr[([n] \backslash C) \cap W \neq \emptyset \mid (W, C, r) \leftarrow \mathsf{ExpASIT}_{\Sigma_{\mathrm{ASIT}}, \mathcal{A}}(\lambda, n)] = \mathrm{negl}(\lambda).$$

5 A Generic Construction of an ASIT from an Aggregate Signature Scheme and a DTT

In this section, we present our generic construction of an ASIT scheme based on an aggregate signature scheme and a DTT.

5.1 Construction

Let $\Sigma_{\mathrm{AS}} = (\mathsf{KeyGen}, \mathsf{Sign}, \mathsf{Verify}, \mathsf{Agg}, , \mathsf{AggVerify})$ be an aggregate signature scheme, and let $\Sigma_{\mathrm{DTT}} = (\mathsf{Initialize}, \mathsf{Trace})$ be a DTT. Using Σ_{AS} and Σ_{DTT} as building blocks, we construct an ASIT scheme $\Sigma_{\mathrm{ASIT}} = (\mathsf{KeyGen}, \mathsf{Sign}, \mathsf{Verify}, \mathsf{Agg}, \mathsf{PartVerify}, \mathsf{Trace})$ as described in Fig. 3.

A verifier in Σ_{ASIT} maintains an internal state and a user partition of Σ_{DTT}. The algorithms $\Sigma_{\mathrm{ASIT}}.\mathsf{KeyGen}$, $\Sigma_{\mathrm{ASIT}}.\mathsf{Sign}$ and $\Sigma_{\mathrm{ASIT}}.\mathsf{Verify}$ are the same as those in Σ_{AS}. The verifier initially executes $\Sigma_{\mathrm{DTT}}.\mathsf{Initialize}$, and in subsequent rounds the aggregator execute $\Sigma_{\mathrm{AS}}.\mathsf{Agg}$ based on the verifier's feedback from the previous round. The algorithm $\Sigma_{\mathrm{ASIT}}.\mathsf{Agg}$ generates aggregate signatures for each subset of the user partition generated by the use of Σ_{DTT}. When $\Sigma_{\mathrm{ASIT}}.\mathsf{Trace}$ finds that an invalid signature is contained in τ, Σ_{ASIT} uses the index of the corresponding subset in the user partition to run $\Sigma_{\mathrm{DTT}}.\mathsf{Trace}$ (and does not verify the rest of the aggregate signatures).

Theorem 3 (Correctness of $\Sigma_{\mathrm{ASIT}}.\mathsf{Trace}$). *If Σ_{AS} satisfies correctness, then $\Sigma_{\mathrm{ASIT}}.\mathsf{Trace}$ also satisfies correctness.*

$\mathsf{KeyGen}(1^\lambda)$:
  $(\mathsf{pk}, \mathsf{sk}) \leftarrow \Sigma_{\mathrm{AS}}.\mathsf{KeyGen}(1^\lambda)$
  return $(\mathsf{pk}, \mathsf{sk})$

$\mathsf{Sign}(\mathsf{sk}, m)$:
  $\sigma \leftarrow \Sigma_{\mathrm{AS}}.\mathsf{Sign}(\mathsf{sk}, m)$
  return σ

$\mathsf{Verify}(\mathsf{pk}, m, \sigma)$:
  $v \leftarrow \Sigma_{\mathrm{AS}}.\mathsf{Verify}(\mathsf{pk}, m, \sigma)$
  return v

$\mathsf{Agg}(f, \{(\mathsf{pk}_i, m_i, \sigma_i)\}_{i \in [n]})$:
  if $f = \epsilon$ **then**
    $(\alpha, P) \leftarrow \Sigma_{\mathrm{DTT}}.\mathsf{Initialize}(1^\lambda, 1^n)$
  else $P := f$
  parse $(S_i)_{i \in [|P|]} \leftarrow P$
  for $j := 1$ to $|P|$ **do**
    $\tau_j \leftarrow \Sigma_{\mathrm{AS}}.\mathsf{Agg}(\{(\mathsf{pk}_i, m_i, \sigma_i)\}_{i \in S_j})$
  return $\tau := (\tau_j)_{j \in [|P|]}$

$\mathsf{PartVerify}(\beta, \{(\mathsf{pk}_j, m_j)\}_{j \in [n]}, \tau, i)$:
  if $\beta = \epsilon$ **then**
    $(\alpha, P) \leftarrow \Sigma_{\mathrm{DTT}}.\mathsf{Initialize}(1^\lambda, 1^n)$
  else parse $(\alpha, P) \leftarrow \beta$
  parse $(S_i)_{i \in [|P|]} \leftarrow P$ and $(\tau_i)_{i \in [|\tau|]} \leftarrow \tau$
  find i' s.t. $i \in S_{i'}$
  $v \leftarrow \Sigma_{\mathrm{AS}}.\mathsf{AggVerify}(\{(\mathsf{pk}_j, m_j)\}_{j \in S_{i'}}, \tau_{i'})$
  return v

$\mathsf{Trace}(\beta, \{(\mathsf{pk}_i, m_i)\}_{i \in [n]}, \tau)$:
  if $\beta = \epsilon$ **then**
    $(\alpha, P) \leftarrow \Sigma_{\mathrm{DTT}}.\mathsf{Initialize}(1^\lambda, 1^n)$
  else parse $(\alpha, P) \leftarrow \beta$
  parse $(S_i)_{i \in [|P|]} \leftarrow P$ and $(\tau_i)_{i \in [|\tau|]} \leftarrow \tau$
  $f' := P;\ \beta' := (\alpha, P);\ V := \emptyset$
  for $i := 1$ to $|\tau|$ **do**
    $v \leftarrow \Sigma_{\mathrm{AS}}.\mathsf{AggVerify}(\{(\mathsf{pk}_j, m_j)\}_{j \in S_i}, \tau_i)$
    if $v = 0$ **then**
      $(\alpha', P', V) \leftarrow \Sigma_{\mathrm{DTT}}.\mathsf{Trace}(\alpha, i)$
      $f' := P';\ \beta' := (\alpha', P')$
      break (†)
  return (β', f', V)

Fig. 3. Our generic construction of an ASIT scheme Σ_{ASIT} from an aggregate signature scheme Σ_{AS} and a DTT Σ_{DTT}. (†) End the **for** loop and proceed to the next line.

Proof Observe that an output of $\Sigma_{\mathrm{ASIT}}.\mathsf{Agg}$ consists of multiple (polynomially many) aggregate signatures of the underlying scheme $\Sigma_{\mathrm{AS}}.\mathsf{Agg}$. Furthermore, $\Sigma_{\mathrm{ASIT}}.\mathsf{Trace}$ outputs a traced user set $V \neq \emptyset$ if and only if $\Sigma_{\mathrm{AS}}.\mathsf{AggVerify}$ outputs 0. Since each algorithm in $\mathsf{ExpASIT}^{\mathrm{Trace}}_{\Sigma_{\mathrm{ASIT}}}$ is executed honestly and Σ_{AS} is correct, the probability that $\mathsf{ExpASIT}^{\mathrm{Trace}}_{\Sigma_{\mathrm{ASIT}}}$ outputs $V \neq \emptyset$ is 0, which guarantees the correctness of $\Sigma_{\mathrm{ASIT}}.\mathsf{Trace}$. □

Theorem 4 (Correctness of $\Sigma_{\mathrm{ASIT}}.\mathsf{PartVerify}$). *If Σ_{AS} satisfies correctness, then $\Sigma_{\mathrm{ASIT}}.\mathsf{PartVerify}$ also satisfies correctness.*

Proof. Observe that an output of $\Sigma_{\mathrm{ASIT}}.\mathsf{Agg}$ consists of multiple (polynomially many) aggregate signatures of the underlying scheme $\Sigma_{\mathrm{AS}}.\mathsf{Agg}$, and an output of $\Sigma_{\mathrm{ASIT}}.\mathsf{PartVerify}$ is that of $\Sigma_{\mathrm{AS}}.\mathsf{AggVerify}$. Since each algorithm in $\mathsf{ExpASIT}^{\mathrm{PartVrf}}_{\Sigma_{\mathrm{ASIT}}}$ is executed honestly and Σ_{AS} is correct, $\mathsf{ExpASIT}^{\mathrm{PartVrf}}_{\Sigma_{\mathrm{ASIT}}}$ outputs 1 with probability 1, which guarantees the correctness of $\Sigma_{\mathrm{ASIT}}.\mathsf{PartVerify}$. □

5.2 Security Proofs

EUF-CMA Security. We first show the EUF-CMA security of Σ_{ASIT}.

Theorem 5. *If Σ_{AS} satisfies EUF-CMA security, then Σ_{ASIT} satisfies EUF-CMA security.*

Proof. We assume for contradiction that there exists a PPT adversary $\mathcal{A}_{ASIT}$ that breaks EUF-CMA security of Σ_{ASIT} with non-negligible probability, and construct a PPT adversary $\mathcal{A}_{AS}$ that breaks EUF-CMA security of Σ_{AS}. We first describe how our adversary $\mathcal{A}_{AS}$ works in the experiment $\mathsf{ExpAS}^{\mathrm{EUF\text{-}CMA}}_{\Sigma_{\mathrm{AS}},\mathcal{A}_{AS}}$, and then show that $\mathcal{A}_{AS}$ indeed breaks EUF-CMA security of Σ_{AS}.

$\mathcal{A}_{AS}$'s experiment generates $(\mathsf{pk}_i, \mathsf{sk}_i) \leftarrow \Sigma_{\mathrm{AS}}.\mathsf{KeyGen}(\lambda)$ $(i \in [n])$, gives pk_1 and $\{(\mathsf{pk}_i, \mathsf{sk}_i)\}_{i\in[n]\setminus\{1\}}$ to $\mathcal{A}_{AS}$, and sets $Q := \emptyset$. Next, $\mathcal{A}_{AS}$ sets $W_1 := \emptyset$. Then, $\mathcal{A}_{AS}$, who is given access to the signing oracle $\Sigma_{\mathrm{AS}}.\mathsf{Sign}(\mathsf{sk}_1, \cdot)$, runs $\mathcal{A}_{ASIT}^{O_S,O_V}(\mathsf{pk}_1, \{(\mathsf{pk}_i, \mathsf{sk}_i)\}_{i\in[n]\setminus\{1\}})$ with simulating O_S and O_V as follows.

O_S: When $\mathcal{A}_{ASIT}$ makes an O_S-query m, $\mathcal{A}_{AS}$ makes a signing query m to its own oracle, receives σ from the signing oracle, and returns σ to $\mathcal{A}_{ASIT}$. $\mathcal{A}_{AS}$ also updates $Q \leftarrow Q \cup \{m\}$.

O_V: When $\mathcal{A}_{ASIT}$ makes a query $(\{(i, m_{i,t})\}_{i\in I_t}, \tau_t)$ to O_V, $\mathcal{A}_{AS}$ responds as follows (where we implicitly assume that $I_t \subseteq [n]$):
- If $\Sigma_{\mathrm{ASIT}}.\mathsf{PartVerify}(\beta_t, \{(\mathsf{pk}_i, m_{i,t})\}_{i\in I_t}, \tau_t, 1) = 1$, $1 \notin W_t$, and $m_{1,t} \notin Q$, then halt the simulation, output τ_t, $\{m_{i,t}\}_{i\in I_t}$ and $S := I_t$ to $\mathcal{A}_{AS}$'s EUF-CMA experiment, and terminate.
- Otherwise, execute $(\beta_{t+1}, f_t, V_t) \leftarrow \Sigma_{\mathrm{ASIT}}.\mathsf{Trace}(\beta_t, \{(\mathsf{pk}_i, m_{i,t})\}_{i\in I_t}, \tau_t)$, return (f_t, V_t) to $\mathcal{A}_{ASIT}$, and set $W_{t+1} = W_t \cup V_t$ and $t \leftarrow t + 1$.

When $\mathcal{A}_{ASIT}$ halts, $\mathcal{A}_{AS}$ also halts. (Note that $\mathcal{A}_{AS}$ perfectly simulates the EUF-CMA experiment for $\mathcal{A}_{ASIT}$.)

We argue that $\mathcal{A}_{AS}$ satisfies the winning condition in the EUF-CMA experiment with non-negligible probability. Suppose that $\mathcal{A}_{AS}$ outputs τ_t, $\{m_{i,t}\}_{i\in I_t}$ and S (i.e., $\mathcal{A}_{ASIT}$ makes a query to O_V on $(\{(i, m_{i,t})\}_{i\in I_t}, \tau_t)$ such that $\Sigma_{\mathrm{ASIT}}.\mathsf{PartVerify}(\beta_t, \{(\mathsf{pk}_i, m_{i,t})\}_{i\in I_t}, \tau_t, 1) = 1$, $1 \notin W_t$ and $m_{1,t} \notin Q$). Since $\Sigma_{\mathrm{ASIT}}.\mathsf{PartVerify}(\beta_t, \{(\mathsf{pk}_i, m_{i,t})\}_{i\in I_t}, \tau_t, 1) = 1$, it holds that $1 \in S \subseteq [n]$. Thus, $\mathcal{A}_{AS}$ wins in this case. Observe that if $\mathcal{A}_{ASIT}$ makes such a query, it means that $\mathcal{A}_{ASIT}$ breaks the EUF-CMA security of Σ_{ASIT}. Hence, if $\mathcal{A}_{ASIT}$ breaks the EUF-CMA security of Σ_{ASIT} with non-negligible probability, then $\mathcal{A}_{AS}$ also breaks the EUF-CMA security of Σ_{AS} with non-negligible probability. □

***R*-Identifiability and Correctness.** Here, we show R-identifiability and correctness of Σ_{ASIT}. Note that the correctness of $\Sigma_{\mathrm{ASIT}}.\mathsf{Trace}$ and $\Sigma_{\mathrm{ASIT}}.\mathsf{PartVerify}$ are already done.

Theorem 6. *If Σ_{DTT} satisfies R-identifiability, then Σ_{ASIT} satisfies R-identifiability.*

Proof. To prove the theorem, we demonstrate security reductions from Σ_{ASIT} to Σ_{DTT}. In what follows, we describe the adversary $\mathcal{A}_{DTT}$ in $\mathsf{ExpDTT}_{\Sigma_{\mathrm{DTT}},\mathcal{A}_{DTT}}$ that simulates the experiment $\mathsf{ExpASIT}^{\mathrm{Trace}}_{\Sigma_{\mathrm{ASIT}},\mathcal{A}_{ASIT}}$ for an adversary $\mathcal{A}_{ASIT}$.

$\mathcal{A}_{DTT}$'s experiment generates $(\alpha_1, P_1) \leftarrow \Sigma_{\mathrm{DTT}}.\mathsf{Initialize}(1^\lambda, 1^n)$, and gives (α_1, P_1) to $\mathcal{A}_{DTT}$. $\mathcal{A}_{DTT}$ first runs $(\mathsf{pk}_i, \mathsf{sk}_i) \leftarrow \Sigma_{\mathrm{ASIT}}.\mathsf{KeyGen}(1^\lambda)$ for $i \in [n]$, and then gives $\{(\mathsf{pk}_i, \mathsf{sk}_i)\}_{i\in[n]}$ to $\mathcal{A}_{ASIT}$, which in turn outputs the set of users $C \subseteq [n]$. Then, $\mathcal{A}_{DTT}$ outputs C to $\mathcal{A}_{DTT}$'s experiment as a traitor set. $\mathcal{A}_{DTT}$

then sets $t' := 1$, $r := 0$, $W_1 := \emptyset$, $\beta_1 := \epsilon$, $f_0 := \epsilon$, $I_1 := [n]$, and $J_1 := C$, and continues the execution of $\mathcal{A}_{ASIT}$ that now may start making O_T queries. When $\mathcal{A}_{ASIT}$ makes an O_T-query $(\{m_i\}_{i \in I_t}, \{(m_{j,t}, \sigma_{j,t})\}_{j \in J_t})$, $\mathcal{A}_{DTT}$ proceed as follows:

1. If there exists $j \in J_t$ such that $\Sigma_{\mathrm{ASIT}}.\mathsf{Verify}(\mathsf{pk}_j, m_{j,t}, \sigma_{j,t}) = 0$, then $r \leftarrow r+1$.
2. For every $i \in I_t$, compute $\sigma_{i,t} \leftarrow \Sigma_{\mathrm{ASIT}}.\mathsf{Sign}(\mathsf{sk}_i, m_{i,t})$.
3. Compute $\tau_t \leftarrow \Sigma_{\mathrm{ASIT}}.\mathsf{Agg}(f_{t-1}, \{(\mathsf{pk}_i, m_{i,t}, \sigma_{i,t})\}_{i \in I_t \cup J_t})$.
4. Simulate $(\beta_{t+1}, f_t, V_t) \leftarrow \Sigma_{\mathrm{ASIT}}.\mathsf{Trace}(\beta_t, \{(\mathsf{pk}_i, m_{i,t})\}_{i \in I_t \cup J_t}, \tau_t)$ where when $\Sigma_{\mathrm{DTT}}.\mathsf{Trace}(\alpha_t, i)$ needs to be executed, $\mathcal{A}_{DTT}$ makes a query i to $\mathcal{A}_{DTT}$'s own tracing oracle O_T to obtain $(\alpha_{t+1}, P_{t+1}, V_t)$ instead of running $\Sigma_{\mathrm{DTT}}.\mathsf{Trace}(\alpha_t, i)$ by itself. Note that in our construction Σ_{ASIT}, the update of the internal state $\beta = (\alpha, P)$ occurs only when $\Sigma_{\mathrm{DTT}}.\mathsf{Trace}(\alpha, i)$ is executed, and thus the internal state used by $\mathcal{A}_{DTT}$ to simulate the tracing oracle for $\mathcal{A}_{ASIT}$ and the internal state used in $\mathcal{A}_{DTT}$'s tracing oracle are always synchronized.
5. Return (f_t, V_t) to $\mathcal{A}_{ASIT}$, and set $W_{t+1} \leftarrow W_t \cup V_t$, $I_{t+1} \leftarrow I_t \setminus W_t$, $J_{t+1} \leftarrow C \setminus W_t$, and $t \leftarrow t+1$.

When $\mathcal{A}_{ASIT}$ halts, $\mathcal{A}_{DTT}$ also halts. (Note that $\mathcal{A}_{DTT}$ correctly simulates the tracing oracle O_T for $\mathcal{A}_{ASIT}$. Furthermore, both $\mathcal{A}_{DTT}$ and $\mathcal{A}_{ASIT}$ run on the same traitor set C.)

Observe that $\mathcal{A}_{DTT}$ makes a query to O_T if and only if there exists $j \in J_t$ such that $\Sigma_{\mathrm{ASIT}}.\mathsf{Verify}(\mathsf{pk}_j, m_{j,t}, \sigma_{j,t}) = 0$, due to the design of $\Sigma_{\mathrm{ASIT}}.\mathsf{Trace}$. Thus, letting t' denote the counter denoting the number of O_T queries in $\mathcal{A}_{DTT}$'s R-identifiability experiment, it holds that $t' = r$ when $\mathcal{A}_{DTT}$ halts the simulation of $\mathcal{A}_{ASIT}$'s R-identifiability experiment. Obviously, if $\mathcal{A}_{ASIT}$ results in a set $W \notin C$, then so does $\mathcal{A}_{DTT}$. Therefore, if there exists a PPT adversary $\mathcal{A}_{ASIT}$ that breaks the R-identifiability of Σ_{ASIT}, then there exists a PPT adversary $\mathcal{A}_{DTT}$ that violates the R-identifiability of Σ_{DTT}. □

Theorem 7. *If Σ_{DTT} satisfies completeness, then Σ_{ASIT} satisfies correctness.*

Proof. (of Theorem 7) Given an adversary $\mathcal{A}_{ASIT}$ attacking the correctness of Σ_{ASIT}, we consider exactly the same reduction algorithm $\mathcal{A}_{DTT}$ as in the proof of Theorem 6. Obviously, if $\mathcal{A}_{ASIT}$ results in a set W_t such that $([n] \setminus C) \cap W_t \neq \emptyset$, then so does $\mathcal{A}_{DTT}$. Therefore, the existence of such $\mathcal{A}_{ASIT}$ means the existence of a PPT adversary $\mathcal{A}_{DTT}$ that violates the completeness of Σ_{DTT}. □

6 Comparison

We compare our schemes with the existing schemes by Hartung et al. [HKK+16] which we denote by HKK^+, and by Sato et al. [SSM20]. In [HKK+16], they proposed a so-called a fault-tolerant signature scheme, which can be understood as an ASIT scheme with a one-round tracing algorithm. However, since this scheme can be trivially extended to a multi-round setting, for the comparison in this section, we use such this extension which we hereafter refer to as $\mathsf{multi\text{-}HKK}^+$.

Table 1. Comparison among existing schemes and proposed schemes. Rounds (R) is the maximum number of rounds that is necessary to trace all users providing invalid signatures, and Sigs per round (max) is the maximum number of signatures that are aggregated (and thus corresponds to the partition of the user set) in a single round. Static and Dynamic represent statically traceable and dynamically traceable, respectively. Each value represents the following: n is the number of users, and d is the number of users providing invalid signatures.

Scheme	Rounds (R)	Sigs per round (max)	Static	Dynamic
multi-HKK$^+$	$2d+1$	$2d+1$ (fixed)	✓	?
Sato et al. [SSM20]	$d\log_2 n + d$	$2d+1$	✓	?
AS-FT-2	$d\log_2 n + d$	$2d+1$	✓	✓
AS-FT-3	$2 \cdot 3^d d\log_2 n + d$	$d+1$	✓	✓

For completeness, we give the description of multi-HKK$^+$ in Appendix A. We remark that HKK$^+$ is able to detect at most d invalid signatures in a single round, where d is a fixed value hard-wired in the scheme. However, the correctness of HKK$^+$ is compromised if more than d invalid signatures are involved. multi-HKK$^+$ inherits this restricted form of correctness. AS-FT-2 and AS-FT-3 denote the ASIT schemes obtained from our generic construction by instantiating the underlying DTT with FT-2 and FT-3, respectively.

Table 1 shows the comparison among these schemes in terms of the number of communication rounds, the maximum number of transmitted signatures per round, and the types of traceability that each scheme achieves: An ASIT scheme is *statically traceable* if it satisfies R-identifiability for some R and correctness in a setting where the adversary generates invalid signatures for all users in C (the adversarial set of users) in every round. In contrast, an ASIT scheme is *dynamically traceable* if it satisfies both of the security requirements as defined in Sect. 4.2 where the adversary may adaptively decide which user in C generates an invalid signature in each round.

As indicated in Table 1, multi-HKK$^+$ and the scheme in [SSM20] are statically traceable, but it is unclear if they are dynamically traceable. The maximum numbers of signatures per round of these two schemes are the same ($2d+1$), but it is constantly $2d+1$ in every round in multi-HKK$^+$, while it can vary from 1 to $2d+1$ as the tracing proceeds in [SSM20]. Comparing [SSM20] and AS-FT-2, the number of rounds and the number of signatures per round are the same, but AS-FT-2 is traceable for both static and dynamic adversaries, while the dynamic traceability of [SSM20] is unclear.

Our schemes are able to trace both dynamic and static adversaries, and the number of rounds required for tracing does not increase compared to the existing method. We remark that the number of rounds and signatures of AS-FT-2 and AS-FT-3 are due to Theorems 1 and 2, respectively. Therefore, our proposed schemes are more suitable for practical usage scenario (e.g. sensor networks) for

$\mathsf{KeyGen}(1^\lambda)$:
$(\mathsf{pk}, \mathsf{sk}) \leftarrow \Sigma_{\mathrm{AS}}.\mathsf{KeyGen}(1^\lambda)$
return $(\mathsf{pk}, \mathsf{sk})$
$\mathsf{Sign}(\mathsf{sk}, m)$:
$\sigma \leftarrow \Sigma_{\mathrm{AS}}.\mathsf{Sign}(\mathsf{sk}, m)$
return σ
$\mathsf{Verify}(\mathsf{pk}, m, \sigma)$:
$v \leftarrow \Sigma_{\mathrm{AS}}.\mathsf{Verify}(\mathsf{pk}, m, \sigma)$
return v
$\mathsf{Agg}(f, \{(\mathsf{pk}_i, m_i, \sigma_i)\}_{i\in[n]})$:
if $f = \epsilon$ **then**
$P := [n]$
else $P := f$
parse $(S_i)_{i\in[\lvert P\rvert]} \leftarrow P$
for $j := 1$ to $\lvert P\rvert$ **do**
$\tau_j \leftarrow \Sigma_{\mathrm{AS}}.\mathsf{Agg}(\{(\mathsf{pk}_i, m_i, \sigma_i)\}_{i\in S_j})$
return $\tau := (\tau_j)_{j\in[\lvert P\rvert]}$
	$\mathsf{PartVerify}(\beta, \{(\mathsf{pk}_j, m_j)\}_{j\in[n]}, \tau, i)$:
	parse $(f, W, t) \leftarrow \beta$
	parse $(S_i)_{i\in[\lvert P\rvert]} \leftarrow P$; $(\tau_i)_{i\in[\lvert\tau\rvert]} \leftarrow \tau$
	find i' s.t. $i \in S_{i'}$
	$v \leftarrow \Sigma_{\mathrm{AS}}.\mathsf{AggVerify}(\{(\mathsf{pk}_j, m_j)\}_{j\in S_{i'}}, \tau_{i'})$
	return v
	$\mathsf{Trace}(\beta, \{(\mathsf{pk}_i, m_i)\}_{i\in[n]}, \tau)$:
	if $\beta = \epsilon$ **then**
	$P := \emptyset$, $W := [n]$, $t := 0$
	else parse $(P, W, t) \leftarrow \beta$
	parse $(S_i)_{i\in[\lvert P\rvert]} \leftarrow P$ and $(\tau_i)_{i\in[\lvert\tau\rvert]} \leftarrow \tau$
	for $i := 1$ to $\lvert\tau\rvert$ **do**
	$v \leftarrow \Sigma_{\mathrm{AS}}.\mathsf{AggVerify}(\{(\mathsf{pk}_j, m_j)\}_{j\in S_i}, \tau_i)$
	$t \leftarrow t + 1$
	if $t = q$ **then**
	$V := W \setminus \bigcup_{v_i=1} S_i$
	else $V := \emptyset$; $W' := W \setminus \bigcup_{v_i=1} S_i$
	$f' \leftarrow (T_{qt}, \ldots, T_{qt+(q-1)})$; $\beta' \leftarrow (f', W', t)$
	return (β', f', V)

Fig. 4. The ASIT scheme multi-HKK$^+$ based on an ordinary aggregate signature scheme Σ_{AS} and a cover free family.

all situations where invalid signatures could be generated constantly by dynamically determined users/devices.

Acknowledgement. This paper is based on results obtained from a project commissioned by the New Energy and Industrial Technology Development Organization (NEDO). The third author was supported by JSPS KAKENHI Grant Number JP18K18055.

A multi-HKK$^+$

Here, we give the description of multi-HKK$^+$ that is constructed based on an ordinary aggregate signature scheme Σ_{AS} and a cover free family. Recall that a d-cover free family (d-CFF) $\mathcal{F} = (\mathcal{S}, \mathcal{B})$ consists of a set $\mathcal{S}$ of m elements and a set $\mathcal{B}$ of n subsets of $\mathcal{S}$, where $d < m < n$, such that for any d subsets $B_{i_1}, \ldots, B_{i_d} \in \mathcal{B}$ and for all distinct $B \in \mathcal{B} \setminus \{B_{i_1}, \ldots, B_{i_d}\}$, it holds that $B \notin \bigcup_{j\in[d]} B_{i_j}$.

Let d be an integer such that there exists a prime $q = 2d+1$. Let $\mathcal{F} = (\mathcal{S}, \mathcal{B})$ be a d-CFF based on quadratic polynomials where $\mathcal{S}$ and $\mathcal{B}$ are defined as follows:

$$\mathcal{S} := \{(x_i, y_i) : i = 0, \ldots, q^2 - 1\} \text{ where } (x_i, y_i) := (\lfloor i/q \rfloor, i \bmod q).$$
$$\mathcal{B} := \{B_{f_0}, \ldots, B_{f_{q^3-1}}\} \text{ where } B_{f_j} := \{(0, f_j(0)), \ldots, (q-1, f_j(q-1))\}$$
$$\text{and } f_j(X) := (\lfloor j/q^2 \rfloor)X^2 + (\lfloor (j \bmod q^2)/q \rfloor)X + (j \bmod q).$$

Figure 4 describes multi-HKK$^+$ where $T_i = \{j \in \{0, \ldots, q^{k+1} - 1\} \mid f_j(x_i) = y_i\}$ $(i = 0, \ldots, q^2 - 1)$.

References

[AGH10] Ahn, J.H., Green, M., Hohenberger, S.: Synchronized aggregate signatures: new definitions, constructions and applications. In: CCS 2010, pp. 473–484. ACM (2010)

[BGLS03] Boneh, D., Gentry, C., Lynn, B., Shacham, H.: Aggregate and verifiably encrypted signatures from bilinear maps. In: Biham, E. (ed.) EUROCRYPT 2003. LNCS, vol. 2656, pp. 416–432. Springer, Heidelberg (2003). https://doi.org/10.1007/3-540-39200-9_26

[FT99] Fiat, A., Tassa, T.: Dynamic traitor tracing. In: Wiener, M. (ed.) CRYPTO 1999. LNCS, vol. 1666, pp. 354–371. Springer, Heidelberg (1999). https://doi.org/10.1007/3-540-48405-1_23

[GLOW12] Gerbush, M., Lewko, A., O'Neill, A., Waters, B.: Dual form signatures: an approach for proving security from static assumptions. In: Wang, X., Sako, K. (eds.) ASIACRYPT 2012. LNCS, vol. 7658, pp. 25–42. Springer, Heidelberg (2012). https://doi.org/10.1007/978-3-642-34961-4_4

[GR06] Gentry, C., Ramzan, Z.: Identity-based aggregate signatures. In: Yung, M., Dodis, Y., Kiayias, A., Malkin, T. (eds.) PKC 2006. LNCS, vol. 3958, pp. 257–273. Springer, Heidelberg (2006). https://doi.org/10.1007/11745853_17

[HKK+16] Hartung, G., Kaidel, B., Koch, A., Koch, J., Rupp, A.: Fault-tolerant aggregate signatures. In: Cheng, C.-M., Chung, K.-M., Persiano, G., Yang, B.-Y. (eds.) PKC 2016. LNCS, vol. 9614, pp. 331–356. Springer, Heidelberg (2016). https://doi.org/10.1007/978-3-662-49384-7_13

[HSW13] Hohenberger, S., Sahai, A., Waters, B.: Full domain hash from (leveled) multilinear maps and identity-based aggregate signatures. In: Canetti, R., Garay, J.A. (eds.) CRYPTO 2013. LNCS, vol. 8042, pp. 494–512. Springer, Heidelberg (2013). https://doi.org/10.1007/978-3-642-40041-4_27

[LLY15] Lee, K., Lee, D.H., Yung, M.: Sequential aggregate signatures with short public keys without random oracles. Theor. Comput. Sci. **579**, 100–125 (2015)

[LMRS04] Lysyanskaya, A., Micali, S., Reyzin, L., Shacham, H.: Sequential aggregate signatures from trapdoor permutations. In: Cachin, C., Camenisch, J.L. (eds.) EUROCRYPT 2004. LNCS, vol. 3027, pp. 74–90. Springer, Heidelberg (2004). https://doi.org/10.1007/978-3-540-24676-3_5

[LOS+06] Lu, S., Ostrovsky, R., Sahai, A., Shacham, H., Waters, B.: Sequential aggregate signatures and multisignatures without random oracles. In: Vaudenay, S. (ed.) EUROCRYPT 2006. LNCS, vol. 4004, pp. 465–485. Springer, Heidelberg (2006). https://doi.org/10.1007/11761679_28

[Mak20] Makarov, A.: A survey of aggregate signature applications. In: Misyurin, S.Y., Arakelian, V., Avetisyan, A.I. (eds.) Advanced Technologies in Robotics and Intelligent Systems. MMS, vol. 80, pp. 309–317. Springer, Cham (2020). https://doi.org/10.1007/978-3-030-33491-8_37

[Nev08] Neven, G.: Efficient sequential aggregate signed data. In: Smart, N. (ed.) EUROCRYPT 2008. LNCS, vol. 4965, pp. 52–69. Springer, Heidelberg (2008). https://doi.org/10.1007/978-3-540-78967-3_4

[SS19] Sato, S., Shikata, J.: Interactive aggregate message authentication scheme with detecting functionality. In: Barolli, L., Takizawa, M., Xhafa, F., Enokido, T. (eds.) AINA 2019. AISC, vol. 926, pp. 1316–1328. Springer, Cham (2020). https://doi.org/10.1007/978-3-030-15032-7_110

[SS20] Sato, S., Shikata, J.: Interactive aggregate message authentication equipped with detecting functionality from adaptive group testing. IACR Cryptology ePrint Archive: Report 2020/1218 (2020)

[SSM20] Sato, S., Shikata, J., Matsumoto, T.: Aggregate signature with detecting functionality from group testing. IACR Cryptology ePrint Archive: Report 2020/1219 (2020)

Combating the OS-Level Malware in Mobile Devices by Leveraging Isolation and Steganography

Niusen Chen, Wen Xie, and Bo Chen(✉)

Department of Computer Science, Michigan Technological University, Houghton, USA
{niusenc,wenxie,bchen}@mtu.edu

Abstract. Detecting the OS-level malware (e.g., rootkit) is an especially challenging problem, as this type of malware can compromise the OS, and can then easily hide their intrusion behaviors or directly subvert the traditional malware detectors running in either the user or the kernel space. In this work, we propose mobiDOM to solve this problem for mobile computing devices. The key idea of mobiDOM is to securely detect the OS-level malware by fully utilizing the existing secure features of a mobile device in the hardware. Specifically, we integrate a malware detector in the flash translation layer (FTL), a firmware layer embedded into the external flash storage which is inaccessible to the OS; in addition, we build a trusted application in the Arm TrustZone secure world, which acts as a user-level controller of the malware detector. The FTL-based malware detector and the TrustZone-based controller communicate with each other stealthily via steganography. Security analysis and experimental evaluation confirm that mobiDOM can securely and effectively detect the OS-level malware.

Keywords: OS-level malware · Detection · Hardware isolation · Flash translation layer · TrustZone · Steganography

1 Introduction

We have been witnessing a surge of malware for mobile devices in the past few years [23]. The malware intrudes into a victim mobile device, stealing personally private or even mission critical data, corrupting the local storage [24], or controlling the entire victim device. Especially, there is one type of strong malware (e.g., rootkit) which is able to compromise the entire operating system of the device, obtaining the root privilege. This type of OS-level malware is extremely difficult to be combated, since it can easily subvert any traditional anti-malware software or tools running in the user/kernel space [6,12,14,15,21,30], by leveraging its high privilege.

To combat the OS-level malware, a first step is to detect them once they are present in the victim mobile devices. This requires a malware detector, which can monitor the system and, once any abnormal activities happen, the malware

J. Zhou et al. (Eds.): ACNS 2021 Workshops, LNCS 12809, pp. 397–413, 2021.
https://doi.org/10.1007/978-3-030-81645-2_23

detector will make a decision and inform the user (e.g., via a user app) if it reaches a "malware detected" decision. It turns out that the malware detector cannot simply run in the normal execution environment of the device to avoid being compromised by the OS-level malware. In addition, the user app which interacts with both the end users and the malware detector should not be compromised by the OS-level malware either. Therefore, a key idea towards a secure design is to place both the malware detector and the user app to an execution environment which is isolated from the regular OS and hence the OS-level malware.

Compared to traditional desktops/laptops, mobile computing devices today are equipped with unique hardware features: 1) They usually use ARM processors which have reduced circuit complexity and low power consumption and, ARM processors have integrated **TrustZone**, a hardware security feature, into any Cortex-A processor (built on the Armv7-A and Armv8-A architecture) and Cortex-M processors (built on the Armv8-M architecture). TrustZone enables the establishment of a trusted execution environment that is hardware separated from the normal insecure execution environment. 2) They typically use flash storage media instead of hard disk drives (HDD) for external storage. For example, smartphones, tablets, IoT devices extensively use microSD, eMMC, or UFS cards. Different from HDDs, flash memory exhibits different physical nature and traditional file systems built for HDDs cannot directly be used on them. To bridge this gap, a new flash translation layer (**FTL**) is usually incorporated into the flash storage media to transparently handle the unique nature of flash, exposing an HDD-like interface externally.

Leveraging the unique hardware features of mobile devices, we have designed mobiDOM, the first scheme which can securely and effectively Detect the OS-level Malware in the mobile devices. Our insights are three-fold: First, we integrate the malware detector into the FTL. This new design is advantageous because: 1) the OS-level malware will not be able to subvert the malware detector located in the FTL which is isolated by the flash storage hardware and remains transparent to the OS (*security*); and 2) the malware usually needs to perform I/Os on the external storage, and such I/Os may exhibit some unique behaviors which can be observed in the FTL as confirmed in our experiments using real-world malware samples (*effectiveness*). Second, we introduce a user-level controller which can allow the end user to control the malware detector located in the FTL. To prevent the controller from being subverted by the OS-level malware, we separate its functionality and move the critical component into the "trusted execution environment" (i.e., a secure world) established by TrustZone. In this way, the controller is secure and is able to work with the malware detector correctly. Third, to prevent the malware from noticing the communication between the malware detector (staying in the FTL) and the controller (the key component is staying in the secure world), we leverage steganography, so that the controller and the malware detector can communicate stealthily via the regular I/Os performed on the external storage.

Contributions. Major contributions of this work are:

- We have proposed the first framework (mobiDOM) which can securely detect the OS-level malware, utilizing both the isolation environments provided by main-stream mobile computing devices as well as the steganography technique.
- We have developed a prototype of mobiDOM, and ported it to a real-world testbed to assess its performance. We have also assessed the effectiveness of our FTL-based malware detector by collecting real-world malware samples, running it in our testbed to capture the I/O traces in the FTL, and using the I/O traces for training and testing the malware detector.
- We also analyze the security of mobiDOM.

2 Background

2.1 Flash Memory

Flash memory especially NAND flash has been extensively used as the mass storage of main-stream mobile computing devices, in form of SD/miniSD/microSD cards, MMC cards, and UFS cards. Compared to traditional mechanical disk drives (e.g., hard disk drives), a flash storage medium removes all the mechanical components, and is electrically erasable and re-programmable. Therefore, it usually has much higher I/O throughput with much lower noise. The NAND flash is usually divided into blocks, with typical block sizes 16 KB, 128 KB, 256 KB, or 512 KB. Each block consists of pages, each of which can be 512 B, 2 KB, or 4 KB in size. In general, the read/write operations in NAND flash are performed on the basis of pages, while the erase operations are performed on the basis of blocks.

NAND flash exhibits a few unique characteristics: First, it follows an erase-then-write design. In other words, a flash block needs to be erased first before it can be re-programmed. Therefore, to modify the data stored in a page, we need to first erase the encompassing block, which requires copying out valid data in this block, erasing the block, and writing the data back, leading to significant write amplification. To mitigate the write amplification, flash memory usually uses an out-of-place instead of in-place update strategy. Second, each flash block only allows a limited number of program-erase (P/E) cycles and, if a flash block is programmed/erased too frequently, it will turn "bad" and cannot store data correctly. Therefore, wear leveling is needed to distribute P/Es evenly across the entire flash. Third, reading/writing a flash memory cell frequently may cause its nearby cells in the same block to change over time, causing read/write disturb errors.

Flash Translation Layer (FTL). Existing flash storage media usually can be used as block devices just like HDDs. This is because, they usually integrate a flash translation layer (FTL), to transparently handle the special nature of NAND flash, exposing a block-access interface. In this way, traditional block-based file systems (e.g., EXT, FAT, and NTFS) can be directly deployed on top of flash storage media. The FTL usually implements four key functions:

address translation, garbage collection, wear leveling and bad block management. Address translation manages the mappings between the block addresses and the actual flash memory addresses. Garbage collection periodically reclaims the flash blocks which store invalid data (the data are invalidated due to the out-of-place update). Wear leveling ensures that programmings/erasures are distributed evenly across the flash. Bad block management handles those blocks which occasionally turn "bad", so that they will not be used to store valid data.

2.2 ARM TrustZone

The TrustZone security extensions are available in ARM Cortex-A processors (or processors built on the Armv7-A and Armv8-A architecture), as well as ARM Cortex-M processors (built on the Armv8-M architecture). Its core idea is to create two execution environments which run simultaneously on a single processor: a secure execution environment (i.e., the *secure world*) which can be used to run sensitive applications, and a non-secure execution environment (i.e., the *normal world*) which can be used to run non-sensitive applications. Each world operates independently when using the same processor and, switching between them is orthogonal to all other capabilities of the processor. Memory/peripherals are aware of the corresponding world of the core and, applications running in the normal world cannot have access to the memory space of the secure world.

2.3 Steganography

Steganography in communication allows a sender to send a seemingly innocuous message, which conceals some critical information, to a receiver. In this way, the critical message can be delivered to the receiver stealthily, i.e., without being noticed by the adversary staying in the middle. Compared to cryptography which protects the content of critical messages (e.g., via encryption), steganography is more advantageous since it essentially conceals the fact that a critical message is being sent as well as protects the corresponding content.

3 System and Adversarial Model

3.1 System Model

We consider a mobile computing device which is equipped with an ARM processor (with TrustZone feature enabled) and a flash-based block device as external storage (e.g., a miniSD/microSD card, eMMC card, or UFS card). This type of mobile devices can be found widely in real world, including smartphones, tablets, wearable devices, etc. A general architecture of the device is shown in Fig. 1. By leveraging TrustZone, we can create a secure world in the mobile device, in which there is a small trusted operating system, with trusted applications (**TA**) running on top of it. In the normal world of the mobile device, there is a rich operating system, with regular applications running on top of it. The external flash storage is used as a block device since the FTL transparently handles the unique nature of NAND flash, exposing a block access interface externally. We assume there are N data blocks on the block layer which are usable by the OS. Note that the size of a data block is equal to the size of a flash page, and if the flash page is 2 KB, each data block will consist of 4 512-byte sectors.

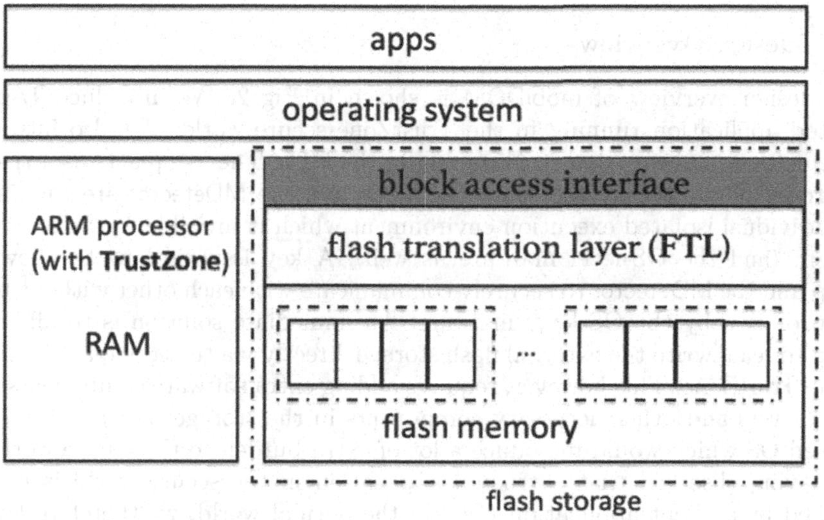

Fig. 1. The architecture of a mobile device

3.2 Adversarial Model

We consider the OS-level malware which is able to compromise the regular rich operating system (in the normal world) of a victim mobile computing device, e.g., by exploiting the system vulnerabilities and escalating the privilege. By compromising the OS, the malware is able to subvert any malware detection tools which run in either the application level or the system level of the normal world. Note that the malware in real world is highly heterogeneous in behaviors, and we only target the malware (e.g., computer viruses, ransomware, etc.) which will perform abnormal/suspicious I/Os on the external storage.

We rely on a few assumptions: First, the malware is assumed to be not able to compromise the trusted OS and TAs running in the TrustZone secure world, which is a reasonable assumption in the domain of TrustZone technologies [13]. The malware is also assumed to be not able to hack into the FTL, which only provides a limited set of block access interfaces externally to the OS. Second, we assume that the malware will not perform DoS attacks, e.g., blocking regular (or seemingly regular) communications between TAs running in the secure world and applications running in the normal world, or blocking I/Os performed by

TAs on the external flash storage device. This assumption is reasonable because: if the malware blocks the communications or I/Os, the TAs in the secure world will detect such an anomaly trivially and notify the user. However, the malware may view, modify or replay the communicated messages and remain undetected.

4 Design

4.1 Design Overview

The design overview of mobiDOM is shown in Fig. 2. We introduce TApp, a trusted application running in the TrustZone secure world. We also introduce MDetector, a malware detector running in the FTL. The TApp acts as a trusted controller of the MDetector. Both the TApp and the MDetector are running in an individual isolated execution environment which is invisible to the operating system (and the OS-level malware as well). A key issue is how to allow the TApp and the MDetector to securely communicate with each other without being compromised by the OS-level malware. An immediate solution is to allow the TApp to read/write the external flash storage directly via the trusted OS running in the TrustZone. This however, requires adding extra software components (i.e., disk drivers and other necessary components in the storage path) to the small trusted OS which would introduce a lot of extra burden to the secure world.

Having observed that a trusted application in the secure world is usually invoked by a client application (CA) in the normal world, we therefore let the TApp use the CA as a proxy[1] to communicate with the MDetector, taking advantage of the rich OS in the normal world. To protect the communication between the TApp and the MDetector, we leverage steganography. Specifically, the secret messages being communicated between the TApp and the MDetector are hidden in the (seemingly) normal I/Os issued by the TApp on the flash storage device (via CA as a proxy). This is advantageous in a few aspects: First, since the secret communicated messages between the TApp and the MDetector are hidden in the normal I/Os, and their confidentiality can be ensured. Second, the integrity of the secret communicated messages can be also ensured since if the malware manipulates the I/Os, the secret messages will not be extracted correctly by the receiver and the receiver will notice that. Third, the steganography technique essentially hides the fact that some secret messages are exchanged, and therefore, the malware is not able to notice the existence of this cover communication.

A few challenges need to be addressed. First, how can we hide the secret messages (e.g., start, stop, query command issued by the TApp to the MDetector) into the regular I/Os? Our idea is, when the TApp performs a write request on the external storage, we randomly select a portion of bits from the write request to embed a secret message. Note that: 1) Each write request is usually a few KBs in size,

[1] The OS-level malware will neither perform DoS attacks nor block/delay regular communications and I/Os to avoid being noticed by the user (Sect. 3.2), and hence the CA will always provide this proxy service correctly.

and the secret message is 100+ bits[2]; in other words, only a tiny portion (e.g., less than 1%) of each write quest has been changed, creating a message which hides the secret message (we call this newly generated message the "steg-message"). This tiny modification will not be alerted by the adversary. 2) The write requests originally issued by the TApp on the external storage are always "cover messages" and allow being altered. 3) The adversary will not be able to access the TrustZone secure world, and hence will not be able to check out the original cover messages. Therefore, the adversary is not able to detect the existence of steganography by comparing the steg-messages with the corresponding cover messages.

Second, how can the MDetector securely convey a response back to the TApp? An immediate solution is that the MDetector modifies the data stored in a flash page to encode a secret response, and the TApp performs a read request on a location of the external storage which is mapped to this page. This immediate solution unfortunately is insecure, since the adversary can have access to the external storage beforehand, and obtain the original data stored in this page and, by comparing the original data with the data after being modified by the MDetector, the adversary can easily identify the existence of steganography. A key observation toward resolving this challenge is that, all the responses sent by the MDetector to the TApp are used to indicate a binary (0 or 1) result, e.g., the command (start or stop) is successfully performed (1) or not (0), or the malware is detected (1) or not (0). Specifically, after the TApp has sent a secret command to the MDetector by performing a write request (which stealthily encodes the secret command) on a random location, the TApp will immediately read the same location. If the read request is returned normally, it will indicate 0; otherwise, if the read request is returned with extra delay, it will indicate 1. Note that: 1) The extra delay should be a secret and dynamic value. The TApp can pick this delay value each time when sending a secret command, and treat it as a part of the secret command. 2) The extra delay can be plausibly denied as the normal system delay, since it happens rarely, e.g., it only happens when the MDetector starts to work, stops working, or has detected the malware.

4.2 Design Details

Let κ and l be security parameters. n is the size of a data block (in terms of bits), and s be the size of the messages (in terms of bits) communicated between the TApp and the MDetector. To avoid disturbing the regular workloads of the system, we reserve an area at the end of the block layer for the communication between TApp and the MDetector. The reserved area has $d \cdot N$ data blocks, with $d << 1$ and $d > 0$. Note that this reserved area does not lead to the compromise of steganography, as having a reserved area is pretty common, e.g., a swap space, a space for backup purpose, or a reserved space for a hidden volume [10,22]. We choose a pseudo-random function (PRF) f and a pseudo-random permutation π, defined as follows:

[2] To prevent the adversary from guessing the secret message, we should use enough bits to represent it, and 100+ bits should be secure enough.

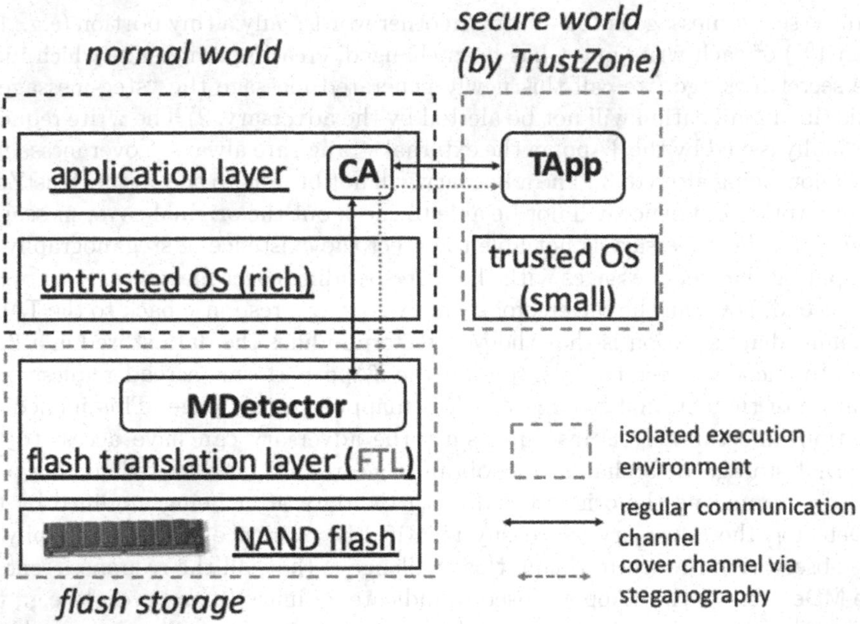

Fig. 2. The design overview of mobiDOM

f: $\{0,1\}^\kappa \times \{0,1\}^* \rightarrow \{0,1\}^l$;
π: $\{0,1\}^\kappa \times \{0,1\}^{log_2^n} \rightarrow \{0,1\}^{log_2^n}$.

Cover Channel Between TApp and MDetector via Steganography. The TApp and the MDetector independently maintain 2 secret keys k_1 and k_2, as well as a counter which will be initialized as 0 during system initialization. We define three secret messages[3]: *START*, *STOP*, and *QUERY*, which are communicated stealthily between the TApp and the MDetector via the steganography:

- START: The TApp uses this message to inform the MDetector to start the malware detection process. Note that the TApp will ask the CA to perform a regular write of DATA on a chosen data block of the block layer, and the DATA conceals the "START" message.
- STOP: The TApp uses this message to inform the MDetector to stop the malware detection process. Similarly, the TApp will ask the CA to perform a regular write of DATA which conceals the "STOP" message.
- QUERY: Periodically, the TApp sends a query (malware is detected or not) to the MDetector. The TApp will ask the CA to perform a regular write of DATA which conceals the "QUERY" message.

Note that each secret message is a collection of s bits determined during the initialization which is only known to the TApp and the MDetector, and s should be large enough to prevent brute-force attacks.

[3] mobiDOM only defines three basic messages to enable the basic functionality, but it can be easily extended to support extra communicated messages.

To start the malware detection, the TApp works as follows: It will generate DATA, pick a delay value, and encode the START message and the *delay* value into it, by running the Encode algorithm (Algorithm 1) using $START||delay$, DATA, k_1, counter as input, generating the stegDATA (corresponding to the "steg-message"). The TApp then runs Algorithm 3 using key k_2, counter, N as input, generating a random location j. The TApp further asks the CA to perform a write of stegDATA on block location j. The MDetector works as follows: It will monitor the write on the page corresponding to data block j (by applying Algorithm 3 using key k_2, counter, N as input, the MDetector can generate j), obtaining the stegDATA. It will then decode the stegDATA, by applying the Decode algorithm (Algorithm 2) using key k_1 and counter as input. It will further check whether the resulting decoded message contains the START message or not. If START is found, it will extract the *delay* value from the decoded message, start the malware detection, and add an artificial delay (determined by the extracted *delay* value) to the read request on the flash page corresponding to data block j. After having measured the read delay on the data block j, the TApp knows that the malware detection has been started successfully. Both the TApp and the MDetector will increase the stored counter by 1. To stop the malware detection, a similar process in both the TApp and the MDetector will be followed except that the secret message is replaced by STOP. Periodically, the TApp checks with the MDetector whether the malware has been detected or not using the QUERY message. The time interval for the this periodical check is a trade-off between the performance overhead and the delay of malware detection. In addition, the process for each check in both the TApp and the MDetector is similar to that for starting the malware detection, except that: 1) If no malware has been detected, the MDetector will not add an artificial delay to the read request on the flash page corresponding to data block j. This is advantageous, since the detected malware is a rarely happening event and most queries will not result in read delay. 2) Regardless whether the malware is detected or not, the counter in both the TApp and the MDetector will be increased by 1. In this way, the secret QUERY message will embedded differently each time, preventing the adversary from noticing the existence of steganography by comparing multiple subsequent write requests.

Algorithm 1: Encode

Input: MESSAGE, DATA, key k, counter
Output: stegDATA
View MESSAGE as a collection of t bits
View DATA as a collection of n bits
for $i = 1 : t$ **do**
  $j = \pi_k(counter||i)$
  $DATA[j-1] = MESSAGE[i-1]$
return DATA

Algorithm 2: Decode

Input: stegDATA, key k, counter
Output: MESSAGE
View stegDATA as a collection of n bits
for $i = 1 : t$ **do**
  $j = \pi_k(counter||i)$
  $MESSAGE[i-1] = stegDATA[j-1]$
return MESSAGE

Algorithm 3: Generate a random location in the reserved area

Input: key k, counter, N, d
Output: a random location in the reserved area
$j = (1-d) \cdot N + f_k(counter)\%(dN)$ **return** j

Malware Detection in the FTL. The idea of our FTL-based malware detector (MDetector) is to detect the malware in the FTL by analyzing the access on the flash storage caused by software (malicious or not) running at the upper layers (i.e., the application or the OS layer). The key observation is that, the malware running at the upper layers may exhibit some unique access behaviors in the FTL [29] and, by capturing those behaviors, we may detect the malware. The advantage of MDetector is clear, since even if the malware can compromise the OS, it cannot compromise our MDetector which has been isolated from the OS at the hardware level. To function correctly, the MDetector relies on a classifier, which is able to classify any software as malicious and non-malicious in real time. The classifier should be trained using the set of pre-collected malware. Once the classifier has been trained and loaded, MDetector will monitor all the I/O requests issued from the upper layers, analyze them in real time, and decide whether there is malware present. Once any malware is identified, the MDetector will work with the TApp to get the user aware of the instance.

5 Discussion and Analysis

5.1 Discussion

Security of TrustZone. mobiDOM relies on an implied assumption that TrustZone itself is secure. This seems to be a widely acceptable assumption in the domain of TrustZone-based solutions [13]. There have been various attacks against TrustZone however, e.g., side-channel attacks [9,20], CLKSCREW attacks [25], hardware-fault injection attacks [19], etc. Enhancing security of TrustZone has been actively taken care of in the literature [27] and is not the focus of this work.

Defending Against other Types of OS-Level Malware. Malware detection in the mobile devices has been a very challenging task because of the heterogeneity and diversity of the malware in the wild. This turns out to be even more challenging when the malware can obtain the OS-level privilege. mobiDOM can only defend against a special type of OS-level malware which causes abnormal I/Os on the external storage media. For other types of OS-level malware, a potential solution is to run the malware detector in an isolated execution environment, which will then access the main memory of the normal world periodically (e.g., via direct memory access). We will further explore this in the future work.

Towards Making mobiDOM more Practical. One practical issue is to keep the FTL lightweight, since it is a thin firmware layer managed by less powerful processors and RAM. When integrating the malware detector into the FTL, a significant concern lies in the performance of ML-based detection. An option towards improving the performance would be conducting a model prunning [31], which can help increase inference speed and decrease storage size of the ML model; additionally, upon initializing mobiDOM, the ML model can be loaded into the RAM for malware detection later. Another practical issue is to manage interference of I/Os among regular software as well as multiple malware, which may perform I/Os simultaneously. Our experimental results in Sect. 6 only capture the scenario in which there is only one piece of malware running in the system. We will further investigate such interference in our future work.

5.2 Security Analysis

There are 3 major components in mobiDOM: the TApp, the MDetector and the communication messages between the TApp and the MDetector (Via the CA).

The security of the TApp is ensured by ARM TrustZone secure world. Without being able to compromise the TrustZone, the adversary is not able to compromise the TApp even if it can compromise the OS. In addition, the adversary will not be able to identify the existence of the TApp in the TrustZone secure world, since the TApp simply writes/reads data to/from the external flash storage (via the CA), which is pretty regular for any trusted applications running in the TrustZone.

The security of the MDetector is ensured by the FTL. Due to the isolation of the FTL in the hardware level, the adversary will not be able to compromise the FTL, even if it can compromise the OS. Therefore, the malware will not be able to notice the existence of MDetector, let alone to compromise it.

The communication messages between the TApp and the MDetector can be protected as analyzed in the following. First, their confidentiality can be ensured by staying hidden among regular I/Os via steganography. Specifically, the secret command messages from the TApp to the MDetector (START, STOP, QUERY) are hidden in the regular write requests on the external storage, which will be invisible to and hence unnoticeable by the adversary. In addition, the response messages are conveyed back from the MDetector to the TApp via read delays and, since the delay time is a one-time secret value, the adversary cannot interpret anything from such delays, which can be plausibly denied as occasional system delays (considering the delays in mobiDOM only happen when starting/stopping the malware or having detected the malware). In addition, the existence of CA will not give the adversary any advantage of inferring the existence of mobiDOM since it is pretty common for the TrustZone-based applications to have CAs running in the normal world to communicate with TAs located in the TrustZone secure world. Second, the integrity of the communication messages can be ensured. If the adversary modifies or replays the messages sent from the TApp to the MDetector, the MDetector can easily detect it since the secret command messages cannot be extracted successfully; if the adversary delays the communication messages sent from the TApp to the MDetector or the read responses from the MDetector to the TApp, the TApp can notice it considering the actual delay time in mobiDOM is a one-time secret value. Note that we do not consider DoS attacks in which the adversary blocks the communication messages or I/Os.

6 Implementation and Experimental Evaluation

To construct a mobile computing device following the architecture in Fig. 1, we used two electronic development boards to build the testbed: 1) a Raspberry Pi [4] (version 3 Model B, with Quad Core 1.2 GHz Broadcom BCM2837 64bit CPU, 1 GB RAM) which is used as the host computing device, and 2) a USB header development prototype board LPC-H3131 [17] (with ARM9 32-bit ARM926EJ-S 180 Mhz, 32 MB SDRAM, and 512 MB NAND flash) which is used as the external flash storage. The LPC-H3131 is connected to the Raspberry Pi via a USB2.0 interface (Fig. 3). We have ported OP-TEE (Open Portable Trusted Execution Environment) [3] to the Raspberry Pi to facilitate the development of TrustZone applications. The TApp has been implemented into the TrustZone secure world as a trusted application (TA). In addition, we have ported [26] an open-source flash controller (FTL) OpenNFM [11] to LPC-H3131 and, after OpenNFM has been ported, the LPC-H3131 can be used as a flash-based block device by the host computing device via the USB2.0 interface. We have modified OpenNFM to support the communication between the TApp and the MDetector via steganography. In addition, a client application (CA) has also been built which runs in the normal world as a proxy for communication. For pseudo-random function, we used HMAC-SHA1, in which the size of the output hash value is 160-bit (i.e., l) and the key size is 128-bit (i.e., κ). The size of the secret message is 128-bit (i.e., s). N is approximately 250,000 (in terms of 2KB data blocks). To further optimize[4] the performance in TrustZone secure world a bit, we have pre-computed the PRF/PRP values and stored them in the memory of the secure world during initialization.

Evaluating the Communication Between the TApp and the MDetector. To assess the time required to execute a command (START, STOP, QUERY) issued

[4] Note that currently we have successfully created the testbed using the Raspberry Pi which: 1) successfully connects to our LPC-H3131 via USB2.0 and, 2) supports Arm TrustZone. However, Raspberry Pi is very poor in performance as observed in our experiments. We are testing new electronic development boards including BD-SL-i.MX6 [1] to build a more powerful testbed.

Fig. 3. The testbed for mobiDOM

by the TApp to the MDetector, we have evaluated four cases: 1) no extra delay is added; and 2) 1-s delay is added; and 3) 3-s delay is added; and 5-s delay is added. We have measured 20 times for each case. Note that the performance of the Raspberry Pi will suffer due to temperature (known as thermal throttling) and, if the CPU temperature exceeds 60 C (but should be below 85 °C for it to work properly), the system will automatically throttle the processor. Our experiment results are shown in Fig. 4. We can observe that: First, without adding any extra delay, it takes around 5 s to execute a command. The overhead mainly includes: encoding a secret message into the stegDATA (in the TrustZone secure world), writing the stegDATA to a flash page (in the normal world), extracting the secret message from the stegDATA (in the FTL), and reading the stegDATA from the flash page (in the normal world). A major time consumption comes from the Raspberry Pi since it significantly slows down when reaching 75 °C. Note that this case is applied to three scenarios: 1) The START command is issued by the TApp, but the MDetector cannot successfully start the malware detection; 2) The STOP command is issued by the TApp, but the MDetector cannot successfully stop the malware detection; 3) The QUERY command is issued by the TApp, and no malware has been detected by the MDetector. Second, after adding different delays (1 s, 3 s, 5 s) in the FTL, the time required for executing a command can be easily differentiated from that no extra delay is added. This justifies the effectiveness of mobiDOM in conveying a response from the MDetector back to the TApp stealthily by adding extra delays. Note that this case is applied to three scenarios: 1) The START command is issued by the TApp, and the MDetector successfully starts the malware detection; 2) The STOP command is issued by the TApp, and the MDetector successfully stops the malware detection; 3) The QUERY command is issued by the TApp, and the MDetector has detected some malware.

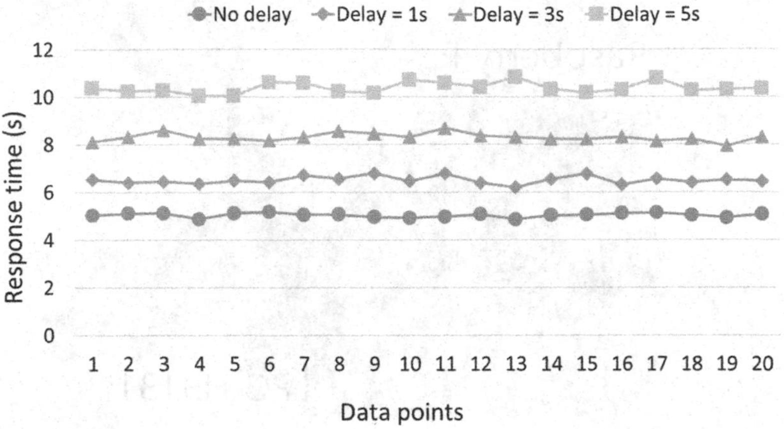

Fig. 4. Time for executing a command (START, QUERY, STOP) with/without adding delays. The CPU temperature is around 75 °C.

Evaluating the Effectiveness of Malware Detection in the FTL. To understand the effectiveness of detecting malware in the FTL, we have collected 96 malware samples (mainly from VirusTotal [5]) and 36 benign software samples (including compression/encryption/deletion software, etc. which will cause I/Os to the external storage). For each sample, we manually ran it in a computer, which was connected to the LPC-H3131 via the USB, and collected the I/O traces (the entire dataset is available in [2]) in the FTL into a trace file. Note that after running each malware sample, we need to restore the entire system to the initial clean state. We used k-Nearest Neighbors (kNN), a supervised machine learning algorithm for classification. We chose k as 1. Our training set contains the I/O traces from 80 malware samples and 30 benign software samples. To test the effectiveness of the malware detection, we used the I/O traces from the remaining 16 malware samples and 6 benign software samples. For each trace file, we selected the first 30 I/O traces, which can be viewed as a three dimensional sequence. Also, we used the dynamic time warping method as the distance metric in kNN.

The experimental results are shown in Table 1. We can observe that: 1) The detection accuracy is 91%, which can justify the effectiveness of our FTL-based malware detector. 2) The false positive rate and the false negative rate are 33% and 0%, respectively. The low false negative rate indicates that our malware detector does not miss any malware if present. The false positive rate seems a little high in our malware detection. The reason is that, in our experiments, we have deliberately chosen those benign software samples which exhibit some similar patterns to the collected malware. However, in practice, most of the benign software may not exhibit such similar patterns.

Table 1. Detection results

Accuracy	False negative rate	False positive rate
91%	0%	33%

7 Related Work

Aafer et al. [6] propose to detect Android malware by relying on critical API calls, their package level information, and their parameters. Zhang et al. [30] propose a semantic-based malware classification to accurately detect both zero-day malware and unknown variants of known malware families, in which they model program semantics with weighted contextual API dependency graphs. For ransomware, existing detection approaches mainly monitor typical file system activities [12,14,15,21] or analyze cryptographic primitives [12,15,16]. For example, Unveil [14] generates an artificial user environment and monitors desktop lockers, file access patterns and I/O data entropy; CryptoDrop [21] observes file type changes and measures file modifications using a similarity-preserving hash function and Shannon entropy to detect ransomware. The aforementioned malware detection mechanisms work under the assumption that the malware cannot obtain the OS privilege, which is unfortunately not truc for the OS-level malwarc.

MimosaFTL [28], SSD-Insider [7,8], Amoeba [18] tried to detect the ransomware in the FTL. The major differences between them and mobiDOM are: First, mobiDOM is a general detection framework for any malware which causes abnormal I/Os on the external storage, rather than a specific framework for ransomware. Second, as a general malware detection framework, mobiDOM securely works with the user-level app, which is necessary for further actions after malware is detected. This is possible by leveraging both the ARM TrustZone (ensuring the security of the app) and the Steganography (ensuring the security of the communication between the malware detector and the user app) technique. On the contrary, the existing detection frameworks [7,8,18,28] are specific for device-level data recovery and do not interact with user apps.

8 Conclusion

In this work, we have designed mobiDOM, a framework for combating the strong OS-level malware by smartly taking advantage of the existing secure features of mobile devices at the hardware level. Security analysis and experimental evaluation justify both the security and the effectiveness of mobiDOM.

Acknowledgment. This work was supported by US National Science Foundation under grant number 1938130-CNS, 1928349-CNS, and 2043022-DGE.

References

1. BD-SL-i.MX6. https://boundarydevices.com/product/bd-sl-i-mx6/
2. Malware I/O Traces On Nand flash (MITON) V0.2. https://snp.cs.mtu.edu/research/drm2/MITON-V0.2.zip
3. Open Portable Trusted Execution Environment. https://www.op-tee.org/
4. Raspberry Pi 3 Model B. https://www.raspberrypi.org/products/raspberry-pi-3-model-b/
5. VirusTotal. https://www.virustotal.com/. Accessed 17 May 2019
6. Aafer, Y., Du, W., Yin, H.: DroidAPIMiner: mining API-level features for robust malware detection in android. In: Zia, T., Zomaya, A., Varadharajan, V., Mao, M. (eds.) SecureComm 2013. LNICST, vol. 127, pp. 86–103. Springer, Cham (2013). https://doi.org/10.1007/978-3-319-04283-1_6
7. Baek, S., Jung, Y., Mohaisen, A., Lee, S., Nyang, D.: SSD-insider: internal defense of solid-state drive against ransomware with perfect data recovery. In: ICDCS. IEEE (2018)
8. Baek, S., Jung, Y., Mohaisen, A., Lee, S., Nyang, D.: SSD-assisted ransomware detection and data recovery techniques. IEEE Trans. Comput. (2020)
9. Bukasa, S.K., Lashermes, R., Le Bouder, H., Lanet, J.-L., Legay, A.: How TrustZone could be bypassed: side-channel attacks on a modern system-on-chip. In: Hancke, G.P., Damiani, E. (eds.) WISTP 2017. LNCS, vol. 10741, pp. 93–109. Springer, Cham (2018). https://doi.org/10.1007/978-3-319-93524-9_6
10. Chang, B., Wang, Z., Chen, B., Zhang, F.: Mobipluto: file system friendly deniable storage for mobile devices. In: Proceedings of the 31st Annual Computer Security Applications Conference, pp. 381–390. ACM (2015)
11. Google Code. Opennfm (2011). https://code.google.com/p/opennfm/. Accessed 17 May 2019
12. Continella, A.: Shieldfs: a self-healing, ransomware-aware filesystem. In: Proceedings of the 32nd Annual Conference on Computer Security Applications, pp. 336–347. ACM (2016)
13. Guan, L., et al.: Supporting transparent snapshot for bare-metal malware analysis on mobile devices. In: Proceedings of the 33rd Annual Computer Security Applications Conference, pp. 339–349. ACM (2017)
14. Kharraz, A., Arshad, S., Mulliner, C., Robertson, W., Kirda, E.: Unveil: a large-scale, automated approach to detecting ransomware. In: 25th USENIX Security Symposium (USENIX Security 16), pp. 757–772 (2016)
15. Kharraz, A., Robertson, W., Balzarotti, D., Bilge, L., Kirda, E.: Cutting the Gordian knot: a look under the hood of ransomware attacks. In: Almgren, M., Gulisano, V., Maggi, F. (eds.) DIMVA 2015. LNCS, vol. 9148, pp. 3–24. Springer, Cham (2015). https://doi.org/10.1007/978-3-319-20550-2_1
16. Kolodenker, E., Koch, W., Stringhini, G., Egele, M.: Paybreak: defense against cryptographic ransomware. In: Proceedings of the 2017 ACM on Asia Conference on Computer and Communications Security, pp. 599–611. ACM (2017)
17. Mantech. Lpc-h3131 (2017). https://www.olimex.com/Products/ARM/NXP/LPC-H3131/. Accessed 17 May 2019
18. Min, D., et al.: Amoeba: an autonomous backup and recovery SSD for ransomware attack defense. IEEE Comput. Archit. Lett. **17**(2), 245–248 (2018)

19. Qiu, P., Wang, D., Lyu, Y., Qu, G.: Voltjockey: breaching trustzone by software-controlled voltage manipulation over multi-core frequencies. In: Proceedings of the 2019 ACM SIGSAC Conference on Computer and Communications Security, pp. 195–209 (2019)
20. Ryan, K.: Hardware-backed heist: extracting ECDSA keys from Qualcomm's Trustzone. In: Proceedings of the 2019 ACM SIGSAC Conference on Computer and Communications Security, pp. 181–194 (2019)
21. Scaife, N., Carter, H., Traynor, P., Butler, K.R.B.: Cryptolock (and drop it): stopping ransomware attacks on user data. In: 2016 IEEE 36th International Conference on Distributed Computing Systems (ICDCS), pp. 303–312. IEEE (2016)
22. Skillen, A., Mannan, M.: On implementing deniable storage encryption for mobile devices. In: 20th Annual Network and Distributed System Security Symposium, NDSS 2013, San Diego, California, USA, 24–27 February 2013
23. Statista. Development of new android malware worldwide from June 2016 to March 2020 (2020). https://www.statista.com/statistics/680705/global-android-malware-volume/
24. Subedi, K.P., Budhathoki, D.R., Chen, B., Dasgupta, D.: Rds3: ransomware defense strategy by using stealthily spare space. In: 2017 IEEE Symposium Series on Computational Intelligence (SSCI). IEEE (2017)
25. Tang, A., Sethumadhavan, S., Stolfo, S.: {CLKSCREW}: exposing the perils of security-oblivious energy management. In: 26th {USENIX} Security Symposium ({USENIX} Security 17), pp. 1057–1074 (2017)
26. Tankasala, D., Chen, N., Chen, B.: A step-by-step guideline for creating a testbed for flash memory research via lpc-h3131 and opennfm (2020)
27. Wan, S., Sun, M., Sun, K., Zhang, N., He, X.: Rustee: developing memory-safe arm trustzone applications. In: Annual Computer Security Applications Conference, pp. 442–453 (2020)
28. Wang, P., Jia, S., Chen, B., Xia, L., Liu, P.: Mimosaftl: adding secure and practical ransomware defense strategy to flash translation layer. In: CODASPY. ACM (2019)
29. Xie, W., Chen, N., Chen, B.: Poster: Incorporating malware detection into flash translation layer
30. Zhang, M., Duan, Y., Yin, H., Zhao, Z.: Semantics-aware android malware classification using weighted contextual API dependency graphs. In: CCS. ACM (2014)
31. Zhu, M., Gupta, S.: To prune, or not to prune: exploring the efficacy of pruning for model compression. arXiv preprint arXiv:1710.01878 (2017)

19. Chen, [illegible], Wang, [illegible]: On [illegible] hacking [illegible] by software [illegible] In: Proceedings of the [illegible] ACM Conference on [illegible] Communications Security, pp. [illegible] (2019)
20. [illegible]: [illegible] In: Proceedings of [illegible] ACM [illegible] Conference on Computer and Communications Security [illegible] (2[illegible])
21. [illegible] International Conference [illegible] (20[illegible])
22. [illegible] In: [illegible] Network and Distributed System Security Symposium [illegible] (20[illegible])
23. [illegible] Development [illegible] malware [illegible] (2020)
24. [illegible] In: 2017 IEEE Symposium [illegible] (2017)
25. [illegible] In: [illegible] USENIX Security Symposium (USENIX Security) [illegible] (20[illegible])
26. [illegible] (2020)
27. [illegible] development [illegible] In: [illegible] (20[illegible])
28. [illegible] In: [illegible] ACM (2019)
29. [illegible] detection [illegible]
30. [illegible] (201[illegible])
31. [illegible] (20[illegible])

SecMT - Security in Mobile Technologies

Pass-As-You-Go: A Direct Anonymous Attestation-Based Untraceable Contactless Transit Pass

Aïda Diop[1(✉)], Nicolas Desmoulins[2], and Jacques Traoré[2]

[1] Ericsson, Massy, France
aida.abdou.diop@ericsson.com
[2] Orange, Caen, France
{nicolas.desmoulins,jacques.traore}@orange.com

Abstract. The secure deployment of NFC-enabled digital services, such as electronic payment, electronic identification (eID), and mobile transit passes in public transportation, is enabled by the trusted execution environment in smartphones, namely the SIM card. A user's authentication and identification credentials are stored in the SIM card, which provides a secure enclave for credential storage and secure authentication operations. The unique identifier assigned to each user leads to important privacy concerns. Indeed, in the case of mobile transit passes, the accountability of users to use a valid and unique transport pass should not undermine the privacy of commuters on the network, notably by disclosing their identities at each pass validation, or by revealing information on their personal mobility patterns.

In this paper, we leverage the use of provably secure and privacy-enhancing cryptographic schemes to build a privacy-preserving mobile transit pass protocol. Notably, we introduce a novel and highly efficient Direct Anonymous Attestation (DAA) scheme as the building block of our construction. Direct Anonymous Attestation is a group signature variant, which enables members of a particular group to anonymously sign on behalf of the group. As opposed to group signatures, the anonymity of DAA signatures cannot be revoked. In addition signatures generated by the same signer can be linked with respect to a linkability parameter. Our construction is an instantiation of a DAA variant, namely pre-DAA, which can be implemented in environments as constrained as SIM cards. We prove the security of our pre-DAA scheme in the random oracle model (ROM), under a variant of the non-interactive q—Strong Diffie-Hellman (q—SDH) assumption. Our pre-DAA scheme, which is of independent interest, is used to design Pass-As-You-Go (PAYGO), an efficient and privacy-preserving mobile transit pass protocol.

We prove the efficiency of our protocol by implementing the solution on a Global Platform-compliant Java card 2.2.2 SIM card. The performance results notably show that PAYGO complies with the stringent timing requirements put forth by Transport Operators for pass validation at station terminals.

J. Zhou et al. (Eds.): ACNS 2021 Workshops, LNCS 12809, pp. 417–435, 2021.
https://doi.org/10.1007/978-3-030-81645-2_24

Keywords: Direct anonymous attestation · Untraceability · Mobile transit pass

1 Introduction

Mobile transport passes enable the efficient and secure deployment of the traditional transit pass using Near Field Communication (NFC) technology. A transit pass is a ticket which allows passengers to take a pre-purchased or unlimited amount of trips within a fixed period of time. The new generation of transit passes allows users to store their credentials directly in their smartphones [22], specifically in the secure Subscriber Identity Module (SIM) card. The technology presents a number of benefits for transport operators, including low maintenance costs, protection against fair evasion (also known as anti-passback), and more importantly, the generation of mobility data on commuters' itineraries in order to anticipate peak hours, to improve traffic flow, and provide accurate information on the state of the traffic. Such operations however should not compromise the privacy of users, notably by linking pass validations for a given user, which allows tracing commuters based on their position at a given time. In addition to the privacy requirements, stringent efficiency requirements for the transport case are to be factored in when designing secure access control protocols. Notably, in order to avoid congestion in front of turnstiles, the pass validation step should take less than 300 milliseconds (ms) [25].

PAYGO. Privacy-preserving solutions for transit passes have so far addressed the anonymity issue [18,20,36], while neglecting the trip unlinkability property. Solutions which have addressed the latter issue, still suffer from efficiency issues, leading to the delegation of computationally expensive secure operations to the mobile phone [19].

We present in this paper Pass-As-You-Go (PAYGO), an NFC-enabled transport service, which enables the anonymous validation of transit passes, while preserving the unlinkability of each validation. Our solution leverages the anonymity and controlled linkability properties of a Direct Anonymous Attestation (DAA) scheme. PAYGO thus provides provably secure and privacy-friendly authentications, as well as the untraceability of users, while enforcing their responsibility. To achieve these properties, we present a new DAA scheme which improves upon existing DAA schemes both in terms of security and efficiency. Our DAA scheme is a stand-alone variant of standard DAA constructions, (also known as pre-DAA). In this case, our scheme is efficient enough to be executed by an element as constrained as a SIM card. As the SIM card performs all the computations required during the validation phase. In addition, the stand-alone authentication by the SIM card implies that the pass validation still works when the phone is switched off or even when the user runs out of battery power (in both cases the NFC SIM card will be powered by the reader via NFC). Our DAA scheme implies that a user is able to validate a transit pass whilst remaining anonymous, even when faced with a malicious transport operator. In addition, pass validations by the same user are unlinkable, provided that they are not performed during a short (predetermined) time span (e.g. 10 min). Otherwise, both validations would be linkable in order to detect fair evasion (i.e. to detect a malicious user passing back his transit pass to a second person who wants to gain access to the public transport system). PAYGO is suitable for monthly or yearly subscriptions, whereby a user with valid credentials (allowing him to travel freely in a delimited zone for example) can validate his pass an unlimited amount of times, provided that the appropriate time span is observed between each validation.

The paper is structured as follows: Sect. 2 discusses related work on privacy-preserving NFC mobile ticketing, more specifically protocols which are based on provably secure cryptographic schemes such as DAAs. Section 3 presents the cryptographic building blocks and assumptions. In Sect. 4, we introduce our novel pre-DAA construction. In Sect. 5, we present the design for our privacy-preserving mobile transit pass protocol named PAYGO. We then evaluate the efficiency of PAYGO in Sect. 6, before concluding in Sect. 7.

2 Related Work

The cryptographic framework for a secure transport service was first discussed by Heydt-Benjamin et al. [27]. They establish the functional, security, and privacy properties inherent to such services. A number of mobile transit pass solutions have since been proposed [18,20,33,34,36], each presenting limitations that we briefly describe in this section.

Initially, solutions employing cryptographic protocols for secure smart ticketing defined an incomplete privacy model, whereby the user remains anonymous with regards to any outside entity, but not the transport operator [20,34,36]. A more complete model must however include the unlinkability of trips in order to avoid tracing users across the transport network, whilst preserving the ability to link validations when users attempt to fraudulently use their transit pass for multiple validations at the same station (anti-passback property). Privacy-preserving solutions addressing both anonymity and unlinkability have since been proposed, based public-key cryptographic schemes such as set-membership proofs [2], and Direct Anonymous Attestation [19]. Arfaoui et al. [2] proposed an m-ticketing system where users store a set of tickets directly into their smartphones. It does not however address the case of transit passes, where users obtain long term credentials that are valid for an unlimited number of trips, depending on the subscription plan. The unlinkability property for such cases is therefore not addressed. Desmoulins et al. [19] proposed a transit pass solution based on Direct Anonymous Attestation [9], which meets the required anonymity and unlinkability properties. Their validation step however requires delegating part of the validation computation to the mobile phone processor, due to the limited computational capabilities of the secure element. This constraint introduces privacy concerns, as a compromised smartphone may disclose information that enables tracing the user on the transport network. In addition, a key functional requirement for NFC mobile transport services is the ability to use the transit pass even in the case where the phone is switched off, or if its battery is empty. This property can only be achieved by using a stand-alone authentication scheme, which can be solely undertaken by the NFC SIM card which, in the event that the smartphone battery is empty, will be indirectly powered by the NFC reader. The efficiency requirement specifying that the pass validation time must not exceed 300 ms [25] introduces further challenges when designing said stand-alone solution.

PAYGO provides a solution which meets both these stringent privacy and efficiency requirements, by leveraging the properties of a new pre-DAA construction.

3 Preliminaries

In this section we introduce the cryptographic building blocks used in the design of our pre-DAA scheme and the PAYGO protocol.

3.1 Bilinear Maps

Bilinear groups are a set of three cyclic groups $\mathbb{G}_1$, $\mathbb{G}_2$ and $\mathbb{G}_T$ of prime order p, along with a bilinear map (or pairing) defined as $e : \mathbb{G}_1 \times \mathbb{G}_2 \rightarrow \mathbb{G}_T$, which satisfies the following properties[1]:

- For $g_1 \in \mathbb{G}_1$, $g_2 \in \mathbb{G}_2$ and $(a, b) \in \mathbb{Z}_p^2$, $e(g_1^a, g_2^b) = e(g_1, g_2)^{ab}$
- For all g_1, g_2 generators of $\mathbb{G}_1, \mathbb{G}_2$ respectively, $e(g_1, g_2)$ generates $\mathbb{G}_T$
- There is an efficient algorithm $\mathcal{G}(1^t)$ that outputs the description of a bilinear map $(p, \mathbb{G}_1, \mathbb{G}_2, \mathbb{G}_T, e, g_1, g_2)$, and $e(g_1, g_2)$ is efficiently computable.

Glabraith, Paterson, and Smart [23] classified bilinear maps in three types depending on the existence (or lack thereof) of computable isomorphism(s) between $\mathbb{G}_1$ and $\mathbb{G}_2$. For type I pairings, there exists computable isomorphisms $\phi_1 : \mathbb{G}_1 \rightarrow \mathbb{G}_2$ and $\phi_2 : \mathbb{G}_2 \rightarrow \mathbb{G}_1$. For type II pairings, there exists a computable isomorphism $\phi : \mathbb{G}_1 \rightarrow \mathbb{G}_2$ but none in the other direction. Finally, for type III pairings, there exists no efficiently computable isomorphism between $\mathbb{G}_1$ and $\mathbb{G}_2$. Type III pairings are known to perform better than type I and II pairings. We make use of type III pairings in the remaining of this paper.

3.2 Extended Pointcheval-Sanders Signature Scheme

Our pre-DAA scheme makes use of the extended Pointcheval-Sanders Signature scheme (EPS) [16] to issue credentials to users. EPS is a simple variant of the basic Pointcheval-Sanders signature scheme [30] (only the public key differs between these two schemes). Let $e : \mathbb{G}_1 \times \mathbb{G}_2 \rightarrow \mathbb{G}_T$ be a type-3 pairing with $\mathbb{G}_1, \mathbb{G}_2, \mathbb{G}_T$ of prime order p, and $\mathbb{G}_1^* = G_1 \backslash 1_{\mathbb{G}_1}$. Let h (respectively $\tilde{h}$) be a random generator of $\mathbb{G}_1$ (respectively $\mathbb{G}_2$). The signer selects $x_0, x_1 \xleftarrow{\$} \mathbb{Z}_p^*$, sets her secret key $sk = (x_0, x_1)$, and defines the corresponding public key $pk = (h, \tilde{h}, X_1 = h^{x_1}, \tilde{X}_0 = \tilde{h}^{x_0}, \tilde{X}_1 = \tilde{h}^{x_1})$. To sign a message $m \in \mathbb{Z}_p$, the

[1] Throughout this paper, for simplicity, we will use the multiplicative notation for the binary operations in $\mathbb{G}_1$ and $\mathbb{G}_2$.

signer selects $b \xleftarrow{\$} \mathbb{Z}_p^*$ and computes $u = h^b$ and $u' = u^{x_0 + m x_1}$. The signature is valid if $u \neq 1_{\mathbb{G}_1}$ and $e(u, \tilde{X}_0 \tilde{X}_1^m) = e(u', \tilde{h})$.

The standard security notion for a signature scheme is existential unforgeability under chosen message attacks (EUF-CMA) [24]. This notion captures the idea that it is hard, even given access to a signing oracle, to output a valid pair (m, σ) for a message m which was never queried to the signing oracle. We will consider in our security proofs a weaker security notion, namely existential unforgeability under weak chosen message attacks (EUF-wCMA) [8], in which the adversary has to provide the list of messages $m_1, ..., m_q$ to the challenger prior to receiving the public key pk.

3.3 Signatures of Knowledge

A Zero-Knowledge Proof of Knowledge (ZKPK) is an interactive protocol between a prover $\mathcal{P}$ and a verifier $\mathcal{V}$, where the prover attempts to convince the verifier of the knowledge of some secrets verifying a given statement, without revealing any information about said secrets. In our constructions, we use as building blocks *non-interactive* zero-knowledge proofs of knowledge (or signatures of knowledge), obtained with a heuristic transformations such as Fiat-Shamir [21]. We use the Camenisch-Stadler notation [15], whereby $\pi := SoK\{\alpha, \beta : y = g^\alpha \wedge z = g^\beta\}[m]$ denotes a signature of knowledge of secrets α, β, verifying the statement on the right side of the colon. The signature of knowledge itself is generated on message m.

In the random oracle model (ROM) [5], one can use the forking lemma [32] to extract the secrets from such a signature of knowledge if correct care is taken that the prover can indeed be efficiently rewound. Moreover in the ROM one can simulate such signatures of knowledge for unknown secrets [32].

3.4 Paillier Cryptosystem

The Paillier Cryptosystem [29] is defined as follows: Let a, b be two large primes such that $a, b > 2$, $a \nmid (b-1)$ and $b \nmid (a-1)$. Let $n = ab$, and $\lambda = lcm(a-1, b-1)$, and $g_P = (1+n)$. The public key pk_{Pai} is defined as $pk_{Pai} = (n, g_P)$, and the secret key sk_{Pai} is defined as $sk_{Pai} = (\lambda)$. To encrypt a message $m \in \mathbb{Z}_n$, a user selects $r \in \mathbb{Z}_n^*$, and computes the ciphertext $C_{Pai} = g_P^m \cdot r^n \bmod n^2$. Decryption is performed by computing $\frac{L(c^\lambda \bmod n^2)}{L(g_P^\lambda \bmod n^2)} \bmod n = m$, where the function L is defined as $L(x) = \frac{x-1}{n}$.

3.5 Computational Complexity Assumptions

The security (namely the *non-frameability* and *anonymity* properties) of our new pre-DAA scheme relies on the following assumptions.

Definition 1 (One-More Discrete Logarithm (OMDL)) Assumption [4]). *Let $\mathbb{G}$ be a cyclic group of prime order p, h a random generator of $\mathbb{G}$, $\mathcal{O}_1$ a challenge* *oracle that returns a random element* $Y_i \in \mathbb{G}$ *when queried, and a discrete logarithm oracle* $\mathcal{O}_2$. *The One-More Discrete Logarithm (OMDL) assumption states that after* t *queries to the* $\mathcal{O}_1$ *(where* t *is chosen by the adversary), and at most* $t-1$ *queries to* $\mathcal{O}_2$*, the adversary has negligible probability in recovering the discrete logarithms of all received* t *elements* Y_i.

Definition 2 (XDH (eXternal Diffie-Hellman) Assumption). *Let* $\mathbb{G}_1, \mathbb{G}_2$ *and* $\mathbb{G}_T$ *be three cyclic groups of prime order* p*, and* $e : \mathbb{G}_1 \times \mathbb{G}_2 \rightarrow \mathbb{G}_T$ *a type 3 bilinear map [23]. The eXternal Diffie-Hellman (XDH) assumption states that the DDH assumption holds in* $\mathbb{G}_1$.

The unforgeability (a.k.a *traceability*) of our pre-DAA scheme relies on the EUF-wCMA security of the EPS signature scheme. The EPS scheme achieves EUF-wCMA security under the q—MSDH assumption[2] (see Lemma 1 of [16]), a variant of the classical q—SDH assumption [7] in type 3 bilinear groups, introduced by Pointcheval and Sanders [31]. The q—MSDH assumption is defined as follows:

Definition 3 (q—MSDH assumption). *Let* $(p, \mathbb{G}_1, \mathbb{G}_2, \mathbb{G}_T, e)$ *a bilinear group of type 3, with* g *(resp.* $\tilde{g}$*) a generator of* $\mathbb{G}_1$ *(resp.* $\mathbb{G}_2$*). Given* $\{g^{x^i}, \tilde{g}^{x^i}\}_{i=0}^{q}$ *and* $(g^a, \tilde{g}^a, \tilde{g}^{a \cdot x})$*, for* $a, x \xleftarrow{\$} \mathbb{Z}_p^*$*, no adversary can output a tuple* $(w, P, h^{\frac{1}{x+w}}, h^{\frac{a}{P(x)}})$ *for some* $h \in \mathbb{G}_1^*$*, where* P *is a polynomial of degree at most* q *and* w *is a scalar such that* $(X + w)$ *and* $P(X)$ *are relatively prime.*

4 Direct Anonymous Attestation

The cryptographic building block of our novel mobile transit pass is a widely deployed privacy-preserving cryptographic scheme, namely Direct Anonymous Attestation.

4.1 Related Work

Direct Anonymous Attestation (DAA) is an anonymous digital group signature scheme which provides privacy-preserving authentication for computer systems and devices. DAA signatures are not traceable, but signatures generated by the same platform can be linked using an auxiliary value called the *basename*. The first RSA-based scheme introduced by Brickell, Camenisch and Chen [9] was standardized in the Trusted Platform Module (TPM) 1.2 specification and the ISO 20008-2 standard [1]. Subsequently, more efficient DAA schemes based on elliptic curves and bilinear groups, namely ECC-DAA schemes, were then proposed [6,10–14,17,28,37,38], and [17] is also standardized in ISO/IEC 20008-2 [1].

[2] where q corresponds to the number of queries to the signing oracle.

4.2 Our Pre-DAA Scheme

In this section, we design an efficient pre-DAA scheme where both the pre-DAA signing key verification and the signature generation, can be solely undertaken by the computationally constrained secure element. Our pre-DAA scheme is suitable for applications where a computationally constrained element (such as a SIM card), must anonymously authenticate itself to a third party, with the additional property that its signatures can only be linked under strict and pre-determined circumstances. Indeed, the linkability of signatures is determined via the basename parameter (bsn), the use of which is to be specified for each application. We detail the different algorithms of our scheme as follows:

Setup. Let $\mathbb{G}_1, \mathbb{G}_2$, and $\mathbb{G}_T$ be three bilinear groups of prime order p. This algorithm selects $e : \mathbb{G}_1 \times \mathbb{G}_2 \rightarrow \mathbb{G}_T$ a type 3 bilinear map. It then selects three generators $g, h \xleftarrow{\$} \mathbb{G}_1$ and $\tilde{h} \xleftarrow{\$} \mathbb{G}_2$. It selects two hash functions: $\mathcal{H} : \{0,1\}^* \rightarrow \mathbb{G}_1$, modeled as a random oracle in the security analysis, and $\mathcal{H}_1 : \{0,1\}^* \rightarrow \mathbb{Z}_p$. It then outputs the public parameters $pp = (p, \mathbb{G}_1, \mathbb{G}_2, \mathbb{G}_T, g, h, \tilde{h}, \mathcal{H}, \mathcal{H}_1, e)$.

Keygen. The issuer $\mathcal{I}$ selects $x_0, x_1 \xleftarrow{\$} \mathbb{Z}_p^*$, and sets his secret key $gmsk = (x_0, x_1)$. He also defines the corresponding public key $gmpk = (C_{x_0} = g^{x_0} h^{\tilde{x}_0}, X_1 = h^{x_1}, \tilde{X}_0 = \tilde{h}^{x_0}, \tilde{X}_1 = \tilde{h}^{x_1})$ where $\tilde{x}_0 \xleftarrow{\$} \mathbb{Z}_p^*$. He generates a zero-knowledge signature of knowledge π on his private key (x_0, x_1), defined as $\pi = SoK\{\alpha, \beta, \gamma : C_{x_0} = g^\alpha h^\beta, X_1 = h^\gamma, \tilde{X}_0 = \tilde{h}^\alpha, \tilde{X}_1 = \tilde{h}^\gamma\}[m_0]$ where m_0 is the empty string. The proof of knowledge on $\mathcal{I}$'s secret keys prevents impersonation attacks. $\mathcal{I}$ generates an additional ECDSA signature [35] on C_{x_0}, X_1, π, which is verified by the secure element $\mathcal{SE}$ as soon as $gmpk$ is deployed. $\mathcal{SE}$ is deployed with an endorsement key pair (esk/epk) of a public-key signature scheme Sign which is EUF-CMA, and is used in the authentication step with the issuer. Finally, $\mathcal{SE}$ selects a private key $s_1 \xleftarrow{\$} \mathbb{Z}_p^*$ as its secret key.

Join-Issue. This interactive protocol runs between the secure element $\mathcal{SE}$ with unique identifier ID_U and the issuer $\mathcal{I}$. During the Join execution, $\mathcal{SE}$ first computes a hiding commitment its secret key s_1 as follows: $C_{s_1} = X_1^{s_1}$. It then builds a zero-knowledge signature of knowledge π of s_1 defined as follows: $\pi_1 = SoK\{\alpha : C_{s_1} = X_1^\alpha\}[m_0]$. It computes a signature $\mathcal{S} = Sign_{esk_i}(C_{s_1})$ of the commitment, and sends $(C_{s_1}, \pi_1, \mathcal{S})$ to the issuer. Upon receiving $(C_{s_1}, \pi_1, \mathcal{S})$, $\mathcal{I}$ checks that $C_{s_1} \neq 1$, checks the validity of $\mathcal{S}$, and the validity of π_1. He then selects $b, s_2 \xleftarrow{\$} \mathbb{Z}_p^*$, and generates $\mathcal{SE}$'s group signing key (u, u') as follows: $u = h^b, u' = u^{x_0}[C_{s_1} X_1^{s_2}]^b = u^{x_0 + x_1(s_1+s_2)}$. $\mathcal{I}$ builds a zero-knowledge signature of knowledge π_2 of $b, x_0, \tilde{x}_0$ defined as follows: $\pi_2 = SoK\{\alpha, \beta, \gamma, \mu : u = h^\alpha \wedge u' = u^\beta [C_{s_1} \cdot C_{s_2}]^\alpha \wedge C_{x_0} = g^\beta h^\gamma \wedge C_{s_2} = X_1^\mu\}[m_0]$, where $C_{s_2} = X_1^{s_2}$. It sends $\mathcal{SE}$ its group signing key (u, u'), as well as C_{s_2} and π_2. Upon receiving $((u, u'), C_{s_2}, \pi_2)$, $\mathcal{SE}$ checks the validity of π_2. If $C_{s_1} \cdot C_{s_2} = 1$, it aborts. Otherwise, it computes a signature $\sigma_0 = Sign_{esk_i}(C_{s_2}, u, u', \pi_2)$ and sends σ_0 to the issuer. The issuer verifies σ_0 and finally sends back s_2 if the verification is successful. The secure element checks that $C_{s_2} = X_1^{s_2}$, and sets $s = s_1 + s_2 \pmod{p}$ and $gsk = (u, u')$.

The issuer stores the values (ID_U, C_s, σ_0) in the register REG, where $C_s = C_{s_1} \cdot C_{s_2}$.

Sign. Upon receiving the challenge Ch and the basename bsn from the verifier, $\mathcal{SE}$ selects $l \xleftarrow{\$} \mathbb{Z}_p^*$ and computes a randomized version (w, w') of the credentials (u, u') where $w = u^l$ and $w' = (u')^l$. It then computes $c = w^s$. Finally, it computes a tag $T = \mathcal{H}(bsn)^s$ on the basename, and build a zero-knowledge signature of knowledge $\pi_3 = SoK\{\alpha : c = w^\alpha \wedge T = \mathcal{H}(bsn)^\alpha\}[Ch]$ of a valid PS signature (w, w'), generated on the message s. It defines the signature $\sigma = (w, w', \pi_3, c, T)$.

Verify. Upon receiving σ, the verifier $\mathcal{V}$ first checks that $w \neq 1$ and $T \neq 1$. It then verifies the following equality: $e(w, \tilde{X}_0) \cdot e(c, \tilde{X}_1) = e(w', \tilde{h})$. $\mathcal{V}$ accepts if π_3 is valid and all the previous checks succeed. This last verification step completes the verification of $\mathcal{SE}$'s credentials and its signature.

Identify$_\mathbb{S}$ (σ, m, bsn, sk_i). Return 1 if $T = \mathcal{H}(bsn)^{sk_i}$ and 0 otherwise.

Identify$_\mathbb{T}$ $(\mathbb{T}, sk_i)$. Return 1 if $C_{s_1} \cdot C_{s_2} = X_1^{sk_i}$, where C_{s_1} and C_{s_2} are the two commitments produced during the *Join* protocol associated with the transcript $\mathbb{T}$, and 0 otherwise.

Link. If both σ and σ' verify for m, and m' respectively using the same basename $bsn \neq \perp$, and both σ and σ' were produced by the same user (i.e. the tags $T = T'$), return 1. Otherwise return 0.

5 Pass-As-You-Go: A Privacy-Preserving Mobile Transit Pass Protocol

In this section, we present Pass-As-You-Go (PAYGO), a privacy-preserving mobile transit pass protocol, which allows commuters to remain anonymous and untraceable on public transport networks. In order to avoid tracing of honest users, pass validations can only be linked if there is an attempt to swipe the same pass for two consecutive users (see Sect. 5.5). The secure element is a smart card (e.g. the UICC/SIM card) present in users' smartphones. The SIM stores the user's credentials, performs all secure computations, and communicates with the validator via the NFC controller. PAYGO is based on our pre-DAA scheme detailed in Sect. 4.2. The security and privacy property of our scheme, guarantee the security and privacy requirement of a mobile transit pass. Indeed, the SIM card is able to verify the pre-DAA signing key, and generate signatures, without delegation to the mobile phone, which may be compromised or run out of battery. In addition, the efficiency of our pre-DAA scheme ensures that commuters can validate their transit passes in less than 300 ms, as recommended for mobile transit pass protocols [25].

5.1 Framework

The PAYGO architecture is defined as follows: the transport operator (TO) who manages the transport service acts as the issuer ($\mathcal{I}$). Each user (U) with a smartphone registers for a valid transport pass stored in their SIM card $\mathcal{SE}$, thus becoming part of the group of commuters with a valid pass. Turnstiles at stations are equipped with an NFC-enabled reader (validator), which act as the verifier ($\mathcal{V}$) in the pre-DAA architecture. In PAYGO, the pre-DAA scheme is extended to include a third entity, namely an extractor (E). E represents a third party whose role is to safeguard the privacy of users on public transport networks, notably regarding the transport operator. This allows sharing the revocation capabilities between entities with conflicting interests. Indeed, the extractor and the transport operator must collaborate in order to lift the anonymity and revoke the credentials of a fraudulent user.

PAYGO comprises three main phases:

Setup. In this phase, TO generates the public parameters of the group, as well as the public and private keys for TO and $\mathcal{SE}$. The group in the public transport network is the set of users with a valid transit pass (i.e. users who have *registered* with the transport operator).

Registration. A users obtains the credentials for his transport pass by engaging in an interactive *Registration* protocol with TO. The resulting credentials are stored by $\mathcal{SE}$. During the *Registration* phase, TO and $\mathcal{SE}$ execute the *Join/Issue* protocol of the pre-DAA scheme, which results in $\mathcal{SE}$ obtaining its authentication credentials (i.e. the pre-DAA group signing key).

Validation. During each validation phase, the validator ($\mathcal{V}$) sends a random challenge and a basename to the smartphone, detected via NFC. The basename is used to prevent users from swiping their pass twice, also known as the anti-passback property (see Sect. 5.5). The SIM card uses its credentials to generate a valid pre-DAA signature, thus anonymously authenticating itself. If the authentication process succeeds, $\mathcal{V}$ grants access to the user with pass $\mathcal{SE}$. Access is otherwise denied.

An additional **Revocation** phase addresses cases where a user's credentials are to be revoked, notably upon fraud or clone detection.

5.2 Setup

The *Setup* phase consists in running the *Setup* and *Keygen* algorithms of the pre-DAA scheme. Essentially, this phase allows the transport operator to generate the public parameters, and its public/private key pair ($gmpk, gmsk$). It is also during this phase that $\mathcal{SE}$ generates its secret key s_1. In parallel, TO and E generate the public and private keys (pk_{Pai}, sk_{Pai}) for a threshold Paillier cryptosystem, which is used to extract a secret key from a given commitment during revocation (see Sect. 5.6) using a joint Paillier decryption method [26].

5.3 Registration

SIM card ($\mathcal{SE}$)		**Transport Operator (TO)**
Public input: $pp, gmpk, epk, pk_{Pai}, ID_U$ **Private input:** esk, s_1		**Public input:** $pp, gmpk, epk, pk_{Pai}, ID_U$ **Private input:** $gmsk$, TO's share of sk_{Pai}, REG
Compute $C_{s_1} = X_1^{s_1}$, $\mathcal{S} = Sign_{esk}(C_{s_1})$, and $C_{Pai} = \mathrm{Enc}_{pk_{Pai}}(s_1) = g_P^{s_1} r^n \pmod{n^2}$		
Build $\pi_1 = SoK\{\alpha : C_{s_1} = X_1^{\alpha} \wedge C_{Pai} = g_P^{\alpha} r^n\}[ID_U]$	$\xrightarrow{C_{s_1}, C_{Pai}, \pi_1, \mathcal{S}}$	**Check** $C_{s_1} \neq 1$ and **Verify** $\pi_1, \mathcal{S}$
		Select $b, s_2 \in \mathbb{Z}_p^*$ **Compute** the group signing key $gsk = (u, u')$ where $u = h^b, u' = u^{x_0}[C_{s_1} X_1^{s_2}]^b = u^{x_0 + x_1(s_1+s_2)}$ Build $\pi_2 = SoK\{\alpha, \beta, \gamma, \mu : u = h^{\alpha} \wedge u' = u^{\beta}[C_{s_1} \cdot C_{s_2}]^{\alpha} \wedge C_{x_0} = g^{\beta} h^{\gamma} \wedge C_{s_2} = X_1^{\mu}\}[m_0]$
Verify π_2. **If** $C_{s_1} \cdot C_{s_2} = 1$ **abort**	$\xleftarrow{(u,u'), C_{s_2}, \pi_2}$	where $C_{s_2} = X_1^{s_2}$. **Compute** $C_s = C_{s_1} \cdot C_{s_2}$
Compute $\sigma_0 = Sign_{esk}(C_{s_2}, u, u', \pi_2)$	$\xrightarrow{\sigma_0}$	**Verify** σ_0
Check that $C_{s_2} = X_1^{s_2}$ and **Set** $s = s_1 + s_2$ (mod p)	$\xleftarrow{s_2}$	**Store** $(ID_U, C_s, C_{Pai}, \mathcal{S}, \sigma_0)$ in REG

Fig. 1. PAYGO registration protocol

A user obtains a weekly, monthly, or yearly transport pass subscription by registering with the transport operator. We denote by ID_U a user's identifier, and REG the database where TO stores the unique identifiers of registered user. The technical description of the registration protocol is detailed in Fig. 1. Let us provide the intuition behind our construction. The *registration* phase is an extension of the *Join-Issue* protocol of our pre-DAA scheme. A user (U) (defined here by the corresponding SIM card $\mathcal{SE}$) obtains a blind PS signature [31] (u, u') on his secret key s, where s is jointly computed by $\mathcal{SE}$ and TO: $s = s_1 + s_2$ (mod p), where s_1 is chosen by $\mathcal{SE}$ and is unknown to TO, while s_2 is chosen by TO and is sent to $\mathcal{SE}$ at the end of the *Registration* protocol. In addition, $\mathcal{SE}$ computes C_{Pai}, a Paillier encryption of s_1, which can be retrieved and decrypted by revocation entities. Indeed, using the threshold version of the Paillier cryptosystem allows to reduce trust in the decryption entity, by sharing the decryption capabilities (therefore secret keys) between l entities. Threshold decryption allows any subset t out of l entities to decrypt a ciphertext. During registration, $\mathcal{SE}$ generates a threshold Paillier encryption on his secret s_1 using the Paillier encryption key generated during the *Setup* phase, thus allowing a set of revocation authorities (comprised of TO and E) to jointly decrypt the ciphertext during the *revocation* process.

At the end of the registration phase, TO knows the PS signature (u, u') generated on s (which will be randomized, when used by $\mathcal{SE}$ as his group signing key), while the secret s remains hidden. TO stores the credential (u, u'), as well as $\mathcal{SE}$'s commitments C_{s_1} and C_{Pai} in a private register REG. The registration phase corresponds to the *Join/Issue* protocol of a pre-DAA scheme, at the end of which $\mathcal{SE}$ obtains credentials associated with its secret key s.

5.4 Validation

A user is able to use his pass to anonymously authenticate at access control points. During this pass validation phase, $\mathcal{SE}$ makes use of the *Sign* algorithm of the pre-DAA scheme. Each turnstile is equipped with an NFC-enabled reader ($\mathcal{V}$), which detects the user's mobile via NFC connectivity. Once the connection is established with the transport applet, $\mathcal{V}$ (who corresponds to the verifier in the pre-DAA architecture) sends a random challenge Ch and the basename bsn corresponding to the time period P of the validation. Specifically, the list of basenames are generated in advance by TO and a second revocation authority (E), which we assume will not collude with TO. The basename generation process, as detailed in Sect. 5.4, enables anonymity revocation in the specific case of fraud detection. Said anonymity revocation process requires the joint collaboration of both TO and E, in order to prevent illegitimate or abusive revocations.

Basename Generation. TO and E jointly generate the basenames in advance, for pre-determined time periods P_j. Indeed, this enables the anonymity revocation authorities to initiate the *revocation* process in the case of fraud detection 5.6, as well as to enforce the anti-passback property during *validation* phase 5.5. The basename generation process is described as follows:

1. Depending on the system policy, a time period P_j for $1 \leq j \leq n$ ranges from a few seconds to a few minutes.
2. TO and E respectively generate the following sets of keys $\{sk_{P_j}^{TO}\}_{j=1}^{n}$ and $\{sk_{P_j}^{E}\}_{j=1}^{n}$, where n denotes the maximum number of tags to be generated in a specific period of time (the sets of keys are generated monthly for example). They also generates the corresponding public keys $\{pk_{P_j}^{TO}\}_{j=1}^{n} = \{X_1^{sk_{P_j}^{TO}}\}_{j=1}^{n}$, and $\{pk_{P_j}^{E}\}_{j=1}^{n} = \{X_1^{sk_{P_j}^{E}}\}_{j=1}^{n}$.
3. To compute the basename for time period P_j, TO sends E his share of the basename computation $X_{TO} = X_1^{sk_{P_j}^{TO}}$, as well as the signature of knowledge $\pi_j^{TO} = SoK\{\alpha : X_{TO} = X_1^{\alpha}\}$. Upon receiving X_{TO}, E appends its own secret key as follows: $X_{P_j} = X_{TO}^{sk_{P_j}^{E}}$. The final basename bsn is defined as $bsn = X_{P_j}$.

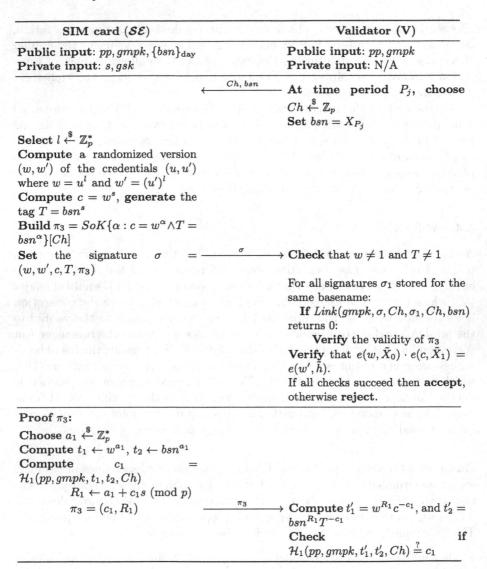

SIM card ($\mathcal{SE}$)		**Validator (V)**
Public input: $pp, gmpk, \{bsn\}_{\text{day}}$ **Private input**: s, gsk		**Public input**: $pp, gmpk$ **Private input**: N/A
	$\xleftarrow{Ch,\, bsn}$	**At time period** P_j, **choose** $Ch \xleftarrow{\$} \mathbb{Z}_p$ **Set** $bsn = X_{P_j}$
Select $l \xleftarrow{\$} \mathbb{Z}_p^*$ **Compute** a randomized version (w, w') of the credentials (u, u') where $w = u^l$ and $w' = (u')^l$ **Compute** $c = w^s$, **generate** the tag $T = bsn^s$ **Build** $\pi_3 = SoK\{\alpha : c = w^\alpha \wedge T = bsn^\alpha\}[Ch]$ **Set** the signature $\sigma = (w, w', c, T, \pi_3)$	$\xrightarrow{\sigma}$	**Check** that $w \neq 1$ and $T \neq 1$ For all signatures σ_1 stored for the same basename: **If** $Link(gmpk, \sigma, Ch, \sigma_1, Ch, bsn)$ returns 0: **Verify** the validity of π_3 **Verify** that $e(w, \tilde{X}_0) \cdot e(c, \tilde{X}_1) = e(w', \tilde{h})$. If all checks succeed then **accept**, otherwise **reject**.
Proof π_3: **Choose** $a_1 \xleftarrow{\$} \mathbb{Z}_p^*$ **Compute** $t_1 \leftarrow w^{a_1}$, $t_2 \leftarrow bsn^{a_1}$ **Compute** $c_1 = \mathcal{H}_1(pp, gmpk, t_1, t_2, Ch)$ $R_1 \leftarrow a_1 + c_1 s \pmod{p}$ $\pi_3 = (c_1, R_1)$	$\xrightarrow{\pi_3}$	**Compute** $t_1' = w^{R_1} c^{-c_1}$, and $t_2' = bsn^{R_1} T^{-c_1}$ **Check** if $\mathcal{H}_1(pp, gmpk, t_1', t_2', Ch) \stackrel{?}{=} c_1$

Fig. 2. PAYGO validation protocol

E also generates the signature of knowledge π_j^E, where $\pi_j^E = SoK\{\alpha : X_{P_j} = X_{TO}^\alpha \wedge pk_{P_j}^E = X_1^\alpha\}$. The signatures of knowledge bind each entity to their part of the basename computation, proving that the values were computed as intended.

Generating the basename in this manner ensures that during the *revocation* process, each entity (TO and E) will be able to retrieve the public commitment of the concerned $\mathcal{SE}$ (see Sect. 5.6). The list of basenames for the day are published and certified, and are thus known to all $\mathcal{SE}$s.

Note. At least one of the two authorities behaves honestly, the *bsn* can thus be a public element of $\mathbb{G}_1$ generated uniformly at random. There is therefore no need to employ a collision resistant hash function to compute the tags T of our underlying pre-DAA scheme. A tag T can simply be equal to $T = bsn^s$ (where s is the private signing key of $\mathcal{SE}$). The security proofs remain valid.

Validation. A user validates his pass by generating an anonymous signature using the credentials obtained in Sect. 5.3. Upon receiving the challenge and basename from the reader $\mathcal{V}$, $\mathcal{SE}$ generates a signature of knowledge on message Ch with respect to *bsn*. The result is an anonymous and basename-dependent linkable signature, which $\mathcal{V}$ is able to verify without lifting the anonymity of U. The detailed description of the *Validation* protocol is presented in Fig. 2. The *validation* phase includes the additional *Link* function of the pre-DAA scheme, which allows to link two signatures to the same user with respect to the same basename. The *Link* function is used to enforce the anti-passback property.

5.5 Anti-passback Property

The anti-passback property of PAYGO denies access to a user who validates his pass twice during a short time period determined by the basename. After each validation, the validator ($\mathcal{V}$) stores the signature σ_1 for basename *bsn* (for time period P_j). If a user generates a signature σ_2 for the same *bsn* (during time period P_j), $\mathcal{V}$ detects passback by running *Link* on σ_1, σ_2 and *bsn*. Indeed, the resulting tags T and T' will be the same for both signatures. For time period P_{j+1}, the basename is renewed, and the signatures generated by the same user are no longer linkable. The frequent and timely update of *bsn* is crucial to the overall untraceability of honest users on the transport network. Their specific generation and management should therefore be optimized accordingly by transport authorities.

5.6 Revocation

The *revocation* phase allows the transport authority to revoke a user's credentials, upon fraud or clone detection. The revocation process is managed by the transport operator (TO) and the external privacy-guarding party (E). Both maintain a secret key-based revocation list Key_{RL}, which stores the secret keys of revoked users. This phase is divided into two sub-phases, namely *Identify* and *Revoke*.

Identify. The first step in the *revocation* procedure allows the transport authority to retrieve the identifier ID_U of the user whose pass is to be revoked. The basename generation procedure described in Sect. 5.4 ensures that revocation authorities, namely TO and E, must collaborate in order to jointly retrieve the identifier of a pass which has issued a given signature. They proceed as follows:

- TO detects two validations which are linked to the same user at different stations in the same time period P_j. This indicates that a clone of the user's pass exists, and triggers the identification process.
- For the concerned signature $\sigma_R = (w_R, w_R', \pi_{3R}, c_R, T_R)$, TO computes $res_{TO} = T_R^{(sk_{P_j}^{TO})^{-1}}$, as well as a signature of knowledge $\pi_{R_1} = SoK\{\alpha : res_{TO} = T_R^{\alpha} \wedge (pk_{P_j}^{TO})^{\alpha} = X_1\}$.
- Upon receiving (res_{TO}, π_R) E verifies π_R, and computes $res = res_{TO}^{(sk_{P_j}^{E})^{-1}}$, as well as a signature of knowledge $\pi_{R_2} = SoK\{\alpha : res = res_{TO}^{\alpha} \wedge (pk_{P_j}^{E})^{\alpha} = X_1\}$.
- The final result res corresponds to the value $X_1^s = C_s$.
- TO retrieves C_s and the corresponding ID_U from REG.

Revoke. Upon recovering ID_U, TO and E jointly decrypt the associated Paillier ciphertext C_{Pai} using a joint Paillier decryption method, such as the one presented in [26]. They retrieve the corresponding secret s. TO stores s in Key_{RL}. Henceforth, the verification step of the validation procedure described in Fig. 2 is modified to include revocation as follows:

1. **Check** that $w \neq 1$ and $T \neq 1$
2. For all signatures σ_1 stored for the same basename:
   If *Link*$(gmpk, \sigma, Ch, \sigma_1, Ch, bsn)$ returns 0:
      Verify the validity of π_3
3. **Verify** that $e(w, \tilde{X}_0) \cdot e(c, \tilde{X}_1) = e(w', \tilde{h})$
4. **Compute** $T_{temp} = X_{P_j}^{s^i}, \forall s^i \in Key_{RL}$
   If $T = T_{temp}$, **reject**
5. Otherwise **accept**

We provide a security analysis of PAYGO in Appendix A.

6 Performance Evaluation

In this section, we then demonstrate the efficiency of PAYGO by implementing the protocol on a standard Java card SIM card, embedded in a Samsung Galaxy S5 NFC-enabled smartphone. The choice of the running platform (a Samsung Galaxy model S5) shows that our protocol performs optimally even using old smartphone models. The SIM card is a Java Card 2.2.2 smart card with a 44MHz ARM processor. The card has 10kB of volatile fast memory (RAM) and 450kB of persistent memory (EEPROM). The only specificity is that the SIM card supports mathematical Application Programming Interfaces (API) for modular arithmetic and arithmetic operations on elliptic curve. Through its own random number generator, the card can also generate its own secret key s_1. The reader used to emulate an NFC-enabled reader at a public transport station is an HID Omnikey contactless reader.

Commands that provide the instructions to generate some pre-computed values are triggered by the PAYGO application on the smartphone, which sends an Application Protocol Data Unit (APDU) command containing the instructions to initiate pre-computation to the SIM whilst the mobile is turned on. The pre-computations consists in the SIM generating multiple randomization values $a_1, l \in \mathbb{Z}_p$ and the corresponding tuples $(w, w', c = w^s, t_1 = w^{a_1})$, which are subsequently stored for later validations. In the implementation of our pre-DAA scheme, we use pairing-friendly Barreto-Naehrig curves [3]. To obtain a security level of 128-bit, the base field prime number p is chosen to be a 256-bit prime.

Table 1 displays the performances obtained from the implementation of our PAYGO protocol. The timings are obtained on an average of 100 tests.

Table 1. PAYGO *Validation* phase timings (min-max) average (ms).

Off-line computation		
Battery On		*Battery Off*
(238-264) 253 ms		*(753-831) 798 ms*
On-line computation		
Sign (SIM card)		Verify (Reader)
Battery on	*Battery Off*	(4–16) 11 ms
(153-167) 162 ms	*(450-472) 462 ms*	
Total On-line computation		
Battery On		*Battery Off*
(157-183) 173 ms		*(455-487) 471 ms*

The implementation is split between an *off-line*, phase which allows the SIM card to perform some pre-computations during the idle time of its processor, and an *on-line* phase for the computations that rely on the values Ch and bsn sent by the terminal. We include the timings for the cases where a SIM has to perform pass validation without being powered by the smartphone ("Battery off"). In such cases, the SIM card performs in "downgraded" mode, due to it being powered by the NFC reader. Such occurrences are however rare, and the timings are only included for completeness purposes. This however demonstrate that a SIM card can authenticate in a standalone manner (without delegating any signature computation to the mobile phone).

The timings obtained for our pre-DAA scheme, show that a computationally constrained SIM card can generate a signature in less than 200 ms. PAYGO is therefore compliant with the stringent efficiency requirements for a contactless transit pass [25].

7 Conclusion

In this paper we introduced PAYGO, a practical pre-DAA-based anonymous transit pass protocol, secure under a non-interactive cryptographic assumption. The protocol is efficient enough for a SIM card to solely execute the entire validation protocol, whilst respecting the timing constraints of NFC-enabled authentication protocols. PAYGO satisfies the privacy and efficiency requirements of mobile transport passes, with security guarantees that are derived from our novel pre-DAA construction.

A Security Analysis of PAYGO

The security of PAYGO mainly relies on the security of the underlying pre-DAA scheme. PAYGO verifies the following security properties:

- **Consistency.** This property captures the notion that valid pass (which obtained valid credentials from the transport operator in a previous registration process) must be granted access by the reader. The PAYGO pass validation is *consistent.* Indeed, a valid credential is a randomized version (w, w') of the group signing key (u, u') obtained during the *registration* process. In the validation process, the reader grants access if the following conditions are met: (1) (w, w') is a valid EPS signature (see Sect. 3.2) on a secret s known to the SIM card (i.e. the group signing key is valid and was obtained during a previous registration process with the transport operator); (2) The same secret is used to generate the tag T. By verifying the previous two conditions, the reader grants access with probability 1.
- **Unforgeability.** It is not be possible for a defrauder to forge the pass credentials, or to modify them in the card. Indeed, in order to forge a signature, a defrauder $\mathcal{A}$ must be able to generate a signature σ that cannot be traced back to a secret key that was queried in a previous *registration* protocol. In the traceability proof of the underlying pre-DAA scheme, we prove that such a forger can be used to construct a second forger against the security of the EPS signature. The EPS signature being proven EUF-wCMA-secure under the q-MSDH assumption ([16], Lemma 1), such a forger succeeds only with negligible probability.
- **Anonymity.** The *anonymity* property of the pre-DAA scheme ensures that PAYGO pass validations are not traceable.
- **Responsibility.** The *non-frameability* property of the pre-DAA scheme ensures that it is unfeasible to assign PAYGO pass validations to a user which has not initiated said validations.
- **Anti-passback.** A defrauder $\mathcal{A}$ validating the same pass consecutively will do so in the same time slot P_j; As described in Sect. 5.5, this results in $\mathcal{A}$ generating two signatures using the same key sk_i with respect to the same basename bsn. The Link function will therefore determine with probability 1 that the two signatures are linked. The anti-passback property is therefore ensured in PAYGO.

References

1. 20008-2, I.: Information technology — security techniques — anonymous digital signatures — part 2: Mechanisms using a group public key. Technical report, ISO/IEC (2013)
2. Arfaoui, G., Lalande, J., Traoré, J., Desmoulins, N., Berthomé, P., Gharout, S.: A practical set-membership proof for privacy-preserving NFC mobile ticketing. PoPETs **2015**(2), 25–45 (2015)
3. Barreto, P.S.L.M., Naehrig, M.: Pairing-friendly elliptic curves of prime order. In: Preneel, B., Tavares, S. (eds.) SAC 2005. LNCS, vol. 3897, pp. 319–331. Springer, Heidelberg (2006). https://doi.org/10.1007/11693383_22
4. Bellare, M., Namprempre, C., Pointcheval, D., Semanko, M.: The one-more-rsa-inversion problems and the security of Chaum's blind signature scheme. J. Cryptol. **16**(3) (2003)
5. Bellare, M., Rogaway, P.: Random oracles are practical: a paradigm for designing efficient protocols. In: Proceedings of the 1st ACM Conference on Computer and Communications Security, pp. 62–73 (1993)
6. Bernhard, D., Fuchsbauer, G., Ghadafi, E., Smart, N.P., Warinschi, B.: Anonymous attestation with user-controlled linkability. Int. J. Inf. Sec. **12**(3), 219–249 (2013)
7. Boneh, D., Boyen, X.: Short signatures without random oracles. In: Cachin, C., Camenisch, J.L. (eds.) EUROCRYPT 2004. LNCS, vol. 3027, pp. 56–73. Springer, Heidelberg (2004). https://doi.org/10.1007/978-3-540-24676-3_4
8. Boneh, D., Boyen, X.: Short signatures without random oracles and the SDH assumption in bilinear groups. J. Cryptol. **21**(2), 149–177 (2008)
9. Brickell, E.F., Camenisch, J., Chen, L.: Direct anonymous attestation. In: Proceedings of the 11th ACM Conference on Computer and Communications Security, CCS 2004, Washington, DC, USA, 25–29 October 2004, pp. 132–145 (2004)
10. Brickell, E., Chen, L., Li, J.: A new direct anonymous attestation scheme from bilinear maps. In: Lipp, P., Sadeghi, A.-R., Koch, K.-M. (eds.) Trust 2008. LNCS, vol. 4968, pp. 166–178. Springer, Heidelberg (2008). https://doi.org/10.1007/978-3-540-68979-9_13
11. Brickell, E., Chen, L., Li, J.: Simplified security notions of direct anonymous attestation and a concrete scheme from pairings. Int. J. Inf. Sec. (2009)
12. Camenisch, J., Drijvers, M., Lehmann, A.: Universally composable direct anonymous attestation. In: Public-Key Cryptography - PKC 2016–19th IACR (2016)
13. Camenisch, J., Drijvers, M., Lehmann, A.: Anonymous attestation using the strong diffie hellman assumption revisited. In: Trust and Trustworthy Computing - 9th International Conference, TRUST 2016, Vienna, Austria, August 29–30, 2016, Proceedings (2016)
14. Camenisch, J., Drijvers, M., Lehmann, A.: Anonymous attestation with subverted TPMs. In: Katz, J., Shacham, H. (eds.) CRYPTO 2017. LNCS, vol. 10403, pp. 427–461. Springer, Cham (2017). https://doi.org/10.1007/978-3-319-63697-9_15
15. Camenisch, J., Stadler, M.: Proof systems for general statements about discrete logarithms. Technical report/Department of Computer Science, ETH Zürich (1997)
16. Canard, S., Pointcheval, D., Santos, Q., Traoré, J.: Privacy-preserving plaintext-equality of low-entropy inputs. In: Preneel, B., Vercauteren, F. (eds.) ACNS 2018. LNCS, vol. 10892, pp. 262–279. Springer, Cham (2018). https://doi.org/10.1007/978-3-319-93387-0_14

17. Chen, L., Page, D., Smart, N.P.: On the design and implementation of an efficient DAA scheme. In: Gollmann, D., Lanet, J.-L., Iguchi-Cartigny, J. (eds.) CARDIS 2010. LNCS, vol. 6035, pp. 223–237. Springer, Heidelberg (2010). https://doi.org/10.1007/978-3-642-12510-2_16
18. Derler, D., Potzmader, K., Winter, J., Dietrich, K.: Anonymous ticketing for NFC-enabled mobile phones. In: Chen, L., Yung, M., Zhu, L. (eds.) INTRUST 2011. LNCS, vol. 7222, pp. 66–83. Springer, Heidelberg (2012). https://doi.org/10.1007/978-3-642-32298-3_5
19. Desmoulins, N., Lescuyer, R., Sanders, O., Traoré, J.: Direct anonymous attestations with dependent basename opening. In: Gritzalis, D., Kiayias, A., Askoxylakis, I. (eds.) CANS 2014. LNCS, vol. 8813, pp. 206–221. Springer, Cham (2014). https://doi.org/10.1007/978-3-319-12280-9_14
20. Ekberg, J.-E., Tamrakar, S.: Mass transit ticketing with NFC mobile phones. In: Chen, L., Yung, M., Zhu, L. (eds.) INTRUST 2011. LNCS, vol. 7222, pp. 48–65. Springer, Heidelberg (2012). https://doi.org/10.1007/978-3-642-32298-3_4
21. Fiat, A., Shamir, A.: How to prove yourself: practical solutions to identification and signature problems. In: Odlyzko, A.M. (ed.) CRYPTO 1986. LNCS, vol. 263, pp. 186–194. Springer, Heidelberg (1987). https://doi.org/10.1007/3-540-47721-7_12
22. Forum, N.: NFC in public transport. https://nfc-forum.org/wp-content/uploads/2013/12/NFC-in-Public-Transport.pdf
23. Galbraith, S.D., Paterson, K.G., Smart, N.P.: Pairings for cryptographers. Discrete Appl. Math. **156**(16), 3113–3121 (2008)
24. Goldwasser, S., Micali, S., Rivest, R.L.: A digital signature scheme secure against adaptive chosen-message attacks. SIAM J. Comput. **17**(2), 281–308 (1988)
25. GSMA: White paper: Mobile NFC in transport (2012)
26. Hazay, C., Mikkelsen, G.L., Rabin, T., Toft, T., Nicolosi, A.A.: Efficient RSA key generation and threshold paillier in the two-party setting. J. Cryptol. **32**(2), 265–323 (2019)
27. Heydt-Benjamin, T.S., Chae, H.-J., Defend, B., Fu, K.: Privacy for public transportation. In: Danezis, G., Golle, P. (eds.) PET 2006. LNCS, vol. 4258, pp. 1–19. Springer, Heidelberg (2006). https://doi.org/10.1007/11957454_1
28. Kumar, V., et al.: Direct anonymous attestation with efficient verifier-local revocation for subscription system. In: Proceedings of the 2018 on Asia Conference on Computer and Communications Security, pp. 567–574 (2018)
29. Paillier, P.: Public-key cryptosystems based on composite degree residuosity classes. In: Stern, J. (ed.) EUROCRYPT 1999. LNCS, vol. 1592, pp. 223–238. Springer, Heidelberg (1999). https://doi.org/10.1007/3-540-48910-X_16
30. Pointcheval, D., Sanders, O.: Short randomizable signatures. In: Cryptographers' Track at the RSA Conference, pp. 111–126 (2016)
31. Pointcheval, D., Sanders, O.: Reassessing security of randomizable signatures. In: Smart, N.P. (ed.) CT-RSA 2018. LNCS, vol. 10808, pp. 319–338. Springer, Cham (2018). https://doi.org/10.1007/978-3-319-76953-0_17
32. Pointcheval, D., Stern, J.: Security arguments for digital signatures and blind signatures. J. Cryptol. **13**(3), 361–396 (2000)
33. Rupp, A., Hinterwälder, G., Baldimtsi, F., Paar, C.: P4R: privacy-preserving prepayments with refunds for transportation systems. In: Sadeghi, A.-R. (ed.) FC 2013. LNCS, vol. 7859, pp. 205–212. Springer, Heidelberg (2013). https://doi.org/10.1007/978-3-642-39884-1_17
34. Sadeghi, A., Visconti, I., Wachsmann, C.: User privacy in transport systems based on RFID e-tickets. In: Proceedings of the 1st International Workshop on Privacy in Location-Based Applications, 9 October 2008 (2008)

35. N.I. of Standards, Technology: Digital signature standard (DSS) (2009)
36. Tamrakar, S., Ekberg, J.-E.: Tapping and tripping with NFC. In: Huth, M., Asokan, N., Čapkun, S., Flechais, I., Coles-Kemp, L. (eds.) Trust 2013. LNCS, vol. 7904, pp. 115–132. Springer, Heidelberg (2013). https://doi.org/10.1007/978-3-642-38908-5_9
37. Wesemeyer, S., Newton, C.J., Treharne, H., Chen, L., Sasse, R., Whitefield, J.: Formal analysis and implementation of a tpm 2.0-based direct anonymous attestation scheme (2019)
38. Yang, K., Chen, L., Zhang, Z., Newton, C., Yang, B., Xi, L.: Direct anonymous attestation with optimal tpm signing efficiency. IACR Cryptol. ePrint Arch. p. 1128 (2018)

SiMLA - Security in Machine Learning and Its Applications

Towards Demystifying Adversarial Robustness of Binarized Neural Networks

Zihao Qin[1,2], Hsiao-Ying Lin[2(✉)], and Jie Shi[2]

[1] Nanyang Technological University, Singapore, Singapore
QINZ0003@e.ntu.edu.sg
[2] Huawei International, Singapore, Singapore
{lin.hsiao.ying,shi.jie1}@huawei.com

Abstract. Quantized neural networks are proposed for reduced computation and memory costs. When quantized neural networks are designed for edge or terminal devices, they may be more vulnerable to adversarial perturbations. We focus on the extreme cases, i.e. binarized neural networks (BNNs) where weights and activations are binarized, and investigate their adversarial robustness. Six different binarized neural networks are considered with their full-precision counterpart as the baseline. We conduct the first empirical study on adversarial robustness over various BNNs in terms of their naive adversarial robustness, the effectiveness of adversarial training on BNNs, and explore attack transferability among BNNs. Our analysis provides quantitative study on how BNNs perform in terms of model accuracy and adversarial robustness.

Keywords: Adversarial robustness · Binarized neural network · Adversarial training · Attack transferability

1 Introduction

Deep neural networks (DNN) have shown impressive performance on various tasks, such as image classification, object detection, and language translation. As DNN-based systems achieve significant performance success in services and applications, yet security concerns also gain more attentions since researchers find systematic means of attack. One major concern is evasion attacks. Evasion attacks generate adversarial examples which are data samples with imperceptible adversarial perturbations to humans but effective enough to mislead DNN-based systems to deliver incorrect output. This may bring harmful consequences. Adversarial robustness captures how strong the DNN is against evasion attacks, such as Fast Gradient Sign Method (FGSM) [9] and Projected Gradient Descent (PGD) [15]. One of the most effective defenses against evasion attacks is adversarial training where the training dataset includes adversarial examples.

While DNN-based services and systems expand broadly over different domains, there remains a challenge applying DNN in resource-limited environments, such as edge-devices, standalone embedded systems, and industrial

J. Zhou et al. (Eds.): ACNS 2021 Workshops, LNCS 12809, pp. 439–462, 2021.
https://doi.org/10.1007/978-3-030-81645-2_25

low-bitwidth microcontrollers. Take an image classification task as an example. A ResNet101 network which performs the classification task on ImageNet dataset has size about 170 MiB while special purpose microcontrollers may only have 256 MiB RAM or less. By applying binary quantizations which convert network parameters into binary values, the model size can be reduced to less than 7 MiB (about more than 25 times smaller by a conservative estimation). The small size of the model also opens the potential of running models in trusted execution environment even in edge-devices. For example, applications in trusted execution environments are constrained to about 7 MiB of secure memory [20].

Two major approaches are proposed for model compression. The first one is to reduce the number of parameters in neural networks, such as SqueezeNet [11] and network pruning [10]. The second approach is quantization, which reduces the bit-width of parameters. Conventionally, parameters are presented as 32-bit floating points. By quantization, they are reduced to less bit-width fixed points. For instance, TensorFlow Lite deploys pre-trained models to mobile or embedded devices via model compression techniques and 8-bit post-training weights quantization. Binary quantizer is the extreme case of quantization. Binary quantizers vary depending on how forward and backward functions are designed. We focus on fully binarized neural networks (BNNs) where binarization covers both weights and activations and aim at answering the main questions:

Do binarized neural networks offer superior adversarial robustness than full-precision counterparts do? And why?

Existing research works on evaluating adversarial robustness of BNNs have diverse results. Bernhard et al. [2] analyzed adversarial robustness on quantized neural networks and indicated that quantization itself offers poor protection against adversarial examples. Similarly, Lin et al. [13] indicated that quantization amplifies input error over layers so gives inferior robustness. On the other side, Galloway et al. [7] conducted empirical evaluations and indicated that stochastic quantization may be a possible defense against iterative attacks. To demystify this phenomenon and dive deeper for adversarial robustness of BNNs, we conduct the first empirical study on various BNNs. Three sets of adaptive experiments are performed to analyze BNNs. We evaluate the naive adversarial robustness, the effectiveness of adversarial training, and attack transferability among BNNs and their full-precision counterpart.

Derived from experimental results, we characterize that adversarial robustness of BNNs highly depends on what binary quantizer is used. Specifically, we identify that SignSwish, StocSwish and stochastic quantizers offer superior and stable robustness against FGSM and PGD attacks. Our experiments are conducted on MNIST and Fashion-MNIST. Our contributions are summarized in the following:

- We conduct the first evaluation on adversarial robustness of six binary quantizers, including our newly-proposed StocSwish quantizer, and conclude that superior robustness is not a universal feature of all BNNs. Specifically, we identify SignSwish, StocSwish and stochastic quantizers outperform others in terms of robustness against FGSM and PGD attacks.

- We conduct the first validation study of adversarial training on various BNNs against FGSM and PGD attacks. Results quantitatively validate the effectiveness of adversarial training on deterministic and stochastic binary quantizers, but not on SignSwish and StocSwish binary quantizers. The use of Swish function may limit the effectiveness of adversarial training.
- We conduct the first empirical study of attack transferability among the six binary quantizers and their full-precision counterpart. Specifically, we identify SignSwish, StocSwish and stochastic quantizers outperform others in terms of robustness against transferred adversarial examples.
- We characterize the newly-composed StocSwish quantizer that it has a stable robustness property against attacks with different perturbation levels and has superior robustness even without adversarial training.

2 Literature Review and Preliminary

2.1 Binarized Neural Networks

Figure 1 gives a high-level view of layers in a quantized neural network in forward and backward processes. The forward process is used in both model training and inference. The backward process is only used for model training, i.e. backward propagation. BNNs are constructed with binary quantizers.

Early BNNs [4] are proposed where only weights are constrained to binary values, e.g. $\{-1, +1\}$. Later on, some BNNs are proposed with both binarized weights and activations [5]. During the forward process, activations and weights of each intermediate layer are binarized through a forward function q. For the backward process for backward propagation, since the derivative of a binary forward function is zero almost everywhere, estimators or approximations are used.

We refer a binary quantizer as a combination of forward and backward functions. Since we only focus on binary quantizers in this study, for simplicity, we call them quantizers in short. Deterministic and stochastic quantizers are proposed in one of the earliest work of BNNs [5]. Followed by their innovation in BNNs, extensive studies and improvement on binary quantizers are proposed mainly for remedying the accuracy gap between BNNs and full precision networks. Figure 2 is a brief review of BNNs. Some existing surveys [18, 19] on BNNs are available for a more comprehensive overview.

Recently, adversarial robustness of BNNs is getting more attentions motivated by their significant business potential. Galloway et al. [7] are ones of the earliest researchers trying to evaluate adversarial robustness of BNNs. They conducted evaluations on stochastic quantizers with MNIST dataset under both FGSM and PGD attacks. Their results yield insights that stochastic quantizer provides certain robustness to the network. Panda et al. [17] considered both input quantization and parameter quantization. They evaluated XNOR-net under FGSM attacks. Their experimental results on MNIST show that quantization gives some robustness, yet results on CIFAR-10 do not. Lin et al. [13] explored the correlation of quantization and robustness. Their results indicate

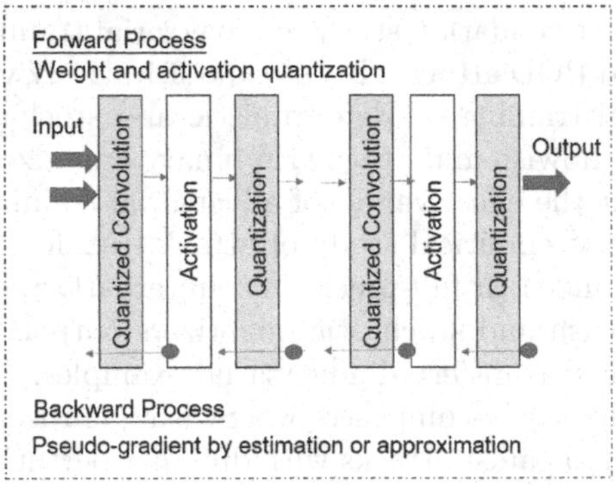

Fig. 1. Forward and backward processed of layers in quantized neural networks.

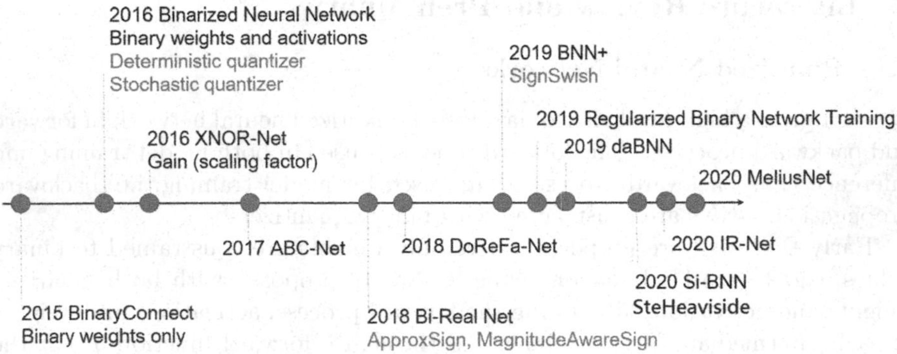

Fig. 2. The footprint of BNNs with some quantizers.

that quantization would amplify input perturbation and hence give inferior robustness. Bernhard et al. [2] evaluated deterministic quantizer by various attacks on CIFAR-10 and SVHN. Their results yield a conclusion that quantization itself gives poor adversarial robustness.

2.2 Binary Quantizers

To understand whether binary quantizers contribute to adversarial robustness, six binary quantizers are analyzed in our investigation. They are introduced as follows, including our newly-composed StocSwish quantizer. We also visualize them in 2D-plots in Appendix A.1.

Deterministic Quantizer. Courbariaux et al. [5] proposed using deterministic quantization and straight-through-estimator (STE) for training BNNs. The resulting BNNs achieve competitive accuracy on standard deep learning datasets.

Deterministic quantizer has a deterministic forward quantization (or a sign function):

$$q(x) = \begin{cases} -1, x < 0 \\ 1, \quad x \geq 0 \end{cases} \tag{1}$$

The backward pass is designed as STE, also called a rectangular function, which can be considered as the derivative of a clip function:

$$\frac{\partial q(x)}{\partial x} = \begin{cases} 1 \text{ , } |x| \leq 1 \\ 0 \text{ , } |x| > 1 \end{cases} \tag{2}$$

Stochastic Quantizer. Stochastic quantizer was proposed in [5] along with deterministic quantization. Yet stochastic quantizer is considered less practical in embedded systems due to the need of randomness. Activations and weights in the forward pass of stochastic quantizer are randomly sampled from a Bernoulli distribution with probability p given by *hard sigmoid* function σ passed by real-valued inputs x:

$$q(x) = \begin{cases} +1, \text{ with probability } p = \sigma(x) \\ -1, \text{ with probability } (1-p) \end{cases} \tag{3}$$

$$\sigma(x) = max(0, min(1, \frac{x+1}{2})) \tag{4}$$

ApproxSign Quantizer. The STE used in deterministic quantizer can be considered as the derivative of a clip function. Liu et al. [14] propose ApproxSign as a better approximation of sign function than clip function by introducing differentiability. Therefore, they use derivative of ApproxSign to replace STE during the backward pass. An ApproxSign quantizer uses the same forward pass as in Eq. 1, while its gradient is estimated using the triangle-shaped derivative of ApproxSign function:

$$\frac{\partial q(x)}{\partial x} = \begin{cases} (2 - 2|x|) & |x| \leq 1 \\ 0 & |x| > 1 \end{cases} \tag{5}$$

MagnitudeAwareSign Quantizer. Liu et al. [14] propose Bi-Real Net where MagnitudeAwareSign quantizer is used to better capture the gradients of weights when also taking magnitude of weights into consideration. Although in [14] MagnitudeAwareSign and ApproxSign are used together for weights and activations, we investigate their adversarial robustness separately.

SignSwish Quantizer. To improve model accuracy, Darabi et al. [6] propose BNN+ where the approximation of derivative of the sign function is improved by using the second derivative of the Swish function. It is worth to mention that the derivative of the Swish function is an approximation of ReLU. Hence, interesting,

BNN+ approximates the derivative of the sign function by approximating the derivative of ReLU. SignSwish qunatizer uses the sign function as its forward pass, and a tunable hyper-parameter β in the backward pass as follows:

$$\frac{\partial q_\beta(x)}{\partial x} = \frac{\beta\left\{2 - \beta x \tanh(\frac{\beta x}{2})\right\}}{1 + \cosh(\beta x)} \tag{6}$$

β is used to control how fast the function approaches horizontal asymptotes at $+1$ and -1. Later in our experiments, we set it to be 5 as in [6].

StocSwish. Existing quantizers are proposed for improving model accuracy. None of them is proposed with an objective of robustness. From initial experimental results, we notice that stochastic and SignSwish quantizers offers superior robustness than others. We hypothesize that the combination may yield a good balance. Hence, we propose StocSwish quantizer where the forward process is stochastic as shown in Eq. 3 and the backward process is the second derivative of Swish function as shown in Eq. 6. In a later section, experimental results provide positive evidences on our hypothesis.

2.3 Adversarial Robustness

Adversarial robustness of neural networks captures how strong a neural network is against adversarial examples. Adversarial examples are crafted data samples aiming at misleading the addressed neural network. We focus on the adversarial robustness against FGSM and PGD attacks in untargeted version.

FGSM [9] generates adversarial examples by maximizing the loss function $L(\theta, x, y)$ of a target model on the benign inputs x and their corresponding targets y. θ is the parameters of the target model. Modified inputs $x' = x + \eta$ simply take one-step perturbations η along the direction of the gradient of $L(\theta, x, y)$.

$$x' = x + \epsilon \cdot sign(\nabla_x L(\theta, x, y)) \tag{7}$$

where ϵ is the magnitude of perturbations.

PGD attack [15] is a more powerful multi-step variant of single-step FGSM. Instead of taking one-step, it iteratively updates along the direction of gradient of loss function L within the maximum number of iterations. S is a set of allowed perturbations.

$$x_{t+1} = \prod_{x+S} (x_t + \epsilon \cdot sign(\nabla_x L(\theta, x, y))) \tag{8}$$

PGD attack has been proved as a general first-order attack and one of the strongest attacks. Hence, we choose it as a strong opponent to evaluate BNNs.

2.4 Adversarial Training

Adversarial training is one of the most successful defense strategy up-to-date against evasion attacks. There are several methods to perform adversarial training, while the basic principle is to inject adversarial examples into the training

Table 1. Model architectures and model sizes in our experiments. The size of BNN is more than 25 times smaller than the full-precision counterpart.

Model architecture			
Full precision network		Binarized neural network	
Conv2D	(32, 3, 3, 1)	QuantConv2D	(32, 3, 3, 1)
MaxPooling	(2, 2)	MaxPooling	(2, 2)
Conv2D	(64, 3, 3, 1)	QuantConv2D	(64, 3, 3, 1)
Conv2D	(64, 3, 3, 1)	QuantConv2D	(64, 3, 3, 1)
MaxPooling	(2, 2)	MaxPooling	(2, 2)
Dense	64	QuantDense	64
Dense	10	QuantDense	10
Softmax	–	Softmax	–
Model size			
477.29 KiB		17.61 KiB	

datasets of a model, i.e. data augmentation. Training on one-step adversarial examples, such as FGSM, would only strengthen the model's robustness against non-iterative attacks, but remains vulnerable against iterative ones such as PGD. Hence, Madry et al. [15] proposed injecting adversarial examples generated by PGD into the training dataset. Their results achieve state-of-the-art robustness on MNIST and CIFAR-10 datasets.

3 Adversarial Robustness Experiments

We investigate adversarial robustness of BNNs by empirically evaluating their accuracy under FGSM and PGD attacks. The core question we would like to answer is that "whether BNNs offer superior adversarial robustness than a full-precision network?" To do so, we adaptively conduct three sets of experiments. Each of them consists of robustness evaluation against FGSM and PGD attacks.

3.1 Experiment Design and Setup

The first set of experiments aims at evaluating adversarial robustness of the six binary quantizers. A full-precision counterpart is included as a baseline for comparison. Model accuracy is measured for clean input and perturbed input generated by FGSM and PGD attacks. Results of the first set of experiments would indicate which quantizer performs better initially without adversarial training. Following the first set, the second set of experiments is conducted on adversarial-trained networks. From the second set of experiment, the effectiveness of adversarial training on BNNs can be analyzed. The third set of experiments is attack transferability. Adversarial examples are generated from the source model and then evaluated on the target model. Putting together results of all three sets of experiments, certain quantizers are expected to stand out for their superior robustness features.

We take MNIST and Fashion-MNIST datasets in our experiments for cross-checking observed tendency. MNIST contains images of gray-scale hand-written digits, while the slightly more challenging Fashion-MNIST is a collection of gray-scale images of clothes and shoes. Both MNIST and Fashion-MNIST contains a training set of size $(60000, 28, 28)$ and a test set of size $(10000, 28, 28)$. We normalize each sample of data into range $[-1, 1]$.

In Table 1, we depict the LeNet-like model architecture used in our experiments [12]. We use exactly the same architectures for both full precision networks and BNNs, while quantizer is deployed in each quantized layer, such as QuantConv2D and QuantDense, for quantization of activations and weights of intermediate layers. It is worth mentioning that we do not binarize the input for the first layer, as it hurts accuracy much more severely than other layers in the neural network.

We conduct experiments on six different quantizers: deterministic quantizer, ApproxSign quantizer, SignSwish quantizer, MagnitudeAwareSign quantizer, stochastic quantizer and our StocSwish quantizer. All the six quantizers are evaluated on both MNIST and Fashion-MNIST datasets.

Benign accuracy is evaluated on clean test set. *Adversarial accuracy* is evaluated on adversarial examples. *Relative accuracy drop* is defined as the percentage decrease of model's adversarial accuracy with respect to its benign accuracy. It is also called *stress* in [21]. Relative accuracy drop is used to quantify the stability of adversarial robustness over different levels of perturbations. We use the entire test dataset to generate adversarial examples with different perturbation levels of ϵ for both FGSM and PGD. Intuitively, the higher adversarial accuracy is, the better the robustness is. A common maximum magnitude of perturbations imperceptible for human is $\epsilon = 0.3$ [7], while we choose ϵ up to 0.5 to cover more extreme cases. The maximum number of iterations for PGD attack is set to 100.

For adversarial training, we augment the training dataset with the set of adversarial examples, on which we then train our model. We employ 20 iterations of PGD attack with $\epsilon = 0.3$ to generate a set of adversarial examples with the same size as the training set.

We measure attack transferability by the adversarial accuracy among all six quantizers and the full-precision counterpart on Fashion-MNIST against FGSM and PGD, respectively. Different perturbation levels are taken into consideration. The higher adversarial accuracy is, the lower the attack transferability is.

We implement BNNs using Keras [3] and TensorFlow [1] for deep learning framework. For quantizations, we use BNN-targeted framework Larq [8]. For FGSM and PGD implementations, we use Adversarial Robustness Toolbox [16].

3.2 Some Binary Quantizers Advance Robustness

In the first set of experiments, adversarial robustness of the six quantizers and the full-precision counterpart are evaluated on MNIST and Fashion-MNIST against FGSM and PGD attacks. We present our experimental results as follows.

Table 2. Benign and adversarial accuracy of the full-precision network and BNNs without adversarial training on MNIST under FGSM attack with relative accuracy drop. "MAS" stands for "MagnitudeAwareSign" quantizer. For each accuracy column, the highest value is underlined. For each column of relative accuracy drop, the lowest value is underlined.

		Adversarial accuracy					Relative accuracy drop				
Quantizers	Benign	$\epsilon = 0.1$	$\epsilon = 0.2$	$\epsilon = 0.3$	$\epsilon = 0.4$	$\epsilon = 0.5$	$\epsilon = 0.1$	$\epsilon = 0.2$	$\epsilon = 0.3$	$\epsilon = 0.4$	$\epsilon = 0.5$
Full Precision	**98.8**	93.7	77.9	57.5	39.4	27.7	5.16%	21.15%	41.8%	60.12%	71.96%
Deterministic	97.1	89.8	68.0	48.5	30.6	22.0	7.52%	29.97%	50.05%	68.49%	77.34%
ApproxSign	96.8	79.6	56.3	38.5	27.8	20.4	17.77%	41.84%	60.23%	71.28%	78.93%
SignSwish	98.0	92.5	**86.9**	**76.3**	**67.8**	**55.5**	5.61%	11.33%	**22.14%**	**30.82%**	**43.37%**
MAS	96.3	**94.5**	85.6	69.9	46.6	28.6	**1.87%**	**11.11%**	27.41%	51.61%	70.30%
Stochastic	93.3	88.2	77.3	60.1	41.3	28.1	5.47%	17.15%	35.58%	55.73%	69.88%
StocSwish	83.8	79.8	72.7	64.5	53.7	44.0	4.77%	13.25%	23.03%	35.92%	47.49%

Table 3. Benign and adversarial accuracy of the full-precision network and BNNs without adversarial training on MNIST under PGD attack with relative accuracy drop.

		Adversarial accuracy					Relative accuracy drop				
Quantizers	Benign	$\epsilon = 0.1$	$\epsilon = 0.2$	$\epsilon = 0.3$	$\epsilon = 0.4$	$\epsilon = 0.5$	$\epsilon = 0.1$	$\epsilon = 0.2$	$\epsilon = 0.3$	$\epsilon = 0.4$	$\epsilon = 0.5$
Full Precision	**98.8**	**95.5**	80.7	47.6	14.2	3.2	**3.34%**	18.32%	51.82%	85.63%	96.76%
Deterministic	97.1	86.6	45.4	14.7	3.9	1.5	10.81%	53.24%	84.86%	95.98%	98.46%
ApproxSign	96.8	52.1	20.8	8.2	2.8	1.2	46.18%	78.51%	91.53%	97.11%	98.76%
SignSwish	98.0	41.2	18.1	6.8	3.1	1.8	57.96%	81.53%	93.06%	96.84%	98.16%
MAS	96.3	89.6	77.0	52.4	31.6	19.6	6.96%	20.04%	45.59%	67.19%	79.65%
Stochastic	93.3	89.0	**80.8**	64.3	43.9	25.9	4.61%	13.40%	31.08%	52.95%	72.24%
StocSwish	83.8	81.0	74.8	**68.6**	**57.7**	**45.0**	**3.34%**	**10.74%**	**18.14%**	**31.15%**	**46.30%**

We summarize model accuracy of full precision network and BNNs on MNIST and Fashion-MNIST under FGSM and PGD attacks in Table 2, Table 3, Table 4 and Table 5, respectively. Recall that relative accuracy drop is the ratio of the difference of benign accuracy and adversarial accuracy over benign accuracy. It captures the stability of the addressed network under attacks.

We observe the consistent tendency on MNIST and Fashion-MNIST. Since the accuracy gap between BNNs and the full-precision network is more obvious on Fashion-MNIST, we focus on observing results of Fashion-MNIST for simplicity. The difference between benign accuracy of full-precision network and BNNs indicates how much accuracy is sacrificed for efficiency from binarization.

With the focus on results under FGSM attack, the variation of benign accuracy and adversarial accuracy among different quantizers can be observed. As shown in Fig. 3a, we observe a distinguishable tendency that the full precision network becomes very vulnerable on Fashion-MNIST under FGSM attacks, while SignSwish and StocSwish quantizers demonstrate superior robustness among all other networks. Moreover, the relative accuracy drop of SignSwish quantizer is much less than that of most other candidates especially at large ϵ values, which indicates a feature of stability. StocSwish quantizer also presents strong robustness at large values of ϵ, while its performance at low levels of perturbation seems

Table 4. Benign and adversarial accuracy of the full-precision network and BNNs without adversarial training on Fashion-MNIST under FGSM attack with relative accuracy drop.

		Adversarial accuracy					Relative accuracy drop				
Quantizers	Benign	$\epsilon = 0.1$	$\epsilon = 0.2$	$\epsilon = 0.3$	$\epsilon = 0.4$	$\epsilon = 0.5$	$\epsilon = 0.1$	$\epsilon = 0.2$	$\epsilon = 0.3$	$\epsilon = 0.4$	$\epsilon = 0.5$
Full Precision	**90.3**	66.8	64.4	63.7	**63.1**	**62.5**	23.53%	25.88%	26.56%	27.23%	27.78%
Deterministic	84.2	56.9	42.1	32.5	23.5	20.1	32.42%	50.00%	61.40%	72.09%	76.13%
ApproxSign	84.6	46.8	35.4	28.7	25.1	20.9	44.68%	58.16%	66.08%	70.33%	75.30%
SignSwish	87.9	**72.6**	**67.9**	**64.5**	60.4	56.1	17.41%	22.75%	26.62%	31.29%	36.18%
MAS	81.9	52.9	39.2	25.0	17.6	17.1	35.41%	52.14%	69.47%	78.51%	79.12%
Stochastic	77.6	69.3	56.1	43.9	32.2	24.7	10.70%	27.71%	43.43%	58.51%	68.17%
StocSwish	71.3	70.3	67.8	64.0	60.0	53.4	**1.40%**	**4.91%**	**10.24%**	**15.85%**	**25.11%**

Table 5. Benign and adversarial accuracy of the full-precision network and BNNs without adversarial training on Fashion-MNIST under PGD attack with relative accuracy drop.

		Adversarial accuracy					Relative accuracy drop				
Quantizers	Benign	$\epsilon = 0.1$	$\epsilon = 0.2$	$\epsilon = 0.3$	$\epsilon = 0.4$	$\epsilon = 0.5$	$\epsilon = 0.1$	$\epsilon = 0.2$	$\epsilon = 0.3$	$\epsilon = 0.4$	$\epsilon = 0.5$
Full Precision	**90.3**	54.3	40.5	29.2	21.6	17.2	35.99%	49.82%	61.12%	68.74%	73.07%
Deterministic	84.2	53.4	33.3	18.7	10.3	7.8	36.58%	60.45%	77.79%	87.77%	90.74%
ApproxSign	84.6	37.2	20.5	11.7	8.4	7.6	56.03%	75.77%	86.17%	90.07%	91.02%
SignSwish	87.9	44.1	26.6	16.9	12.6	10.2	49.83%	69.74%	80.77%	85.67%	88.40%
MAS	81.9	58.4	35.8	21.2	15.1	12.3	28.69%	56.29%	74.11%	81.56%	84.98%
Stochastic	77.6	**71.8**	57.7	40.0	24.6	14.5	7.47%	25.64%	48.45%	68.30%	81.31%
StocSwish	71.3	70.0	**68.3**	**65.7**	**62.1**	**57.5**	**1.82%**	**4.21%**	**7.85%**	**12.90%**	**19.35%**

to be limited by its benign accuracy. We identify that SignSwish and StocSwish quantizers are more robust against FGSM attack, especially at high levels of perturbations.

With the focus on results under PGD attack, most of addressed networks are vulnerable except StocSwish and stochastic quantizers. As shown in Fig. 3b, StocSwish and stochastic quantizers show competitive adversarial accuracy against PGD attack especially against large magnitudes of perturbation.

Putting results under FGSM and PGD attacks together, we observe that although SignSwish and stochastic quantizers are robust against FGSM and PGD respectively, they remain vulnerable against the other attack. However, StocSwish quantizer maintains relatively better performance simultaneously against both attacks. Moreover, relative accuracy drop offers a view that adversarial robustness of StocSwish quantizer is the most stable among all other candidates against both FGSM and PGD.

3.3 Adversarial Training Is Effective for Some BNNs

To further investigate the robustness effectiveness from adversarial training on BNNs, the second set of experiments is conducted on deterministic, stochastic, SignSwish and StocSwish quantizers. Adversarial accuracy is evaluated on adversarial trained models. Experimental results on MNIST and Fashion-MNIST are

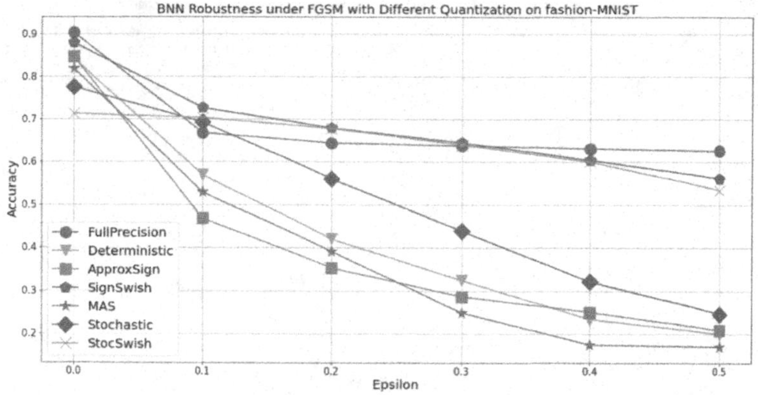

(a)

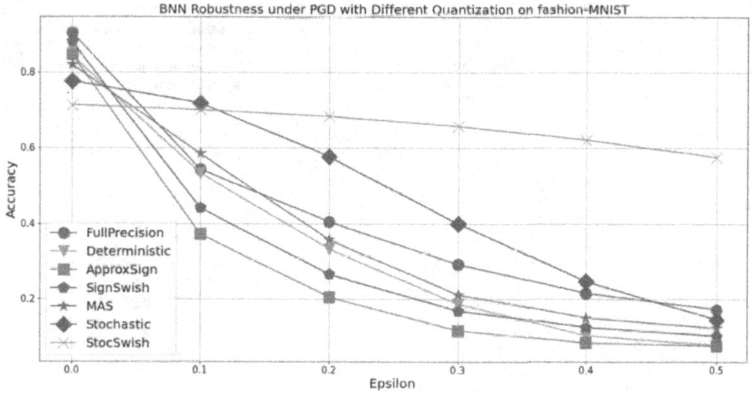

(b)

Fig. 3. Benign and adversarial accuracy of BNNs under (a) FGSM attack and (b) PGD attack on Fashion-MNIST.

summarized in Table 6. It is worth to mention that we find SignSwish and StocSwish quantizers both struggle to obtain robustness from adversarial training. We hypothesize that by using the second derivative Swish function as the backward process may limit the effectiveness of adversarial training. We also observe that adversarial training works well for deterministic and stochastic quantizers. We take deterministic and StocSwish quantizers as representatives and illustrate the effectiveness of adversarial training on them in Fig. 4. Results of SignSwish and stochastic quantizers are illustrated in Appendix A.3.

With the focus on results against FGSM on MNIST and Fashion-MNIST, and putting together results without adversarial training in Table 2, Table 4 and with adversarial training in Table 6, deterministic and stochastic quantizers obtain robustness improvement. We observe that SignSwish and StocSwish quantizers do not always gain robustness improvement from adversarial training and

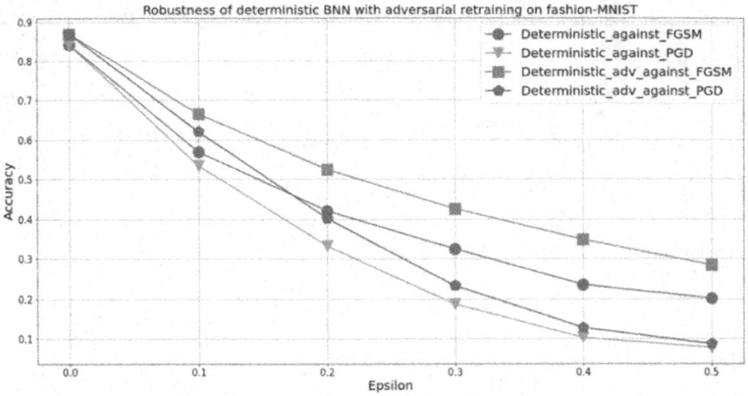

(a)

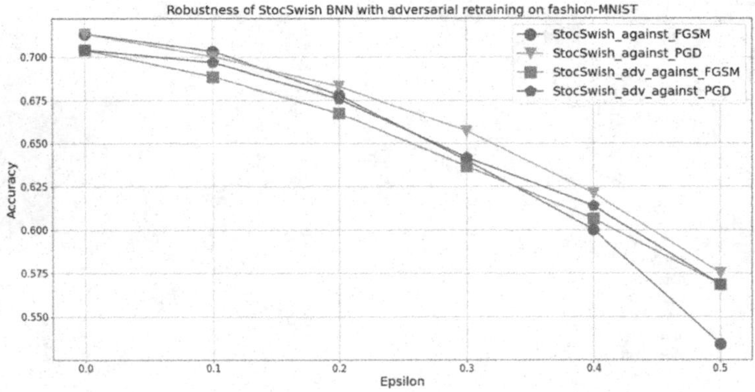

(b)

Fig. 4. Adversarial training on deterministic and StocSwish quantizers against FGSM and PGD

sometimes even get negative impact. However, SignSwish and StocSwish quantizers still outperform other candidates against FGSM attack no matter with or without adversarial training.

With the focus on results against PGD on MNIST and Fashion-MNIST, and putting together results without adversarial training in Table 3, Table 5 and with adversarial training in Table 6, BNNs obtain more robustness improvement from adversarial training against PGD than FGSM attack. Moreover, stochastic quantizer stands out due to the non-negligible robustness improvement via adversarial training.

Table 6. Adversarial robustness of BNNs with adversarial training tested at $\epsilon = 0.1/0.2/0.3/0.4/0.5$. For each column, the highest value is underlined.

			FGSM					PGD				
Dataset	Quantizers	Benign	$\epsilon = 0.1$	$\epsilon = 0.2$	$\epsilon = 0.3$	$\epsilon = 0.4$	$\epsilon = 0.5$	$\epsilon = 0.1$	$\epsilon = 0.2$	$\epsilon = 0.3$	$\epsilon = 0.4$	$\epsilon = 0.5$
MNIST	Deterministic	96.8	93.4	81.0	62.7	41.4	29.7	**94.1**	82.7	57.0	27.4	10.4
	SignSwish	98.8	**95.5**	**93.9**	**91.8**	**88.9**	**77.2**	88.0	64.9	40.8	26.0	17.2
	Stochastic	95.1	92.2	86.5	76.4	61.9	47.2	93.1	**88.1**	78.7	60.9	40.0
	StocSwish	88	85.41	83.32	77.71	73.09	64.75	86.95	83.44	**79.24**	**73.74**	**65.43**
Fashion-MNIST	Deterministic	86.9	66.5	52.5	42.6	34.8	28.4	62.0	40.2	23.3	12.8	8.7
	SignSwish	87.6	**71.6**	66.0	60.9	56.5	52.5	56.1	36.7	25.3	17.9	12.8
	Stochastic	80.3	71.5	57.5	44.2	33.6	25.7	**73.1**	60.5	45.1	31.7	20.7
	StocSwish	70.38	68.85	**66.73**	**63.66**	**60.63**	**56.85**	69.66	**67.57**	**64.17**	**61.37**	**56.84**

3.4 Attack Transferability

We conduct attack transferability experiments on Fashion-MNIST against FGSM and PGD attacks with the magnitude of perturbations ϵ from 0.1 to 0.5. Since the result tendency on the same attack are consistent among different perturbation magnitudes, we summarize results with $\epsilon = 0.3$ under FGSM and PGD attacks in Fig. 5. Other results are illustrated in Appendix A.4. The metrics are the adversarial accuracy of the target model on adversarial examples generated from other source models. The higher the adversarial accuracy is, the lower the transferability is. It can be observed that stochastic, StocSwish and SignSwish quantizers outperform others in general. These observations highly align with the experimental results on the naive adversarial robustness of these quantizers. In addition, it is worth to note that

- Adversarial examples from the full-precision networks and StocSwish quantizer do not work well on other quantizers.
- Adversarial examples from deterministic and stochastic quantizers tend to have strong transferability to other quantizers.
- MAS quantizer is super sensitive to transferred adversarial examples.

4 Analysis and Discussion

We integrate and analyze all experimental results to study adversarial robustness of BNNs. We also discuss potential research directions.

4.1 Adversarial Robustness with and Without Adversarial Training

Based on our empirical experiments on adversarial robustness with and without adversarial training, we conclude that robustness is an individual feature of specific quantizers and adversarial training is very effective for some-but-not-all BNNs. Moreover, we summarize our observations in three highlights:

- SignSwish quantizer presents competitive adversarial robustness against FGSM attack, no matter with or without adversarial training. It is worth noting that SignSwish quantizer has better robustness than deterministic quantizer with adversarial training.
- Stochastic quantizer provides BNNs with superior adversarial robustness against PGD attack. Again, it has better robustness than deterministic quantizer with adversarial training.
- StocSwish quantizer effectively combines advantages of SignSwish and stochastic quantizers and offers stable accuracy simultaneously against both FGSM and PGD attacks at a cost of benign accuracy.

These experimental results also explain a false sense of contradiction from existing research works. For those claiming quantization gives robustness and the others claiming quantization reduces robustness, they are all correct. The phenomenon of robustness depends on which binary quantizer is implemented.

4.2 Robustness, Binary Quantizations and Attack Transferability

Previous studies states that quantizations introduce gradient masking effect [7] and hence the resulting models may have a false sense of robustness. However, from our empirical study, not every binary quantizer enjoys a superior robustness than the full-precision model. It implies that there are other factors than quantization impacting the model's robustness. Since random processes might introduce gradient masking effect, we hypothesize that the Swish function contributes to robustness. Further study is required to verify this hypothesis.

We observe attack transferability from full-precision networks to BNNs and vice versa. Adversarial examples from BNNs work better on full-precision networks when $\epsilon \leq 3$. On the other hand, we see adversarial examples from full-precision networks do not work well on binary quantizers. It shows how different BNNs work from full-precision ones do. Hence, it is more appropriate to evaluate BNNs by adversarial examples from BNNs rather than from full-precision networks. From our empirical study, we would also recommend deterministic and stochastic quantizers as the source models to generate adversarial examples since they provide better attack transferability.

4.3 Dive Deeper on Focused Quantizers

To find the reason for robustness of SignSwish and stochastic quantizers, we further investigate their robustness feature by referring to their differences of quantizations and output distributions. We take deterministic quantizer as a baseline for comparison.

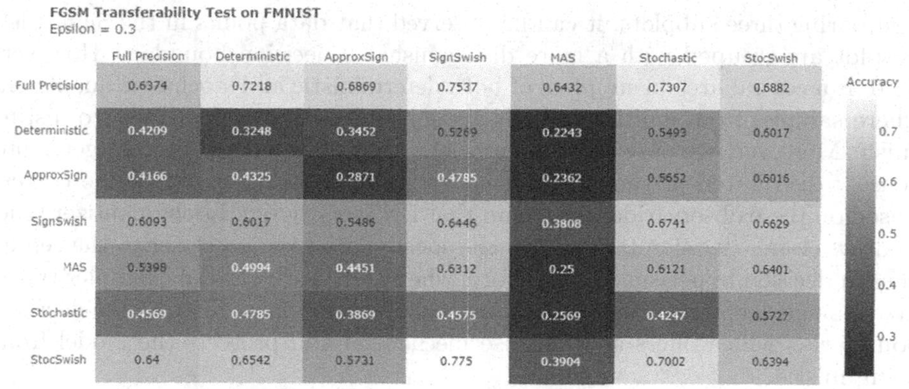

(a)

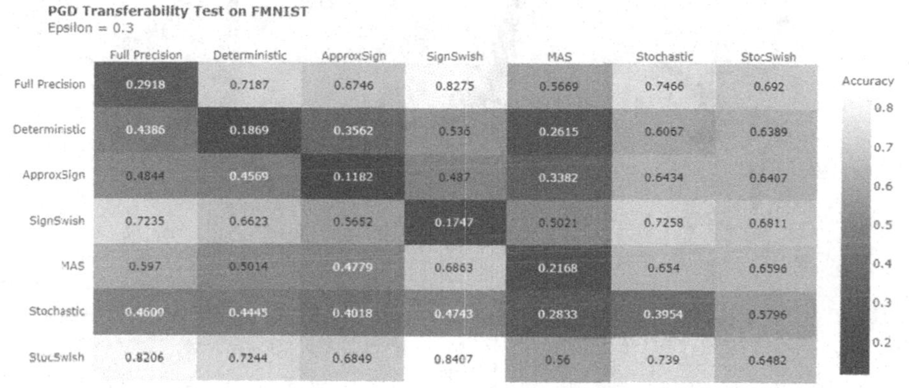

(b)

Fig. 5. FGSM and PGD attack transferability among models with $\epsilon = 0.3$. The x-axis is the source model and the y-axis is the target model.

We input benign test images to each trained BNN with SignSwish, deterministic and stochastic quantizers, respectively. The output for each set is a 10000×10 tensor and we apply principal components analysis (PCA) to reduce the dimension to 3 for more convenient visualization. Figure 6 shows the 3D scattering plot for the outputs of each of the three quantizers after dimension reduction. Each color represents data samples that belong to the same class.

Comparing three subplots, it can be observed that data points in the SignSwish subplot are grouped with a more distinguishable decision boundary. However, there is a central area in subplots of both deterministic and stochastic quantizers where samples from multiple classes are mixed together and difficult to distinguish. Moreover, we observe in SignSwish subplot that data samples get more densely distributed at the tips of each group while being sparse in the center. Based on these observations, we claim that BNNs with SignSwish quantizer tend to draw clearer decision boundaries and locate data samples closer to the center of each decision hyper-space. Therefore, when FGSM adversarial examples try to take a single-step perturbation, it is more difficult for them to cross the decision boundaries, which offers as a defense mechanism and protects the model from being misled.

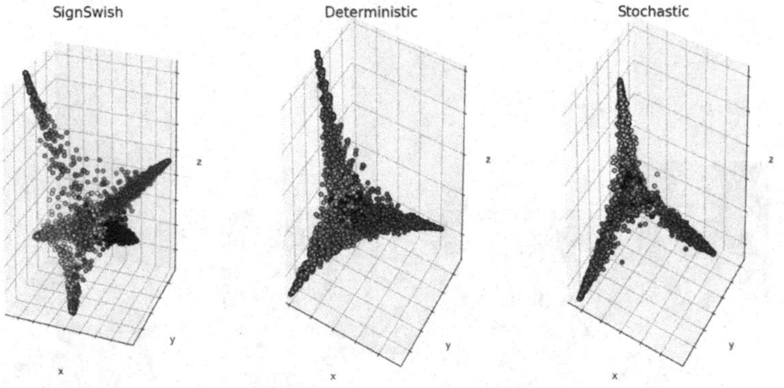

Fig. 6. 3D-scattering plot of outputs reduced by PCA.

4.4 Future Work

Our current work and extensive experimental results on robustness of various quantizers on MNIST and Fashion-MNIST serve as the first step to understand and improve robustness of quantizers. They can speak for data from a well-controller environment, such as data from industrial automation product lines. More datasets may be evaluated for reflecting potential results in extended scenarios.

We adopt adversarial training as the defense and validate its effectiveness on BNNs. Other defense technology can be further explored. Recently, Lipschitz regularization has also shown convincing results [13] on improving robustness for DNN in general. One potential direction for BNNs is to apply Lipschitz regularization on various binary quantizers.

Although we evaluate adversarial robustness by adversarial accuracy under FGSM and PGD attacks, there are other ways to do so. One example is CLEVER score (Cross Lipschitz Extreme Value for nEtwork Robustness) [22,23]. CLEVER score is an attack-independent robustness metrics for deep neural networks. It gives a lower bound on the minimal distortion required for an adversarial example. By adopting different robustness metrics, it may open another pathway to demystify robustness of BNNs.

5 Conclusion

In this paper, we present the first empirical study on adversarial robustness of BNNs from the perspectives of binary quantizers. We identify that adversarial robustness, instead of being a universal feature of binarization, is tailored to specific quantizers. BNNs with SignSwish and stochastic quantizers may offer superior robustness than full precision networks against FGSM and PGD attacks. Moreover, our newly-proposed StocSwish quantizer nicely merges good robustness features of SignSwish and stochastic quantizers with some cost in benign accuracy. We quantitatively validate the effectiveness of adversarial training on BNNs. We observe that adversarial training have limited effect on SignSwish and StocSwish quantizers. Attack transferability experiments show how different a full-precision network works from BNNs by limited attack transferability from the full-precision networks to BNNs. And again, SignSwish, StocSwish and stochastic quantizers show superior robustness. With increasing attention on designing BNNs and developing BNN applications, our work demonstrates a novel perspective to get deeper understanding on adversarial robustness of BNNs.

A Appendix

A.1 Visualize Binary Quantizers

Figure 7 shows some binary quantizers for visually demonstrating functions in two-dimensional plots.

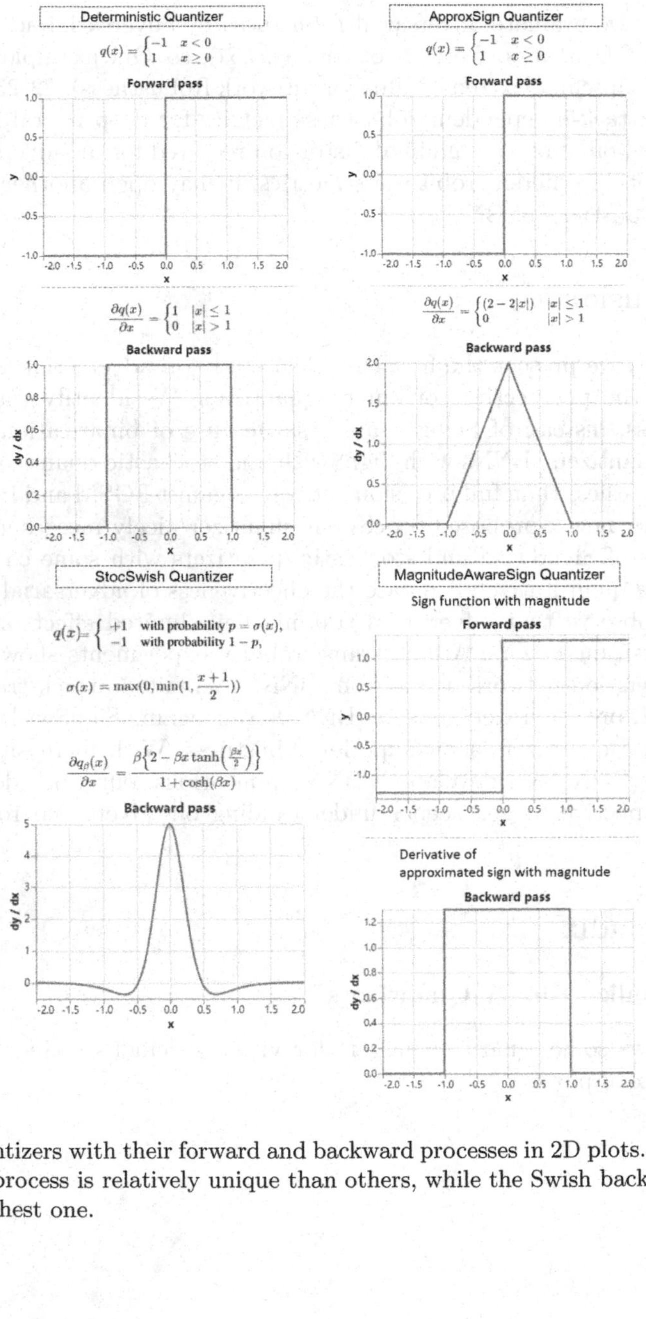

Fig. 7. Quantizers with their forward and backward processes in 2D plots. The stochastic forward process is relatively unique than others, while the Swish backward process is the smoothest one.

A.2 Naive Adversarial Robustness

Here we represent adversarial accuracy of BNNs on MNIST against FGSM and PGD, respectively, in Fig. 8.

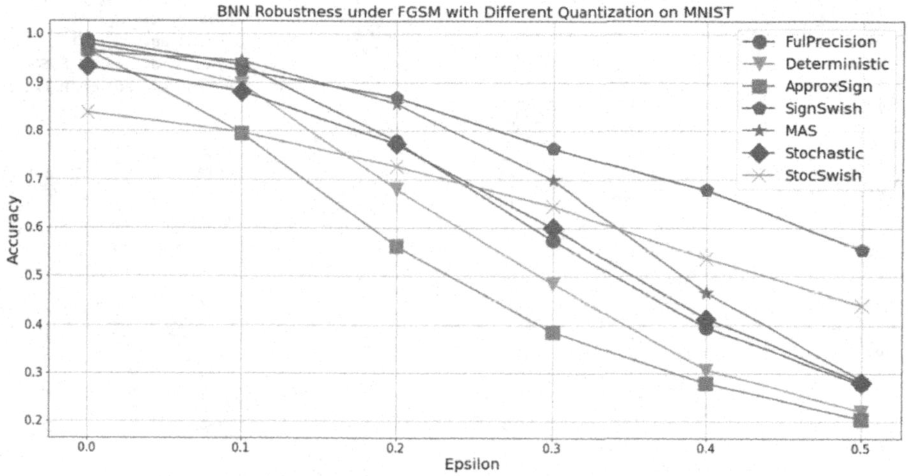

(a)

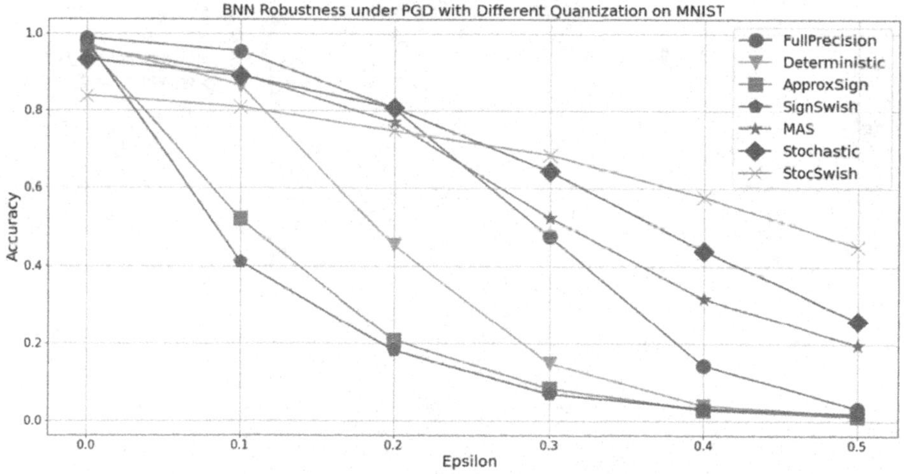

(b)

Fig. 8. Benign and adversarial accuracy of BNNs under (a) FGSM attack and (b) PGD attack on MNIST. "MAS" stands for "MagnitudeAwareSign" quantizer. Results of SignSwish, StocSwish and stochastic quantizers stand out.

A.3 Adversarial Training

Here we show experimental results of adversarial training for SignSwish and stochastic quantizers in Fig. 9.

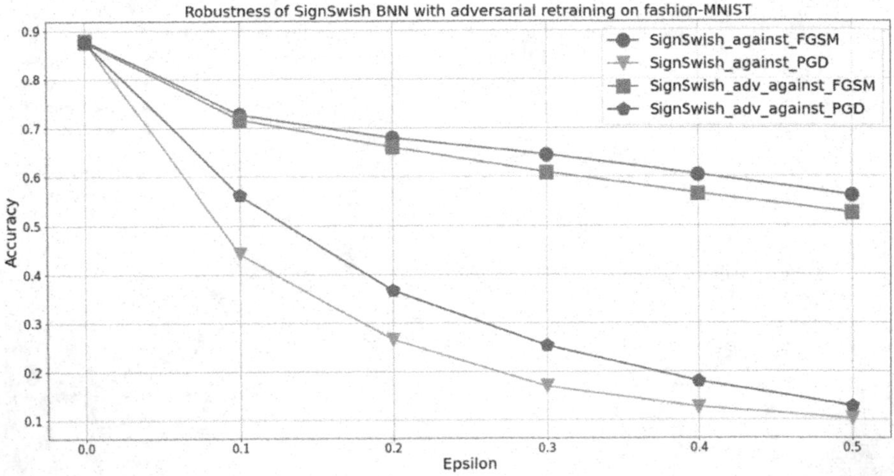

(a)

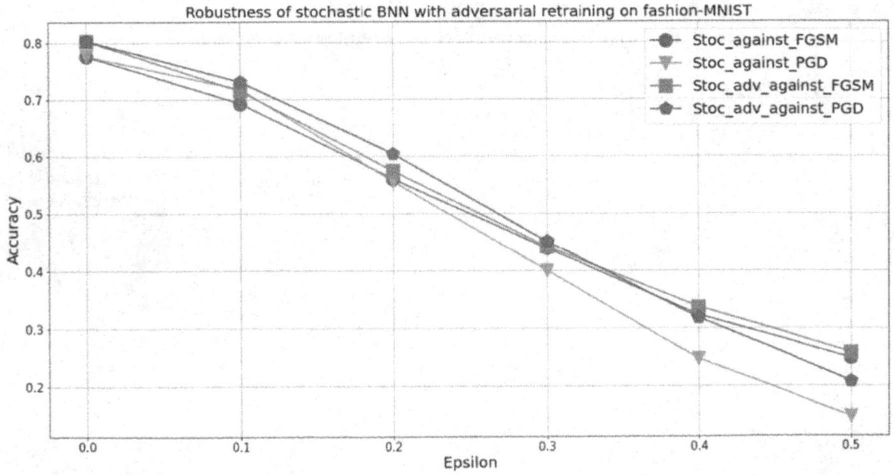

(b)

Fig. 9. Adversarial training on SignSwish and stochastic quantizers against FGSM and PGD

A.4 Attack Transferability

Here we demonstrate experimental results of attack transferability for FGSM and PGD in Fig. 10 and Fig. 11, respectively.

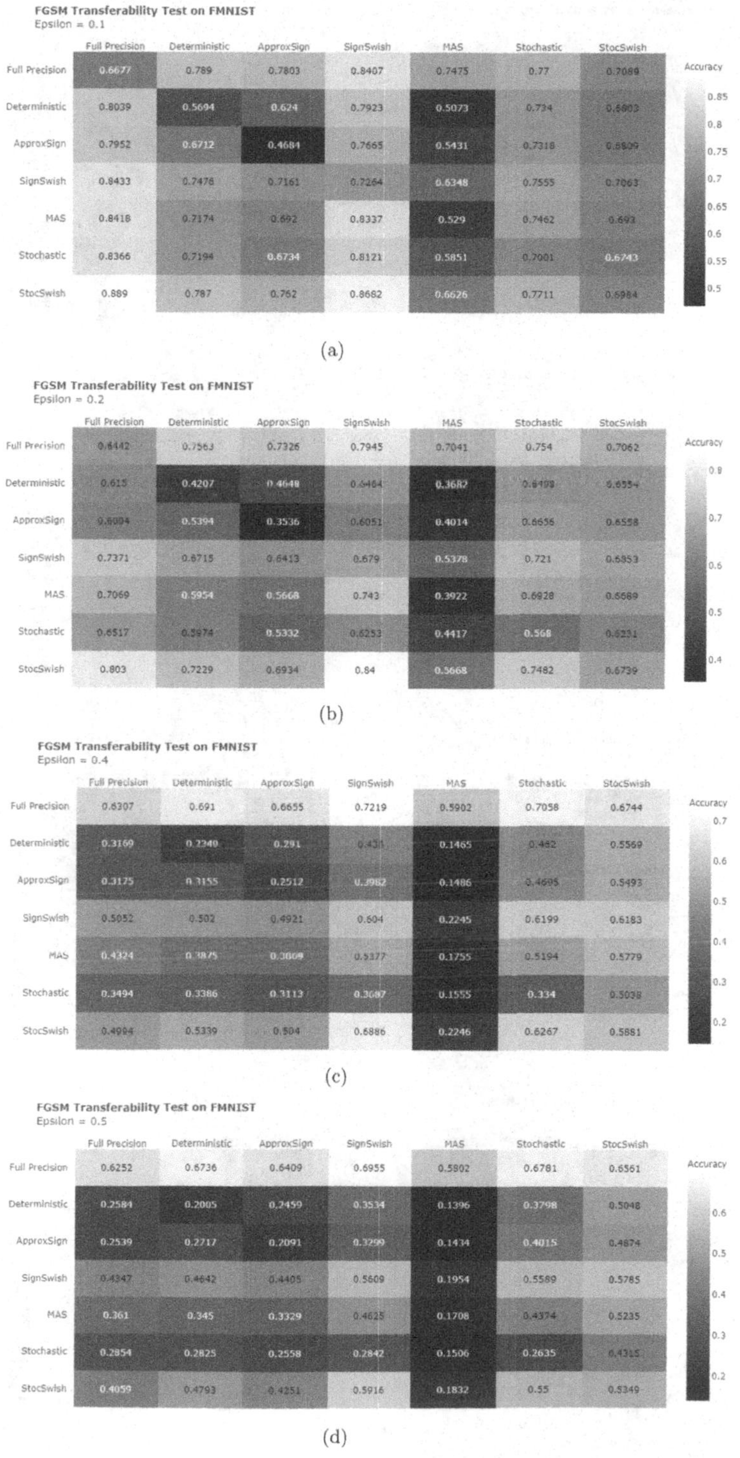

Fig. 10. FGSM attack transferability among models with 4 different perturbation levels, i.e. $\epsilon = 0.1, 0.2, 0.4$ and 0.5.

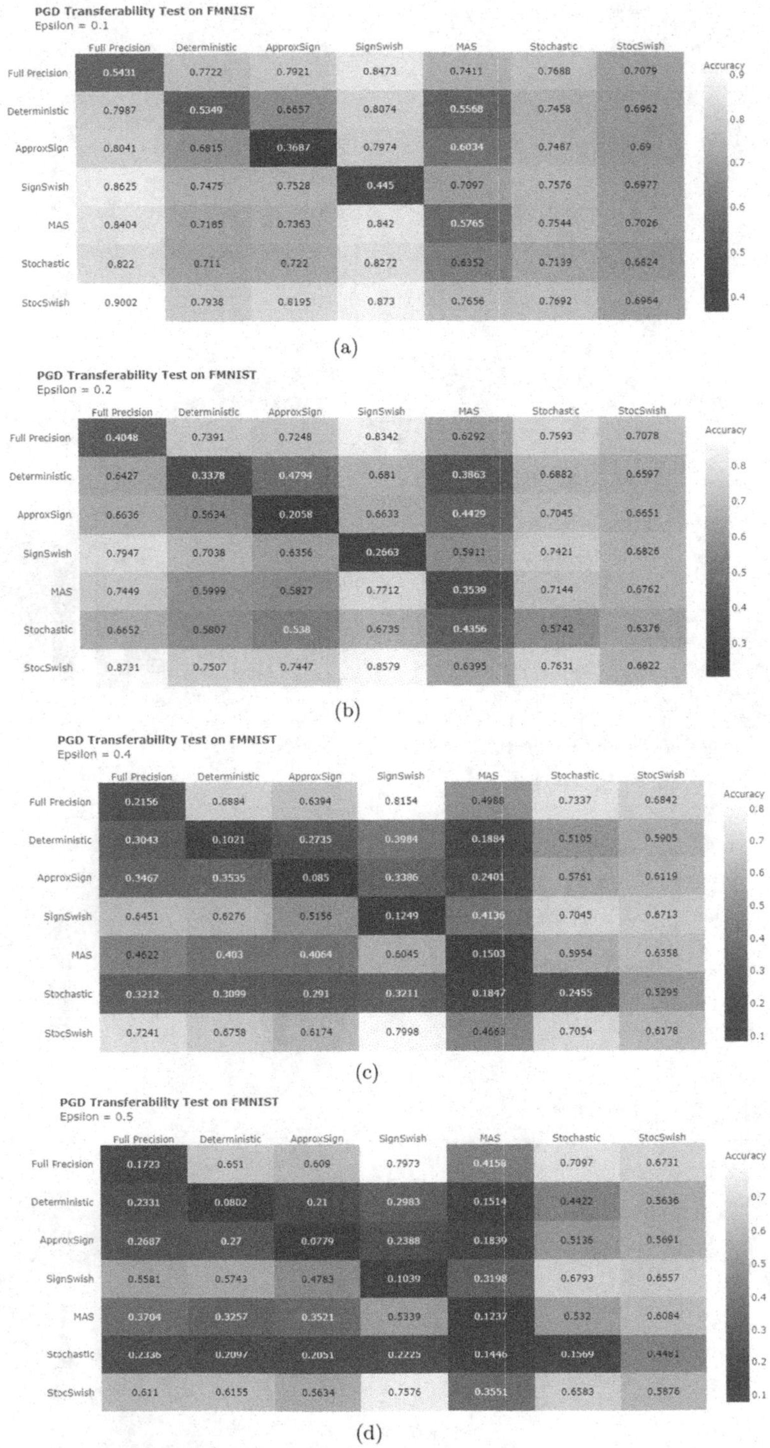

Fig. 11. PGD attack transferability among models with four perturbation levels, i.e. $\epsilon = 0.1, 0.2, 0.4$ and 0.5.

References

1. Abadi, M., et al.: TensorFlow: large-scale machine learning on heterogeneous systems (2015). Software available from tensorflow.org
2. Bernhard, R., Moellic, P., Dutertre, J.: Impact of low-bitwidth quantization on the adversarial robustness for embedded neural networks. In: 2019 International Conference on Cyberworlds (CW), pp. 308–315 (2019)
3. Chollet, F.: keras (2015). https://github.com/fchollet/keras
4. Courbariaux, M., Bengio, Y., David, J.: BinaryConnect: training deep neural networks with binary weights during propagations. In: Advances in Neural Information Processing Systems 28. Curran Associates, Inc. (2015)
5. Courbariaux, M., Hubara, I., Soudry, D., El-Yaniv, R., Bengio, Y.: Binarized neural networks. In: Proceedings of the 30th International Conference on Neural Information Processing Systems, pp. 4114–4122 (2016)
6. Darabi, S., Belbahri, M., Courbariaux, M., Nia, V.P.: BNN+: improved binary network training (2019)
7. Galloway, A., Taylor, G.W., Moussa, M.: Attacking binarized neural networks. In: International Conference on Learning Representations (2018)
8. Geiger, L., Team, P.: Larq: an open-source library for training binarized neural networks. J. Open Source Soft. (45), 1746 (2020)
9. Goodfellow, I., Shlens, J., Szegedy, C.: Explaining and harnessing adversarial examples. In: International Conference on Learning Representations (2015)
10. Han, S., Pool, J., Tran, J., Dally, W.: Learning both weights and connections for efficient neural network. In: Advances in Neural Information Processing Systems 28, pp. 1135–1143. Curran Associates, Inc. (2015)
11. Iandola, F.N., Moskewicz, M.W., Ashraf, K., Han, S., Dally, W.J., Keutzer, K.: Squeezenet: Alexnet-level accuracy with 50x fewer parameters and <1 mb model size. CoRR (2016)
12. LeCun, Y., Bottou, L., Bengio, Y., Haffner, P.: Gradient-based learning applied to document recognition. In: Proceedings of the IEEE, pp. 2278–2324 (1998)
13. Lin, J., Gan, C., Han, S.: Defensive quantization: when efficiency meets robustness. In: International Conference on Learning Representations (2019)
14. Liu, Z., Wu, B., Luo, W., Yang, X., Liu, W., Cheng, K.-T.: Bi-real net: enhancing the performance of 1-bit CNNs with improved representational capability and advanced training algorithm. In: Ferrari, V., Hebert, M., Sminchisescu, C., Weiss, Y. (eds.) ECCV 2018. LNCS, vol. 11219, pp. 747–763. Springer, Cham (2018). https://doi.org/10.1007/978-3-030-01267-0_44
15. Madry, A., Makelov, A., Schmidt, L., Tsipras, D., Vladu, A.: Towards deep learning models resistant to adversarial attacks. In: International Conference on Learning Representations (2018)
16. Nicolae, M., et al.: Adversarial robustness toolbox v1.0.0. CoRR (2019). https://arxiv.org/abs/1807.01069v4
17. Panda, P., Chakraborty, I., Roy, K.: Discretization based solutions for secure machine learning against adversarial attacks. CoRR (2019)
18. Qin, H., Gong, R., Liu, X., Bai, X., Song, J., Sebe, N.: Binary neural networks: a survey. Pattern Recogn., 107281 (2020)
19. Simons, T., Lee, D.J.: A review of binarized neural networks. Electronics, 661 (2019)
20. VanNostrand, P.M., Kyriazis, I., Cheng, M., Guo, T., Walls, R.J.: Confidential deep learning: executing proprietary models on untrusted devices. CoRR (2019)

21. Vemparala, M.R., et al.: Breakingbed - breaking binary and efficient deep neural networks by adversarial attacks (2021)
22. Weng, T., Zhang, H., Chen, P., Lozano, A.C., Hsieh, C., Daniel, L.: On extensions of clever: a neural network robustness evaluation algorithm. In: 2018 IEEE Global Conference on Signal and Information Processing, GlobalSIP 2018, Anaheim, CA, USA, 26–29 November 2018, pp. 1159–1163 (2018)
23. Weng, T., et al.: Evaluating the robustness of neural networks: an extreme value theory approach. In: 6th International Conference on Learning Representations, ICLR 2018, Vancouver, BC, Canada, 30 April–3 May 2018, Conference Track Proceedings (2018)

Kryptonite: An Adversarial Attack Using Regional Focus

Yogesh Kulkarni and Krisha Bhambani(✉)

Department of Computer Engineering, Pune Institute of Computer Technology, Pune, India

Abstract. With the Rise of Adversarial Machine Learning and increasingly robust adversarial attacks, the security of applications utilizing the power of Machine Learning has been questioned. Over the past few years, applications of Deep Learning using Deep Neural Networks(DNN) in several fields including Medical Diagnosis, Security Systems, Virtual Assistants, etc. have become extremely commonplace, and hence become more exposed and susceptible to attack. In this paper, we present a novel study analyzing the weaknesses in the security of deep learning systems. We propose 'Kryptonite', an adversarial attack on images. We explicitly extract the Region of Interest (RoI) for the images and use it to add imperceptible adversarial perturbations to images to fool the DNN. We test our attack on several DNN's and compare our results with state of the art adversarial attacks like Fast Gradient Sign Method (FGSM), DeepFool (DF), Momentum Iterative Fast Gradient Sign Method (MIFGSM), and Projected Gradient Descent (PGD). The results obtained by us cause a maximum drop in network accuracy while yielding minimum possible perturbation and in considerably less amount of time per sample. We thoroughly evaluate our attack against three adversarial defence techniques and the promising results showcase the efficacy of our attack.

Keywords: Adversarial Machine Learning · Adversarial attack · Image classification

1 Introduction

Significant progress in the field of artificial intelligence has caused its use to be almost ubiquitous. From security and safety systems to autonomous cars and health care systems, incredible strides have been made to create efficient neural nets, however, they remain constantly vulnerable to adversarial attacks. Even though certain object detectors, classifiers, etc., have reached near human accuracy, it has been found that they can be easily fooled by small, almost unnoticeable modifications in images. As our reliance on artificial intelligence systems increases, the possible impact of their failure also increases tremendously. We need to ensure that these networks work in the most proper manner. New and

Y. Kulkarni and K. Bhambani—Equal Contribution.

J. Zhou et al. (Eds.): ACNS 2021 Workshops, LNCS 12809, pp. 463–481, 2021.
https://doi.org/10.1007/978-3-030-81645-2_26

more advanced attacks, where imperceptible perturbations are being added to disrupt the working of these networks are being made, against which existing defences are rendered useless. Hence, analysing every possible weakness in networks that make them susceptible to attack, is the need of the hour.

Let us consider image specific tasks like image classification, object detection, etc. To accomplish these tasks, neural networks try to identify features characteristic to particular classes in the training set to best determine the result. An ideal adversarial attack is of course one that causes effective misclassification with minimum distortion.

When a human attempts to classify objects in an image, their attention is inevitably drawn to the main region of interest, the object itself [1]. It stands to reason, that modifying this object may cause ambiguity in analysing the image. We use this same reasoning in the adversarial attack we present here.

In this paper, we emphasize more on medical datasets. Most medical datasets including MRIs, X-rays, etc. all contain a very specific, well-defined region of interest that can be analysed to detect and classify ailments. It has also been found that medical datasets are more vulnerable to adversarial attacks [2]. The inspiration for this attack is possible unexplored vulnerability of perturbations in a region of interest, since most adversarial attacks are fairly antagonistic to it. Medical datasets were hence chosen for experimentation of the attack for two reasons. The first reason for doing so is to demonstrate threats on a real life application of deep learning. The second reason is that because the region of interest here can be easily extracted, monitored, and modified.

In this attack, we aim to monitor and encourage changes especially in the region of interest of the image in order to constrain the noise as much as possible to a particular area of the image. In order to prevent excessive changes in pixel values in a specific area, the perturbations are constrained. In most cases, this method effectively manages to fool the classifier with the addition of minimum noise. This attack hides in plain sight, and infected pixels cannot be easily identified, unlike other constricted attacks that use adversarial patches, which make it obvious to viewers that an image is adulterated. We also find that attacking this region of interest mitigates the effectiveness of state of the art defences, as compared to their effect on other attacks.

To summarise the contribution to research presented in this paper:

- We propose a highly efficient and accurate, three-step RoI extraction algorithm built upon Otsu's method of image thresholding, image dilation using predefined kernel and finally extract RoI using the contour of lesion/tumor found using Topological Structural Analysis.
- We propose Kryptonite, a white-box, non-targeted adversarial attack, that exploits a proposed area of weakness.
- We compare our proposed attack with the existing state of the art attacks based on Receiver Operating Characteristic Curve (ROC), and perturbation size.
- We analyse the comparison of the impact of various state of the art defences on the proposed attack with other attacks.

– We aim to show the advantages of localising an attack in an image.

The remainder of the paper is structured as follows: Sect. 2 talks about related work. Section 3 elaborates on the dataset and network architecture used. Section 4 provides an overview of our proposed attack. In Sect. 5 the proposed methodology for RoI extraction and Kryptonite is discussed. Section 6 highlights our obtained results, Sect. 7 highlights the limitations of our study and Sect. 8 concludes the paper with the scope of further research and improvement.

2 Related Work

2.1 Adversarial Attacks

FGSM. The Fast Gradient Sign Method proposed by [3] uses a method where a given loss function J(x, y), which is almost always cross-entropy loss that the target network is trained on, is maximised, and the sign of the gradient obtained is used to control the added perturbation of adjustable magnitude in L_∞ norm.

$$x* = x + \epsilon.sign(\nabla_x J(x, y)) \tag{1}$$

I- FGSM. The proposed Iterative Fast Gradient Sign Method proposed by [4] is a simple, but a greatly effective improvement over the simple FGSM attack. It uses the observation that for any input image x, the gradient of the adopted loss function is continuously changing. Hence in every iteration, a perturbation is generated that is optimal for the current gradient obtained. Here, a clip function is used to control the size of the final perturbation and restrict it to the original constraint ϵ.

$$x*_{t+1} = Clip_{x,\epsilon}\{x*_t + \alpha.sign(\nabla_x J(x*_t, y))\} \tag{2}$$

Projected Gradient Descent proposed by [5] is a variation of FGSM where the constraint $\alpha.T = \epsilon$ does not exist. Instead, to constrain perturbations, the adversarial samples are "projected" to their benign counterparts. Images in PGD are updated as follows:

$$x*_{t+1} = Proj\{x*_t + \alpha.sign(\nabla_x J(x*_t, y))\} \tag{3}$$

PGD is more powerful than FGSM but it is slower than FGSM as it calculates gradients for numerous iterations.

MI- FGSM. Momentum Iterative Attack proposed by [6] is a version of I-FGSM that uses the technique of memorization of previous gradients to optimise the iterative process and find the most effective perturbation. This helps to stabilise update directions and escape local minima that may yield poor, less-than-ideal perturbations.

$$g_{t+1} = \mu * g_t + \frac{\nabla_x J(x, y))}{||\nabla_x J(x, y))||_1} \tag{4}$$

$$x*_{t+1} = Clip_{x,\epsilon}\{x*_t + \alpha.sign(g_{t+1})\} \tag{5}$$

DeepFool. DeepFool proposed by [7] is an adversarial attack based on the assumption that the neural networks are linear, and that the various classes are essentially separated by a hyperplane. Here, imperceptible perturbations are added to take a step forward to push the sample to be classified over the decision boundary. Since most neural networks are not linear, this is done iteratively until the adversarial example is optimally constructed. In this paper, we use the L_∞ version of the attack.

2.2 Adversarial Attacks and Defences on Medical Imaging

The intensive research in [2] showed adversarial attacks on medical images are *easy* to detect, we *improved* upon their research by exploiting image regions and producing more erroneous adversarial features which easily fool DNN's and anomaly detectors. An Ensemble of multiple Convolutional Neural Network's (CNN) and inclusion of adversarial images while training was proposed in [8] for mitigating adversarial attacks against *simpler* FGSM and One - Pixel attacks but the inclusion of adversarial images while training may *not* provide resilience as shown later in Table 5. DL systems in production consist of complex data pipelines, therefore, the addition of new component as proposed in [9] for detection of adversarial attacks on medical images would be *arduous*, also as proved by Carlini and Wagner in [10] the proposed unsupervised statistical anomaly detection technique can easily be evaded when an adversary targets a specific defence which is a white box adversary in this case. A novel adversarial bias field attack was proposed by [11] for chest X-ray classification systems, which generated more realistic adversarial samples by adding smooth perturbations instead of noises but the attack success rate was *less* than noise-based adversarial attacks.

2.3 Analysis of Related Attacks

There have been very few attacks focused on modifying a constrained area of an image. One such attack is mentioned in [12], which essentially uses gradient information to adjust the trust region, within a continuously adaptive radius. With this, the extent of the added noise in the image is restricted, however, the *JumpReLU* defence proposed by [13] has provided resilience to this attack as well. Another attack in this category is the localized BIM attack proposed by [14], wherein the final perturbations were hard to detect yet *efficacy of the proposed attack is questionable* as the attack has more emphasis on minimal human perceptibility and the paper lacks evaluation with existing adversarial attacks in terms of drop in network accuracy. We hence believe our attack is a novel, efficient and effective addition to this limited class of families.

3 Dataset and Model Architecture

We have presented results for 2 datasets and 4 neural nets in this paper. The first dataset is the Melanoma dataset, whereas the other dataset is the MRI dataset.

Table 1. CNN architecture.

Layers	Parameters
Input	126 × 126 × 1
Conv1 + ReLU	50 × 3 × 3, pad = same, stride = 1
Conv2 + ReLU	75 × 3 × 3, pad = same, stride = 1
Max Pool 1	2 × 2, stride 2, pad = 0
Dropout	0.25
Conv3 + ReLU	125 × 3 × 3, pad = same, stride = 1
Max Pool 2	2 × 2, stride 2, pad = 0
Dropout	0.25
FC1 + ReLU	500
Dropout	0.4
FC2 + ReLU	250
Dropout	0.3
FC3 + Sigmoid	1
Total Parameters	60, 307, 326

The first medical dataset we have used is the 2020 ISIC Challenge Dataset [15] containing 33,126 dermoscopic training images having unique benign and malignant lesions from over 2,000 patients. We split the data into training, validation and testing sets having 20,000, 6,576 and 6,550 samples respectively. We generated adversarial samples from the test set. Data augmentations the images went through include cutout, hue saturation, addition of Gaussian noise, motion or median blur, optical or grid distortion, as well as rotation and flipping. We have used EfficentNet-B5 [16] and ResNeXt-50 [17] as these architectures are extremely complex, and often yield state of the art results for biomedical imaging datasets as seen in Table 3.

The second dataset we have used is the MRI dataset [18]. Here we aim to identify whether a given MRI of a brain has a tumor or not, and classify it respectively. The original training set contains 253 images of MRI scans out of which 155 have a tumour and 98 do not. We augment the dataset to generate 2065 images out of which 1200 are used for training the neural network, 365 are used for validation and 500 are used for testing. To classify images for this dataset, we have used the VGG16 [19] neural network, which gives near state of the art results. The second network we use to execute this task is a custom convolutional neural network. The architecture for the same is provided in Table 1. This also yields fairly accurate classification results, as shown later in Table 4.

4 Attack Overview

4.1 Threat Model

Today, several effective defences have been created to avoid attacks, however, attacks to circumvent these defences are being continuously created. For example, the CW attack [20] was able to render defensive distillation almost useless.

It is important to analyse the vulnerability of any image, which is what we aim to do with Kryptonite. A vulnerability we exploit through the attack Kryptonite is one that has been largely ignored by several attacks, and hence defences: the region of interest. For this attack we assume that the attacker *has access to every aspect* of the architecture of the network and its parameters, and hence assume this attack is *white box*. Kryptonite launches its attack by focusing mainly on the region of interest. In most cases, this method effectively manages to fool the classifier with the addition of minimum noise.

Kryptonite belongs to a class of iterative gradient based attacks, and it aims to show the ways in which the effectiveness of an attack can be improved by localising it. We have hence compared Kryptonite to such attacks in terms of drop in accuracy, effectiveness, efficiency, and resilience to state of the art defences, and found that focusing on a region of interest indeed improves performance on all fronts.

4.2 Metrics Used

The distance metric we have chosen to use to evaluate and perform this attack is the L_p norm metric. L_p distance is expressed as:

$$||x - x'||_p = (\sum_{i=1}^{n} |x - x'|)^{1/p} \tag{6}$$

The metric is used to limit the maximum change in pixel values, and evaluate the size of the perturbation by measuring the Euclidean distance between the original and perturbed image.

5 Proposed Methodology

5.1 Extracting Region of Interest

The Region of Interest extractor consists of the following modules:

OTSU Thresholding Method. We use the methodology given in [21] to binarize the image based on pixel intensities and separate the pixels into classes, foreground and background. We minimize the weighted within-class variance in search of optimal threshold which is given below:

$$\sigma_w^2(t) = \omega_0(t)\sigma_0^2(t) + \omega_1(t)\sigma_1^2(t) \tag{7}$$

In the above equation ω_0 and ω_1 are probabilities of two classes which are separated by threshold t, and σ_0^2 and σ_1^2 are the variances for these two classes. For L bins of the histogram we compute the class probability $\omega_{0,1}(t)$ as follows:

Algorithm 1: OTSU Thresholding

Input: Grayscale image

Output: Intensity Threshold

1. For each intensity level compute histogram and intensity level probabilities.
2. Initialize $\omega_i(0)$ and $\mu_i(0)$.
3. **for** *threshold* $t = 1, ...upto\ max(intensity)$ **do**
4.   update ω_i and μ_i;
5.   Compute $\sigma_b^2(t)$;
6. **end**
7. return $\max(\sigma_b^2(t))$ which corresponds to final threshold value.

$$\omega_0(t) = \sum_{i=0}^{t-1} p(i) \tag{8}$$

$$\omega_1(t) = \sum_{i=t}^{L-1} p(i) \tag{9}$$

We minimize the intra-class variance as follows:

$$\begin{aligned} \sigma_b^2(t) &= \sigma^2 - \sigma_w^2(t) = \omega_0 \left(\mu_0 - \mu_T\right)^2 + \omega_1 \left(\mu_1 - \mu_T\right)^2 \\ &= \omega_0(t)\omega_1(t)\left[\mu_0(t) - \mu_1(t)\right]^2 \end{aligned} \tag{10}$$

The above expression is expressed in terms of class probabilities ω and the class means μ, and the class means are defined as follows:

$$\mu_0(t) = \frac{\sum_{i=0}^{t-1} ip(i)}{\omega_0(t)} \tag{11}$$

$$\mu_1(t) = \frac{\sum_{i=t}^{L-1} ip(i)}{\omega_1(t)} \tag{12}$$

$$\mu_T = \sum_{i=0}^{L-1} ip(i) \tag{13}$$

We compute the class probabilities and class means iteratively. Algorithm 1 explains briefly the procedure to minimize the weighted within-class variance. As we can see from Fig. 1, the RoI extraction algorithm accurately returns the RoI. The algorithm is simple yet effective and is highly accurate. Although, one can obtain decent results using complex segmentation models such as U - Net [22] by training neural networks on enormous datasets but our method is much simpler and efficient which leads to an stronger region constricted adversarial attack.

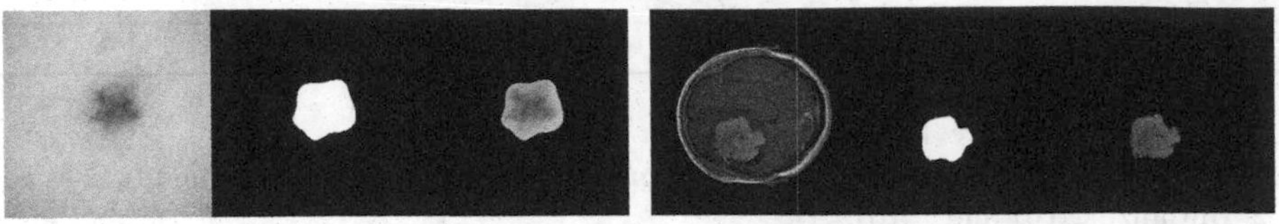

Fig. 1. Process for generation of the RoI on original image, application of OTSU Thresholding and dilation, and finally, derived RoI

Image Dilation. To increase the object area and to accentuate the features we performed image dilation. To achieve the same we performed the following steps:

- We convolve the thresholded image obtained from algorithm 1 with a kernel (matrix of odd size).
- We define the center of the kernel as the anchor point.
- We scan the kernel over the image and calculate the maximum value of the pixel overlapped by the kernel and replace the image pixel at the anchor point position with the maximum value. This would increase the white region in the image and the size of the foreground object.

Topological Structural Analysis. We have utilized the contour tracing algorithm given by Suzuki [23]. The algorithm defines hierarchical relationships among the borders and differentiates between the outer and the hole boundary. As this is an iterative algorithm it connects groups of 1-pixels that surround groups of 0-pixels. Then, a raster scan of the image is performed which locates all possible pixels for a border [24], by detecting whether the pixel has value 1 and the neighboring pixel has value 0. Then a label is assigned to keep track of the border. Then for each new succeeding pixel, it is either added to an existing border or a new border with a new label. If two border segments connect then we reassign labels of pixels to form one border. We return the contour obtained for skin lesion and the pixels inside it. For a $512 \times 512 \times 3$ image from [15], RoI extraction took 1.99 ms whereas for $126 \times 126 \times 1$ grayscale image from [18], RoI extraction took 0.88 ms.

Our proposed RoI extraction algorithm performs perfectly for images having distinct contour lines but noisy images or images having no contour lines surrounding the RoI, our algorithm returns *arbitrary* RoI.

5.2 Kryptonite

Kryptonite comes under a class of momentum iterative gradient-based methods, and hence is compared to similar attacks in this paper. Kryptonite is essentially an adversarial attack proposed to improve adversarial attacks boosted by momentum even further, by monitoring the changes observed specifically in the region of interest. Kryptonite uses a region of interest extractor(ρ) that specifically monitors these features to evaluate the progress(P) of the attack. The

Algorithm 2: Kryptonite adversarial attack

Input: Image x, Classifier f with loss function J, Region of Interest Extractor ρ, Size of perturbation ϵ, Iterations T, Decay Weight ω, Initial decay factor μ_0

Output: Perturbation x* clipped as $\|x * -x\|_\infty \leqslant \epsilon$

Initialize $g_0 = 0, x{*}_0 = x$ and $\alpha = \frac{\epsilon}{T}$.

for *threshold* t = *0 to (T-1)* **do**

  Input $x{*}_t$ to f and retrieve $\nabla_x J(x, y)$.

  Update g_{t+1} by accumulating the velocity vector in the gradient direction:

$$g_{t+1} = \mu_t * g_t + \frac{\nabla_x J(x, y))}{||\nabla_x J(x, y))||_1}$$

  Update $x{*}_{t+1}$ by applying sign gradient:

$$x{*}_{t+1} = Clip_{x,\epsilon}\{x *_t + \alpha.sign(g_{t+1})\}$$

  Calculate progress P:

$$P = \|\rho(x{*}_{t+1}) - \rho(x{*}_t)\|_2$$

  Update decay factor:

$$\mu_{t+1} = \frac{1}{P} * \omega$$

end

return $x{*}_{T-1}$

change of these features is used to optimise the momentum applied to simple Iterative Fast Gradient Sign Method. Essentially, this network aims to demonstrate the increased susceptibility of the images, by monitoring the region of interest. Momentum is a method used to optimise the efficiency of gradient descent and provide a certain acceleration to the algorithm to help it easily navigate through local minima, and other hurdles effectively.

Kryptonite uses the region of interest(ρ) method to evaluate the attack's exact progress(P) as:

$$P = \|\rho(x{*}_{t+1}) - \rho(x{*}_t)\|_2 \tag{14}$$

This progress in the absolute area of interest is used to determine the decay factor for the next iteration. The decay factor can be written as:

$$\mu_{t+1} = \frac{1}{P} * \omega \tag{15}$$

Where ω is the decay weight. This is a hyper parameter to be specified by the user according to the network requirements. If this hyper parameter is too small, the network will be caused to act like Iterative Fast Gradient Sign Method. If the gradient is too large, the inertia of the attack would increase which would not allow any significant progress to be made.

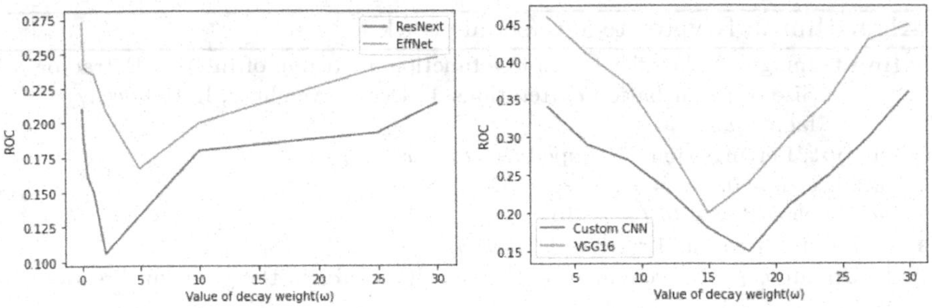

(a) Dermatology Dataset (b) Radiology Dataset

Fig. 2. Comparison of ROC score to variation in decay wt.

The gradient is then updated using this newly obtained decay factor in a similar way as that used in MI-FGSM.

$$g_{t+1} = \mu_t * g_t + \frac{\nabla_x J(x,y))}{||\nabla_x J(x,y))||_1} \tag{16}$$

This updated gradient is used to assess the optimal perturbation to add to the original image.

$$x*_{t+1} = x*_t + \alpha.sign(g_{t+1}) \tag{17}$$

6 Results

6.1 Attack

We perform all attacks in the white-box setting. We used the Cleverhans library [25] for the implementation of the attack algorithms. The optimal hyper parameters for all the attack algorithms are provided in Table 2. These parameters were chosen by monitoring network accuracy, perturbation size and actual

Table 2. Optimal Hyper Parameters for all the attacks for the given two datasets.

Melanoma	Epsilon		Iterations		Alpha		Decay Factor		Overshoot	
	EffNet	ResNext	EffNet	ResNext	EffNet	ResNext	EffNet	ResNext	EffNet	ResNext
FGSM	0.08	0.07	–	–	–	–	–	–	–	–
DeepFool	–	–	60	45	–	–	–	–	0.07	0.04
PGD	0.04	0.03	16	12	0.04/16	0.03/12	–	–	–	–
MIFGSM	0.03	0.01	10	7	0.04/10	0.02/7	1.5	1	–	–
KRYPTONITE	0.01	0.007	15	5	0.01/15	0.007/5	*0.5	*1	–	–
MRI	Epsilon		Iterations		Alpha		Decay Factor		Overshoot	
	CNN	VGG16	CNN	VGG16	CNN	VGG16	CNN	VGG16	CNN	VGG16
FGSM	0.1	0.15	–	–	–	–	–	–	–	–
DeepFool	–	–	50	65	–	–	–	–	0.06	0.08
PGD	0.03	0.05	20	12	0.03/20	0.05/12	–	–	–	–
MIFGSM	0.02	0.03	12	15	0.02/12	0.03/15	0.5	1	–	–
KRYPTONITE	0.02	0.04	16	20	0.02/16	0.04/20	*0.5	*0.7	–	–

* Inital decay factor for Kryptonite

Table 3. The table below shows the average of network accuracy after conducting the experiment five times on the Dermatology Dataset.

Samples	Effnet		ResNext	
	Accuracy	Size of Pert.	Accuracy	Size of Pert.
CLEAN	0.881	–	0.890	–
FGSM	0.442	5.2%/5.9%	0.391	4.7%/5.5%
DeepFool	0.419	1.5%/2.3%	0.406	1.2%/1.4%
PGD	0.273	2.3%/2.8%	0.206	1.9%/2.5%
MIFGSM	0.229	2.6%/3.0%	0.187	2.4%/2.9%
KRYPTONITE	**0.155**	1.7%/2.2%	**0.114**	1.5%/1.7%

Size of perturbation is expressed as a percentage of added perturbation to image measured using the standard L_2 norm. The value of the left of the slash is average case percentage perturbation, and to the right is the worst case percentage perturbation.

Table 4. The table below shows the average of network accuracy after conducting the experiment six times on the Radiology Dataset.

Samples	Custom CNN		VGG16	
	Accuracy	Size of Pert.	Accuracy	Size of Pert.
CLEAN	0.942	–	0.966	–
FGSM	0.474	7.0%/7.6%	0.490	7.3%/7.8%
DeepFool	0.379	1.8%/2.5%	0.399	2.1%/2.9%
PGD	0.229	2.5%/3.0%	0.293	2.6%/3.1%
MIFGSM	0.161	2.8%/3.4%	0.247	3.0%/3.7%
KRYPTONITE	**0.147**	1.9%/2.6%	**0.216**	2.0%/2.7%

Size of perturbation is expressed as a percentage of added perturbation to image measured using the standard L_2 norm. The value of the left of the slash is average case percentage perturbation, and to the right is the worst case percentage perturbation.

perceptibility of perturbations to the naked eye. A small increment to optimal values of epsilon or increasing the number of iterations will lead to further drop in accuracy but increase perturbation size and also the final adversarial image may look like an image someone has tampered with. Furthermore, The optimal decay weight for kryptonite can be observed from Fig. 2. As can be observed from Fig. 2, this parameter makes a great difference to the reduction in ROC score, and the optimal value must be chosen for the best results.

All of our experiments were conducted on the Radiology and the Dermatology datasets and we chose to fool four neural networks that provided the best results for the classification of these images. In Table 3 we see the ROC scores for the networks EfficientNet and ResNext, on clean samples, and with the adversarial samples generated using the attacks FGSM, DeepFool, PGD, MIFGSM, and Kryptonite respectively for the dermatology (Melanoma) dataset. All of

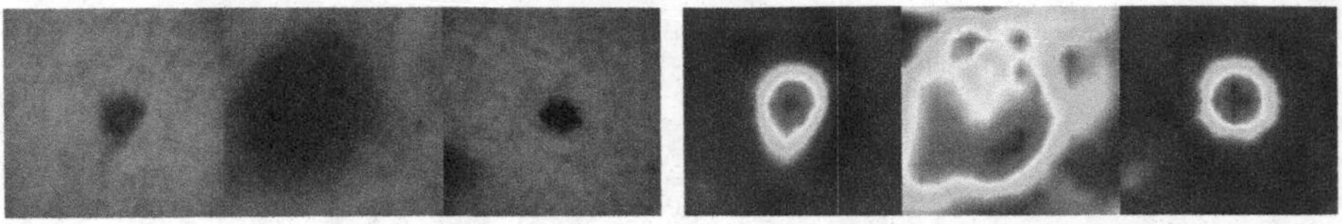

Fig. 3. Grad-CAM for Melanoma (kryptonite sample)

the results obtained are the average ROC scores from the five trials conducted. From Table 3 we can see that ResNext is *more vulnerable* to adversarial samples in comparison to EffNet. We note that due to the inherent assumption of Deepfool that neural networks are all but linear it fails to outperform other iterative attacks on these datasets.

Our proposed attack as can be seen from Table 3 caused *max drop* in network accuracy. We have utilized the Gradient-weighted Class Activation Mapping (Grad-CAM) technique [26] which is used to find the most important regions for any given input image which affect the network output the most. From Grad-CAM image shown in Fig. 3 we can see that the classifier takes into consideration the lesion for making its prediction. Now, since kryptonite constricts its focus as much as it can on the region of interest which is the lesion for this dataset, the classifier becomes more vulnerable when an adversarial attack targets the region on which the classification most depends on, leading to the best misclassifcation rate.

Furthermore, kryptonite *does not* push the attention completely away from lesion in the final adversarial sample. On the contrary, the other attacks distract the classifier towards the regions completely *irrelevant* for the classification which though leads to a significant drop in network accuracy but in our rigorous experiments we have seen that in kryptonite wherein all the adversarial perturbations are all but concentrated inside a fixed region (of highest interest to classifier) cause the *max* misclassification rate. This is because in comparison to other adversarial samples wherein the perturbations are spread throughout the image, the classifier randomly selects the region and uses it as an important region for classification. On the other hand, a classifier fed with a kryptonite sample will always choose the lesion for classification which indeed has all of the perturbations leading to the highest drop in network accuracy.

On similar lines for the MRI dataset we can infer from Table 4 that the Custom Convolutional Neural Network is more vulnerable to adversarial samples in comparison to VGG16 network. All of the results obtained are the average ROC scores from the six trials conducted. From the Grad-CAM images in Fig. 4

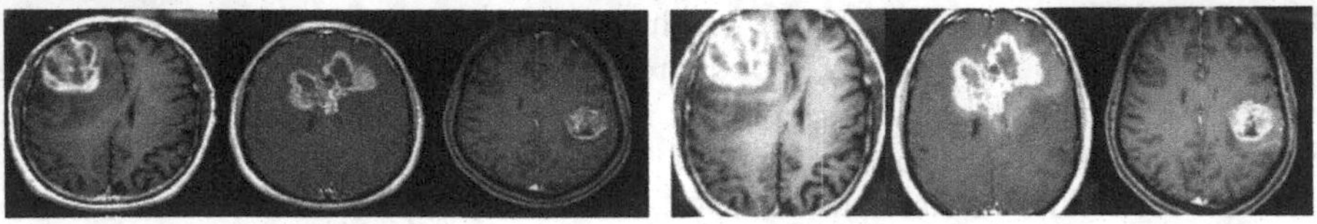

Fig. 4. Grad-CAM for MRI (kryptonite sample)

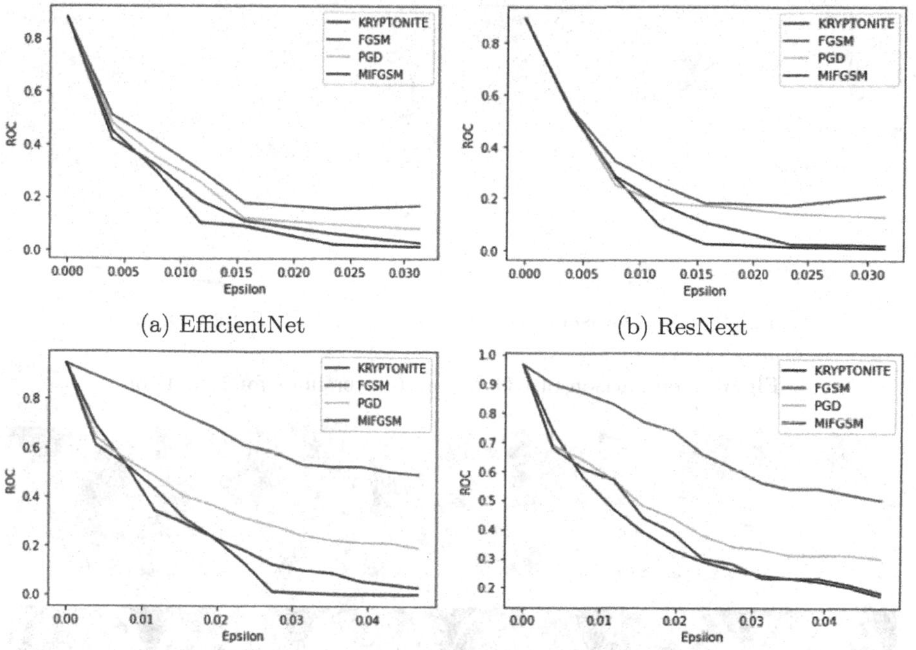

(a) EfficientNet (b) ResNext

(c) Custom CNN (d) VGG16

Fig. 5. Comparison of ROC score to constrain ϵ

we can see that for a given grayscale MRI image having a tumour, the region occupied by the tumor is most important for a classifier. In our rigorous study we found out that kryptonite restricted perturbations only to the tumour leading to malign samples being classified as benign and consequently leading to highest misclassification rates.

In Fig. 5, it is seen that Kryptonite lowers the ROC score of all the networks tested upon better than any other attacks presented almost consistently, for perturbation sizes constrained by the hyperparameter ϵ, and ultimately drops the score of generated samples to 0. Also, for DeepFool we noticed a weak negative correlation between the overshoot parameter and ROC score such that a step wise increase in that parameter led to a linear decrease in ROC score as shown in Fig. 6.

6.2 Perturbation Size

Since having the highest drop in network accuracy is not the only criterion for a strong adversarial attack, as we can see from Fig. 7 that the final kryptonite adversarial sample pertubations are almost imperceptible and looks very similar to the clean sample to a naked eye.

In the Tables 3 and 4, we can observe the average and worse case perturbation size for each of the attack and the corresponding network accuracy

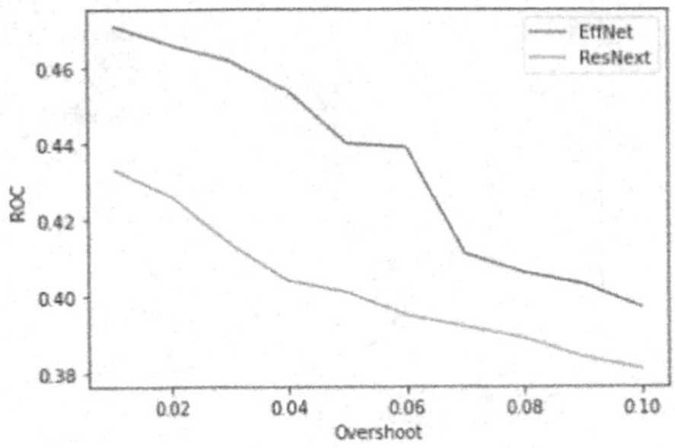

(a) Melanoma Dataset

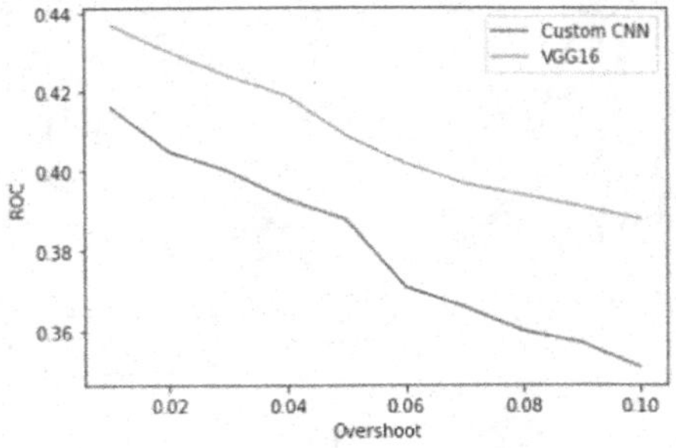

(b) Radiology Dataset

Fig. 6. Comparison of ROC score to overshoot for DeepFool

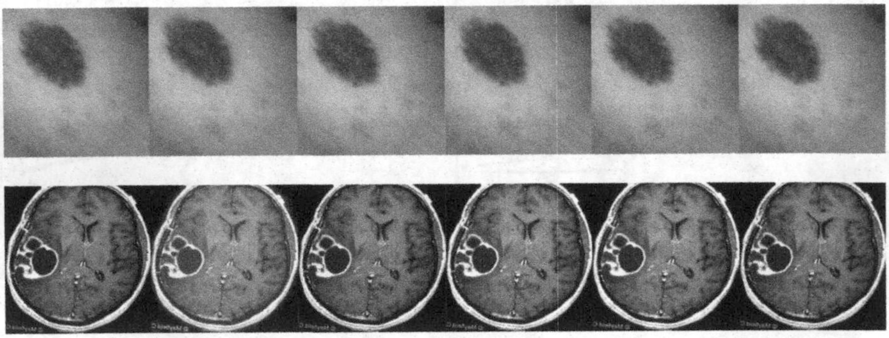

Fig. 7. Comparison of Clean, FGSM, DeepFool, MIFGSM, PGD and Kryptonite sample

(at average perturbation level). Furthermore, we note that DeepFool provides the minimal perturbations as it was designed to do so but kryptonite is a powerful alternative as well with highly respectable perturbation sizes in comparison to DeepFool and *highest* drop in network accuracy. As mentioned before kryptonite ensures the classifier uses the lesion/tumor for classification, consequently, *smaller* perturbations to the same cause high misclassification rates as can be seen from Fig. 5.

6.3 Adversarial Defence for Kryptonite

We have evaluated our proposed method on three types of adversarial defence, the detailed results and analysis is provided in Table 5. These include Adversarial Training [3], Pixel Deflection (PD) [27] and Defensive Distillation (DD) [28]. The results are an average of five rigorous trials conducted. The *JumpReLU* defence [13] was easily broken with increasing perturbation size, hence, was avoided in this study.

Table 5. The table below shows the average (5 trials conducted) of adversarial defence results for the proposed attack. The metrics on the left of the slash represent accuracy of the model with adversarial samples as input. The metrics on the right of the slash represents the accuracy on clean samples.

Melanoma	FGSM		DeepFool		PGD		MIFGSM		Our's	
	EffNet	ResNext	EffNet	ResNext	EffNet	ResNext	EffNet	ResNext	EffNet	ResNext
Adv.Train (FGSM)	0.71/0.82	0.79/0.86	0.48/0.82	0.54/0.86	0.29/0.82	0.33/0.86	0.28/0.82	0.29/0.86	0.19/0.82	0.27/0.86
Adv.Train (DeepFool)	0.69/0.84	0.73/0.85	0.78/0.84	0.80/0.85	0.46/0.84	0.47/0.85	0.40/0.84	0.44/0.85	0.31/0.84	0.32/0.85
Adv.Train (PGD)	**0.73**/0.76	**0.75**/0.78	**0.73**/0.76	**0.74**/0.78	0.67/0.76	0.70/0.78	0.64/0.76	**0.69**/0.78	0.58/0.76	0.60/0.78
Adv.Train (MIFGSM)	**0.62**/0.65	**0.66**/0.68	**0.59**/0.65	**0.60**/0.68	**0.58**/0.65	0.58/0.68	0.51/0.65	0.55/0.68	0.47/0.65	0.52/0.68
Adv.Train (Our's)	**0.69**/0.72	**0.70**/0.74	**0.65**/0.72	**0.66**/0.74	0.62/0.72	**0.65**/0.74	0.59/0.72	**0.65**/0.74	0.57/0.72	0.62/0.74
PD	**0.49**/0.56	**0.50**/0.59	0.44/0.56	0.48/0.59	0.39/0.56	0.41/0.59	0.30/0.56	0.33/0.59	0.20/0.56	0.23/0.59
DD	**0.85**/0.86	**0.85**/0.88	**0.83**/0.86	**0.84**/0.88	**0.77**/0.86	**0.80**/0.88	0.74/0.86	**0.79**/0.88	0.70/0.86	0.73/0.88
MRI	FGSM		DeepFool		PGD		MIFGSM		Our's	
	CNN	VGG16	CNN	VGG16	CNN	VGG16	CNN	VGG16	CNN	VGG16
Adv.Train (FGSM)	0.81/0.88	0.84/0.93	0.42/0.88	0.47/0.93	0.38/0.88	0.41/0.93	0.24/0.88	0.30/0.93	0.18/0.88	0.23/0.93
Adv.Train (DeepFool)	0.79/0.90	**0.86**/0.91	0.76/0.90	0.78/0.91	0.43/0.90	0.50/0.91	0.25/0.90	0.33/0.91	0.17/0.90	0.25/0.91
Adv.Train (PGD)	**0.80**/0.83	**0.82**/0.84	**0.78**/0.83	**0.79**/0.84	0.71/0.83	0.75/0.84	0.66/0.83	0.70/0.84	0.57/0.83	0.63/0.84
Adv.Train (MIFGSM)	**0.74**/0.76	**0.75**/0.79	**0.67**/0.76	0.69/0.79	0.56/0.76	0.62/0.79	0.69/0.76	0.73/0.79	0.44/0.76	0.49/0.79
Adv.Train (Our's)	**0.80**/0.82	**0.81**/0.85	**0.76**/0.82	**0.78**/0.85	**0.73**/0.82	**0.76**/0.85	0.68/0.82	0.69/0.85	0.64/0.82	0.69/0.85
PD	**0.51**/0.60	**0.60**/0.67	**0.53**/0.60	**0.63**/0.67	0.47/0.60	0.53/0.67	0.46/0.60	0.51/0.67	0.16/0.60	0.19/0.67
DD	**0.92**/0.93	**0.94**/0.96	**0.89**/0.93	**0.93**/0.96	**0.86**/0.93	**0.89**/0.96	**0.84**/0.93	0.85/0.96	0.79/0.93	0.84/0.96

In the table above values mentioned in bold font indicate resilience to a particular attack. We have chosen a drop of less than 10% in accuracy from the original accuracy of a particular network on clean samples as a sign of robustness or resilience to a particular attack.
For example, consider PGD Adversarial Training for Melanoma dataset performed on ResNext network. Now attacking this network with MIFGSM adversarial samples results in an accuracy of 69% which is a less than 10% drop from the accuracy on clean samples (78%). Hence, we say that performing PGD adversarial training on ResNext makes it robust to MIFGSM.
If an adversarial training defence trained on a particular attack is implemented on a network to counter the same attack, the effectiveness of the implemented defence does not indicate any kind of robustness.

Adversarial Training. We performed adversarial training using each of the attack algorithms using both of our datasets on their respective classifiers. To ensure the classifier does not fail to classify on clean samples we trained the classifiers on complete training data which included 65% adversarial samples and 35% clean samples. All the adversarial attacks were kept at their optimal parameters while evaluating defence as well. As we can see from Table 5 re - training classifiers using FGSM and DeepFool did not help much in making them more robust against adversaries. On the other hand, PGD adversarial training which is considered the best was able to provide robustness against FGSM, DeepFool and even MIFGSM (for ResNext). We noticed that PGD adversarial training was really slow as compared to others. Adversarial training done using MIFGSM helped make the classifiers robust against FGSM, DeepFool and PGD (for EffNet). Furthermore, adversarial training performed using the samples generated by our proposed method show that we were able to make our classifiers robust to FGSM, DeepFool, PGD (excluding EffNet case) and even MIFGSM (for ResNext). In terms of accuracy on clean images, a classifier trained using DeepFool samples performs the best owing to its small perturbation size but this does not ensure robustness whereas using PGD or Kryptonite adversarial training though we lose out a bit on accuracy on clean images we still have a higher chance towards resilience to adversaries. Adversarial training gives a *false* sense of security [29] and for very large scale datasets it seems impractical to re - train the huge neural nets just for certain amount of robustness. Furthermore, the robustness achieved through this method seems limited as we can infer from Table 5 that this method could not bring robustness towards our proposed attack. Another observation made was that going beyond optimal parameters resulted in breaking this defence at the cost of perceptible perturbations.

Pixel Deflection. In this method proposed by [27], we randomly select a pixel and replace that pixel with another randomly selected pixel, this process the authors have called as pixel deflection (PD). Then, we use a Robust Class Activation Map (RCAM) to select pixel which is least important for classification and deflect that pixel. The added noise is then removed using Wavelet Denoising (WD). The authors of this defence base their intuition on the fact that adversarial attacks are *antagonistic* to region's of interest but for kryptonite region of interest is everything. Hence, as we can see from Table 5, this defence *struggles* to provide any kind of resilience towards our proposed attack. Another observation was that this method led to a big drop of network accuracy on clean images. The parameter deflections was set at 120, 100, 100, 80 for the networks EffNet, ResNext, CNN and VGG16 respectively. Pixel Deflection performs the best in terms of computational efficiency but with increasing ϵ this approach failed as well. Also, we found out that in some cases the amount of noise even after performing Wavelet Denoising was really high which lead to poor classification performance on clean images as information critical to the classifier got deflected as well.

Defensive Distillation. Proposed by [28], the idea is to train a neural network having a softmax output layer at some temperature T using the hard or discrete labels. Then, the obtained class probabilities or soft labels are used to train another neural network with the same architecture as the original one which is called a distilled network. In our experiments the parameter T was set at 10, 15, 20 and 20 for the classifiers EffNet, ResNext, CNN and VGG16 respectively. From Table 5 we can see that this defence provides very good resilience to all of the attacks at the same time also retains accuracy on clean samples but this idea just makes the *generation* of adversarial samples difficult. Secondly, it has been shown by Carlini in [30] that distillation can be easily broken. In our preliminary testing using the method proposed by [30], we saw a misclassification rate of a respectable 64% for our proposed method. Also, increasing perturbation size to perceptible levels led to an increased misclassification rate for this method of defence. Defensive distillation hides the gradient, making it tough for us to find adversarial samples. We found out that this method flattens out the model completely in comparison to adversarial training. Furthermore, in our preliminary black - box testing wherein we attacked a distilled model using adversarial samples generated by another model having similar architecture, our attack produced a misclassification rate of 79% (conducted on the MRI dataset). Furthermore,

Table 6. The table below shows the average of time (10 trials conducted) required to generate a single adversarial sample (in seconds) with all the hyper parameters of the attacks at their optimal values.

Attack	Melanoma		MRI	
	EffNet	ResNext	CNN	VGG16
FGSM	0.23	0.19	0.11	0.14
DeepFool	0.96	0.90	0.84	0.87
PGD	0.75	0.70	0.61	0.64
MIFGSM	0.43	0.41	0.32	0.35
KRYPTONITE	0.44	0.41	0.31	0.35

we plan to implement more advanced defence and adversarial sample detection techniques for this proposed attack.

6.4 Time Efficiency Comparison

Table 6 shows the efficiency of our proposed attack. Though FGSM takes the least amount of time to generate an adversarial sample, its a comparatively weak attack as shown before. Furthermore, we are performing better in terms of efficiency in comparison to PGD and DeepFool attacks. These results further extend towards adversarial training as well with PGD and DeepFool being the slowest, FGSM the fastest while, MIFGSM and our proposed method perform similarly.

7 Limitations of the Study and Future Work

The attack presented in this study has only been evaluated upon certain medical datasets due to difficulties in generalising the attack. A limitation of our attack is that identifying a region of interest for more elaborate images is challenging. In the future, we hope to advance the scope of this algorithm to identify regions of interest for diverse images and hence present results for standard datasets. We also hope to motivate the creation of a more robust defence in order to protect the main region of interest.

8 Conclusion

In this paper we have presented the adversarial attack Kryptonite, which is used to find the most optimal perturbation that can be added to an image in order to encourage a network to make an incorrect prediction. This attack that hides in plain sight, uses the changes in a region of interest to find the least possible added noise in a constricted region to fool a given network. The effectiveness of this attack, as seen with the given empirical evidence, shows that the region of interest of an image is a major vulnerability in an image that can be exploited. Furthermore, it is seen that more changes constricted to this region can mitigate the effectiveness of some state of the art defences, as compared to those attacks that are more antagonistic to the region of interest. We have hence shown that localising the added perturbation makes an attack more robust.

References

1. Carrasco, M.: Visual attention: the past 25 years. Vis. Res. **51**(13), 1484–1525 (2011)
2. Ma, X., Niu, Y., Gu, L., Wang, Y., Zhao, Y., et al.: Understanding adversarial attacks on deep learning based medical image analysis systems. Pattern Recogn. **110**, 107332 (2021)
3. Goodfellow, I.J., Shlens, J., Christian, S.: Explaining and harnessing adversarial examples. In: International Conference on Learning Representations (2015)
4. Alexey, K., Goodfellow, I., Bengio, S.: Adversarial machine learning at scale. In: International Conference on Learning Representations (2017)
5. Madry, A., Makelov, A., Schmidt, L., Tsipras, D., et al.: Towards deep learning models resistant to adversarial attacks. In: International Conference on Learning Representations (2018)
6. Dong, Y., Liao, F., Pang, T., Su, H., et al.: Boosting adversarial attacks with momentum. In: IEEE/CVF Conference on Computer Vision and Pattern Recognition, pp. 9185–9193 (2018)
7. Dezfooli, S.M., Fawzi, A., Frossard, P.: DeepFool: a simple and accurate method to fool deep neural networks. In: IEEE/CVF Conference on Computer Vision and Pattern Recognition, pp. 2574–2582 (2016)
8. Paul, R., Schabath, M., Gillies, R., Hall, L., Goldgof, D.: Mitigating adversarial attacks on medical image understanding systems. In: 2020 IEEE 17th International Symposium on Biomedical Imaging, pp. 1517–1521 (2020)
9. Li, X., Zhu, D.: Robust detection of adversarial attacks on medical images. In: 2020 IEEE 17th International Symposium on Biomedical Imaging, pp. 1154–1158 (2020)
10. Carlini, N., Wagner, D.: Adversarial examples are not easily detected: bypassing ten detection methods. In: Proceedings of the 10th ACM Workshop on Artificial Intelligence and Security, pp. 3–14 (2017)
11. Tian, B., Guo, Q., Juefei-Xu, F., Le Chan, W., et al.: Bias field poses a threat to DNN-based X-Ray recognition. arXiv preprint arXiv:2009.09247 (2020)
12. Yao, Z., Gholami, A., Xu, P., Keutzer, K., Mahoney, M.W.: Trust region based adversarial attack on neural networks. In: IEEE/CVF Conference on Computer Vision and Pattern Recognition, pp. 11342–11351 (2019)
13. Erichson, N.B., Yao, Z., Mahoney, M.W.: Jumprelu: a retrofit defense strategy for adversarial attacks. In: Proceedings of the 9th International Conference on Pattern Recognition Applications and Methods, pp. 103–114 (2020)
14. Göpfert, J.P., Artelt, A., Wersing, H., Hammer, B.: Adversarial attacks hidden in plain sight. In: Advances in Intelligent Data Analysis (2020)
15. Rotemberg, V., Kurtansky, N., Betz-Stablein, B., Caffery, L., et al.: A patient-centric dataset of images and metadata for identifying melanomas using clinical context. Sci. Data **8** 1–34 (2021)

16. Tan, M., Le, Q.V.: Efficient net: rethinking model scaling for convolutional neural networks. In: International Conference on Machine Learning (2019)
17. Xie, S., Girshick, R., Dollár, P., Tu, Z., et al.: Aggregated residual transformations for deep neural networks. In: IEEE/CVF Conference on Computer Vision and Pattern Recognition, pp. 5987–5995 (2017)
18. https://www.kaggle.com/navoneel/brain-mri-images-for-brain-tumor-detection
19. Simonyan, K., Zisserman, A.: Very deep convolutional networks for large-scale image recognition. arXiv preprint arXiv:1409.1556 (2014)
20. Carlini, N., Wagner, D.: Towards evaluating the robustness of neural networks. In: IEEE Symposium on Security and Privacy, pp. 39–57 (2017)
21. Otsu, N.: A threshold selection method from gray-level histograms. IEEE Trans. Syst. Man Cybern. **9**, 62–66 (1979)
22. Ronneberger, O., Fischer, P., Brox, T.: U-Net: convolutional networks for biomedical image segmentation. In: Navab, N., Hornegger, J., Wells, W.M., Frangi, A.F. (eds.) MICCAI 2015. LNCS, vol. 9351, pp. 234–241. Springer, Cham (2015). https://doi.org/10.1007/978-3-319-24574-4_28
23. Satoshi, S., KeiichiA, N.: Topological structural analysis of digitized binary images by border following. In: Computer Vision, Graphics, and Image Processing, vol. 30(1), pp. 32–46 (1985)
24. Geis, T.: Using computer vision to play super hexagon (2016)
25. Papernot, N., Faghri, F., Carlini, N., Goodfellow, I., Feinman, R., et al.: Technical report on the cleverhans v2. 1.0 adversarial examples library. arXiv preprint arXiv:1610.00768 (2016
26. Selvaraju, R.R., Cogswell, M., Das, A., Vedantam, R., Parikh, D., et al.: Grad-CAM: visual explanations from deep networks via gradient-based localization. In: IEEE/CVF Conference on Computer Vision and Pattern Recognition, pp. 618–626 (2017)
27. Prakash, A., Moran, N., Garber, S., DiLillo, A., Storer, J.: Deflecting adversarial attacks with pixel deflection. In: IEEE/CVF Conference on Computer Vision and Pattern Recognition, pp. 8571–8580 (2018)
28. Papernot, N., McDaniel, P., Wu, X., Jha, S., Swami, A.: Distillation as a defense to adversarial perturbations against deep neural networks. In: IEEE Symposium on Security and Privacy, pp. 582–597 (2016)
29. Athalye, A., Carlini, N., Wagner, D.: Obfuscated gradients give a false sense of security: Circumventing defenses to adversarial examples. In: International Conference on Machine Learning, pp. 274–283, PMLR (2018)
30. Carlini, N., Wagner, D.: Defensive distillation is not robust to adversarial examples. arXiv preprint arXiv:1607.04311 (2016)

Posters

POSTER: Resistance Analysis of Two AES-Like Against the Boomerang Attack

Laetitia Debesse[1(✉)], Sihem Mesnager[2,3], and Mounira Msahli[4]

[1] ENSTA Paris, Institut Polytechnique de Paris, 91120 Palaiseau, France
laetitia.debesse@ensta-paris.fr
[2] Department of Mathematics, University of Paris VIII, 93526 Saint-Denis, France
smesnager@univ-paris8.fr
[3] University Sorbonne Paris Cité, LAGA, UMR 7539, CNRS, 93430 Villetaneuse, France
[4] LTCI, Telecom Paris, Institut Polytechnique de Paris, 91120 Palaiseau, France
mounira.msahli@telecom-paris.fr

Abstract. Introduced by Carlos Cid et al. in EUROCRYPT 2018, boomerang uniformity is an essential tool to handle and analyze vectorial functions (S-boxes) to resist boomerang attacks. This mathematical tool quantifies the resistance against differential cryptanalysis, which is highly dependent on the non-linearity features of the S-box. This poster gives a brief analysis examining three AES S-Box's resistance to the boomerang attack. We used the boomerang Uniformity as a theoretical tool, and we tested the implementation of the boomerang attack to three S-Box over 500 keys. All three S-boxes share the same boomerang uniformity, and the probability of success of the attack is similar.

Keywords: Block cipher · AES · Boomerang attack · Boomerang uniformity · Differential cryptanalysis · Symmetric cryptography

1 Introduction

The boomerang attack is a method for the cryptanalysis of block ciphers based on differential cryptanalysis. The attack was published in 1999 by D. Wagner [8], who used it to break the COCONUT98 cipher. This attack was implemented and tested on the AES in 2018 by O. Dunkelman et al. [6]. It can be applied under chosen-ciphertext and plaintext to block ciphers E that can be separated into two independent sub-ciphers $E = E_0 \circ E_1$. Let $\mathbb{F}_2^n$ be the n-dimensional vector space over the finite field $\mathbb{F}_2 = \{0, 1\}$. To avoid confusion, we denote the sum over $\mathbb{Z}$ by $+$, and the sum over $\mathbb{F}_2$ by $\oplus$. Let n and m be two positive integers. An (n, m)-vectorial Boolean function F is any mapping $F : \mathbb{F}_{2^n} \to \mathbb{F}_{2^m}$. In symmetric cryptography, vectorial Boolean functions are called *S-boxes* (substitution-boxes). They are fundamental parts of block ciphers by providing confusion (a requirement already mentioned by C. Shannon) to withstand known (and hopefully future) attacks. Several researchers have defined various properties which

J. Zhou et al. (Eds.): ACNS 2021 Workshops, LNCS 12809, pp. 485–489, 2021.
https://doi.org/10.1007/978-3-030-81645-2_27

measure the resistance of an (n, m)-function to different kinds of cryptanalysis, including nonlinearity, differential uniformity, boomerang uniformity (see definition below), algebraic degree, and so forth. Let α, α', β, β', γ, γ', δ, P, P', C, C', D, D', Q, Q' be elements in $\mathbb{F}_2^n$, E_0 and E_1 be two (n, n)-functions defined over $\mathbb{F}_2^n$ [8] (Fig. 1).

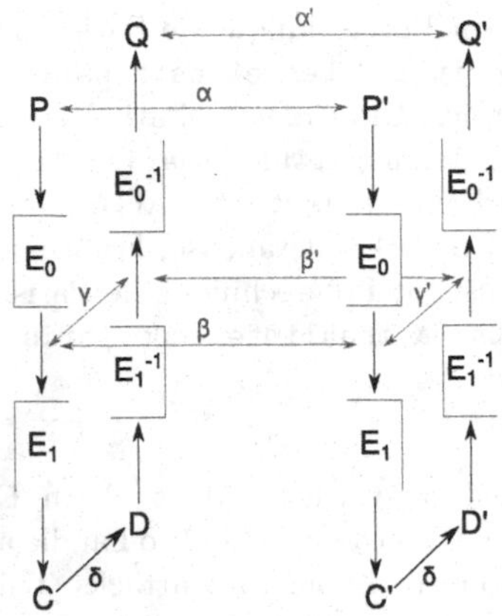

Fig. 1. The boomerang attack on block cipher E.

To more accurately evaluate the probability of generating a right quartet in boomerang-style attacks, C. Cid et al. [4] defined in 2018 a new mathematical tool called the Boomerang Connectivity Table (BCT).

Let S be an invertible (n, n)-function (that is, $x \mapsto S(x)$ induces a bijection) and S^{-1} its computational inverse. The BCT is the two-dimensional table where the entry at the row $\alpha \in \mathbb{F}_2^n$ and the column $\alpha_1 \in \mathbb{F}_2^n$ is defined by

$$\mathrm{BCT}_S(\alpha, \alpha_1) = \#\left\{x \in \mathbb{F}_2^n, S^{-1}\left(S(x) \oplus \alpha_1\right) + S^{-1}\left(S(x \oplus \alpha) \oplus \alpha_1\right) = \alpha\right\}. \quad (1)$$

The boomerang uniformity [3] of S denoted by β_S, is the highest value in the BCT without considering the row and the column of index 0:

$$\beta_S = \max_{(\alpha,\alpha_1)\in(\mathbb{F}_2^n)^2\setminus\{0\}} \mathrm{BCT}_S(\alpha, \alpha_1).$$

The lowest possible value for the boomerang uniformity of an S-box S, the better resistance to the boomerang attack of the block-cipher involving S. The studied block cipher in this project is the AES-256 (Advanced Encryption Standard), a block cipher in 14 rounds with a symmetric key of 256 bits. The key is derived into sub-keys for each turn of the encryption, and the text is stored in a state of 4×4 bytes. One round consists of four operations:

- SubBytes Transformation: it is a nonlinear transformation of the state and is represented by the S-box;
- ShiftRows Transformation: it is a circular shift on the rows of the state;

- Mixcolumns Transformation: it is a linear transformation of the state;
- Addroundkey Transformation: it is a transformation of the state by XORing a 128-bit key.

In 2011, J. Cui et al. [5] and then in 2020, A. Nitaj et al. [7] introduced two new S-boxes for the AES. The authors have studied the cryptographic properties of their S-boxes against several kinds of classical known attacks. However, despite that the boomerang attack exists at that time, the authors of [5,7] have not studied their behavior S-boxes to the boomerang attack. The objective of this work is to complete this gap. To this end, we shall analyze the corresponding S-boxes and quantify their resistance against the boomerang attack (in particular, using a simulation provided by O. Dunkelman [6]). The poster is organized as follows. In Sect. 2, which is the core of the poster, we shall focus on studying the S-boxes given in [5,7] from the boomerang cryptanalysis and present our implementation and results.

2 Our Contribution

Although the resistance against the boomerang attack of the Rijndael S-box was studied by O. Dunkelman et al. [6], the resistance of the J. Cui et al. and A. Nitaj et al. S-boxes were not. This is why we developed a script to calculate the boomerang connectivity table of substitutions in Python.

To verify our script that calculates the boomerang uniformity, we performed the same calculations using PEIGEN. The PEIGEN tool can calculate properties of S-boxes [1]. The results obtained confirmed the validity of our script. The maximum value of the BCT of Rijndael, Jie Cui et al. and Nitaj et al. S-boxes is 6, which precisely corresponds to the boomerang uniformity. All three S-boxes have, therefore, the same boomerang uniformity. It means that they all have an equivalent resistance against the boomerang attack.

The methodology used to apply the boomerang attack implemented by O. Dunkelman et al. to the two other s-boxes will be explained below.

The hypothesis used in the implementation of the article [6] were kept. An improvement of the boomerang attack called the retracing boomerang attack is used, and plaintexts are generated using structures both in order to increase the probability of success of the attack. It is applied to AES-256 reduced to 5 rounds, and the operation Addroundkey is not applied for the last round. We tested every cipher with the same 500 keys.

We had to modify the boomerang attack of O. Dunkelman et al. We changed the AES of the implementation for Gabriel Martin Blazquez's one to change the S-box used for encryption [2].

After we ran the three simulations using each S-boxes in the AES, the results were presented into a graph. The x-axis represents the number of plaintexts used to retrieve the key, and on the y-axis, the probability of success of the attack. The blue, red, green curves represent respectively the results of the Rijndael, J. Cui, et al. and A. Nitaj et al. S-boxes (Fig. 2).

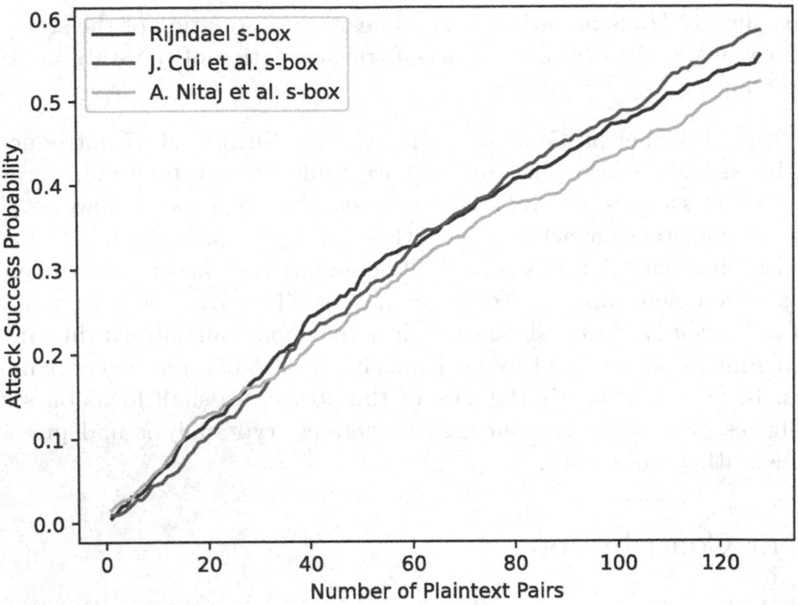

Fig. 2. The probability of success of the boomerang attack on the AES using different S-boxes

The probability of success of the three S-boxes rises steadily. J. Cui et al. get to a 60% while the Rijndael get to a 55% and the A. Nitaj et al. get to a 50% for 120 plaintexts. We observe a slight improvement in practice with the A. Nitaj et al. S-box. With the introduction of their s-box, J. Cui et al. increased the resistance to algebraic attack, but the results show that it decreased the resistance to boomerang attack.

Conclusions

In this poster, the resistance to boomerang attacks of three S-boxes is compared. Firstly, the S-boxes are introduced and theoretically analyzed using the Boomerang Connectivity Table. Their BCT share the same maximum value; they all have the same resistance against boomerang attacks. Then, their resistance is tested with an implementation of the boomerang attack. They got close results. The use of these three S-boxes does not drastically change the resistance to the boomerang attack of the AES.

Future work can focus on changing parameters of the homographic function used by A. Nitaj et al. and investigate their correlation with resistance to the boomerang attack. This work can be expanded to the study of other S-boxes, for instance, lightweight S-boxes. Moreover, increasing the number of rounds of the AES would help to confirm the implementation results. Finally, studying the new notion of the c-boomerang uniformity where $c \in \mathbb{F}_{2^8} \setminus \{0, 1\}$ on the AES could also be an interesting future work even though the former mathematical parameter has not been yet justified from the cryptanalysis point of view.

References

1. Bao, Z., Guo, J., Ling, S., Sasaki, Y.: PEIGEN - a platform for evaluation, implementation, and generation of s-boxes. IACR Trans. Symmetric Cryptol. **2019**(1), 330–394 (2019). https://doi.org/10.13154/tosc.v2019.i1.330-394. https://tosc.iacr.org/index.php/ToSC/article/view/7406
2. Blazquez, G.M.: AES (2019). https://github.com/gabrielmbmb/aes
3. Boura, C., Canteaut., A.: On the boomerang uniformity of cryptographic s-boxes. IACR Trans. Symmetric Cryptol. **3**, 290–310 (2018)
4. Cid, C., Huang, T., Peyrin, T., Sasaki, Yu., Song, L.: Boomerang connectivity table: a new cryptanalysis tool. In: Nielsen, J.B., Rijmen, V. (eds.) EUROCRYPT 2018. LNCS, vol. 10821, pp. 683–714. Springer, Cham (2018). https://doi.org/10.1007/978-3-319-78375-8_22
5. Cui, J., Huang, L., Zhong, H., Chang, C., Yang, W.: An improved AES S-box and its performance analysis. Int. J. Innovative Comput. Inf. Control **7**(5), 2291–2302 (2011)
6. Dunkelman, O., Keller, N., Ronen, E., Shamir, A.: The retracing boomerang attack. In: Annual International Conference on the Theory and Applications of Cryptographic Techniques, pp. 280–309. Springer (2020)
7. Nitaj, A., Susilo, W., Tonien, J.: A new improved AES S-box with enhanced properties (2020)
8. Wagner, D.: The boomerang attack. In: Knudsen, L. (ed.) FSE 1999. LNCS, vol. 1636, pp. 156–170. Springer, Heidelberg (1999). https://doi.org/10.1007/3-540-48519-8_12

POSTER: LHSA: Lightweight Hardware Security Arbitrator

Yongjin Kim(✉)

Twitter Inc., Seattle, WA, USA

Abstract. Hardware security components provide a Root-of-Trust (RoT) environment for critical system operations and bring in a substantially high level of security guarantee since it is protected from various software-based vulnerabilities and side channel attacks. There are a few state-of-art hardware security components which are prevalent in modern digital devices such as crypto engines, key management cores, and random number generators among others. However, most hardware security components are not exposed to end-user applications and their usage and benefits are severely limited by the policies imposed by device vendors. The reason behind the strict restriction is to reduce the attack surface and harden the hardware security components. However, application is the most vulnerable attack surface and requires utmost protection. Hence, it is imperative to provide a secure mechanism through which applications can fully leverage the hardware security components. In this paper, we propose the Lightweight Hardware Security Arbitrator (LHSA) which opens up a path for applications to fully utilize hardware security components without jeopardizing hardware security hardening. LHSA creates virtualized hardware security components for each application and applications can utilize the full hardware security functionalities in a securely isolated environment. We have built a prototype using a commodity Windows platform on ARM SoC (System-on-Chip) environment and we demonstrate its practicality and security benefits.

Keywords: Hardware security · Root of trust

1 Introduction

In modern digital devices, vendors strive to provide fundamental pieces of security guarantees by utilizing hardware security components. The hardware security components serve as a root of trust upon which all security measures of systems put trust on. For example, in ARM-based chipset systems, TrustZone [1] provides a hardware-backed protection environment which isolates the secure world from the normal world through CPU operation mode switching. Vendors put additional hardware features on top of TrustZone such as a key management core, crypto engine, or random number generator among others to strengthen hardware-level protection. By performing sensitive operations such as secure

J. Zhou et al. (Eds.): ACNS 2021 Workshops, LNCS 12809, pp. 490–494, 2021.
https://doi.org/10.1007/978-3-030-81645-2_28

boot and key management inside TrustZone along with the specialized hardware security components, we can prevent nefarious code from compromising critical system resources. Unfortunately, the hardware security features that are available in most modern commodity digital devices bring nearly zero benefits to application developers and end users due to strictly restricted deployment policies imposed by device vendors. Hardware security components are tightly coupled with each device vendor and require high costs for their integration. The reason behind this restriction on hardware security component usage is that any vulnerable or malicious trusted application inside a hardware security operation environment can compromise the fundamental system9́2s security posture [2]. Hence, deploying a trusted application requires mutual trust between device vendor and application developer. More specifically, each normal world application requires a counterpart trusted application inside the secure world to utilizes hardware security components. All application developers should go through rigorous integration processes with each device vendor to integrate the trusted application. Ironically, this strict process has resulted in a drastic increase of TrustZone code size and related attack surface. In this paper, we introduce LHSA architecture which allows applications to transparently utilize hardware security components as simply as system function calls. Some noteworthy LHSA features are (1) LHSA abstracts out complexity and provides a transparent way for applications to utilize hardware security components. (2) We eliminate the need of device vendor involvement for each application to access hardware security features. (3) Each application is assigned with its own virtualized hardware security component in a securely isolated way. (4) We take a defense-in-depth approach so that a compromise of the application or LHSA itself cannot cause system-wide hardware security functionality failure. We use ARM SoC's TrustZone environment and associated hardware security components to apply our LHSA architecture in this paper. However, note that our LHSA design can be broadly applied to any other hardware security architectures. Our paper is organized as follows. In Sect. 2, we introduce the overall architecture of LHSA. Then, we show our prototype implementation and its analysis in Sect. 3 and conclude our paper in Sect. 4.

2 Lightweight Hardware Arbitrator (LHSA)

2.1 Architecture

We aim to provide a transparent and secure interface for end-user applications to fully utilize hardware security components. To achieve this goal, we need to satisfy the following requirements.

- LHSA should fully expose hardware security functionalities to end user applications.
- Hardware-level complexity should be hidden and applications should be able to utilize hardware security components in a transparent way.

- Instances inside LHSA should be isolated so that user-space applications cannot tamper with each other.
- Compromise of LHSA should not cause system-wide hardware security compromise.

In traditional TrustZone architecture (Fig. 1(a)), each user-space application requires a corresponding trusted application in the secure world. The trusted application utilizes security hardware functionalities through trusted kernel calls inside the TrustZone. Device vendors should be involved to develop and materialize a trusted application. To overcome the inefficiency and complexity around the secure application development echo system, we introduce the LHSA architecture as shown in Fig. 1(b). LHSA consists of two parts, namely the LHSA dispatcher/listener in the normal world and the LHSA common trustlet in the secure world. By having a common interface and trustlet, we can eliminate the need of individual trust application development and associated cost and overhead. In addition, the LHSA dispatcher/listener is protected inside a hypervisor-based isolated environment and it abstracts out hardware security functionalities. LHSA maintains minimal state information for applications inside secure storage so that each application can utilize its own virtualized hardware security components in a seamless and secure way.

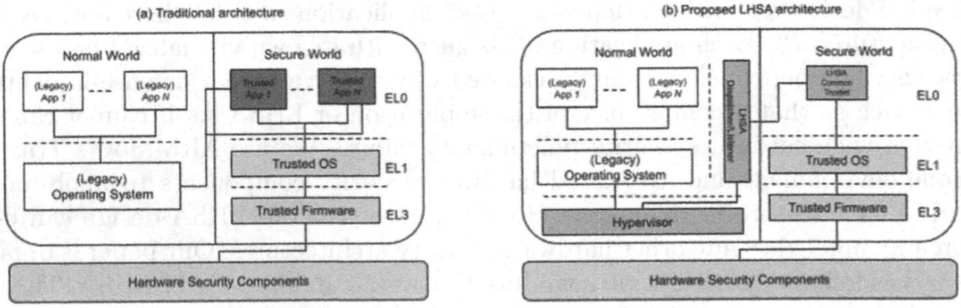

Fig. 1. Comparison between traditional and LHSA Architectures

2.2 Hardware Security Component Virtualization

LHSA performs arbitration tasks for each application to virtualize hardware security components transparently. It maintains minimal state information to isolate application processes. We show specific virtualization tasks in the following.

- Key Manager: The key manager performs application-specific key derivation from the device's master hardware key (K_m) that is protected in the secure fuse. The derivation is based on the application's context (context_i) and label (label_i), which are passed from caller. In addition, the LHSA key manager adds a UUID (Universally Unique IDentifier) in the key derivation process to enforce uniqueness and randomness in each application92s key derivation. The mapping between UUID and corresponding process identification is the minimal state information that LHSA should securely store. Through this enforced isolation, LHSA prevents malicious applications from impersonating and accessing another application's derived key.

$$K_i = KDF(K_m, \text{context}_i \mid\mid \text{label}_i \mid\mid \text{UUID}_i) \tag{1}$$

- Crypto Engine: The LHSA dispatcher passes input data and output data pointers $(\text{input}_i, \text{output}_i)$ to the LHSA common trustlet along with an application specific key (K_i) to perform hardware-based crypto operation on behalf of the end-user application. The LHSA common trustlet calls a crypto driver inside the TrustZone kernel for crypto operation by the crypto engine hardware. The result is returned to the LHSA listener once the operation is done.

$$\text{EncData}_i = E(K_i, \text{input}_i, \text{output}_i) \tag{2}$$

- Random Number Generator: To avoid excessive direct access to a hardware-based entropy source, which can cause a denial of service attack, LHSA leverages a DRBG (Deterministic Random Bit Generator) function that uses HMAC-SHA256 and generates random numbers based on a hardware-provided seed for each application (S_i). The seed and intermediate DRBG state information are the minimal pieces of information that LHSA keeps for each application.

$$\text{Rand}_i = DRBG(S_i \mid\mid \text{UUID}_i) \tag{3}$$

- Secure Storage: Secure storage is hardware-specific encrypted storage. We encrypt application data using an application-specific key which is derived from the device's master hardware key so that it can only be decrypted in the same device. We utilize KDF and UUID as follows.

$$\text{EncStorage}_i = E(KDF(K_m, \text{context}_i \mid\mid \text{label}_i \mid\mid \text{UUID}_i), \text{input}_i, \text{output}_i) \tag{4}$$

3 Prototype Analysis

We implemented a prototype of LHSA architecture utilizing Microsoft's Virtualization Based Security (VBS) [3] for the LHSA dispatcher/listener. The LHSA common trustlet was implemented inside an ARM-based TrustZone in a 2.2 GHz Cortex-A57 mobile processor. The hardware security components included in the OEM's device are a crypto engine, CSPRNG (Cryptographically Secure Pseudo Random Number Generator) core, key management core, and secure fuse. We ran performance evaluation for each LHSA functionality, namely DRBG, KDF, data encryption, and secure storage. As shown in Fig. 2, DRBG and KDF performance overhead was insignificant (less than 50 μsec) since the operation is based on HMAC-SHA256 which is computationally light-weight. In addition, communication overhead between the LHSA dispatcher/listener component and the LHSA common trustlet was within an acceptable range. We have also done performance tests for data encryption through a crypto engine and secure storage operation for a 32 Kbyte data block. The performance overhead incurred by the LHSA architecture was not significant since KDF and DRBG, which are the core components for data encryption inside the LHSA dispatcher/listener, were computationally efficient.

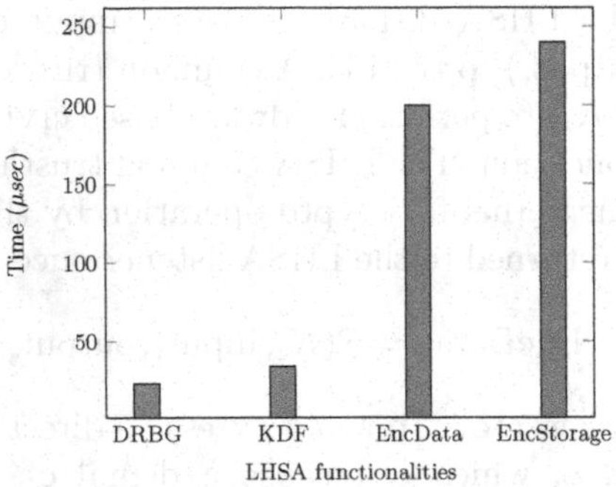

Fig. 2. Performance of each LHSA functionality

4 Conclusion

We proposed the LHSA architecture which provides a lightweight virtualization of hardware security components for user space applications. LHSA paves a way for applications to fully leverage hardware security components without increasing the attack surface in the system's root of trust. We have implemented the LHSA prototype using a commodity device and operation system and demonstrated that we can achieve our goal - *to provide a transparent interface for end-user applications to fully utilize hardware security components without degrading performance or sacrificing security significantly.*

References

1. ARM Limited: GlobalPlatform TEE & ARM TrustZone technology: Building security into your platform. https://pdfs.semanticscholar.org/presentation/7b94/63d58a2d4ec9724c5933419be6f08754ce86.pdf
2. Brasser, F., Gens, D., Jauernig, P., Sadeghi, A., Stapf, E.: SANCTUARY: ARMing TrustZone with User-space Enclaves. In: Network and Distributed System Security Symposium, February 2019
3. Microsoft. Isolated User Mode (IUM) Processes. https://docs.microsoft.com/en-us/windows/desktop/procthread/isolated-user-mode-ium-processes

POSTER: Another Look at Boyar-Peralta's Algorithm

Anubhab Baksi[1(✉)], Banashri Karmakar[2], and Vishnu Asutosh Dasu[3]

[1] Nanyang Technological University, Singapore, Singapore
anubhab001@e.ntu.edu.sg
[2] Indian Institute of Technology, Bhilai, India
banashrik@iitbhilai.ac.in
[3] TCS Research and Innovation, Hyderabad, India
vishnu.dasu1@tcs.com

Abstract. A linear layer, which is basically a binary non-singular matrix, is an integral part of cipher construction. As a result, optimising it for device implementation is an important research direction. The Boyar-Peralta's algorithm (Eprint'09) is one such common algorithm, which offers significant improvement compared to the straightforward implementation. This algorithm only returns implementation with XOR2 gates. In this work, we show an extension so that now XOR3 gates are also supported. In other words, our variant of the Boyar-Peralta's algorithm now give an implementation using XOR2 and XOR3 in the logic library.

1 Introduction

With the rapid growth of lightweight cryptography in recent times, it becomes essential to reduce the cost of the cipher components. The linear layer spreads the diffusion to the entire state in modern ciphers, thus constituting an integral part in cipher construction. A linear layer can be expressed as a binary non-singular matrix (e.g., `AES MixColumn` can be expressed as a 32×32 binary non-singular matrix), it can be implemented using assignment operations (software) or wiring (hardware) with XOR gates only.

The Boyar-Peralta's algorithm is an important step in this direction, which aims at finding efficient implementation of a given linear layer by using XOR2 gates only. In this work, we show how XOR3 gate can be supported in the Boyar-Peralta algorithm [BP09], on top of the existing support for the XOR2 gate. Thus, our variant can efficiently make use of the cases when XOR2 and XOR3 gates are available in the library. To the best of our knowledge, our work is the first open-source[1] project to achieve this, since other open-source projects (like [TP19,XZL+20]) only consider XOR2.

[1] Available at https://bitbucket.org/anubhab001/boyar-peralta-xor3/.

J. Zhou et al. (Eds.): ACNS 2021 Workshops, LNCS 12809, pp. 495–499, 2021.
https://doi.org/10.1007/978-3-030-81645-2_29

2 Boyar-Peralta's Algorithm and Its Variants

Before proceeding further, we describe the basic work-flow of the Boyar-Peralta's algorithm [BP09] (Sect. 2.1). Over the years, multiple variants of this algorithm are proposed, a summary of which is given thereafter (Sect. 2.2). Here we follow the XOR notions (viz., b_1, b_2, s_1) given in [BKD+21]. For clarity, those are described next.

Definition 1 (*d*-XOR Count). *The d-XOR count of the binary matrix* $M^{m \times n}$ *is defined as* $d(M) = \mathrm{HW}(M) - m$, *where* $\mathrm{HW}(\cdot)$ *denotes the Hamming weight.*

Definition 2 (ϵ-addition Matrix). *Let* $I^{n \times n}$ *be the identity matrix and* $E_{i,j}^{n \times n}$ *be null matrix except for* $E[i,j] = 1$ *for some* i, j *over* $\mathbb{F}_2$. *Then* $A_\epsilon = I + E_{i,j_1} + \cdots + E_{i,j_\epsilon}$ *for distinct* $\{i, j_1, \ldots, j_\epsilon\}$, *is defined an* ϵ*-addition matrix where* $\epsilon \geq 1$.

Definition 3 (s_ϵ-XOR Count). *Given a cost vector* $c = [c_0, c_1, \ldots, c_\epsilon]$ *where* $\epsilon \geq 1$ *and* $c_i \geq 0\ \forall i$, *the* s_ϵ*-XOR count, of the non-singular matrix* $M^{n \times n}$ *over* $\mathbb{F}_2$, *is defined as* $\min(c_0 + c_1 e_1 + \cdots + c_\epsilon e_\epsilon)$, *provided* M *can be expressed as a product of the factor matrices from the multi-set (with the given multiplicity) in any order:* $[P, \underbrace{A_1, \ldots, A_1}_{e_1 \text{ times}}, \ldots, \underbrace{A_\epsilon, \ldots, A_\epsilon}_{e_\epsilon \text{ times}}]$, *where* $A_\epsilon^{n \times n}$*'s are* ϵ*-addition matrices, and* $P^{n \times n}$ *is a permutation matrix. Here* c_0 *is the cost for* P, *and equals to* 0 *if* P *is identity.*

2.1 Basic Work-Flow of Boyar-Peralta Algorithm

The Boyar-Peralta algorithm [BP09] attempts to implement b_1 with the cost vector $[0, 1]$ for the binary matrix $M^{m \times n}$. The algorithm works as follows. Initially, two vectors called the *Base* vector of size n and *Dist* vector of size m are created. The *Dist* vector is initially assigned one less than the Hamming weight of each row and the *Base* vector contains all the input variables, i.e., $x_1, x_2, \ldots, x_n$. At any given point, the *Dist* vector for a given row represents the number of elements from the *Base* vector that need to be combined to generate the implementation of that particular row and the *Base* vector contains the implementations that have been generated so far. The following steps are then performed until the sum of all elements of the *Dist* vector are 0, i.e., 0 operations are required to implement all the rows of the input matrix.

1. Generate all $\binom{n}{2}$ combinations of the *Base* vector elements and compute their sum. Create a copy of the *Dist* vector for each combination. This will be called *DistC* for each combination.
2. For each combination, determine whether it is possible to reduce *DistC*$[i]$ by 1, where $i \in [1, m]$. To put it explicitly, determine whether it is possible to implement the sum of the ith row of M and the combination using *DistC*$[i] - 1$ elements of the *Base* vector. If it is possible to do so, set *DistC*$[i]$ to *DistC*$[i] -$ 1. If it is not possible, leave *DistC*$[i]$ as is.

3. Determine the most suitable combination (based on a defined heuristic) to be added to the *Base* vector. Set the *Dist* vector with the *DistC* vector of the selected combination.
4. If any element $Dist[i] = 1$, this means that the ith row of M can be implemented by adding two elements of the *Base* vector. Check every pair of elements in the *Base* vector to determine which pair when summed will be equal to the ith row of M. Once this pair has been found, set $Dist[i]$ to 0.
5. Repeat until $Dist[i] = 0$ for all i.

Remark 1. $Dist[i]$ at each step of the Boyar-Peralta algorithm contains the number of elements of the *Base* vector which need to be summed to equal to the ith row of M.

2.2 Variants of Boyar-Peralta Algorithm

Recently, three variants of the original Boyar-Peralta algorithm have been proposed [Max19, BFI19, TP19]. The authors of [BFI19] used random row and column permutations of the target matrix before feeding to the original Boyar-Peralta program. They reported b_1 cost of 95. In another direction, the authors of [TP19] proposed three types of randomization, all are internal to the algorithm and reported b_1 cost of 94. The best implementation using the Boyar-Peralta algorithm family was reported in [Max19] with a b_1 cost of 92. An overview of notable works that have implemented `AES MixColumn` can be found in Table 1, including our result (Sect. 3).

Table 1. Summary of `AES MixColumn` implementations

	Representation	# XOR2	# XOR3	Depth
Banik, Funabiki, Isobe [BFI19]	b_1	95	–	6
	b_2	39	28	N/A
Tan, Peyrin [TP19]	b_1	94	–	9
Maximov [Max19]	b_1	92	–	6
Xiang, Zeng, Lin, Bao, Zhang [XZL+20]	s_1	92	–	6
Ours	b_2	21	42	6

3 Incorporating XOR3 (b_2) Support for Boyar-Peralta Algorithm

To the best of our knowledge, the only attempt on b_2 is reported in [BFI19], where the authors used an MILP based approach. It may be noted that, this MILP based approach only considers the XOR2 and XOR3 operations, but do not take into account the cost vector (their approach returns the same implementation regardless of the cost vector). To this effect, here we attempt to modify the

Boyar-Peralta algorithm to incorporate XOR3 support which will make use of the relative cost vector.

As the source code for [TP19] is available[2], we decided to implement our approach (which is described next) on top of it. In particular, we choose the RNBP variant due to its efficiency over the other variants proposed in [TP19]. Also, we used random row and column permutations to the matrix before feed it to the program, following [BFI19].

3.1 Modelling

We assume a cost vector is given. Initialization of the *Base* vector and *Dist* vector is identical to the original algorithm as described in Sect. 2.1. The following steps highlight the changes made:

1. Generate all $\binom{n}{2}$ pairs and $\binom{n}{3}$ triplets of the *Base* vector elements and compute their sum over GF(2). The pairs represent XOR2 combinations and the triplets represent XOR3 combinations. For each combination, assign the corresponding cost from the cost vector.
2. For each of the XOR2 combinations, determine whether it is possible to reduce $DistC[i]$ by 1. Similarly, for each of the XOR3 combinations, first check it is possible to reduce $DistC[i]$ by 2; if it is not, then check if $DistC[i]$ can be reduced by 1. If $DistC[i]$ cannot be changed, leave it as is.
3. Based on the defined heuristic, determine the most suitable combination to be added to the *Base* vector. Unlike the original Boyar-Peralta algorithm, the heuristic would account for the distance vector, *DistC*, and the cost of the combination.
4. If $Dist[i] = 1$ or $Dist[i] = 2$, then the ith row of M can be implemented by adding two or three elements of the *Base* vector respectively, i.e., either XOR2 or XOR3 operations. Check every pair/triplet of the *Base* vector to determine the elements which sum to $M[i]$. Once these elements have been found, set $Dist[i]$ to 0 and add $M[i]$ to the *Base* vector.
5. Repeat until $Dist[i] = 0$ for all i.

3.2 Result

We applied the above algorithm on `AES MixColumn` matrix (with encoding compatible to that of [TP19]) and found the following result with gate count 63 (XOR2: 21, XOR3: 42):

$t0 = x24 + x0$
$t1 = x8 + x16$
$t2 = x24 + x16$
$t3 = x8 + x0$
$t4 = x29 + x5 + x22$
$y13 = x21 + x14 + t4$
$y21 = x30 + x13 + t4$
$t7 = x22 + x6$
$t8 = x3 + x10 + x18$
$y2 = x26 + x11 + t8$
$y26 = x27 + x2 + t8$
$t11 = x19 + x3$
$t12 = x9 + x2 + x17$
$y1 = x25 + x10 + t12$
$y25 = x26 + x1 + t12$

[2] https://github.com/thomaspeyrin/XORreduce.

$t15 = x9 + x18 + y1$	$t31 = x25 + x0 + t1$	$t47 = x27 + x10 + t45$
$y9 = x1 + x2 + t15$	$y24 = x1 + t31$	$y10 = x11 + t47$
$y17 = x10 + y25 + t15$	$y16 = x17 + t2 + t31$	$t49 = x5 + t0 + t18$
$t18 = x4 + x29 + x12$	$t34 = x23 + x22 + y7$	$y28 = x20 + t49$
$t19 = x20 + x28 + x13$	$y14 = t26 + t34$	$t51 = x5 + x13 + t7$
$t20 = x7 + x31$	$t36 = x4 + x11 + t11$	$y5 = y13 + t51$
$y15 = x23 + t1 + t20$	$y27 = x28 + t0 + t36$	$t53 = x21 + x28 + t18$
$y23 = x15 + t2 + t20$	$t38 = x27 + x3 + x12$	$y20 = t2 + t53$
$t23 = x7 + t3 + y15$	$y3 = t3 + t36 + t38$	$t55 = x21 + t1 + t19$
$y7 = x15 + t1 + t23$	$t40 = x19 + x20 + t1$	$y12 = x4 + t55$
$y31 = y23 + t23$	$y11 = t38 + t40$	$t57 = x5 + t3 + t19$
$t26 = x30 + x6 + t23$	$t42 = x14 + t20$	$y4 = x12 + t57$
$y22 = x14 + t0 + t26$	$y6 = x30 + t34 + t42$	$t59 = x21 + x22 + t51$
$t28 = x9 + x0 + t2$	$y30 = t0 + t7 + t42$	$y29 = x30 + t59$
$y0 = x1 + t3 + t28$	$t45 = x26 + y26 + t11$	$t61 = x27 + y27 + t40$
$y8 = x17 + t28$	$y18 = x18 + t45$	$y19 = x4 + t3 + t61$

Here our result outperforms the result from [BFI19], where the XOR cost of `AES MixColumn` matrix is 67 (XOR2: 39, XOR3: 28). If XOR3 is available in the logic library and it has the same cost as XOR2, then our result would yield lower cost.

4 Conclusion

Our work shows a natural extension to the Boyar-Peralta's algorithm [BP09]. With minimal alteration to an open-source source code, we show how XOR3 support can be incorporated. Our work is probably the first open-source project to do so.

References

[BFI19] Banik, S., Funabiki, Y., Isobe, T.: More results on shortest linear programs. Cryptology ePrint Archive, Report 2019/856 (2019). https://eprint.iacr.org/2019/856

[BKD+21] Baksi, A., Karmakar, B., Dasu, V.A., Saha, D., Chattopadhyay, A.: Further insights on implementation of the linear layer, SILC Workshop - Security and Implementation of Lightweight Cryptography (2021)

[BP09] Boyar, J., Peralta, R.: New logic minimization techniques with applications to cryptology. Cryptology ePrint Archive, Report 2009/191 (2009). https://eprint.iacr.org/2009/191

[Max19] Maximov, A.: aes mixcolumn with 92 xor gates. Cryptology ePrint Archive, Report 2019/833 (2019). https://eprint.iacr.org/2019/833

[TP19] Tan, Q.Q., Peyrin, T.: Improved heuristics for short linear programs. Cryptology ePrint Archive, Report 2019/847 (2019). https://eprint.iacr.org/2019/847

[XZL+20] Xiang, Z., Zeng, X., Lin, D., Bao, Z., Zhang, S.: Optimizing implementations of linear layers. Cryptology ePrint Archive, Report 2020/903 (2020). https://eprint.iacr.org/2020/903

POSTER: Optimizing Device Implementation of Linear Layers with Automated Tools

Anubhab Baksi[1(✉)], Banashri Karmakar[2], and Vishnu Asutosh Dasu[3]

[1] Nanyang Technological University, Singapore, Singapore
anubhab001@e.ntu.edu.sg

[2] Indian Institute of Technology, Bhilai, Bhilai, India
banashrik@iitbhilai.ac.in

[3] TCS Research and Innovation, Hyderabad, India
vishnu.dasu1@tcs.com

Abstract. The linear layer (which can be equivalently expressed as a binary non-singular matrix) is an essential component in modern cipher construction. Thus a low-cost implementation of the linear layer is needed in order to reduce the cost for the overall cipher implementation. In this work, we propose new modelling based on Satisfiability Modulo Theory (SMT) and Mixed Integer Linear Programming (MILP) which can find the optimal linear layer given certain conditions (such as, the dimension of the matrix). Our modelling automates the process of finding good linear layers.

1 Introduction

Given the current era of lightweight cryptography, there is a need to optimise the linear layer for device implementation. Since a linear layer can be written as a binary non-singular matrix (e.g., `AES MixColumn` can be expressed as a 32×32 binary non-singular matrix), it can be implemented using only XOR gates.

In recent times, there are a number of attempts to implement a given linear layer with reduced cost; and also finding linear layers with good cryptographic properties which can be implemented with low cost. Our work combines both the directions through an automated modelling that can find linear layers by optimizing certain constraints or can find optimal implementation of a given linear layer with respect to certain constraints. Our proposed models are compatible with Satisfiability Modulo Theory (SMT) or Mixed Integer Linear Programming (MILP), and any standard SMT or MILP solver can be used in the process.

2 Automated Modelling for s_1 XOR and s_2 XOR

Three notions of XOR count, namely d, s_1 and s_2 are considered here. The s_1 and s_2 notions are adopted from [BKD+21], and given next for reference. Our source codes are available online[1].

[1] https://bitbucket.org/anubhab001/linear-layer-smt/.

J. Zhou et al. (Eds.): ACNS 2021 Workshops, LNCS 12809, pp. 500–504, 2021.
https://doi.org/10.1007/978-3-030-81645-2_30

Definition 1 (d-XOR Count). *The d-XOR count of the binary matrix $M^{m\times n}$ is defined as $d(M) = \mathrm{HW}(M) - m$, where $\mathrm{HW}(\cdot)$ denotes the Hamming weight.*

Definition 2 (ϵ-addition Matrix). *Let $I^{n\times n}$ be the identity matrix and $E_{i,j}^{n\times n}$ be null matrix except for $E[i,j] = 1$ for some i, j over $\mathbb{F}_2$. Then $A_\epsilon = I + E_{i,j_1} + \cdots + E_{i,j_\epsilon}$ for distinct $\{i, j_1, \ldots, j_\epsilon\}$, is defined an ϵ-addition matrix where $\epsilon \geq 1$.*

Definition 3 ((s_ϵ-XOR Count). *Given a cost vector $c = [c_0, c_1, \ldots, c_\epsilon]$ where $\epsilon \geq 1$ and $c_i \geq 0\ \forall i$, the s_ϵ-XOR count, of the non-singular matrix $M^{n\times n}$ over $\mathbb{F}_2$, is defined as $\min(c_0 + c_1 e_1 + \cdots + c_\epsilon e_\epsilon)$, provided M can be expressed as a product of the factor matrices from the multi-set (with the given multiplicity) in any order: $[P, \underbrace{A_1, \ldots, A_1}_{e_1 \text{ times}}, \ldots, \underbrace{A_\epsilon, \ldots, A_\epsilon}_{e_\epsilon \text{ times}}]$, where $A_\epsilon^{n\times n}$'s are ϵ-addition matrices, and $P^{n\times n}$ is a permutation matrix. Here c_0 is the cost for P, and equals to 0 if P is identity.*

Basic Structure

For the modelling, we create a system of symbolic matrices, which are multiplied in sequence to produce M. We start with a number (say, m) of $n \times n$ matrices. Each matrix, M_k for $k = 0 \cdots (m-1)$ is represented as:

$$M_k = \begin{bmatrix} 1 & x_{0,1,k} & x_{0,2,k} & \cdots & x_{0,n-1,k} \\ x_{1,0,k} & 1 & x_{1,2,k} & \cdots & x_{1,n-1,k} \\ \vdots & \vdots & \vdots & \ddots & \vdots \\ x_{n-1,0,k} & x_{n-1,1,k} & x_{n-1,2,k} & \cdots & 1 \end{bmatrix},$$

where each $x_{i,j,k}$ is of type binary.

To keep the algebraic degree in check, we assign a new temporary variable, t_l to each quadratic term (e.g., $t_0 = x_{0,2,1} \cdot x_{1,3,2}$); and use t_l's for further computation. We avoid having any constraint with algebraic degree more than 2 because that might slow down the solution process [BMS]. Examples can be found in [BKD+21].

2.1 Optimization for Cost

Modelling s_1-XOR (Satisfiability Variant)

1. We allow each of the factor matrices, M_k, to be either permutation or addition. The characterization for an addition matrix is,
   (a) All diagonal elements are 1, similar to the identity matrix, i.e., $x_{i,j,k} = 1$ where $0 \leq i, j \leq n-1, i = j$.
   (b) The arithmetic sum of all non-diagonal elements is 1.
2. Similarly, the characterization of a permutation matrix is given by: The arithmetic sum of each row (respectively, column) is 1.
3. We equate the product of all the m matrices to the target matrix, M. This will give the constraints for SMT/MILP.

Modelling s_2-XOR (Optimization Variant). The modelling of s_2-XOR follows from s_1-XOR.

1. For each factor matrix $M_k^{n\times n}$, except the first (which is a permutation matrix), we create two binary variables $q_{k,2}, q_{k,3}$ with $q_{k,2} + q_{k,3} \leq 1$. This is to indicate a factor matrix can be either a permutation or an addition matrix with XOR2 ($q_{k,2}$) or an addition matrix with XOR3 ($q_{k,3}$). If $q_{k,2}, q_{k,3}$ are both 0, it is a permutation matrix; if $q_{k,2} = 1, q_{k,3} = 0$, it is an addition matrix with XOR2; if $q_{k,2} = 0, q_{k,3} = 1$, it is an addition matrix with XOR3.
2. If sum of non-diagonal elements is greater than 0, it has to trigger exactly one of $q_{k,2}$ and $q_{k,3}$. Also that sum can be at most 2. This is modelled as, $\sum_{i,j=0}^{i,j\leq n-1} x_{i,j,k} - n = q_{k,2} + 2q_{k,3}$.
3. An addition matrix with XOR3 (2-addition matrix from Definition 2) is characterised as, an identity matrix except the sum of all non-diagonal elements in one particular row is 2. To capture this, each row has to be checked individually.
   (a) For the ith row of the matrix M_k, create a binary variable $r_{i,k}$. This variable is 1 if the corresponding sum of non-diagonal elements is 2; otherwise it is 0.
   (b) There has to be exactly one row with $r_{i,k} = 1$ given $q_{k,3} = 1$, so set $\sum_{i=0}^{n-1} r_{i,k} = q_{k,3}$.
   (c) The sum of all elements in one row except the element in the diagonal has to be 2; and the same for rest of the rows is 0: $\sum_{j=0;j\neq i}^{j\leq n-1} x_{i,j} \leq 2r_{i,k} + q_{k,2}$ for each $i = 0 \cdots n-1$.
4. Given a cost vector $c = [c_1, c_2]$, where c_1 and c_2 represent the cost of XOR2 and XOR3 gates respectively, the objective function will be: Minimize $\sum_{k=0}^{m-1} c_1 \times q_{k,2} + c_2 \times q_{k,3}$

2.2 Optimization for Depth

To optimize for the depth, a new integer variable $d_{i,k}$ for row i and for matrix M_k is to be created. This will keep track of the depth incurred over the array of matrices.

Modelling s_1-XOR (Satisfiability Variant)

1. We take the rightmost matrix as a permutation, and rest all are addition matrices.
2. We create integer variables $d_{i,k}$ (≥ 0) for row $i = 0 \cdots n-1$, and set $d_{i,m-1} = 0$ for all i. Although the last permutation may take clock cycles, we do not count it here for simplicity.
3. For all i and all j, ($i \neq j$) and $0 \leq k \geq m-1$; if $x_{i,j,k} = 1$, then $d_{i,k} = \max(d_{i,k+1}, d_{j,k+1}) + 1$; if $x_{i,j,k} = 0$, then $d_{i,k} = d_{i,k+1}$. As we can't write if-else clause in MILP constraints, so to realize the above constraint, we set: $d_{i,k} \geq d_{i,k+1}$, $Q(x_{i,j,k} - 1) \leq d_{i,k} - \max(d_{i,k+1}, d_{j,k+1}) - 1$, where Q is a suitably chosen large constant. Twice the dimension of the matrix should suffice as Q.

4. For a given d (starting from 0 and growing by 1 at each iteration until the model is satisfied), a new constraint is inserted in the corresponding MILP instance: $d \leq \max(d_{0,0}, d_{1,0} \cdots d_{n-1,0})$.

Here, we fix a d, and create the MILP instance with a suitable number of factor matrices. If not satisfied, then we increment d (keeping the same number of factor matrices) and check again.

There exists an equivalent optimization variant of the above model. Here the leftmost matrix is again a permutation matrix and the rest are either permutation or addition. Since we want the depth of the circuit to be minimum, we set the objective function to: Minimize $\max(d_{0,0}, d_{1,0} \cdots d_{n-1,0})$.

Example 1. Consider, $M_{8\times 8} = [[\texttt{18}], [\texttt{09}], [\texttt{8c}], [\texttt{77}], [\texttt{07}], [\texttt{14}], [\texttt{a5}], [\texttt{1c}]]$. It can be shown that, $M = A_1^{(6,2)} \cdot A_1^{(6,1)} \cdot A_1^{(7,0)} \cdot A_1^{(3,4)} \cdot A_1^{(5,7)} \cdot A_1^{(0,5)} \cdot A_1^{(2,0)} \cdot A_1^{(3,6)} \cdot A_1^{(3,5)} \cdot A_1^{(2,7)} \cdot A_1^{(1,0)} \cdot A_1^{(4,1)} \cdot A_1^{(4,7)} \cdot P$, where $P_{8\times 8} = [[\texttt{08}], [\texttt{01}], [\texttt{80}], [\texttt{40}], [\texttt{02}], [\texttt{10}], [\texttt{20}], [\texttt{04}]]$ is a permutation matrix and $A_1^{(i,j)} = I + E_{i,j}$ is an addition matrix. This factorization of M is obtained through our depth optimization model. This has the depth of 3, and the s_1 cost of 13. Hence we conclude that for this matrix, the least possible depth is 3, and the least s_1 cost for this depth is 13.

2.3 Modelling Branch Number

Here our main goal is to find matrices with higher differential branch number (denoted by, *dbn*) and/or with higher linear branch number (*lbn*). The MILP instance takes either of *dbn*, *lbn* or both as input. The left hand side (i.e., the products of the matrices) is not imposed any restriction. Instead, the target matrix is to satisfy certain constraints.

1. We start with m (say, 2) matrices initially of which the leftmost matrix is a permutation and the rest are addition matrices (A_1). These matrices follow the constraints as discussed earlier.
2. The target matrix is denoted by Y and its elements by $y_{i,j}$ for $i, j = 0, \cdots, n-1$. We multiply m factor matrices and equate the product with Y.
3. For all non-null vector v of length n, which is denoted by $(v_0, v_1, \ldots, v_{n-1})$, we perform the following:
   (a) Compute Yv and denote its elements by $(yv_0, yv_1, \ldots, yv_{n-1})$.
   (b) We assign $\sum_{i=0}^{n-1} v_i + \sum_{i=0}^{n-1} yv_i \geq dbn$.
   Therefore there will be $2^n - 1$ constraints for v. This completes the modelling for differential branch number.
4. For linear branch number modelling (on top of differential branch number), additional $2^n - 1$ constraints will be needed. This time the transpose of Y is of interest. For all non-null vector v of length n, which is denoted by $(v_0, v_1, \ldots, v_{n-1})$, we perform the following:
   (a) We find $Y^\top v$ and denote its elements by $(ytv_0, ytv_1, \ldots, ytv_{n-1})$.
   (b) We assign $\sum_{i=0}^{n-1} v_i + \sum_{i=0}^{n-1} ytv_i \geq lbn$.
5. If the model is not satisfied for a given m, we increase the value of m by 1 and then again repeat the above procedures until the model is satisfied.

2.4 Modelling MDS Matrix with Minimum D-XOR

Here we propose the MILP modelling of MDS matrices, defined over higher order field, with minimum d-XOR count. Here our main goal is to find an $k \times k$ MDS matrix, defined over $\mathrm{GL}(n, \mathbb{F}_2)$, with minimum d-XOR count. Any such MDX matrix has the maximum branch number, i.e., $k+1$ and this property of MDS matrices has been used in this model. Moreover, each such MDS matrix can be converted into a $kn \times kn$ binary matrix, as shown below:

$$M = \begin{bmatrix} [\,]_{n\times n} & [\,]_{n\times n} & \cdots & [\,]_{n\times n} \\ [\,]_{n\times n} & [\,]_{n\times n} & \cdots & [\,]_{n\times n} \\ \vdots & \vdots & \ddots & \vdots \\ [\,]_{n\times n} & [\,]_{n\times n} & \cdots & [\,]_{n\times n} \end{bmatrix}_{k\times k} = \begin{bmatrix} m_{0,0} & m_{0,1} & \cdots & m_{0,kn-1} \\ m_{1,0} & m_{1,1} & \cdots & m_{1,kn-1} \\ \vdots & \vdots & \ddots & \vdots \\ m_{kn-1,0} & m_{kn-1,1} & \cdots & m_{kn-1,kn-1} \end{bmatrix}_{kn\times kn}.$$

1. Take 2 column vectors, $X = [x_0, x_1, \cdots, x_{kn-1}]^T$ and $Y = [y_0, y_1, \cdots, y_{kn-1}]^T$ and add the following constraint in the model: $M \cdot X = Y$.
2. To model the branch number constraint, we introduce new variables.
   (a) $QX_0 = \max(x_0, \cdots, x_{n-1})$, $QX_1 = \max(x_n, \cdots, x_{2n-1})$ and so on. In general, $QX_i = \max(x_{i\cdot n}, \cdots, x_{((i+1)\cdot n)-1})$. There are k such variables.
   (b) $QY_0 = \max(y_0, \cdots, y_{n-1})$, $QY_1 = \max(y_n, \cdots, y_{2n-1})$ and so on. In general, $QY_i = \max(y_{i\cdot n}, \cdots, y_{((i+1)\cdot n)-1})$. There are k such variables.
3. Now, we add the constraint for maximum branch number. For every non-null X, $\sum_{i=0}^{k-1} QX_i + \sum_{i=0}^{k-1} QY_i \geq k+1$.
4. Finally, we add the optimization constraint for minimum d-XOR. minimize $\left(\sum_{i,j=0}^{kn-1} m_{i,j}\right) - kn$.
5. For a given k and n, this model generates the MDS matrix, with minimum d-XOR, as output.

Example 2. We ran our MILP model to find the 3×3 MDS matrix, defined over $\mathrm{GL}(2, \mathbb{F}_2)$, with minimum d-XOR count. The model produced the following matrix M as output, which has d-XOR count 15: $M = [[\texttt{2D}], [\texttt{16}], [\texttt{19}], [\texttt{27}], [\texttt{35}], [\texttt{2A}]]$.

3 Conclusion

Our work shows automated modelling methods which can find optimal linear layers by converting it to an SMT or MILP problem. This kind of modelling can be useful in the future to construct more lightweight ciphers or improving benchmarks for existing ciphers.

References

[BKD+21] Baksi, A., Karmakar, B., Dasu, V.A., Saha, D., Chattopadhyay, A.: Further insights on implementation of the linear layer. In: SILC Workshop - Security and Implementation of Lightweight Cryptography (2021)

[BMS] Baksi, A., Maitra, S., Sarkar, S.: An improved slide attack on trivium. IPSI BgD Trans. Adv. Res. (2015). http://vipsi.org/ipsi/journals/journals/papers/tar/2015jan/p1.pdf

Short Paper

Long-term Availability of Crypto Currencies Security and Privacy Against Quantum-Attacks

Kouichi Sakurai

Department of Informatics, Kyushu University
sakurai@inf.kyushu-u.ac.jp

Abstract. Currently, post quantum cryptography has been applied to blockchains and distributed ledgers, including virtual currencies, for achieving their long-term security. Whereas we discuss the issues of how well these security evaluations have been investigated whether quantum safety can really be expected, and whether privacy is in addition to security.

Keywords: Crypto currency Distributed ledger · Post quantum cryptography · Long-term security · Everlasting privacy

1 Background and Motivation

The current standard hash function SHA2 system and the public key cryptography ECDSA, which are used for the exiting crypto currencies including BITCOIN, may not guarantee long-term use for 10 years or more due to risk of cryptographic compromise. While new virtual currencies using quantum cryptography are also appeared (e.g. DapCash), and researchers are developing sophisticated techniques for enhancing distributed ledgers' security against quantum attacks [ZZHA].

Abelian [Abel], proposed by cryptographic team Wong et al. adapts a ring signature with lattice-based cryptography for quantum security, and claims a three-step privacy function that takes auditability into consideration, as a fusion of existing technologies, and the privacy level seems to follow Zcash and MONERO. Whereas, another crypto currency, Aidos kuneen [Aido] claims quantum safety, also emphasizes anonymity, however may exclude audit transparency and traceability.

2 Technical Issues

Currently, even the realization of blind signature lattice-based cryptography is struggling with design and attack [HKLN] by leading researchers. Now we have many challenging issues around post quantum cryptographic protocols: is it feasible to design

Part of this research is supported by JSPS Grant-in-Aid for Scientific Research JP18H03240. And the author is also working with Advanced Telecommunications Research Institute International (ATR).

J. Zhou et al. (Eds.): ACNS 2021 Workshops, LNCS 12809, pp. 507–509, 2021.
https://doi.org/10.1007/978-3-030-81645-2

based on other principles such as multi-variables or code based cryptography, or is it possible to compose the privacy protocols, which have been constructed on the conventional pairing techniques, with lattice cryptography? Etc.

3 Evaluation of Super-Long-Term Security

The security compromise of SHA-2 and even SHA-3 has already been discussed based on the prediction of the progress of classical computers, as the private key cryptosystems DES and AES. Also, with the advent of quantum computers, quantum (in)security of many cryptographic algorithms (RSA, ECDSA, AES, SHA2) is also being researched, and new quantum cryptographic algorithms are being designed, analyzed, and to be standardized [NIST]. A question is, however, how long we can evaluate cryptographic technology for ultra-long-term use, for 50 years or 100 years or more longer. J. Buchmann et al. [BMV, BGB, IWAP] take the initiative in this super-long term security issue.

4 Future Research Topics

Cryptography is compromised when quantum computing becomes a reality, and the design and analysis of quantum-safe algorithms as a countermeasure has advanced to the timetable of standardization under the initiative of some government projects On the other hand, the design and analysis of the protocol using the quantum-resistant algorithm based on lattice and coding theory has just begun, and future mathematical and computer science research would be more expected.

We shall note that the compromise of cryptographic algorithms is mainly(only) due to the effect of technological advances such as the improvement of computer performance and the advent of quantum computers, whereas privacy is also affected by the national and social systems even at this point. [PvsS, BEHE].

Our research shall be going to resolve those issues by designing more flexible systems with blockchain, distributed ledger and smart contract.

References

[ZZHA] Zhang, H., Zhang, F., Tian, H., Au, M.H.: Anonymous post-quantum cryptocash. In: FC (2018)

[Abel] Abelian: https://www.abelianfoundation.org

[Aido] Kuneen, A.: https://aidoskuneen.com

[HKLN] Hauck, E., Kiltz, E., Loss, J., Nguyen, N.K.: Lattice-based blind signatures. Revisited CRYPTO (2020)

[NIST] NIST/PQC: https://csrc.nist.gov/projects/post-quantum-cryptography

[BMV] Buchmann, J., May, A., Vollmer, U.: Perspectives for cryptographic long-term security. Comm. ACM (2006)

[BGB] Buldas, A., Geihs, M., Buchmann, J.: Long-term secure time-stamping using preimage-aware hash functions - (short version). In: ProvSec (2017)

[IWAP] Takagi, T., Buchmann, J.: Panel A: on long-term security of public-key technology chairperson and a panelist. In: IWAP (2004) (Fukuoka, Japan)

[PvsS] Privacy and Security: What's the Difference? (March 5, 2019). https://it.umn.edu/news-alerts/news/privacy-security-whats-difference

[BEHE] Buocza, T., Ehrke-Rabel, T., Hödl, E., Eisenberger, I.: Bitcoin and the GDPR: allocating responsibility in distributed networks. Comput. Law Secur. Rev. 35(2), 182–198 (2019)

[MQU] Mueller-Quade, J., Unruh, D.: Long-Term Security and Universal Composability. Eprint 2006/422, TCC (2007)

[Unr] Unruh, D.: Everlasting Multi-party Computation. ePrint 2012, CR2013, JoC 2018

[TvT] Trinh, T.V.: How to protect blosckchain systems from quantum computer attacks. Department of Informatics Faculty of mathematics and natural sciences, University of Oslo Autumn (2020)

[GPZ] Grontas, P., Pagourtzis, A., Zacharakis, A.: Security models for everlasting privacy. E-Vote-ID (2019)

Author Index

Printed in the United States
by Baker & Taylor Publisher Services